S0-EKL-560

GORDON PAPE'S
1999 BUYER'S GUIDE TO
MUTUAL
FUNDS

PRENTICE HALL CANADA INC., SCARBOROUGH, ONTARIO

Canadian Cataloguing in Publication Data

Pape, Gordon, 1936–   .
    Gordon Pape's ... buyer's guide to mutual funds

Annual.
1993–
Continued: Pape, Gordon, 1936–   . Gordon Pape's
guide to mutual funds, ISSN 1193-9710.
ISSN 1193-9729
ISBN 0-13-974973-X (1999)

1. Mutual funds—Canada—Handbooks, manuals, etc. I. Title.
II. Title: Mutual funds. III. Title: Gordon Pape's buyer's guide to
mutual funds.
HG4530.P3 332.63'27 C93-030840-9

Prentice-Hall, Inc., Upper Saddle River, New Jersey
Prentice-Hall International (UK) Limited, London
Prentice-Hall of Australia, Pty. Limited, Sydney
Prentice-Hall Hispanoamericana, S.A., Mexico City
Prentice-Hall of India Private Limited, New Delhi
Prentice-Hall of Japan, Inc., Tokyo
Simon & Schuster Southeast Asia Private Limited, Singapore
Editora Prentice-Hall do Brasil, Ltda., Rio de Janeiro

ISBN 0-13-974973-X

MANAGING EDITOR: Robert Harris
PRODUCTION EDITOR: Kelly Dickson
COPY EDITOR: Reni Walker
PRODUCTION COORDINATOR: Shannon Potts
COVER DESIGN: Sarah Battersby
COVER IMAGE: Michael Custode
PAGE LAYOUT: Artplus Limited/Valerie Bateman

1 2 3 4 5 WC 02 01 00 99 98

Printed and bound in Canada.

Visit the Prentice Hall Canada Web site! Send us your comments,
browse our catalogues, and more at www.phcanada.com.

Every reasonable effort has been made to obtain permissions for all
articles and data used in this edition. If errors or omissions have
occurred, they will be corrected in future editions provided written
notification has been received by the publisher.

ALSO BY GORDON PAPE

INVESTMENT ADVICE

Building Wealth in the '90s
Low-Risk Investing in the '90s
Retiring Wealthy
Gordon Pape's 1999 Buyer's Guide to RRSPs
Making Money in Mutual Funds
The Canadian Mortgage Book
(with Bruce MacDougall)
The Best of Pape's Notes
Head Start
(with Frank Jones)

CONSUMER ADVICE

Gordon Pape's International Shopping Guide
(with Deborah Pape)

HUMOUR

The $50,000 Stove Handle

FICTION

(With Tony Aspler)
Chain Reaction
The Scorpion Sanction
The Music Wars

NON-FICTION

(With Donna Gabeline and Dane Lanken)
Montreal at the Crossroads

VISIT THE GORDON PAPE WEB SITE
(www.gordonpape.com)
for
CBC radio transcripts
Gordon Pape's e-mail newsletter
Mutual Fund Minute commentary
Answers to your financial questions
Book excerpts
Seminar dates and locations
And much more

CONTENTS

INTRODUCTION

Every year, this book gets larger as the number of mutual funds in Canada continues to grow. And every year I face a hard decision — should I pare back this *Buyer's Guide*, perhaps by focusing on just a few select funds as other books of this kind do? It's tempting, both for me (less work) and for the publisher (smaller books equal less cost). But the answer has consistently been no, we will not cut back. And it will continue to be that way for as long as my staff and I are capable of maintaining the high editorial standard we have always tried to bring to this book.

The reason for my insistence on keeping the encyclopedic character of this annual *Buyer's Guide* is simple. No one else does it. It's all well and good for a writer to pick out a few top funds, but what about all the others? Suppose you want to make some switches within a family? What are the best alternatives? How good are the funds in your portfolio that may not rank on the "Best Of" lists? Are they decent yeoman performers, or are they losers that should be dumped out? Which funds are the potential stars of the future, the ones that haven't made it to the top yet but are on the way?

These are all important questions for investors that can only be answered by looking at the entire fund universe — not just a chosen few.

That's a roundabout way of apologizing for the fact that this book continues to get more bulky every year. It used to fit comfortably in a coat pocket, but now I'm afraid it would have to be an awfully large coat. This year's edition contains ratings and reviews for more than 900 mutual funds, up from about 750 last year.

But what we've lost in convenience, I hope we've more than made up for in terms of information. If you want to know about a mutual fund and it has been in business more than three years, you'll find it in these pages. And it will continue to be that way for as long as possible. That's a promise.

As a fund investor, I don't have to tell you how rapidly things change in this business. Since last year's *Buyer's Guide* came out, a total of 217 funds have experienced a rating change — 119 moving up, 98 receiving a demotion. Plus, we have about 150 brand-new entries this year. That's why it's so important not to rely on old editions to make investment decisions. Last year's $$$ winner may be this year's $ dog because of a managerial change, or a different economic climate, or for any one of a dozen other reasons.

Although I keep this *Buyer's Guide* as current as possible, it is only published once a year. If you're an active mutual funds investor and would like to be kept up to date on new developments and opportunities, you may wish to subscribe to my monthly newsletter, *Gordon Pape's Mutual Funds Update*. It's devoted exclusively to mutual funds and contains updates on my recommendations, portfolio suggestions, articles on new funds, best fund picks, and more. You'll find a card in the book with a special subscription offer. *Mutual Funds Update* is now available in both a traditional paper-and-ink newsletter format and in an electronic edition.

If you have access to the Internet, there's a brand-new way to keep on top of my latest fund ratings. It's my On-Line Mutual Funds Database, which covers all the funds listed in this book and is constantly being updated. New funds are added as they pass their third anniversary and existing funds are reviewed periodically and their ratings adjusted when appropriate. The Database is available on an annual subscription basis through my web site (http://www. gordonpape.com).

In closing, I would like to thank all those who have helped make this year's edition a reality. They include:

Deborah Kerbel, my assistant editor, who gathers all the raw material for this book, organizes my files, compiles the statistical information, keeps the On-Line Database up to date, and does just about everything else to keep this operation going, except make my coffee. (That's my job.)

Thomas Kingissepp, Vice President, Ernst & Young Investment Advisers Inc., for supplying us once again this year with the tax information that is so important in many fund purchase decisions.

Wilfred Vos of Altamira Investment Services, who created and continues to fine-tune that company's valuable All Time Periods (ATP) performance analysis, which brings a new dimension to historical risk/return evaluation. Also, thanks to Altamira for again allowing me to make use of their data in my ratings assessments.

Robert Harris and Hart Hillman of Prentice Hall Canada for their ongoing support and assistance in this increasingly massive project, as well as all the other people at Prentice Hall — designers, editors, production people and more — who bring everything together.

And finally, once again my thanks to the many people in the mutual funds industry who take the time and effort to supply us with the detailed information we need to make a book like this possible. Your help is greatly appreciated, not just by us but by all the people who will be able to make better-informed investment decisions as a result of what they read in these pages.

GORDON PAPE
Toronto, Ontario

THE YEAR AHEAD

It's been a rough period for mutual fund investors. 1998 opened on a positive note, and markets moved to new record highs through the spring and early summer. But the storm clouds kept gathering in other parts of the world. Japan officially fell into a recession and their leadership seemed paralyzed to take meaningful action. In other parts of Asia, the economic woes deepened as currencies were devalued and stock markets fell to lows not seen in a decade.

In May, the Asian contagion leaped the Pacific and began to vent its rage on Latin America. Mutual funds that specialize in that region went into a tailspin and started to give back many of the big gains they had made over the previous 18 months.

European and North American stock markets continued to surge in the face of all this bad news, but time was running out.

The dramatic mid-summer events in Russia were the proverbial straw that broke the camel's back. On a world scale, Russia is an insignificant player. But the spectacle of a plunging ruble, of an apparently powerless president, of a squabbling legislature, of lineups at banks and food stores, and of potentially worse to come finally hit home in the U.S. and Canada. Stock markets began to wilt in July and by August the rout was on. By the time September dawned, the Dow had lost more than 15% in a chaotic month that culminated with the second-biggest one-day drop ever. The TSE 300 did even worse, losing more than 20%. And there was no sign that the carnage was over.

Regular readers of this book should not have been surprised. Last year I wrote: "A high degree of prudence is warranted in structuring your mutual fund portfolio, particularly if it is held in a registered plan. You've enjoyed some very healthy gains for a long period of time. You don't want to give a big chunk of them back now, if you can possibly avoid doing so."

I then recommended a defensive portfolio mix that consisted of 10% cash, 40% fixed-income funds, 15% balanced funds, and just 35% equity funds. If you followed that advice, you were well insulated from the worst of the summer market madness.

So what now? As this is written, on Labour Day 1998, the markets are still in turmoil. There appears to be a good possibility that we have entered a bear market that could last for several months. We will come out of it, of course. We always do. But the timing is uncertain.

In such circumstances, the first priority of the mutual fund investor should be to protect capital. This is not a time to be thinking about double-digit profits. Rather, it is a time for caution and for avoiding undue exposure to the more volatile areas of the market. So, although there are great bargains now available in regions like the Far East, I don't advise jumping in just yet. Wait until a clear recovery pattern has been established. Better to leave the first 15% of a market advance on the table than to be caught by a temporary bounce that turns out to be only the precursor to further declines.

Events such as we experienced in the summer of '98 offer an opportunity to take stock of your investment personality. How did you feel when the markets came crashing down? Were you sanguine about it all, secure in the knowledge that you had a well-balanced fund portfolio that would see you comfortably through the hard times? Or were you uptight, edgy, nervous, and worried? If so, there's a strong message there: Your portfolio is not right for your risk tolerance level. Act now to reduce its anxiety quotient so that the next time something like this happens you won't lie awake nights.

The market tumble also brought home to many people the psychological trauma of leveraged investing. It's great to ride along on borrowed money when markets are moving steadily up. Your profits multiply and you look like a financial genius to family and friends. But when markets fall, a leveraged strategy can lead to disaster. The unit value of funds being used as loan security may fall below the outstanding balance of the loan, prompting the lender to demand partial repayment or more collateral. That can lead to a personal financial crisis that could have serious consequences. Remember this the next time bull market euphoria prompts you to rush out and borrow heavily.

For the year ahead, I continue to recommend a defensive position, especially for registered plans. Here's a mix to use as a base:

10% — Money market funds. A mix of Canadian and U.S. dollar funds will act as a hedge against currency fluctuations.

10% — Short-term bond funds and/or mortgage funds. Short-term bond funds hold securities with a maturity of no more than five years. Along with mortgage funds, they are excellent defensive investments.

20% — Regular bond funds. If stock market jitters continue through the fall and winter, the chances are that worldwide interest rates will decline, led by the U.S. That would generate excellent profits for bond funds.

10% — High-yield fixed-income funds. This would include high-yield bond funds and funds that specialize in royalty income trusts and REITs. They were battered last year but we should see some recovery in '99.

15% — Balanced funds. Look especially at some of the $$$$ balanced funds in this year's edition.

10% — Canadian equity funds. Our stock markets will not do particularly well unless commodity prices stage a comeback.

15% — U.S. equity funds. They're the best place for your equity positions in rough markets.

10% — International equity funds. Choose funds with a broad global mandate as opposed to those that focus on a specific country or area.

If stock markets recover and have a boom year, make appropriate adjustments. But if the markets continue to flounder, this type of asset allocation will work well.

Remember that, over the long haul, an average annual gain of between 10% and 12% is excellent for a mutual funds portfolio. Don't get greedy.

TAXES AND YOUR FUNDS

Canadian tax rates have eased a bit for lower- to middle-income people, but they are still very high by international standards. So one of the most important criteria in selecting a mutual funds portfolio continues to be the amount of money you'll end up with in your pocket at the end of the day. Surprisingly, many investors give little or no consideration to the tax consequences of their actions until it's too late to do much about it.

You're liable for taxes on any profits you make from your mutual fund investments, whether as a capital gain, as a dividend cheque from the mutual fund company, or by having any distributions reinvested in additional fund units. But there are several ways to reduce the tax burden, if you know how.

The easiest way to cut taxes is to hold your mutual fund investments in some sort of tax shelter, such as a registered retirement savings plan (RRSP) or a registered retirement income fund (RRIF). Most Canadian mutual funds are eligible for such treatment, either without restriction or under the foreign content rules (no more than 20% of the book value of your RRSP or RRIF can consist of foreign investments).

If you can't tax shelter your mutual fund investments, there are other ways to reduce Revenue Canada's bite by selecting your investments wisely. The corporate structure of the mutual fund you purchase will also have an effect on the taxes you pay so you should be aware of what it is (most investors never bother to check).

There are two types of mutual fund structures:

Mutual fund trusts: This is the most common. A mutual fund trust will distribute all the income it takes in to unitholders in the form it received the money, so that the fund itself does not have to pay any taxes. This means any capital gains earned by the fund come to you as such, as do dividends, interest, rental income, etc. You'll receive a T3 supplementary form from the fund each year, showing the origin of all income distributed to you. For example, you may have received $1,000 from a fund last year, of which $500 represented your share of its total realized capital gains, $300 your share of dividends from taxable Canadian companies, and $200 your share of interest earned by the fund. Each of these individual amounts will be shown in a box on the T3 supplementary and each must be declared separately on your tax return at the appropriate line.

Mutual fund corporations: In this case, the fund itself is taxable on the income it receives from all sources. Once all taxes have been paid, the fund declares a dividend for distribution to shareholders. This means any income you receive from the fund (except for capital gains, which are treated separately) is in the form of a dividend from a taxable Canadian corporation, and is therefore eligible for the dividend tax credit. It doesn't matter whether the fund originally received the income in the form of interest, foreign dividends, or whatever — in your hands, it's all the same. The net result probably won't be any tax saving, since the fund has already paid appropriate taxes on the income before distributing the profits to shareholders. But it greatly simplifies the tax reporting of your income.

Now, here's a rundown of the types of profits your mutual funds may generate and the tax implications of each. As you'll see, in some cases the treatment will be different depending on whether the fund is structured as a trust or a corporation. Remember that fund units held inside a registered plan do not attract tax.

Capital gains: Whenever you sell units in a mutual fund for a higher price than you originally paid, you've made a capital gain. However, the amount subject to tax will be affected by several factors. These include:

LOAD CHARGES — If you paid a commission to purchase the fund, this amount can be added to your purchase price for tax purposes, producing a higher "adjusted cost base."

DISPOSITION COSTS — Any expenses associated with the sale of your units, such as a redemption fee, can be subtracted from the proceeds of the sale before calculating the tax owed.

REINVESTED DISTRIBUTIONS — If you have directed that distributions from the fund be used to purchase additional units, these amounts can be added to the adjusted cost base.

Here's how some of these costs would affect your tax payable. Suppose, for example, you bought 100 shares in a no-load fund for $10 each (total $1,000) and later sold them for $15 each (total $1,500). You would have a taxable capital gain of $500. However, if you paid a front-end load of 5%, you would add $50 to the amount of your original investment, producing an adjusted cost base of $1,050 and reducing the capital gain to $450. If you were charged a $25 fee for closing your account, you would subtract this from the gross proceeds of the sale, reducing the net amount to $1,475 and the amount subject to tax to $425.

Note that you must sell or otherwise dispose of your units (such as by contributing them to a self-directed RRSP or exchanging them for units in another fund) to trigger the tax liability. Unrealized capital gains are not taxed. The first 25% of any capital gain is free; the balance is added to your income and taxed accordingly.

Capital gains distributions: Even if you don't sell your fund units, you may be credited with capital gains for tax purposes if the fund distributes some of the profits it makes from the sale of securities to unitholders. These will be indicated in Box 21 of the T3 supplementary slip. These capital gains are treated the same way for tax purposes as those explained above.

Dividends (Canadian): Any dividends from taxable Canadian corporations that are distributed to you must be declared for tax purposes. However, you'll be allowed to claim the dividend tax credit in connection with these payments, thus reducing the tax impact. If your fund is a trust, you'll find the actual amount of dividends credited to you in Box 23 of the T3 supplementary slip. The taxable amount of dividends eligible for the dividend tax credit appears in Box 32 and the amount of dividend tax credit you can claim will be shown in Box 39.

Dividends (foreign): If your mutual fund is a corporation, you don't have to concern yourself with this type of income. All the tax implications will be dealt with at the corporate level before distributions are made. If your fund is a trust, it's a different story. Any dividends from foreign sources will be shown separately on your T3 supplementary, as will any tax withheld at source. Taxes withheld by another country may be eligible for a foreign tax credit on your Canadian return. This won't be the case, however, if your mutual fund is being held in a RRIF or RRSP. Any foreign withholding tax paid in that situation is lost — you have no recourse under current tax regulations. However, recent amendments to the Canada-U.S. Tax Treaty have ended the requirement that tax be withheld on dividends paid to registered plans from U.S. companies, the main source of this problem in the past.

Note that dividends from foreign corporations received outside a registered plan are not eligible for the dividend tax credit.

Interest: Any interest income credited to you by a mutual fund trust will be shown in Box 26 of the T3 supplementary, headed "Other Income". This income will be subject to tax at your marginal rate (the rate you pay on the last dollar you earn) and is not eligible for any special tax treatment.

Rental income: If you own units in a real estate fund (either closed or open-end), some of the income you receive may be from rents. This income is eligible for special treatment because capital cost allowance (CCA) may be used to shelter part or all of it from tax. The mutual fund company will normally make the necessary calculations on your behalf. However, you should be aware that any tax advantages gained in this way may be partially offset when you sell your units in the fund. Ask for full details from the mutual fund company before investing.

You'll pay tax at different rates depending on the type of distribution you receive from the mutual fund company. The applicable tax rates in all brackets for dividends, interest, and capital gains are below. They were prepared by Thomas Kingissepp, Vice President, Ernst & Young Investment Advisers Inc., and are reproduced here with permission.

All rates assume the investment income is being earned on top of a base salary. They include federal and provincial income taxes, surtaxes, and provincial tax reductions. The basic personal tax credit is allowed for in the calculation.

Tax on capital gains, when applicable, is only paid on 75% of the total gain. The rates shown below take that into account and represent the effective rate for the full capital gain.

Dividend rates apply to the actual amount of dividends received from taxable Canadian corporations, not the grossed-up amount.

SPECIAL TIP: If you'd like a precise analysis of your tax situation and have access to the Internet, log on to the Ernst & Young web site (www.eycan.com) and go to the tax page. You'll find a special Personal Tax Calculator. Enter your estimated taxable income and your province of residence and it will determine your approximate tax liability and tell you your marginal tax rate for regular income, dividends, and capital gains. The section also offers an RRSP Tax Calculator and a weekly column, EY Tax Mailbag. It's a free service.

1998 MARGINAL TAX RATES

BRITISH COLUMBIA

TAXABLE INCOME	INTEREST	DIVIDENDS	CAPITAL GAINS
$6,707 to $6,956	25.84%	6.97%	19.38%
6,957 to 19,456*	26.36%	7.61%	19.77%
19,457 to 29,590	25.84%	6.97%	19.38%
29,591 to 46,514	39.52%	24.07%	29.64%
46,515 to 54,829	40.69%	24.78%	30.52%
54,830 to 59,180	44.63%	27.18%	33.47%
59,181 to 62,192	49.78%	33.61%	37.33%
62,193 to 78,222	50.36%	34.01%	37.77%
78,223 and up	54.17%	36.58%	40.62%

ALBERTA

TAXABLE INCOME	INTEREST	DIVIDENDS	CAPITAL GAINS
$6,707 to $6,956	17.26%	4.65%	12.94%
6,957 to 9,824	17.60%	5.08%	13.20%
9,825 to 16,877*	29.79%	9.33%	22.35%
16,878 to 19,456*	25.73%	7.91%	19.30%
19,457 to 29,590	25.24%	7.29%	18.93%
29,591 to 45,058	38.33%	23.66%	28.75%
45,059 to 46,514	39.25%	24.22%	29.43%
46,515 to 59,180	40.42%	24.93%	30.31%
59,181 to 62,192	45.02%	30.69%	33.77%
62,193 and up	45.60%	31.08%	34.20%

SASKATCHEWAN

TAXABLE INCOME	INTEREST	DIVIDENDS	CAPITAL GAINS
$6,707 to $6,956	17.26%	4.65%	12.94%
6,957 to 7,327	17.60%	5.08%	13.20%
7,328 to 10,000*	28.06%	10.04%	21.04%
10,001 to 14,000*	33.10%	16.41%	24.82%
14,001 to 19,456*	28.10%	10.04%	21.07%
19,457 to 19,727	27.59%	9.40%	20.69%
19,728 to 29,590	28.62%	9.87%	21.46%
29,591 to 39,638	42.60%	27.36%	31.95%
39,639 to 46,514	44.82%	28.89%	33.61%
46,515 to 59,180	45.99%	29.61%	34.49%
59,181 to 62,192	51.00%	35.88%	38.25%
62,193 and up	51.58%	36.27%	38.69%

MANITOBA

TAXABLE INCOME	INTEREST	DIVIDENDS	CAPITAL GAINS
$6,707 to $6,956	17.26%	4.65%	12.94%
6,957 to 7,970	17.60%	5.08%	13.20%
7,971 to 19,456*	30.44%	12.64%	22.83%
19,457 to 21,500*	29.92%	11.99%	22.44%
21,501 to 29,590	27.92%	9.49%	20.94%
29,591 to 30,000	41.65%	26.65%	31.24%
30,001 to 46,514	43.65%	29.15%	32.74%
46,515 to 59,180	44.82%	29.86%	33.61%
59,181 to 62,192	49.53%	35.75%	37.15%
62,193 and up	50.11%	36.14%	37.58%

ONTARIO

TAXABLE INCOME	INTEREST	DIVIDENDS	CAPITAL GAINS
$6,707 to $6,956	17.26%	4.65%	12.94%
6,957 to 8,774	17.60%	5.08%	13.20%
8,775 to 11,041*	31.76%	9.37%	23.82%
11,042 to 19,456*	25.01%	7.22%	18.76%
19,457 to 29,590	24.52%	6.61%	18.39%
29,591 to 46,514	37.51%	22.84%	28.13%
46,515 to 50,960	38.68%	23.55%	29.01%
50,961 to 59,180	40.90%	24.91%	30.67%
59,181 to 61,175	45.62%	30.80%	34.21%
61,176 to 62,192	49.71%	33.57%	37.28%
62,193 and up	50.29%	33.96%	37.72%

QUEBEC

TAXABLE INCOME	INTEREST	DIVIDENDS	CAPITAL GAINS
$6,707 to $6,785	14.45%	3.90%	10.84%
6,786 to 6,956	34.51%	17.85%	25.88%
6,957 to 19,456*	34.80%	18.21%	26.10%
19,457 to 25,000	34.51%	17.85%	25.88%
25,001 to 29,590 .	37.52%	21.61%	28.14%
29,591 to 46,514	45.08%	31.17%	33.81%
46,515 to 50,000	46.34%	31.89%	34.76%
50,001 to 59,180	49.35%	35.65%	37.01%
59,181 to 62,192	52.04%	39.00%	39.03%
62,193 and up	52.62%	39.40%	39.47%

NOVA SCOTIA

TAXABLE INCOME	INTEREST	DIVIDENDS	CAPITAL GAINS
$6,707 to $6,956	17.26%	4.65%	12.94%
6,957 to 9,720	17.60%	5.08%	13.20%
9,721 to 15,000*	27.57%	7.96%	20.68%
15,001 to 19,456*	32.57%	14.21%	24.43%
19,457 to 21,000*	32.03%	13.54%	24.02%
21,001 to 29,590	27.03%	7.29%	20.27%
29,591 to 46,514	41.34%	25.18%	31.01%
46,515 to 59,180	42.51%	25.89%	31.88%
59,181 to 62,192	47.42%	32.02%	35.56%
62,193 to 79,060	48.00%	32.41%	36.00%
79,061 and up	49.66%	33.54%	37.25%

NEW BRUNSWICK

TAXABLE INCOME	INTEREST	DIVIDENDS	CAPITAL GAINS
$6,707 to $6,956	27.63%	7.45%	20.72%
6,957 to 19,456*	28.18%	8.14%	21.13%
19,457 to 29,590	27.63%	7.45%	20.72%
29,591 to 46,514	42.25%	25.73%	31.69%
46,515 to 59,180	43.42%	26.44%	32.57%
59,181 to 62,192	48.43%	32.70%	36.32%
62,193 to 95,404	49.01%	33.10%	36.76%
95,405 and up	50.43%	34.05%	37.82%

PRINCE EDWARD ISLAND

TAXABLE INCOME	INTEREST	DIVIDENDS	CAPITAL GAINS
$6,707 to $6,956	27.37%	4.65%	20.53%
6,957 to 19,456*	27.92%	8.06%	20.94%
19,457 to 29,590	27.37%	7.38%	20.53%
29,591 to 46,514	41.86%	25.49%	31.40%
46,515 to 48,077	43.03%	26.20%	32.27%
48,078 to 59,180	44.58%	27.15%	33.43%
59,181 to 62,192	49.72%	33.58%	37.29%
62,193 and up	50.30%	33.97%	37.73%

NEWFOUNDLAND

TAXABLE INCOME	INTEREST	DIVIDENDS	CAPITAL GAINS
$6,707 to $6,956	28.99%	7.81%	21.74%
6,957 to 19,456*	29.56%	8.54%	22.17%
19,457 to 29,590	28.99%	7.81%	21.74%
29,591 to 46,514	44.33%	27.00%	33.25%
46,515 to 58,500	45.50%	27.71%	34.13%
58,501 to 59,180	47.29%	28.80%	35.47%
59,181 to 62,192	52.75%	35.62%	39.56%
62,193 and up	53.33%	36.01%	40.00%

NORTHWEST TERRITORIES

TAXABLE INCOME	INTEREST	DIVIDENDS	CAPITAL GAINS
$6,707 to $6,956	24.91%	6.71%	18.68%
6,957 to 19,456*	25.40%	7.34%	19.05%
19,457 to 29,590	24.91%	6.71%	18.68%
29,591 to 46,514	38.09%	23.20%	28.57%
46,515 to 59,180	39.26%	23.91%	29.45%
59,181 to 62,192	43.79%	29.57%	32.84%
62,193 and up	44.37%	29.96%	33.28%

YUKON TERRITORY

TAXABLE INCOME	INTEREST	DIVIDENDS	CAPITAL GAINS
$6,707 to $6,956	25.76%	6.94%	25.76%
6,957 to 19,456*	26.27%	7.59%	26.27%
19,457 to 29,590	25.76%	6.94%	25.76%
29,591 to 46,514	39.39%	23.99%	39.39%
46,515 to 59,180	40.56%	24.70%	40.56%
59,181 to 60,469	45.24%	30.55%	45.24%
60,470 to 62,192	45.97%	31.04%	45.97%
62,193 and up	46.55%	31.43%	46.55%

* Higher marginal income tax bracket results from the recapture of provincial tax reductions allowed at lower levels of income.

There are a few other important tax considerations to remember when buying mutual funds:

Make sure your registered and non-registered portfolios are structured so you pay the least possible tax. As a general rule, you should hold fixed income and money market mutual funds (those that are designed to generate interest) inside a registered plan, such as an RRSP or RRIF. That's because interest income is taxed at the highest rate, as you can see from the above tables. Keep equity, dividend, and real estate funds outside the registered plan, since profits earned by these types of funds are taxed more favourably. If your money is being professionally managed, check to see these basic tax guidelines are being observed. I recently came across a case where an Edmonton investment house had replicated exactly the same portfolio in a client's registered and non-registered account. As a result, the customer was paying several thousand dollars a year in unnecessary taxes.

A Willowdale, Ontario reader recently wrote to ask how maintaining tax-effective registered and non-registered portfolios could be done in an easy way.

"I try to save outside my RRSP (for a house, car, etc.) but you recommend income and mortgage funds for this purpose since they are better suited for short-term goals," he says. "Equities, on the other hand, are too volatile for short-term savings. But they are more tax-effective than interest-bearing investments outside an RRSP. How does an investor deal with these conflicts?"

In this kind of situation, I recommend investing in conservatively managed equity mutual funds outside the RRSP and keeping the savings component (e.g., the mortgage fund) inside a self-directed plan. Then, when you need the money, you can swap your equity units for the mortgage units inside the fund, sell the mortgage units and use the cash for buying the house or whatever. However, you'll have to pay tax on any capital gains in the equity units at that point. See the next tip.

Remember that switching from one fund to another may trigger a tax liability. Revenue Canada takes the position that a switch is the same as a sale. If you've made a capital gain on the fund you're leaving, that profit will be subject to tax at the capital gains rate when you file your next return. Obviously, this won't apply if the switch takes place within an RRSP or RRIF. A few fund groups offer "umbrella" funds, which allow you to switch from one "section" of the fund to another without triggering a capital gain. AGF, C.I., Synergy, and AIM GT use this approach for some of their funds. However, the tax-deferral is only temporary. When you eventually sell your units in the umbrella fund, taxes will have to be paid.

Buying funds at year-end may cause tax problems. Many funds make an annual profit distribution at year-end to unitholders of record on December 31. If you buy into the fund a few days before, you'll receive the same payment as someone who has owned it all year. Sounds great? It's not. As Midland Walwyn (now Merrill Lynch) financial advisor Stanley Tepner pointed out in *The Globe and Mail,* you end up paying tax on money you didn't earn. Here's how. Suppose you own 1,000 fund units, which you just bought. They are valued at $10 each on December 31. The total value of your investment therefore equals $10,000. The fund manager declares a $1 distribution. You receive a cheque for $1,000. Because this is an open-end fund, the net asset value of the units is adjusted to $9, reflecting the dis-tribution payment. You still have $10,000 in assets — only now you have to pay tax on $1,000 of that amount. You're out of pocket several hundred dollars, just because you bought in at the wrong time. The solution? Buy new units after the first of the year or choose funds that make distrib-utions more frequently, thereby minimizing this effect.

Thomas Kingissepp of Ernst & Young offers this addi-tional advice: "What is often overlooked is that the tax problem with buying mutual funds is a timing issue, not an additional tax. The distribution to the investor that gives rise to the tax is reinvested into additional units of the mutual fund. Thus, the investor's total cost base in the mutual fund has been increased and the investor will con-sequently have a smaller capital gain or a larger capital loss in the future when all of the units of the mutual fund are sold or transferred to an RRSP.

"Thus, the impact of the tax on the distribution increases the longer the investor holds the mutual fund and the longer the investor has to wait to obtain the tax benefit of the increased tax cost base. Conversely, a shorter holding period might mean that the impact of this tax is lessened. Thus, consider the magnitude of investment returns given up by waiting to buy until after the distribution, your expected holding period, purchases throughout the year as well as purchases after the first of the year, and funds that make more frequent distributions."

HOW TO USE THE MUTUAL FUND RATINGS

The ratings on the pages that follow are designed to help you Identify those mutual funds that may be most suitable for your personal investing strategy. They should not be interpreted as buy or sell recommendations! Because of publishing deadlines, these ratings were compiled in August and September, 1998. Conditions may have changed significantly since then, so you should consult an investment advisor before making any final decisions. You should also obtain a copy of the simplified prospectus (the document that provides all the information about the fund and its management) and study it carefully before going ahead. For ongoing mutual funds information, you may wish to subscribe to my special newsletter, *Gordon Pape's Mutual Funds Update.* Mutual fund information can also be obtained at my Internet site (www.gordonpape.com).

My Investment Ratings take into account a number of factors. These include:

Risk level. Most investors, myself included, are uncomfortable with a high degree of risk in the mutual funds they purchase, so this weighs heavily in my ratings. A higher risk investment, even one that has a good performance record, will generally receive a lower rating than an investment that may not promise as good a return but that is less risk-prone. Note that risk levels are relative within each fund category. Equity funds, for example, are generally higher risk than fixed-income funds. So a medium-risk equity fund (expressed as → in the summary line) will have a higher degree of risk than a medium-risk fixed-income fund.

Performance record. While previous performance is no guarantee of a fund's future success, it's a far better indicator than throwing darts at a board. Because I regard performance records as being particularly important in judging the suitability of mutual funds, no fund that has been in existence for less than three years is included in the ratings. Mutual fund performance ratings are based on results for the period ending June 30, 1998. My information sources include data compiled by *The Financial Post, The Globe and Mail Report on Business*, Southam's *Mutual Fund SourceBook*, plus the mutual fund companies themselves.

This year I have again drawn on data prepared by Wilfred Vos of Altamira Investment Services, using the All Time Periods (ATP) analysis he has developed. This system goes much deeper into the historical performance of funds than the statistics quoted in the business press. To do this, each fund is assessed in terms of rolling one-month periods. The ATP system provides a full range of possible investment returns over the selected time frame, compared to the traditional reporting method that only shows one set of returns for any given period.

The Vos system also measures each fund against its peer group on the basis of performance, risk, and total balance over the past three years. These ratings are arrived at through the use of a range of variables. For example, the performance rating looks at seven variables, including such indicators as the quartile performance of a fund on an on-going basis, its average monthly rate of return, its average percentile ranking, etc. The risk measurement considers such factors as the frequency with which the fund posts gains over a one-month period, the worst monthly return, the sum of all negative monthly losses for the period being assessed, volatility compared to others in the group, etc.

I have not reproduced all the numbers from ATP because of space considerations, but they have been factored into my individual fund ratings, particularly as they relate to relative risk.

Trend pattern. Remember the old question, "But what have you done for me lately?" It applies to mutual funds too. Funds that are performing well now are given an edge over those that have done well in the past but are struggling today. This means that a fund with a strong performance over the past five years would rank higher than one that did well five to 10 years ago but has tailed off recently. My main source of information on trend performance is Southam's *Mutual Fund SourceBook* and the ATP analysis.

Economic conditions. Certain mutual funds perform better under specific economic conditions. My ratings take this into account, based on economic conditions as they were anticipated to develop in late summer, 1998.

Costs. High costs will impact negatively on the rating of a fund. A low cost fund earns Brownie points. In cases where a front-end load (commission) is charged, assume the fee is negotiable unless the entry specifically states otherwise. Regardless of the posted commission scale, you should not pay more than 4% when purchasing a fund with a negotiable fee, even if the amount you're investing is small. Discount brokers will charge less. As for management fees, which come directly out of investors' pockets, you'll find the management expense ratio (MER) for every fund that's rated. This allows you to compare the hidden cost of all the funds. Wherever possible, I've used the MERs published in the fund company's latest annual report or in the prospectus. Note that MERs usually don't include GST, which adds an extra 7%. So a fund with a 2% MER actually pays out 2.14%.

Management. The strength of a fund manager has been taken into account in the rating, as well as his or her tenure with the fund. As well, I've included in each rating the name of the fund manager and the year he or she took over, if it could be obtained. Note that in some cases, companies refuse to give the name of a lead manager, claiming the decisions are made by a team. We've complied with this in the reviews, since we don't have much choice. But it has been my experience that in business every team has a leader. Hopefully, these firms will acknowledge this in future editions. You will also find some cases in which a corporation is shown as manager, rather than an individual. Here again I encourage all funds to provide the names of real people in the future. Investors have a right to know when a key person moves on.

Personal experience. Over the years, I've found that some funds have performed better for me than others. I've tossed these personal preferences into the ratings stew as well.

I've attempted to include as many of the more than 1,500 Canadian mutual funds as possible. Excluded are those funds with a performance record of less than three years, funds that are only open to a specific group of people (e.g., doctors, teachers, public servants), and a few funds about which I have been unable to obtain adequate information (occasionally we run into a fund company that doesn't like to provide information to independent guides such as this).

You'll find a separate section on "segregated" funds. These are identified by an "S" in the ratings. Segregated funds are operated by life insurance companies. You'll find an explanation of how they differ from regular mutual funds at the beginning of the section.

Reference in the ratings to "compound average annual rates of return" refers to the amount by which a fund would have grown each year over the period, assuming all dividends, interest, and capital gains were reinvested. Thus, a fund that is said to have an average annual compound rate of return of 15% over 10 years is one in which $1,000 invested a decade ago would have grown at an average annual rate of 15%. All figures are based on results for the year ending June 30, 1998.

Rates of return of one year or less are simple rates of return — how much your money would have increased in value since you made the investment.

Load charges are not taken into account in any of these calculations since they will vary from one investor to another.

Note that not all mutual funds are sold in every province. Consult a sales representative in your area to determine whether a fund you're interested in is available.

Each entry is introduced with a series of symbols. Here's how to interpret them.

OVERALL SUITABILITY

$ BELOW AVERAGE OR HIGHER THAN ACCEPTABLE RISK. THERE ARE BETTER CHOICES AVAILABLE.

$$ AVERAGE. RETURNS WILL LIKELY BE ABOUT AVERAGE FOR THE CATEGORY, OR THE FUND MAY HAVE A HIGHER COST OR RISK LEVEL.

$$$ ABOVE AVERAGE. SHOULD BE SERIOUSLY CONSIDERED.

$$$$ SUPERIOR. SHOULD CONSISTENTLY PERFORM IN THE TOP QUARTILE OF ITS CATEGORY.

RISK LEVEL

↑   HIGH. SUITABLE ONLY FOR INVESTORS WILLING TO ACCEPT ABOVE-AVERAGE RISK FOR A FUND OF ITS TYPE.

→   MEDIUM. SOME DEGREE OF RISK INVOLVED.

↓   LOW. MINIMAL RISK FOR A FUND OF ITS TYPE.

ASSET TYPE

C   CASH OR CASH EQUIVALENT.

FI   FIXED INCOME.

G   GROWTH.

FI/G   BALANCED.

G/FI   BALANCED, WITH A GROWTH BIAS.

CHARACTERISTICS

FRONT-END LOAD.

*   BACK-END LOAD.

#/*   OPTIONAL FRONT- OR BACK-END LOAD.

#/*/No   FRONT-END, BACK-END, AND NO-LOAD OPTIONS.

#&*	FRONT- AND BACK-END LOADS APPLICABLE.
No	NO LOAD.
S	SEGREGATED FUND OF AN INSURANCE COMPANY.
RSP	FULLY ELIGIBLE FOR RRSPs AND RRIFs, WITHOUT RESTRICTION.
£	FOREIGN PROPERTY IN RRSPs AND RRIFs. LIMITS APPLY.
MER	MANAGEMENT EXPENSE RATIO

MUTUAL FUND TYPES

CE	CANADIAN EQUITY. INVESTS PRIMARILY IN STOCKS OF CANADIAN MID-SIZE TO LARGE COMPANIES.
CSC	CANADIAN SMALL CAP. INVESTS PRIMARILY IN STOCKS OF SMALLER CANADIAN FIRMS.
USE	U.S. EQUITY. SPECIALIZES IN STOCKS OF LARGER AMERICAN COMPANIES OR OFFERS A DIVERSIFIED PORTFOLIO.
USSC	U.S. SMALL CAP. SPECIALIZES IN SMALLER AMERICAN CORPORATIONS.
IE	INTERNATIONAL EQUITY. INVESTS IN INTERNATIONAL STOCKS FROM ONE OR SEVERAL COUNTRIES.
AE	AMERICAS EQUITY. INVESTS IN STOCKS FROM TWO OR MORE COUNTRIES IN NORTH AND/OR SOUTH AMERICA. MAY INCLUDE SOME U.S. HOLDINGS.
FEE	FAR EAST EQUITY. INVESTS MAINLY IN ASIAN STOCKS.
EE	EUROPEAN EQUITY. INVESTS IN EUROPEAN STOCKS.
EME	EMERGING MARKETS EQUITY. INVESTS IN STOCKS FROM DEVELOPING COUNTRIES.
CB	CANADIAN BOND. INVESTS PRIMARILY IN CANADIAN DOL-LAR BONDS AND DEBENTURES WITH MATURITIES OF MORE THAN ONE YEAR.
IB	INTERNATIONAL BOND. INVESTS IN BONDS AND DEBEN-TURES DENOMINATED IN FOREIGN CURRENCIES.
M	MORTGAGE. INVESTS MAINLY IN RESIDENTIAL FIRST MORTGAGES.

B/M	BOND/MORTGAGE. INVESTS IN A COMBINATION OF BONDS AND RESIDENTIAL MORTGAGES AND/OR MORTGAGE-BACKED SECURITIES.
CBAL	CANADIAN BALANCED. INVESTS IN A BLEND OF CANADIAN EQUITIES AND DEBT SECURITIES.
IBAL	INTERNATIONAL BALANCED. INVESTS IN A BLEND OF FOREIGN EQUITIES AND DEBT SECURITIES.
PM	PRECIOUS METALS. INVESTS IN GOLD, PRECIOUS METALS, AND SHARES IN MINING COMPANIES.
D	DERIVATIVES. INVESTS PRIMARILY IN FUTURES, OPTIONS, AND OTHER TYPES OF DERIVATIVES.
RE	REAL ESTATE. INVESTS PRIMARILY IN COMMERCIAL REAL ESTATE.
SEC	SECTOR. INVESTS IN A SPECIFIC AREA OF THE ECONOMY.
CMM	CANADIAN MONEY MARKET. INVESTS IN CANADIAN SHORT-TERM DEBT SECURITIES SUCH AS TREASURY BILLS.
IMM	INTERNATIONAL MONEY MARKET. INVESTS IN SHORT-TERM SECURITIES DENOMINATED IN FOREIGN CURRENCIES, USUALLY U.S. DOLLARS.
LAB	LABOUR-SPONSORED VENTURE CAPITAL FUND.

MUTUAL FUNDS —
INTRODUCTION

The pages that follow contain information about most of the mutual fund companies in Canada as well as ratings and reviews of all the funds in each group that have a track record of at least three years. The companies are listed in alphabetical order.

The number of mutual fund firms continues to grow each year. At the end of August, 1998 our database showed a total of 138 companies that were actively marketing mutual funds to the Canadian public. If a company is not included in this year's edition, it's because they did not supply us with the necessary background material (prospectus, financial reports, etc.) or because their funds are only open to a specific group of investors, such as teachers.

This year's *Buyer's Guide* contains reviews and ratings for more than 900 funds. Regular mutual funds are listed by family name in the pages that follow. Segregated funds and labour-sponsored venture capital funds appear in their own sections.

To help you identify the top-rated funds quickly, their names appear in coloured type.

ABC FUNDS

THE COMPANY

This is a small operation that has produced good results for its investors. The guiding genius is Irwin Michael, an MBA from the prestigious Wharton School of Finance who believes in taking a simple, down-to-earth approach to value investing. The results speak for themselves. Despite a so-so year in '97–'98, his ABC Fully Managed Fund has been the top performer in the Canadian balanced fund category by a wide margin over the past decade. His ABC Fundamental Value Fund holds that distinction over the past five years in the diversified Canadian equity fund class, if AIC Advantage Fund is classified in the Sector category (which some data compilers are now doing). Otherwise, the ABC entry drops to the number-two spot — still highly respectable. To add some icing to the cake, these funds have a history of outperforming in down markets, which means your risk is reduced.

Michael and his colleagues spend most of their working hours poring over balance sheets and income statements, looking for hidden value within a company. They have shown themselves to be especially adept at identifying companies that are ripe for takeover bids, such as Harmac Pacific and Schneider's. None of the funds in the group has ever used options, futures, or other derivatives.

Unfortunately, you need a lot of money to invest here. The minimum amount required to open an account is $150,000 (which can be split between spouses) and even then Michael may not accept your cash if he feels it represents too large a percentage of your total net worth (if things turn sour, he doesn't want to be responsible for wiping out an investor). But if you have the entry price and pass his admission test, you won't find a much better place to stash some of your savings for long-term growth. And once you're in, you get first-class attention. The manager is accessible by phone, and the firm offers monthly in-house briefings for its investors to keep them up to date on what's happening.

Note: The ABC American-Value Fund has been the strongest performer in this group over the past two years, however it is still too young to qualify for a formal rating.

THE DETAILS

NUMBER OF FUNDS:	3
ASSETS UNDER MANAGEMENT:	$450 MILLION
LOAD CHARGE:	NONE
SWITCHING CHARGE:	NONE
WHERE SOLD:	ACROSS CANADA
HOW SOLD:	DIRECTLY THROUGH MANAGER, OR THROUGH BROKERS AND PLANNERS
PHONE NUMBER:	1-888-OPEN-ABC OR (416) 365-9696
WEB SITE ADDRESS:	WWW.ABCFUNDS.COM
E-MAIL ADDRESS:	IAMICH@ABCFUNDS.COM

FUND SUMMARY

$$$$ - FULLY MANAGED, FUNDAMENTAL VALUE
$$$ - NONE
$$ - NONE
$ - NONE
NR - AMERICAN VALUE
BEST CHOICES: FULLY MANAGED, FUNDAMENTAL VALUE
BEST FOR RRSPs: FULLY MANAGED
BEST UNRATEDS: AMERICAN VALUE

FUND RATINGS

CANADIAN EQUITY FUNDS

ABC FUNDAMENTAL VALUE FUND $$$$ ↓ G No RSP CE

Manager: Irwin Michael, since inception (1989)

MER: 2.00%

This fund made a decent return for investors last year. But the performance wasn't up to Irwin Michael's usual standards, in large part because of a heavy portfolio weighting towards the underperforming resource sector. During the first half of '98, over 19% of the portfolio was in forestry issues, about 15% in minerals and precious metals, and almost 12% in oil and gas. Those sectors clearly offer good values, but the question is when the market will recognize them. Investors will have to be patient. Other large holdings included Stelco, troubled Moore Corp., takeover target Schneider's, and Astral

Communications. Michael's strategy at this stage is to look for companies that may become takeover targets by U.S. firms seeking to take advantage of the bargains created by the cheap Canadian dollar. As he said in a newsletter to clients: "We conclude now that foreigners, particularly Americans with their overvalued currency, might be starting a 'king's feast' of fundamentally cheap Canadian companies... Our succulent Canadian corporations are ripe to be overrun and bought up by opportunistic entities while we slumber." This fund has an excellent risk/reward profile over the longer term. Wilfred Vos's ATP analysis, prepared for Altamira, shows that over any given five-year investment period since inception (April, 1989), investors have had a 100% chance of earning annual gains in excess of 20% and a zero chance of losing money. So don't be put off by the sub-par short-term numbers. Michael's long-term track record speaks for itself. If you have the money to get in, this one should be high on your buy list.

BALANCED FUNDS

ABC FULLY-MANAGED FUND $$$$ → FI/G No RSP CBAL

Manager: Irwin Michael, since inception (1988)

MER: 2.00%

Here again, an overweighting towards the resource sector in the equity section of the portfolio pulled down returns for the period to June 30/98 to below average for the balanced category. With resource issues taking a beating, especially in the minerals sector, manager Irwin Michael was fortunate to have a few big gainers in other categories, including Astral Communications, Laurentian Bank, and the North West Company. The fund's focus continued to be on the stock markets in the first half of '98, with the fixed-income section of the portfolio down to just 26% of assets, all of which were in Government of Canada bonds. Longer term, this continues to be the best performer in the balanced category, which is why it retains its $$$$ rating despite an off-year. However, be aware that ATP analysis shows this fund to have a higher-than-expected volatility level on a short-term basis. Over any given three-year period, however, the historic chances of losing money are zero.

ACADIA INVESTMENT FUNDS

THE COMPANY

This is a new, small company that only operates in New Brunswick. The funds are mainly sold through Caisses Populaires Acadiennes in that province.

THE DETAILS

NUMBER OF FUNDS:	8
ASSETS UNDER MANAGEMENT:	$31.5 MILLION
LOAD CHARGE:	NONE
SWITCHING CHARGE:	NONE
WHERE SOLD:	NEW BRUNSWICK
HOW SOLD:	THROUGH EMPLOYEES OF FINANCIAL INSTITUTIONS (CAISSES POPULAIRES)
PHONE NUMBER:	(506) 726-4108
WEB SITE ADDRESS:	N/A
E-MAIL ADDRESS:	MARC_HEBERT@ACADIE.NET

FUND SUMMARY

$$$$ - NONE
$$$ - NONE
$$ - BOND
$ - BALANCED, MONEY MARKET, MORTGAGE
NR - ATLANTIC, CANADIAN EQUITY, DIVERSIFIED, INTERNATIONAL EQUITY

BEST CHOICES: BOND
BEST FOR RRSPs: BOND
BEST UNRATEDS: ATLANTIC

FUND RATINGS

BALANCED FUNDS

ACADIA BALANCED FUND　　　　　$ → FI/G No RSP CBAL

Manager: Aldoria Cormier, since inception (1994)

MER: 2.13%

This fund offers a diversified portfolio that had a 45% equity weighting in the first half of '98, along with 28.5%

in bonds and a large cash position (25%). The performance has not been impressive; the fund lost 7.5% in the year to June 30/98 and the three-year average is well below par for the balanced category. Debuts at $.

FIXED INCOME AND MONEY MARKET FUNDS

ACADIA BOND FUND $$ ↓ FI No RSP CB

Manager: Aldoria Cormier, since inception (1994)

MER: 1.86%

This fund invests in a diverse portfolio of corporate and government bonds. As of the first half of '98, all the maturities were for less than 10 years. This has the effect of reducing risk in the event of an upward move in interest rates, but also minimizes capital gains potential. It should not come as a surprise, therefore, that the return for the year to June 30/98 was below average, at 6.5%. Three-year results are about average for the bond category, however. Debuts at $$.

ACADIA MONEY MARKET FUND $ → C No RSP CMM

Manager: Aldoria Cormier, since inception (1994)

MER: 1.36%

This is a tiny fund that was invested mainly in Province of Quebec short-term bonds in the first half of '98. Returns are below average, in part due to a relatively high MER.

ACADIA MORTGAGE FUND $ → FI No RSP M

Manager: Aldoria Cormier, since inception (1994)

MER: 1.81%

The fund invests mainly in first mortgage loans in the province of New Brunswick. Results have been weak; the three-year average annual compound rate of return of 3.7% to June 30/98 is the lowest in the mortgage fund category.

ACKER FINLEY INC.

THE COMPANY

A new player on the mutual fund scene, this Toronto-based company operates a single fund, known as the QSA Canadian Equity Fund. QSA stands for Quantitative Security Analysis, a proprietary stock selection technique that is used to determine the intrinsic business value of a company by means of a mathematical analysis of its balance sheet and the consensus of analysts' earnings estimates, in the context of the current interest rate environment. Sounds interesting, but the fund has not been in operation long enough to make any realistic judgment on the effectiveness of the method from an investor's viewpoint.

THE DETAILS

NUMBER OF FUNDS:	1
ASSETS UNDER MANAGEMENT:	$5 MILLION
LOAD CHARGE:	NONE
SWITCHING CHARGE:	NONE
WHERE SOLD:	EVERYWHERE EXCEPT QUEBEC
HOW SOLD:	BROKERAGE FIRMS
PHONE NUMBER:	(416) 777-9005
WEB SITE ADDRESS:	WWW.QSAQUANTS.COM
E-MAIL ADDRESS:	SUCCESS@ACKERFINLEY.COM

FUND SUMMARY

$$$$ - NONE
$$$ - NONE
$$ - NONE
$ - NONE
NR - QSA CANADIAN EQUITY

BEST CHOICES: N/A
BEST FOR RRSPs: N/A
BEST UNRATEDS: QSA CANADIAN EQUITY

FUND RATINGS

The QSA Canadian Equity Fund was launched in early 1998, so it is too soon to provide a rating for it.

AGF GROUP

THE COMPANY

This is a company that looks better with each passing year. The integration of the 20/20 funds into the total structure is working well, and new funds are being added as appropriate. Several funds in the group are turning in good results, and the end result is an organization that should not be overlooked when it comes time to make investment decisions.

This is one of Canada's older fund companies, in business since 1957. (In fact, American Growth Fund, the source of the AGF name, was the first mutual fund I ever bought.) Investors must like the changes they've seen in recent years; the company's assets under management increased by more than 30% in the 12 months to June 30/98.

Note that funds with the term "Class" attached are held within an overall umbrella fund. This allows investors to move assets from one "class" to another without triggering taxable capital gains.

Also note that funds that bear the 20/20 designation should be viewed as generally more aggressive in their investment style. AGF-designated funds will be more conservative as a rule.

THE DETAILS

NUMBER OF FUNDS:	39
ASSETS UNDER MANAGEMENT:	$15.3 BILLION
LOAD CHARGE:	FRONT: MAX. 6%; BACK: MAX. 5.5%
SWITCHING CHARGE:	2% MAXIMUM
WHERE SOLD:	ACROSS CANADA
HOW SOLD:	THROUGH BROKERS, DEALERS, AND FINANCIAL PLANNERS
PHONE NUMBER:	(416) 367-3981 OR 1-800-520-0620
WEB SITE ADDRESS:	WWW.AGF.COM
E-MAIL ADDRESS:	TIGER@AGF.COM

FUND SUMMARY

AGF FUNDS

$$$$ - AMERICAN TACTICAL ASSET ALLOCATION

$$$ - AMERICAN GROWTH, CANADIAN BOND, CANADIAN GROWTH, CANADIAN TACTICAL ASSET ALLOCATION, DIVIDEND, EUROPEAN ASSET ALLOCATION, EUROPEAN GROWTH, GERMANY, GLOBAL GOVERNMENT BOND, INTERNATIONAL VALUE, HIGH INCOME, RSP INTERNATIONAL EQUITY ALLOCATION, U.S.$ MONEY MARKET, WORLD BALANCED

$$ - GROWTH EQUITY, JAPAN, RSP GLOBAL BOND, U.S. INCOME, U.S. SHORT TERM HIGH YIELD INCOME, WORLD EQUITY

$ - ASIAN GROWTH, CANADIAN EQUITY, CHINA FOCUS, GROWTH & INCOME, INTERNATIONAL SHORT-TERM INCOME CLASS, MONEY MARKET, SPECIAL U.S.

NR - CANADA CLASS

BEST CHOICES: AMERICAN TACTICAL ASSET ALLOCATION, CANADIAN BOND, DIVIDEND

BEST FOR RRSPs: CANADIAN BOND, CANADIAN TACTICAL ASSET ALLOCATION

BEST UNRATEDS: GERMANY, WORLD EQUITY

20/20 FUNDS

$$$$ - NONE

$$$ - NONE

$$ - AGGRESSIVE GROWTH, RSP AGGRESSIVE EQUITY

$ - CANADIAN RESOURCES, EMERGING MARKETS VALUE, INDIA, LATIN AMERICA, MANAGED FUTURES VALUE

NR - AGGRESSIVE GLOBAL STOCK, RSP AGGRESSIVE SMALLER COMPANIES

BEST CHOICES: CANADIAN RESOURCES, LATIN AMERICA

BEST FOR RRSPs: NONE

BEST UNRATEDS: NONE

FUND RATINGS

AGF FUNDS

CANADIAN EQUITY FUNDS

AGF CANADIAN EQUITY FUND

This fund was to be merged into the companion Canadian Growth Fund (below) at the end of September, 1998, pending unitholder approval.

AGF CANADIAN GROWTH FUND $$$ → G #/* RSP CE

Manager: Martin Hubbes, since 1996

MER: 2.46%

Next to the Dividend Fund, this has been the best performer among AGF's Canadian stock funds over the past couple of years. Like most of the managers in the AGF stable, Martin Hubbes is a bottom-up stock picker. The focus of this fund is on medium to large companies, so it should come as no surprise that household names like Petro-Canada, Royal Bank, and Northern Telecom are sprinkled throughout the portfolio. In the first half of '98, Hubbes was taking profits on high valuation stocks and focusing on finding value in the mid-cap field. I'm impressed by his performance since taking charge, so the fund moves up to $$$ ranking. Formerly the DK Enterprise Fund.

AGF DIVIDEND FUND $$$ → G #/* RSP CE

Managers: Gordon MacDougall, since inception (1985) and Martin Gerber, since 1991

MER: 1.87%

Despite the name, any resemblance between this and a real dividend fund is purely coincidental. The fund throws off virtually no cash flow, which is supposed to be an integral feature of a true dividend fund. In fact, the special study we did for the *Mutual Funds Update* newsletter showed this fund only had a 0.3% cash distribution in '97, among the lowest in the dividend category. Keep that in mind if maximizing the dividend tax credit is your main goal. Also, the cash distributions from this fund show considerable variance from year to year, which is not helpful if you're relying on the income to fund your retirement. I have suggested to AGF that they rename this fund to more accurately reflect its investment style, but so far there has been no action on that. However, this fund does very well on the capital gains side with a portfolio of blue-chip stocks that includes a lot of banks and big industrial companies. The fund is conservatively managed by Gordon MacDougall and Martin Gerber, who are with the investment house of Connor, Clark & Lunn. I suggest you treat this fund as a solid blue-chip entry for risk-averse investors, and make your purchase judgment on that basis. Using that criterion, its performance in recent years would be well above average for Canadian equity funds generally. Formerly known as the 20/20 Dividend Fund and, in the distant past, as the Sunset Convertible Preferred and Dividend Fund.

AGF GROWTH EQUITY FUND $$ ↑ G #/* RSP CE

Manager: Bob Farquharson, since inception (1965)

MER: 2.80%

This is the small- to mid-cap entry from AGF, at least in theory. The manager uses a bottom-up growth strategy and targets those areas of the economy that are expected to outperform the market as a whole. In the first half of '98, Industrial Products and Oil and Gas were his favourite sectors. Returns have been good when compared to other small-cap funds, however the portfolio contains several large holdings that don't fit comfortably into the stated mandate, such as Petrocan and MDS. When compared to more broadly diversified Canadian stock funds, this one is just so-so. The risk profile shows some cause for concern. The ATP analysis, using rolling 10-year periods, shows an historical 28% chance of loss in any given 12-month period, with the worst one-year drop being almost 50%! Of greater concern is the fact there's still an 11% chance of loss after three years and a 4% chance after five years. The portfolio is very large (over 200 securities), which means good diversification, but all those stocks may be difficult to monitor. The assets of the old Corporate Investors Stock Fund were merged into this fund in October, '94.

U.S. AND INTERNATIONAL EQUITY FUNDS

AGF AMERICAN GROWTH CLASS $$$ → G #/* £ USE

Manager: Stephen Rogers, since 1993

MER: 2.79%

This is a blue-chip fund, investing in shares of large, well-established companies with strong fundamentals. It has been on a very good run, thanks in large part to a heavy weighting in technology stocks, which, despite some bumps along the way, have generally done well. Over the past five years, which roughly coincides with Steve Rogers' tenure, investors have earned almost 25% a year from this one. Not many people would be unhappy with that. This fund is suitable for more conservative equity investors, because of its emphasis on large companies. Historic results using the ATP system show only a 1% chance of loss after a three-year holding period, with a 68% probability of an average annual gain of better than 10%. That's an excellent risk/return equation, and it's actually slightly better than a year ago, which demonstrates the consistency of this fund. Recommended for long-term investors seeking steady growth in the U.S. market.

AGF ASIAN GROWTH CLASS $ ↑ G #/* £ FEE

Manager: David Chan, since 1993

MER: 3.03%

Singapore-based David Chan is a bottom-up investor who concentrates on corporate fundamentals. He's wary of the kind of fly-by-night operations that can crop up in Asia and prefers to focus on established companies with good long-term records. The fund invests in southeast Asia; there is no Japanese content. In the first half of '98, Hong Kong was far and away Chan's favourite market, with a 45.9% portfolio weighting. Exposure to the major trouble spots — Korea, Thailand, and Indonesia — was non-existent.

But none of that was enough to withstand the debacle in Asia. Investors in this fund suffered big losses (-53.6% in the year ending June 30/98) and it will likely be some time before we see a significant improvement. Put your money elsewhere for now.

AGF CHINA FOCUS CLASS $ ↑ G #/* £ FEE

Manager: Yuki Aiga (Nomura Asset Management), since 1996

MER: 3.49%

Believe it or not, this fund has lost in the neighbourhood of 10% a year over the past three years, yet still qualifies as an above-average performer in the Far East category. It just shows you how bad things have become, and it will likely be some time before they get better. Despite the name, the fund does not invest exclusively, or even primarily, in China. Rather, its mandate allows the managers to "invest in securities benefiting from growth in China". That's a lot of latitude and the portfolio composition reflects that, with large holdings of Hong Kong and Japanese stocks, as well as Chinese companies. The portfolio is run by Yuki Aiga of Nomura. She took it over in December, '96 although Nomura has been running it from its launch in 1994. I suggest staying on the sidelines here until the Far East situation stabilizes. Don't put this one in an RRSP, it's too volatile. Rating is cut back to $.

AGF EUROPEAN GROWTH CLASS $$$ → G #/* £ EE

Managers: John Arnold and Rory Flynn, since inception (1994)

MER: 3.03%

Last year I was critical of this fund's so-so performance in a hot European market. I must have stirred up somebody, because the fund has been hotter than a chili pepper ever since. Over the year ending June 30/98, it racked up the biggest single gain of any European equity fund available in this country, advancing more than 50%. Don't you wish you'd been there! In the first half of '98, the portfolio was heavily weighted to the U.K. (42% of assets), with France and Spain the only other geographic holdings in double digits. Risk profile is respectable, but this is a young fund that has not been exposed to a European bear market, so don't put too much emphasis on that aspect. Rating moves up to $$$ on the strength of the excellent recent performance.

AGF GERMANY CLASS $$$ → G #/* £ EE

Manager: Nils Wittenhagen (Deutsche Asset Management), since inception (1994)

MER: 2.99%

This is the only European equity fund available in Canada that invests in a single country — in this case, Germany. Single-country funds are by nature higher risk than those with more diversified portfolios. However, Germany's tight economic ties with the EEC limit that risk to some degree in this case. Manager Nils Wittenhagen is based in Frankfurt, so he is certainly in a good position to keep tabs on what is happening in the country. The portfolio tends to favour large corporations (Siemens, Bayer, Daimler-Benz and the like). There are some non-German holdings as well, but they account for less than 20% of the total assets. Good results to date; average annual compound rate of return for the three years to June 30/98 was a terrific 31%. If you want a Germany-specific fund in your portfolio, add it. However, I prefer a more broadly based Europe fund. Debuts with $$$.

AGF INTERNATIONAL VALUE FUND $$$ → G #/* £ IE

Managers: Charles Brandes and Jeff Busby, since 1994

MER: 2.77%

This is one of the stars in the AGF firmament and is a must for anyone who has a portfolio with the company. Charles Brandes is one of America's great value investors, regarded by many as a successor to the legendary Benjamin Graham. He has written his own book on the subject, *Value Investing Today*, and is frequently quoted in the U.S. media. The 20/20 Group, which has since been absorbed into AGF, scored a major coup in getting him to take over this fund in '94, even though they had to change the mandate to do it. Brandes and his San Diego-based team scour the world for good values and the result is a well-diversified portfolio that has churned out returns that are well above the average since he took charge. Formerly known as the 20/20 U.S. Growth Fund and, subsequently, the 20/20 International Value Fund.

AGF JAPAN CLASS $$ ↑ G #/* £ FEE

Manager: Sumio Sakamoto (Nomura Asset Management), since 1996

MER: 3.07%

The best thing that can be said about this fund is that most of its competitors have done worse. Investors have lost money, but not as much as you might expect, given the economic troubles that have plagued Japan. Manager Sumio Sakamoto, who has more than two decades of experience, took over the fund in December, '96 when he returned to Nomura Asset Management, AGF's long-time advisor on this fund, after a lengthy absence. Portfolio emphasis has been on high-tech and export-oriented companies, like Honda, Sony, and Bridgestone. Those are good blue-chip names, and the stocks are excellent value right now. But risk involved in any Japan fund is high at this time. When the recovery sets in, funds like this will explode with huge gains, but there is no way of knowing how long that will take.

AGF RSP INTERNATIONAL EQUITY ALLOCATION FUND $$$ → G #/* RSP IE

Manager: Kathy Taylor (Barclays Global Investors), since inception (1993)

MER: 2.45%

This is a "pseudo-Canadian" fund that's fully eligible for registered plans but invests internationally, through the use of futures contracts on exchange indexes around the globe. Results have generally been better than average for the international category. However, this isn't a fund you'd normally use unless you have reached the 20% foreign content limit in your RRSP. The AGF International Value Fund is my preferred choice if the foreign content rule is not a barrier.

AGF SPECIAL U.S. CLASS $ ↑ G #/* £ USSC

Manager: Stephen Rogers, since 1996
MER: 2.86%

This is the small-cap partner to the American Growth Class. For many years, it was an outstanding performer but recent results have been very weak. In an attempt to revive it, AGF turned over portfolio responsibility to Steve Rogers late in 1996, hoping he could weave some of the same magic that he's displayed with the American Growth Class. So far, we're still waiting, although to be fair the fund did generate a gain over the year ending June 30/98. It just wasn't very much. Give this one a pass for now.

AGF WORLD EQUITY CLASS $$ → G #/* £ IE

Manager: Steve Way, since inception (1995)
MER: 3.07%

This is a value-oriented international fund that may invest up to 25% of its portfolio in emerging markets. Fortunately for investors, manager Steve Way has chosen to play down that aspect of his mandate for now, and emphasized the U.S. and Europe in his geographic mix. The result was a respectable gain of 16.2% for the year to June 30/98. Three-year results are below average, however. This one seems to be improving, but if you're only buying one AGF international fund, I'd choose the International Value Fund at this time.

BALANCED FUNDS

AGF AMERICAN TACTICAL ASSET ALLOCATION FUND $$$$ → FI/G #/* £ IBAL

Manager: Kathy Taylor (Barclays Global Investors), since inception (1988)
MER: 2.56%

The portfolio of this fund is adjusted between U.S. bonds, stocks, and short-term notes according to the dictates of a computerized asset allocation formula developed by the managers, a San Francisco-based company that runs more than $300 billion in assets worldwide. Results have been very good; the fund averaged 15.2% a year for the five years to June 30/98. That was less than the average for pure

U.S. equity funds sold in Canada, but this is a balanced fund with much lower risk. In fact, the safety record of this fund is excellent, according to ATP analysis. There's only a 3% chance of losing money over a one-year period, although month-to-month results show much more volatility. Historically, this fund has stood up very well in bear markets. If you're interested in an asset allocation approach for your U.S. holdings, this one is well worth looking at. This one moved into the top $$$$ rank last year and retains that position.

AGF CANADIAN TACTICAL ASSET ALLOCATION FUND $$$ → FI/G #/* RSP CBAL

Manager: Kathy Taylor (Barclays Global Investors), since 1996

MER: 2.42%

This fund went through a metamorphosis following the takeover of the 20/20 Group by AGF. Out went Connor, Clark & Lunn, who had been running the fund on the basis of a managerial-driven asset mix approach. In came Barclays Global Investors, who use a computer program to make the key asset allocation decisions. The mandate of this fund remains the same: to use asset mix to minimize risk and enhance return. The question was, could the new folks make it work better than their predecessors did? I said at the time that I expected they would, because of the good job the same company has done with the companion American Tactical Asset Allocation Fund. Well, that has turned out to be the case. For the year to June 30/98, this fund advanced 15.5%, comfortably above average for the balanced fund category. A good choice if you want some stock market exposure with reduced risk.

AGF EUROPEAN ASSET ALLOCATION FUND $$$ → G/FI #/* £ IBAL

Manager: Warren Walker (Oechsle International), since inception (1993)

MER: 2.56%

AGF offers two European funds. The difference between this and the European Growth Class is that this is supposed to be an asset allocation fund, offering a blend of bonds and stocks. At least, that's what it says in the prospectus. In reality, this fund was fully invested in stocks throughout 1997 and the first half of 1998. We'll give them the benefit of a doubt for another year and list it as a balanced fund, but if you think you're getting some bond exposure, forget it. I suspect that no one who owns units is complaining too much, however, given the fact the fund turned in a whopping gain of 45.9% for the year ending June 30/98. That's enough to make anyone forget about such fine points as asset mix. But be wary. Since it's clear that this fund can move 100% into a specific asset class, the risk level may be higher than is normally associated with an asset allocation fund.

AGF GROWTH + INCOME FUND $ ↑ G/FI #/* RSP CBAL

Managers: Gerard Ferguson (equities), since 1996; Clive Coombs (bonds), since 1994

MER: 2.50%

This one is slipping. I noted last year that returns had fallen to below average, and that pattern continued through the first half of 1998. There is no obvious reason for this, as the equity side of the fund is not overexposed to the resource sector. But the figures are there to see. Asset mix in the first half of '98 was about 57% in stocks, 24% in bonds, and the balance in cash. As balanced funds go, the risk associated with this fund tends to be higher than normal. Formerly known as Corporate Investors Ltd.

AGF WORLD BALANCED FUND $$$ ↑ G/FI #/* £ IBAL

Managers: John Arnold and Rory Flynn, since 1996

MER: 2.46%

This is yet another of the many 20/20 funds that underwent a managerial and name change following the takeover by AGF. The managers are based in Dublin, which has become something of a mini financial capital in recent years. This fund uses a three-way asset allocation approach, taking asset class, currency mix, and geographic allocation into account. In the first half of '98, the asset mix was heavily weighted towards stocks, which comprised more than 80% of the portfolio. Geographic diversification was good. Results have been improving under the new managerial direction, so we'll move the rating up a notch to $$$.

FIXED INCOME AND MONEY MARKET FUNDS

AGF CANADIAN BOND FUND $$$ → FI #/* RSP CB

Managers: Warren Goldring, since inception (1962); Clive Coombs, since 1984

MER: 1.93%

This fund has been a dependable performer for many years, never sensational but with good, steady returns. This is a conservative fund from a portfolio safety perspective, investing mainly in government issues. In the first half of '98, almost 70% of the assets were in federal government bonds, with 20% in provincial issues and the rest in cash. The fund has had only one down year in the past two decades, losing 8.5% in '94 (a bad year for all bond funds). Latest results, to June 30/98, show a one-year gain of 9.8%, slightly better than average for Canadian bond funds as a group. This continues to be a sound choice in the AGF lineup.

AGF GLOBAL GOVERNMENT BOND FUND $$$ → FI #/* £ IB

Managers: Warren Goldring and Clive Coombs, since inception (1986)

MER: 1.86%

AGF offers two international bond funds: this one, which invests directly in foreign bonds and can therefore only be held as foreign content in RRSPs, and the RSP Global Bond Fund, which is fully eligible for registered plans. This has been the better performer, with a gain of 12.5% for the year to June 30/98 and a good (for this category) 10-year average annual compound rate of return of 8.4%. In the first half of '98, the fund's portfolio was weighted towards the U.S. dollar, with almost 40% of the portfolio denominated in that currency. However, emphasis was shifting towards the Canadian dollar, which the managers felt was oversold and offered upside potential for future gains. As you can see by all this, currency plays are very much a part of the management strategy here. If the managers get it right (and the track record suggests they do so more often than not) investors will benefit. International bond funds have been doing better lately as a result of economic weakness spawned by the Far East's decline and volatile currency movements. This fund is a decent choice in the category, but remember that if you hold it in a registered plan it will chew into your foreign content allocation. If you decide to put it into your RRSP despite this, be careful. This fund pays interest monthly. If you have opted for automatic reinvestment, and hold the fund in an RRSP, the additional units you receive could push you over the foreign content limit. Rating moves up a notch this year.

AGF HIGH INCOME FUND $$$ → FI #/* RSP CB

Manager: Clive Coombs, since inception (1989)

MER: 1.68%

This is one of those funds that is difficult to classify. It was formerly known as the AGF Preferred Income Fund, and operated as a dividend fund with the goal of enabling investors to take maximum advantage of the dividend tax credit. Although it still holds some high-yielding stocks and preferred shares, over 60% of the portfolio was in bonds in the first half of '98, so I have moved it into the fixed-income category. But it's really a kind of hybrid with the main emphasis on income generation. It performs that task quite effectively. A survey of income funds conducted for the *Mutual Funds Update* newsletter showed that in 1997 this fund generated a cash flow return of 6.3%, one of the best we found. Of that, 25% was received as interest and the balance as dividends. Total returns are below those produced by the average Canadian bond fund, but this is not your typical fund so don't use that criterion to judge it. If steady income is a prime concern (the fund pays monthly distributions), this is certainly one to look at. It would be a good fit in a RRIF, where a steady cash stream is required. Note: Ignore returns prior to '94, since the fund was operating under its old mandate before then.

AGF INTERNATIONAL SHORT TERM
INCOME CLASS $ → FI #/* £ IMM

Manager: Clive Coombs, since inception (1994)

MER: 2.69%

The goal of this fund is to invest in an international portfolio of money market instruments, with the intention of providing currency diversification. It has been a weak performer in the international money fund category, with an average annual compound rate of return of just 2.7% for the three years to June 30/98. One of the main problems is a whopping MER that is so far out of line one wonders what AGF is thinking. I certainly would not recommend using any part of the foreign content in your RRSP for this one.

AGF MONEY MARKET ACCOUNT $ ↓ C #/* RSP CMM

Manager: Clive Coombs, since 1984

MER: 1.42%

This fund continues to be a below-average performer in the money market fund category, mainly because its high MER makes it virtually impossible for manager Clive Coombs to keep pace with the competition in a low interest rate environment. It's about time AGF took a close look at this fund (which, amazingly, has over $650 million in it) and gave unitholders a break by trimming the expense ratio to a more competitive level. The fund invests mainly in Canadian T-bills, which gives it a high safety quotient. Do not, under any circumstances, buy this fund as a back-end load. You'll be assessed a redemption fee of as high as 5.5% if you cash in before seven years have passed. Money market funds are short-term holdings by nature, so a redemption fee of that magnitude is out of line. Your redemption fee could exceed several years' worth of profits! Only acquire units if you can get them on the front-end load option at 0%.

AGF RSP GLOBAL BOND FUND $$ → FI #/* RSP IB

Managers: Warren Goldring and Clive Coombs, since inception (1993)

MER: 1.97%

This fund has the same management team as the Global Government Bond Fund, so it shouldn't come as a great surprise that the broad strategies are similar. The difference is that this fund invests only in RRSP-eligible bonds to minimize risk and make the fund fully eligible for registered plans. That's a different direction for this fund, which has gone through several recent name changes — two years ago it was the 20/20 Foreign RSP

Bond Fund and prior to that the Strategic Income Fund and before that Convertible Income Fund. Because of the changes, any results prior to late '93 are not relevant when measuring historical returns because of a mandate change. Since then, results have been slightly better than average for the international bond fund category, although not as good as those of the Global Government Bond Fund. All else being equal, the Global Government Bond Fund is the better choice, but if you need to preserve foreign content room in your RRSP you can use this one instead.

AGF U.S. DOLLAR MONEY MARKET ACCOUNT $$$ ↓ C #/* IMM

Manager: Clive Coombs, since 1988

MER: 0.84%

This fund invests mainly in U.S.-pay Canada T-bills. For the past two years, U.S. dollar money market funds have paid much better returns than Canadian MMFs because of higher short-term interest rates in the U.S. As a result, this fund added 4.7% in the year to June 30/98, while its Canadian-dollar counterpart gained just 2.4%. And that doesn't take into account the additional profit you made on the currency exchange, as the loonie collapsed to its lowest level in history. But keep an eye on Canadian dollar movements if you have money here. If our currency starts to rise, you may want to make a switch. Don't pay any commission to buy this fund; the low return isn't worth it. If the sales rep won't provide it without charge, look for a no-load alternative. Also note that this fund is not eligible for RRSPs, even as foreign content.

AGF U.S. INCOME FUND $$ ↓ FI #/* IB

Manager: Clive Coombs, since inception (1992)

MER: 2.46%

This fund is designed to produce U.S. dollar interest income plus some potential capital gains by investing in U.S. government debt securities, such as bonds and T-bills. This makes for a safe portfolio, suitable for conservative investors who want more U.S. currency exposure. Of course, when and if the Canadian dollar strengthens, that will work against you. Returns have started to look much better, with a 14.8% gain for the year ending June 30/98, thanks to the strength of the U.S. greenback. Not eligible for registered plans.

AGF U.S. SHORT-TERM
HIGH YIELD INCOME FUND $$ → FI #/* £ IB

Managers: Michael Bowen, Tom Krasner, and Tom Ryan (Riverside Capital), since inception (1994)

MER: 2.48%

This short-term bond fund invests mainly in U.S. low grade corporate bonds with maturities out to five years, although it may hold some of longer term. There are also a few preferred shares in the mix. The goal is to produce a better return than U.S. Treasuries. This fund is best suited to investors who want a U.S. dollar fixed-income component in their mix that doesn't carry an undue amount of risk. Returns have been about average for the U.S. bond fund category. The high MER is a detriment, as it is with many AGF fixed-income and money market funds.

20/20 Funds

CANADIAN EQUITY FUNDS

20/20 CANADIAN RESOURCES FUND $ ↑ G #/* RSP SEC

Manager: Bob Farquharson, since 1975

MER: 2.88%

If you've been in this over the long haul (it was originally the AGF Canadian Resources Fund), then you haven't done too badly. But the most positive thing I can say about this fund's recent performance is that some other resource funds have done much worse. Resource stocks, one of the pillars of Canadian markets, have been taking a beating and there are many good values available. The question is, when will they start to come back? A resurgence in Asia and a hint of inflation would help, so keep your eyes open for signs like that. Until then, you're probably best to stand clear. The name change to 20/20 a couple of years ago was intended to reflect the fact that this is a more aggressive, higher risk fund. It is certainly all of that. The veteran Farquharson was heavily weighting the portfolio to oil and gas in the first half of '98, with Suncor and Petro-Canada the top holdings. Warning: The risk element in this fund is very high; even over a 10-year period there is a 15% chance you could be in the red, according to the ATP measurements. Historic odds on an average annual gain of more than 10% over that time are less than one in five.

20/20 MANAGED FUTURES VALUE FUND $ ↑ G #/* RSP D

Manager: John Di Tomasso, since inception (1995)

MER: 3.69%

This is one of the few derivative funds in Canada, investing in a portfolio of commodity futures contracts and options, backed by government T-bills. Results have not been good, so you probably won't be disappointed to learn it has been closed to new investors.

U.S. AND INTERNATIONAL EQUITY FUNDS

20/20 AGGRESSIVE GROWTH FUND $$ ↑ G #/* £ USSC

Manager: Richard Driehaus, since inception (1993)

MER: 2.55%

Richard Driehaus is known as one of the top small-cap stock pickers in the U.S., and it was considered a real coup when 20/20 signed him up for this fund. Initial returns were excellent, but more recent results have been below average for U.S. small-cap entries, although the fund has churned out double-digit profits in the past three years. In the first half of '98, Driehaus was putting the emphasis on consumer cyclicals, seeking to take advantage of the strong U.S. economy and expanding sales, especially in the housing sector. Technology stocks were the other main theme of the portfolio, especially information technology service companies that specialize in fixing Millennium Bug problems. Driehaus is known to be an active trader, so there's a lot of turnover in this portfolio. The latest ATP analysis shows the risk element here is higher than normal, so only investors who can handle volatility should put money here.

20/20 EMERGING MARKETS VALUE FUND $ ↑ G #/* £ EME

Managers: Charles Brandes and Jeff Busby, since 1996

MER: 3.57%

The managers take a value approach to emerging market investing, searching out what they regard as bargain stocks in developing countries. When these markets take off, stocks can shoot up in value overnight, but the opposite is also true, as we have seen recently. Not even the investing acumen of Charles Brandes could stand up to the battering these markets have been taking, and this fund lost 43.8% of its value in the year to June 30/98. And for that investors had to pay a sky-high MER as well! Ouch!

20/20 INDIA FUND $ ↑ G #/* £ FEE

Managers: Asha Waglé and Jay Mitra (Chescor Capital), since inception (1994)

MER: 3.74%

Well now. This fund lost an average of 18% a year over the three years to June 30/98. India has sent shock waves around the world with a series of underground nuclear tests, to which Pakistan responded, setting off fears of an Asian arms race. The U.S. is imposing economic sanctions as are other countries. Private lines of credit are being withdrawn. This is not the kind of scenario that breeds investor confidence, especially in the context of the widespread economic weakness in Asia. Avoid this one.

20/20 LATIN AMERICA FUND $ ↑ G #/* £ AE

Manager: Peter Gruber, since inception (1994)

MER: 3.24%

Peter Gruber is a veteran manager who places big bets on single countries. Not for him the safety of broad diversification; this is very much a roll-the-dice-and-make-it-right kind of style. So in the first half of '98, this fund might more accurately have been named the Brazil Fund, since that's where 75% of the portfolio was concentrated. Unfortunately, the Brazilian stock market was floundering. So whereas a year before happy investors had chuckled all the way to the bank with a huge 67.3% gain, they were in the process of giving back a fair chunk of that money. That's the problem with Latin funds — there is no consistency. One year you're on top of the world, the next you're down the toilet. So if you want to invest here, be prepared for a wild ride. Don't bet the rent and definitely don't put this fund into an RRSP. But if you're looking for a substitute for a trip to Vegas, here it is.

20/20 RSP AGGRESSIVE EQUITY FUND $$ ↑ G #/* RSP CSC

Managers: Bill Anderson and Brendan Kyne, since inception (1993)

MER: 2.45%

As the name suggests, this is an aggressively managed small-cap fund designed for RRSPs. Started off strongly, sagged, and is now recovering. I don't like this type of fund in registered plans because of the above-average risk, so if you have it in an RRSP you may wish to review the situation. Closed to new investors.

AIC GROUP

THE COMPANY

In just a few years, this Hamilton-based firm has rocketed from nowhere to become the talk of the mutual fund world. Its success is grounded in two brilliant strategic moves. One was the decision to focus the portfolio of the original AIC Advantage Fund on shares in the burgeoning mutual funds industry. As the fortunes of companies like Trimark, Investors Group, AGF, C.I., and other publicly traded fund managers zoomed, Advantage Fund investors went along on the dizzying ride.

The other clever strategic move was to base the portfolio of the AIC Value Fund on the investment principles of billionaire Warren Buffett, the so-called oracle of Omaha. This involved investing only in the highest quality businesses in long-term growth sectors and holding them forever. The Value Fund took a large position in Buffett's Berkshire Hathaway company and fleshed that out with purchases of large blocks of shares in many of the core companies Buffett favours: Coca-Cola, Gillette, American Express and the like.

The huge returns generated by both funds as stock markets roared through the mid-'90s captured investor attention and new money rolled in from all directions. The temporary closure of the original AIC Advantage Fund, due to the fact it had reached the legal maximum on many of its key positions, and its replacement by Advantage II (which carries a management expense ratio that's 26 basis points higher) did nothing to stem the cash flow. (Both funds are now open again.) By mid-1998, less than two years after its creation, Advantage II had attracted more than $4 billion in assets.

AIC now has several other funds in its stable, including the relatively new (1994) Diversified Canada Fund, which features a more broadly based portfolio than the Advantage twins. Its three-year returns are almost as good as the original Advantage Fund.

AIC has also tried its hand at international funds. The results are not as spectacular as with its U.S. and Canadian products, but they are respectable nonetheless.

AIC divides its funds into three types:

The Advantage Series: The focus of these funds is financial services companies, although the degree of concentration on that sector has fallen to about 60% in recent years. Nonetheless, the performance of these funds will be tied very closely to financial markets. When they're strong, these funds will do well. When they're weak, the Advantage funds will likely underperform a more diversified portfolio.

The Diversified Series: The portfolios of these funds are more broadly based than those of the Advantage Series. That reduces their potential for explosive returns to some extent, but also cuts the risk in bad markets.

The Income Series: The goal of these funds (Income Equity and American Income Equity) is to focus on tax-efficient, stable monthly cash flow.

Finally, a bit of trivia that some people have asked about: AIC stands for Advantage Investment Counsel, the original name of the company.

THE DETAILS

NUMBER OF FUNDS:	10
ASSETS UNDER MANAGEMENT:	$11 BILLION
LOAD CHARGE:	FRONT: MAX. 6%; BACK: MAX. 6%
SWITCHING CHARGE:	2% MAXIMUM
WHERE SOLD:	ACROSS CANADA
HOW SOLD:	THROUGH LICENSED FINANCIAL ADVISORS
PHONE NUMBER:	1-800-263-2144
WEB SITE ADDRESS:	WWW.AICFUNDS.COM
E-MAIL ADDRESS:	INFO@AICFUNDS.COM

FUND SUMMARY

$$$$ - ADVANTAGE, VALUE
$$$ - DIVERSIFIED CANADA, WORLD EQUITY
$$ - MONEY MARKET
$ - NONE
NR - ADVANTAGE II, AMERICAN ADVANTAGE, AMERICAN INCOME EQUITY, INCOME EQUITY, WORLD ADVANTAGE

BEST CHOICES: ADVANTAGE, VALUE
BEST FOR RRSPs: ADVANTAGE, DIVERSIFIED CANADA
BEST UNRATEDS: ADVANTAGE II

FUND RATINGS

CANADIAN EQUITY FUNDS

AIC ADVANTAGE FUND$$$$ ↑ G #/* RSP CE

Managers: Jonathan Wellum, since 1990; Michael Lee-Chin, since 1987

MER: 2.31%

Wealth management companies of various types (including mutual funds, insurance firms, and brokerages) are the largest segment of this portfolio, representing about 60% of the holdings. But, in a nod towards a degree of diversification, there are other components in the small portfolio (about two dozen stocks) as well, including some media, gold royalty, consumer products, and health care issues, along with shares in Berkshire Hathaway and Coca-Cola as foreign content. It's difficult to believe that the managers can continue to post the high returns they do year after year, but the numbers don't lie. Over the 12 months to June 30/98, this fund added 25.4% to unitholders' value. Granted, that was way down from the incredible gain of 82.9% the year before, but are you really going to complain? Long-term performance is also excellent. The fund was closed to new investors between Sept. 30/96 and Jan. 1/98, but is now open for business again. There's just one point to be aware of with both this fund and the companion Advantage II Fund, which is not rated. Financial services stocks tend to get badly beaten up in market downturns. This fund lost 18.6% in '90 and 12.9% in '94. The ATP analysis shows you have a 23% chance of losing money on this fund in any given year, and a 14% chance of losing more than 10%. However, overall the risk/reward profile of this fund ranks it in the top category according to ATP analysis. The returns are so outstanding that they outweigh the above-average risk in down markets.

AIC DIVERSIFIED CANADA FUND$$$ → G #/* RSP CE

Managers: Jonathan Wellum and Michael Lee-Chin, since inception (1994)

MER: 2.39%

This fund applies the Warren Buffett approach of buying only top-quality companies to the Canadian market. It also offers better industry diversification than the Advantage funds, although it too is top-heavy in financial services (44% of the portfolio in the first half of '98.) That sector has done well and the result has been good gains for investors, with an average annual return of 42.5% for the three years to June 30/98. However, by heavily skewing the portfolio in this way, AIC is negating much of the diversification that was supposed to distinguish this fund from the Advantage funds and give investors an alternative. AIC may want to take a closer look at this situation, because any fund that is so concentrated on a single sector can hardly be called "diversified". This issue hasn't troubled investors so far because of the good performance, but it could emerge as a problem when markets go soft. Don't get me wrong — this is not a bad place for your money, by any means. But it's not what some people may be expecting when they buy in. We'll give this one a debut rating of $$$.

U.S. AND INTERNATIONAL EQUITY FUNDS

AIC VALUE FUND $$$$ ↓ G #/* £ USE

Managers: Neal Murdoch, since 1994 and Michael Lee-Chin, since 1987

MER: 2.44%

This fund, which clones the Warren Buffett style of investing, just keeps rolling along, chalking up great returns in the bull market environment we've experienced in recent years. Advance for the 12 months to June 30/98 was a very good 36.7%, again making it one of the leaders in the U.S. equity fund category. Five-year average annual compound rate of return was 28.1%, best in the peer group. The historical analysis done by Wilfred Vos of Altamira gives this one an A rating on all three counts: performance, risk, and best balance. That's a rare achievement. Over any one-year time frame, there is only a 7% probability of losing money, and the chance of that loss being in excess of 5% is a tiny one percentage point. Over any five-year period, the chance of a loss was nil while you had a 90% chance of gaining more than 15% annually on average. Those are very attractive odds! The combination of a low downside and consistent returns make this one worth a look, especially if you're a Warren Buffett fan. This is a good candidate for the foreign content section of an RRSP. A top-notch entry!

AIC WORLD EQUITY FUND $$$ → G #/* £ IE

Managers: Michael Lee-Chin, since inception (1993), Neal Murdoch, since 1994

MER: 2.70%

This fund marks AIC's attempt to play on a broader stage. Most of the assets are held in non-North American securities, using the same "overweighting in wealth management stocks" strategy that has made the company's other funds so successful. As well, this fund invests in dominant multi-national companies such as adidas (Germany), Nestle (Switzerland), and Cable and Wireless PLC (U.K.). Initial results were weak, although the fund has looked much better over the past two years (it gained 30.4% per year over the two years to June 30/98). I said last year that the rating would be upgraded if results kept improving. They did. It has. AIC's fledgling Emerging Markets fund was merged into this one in mid-'97.

FIXED INCOME AND MONEY MARKET FUNDS

AIC MONEY MARKET FUND $$ → C #/* RSP CMM

Managers: Jonathan Wellum and Michael Lee-Chin, since inception (1994)

MER: 1.00%

This is a run-of-the-mill money fund that invests mainly in commercial paper. It's an okay place to hold cash temporarily, but don't pay any entry or exit fees to buy it.

AIM GT INVESTMENTS

THE COMPANY

On June 1, 1998, the small AIM Funds group (originally the Admax funds) merged with the GT Global funds to form this new enterprise. It looked like a minnow swallows whale story at first glance. The tiny AIM Funds, which few people are familiar with, took over the GT Global operation, absorbing a company that was six times larger in asset terms ($3.1 billion).

The move came as a surprise. GT Global was one of the shooting stars of the Canadian mutual fund firmament, a company that had burgeoned past the $2-billion mark in assets in record time. But that was under the direction of hard-driving Joe Canavan. When he shocked the financial community by stepping down as GT Global president last year, the company was left rudderless. Growth continued, but the spark seemed to be gone.

Meantime, bigger events were transpiring on the international stage, where mergers and acquisitions are running big these days. A London-based company, Invesco PLC, had taken control of a small Canadian fund company, Admax, which was originally founded by Lou Voticky, an ex-Air Canada pilot. Shortly thereafter, Invesco merged with a U.S. mutual fund giant, AIM, which is based in Houston. The Canadian operation took on the AIM name, but not a lot happened beyond that (total assets under management at the time of the merger with GT Global were about $500 million).

AIM and Invesco are controlled by a holding company called Amvescap PLC, which is based in the U.K. Amvescap moved earlier this year to acquire the worldwide assets of GT Global. That purchase had the effect of pulling the two Canadian operations into a single company, to be known as AIM GT Investments. Canada is the only country in which the GT Global name is being retained, at least temporarily — a practical move in light of the fact that it has a much higher brand awareness than AIM has established.

I expect the new organization is going to be a factor to be reckoned with, especially when it comes to international funds. Through its various offshoots, Amvescap now has over $360 billion under management worldwide, making it one of the dozen largest fund companies on the globe. It employs more than 300 money managers and has analysts in 27 offices worldwide, including such out-of-the-way places as Prague.

It will take some time to effect a full merger of the two fund groups (they will all eventually be known as AIM funds). But by the time all is said and done, expect to see a well-integrated operation with a strong Canadian equity side led by Derek Webb from GT, good balanced and fixed-income funds from AIM, and a powerhouse international lineup that will incorporate GT Global's successful specialty funds with some new entries.

The key for investors in the old GT Global funds will be whether there are any managerial changes down the road. Webb is being retained for Canada, and it appears the funds managed out of the San Francisco office of GT will stay the same. Beyond that, it's a matter of wait and see.

THE DETAILS

NUMBER OF FUNDS:	29
ASSETS UNDER MANAGEMENT:	$3.7 BILLION
LOAD CHARGE:	FRONT: MAX. 5%; BACK: MAX. 6%; LOW-LOAD OPTION: 0% FRONT, 2% BACK.
SWITCHING CHARGE:	2% MAXIMUM
WHERE SOLD:	ACROSS CANADA
HOW SOLD:	THROUGH REGISTERED BROKERS, DEALERS, AND FINANCIAL PLANNERS
PHONE NUMBER:	1-800-588-5684
WEB SITE ADDRESS:	WWW.AIMGT.CA
E-MAIL ADDRESS:	FEEDBACK@AIMGT.CA

FUND SUMMARY

$$$$ - NONE
$$$ - AMERICAN PREMIER, CANADA GROWTH, EUROPA, GLOBAL GROWTH & INCOME, GLOBAL HEALTH SCIENCES, GLOBAL TELECOMMUNICATIONS, INTERNATIONAL

$$ - AMERICA GROWTH, CANADIAN BALANCED, CANADIAN
PREMIER, CASH PERFORMANCE, GLOBAL BOND, GLOBAL
INFRASTRUCTURE, GLOBAL RSP INCOME

$ - KOREA, LATIN AMERICA GROWTH, NATURAL RESOURCES,
NIPPON, PACIFIC GROWTH, TIGER

NR - AMERICAN AGGRESSIVE GROWTH, CANADA INCOME,
CANADA VALUE, GLOBAL CANADA MONEY MARKET,
GLOBAL HEALTH CARE, GLOBAL TECHNOLOGY, GLOBAL
THEME, SHORT TERM INCOME "A", SHORT TERM
INCOME "B"

BEST CHOICES: AMERICAN PREMIER, CANADA GROWTH, EUROPA, GLOBAL
GROWTH & INCOME, GLOBAL HEALTH SCIENCES,
INTERNATIONAL

BEST FOR RRSPS: CANADA GROWTH

BEST UNRATEDS: GLOBAL THEME

FUND RATINGS

CANADIAN EQUITY FUNDS

AIM CANADIAN PREMIER FUND $$ → G #/* RSP CE

Managers: Paul Rogge, Clas Olsson, Bob Alley, since 1997

MER: 2.64%

This fund underwent a managerial change in October, '97, after a decision by the company to bring the portfolio responsibility in-house. The managers are with AIM Advisors Inc. and use a bottom-up investment style. The portfolio may invest across the spectrum of small-, medium-, and large-cap stocks. Since the change, the number of stocks held has been increased to provide better diversification and to reduce risk. Resource holdings were reduced, and positions in financial services and industrials increased. Early results show significant improvement in this long-time underperformer. Gain for the six months to June 30/98 was an impressive 18.4%, more than double the average for Canadian equity funds as a group. That performance also helped to pull up the longer term averages to more respectable levels. This looks like a real turnaround situation. Rating moves up to $$ on the strength of this early showing. This fund was previously known as the Admax Canadian Performance Fund.

AIM GT CANADA GROWTH CLASS $$$ → G #/* RSP CE

Manager: Derek Webb, since inception (1994)

MER: 2.47%

This is a growth-oriented fund that invests across the full spectrum of Canadian businesses, as well as offering a foreign content component of at least 15%. Manager Derek Webb has developed his own screen for stock selection and has generally been quite successful. The fund's three-year average annual compound rate of return to June 30/98 was 24%, well above par for diversified Canadian equity funds as a group. The portfolio in the first half of 1998 was heavily weighted towards the financial sector (one-third of assets), otherwise well diversified. A good choice in this group. Originally part of the GT Global Funds.

U.S. AND INTERNATIONAL EQUITY FUNDS

AIM AMERICAN PREMIER FUND $$$ → G #/* £ USE

Managers: Tim Miller, Trent May, since 1996

MER: 2.65%

This fund has gone through so many manifestations that it's hard to keep track. It started as the U.S. Polymetric Performance Fund, using the market timing principles of well-known Canadian newsletter writer and analyst Picton Davies. Unfortunately, it didn't perform well in that guise. After undergoing a couple of name changes (American Growth Fund, American Select Growth Fund), responsibility for the portfolio went in mid-'96 to the Denver-based team of Tim Miller and Trent May, who work for Invesco. Their core focus is on large, high-quality growth companies, such as Microsoft and Pepsico. The results since the management change have been very good, with an average annual compound rate of return of 31.7% for the two years to June 30/98. Rating moves up another notch this year as a result.

AIM EUROPA FUND $$$ → G #/* £ EE

Manager: Steven Chamberlain, since 1996

MER: 2.86%

The previous name of this fund was Admax Europa Performance Fund. It was formerly managed by Hong

Kong-based Regent Pacific, who did a less-than-stellar job with the portfolio. Responsibility now rests in the hands of Invesco's Steven Chamberlain, who is based in London. He uses a top-down country allocation approach, which means identifying those European nations that he expects to out-perform. Specific stock selection is then done on a bottom-up basis. The portfolio emphasis in the first half of '98 was on the U.K., which represented about a third of the assets. Performance has been outstanding under Chamberlain's direction. The fund gained 56.7% in the year ending June 30/98, the best performance of any conventionally managed Europe fund. Another rating increase is the reward.

AIM GLOBAL HEALTH SCIENCES FUND $$$ ↓ G #/* £ SEL

Manager: John Schroer, since 1996

MER: 2.83%

This was one of the first industry sector funds to appear in Canada. The mandate is to invest in the health care indus-try throughout the world, including everything from phar-maceutical manufacturers to nursing homes. This should continue to be a huge growth area as the North American population ages. The fund got off to a quick start, then sagged somewhat following a managerial change in 1996. It now seems to be back on track, however, with a strong 27.9% gain over the year to June 30/98. There are now a number of other competing health funds available, but the latest performance was right up there with the best of them. Safety record to date is quite good for a single indus-try fund. Rating moves to $$$.

AIM GT AMERICA GROWTH CLASS $$ → G #/* £ USE

Manager: Brent Clum, since 1996

MER: 2.86%

This fund was one of the funds that came over to the AIM lineup as a result of the merger with GT Global in mid-1998. It specializes in small- to mid-cap U.S. companies, which are defined as those having a market capitalization of US$5 billion or less. In Canadian terms, a US$5 billion company would be huge, but south of the border it's just a pup. As a result, most of the names in the portfolio will be unfamiliar to a majority of investors, although a few well-known companies make it, such as Hilton Hotels. The portfolio emphasis in the first half of '98 was in the service industry (22% of assets) and technology (21%). Performance has been spotty, although the fund produced a good gain of 32.8% for the year to June 30/98. Longer term results are below average, however. The AIM American Premier Fund has been more consistent recently, although the mandate is somewhat different. It would be the preferred choice at this time.

AIM GT GLOBAL INFRASTRUCTURE CLASS $$ → G #/* £ SEC

Manager: Brian Nelson, since 1997

MER: 2.76%

The mandate of this specialty fund is to invest in companies that design, develop, or provide products and services that are important to a country's infrastructure. This would include transportation companies, telecommunications firms, power companies, construction operations, and the like. The fund invests in both developed and developing countries (e.g., Egypt, Indonesia). This has been the weakest performer among the half-dozen sector funds offered by this group, although you'd still have made money from it. The fund averaged 15.5% annually for the three years to June 30/98, but compared to some of the returns from other sector funds that was small potatoes.

AIM GT GLOBAL NATURAL RESOURCES CLASS $ ↑ G #/* £ SEC

Manager: Derek Webb, since inception (1994)

MER: 2.95%

Natural resources have not been very rewarding for investors in recent years. However, this fund has fared much better than most, with an average annual compound rate of return of 9.1% for the three years to June 30/98. That's because manager Derek Webb has been given a mandate that is more broadly focused than that of most resource funds. He can invest not only in companies that are involved in the exploration and development of natural resources, but also in firms that supply goods and services to such companies. Liberally interpreted, that could be extended to include banks, although there are none of them in the portfolio. There are some chemical companies, however, such as Nova Corp., as well as steel companies (IPSCO) and major integrated oil firms (Petrocan). As far as resource funds are concerned, this one looks better than most. However, I don't think anyone is going to make much money in resource stocks for a while yet, hence the low rating.

AIM GT GLOBAL
TELECOMMUNICATIONS CLASS $$$ → G #/* £ SEC

Manager: Michael Mahoney, since inception (1994)

MER: 2.82%

If you believe that telecommunications is one of the major growth industries of the 21st century, then this is a fund for you. The manager can invest around the world in companies that are involved in the manufacture, sale, or development of telecommunications services or equipment. This mandate opens up the portfolio to both developed countries (55% of the assets are in North America) and emerging nations, such as Russia (3.1% of the portfolio). There are lots of names you'd recognize in the mix (AT&T, Bell International, GTE) and many that will be totally unfamiliar. The result has been a big winner for investors who were in from the start; average annual compound rate of return for the three years to June 30/98 was an impressive 21.2%. However, remember that sector funds may be somewhat more volatile than more broadly based equity funds.

AIM GT LATIN AMERICA GROWTH CLASS $ ↑ G #/* £ AE

Manager: David Manuel, since 1997

MER: 2.86%

If you've been in this fund from the outset, you've done all right, with an average annual compound rate of return of 13.2% for the three years to June 30/98. Now it's time to bail out. Latin American funds went into the tank in the late spring of '98, in what appeared to be a reaction to the Asian contagion. It may take some time for them to recover, so best to stand aside until then. Like most Latin funds, this one is heavily concentrated in Brazil and Mexico, which together made up 70% of the portfolio in the first half of '98. If Mexzil isn't doing well, neither will funds like this.

AIM GT PACIFIC GROWTH CLASS $ ↑ G #/* £ FEE

Manager: Andrew Callender, since 1998

MER: 2.95%

Not even a new manager is going to do this fund any good. The only hope is for recovery in the Asian economies, and that may be some time in coming. The mandate allows the portfolio to hold securities from nations throughout the Far East, including up to 50% in Japanese stocks. However, in the first half of '98, Japan wasn't even represented in the portfolio. Instead, the focus was on Hong Kong, with 35% of the assets, and Australia, with 30%. The major trouble spots of Asia, such as Indonesia and South Korea, weren't in the mix at all. Still, their exclusion wasn't enough to prevent a whopping decline of 48.2% for the year to June 30/98. Stay on the sidelines for now.

AIM INTERNATIONAL FUND $$$ → G #/* £ IE

Manager: Lindsay Davidson, since 1996

MER: 2.76%

This is another fund that was previously run by Hong Kong-based Regent Pacific, and did not do well under their direction. Managerial responsibility was turned over to Invesco's Lindsay Davidson in mid-'96. Perhaps not surprisingly, Davidson, who is Scottish by birth, has switched the focus to value investing, with an emphasis on large-cap stocks. The fund's mandate allows it to invest anywhere in the world, which makes the name a bit misleading (in mutual fund parlance, a fund with the word "international" in the title usually does not invest in its home country or continent). In this case, the largest geographic holding in the portfolio in the first half of '98 was in the U.S. However, investors tend not to quibble about these fine points if the performance is good, and in this case it has been. Average annual return for the two years to June 30/98 (which coincides with Davidson's tenure) was

21.4%, comfortably above average. Also, Davidson's value approach means the fund should be less volatile going forward than it has been in the past. The rating moves up to $$$ on the strength of all this.

AIM KOREA FUND $ ↑ G #/* £ FEE

Manager: Alfred Ho, since 1996

MER: 3.07%

This is Canada's only dedicated Korea fund. Needless to say, its fortunes will reflect those of the South Korean stock market, which has been a disaster zone over the past few years. As you might expect, this fund has been clobbered as a result, and since its mandate is so narrow, there's not much any manager can do but hold on and wait for better times. In the meantime, values are tumbling. This fund dropped a breathtaking 66.2% in the year to June 30/98. If you'd been in for five years, your assets would have fallen by almost 22% annually. This is one of the few funds I've seen that appears to be in danger of going to zero. Look for it to be merged into one of the more broadly based funds in this group before too long.

AIM NIPPON FUND $ ↑ G #/* £ FEE

Managers: James Hegarty and Ritsu Matsushita, since 1996

MER: 3.05%

This is another fund that was previously run by Regent Pacific. It moved to Invesco's Tokyo office in mid-'96. The emphasis is on growth, with large-cap stocks as the mainstay. All Japan funds lost money last year and this one was no exception, dropping 29.5%. If the Japanese stock market ever turns around, this fund will perform well. But that may take some time. Meanwhile, the risk here is higher than average.

AIM TIGER FUND $ ↑ G #/* £ FEE

Managers: Alfred Ho, Sam Lau, Adrian Au, since 1996

MER: 2.96%

This fund specializes in the "Four Tigers" of Asia: Hong Kong, Taiwan, South Korea, and Singapore, and may also hold shares from the "mini-Tigers" (Malaysia, Thailand, the Philippines, and Indonesia), as well as from other Asian markets like Sri Lanka. As with most of the AIM funds, the managerial style is a blend of top-down country allocation and bottom-up growth, with a preference for large-cap stocks. Performance was improving until the Asian economic crisis hit in the fall of '97. Since then, it has been all downhill. The fund lost 55.6% in the year to June 30/98. Stay clear until Asia recovers.

BALANCED FUNDS

AIM CANADIAN BALANCED FUND $$ → G #/* RSP CBAL

Managers: Paul Rogge, Clas Olsson, Bob Alley, since 1997

MER: 2.90%

The new managerial team has only been at the helm a short time but they have already restructured the portfolio. The objective going forward is to maintain a blend of approximately 60% stocks, 40% bonds, with little variation. Equities are selected from the entire universe (no large- or small-cap bias) while the bond segment will be a middle-of-the-road mix of government and corporate issues. Initial results since the changeover have been good; the fund gained 12.2% in the first half of '98. That's very promising. Formerly known as the Admax Asset Allocation Fund.

AIM GT GLOBAL GROWTH & INCOME FUND $$$ → FI/G #/* £ IBAL

Manager: Nick Train, since inception (1994)

MER: 2.87%

This is a great choice for an investor who is looking to add a mix of top-quality international securities to a portfolio. The mandate is to invest in shares of blue-chip companies from around the globe and high-quality government bonds. The result is a portfolio that includes everything from U.S. Treasury notes to shares in companies like Exxon and Cadbury Schweppes. In the first half of '98, the portfolio emphasis was on equities, with bonds and cash accounting for only 35% of the mix. Performance has been extremely good, with returns well above average. Gain for the year to June 30/98 was 26.3%. Recommended.

FIXED INCOME AND MONEY MARKET FUNDS

AIM CASH PERFORMANCE FUND $$ → C #/* RSP CMM

Manager: Karen Dunn Kelley, since 1996

MER: 1.16%

So-so performer that invests mainly in Government of Canada T-bills, with some provincial and corporate notes in the mix as well. Okay if you're already an AIM client and you can get it without any sales commission, otherwise don't bother.

AIM GLOBAL RSP INCOME FUND $$ ↓ FI #/* RSP IB

Manager: Bob Alley, since 1992

MER: 2.27%

The mandate of this fund is to invest in a portfolio of international interest-bearing securities, which may include some dividend-paying equities. However, the portfolio is structured so as to retain full RRSP eligibility. Had been doing quite well, but recent results have slipped a bit, with a 12-month gain of 8.3% to June 30/98. Longer term results are still better than average, however. Good safety record. Formerly known as the Admax World Income Fund.

AIM GT GLOBAL BOND FUND $$ → FI #/* £ IB

Manager: Cheng-Hock Lau, since 1996

MER: 2.45%

This is a true international bond fund with a well-diversified portfolio, including some developing countries issues from nations such as Bulgaria and Croatia. The bulk of the holdings are in highly rated bonds, however, such as U.S. Treasuries and Ginnie Maes. Returns have slipped to below average for the international bond category. Not recommended for RRSPs because it will eat into your precious foreign content. Try the companion Global RSP Income Fund instead.

ALL CANADIAN FUNDS

THE COMPANY

This is a small organization that specializes in value investing, with a focus on fundamentally sound companies whose shares are underpriced or out of favour for some reason. The funds are managed by an investment committee composed of Paul A. Gratton (chairman and CEO of the company), Michael A. Parente (president and CFO), J.C. Stefan Spicer (vice-chairman and chief investment officer), and J.L. Michele Spicer (vice-president, marketing and research).

THE DETAILS

NUMBER OF FUNDS:	4
ASSETS UNDER MANAGEMENT:	$18 MILLION
LOAD CHARGE:	FRONT: MAX. 5%
SWITCHING CHARGE:	2% MAXIMUM
WHERE SOLD:	ONTARIO
HOW SOLD:	DIRECTLY THROUGH THE MANAGER OR THROUGH BROKERS, DEALERS, AND FINANCIAL PLANNERS
PHONE NUMBER:	(905) 648-2025 - J.C. STEFAN SPICER
WEB SITE ADDRESS:	WWW.ALL-CANADIAN.COM
E-MAIL ADDRESS:	S.SPICER@NAS.NET

FUND SUMMARY

$$$$ - NONE
$$$ - NONE
$$ - NONE
$ - CAPITALFUND, COMPOUND FUND, CONSUMERFUND, RESOURCES
NR - NONE
BEST CHOICES: CONSUMERFUND
BEST FOR RRSPS: NONE
BEST UNRATEDS: N/A

FUND RATINGS

CANADIAN EQUITY FUNDS

ALL-CANADIAN CAPITALFUND $ → G # RSP CE

Managers: Committee

MER: 2.00%

The history of this fund dates all the way back to 1954, making it one of the oldest funds in Canada. Unfortunately, it hasn't improved with age. This portfolio has been run very defensively for the past couple of years, with large cash positions (more than 45% entering 1998). That has contributed to the continued below-average performance of the fund. Another negative factor has been the relatively large gold weighting — gold stocks were the largest segment of the equity component of the fund in the first half of '98, and did nothing to contribute to valuations. The net result of all this was a small gain of 4.9% over the 12 months to June 30/98. That was better than the previous year, but still not very good at a time when most Canadian stock funds showed double-digit profits. Longer-term results have also slipped, and are well below the performance of the average Canadian stock fund. This fund doesn't seem to be making much headway. The All-Canadian Compound Fund invests exclusively in units of this fund, and is not active at this time.

ALL-CANADIAN COMPOUND FUND

See entry for All-Canadian CapitalFund.

ALL-CANADIAN CONSUMERFUND $ → G # RSP SEC

Managers: Committee

MER: 2.00%

This is the only fund of its kind in Canada. It focuses on consumer-oriented securities; the small portfolio includes such stocks as Andres Wines, George Weston Ltd., Molson, and the like. The goal of the managers is to seek out undervalued stocks in this sector. Consumer stocks have started to perk up lately, so this fund has recently done better than any other in the group, with a gain of 6.3% for the year to June 30/98. That's still well below the average for Canadian equity funds as a group, however. A 50% cash component entering '98 weighed this one down and for some reason the managers have chosen to add a 4.5% gold weighting as well. I've never seen anyone eating bullion! Had this fund been fully invested in its specialized field, with no gold, it would have done much better. Too much timidity here. One factor this fund has going for it is a good risk profile. Over any three-year period, the chance of losing money is historically zero. Unfortunately, so is the chance of making an average annual profit in excess of 10%.

ALL-CANADIAN RESOURCES CORPORATION $ ↑ G # RSP PM

Managers: Committee

MER: 2.00%

This used to be a broadly based resource fund, but it now concentrates mainly on precious metals, although there are some other types of resource companies in the portfolio (e.g., Imperial Oil). Given the terrible time stocks have endured, it should come as no great surprise to learn that this fund was down an average of 10.3% a year over the three-year period to June 30/98. A lot of retooling is needed here. Formerly called Natural Resources Growth Fund.

ALLSTAR FUND GROUP

THE COMPANY

This is a new Vancouver-based organization that has taken over the former Top Fifty Funds and added a couple of others to the mix as well. The portfolios are directed by American International Group (AIG), an international property and casualty insurance firm that manages assets in excess of US$65 billion.

THE DETAILS

NUMBER OF FUNDS:	4
ASSETS UNDER MANAGEMENT:	$10 MILLION
LOAD CHARGE:	MONEY MARKET - FRONT: MAX. 1.5%
	ALL OTHER FUNDS - FRONT: MAX. 5%
SWITCHING CHARGE:	NONE
WHERE SOLD:	ALBERTA, B.C., MANITOBA, ONTARIO, AND SASKATCHEWAN
HOW SOLD:	THROUGH APPROVED SECURITIES DEALERS
PHONE NUMBER:	(604) 682-6446
WEB SITE ADDRESS:	WWW-MCSL.ALLSTARFUNDS.CA
E-MAIL ADDRESS:	INVEST@ALLSTARFUNDS.CA

FUND SUMMARY

$$$$ - NONE
$$$ - NONE
$$ - AIG CANADIAN EQUITY
$ - ADRIAN DAY GOLD PLUS, MONEY MARKET
NR - AIG ASIAN
BEST CHOICES: AIG CANADIAN EQUITY
BEST FOR RRSPs: AIG CANADIAN EQUITY
BEST UNRATEDS: NONE

FUND RATINGS

CANADIAN EQUITY FUNDS

ALLSTAR AIG CANADIAN EQUITY FUND $$ → G # RSP CE

Manager: Jamie Tucker, since 1995

MER: 2.68%

This is a value-oriented fund, with particular emphasis placed on long-term earnings growth trends, balance sheet strength, and trading liquidity. Performance is improving under the new ownership, although Jamie Tucker actually assumed management responsibility before the transfer was made. The average annual gain of 20.1% for the two years to June 30/98 was above average for the Canadian equity fund category. This could be an interesting turn-around situation to keep an eye on. Another good year will see an upgrade in this rating. Formerly known as the Top 50 Equity Fund.

U.S. AND INTERNATIONAL EQUITY FUNDS

ALLSTAR ADRIAN DAY GOLD PLUS FUND $ ↑ G # £ PM

Manager: Adrian Day, since 1997

MER: 5.28%

This was formerly the Top Fifty U.S. Equity Fund. It has now been transformed into a gold and precious metals fund under the direction of Adrian Day, who is well-known in the U.S. for his newsletter, *Adrian Day's Investment Analyst*. Sadly for investors, the changeover could hardly have come at a worse time, given the recent sagging for-tunes of gold. The fund dropped a whopping 54.2% in value in the year to June 30/98. Day is advising unithold-ers to stick it out, and in the meantime is taking advantage of the weakness in the market to add top-quality compa-nies to the portfolio. But this could be a long slog, and the very high MER doesn't help matters. If you're not in it now, don't be.

FIXED INCOME AND MONEY MARKET FUNDS

ALLSTAR MONEY MARKET FUND $ → C # RSP CMM

Managers: Ian Scott and Tim Coristine, since 1997

MER: 1.15%

This fund was previously known as the Top Fifty T-Bill/Bond Fund. In that guise, its investment mandate was to alternate between Treasury bills and longer term government of Canada bonds. The new name, and the new mandate, only came into operation in 1997. This is now a pure money market fund that holds mainly bankers' acceptances in its portfolio. Maximum front-end load on this one is only 1.5%, but in these days of low interest rates even that is too much. If you can't get it without commission, pass.

ALTAMIRA INVESTMENT SERVICES

THE COMPANY

It has not been a happy time for Altamira. The company, once the darling of the no-load mutual fund set, has lurched from crisis to crisis, losing market share at every step along the way. Think of all the bad things that can happen to a fund company and the chances are Altamira has experienced them. A messy ownership battle. Poor returns on several key funds. The departure of star managers. Problems with securities regulators. Heavy redemptions. For the past two years, it's been nothing but damage control. Things can't get much worse.

And they probably won't. The ownership fight is over, a new CEO is at the helm, and a young, new crop of fund managers is in the process of putting their own stamp on the funds that had been originally built by Frank Mersch, Will Sutherland, Cec Rabin, and friends. It won't be the same Altamira going forward, and the funds may or may not regain the lustre of years past. But the turbulence of recent years should be over. Now it's a case of seeing what the new team is able to accomplish.

THE DETAILS

NUMBER OF FUNDS:	27
ASSETS UNDER MANAGEMENT:	$5.4 BILLION
LOAD CHARGE:	NONE
SWITCHING CHARGE:	NONE
WHERE SOLD:	ACROSS CANADA
HOW SOLD:	DIRECTLY THROUGH THE MANAGER OR THROUGH BROKERS, DEALERS, AND FINANCIAL PLANNERS
PHONE NUMBER:	1-800-263-2824
WEB SITE ADDRESS:	WWW.ALTAMIRA.COM
E-MAIL ADDRESS:	ADVICE@ALTAMIRA.COM

FUND SUMMARY

$$$$ - BOND
$$$ - DIVIDEND, EUROPEAN EQUITY, INCOME, NORTH AMERICAN RECOVERY, SELECT AMERICAN, SPECIAL GROWTH

$$ - Capital Growth, Global Bond, Global Diversified,
Short Term Government Bond, U.S. Larger
Company

$ - AltaFund, Asia Pacific, Balanced, Equity, Global
Discovery, Growth and Income, Japanese
Opportunity, Precious and Strategic Metals,
Resource, Short Term Global Income

NR - Global Small Company, High-Yield Bond, Science and
Technology, Short Term Canadian Income, T-Bill

Best choices: Bond, Dividend, North American Recovery
Best for RRSPs: Bond, Dividend, Income
Best unrateds: Science and Technology, High-Yield Bond

FUND RATINGS

CANADIAN EQUITY FUNDS

ALTAFUND INVESTMENT CORPORATION $ ↑ G No RSP SEC

Manager: David Taylor, since 1995

MER: 2.32%

This Altamira entry is the only fund in the country that
focuses on businesses with a significant presence in
Western Canada. As such, it's strongly oriented to the
resource sector (although not exclusively so) and is there-
fore likely to be more volatile than more broadly based
equity funds. When resource stocks are in favour, this fund
will perform well. When they aren't, watch out — investors
are likely to take a big hit, which is exactly what has hap-
pened recently. In the first half of 1998, almost half the
portfolio was in the resource sector, most of it in oil and gas.
Three guesses what that did to the returns — red ink all
over the place! Even though this isn't a pure resource fund,
you may wish to stay clear of it, at least until conditions start
to improve in the oil patch. Because of the narrow focus of
this fund, the volatility potential is above average.

ALTAMIRA CAPITAL GROWTH FUND $$ → G No RSP CE

Managers: Ian Joseph, since 1994

MER: 2.00%

Altamira offers several Canadian equity funds, so you have to
check carefully to make sure you buy the one that best suits

your goals. This one specializes in blue-chip stocks, with an emphasis on those with high dividend yields. So you'll find a lot of familiar names on the portfolio list: BCE, Thomson Corp., Newbridge, all the big banks, etc. Even though the large-cap segment of the market has performed well, this fund has produced below-average returns over the past three years. The latest results are better, however; gain for the year ending June 30/98 was modestly above the norm at 15.6%. Historical risk level is worse than you might expect for a large-cap fund of this type, although it tends to outperform its peer group in bear markets. Not great, but okay.

ALTAMIRA DIVIDEND FUND $$$ → G/FI No RSP INC

Managers: Ian Joseph, since 1994

MER: 1.56%

This is a pretty good-looking dividend fund, with some decent returns. The portfolio includes high-yielding common stocks (banks, etc.), preferred shares, and some royalty income trusts and REITs. Total returns have been slightly above average for the dividend category, with an average annual compound rate of return of 21.1% for the three years to June 30/98. Cash flow is adequate but not great. Cash on cash yield in 1997 was 2.5%, so don't rely on this fund as your main income generator. Because of the conservative nature of the portfolio, this one is worth considering for your RRSP if you're looking for a relatively low-risk stock fund. One of the better Altamira choices right now. Makes its debut in the *Guide* with a $$$ rating.

ALTAMIRA EQUITY FUND $ → G No RSP CE

Manager: Ian Ainsworth, since 1998

MER: 2.28%

Frank Mersch's sudden departure from this fund and from the Altamira group throws everything here into question. Certainly, the fund has not been doing well in recent years under his direction. But Mersch was a proven stock-picker, and wasn't likely to flounder forever. Now there's a new team in place headed by Ainsworth, who has been running the successful U.S. Larger Company Fund. He is assisted by Sue Coleman, a small-cap specialist, and Shauna Sexsmith, who recently took over the struggling Growth and Income Fund. It will take time for this new team to get its act together, so all we can do is wait and see. Rating is set at $ until some improvement starts to show through.

ALTAMIRA NORTH AMERICAN RECOVERY FUND $$$ → G No RSP CE

Manager: David Taylor, since 1995

MER: 2.30%

This fund went through a rough patch at the end of '97 and into early '98, losing more than 10% of its value in just three months. However, it has since bounced back and is doing better. Over two and three years, this is one of the stronger performers in the Altamira stable and should be seriously considered by anyone who has a portfolio with the company. Manager David Taylor seeks out U.S. and Canadian companies that he feels are undervalued. That hasn't been easy in recent years as stock markets rose to record highs, but Taylor has done a very respectable job with this well-diversified portfolio, which holds stocks ranging from giant corporations like General Motors to tiny, troubled Noble China, a Canadian-based firm that brews Pabst Blue Ribbon beer for the Chinese market. Unfortunately, few Altamira investors have participated in this fund's good gains; it only had about $120 million in assets in mid-'98. Altamira Equity, which hasn't performed anywhere near as well in recent years, was more than 10 times larger!

ALTAMIRA PRECIOUS AND STRATEGIC METAL FUND $ ↑ G No RSP PM

Manager: Craig Porter, since 1998

MER: 2.30%

Oh my! I hope you didn't have any money in this one! All precious metals funds have had it tough and this one didn't escape the carnage, with a loss of 35.6% in the year ending June 30/98. It could have been worse, though. The managers cut back their exposure to gold and added more silver, which did better thanks in part to Warren Buffett's big move on the metal. That helped to propel the fund to a gain of 4.7% in January/98, but by mid-year it was back to its losing ways again. Gold will have its day again (I think), but this probably isn't an area where most investors want to be right now. The exceptions are you folks who like to bottom fish. There's lots of bottom here; I just don't know if we've seen it all yet. Debuts at $. Be careful! This was formerly a Frank Mersch fund but Craig Porter was working with him on it prior to Mersch's sudden departure, so he's not a neophyte.

ALTAMIRA RESOURCE FUND $ ↑ G No RSP SEC

Manager: Craig Porter, since 1998

MER: 2.27%

It's been a bad time for resource funds and this one has suffered along with the rest of them — actually, a little more than the rest since its average losses in recent years have been somewhat worse than the norm. This is one of those rare situations in which even long-term investors are in the red — five-year average annual compound rate of return to June 30/98 was -8.1%. It just goes to show you what a sorry state our resource sector has been in. Resource stocks will come back at some point and when they do the gains will be explosive. It would not surprise me to see this fund gain 40% in one year at that stage. But there's no way of knowing when that will happen. Certainly, as of mid-1998, there was no sign of any comeback in resources on the horizon, with the possible exception of the natural gas sector. So right now this is a fund for gamblers. If you think resources are about to pop, buy some. Otherwise, stand clear. There's a new manager at the helm this year, but Craig Porter was an analyst for this fund for several years prior to assuming the leadership role, so don't expect anything different.

ALTAMIRA SPECIAL GROWTH FUND $$$ ↑ G No RSP CSC

Manager: Susan Coleman, since 1993

MER: 1.80%

This fund specializes in emerging growth companies (capitalization less than $500 million, up from $250 million previously), a tricky and sometimes risky area of investment. Coleman got off to a bad start with a loss of almost 20% in

'94, her first full year at the helm. Things have improved since, however, and the fund has looked much better in recent years with gains somewhat better than average for the small-cap category. As of the first half of '98, the portfolio was well-diversified, with about a fifth of the assets in the industrial products sector, the largest single category. Major holdings included Aber Resources (diamonds in the Northwest Territories), Geac Computer, and Astral Communications (pay TV, movies, etc.). This fund has been looking better and merits a rating increase to $$$. Be aware, though, that there is considerable downside risk. The ATP analysis shows a 17% chance of a loss of more than 10% in any given one-year period, with the worst one-year result being -25.6%. So be prepared to ride out the downturns if you go into this one.

U.S. AND INTERNATIONAL EQUITY FUNDS

ALTAMIRA ASIA PACIFIC FUND $ ↑ G No £ FEE

Manager: Mark Grammer, since 1997

MER: 2.34%

This fund has been through several managerial changes in the past two years. The new boss, Mark Grammer, joined Altamira in December, 1997 with the title of Vice President and Portfolio Manager, International Equities. He's an Asian specialist, but he's really got his work cut out for him here. This fund has a track record that is even worse than most of its competitors, so it's going to be a long slog back. This is one of the few Pacific Rim funds that can invest throughout the entire region, including Japan, and Japanese stocks accounted for almost a quarter of the portfolio in the first half of '98. Performance will improve at some stage, but it may take a while.

ALTAMIRA EUROPEAN EQUITY FUND $$$ → G No £ EE

Manager: Richard Williamson (Banque Pictet), since 1993

MER: 2.32%

Europe has been a happy hunting ground for mutual fund managers in recent years, and this fund has been no exception. It has emerged as one of the bright spots in the

Altamira lineup and if you have an account with that company, it should be on your list. Manager Richard Williamson is with Banque Pictet (Luxembourg). His portfolio is strongly blue chip oriented, sprinkled with world-renowned names like Volkswagen, British Telecom, and Royal Dutch. Results have been steadily improving. Gain for the year to June 30/98 was 40.6%. Three-year record is above average for the European category. Safety record is good, although the fund has only been in existence since 1993 so you can't read too much into that. Rating is upgraded to $$$ on the strength of the good returns.

ALTAMIRA GLOBAL DISCOVERY FUND $ ↑ G No £ EME

Manager: Vincent Fernandez, since 1998

MER: 2.95%

This is Altamira's entry into the emerging markets field and, like most funds in this category, it has struggled since its launch in '94. The good news is that investors who have held on for three years are still modestly in the black, but not by a lot. The current portfolio emphasis is on Latin America, with Mexico and Brazil the heaviest weightings. Other significant holdings are in Malaysia, Portugal (not usually a big player in funds of this type), South Africa (ditto), and Korea. Altamira made a management switch here in April, 1998, bringing the responsibility in-house (it had been with State Street Bank and Trust Company of the U.S.). We'll start it off with a $ rating in its debut in the *Guide* because of the uncertainty in emerging markets and the high risk factor.

ALTAMIRA JAPANESE OPPORTUNITY FUND $ ↑ G No £ FEE

Manager: Mark Grammer, since 1997

MER: 2.37%

Altamira recently named a new manager for this underperforming fund in a bid to turn around its sagging fortunes. It certainly needs help; average annual compound rate of return for the three years to June 30/98 was -5.5%! Granted, it's been a rough period for Japan funds, and some did a lot worse than that. The focus of this fund is on small- to mid-size companies, which means the high risk factor that currently applies to the entire Japanese market is magnified. Perhaps Mark Grammer, who is an Asian specialist, can breathe some life into this one, but the reality is that it all will come down to a turnaround in the Japanese economy. Right now, this is a fund for speculators only.

ALTAMIRA SELECT AMERICAN FUND $$$ → G No £ USSC

Manager: Ken Abrams (Wellington Management), since 1991

MER: 2.28%

This fund specializes in small- to medium-size U.S. companies. That category took it on the chin in the fall as a result of the Far East crisis and a flight to high-quality, large company shares in the U.S. But manager Ken Abrams of Wellington Management managed to weather the storm reasonably well. Despite the setback, the fund ended the 12 months to June 30/98 with a gain of 17.2%. A few U.S. small-cap funds run by competitors are doing much better. Fidelity Small Cap America, for example, was ahead 27.5% over the same time frame. Still, this one hasn't performed badly and the three-year returns are slightly better than average for U.S. small-cap funds as a group according to numbers compiled by *The Financial Post*. We'll leave the rating at $$$ for now and watch for further progress.

ALTAMIRA U.S. LARGER COMPANY FUND $$ → G No £ USE

Manager: Brian Smith, since 1998

MER: 2.30%

Last year I said this large-cap fund should be doing much better. Someone listened because it has since started to live up to its potential, chalking up big gains. However, there is now a new manager at the helm as Ian Ainsworth was promoted to take the lead on the flagship Altamira Equity Fund following the shocking departure of Frank Mersch. The mandate here is to invest in large, well-known, and widely followed U.S. companies. That's exactly the description that best fits the stocks that drove the Dow up and up and up in the mid-'90s. This fund went up too, but, until recently, not to anything like the extent you might have expected, given its focus. Perhaps new manager Brian

Smith can impart more value added. Current portfolio emphasis is on consumer goods and services, and includes names like General Electric, IBM, Gillette, Coca-Cola, and all those other behemoths from south of the border. We'll leave the rating at $$ for now until we can get a handle on how Smith performs.

BALANCED FUNDS

ALTAMIRA BALANCED FUND $ ↑ FI/G No RSP CBAL

Manager: Shauna Sexsmith, since 1997

MER: 2.00%

This began life in '85 as one of the much-publicized Hume funds, managed by a team that included several big names of the day, such as Dr. Morton Shulman and the late Andrew Sarlos. Unfortunately, results didn't live up to expectations and the fund was sold to Altamira Investment Services in '88. Several managers have tried their hand at improving matters without notable success. The latest is Shauna Sexsmith, who assumed responsibility in July, '97. Her initial efforts have been encouraging; the fund gained 11.3% in the year to June 30/98, which was a little above average for the balanced category. Given the change in management, historical results don't count for a lot. It's still too soon to upgrade the rating, given the weak longer term results, but there is promise here. Historical risk rating is poor, but we should see that improve as well. Sexsmith has also assumed responsibility for the Altamira Growth and Income Fund, so it would not be surprising to see a merger announcement at some point in the not-too-distant future.

ALTAMIRA GLOBAL DIVERSIFIED FUND $$ ↑ G No £ IBAL

Managers: Chuck Bastyr, since 1997

MER: 2.00%

Technically, this is supposed to be a balanced fund, investing in a portfolio of stocks, bonds, and short-term securities, so I'm including it in the balanced category. But the portfolio has tended to be weighted heavily toward stocks, so if you're looking for a true international balanced fund, this isn't it, although that may be changing. For years, this was one of the weak links in the Altamira chain. It started to show signs of life a couple of years ago, but has tailed off again. As a result, the team from Wellington Management of Boston that had been running the show since '90 was shown the door and the portfolio responsibility was brought in-house in August, '97. That has resulted in a re-focusing of the investment strategy. Holdings in risky markets like Asia have been cut back. The emphasis is now on quality stocks, especially in the U.S. and Europe. As well, the fund is now starting to look more like a balanced fund, having taken large positions in U.K. government bonds and U.S. T-bills. Results are starting to improve and I have a hunch the new management team may be on the right track. We'll leave the rating at $$ for now, but this could be a candidate for an upgrade next year.

ALTAMIRA GROWTH & INCOME FUND $ ↑ G No RSP CBAL

Manager: Shauna Sexsmith, since 1997

MER: 1.40%

This used to be one of my favourite Altamira funds. For several years it rewarded investors well, but it has fallen on very hard times. Former manager Cec Rabin, who for years ran this as a kind of mother-in-law fund, went off in some strange directions for what traditionally had been a conservatively managed portfolio, adding big holdings in gold and energy. In an effort to turn things around, Altamira brought in Sexsmith in mid-'97 to co-manage. Now she has been handed full responsibility, and Rabin is out. Sexsmith has made some major changes to the portfolio. The gold and energy components have been cut way back and some high-yielding REITs and royalty trusts have been added to the mix. The stock selection is more in line with what you might expect in this type of fund, with lots of banks, utilities, and the like. We're now starting to see some modest improvement in results, but it's like turning an aircraft carrier into the wind. It will take time.

FIXED INCOME AND MONEY MARKET FUNDS

ALTAMIRA BOND FUND $$$$ ↑ FI No RSP CB

Manager: Robert Marcus, since 1991

MER: 1.30%

This has been one of the true bright spots in the Altamira lineup over the past few years. The one-, three-, and five-year returns to mid-'98 were all outstanding, making this the top-performing fund in the Canadian bond category. Marcus brings a more aggressive management style to this fund than you'll find in the companion Altamira Income Fund, which he also now manages following the departure of Will Sutherland. Marcus describes this as a fund for "long-term investors with long-term money" who are prepared to ride out dips in the market, such as the one in 1994 when interest rates suddenly backed up and knocked the stuffing out of bonds. The average duration of Altamira Bond in mid-'98 was 11.2 years. (Duration is a technical measure of the number of years it will take to receive today's present value of a bond in future payments. The longer the duration, the more sensitive a bond portfolio will be to interest rate movements. So a bond fund with a long duration will increase proportionately more in value when interest rates fall, and lose more when rates rise.) As you might expect, all this results in a higher risk factor; historically this fund has a 7% chance of losing money in any given one-year period, and a 30% chance of loss in any given month. It also tends to drop more sharply in bear markets than the average bond fund. Still, there are a lot of Canadian bond funds that are even more risky, without the compensation of superior returns. If you invest with Altamira, this one should definitely be on your list. The $$$$ rating is maintained.

ALTAMIRA GLOBAL BOND FUND $$ → FI No RSP IB

Manager: Robert Marcus, since 1998

MER: 1.81%

This is one of the many international bond funds that is fully eligible for RRSPs/RRIFs. Most of the assets are federal and provincial bonds denominated in foreign currencies, plus issues from such international financial institutions as the World Bank that have also been awarded honourary RRSP status. The performance of international bonds has improved in recent months, in part due to a flight to quality as a result of the financial crisis in Asia. This fund has benefitted accordingly, although longer term results are below average for the international bond category. Following Will Sutherland's departure from Altamira in mid-1998, Robert Marcus assumed overall responsibility for this fund. Rating moves up a notch in recognition of the improved climate for international bonds.

ALTAMIRA INCOME FUND $$$ → FI No RSP CB

Manager: Robert Marcus, since 1998

MER: 1.00%

The surprise departure in mid-'98 of Will Sutherland from this sound performer that he had managed for more than a decade caught investors completely off guard. His replacement, Robert Marcus, has established a great record with Altamira Bond, but this is a very different fund. It is more conservatively managed, focusing on short- to medium-term bonds to limit risk. It's the type of fund that won't blow the lights out in a great bond bull market, but neither will it knock you down and kick you when markets turn sour. Marcus told me immediately after assuming control that he anticipates no problem running the two funds and keeping them completely distinct from one another, however. Each will continue to occupy its own niche, and he has no intention of allowing Altamira Income to change its character. As evidence of this, he cites the fact he had been running Altamira's Pooled Bond Fund for pension clients for two and a half years prior to taking over Altamira Income. Its mandate is virtually the same as that of Altamira Income and both use the Scotia Capital Universe Bond Index as their benchmark. His results with the Pooled Bond Fund over that time were actually better than those achieved by Sutherland with Altamira Income, so this may all work out. I will leave the rating at $$$ for now while we see what happens next.

ALTAMIRA SHORT TERM GLOBAL
INCOME FUND
$ ↑ C No RSP IMM

Manager: Robert Marcus, since 1998

MER: 1.22%

This is one of the new breed of international money funds that invests in a basket of short-term notes denominated in foreign currencies. This makes it fully RRSP eligible. Unlike Canadian and U.S. dollar money market funds, the unit value is not fixed and will fluctuate with exchange rate and interest rate movements. That's why it receives a higher risk rating. For a time, this was the top performing international money market fund in Canada, but returns have slumped lately and it now ranks near the bottom over five years. One of the reasons: a very heavy exposure to the weak Japanese yen in the first quarter of 1998. There is a lot of currency play going on here, and if the manager gets on the wrong side it can cause problems. Robert Marcus assumed overall control for the direction of this fund in mid-'98. Warning: This fund will not be a good place to be if the Canadian dollar stages a major rally.

ALTAMIRA SHORT TERM GOVERNMENT
BOND FUND
$$ ↓ FI No RSP CB

Manager: Frances M. Connelly, since inception (1994)

MER: 1.30%

This is one of those halfway-house funds for investors who want better returns than a money market fund can offer but don't want the risks of a pure bond fund. The manager invests in bonds with a maximum maturity of five years (it used to be three). This policy protects investors from substantial loss in the event of a spike in interest rates. However, you pay a price in the form of lower returns. Just compare this fund's results with those of the Altamira Bond Fund to see what I mean. Return for the 12 months to June 30/98 was just 4.6%. Still, that was a lot better than being in a money market fund. Debut rating is $$.

@RGENTUM MANAGEMENT & RESEARCH CORP.

THE COMPANY

@rgentum is a new fund organization that uses the slogan "Tradition Meets Technology" to describe what it does. The idea is to combine traditional fundamental values with advanced technology to create high-performance investment portfolios through computer selection. Some of the funds are run by outside managers, such as Hillsdale and C.A.S.E. Management. The firm is headed by Fred Pye, a former senior executive with Fidelity. The funds are all too new to be rated.

THE DETAILS

NUMBER OF FUNDS:	7
ASSETS UNDER MANAGEMENT:	$10 MILLION
LOAD CHARGE:	FRONT: MAX. 5%; BACK: MAX. 5.75%
SWITCHING CHARGE:	2% MAXIMUM
WHERE SOLD:	ACROSS CANADA
HOW SOLD:	THROUGH INVESTMENT ADVISORS
PHONE NUMBER:	1-877-274-3688
WEB SITE ADDRESS:	WWW.RGENTUM.COM
E-MAIL ADDRESS:	INFO@RGENTUM.COM

FUND SUMMARY

$$$$ - NONE

$$$ - NONE

$$ - NONE

$ - NONE

NR - CANADIAN EQUITY PORTFOLIO, CANADIAN SMALL COMPANY PORTFOLIO, INCOME PORTFOLIO, INTERNATIONAL MASTER PORTFOLIO, MARKET NEUTRAL PORTFOLIO, SHORT TERM ASSET PORTFOLIO, U.S. MASTER PORTFOLIO

BEST CHOICES: NONE

BEST FOR RRSPS: NONE

BEST UNRATEDS: U.S. MASTER PORTFOLIO

FUND RATINGS

All funds in this group are too new to qualify for a rating.

ARTISAN FUNDS

THE COMPANY

The 15 funds this group offers are actually portfolios of other companies' funds. You'll find funds from such organizations as Fidelity, Dynamic, BPI, C.I. and AGF represented in the various portfolios. So, to illustrate, if you purchase units in the Artisan International Equity Fund, you'll be buying a basket of outside funds that is made up of 40% each in the Fidelity International Portfolio Fund and the Hansberger Value Fund and 10% each in the AGF International Value Fund and the C.I. Emerging Markets Fund.

The weightings in each of the portfolios is determined by the investment counselling firm of Loring Ward, a Winnipeg-based company that was founded in 1987 and which has emerged as a highly innovative firm with a variety of financial products and services.

The Artisan Funds were launched in January, 1998, so all are too new to receive a rating. However, most of the underlying funds in which they invest have been around long enough to qualify, so if you can assess the individual components of each Artisan portfolio on that basis.

THE DETAILS

NUMBER OF FUNDS:	15
ASSETS UNDER MANAGEMENT:	$80 MILLION
LOAD CHARGE:	BACK: MAX. 6%
SWITCHING CHARGE:	N/A
WHERE SOLD:	ACROSS CANADA
HOW SOLD:	THROUGH THE LIMITED DEALER DISTRIBUTION NETWORK
PHONE NUMBER:	1-888-483-0282
WEB SITE ADDRESS:	N/A
E-MAIL ADDRESS:	INFO@LORINGWARD.CA

FUND SUMMARY

$$$$ - NONE
$$$ - NONE
$$ - NONE

$ - NONE

NR - AGGRESSIVE GROWTH, CANADIAN EQUITY, CANADIAN FIXED INCOME, GLOBAL FIXED INCOME, GROWTH, GROWTH & INCOME, INCOME, INTERNATIONAL EQUITY, MAXIMUM GROWTH, RSP AGGRESSIVE GROWTH, RSP GROWTH, RSP GROWTH & INCOME, RSP INCOME, RSP MAXIMUM GROWTH, U.S. EQUITY

BEST CHOICE: N/A
BEST FOR RRSPs: N/A
BEST UNRATEDS: TOO SOON TO JUDGE

FUND RATINGS

The funds in this group have not been in existence for three years, so do not qualify for a rating.

ASSOCIATE INVESTORS GROUP

THE COMPANY

This is an ultra-small organization, offering just one small fund with assets of about $16 million. However, it has the distinction of being the oldest fund in Canada under continuous management (since 1950).

THE DETAILS

NUMBER OF FUNDS:	1
ASSETS UNDER MANAGEMENT:	$16 MILLION
LOAD CHARGE:	NONE
SWITCHING CHARGE:	N/A
WHERE SOLD:	ONTARIO
HOW SOLD:	DIRECTLY THROUGH THE MANAGER OR THROUGH BROKERS, DEALERS, AND FINANCIAL PLANNERS
PHONE NUMBER:	(416) 864-1120 - JACQUELINE FRAZER
WEB SITE ADDRESS:	N/A
E-MAIL ADDRESS:	N/A

FUND SUMMARY

$$$$ - NONE
$$$ - ASSOCIATE INVESTORS
$$ - NONE
$ - NONE
NR - NONE

BEST CHOICE: ASSOCIATE INVESTORS
BEST FOR RRSPs: ASSOCIATE INVESTORS
BEST UNRATEDS: N/A

FUND RATINGS

CANADIAN EQUITY

ASSOCIATE INVESTORS LTD. $$$ ↓ G No RSP CE

Manager: George L. Frazer, since inception (1950)

MER: 1.83%

This venerable fund was a solid if unspectacular performer for many years, then slipped back relative to others in this category for a time. However, it is now back on track, with a vengeance and sports above-average results for all time periods, including an impressive 34.6% gain for the year to June 30/98. The small blue-chip portfolio was heavily oriented to banks and utilities in the first half of '98, two areas that had registered very strong results. The fact that the portfolio held virtually no resource stocks also helped performance. Note that a redemption fee of 1% applies when units are cashed within 90 days of purchase, otherwise there are no load charges. Not many people know about this one, but it's a worthwhile entry for conservative investors. It is one of the few funds to receive a AAA rating (for risk, reward, and balance) from Wilfred Vos's ATP analysis.

ATLAS FUNDS

THE COMPANY

This is the in-house fund group of brokerage firm Merrill Lynch. It has undergone a lot of changes in the past year, including the merger of the Atlas and Hercules fund groups, the merger of a number of funds, and the launch of several new ones. From your point of view, as an investor, one of the key things to understand before you place any money here is the commission structure, which is unlike any other in the industry. Basically, you have three options when you buy an Atlas fund: no-load, front-end load and deferred sales charge. The no-load choice is exactly that, no strings attached. The maximum front-end load is 5%. The deferred sales charge (back-end load) will result in a sales commission of up to 5.5% if you sell within six years of purchasing the units (although you're allowed to redeem 10% of your holdings each year without charge). So, you may ask, why would anyone choose the front-end load or the deferred sales option? The simple answer is, they shouldn't — as long as they know the no-load choice exists. Your financial advisor should tell you that. However, you should be aware that the sales person will receive a much larger up-front commission if you invest through the front or back-end load option. That might conceivably influence a purchase recommendation in some cases. So be alert. If you invest in Atlas (and many more people are) think no-load!

THE DETAILS

NUMBER OF FUNDS:	24
ASSETS UNDER MANAGEMENT:	$2.8 BILLION
LOAD CHARGE:	BACK: MAX. 5.5%, NO-LOAD OPTION AVAILABLE
SWITCHING CHARGE:	0-2% FOR FUNDS PURCHASED WITH THE FRONT-LOAD OPTION; OTHERWISE NO SWITCHING FEES APPLY
WHERE SOLD:	ACROSS CANADA
HOW SOLD:	THROUGH AUTHORIZED FINANCIAL ADVISORS
PHONE NUMBER:	1-800-463-2857
WEB SITE ADDRESS:	WWW.ATLASFUNDS.CA
E-MAIL ADDRESS:	ATLAS.FUNDS@ATLASFUNDS.CA

FUND SUMMARY

$$$$ - NONE

$$$ - AMERICAN LARGE CAP GROWTH, AMERICAN MONEY MARKET, CANADIAN BALANCED, CANADIAN HIGH YIELD BOND, CANADIAN LARGE CAP GROWTH, CANADIAN MONEY MARKET, EUROPEAN VALUE

$$ - AMERICAN ADVANTAGE VALUE, CANADIAN BOND, CANADIAN LARGE CAP VALUE, CANADIAN SMALL CAP VALUE, CANADIAN T-BILL, WORLD BOND

$ - CANADIAN EMERGING GROWTH, GLOBAL VALUE, LATIN AMERICAN VALUE, PACIFIC BASIN VALUE

NR - AMERICAN RSP INDEX, CANADIAN DIVIDEND GROWTH, CANADIAN INCOME TRUST, CANADIAN SMALL CAP GROWTH, INTERNATIONAL EMERGING MARKETS GROWTH, INTERNATIONAL LARGE CAP GROWTH, INTERNATIONAL RSP INDEX

BEST CHOICES: AMERICAN LARGE CAP GROWTH, CANADIAN BALANCED, CANADIAN LARGE CAP GROWTH

BEST FOR RRSPs: CANADIAN BALANCED, CANADIAN LARGE CAP GROWTH

BEST UNRATEDS: AMERICAN RSP INDEX, CANADIAN DIVIDEND GROWTH

FUND RATINGS

CANADIAN EQUITY FUNDS

ATLAS CANADIAN EMERGING GROWTH FUND $ ↑ G #/*/No RSP CSC

Manager: Wayne Deans (Deans, Knight) since inception (1994)

MER: 2.46%

This fund features an emphasis on small- to mid-size companies (market capitalization under $350 million) and the name of Wayne Deans who at one point was the hottest fund manager in Canada. At that time, investors were so keen to put their money here that Atlas had to close the fund for more than a year, re-opening it only in November, 1997. But those heady days are over. Like many other hot managers before him, Deans has been in something of a slump recently and the performance of this fund reflects that. It dropped a whopping 22.1% in value over the 12 months to June 30/98 at a time when most other Canadian small-cap funds were producing good results. You **may** want to stay away from this one until there is evidence **that** Deans has recovered his golden touch.

ATLAS CANADIAN LARGE CAP GROWTH FUND $$$ → G #/*/No RSP CE

Manager: Fred Pynn (Bissett & Associates), since 1994

MER: 2.57%

This fund was an underachiever in previous manifestations but it has been doing well since managerial responsibility was handed over to the small but well-respected Calgary firm of Bissett and Associates. The mandate is to invest in medium to large companies (market cap of $350 million plus) with good growth potential. Manager **Fred** Pynn is a bottom-up stock picker who focuses on fundamentals and good value. Recent portfolio holdings included companies like Northern Telecom, Geac, Magna, and several banks, as well as a large position in TIPs, so this is a fund for blue-chip lovers. Results continue to be very **good** and this has been the strongest performer among the **five** Atlas Canadian stock funds over the past three years **by a** wide margin. If you invest in the Atlas family, this **should** be your first choice among Canadian equity funds. This is an excellent way for people who don't have enough cash **to** invest in the Bissett funds directly (they have a $10,000 minimum) to obtain their management expertise at a bargain price.

ATLAS CANADIAN LARGE CAP VALUE FUND $$ → G #/*/No RSP CE

Manager: Terry Bacinello (Bonavista Asset Management) since 1998

MER: 2.57%

The latest trend in the fund industry is to offer investors choices based on management style. This and the companion Atlas Canadian Large Cap Growth Fund are examples. Both focus on mid- to large-cap stocks but in the case of this fund the selection is made on the basis of valuations. The managers look for companies that are cheap by market standards. Some of his holdings as of Spring 1998 included the banks, Northern Telecom, and BCE Inc., all stocks that had already experienced a good run. This fund got off to a slow start, and performance has lagged well behind that of the Growth Fund. Atlas is hoping that Bacinello, who took over responsibility for the portfolio at the beginning of 1998 from RT Capital Management, can breathe some life into this one. Until that happens, keep your money with Fred Pynn in the Growth Fund.

ATLAS CANADIAN SMALL CAP VALUE FUND $$ → G #/*/No RSP CSC

Manager: Terry Bacinello (Bonavista Asset Management), since 1998

MER: 2.57%

Atlas offers three Canadian small-cap entries: this one, the Atlas Small Cap Growth Fund, and the Atlas Canadian Emerging Growth Fund. All are relatively young (the Growth Fund hasn't been around long enough to earn a rating), and three funds of similar type strikes me as overkill. This one uses a value investing approach to selecting small-cap stocks, a style that I consider questionable in view of the fact that small-cap companies are typically growth plays. Results have been okay but not great. Bacinello is new at this portfolio, having taken over only at the start of 1998 from RT Capital Management. We'll start it off with a $$ rating in its debut, while we wait to see which of these three small-cap funds emerges as the best bet.

U.S. AND INTERNATIONAL EQUITY FUNDS

ATLAS AMERICAN ADVANTAGE VALUE FUND $$ ↓ G #/*/No £ USE

Manager: Richard Glasebrook (Opcap Advisors), since inception (1994)

MER: 2.54%

This fund invests only in BIG companies — those with a market capitalization of US$1 billion and up. The emphasis is on firms with a long earnings history and relatively low risk, so this fund is suited to more conservative equity investors. The portfolio is loaded with stocks you're almost sure to recognize, such as Time Warner, Du Pont, 3M, and Lockheed. Manager Richard Glasebrook is an award-winner money man who runs the successful Oppenheimer Opportunity Value Fund in the United States. He uses a bottom-up approach to stock selection, choosing companies on the basis of fundamental value. Results have been good but not sensational, given the strength of the U.S. market in recent years. Some fund reporting organizations class this as a balanced fund, which makes the performance look better in relative terms. But it's really an equity fund, and as such it has been just so-so.

ATLAS AMERICAN LARGE CAP GROWTH FUND $$$ → G #/*/No £ USE

Manager: Len Racioppo, since inception (1985)

MER: 2.57%

This fund was created in '85 as the Jarislowsky Finsco American Equity Fund. The name was changed in July, '94 when the Atlas group was created and modified again recently to reflect the large-cap orientation of the fund. Management is still in the hands of the well-known Montreal firm of Jarislowsky Fraser, with president Len Racioppo calling the shots. As the name suggests, the portfolio emphasis is on larger U.S. companies; portfolio in the first half of '98 included holdings such as Disney, Exxon, Xerox, and Johnson & Johnson. Big corporate America wasn't a bad place to be in recent years, as the Dow was hitting new records and this fund rewarded its investors accordingly with above-average returns. If you have an Atlas portfolio, this fund should definitely be part of it.

ATLAS EUROPEAN VALUE FUND $$$ → G #/*/No £ EE

Manager: Stephen Burrows (Pictet International) since 1998

MER: 2.71%

The goal of this fund is to search out large European companies that are out of favour with investors for whatever reason. As of the first half of '98, the portfolio was heavily weighted toward the U.K. (about 28%), with Germany, Switzerland, and France the next largest holdings. Interestingly enough,

6.5% of the holdings were in Canada, which wasn't part of Europe the last time I looked. Pictet International, which is based in Geneva, has been managing this fund since it was launched in 1993, but portfolio responsibility recently passed to new hands in the person of senior investment manager, European equities, Stephen Burrows. He has specialized knowledge of some of the often overlooked European markets, such as Austria, Spain, and Scandinavia. Returns have been above average for this fund category, and the fund enjoyed an especially good year over the 12 months to June 30/98 with a gain of 38.4%. A good choice. Formerly known as the Hercules European Value Fund.

ATLAS GLOBAL VALUE FUND $ → G #/*/No £ IE

Manager: Roy Gillson (IAI International), since inception (1990)

MER: 2.75%

The mandate of this fund is to invest in undervalued companies throughout the world, using a bottom-up value selection approach. Although the fund is international in scope, the portfolio was heavily weighted to the U.S. in the first half of '98, with a 45.7% asset allocation. No other country had more than 10.9% (France). This big tilt to the U.S. might lead you to believe that the fund would be generating above-average returns for its category on the strength of the U.S. markets. But that has not been the case. Although it has made money for investors in recent years, returns tend to be on the weak side compared to similar funds offered by competitors. This is not one of the better performers in the Atlas group. Give it a pass. Previously known as the Atlas Global Equity Fund.

ATLAS LATIN AMERICAN VALUE FUND $ ↑G #/*/No £ AE

Managers: Mark Haet (Bankers Trust), since 1997

MER: 2.95%

The emphasis here is on large, undervalued companies, with telecommunications firms and utilities prominent in the portfolio. Brazil and Mexico were the dominant nations by far in the first half of '98, accounting for more than three quarters of the total assets between them. Latin American funds as a group did well in 1996 and 1997, and this one was no exception. However, the markets in that part of the world started to soften in the first half of '98, partially in response to the continuing Far East crisis. If you made some profits here, it may be time to reduce your exposure. Rating is being cut back to $. Formerly the Hercules Latin American Value Fund.

ATLAS PACIFIC BASIN VALUE FUND $ ↑ G #/*/No £ FEE

Manager: William E. Dodge (Marvin & Palmer), since 1997

MER: 2.90%

William Dodge is a well-known stock picker who took over this moribund fund in March, '97 after it had floundered under the direction of Edinburgh Fund Managers PLC. Not even his skills have been able to make it profitable in the face of the free fall in the Far East; however, losses here over the past year have been much less than those incurred by many of the competitors. The portfolio is well diversified and many of the top 10 holdings are blue-chip companies (Fuji, Sony). But Asia is going to be turbulent for a while yet, so hold off for now. Formerly the Hercules Pacific Basin Value Fund.

BALANCED FUNDS

ATLAS CANADIAN
BALANCED FUND $$$ ↓ FI/G #/*/No RSP CBAL

Manager: Len Racioppo, since inception (1984)

MER: 2.21%

This one started life in '84 as the Jarislowsky Finsco Balanced Fund. The name was changed in July, '94; however, the Montreal-based investment firm of Jarislowsky Fraser continues to run the show, under the direction of the firm's president, Len Racioppo. The solid portfolio of blue-chip stocks and high-quality bonds has produced good results for investors in recent years. In the first half of '98, the portfolio was about 50% in stocks, including a U.S. equity position of 20%, thus maximizing foreign content. The balance was in bonds and cash. The fund's one-, three-, and five-year rates of return are comfortably above average for this category. Excellent safety rating for the balanced fund category. If you are only buying one Atlas fund, this would be the best choice because of its excellent diversification. The Atlas Canadian Diversified Fund was merged into this one in October, '96.

FIXED INCOME AND MONEY MARKET FUNDS

ATLAS AMERICAN MONEY MARKET FUND $$$ → C #/*/No £ IMM

Manager: Salomon Brothers Asset Management, since 1994

MER: 1.16%

A good performer in the U.S. money fund category, and a respectable choice if you want to diversify out of the Canadian dollar during down periods such as we experienced in the latter half of '97 and the first half of '98. But when the loonie is on the rise (and it will happen), you don't want to have a lot of your money in this one. Warning: Do not buy this or any other Atlas money market fund under the front- or back-end load options. Any commission is too high in these times of low yields. Choose the no-load option only. Name changed from Finsco U.S. Dollar Money Market Fund in July, '94.

ATLAS CANADIAN BOND FUND $$ ↓ FI #/*/No RSP CB

Manager: Jacob Greydanus (Greydanus Boeckh), since 1994

MER: 1.97%

The management style here is cautious, with a focus on short- to medium-term government and corporate bonds. As of Spring '98, the portfolio was positioned defensively, with no long-term bonds in the mix. This means reduced risk if the bond market should take a tumble. This is not a particularly exciting fund but it offers a decent fixed-income option if you're already investing in this group. It started out as the AMD Fixed Income Fund, became the Finsco Bond Fund, and evolved to the Jarislowsky Finsco Bond Fund before assuming its current name.

ATLAS CANADIAN HIGH
YIELD BOND FUND $$$ ↑ FI #/*/No RSP CB

Manager: Doug Knight (Deans, Knight), since inception (1994)

MER: 1.89%

If you're looking for above-average income from a bond fund in these times of low interest rates, this fund is worth considering. It invests in debt issued by large companies with a relatively low credit rating (B or less). Some of the big names that fall into that category may surprise you: real estate giant TrizecHahn, paper-makers Avenor and Domtar, funeral home operator Loewen Group, and communications companies like Rogers Cantel and Call-Net. Returns have been above average for the bond fund category. However, the nature of the portfolio is such that if the economy went into a slump, there might be a risk of default in some of the holdings. That doesn't appear to be a near-term concern, but if you put any money here keep the possibility in mind for the future.

ATLAS CANADIAN MONEY
MARKET FUND $$$ → C #/*/No RSP CMM

Managers: Salomon Asset Management, since 1994

MER: 1.11%

This is a middle-of-the-road money fund, with decent performance record. The portfolio is almost entirely in corporate notes, with a small percentage of T-bills and short-term bonds. Returns have been much better than those of the companion Canadian T-Bill Fund, so choose this one if you want a money fund from Atlas. Choose the no-load purchase option only. Name changed from Finsco Canadian Money Market Fund in July, '94, at the time management responsibilities were handed to the well-known international house of Salomon Brothers.

ATLAS CANADIAN T-BILL FUND $$ ↓ C #/*/No RSP CMM

Managers: Newcastle Capital Management, since 1997

MER: 1.29%

Brother to the Atlas Canadian Money Market Fund, but with a different manager. The only significant difference is that this one invests primarily in Government of Canada Treasury bills, for slightly better safety. Returns tend to be lower than for the Money Market Fund, in part due to a higher expense ratio. You'll have to decide if the extra safety is worth the reduced return; personally, I'd go for the higher yield.

ATLAS WORLD BOND FUND $$ ↓ FI #/*/No RSP IB

Manager: David Scott (Salomon Brothers), since inception (1993)

MER: 2.06%

This is a 100% RRSP-eligible international bond fund, run by the world-renowned house of Salomon Brothers. Three-year returns are better than average for this category, although more recent results have been weak. Reason: In the first half of '98, the portfolio was 91% exposed to the Canadian dollar, which was sliding against U.S. currency. Formerly the Hercules World Bond Fund. The Hercules Global Short-Term Fund and Emerging Markets Debt Fund were merged into this one in October, '96.

AZURA GROUP

THE COMPANY

A new mutual funds group based in Quebec City. Its six funds are all called "pooled funds" but they are actually open to individual investors as well as to group plans. Minimum investment is $5,000. They are only available in Quebec, and all are too new to qualify for a formal rating.

THE DETAILS

NUMBER OF FUNDS:	6
ASSETS UNDER MANAGEMENT:	$153 MILLION
LOAD CHARGE:	NONE
SWITCHING CHARGE:	NONE
WHERE SOLD:	QUEBEC ONLY
HOW SOLD:	THROUGH REGISTERED BROKERS, DEALERS, AND FINANCIAL PLANNERS
PHONE NUMBER:	(418) 624-3000 OR 1-800-231-6539
WEB SITE ADDRESS:	WWW.AZURA.CA
E-MAIL ADDRESS:	CJACQUES@AZURA.CA

FUND SUMMARY

$$$$ - NONE
$$$ - NONE
$$ - NONE
$ - NONE
NR - AGGRESSIVE GROWTH RSP, BALANCED, BALANCED RSP, CONSERVATIVE, GROWTH, GROWTH RSP

BEST CHOICES: N/A
BEST FOR RRSPS: N/A
BEST UNRATEDS: GROWTH

FUND RATINGS

No funds have been in existence for the three years required to be rated.

BANK OF MONTREAL (FIRST CANADIAN FUNDS)

THE COMPANY

The Bank of Montreal got a relatively late start in modernizing its mutual fund lineup, but it has been coming on strong over the past few years with an aggressive expansion strategy that has involved the creation of many new funds. Their U.S. entries are worth a special look. Most of the managerial chores for the domestic funds are now in the hands of Jones Heward Investment Counsel, which is owned by the Bank.

THE DETAILS

NUMBER OF FUNDS:	25
ASSETS UNDER MANAGEMENT:	$9 BILLION
LOAD CHARGE:	NONE
SWITCHING CHARGE:	NONE
WHERE SOLD:	ACROSS CANADA
HOW SOLD:	THROUGH ANY BANK OF MONTREAL BRANCH, NESBITT BURNS, FIRST CANADIAN FUNDS CALL CENTRE, OR THROUGH INVESTORLINE.
PHONE NUMBER:	1-800-665-7700 1-888-636-6376 (QUEBEC) (416) 956-2271 (TORONTO)
WEB SITE ADDRESS:	WWW.BMO.COM/FCFUNDS/ (ENGLISH) OR WWW.BMO.COM/FONDSM/ (FRENCH)
E-MAIL ADDRESS:	FCFUNDS@BMO.COM (ENGLISH) OR FONDSM@BMO.COM (FRENCH)

FUND SUMMARY

$$$$ - NONE

$$$ - DIVIDEND INCOME, GROWTH, MORTGAGE, NAFTA ADVANTAGE, SPECIAL GROWTH, U.S. GROWTH

$$ - BOND, EQUITY INDEX, EUROPEAN GROWTH, MONEY MARKET, T-BILL

$ - ASSET ALLOCATION, EMERGING MARKETS, FAR EAST GROWTH, INTERNATIONAL BOND, INTERNATIONAL GROWTH, JAPANESE GROWTH, RESOURCE

NR - GLOBAL SCIENCE AND TECHNOLOGY, LATIN AMERICAN
GROWTH, PRECIOUS METALS, PREMIUM MONEY MARKET,
U.S. DOLLAR BOND, U.S. DOLLAR EQUITY INDEX, U.S.
DOLLAR MONEY MARKET, U.S. EQUITY INDEX RSP,
U.S. SPECIAL GROWTH, U.S. VALUE

BEST CHOICES: GROWTH, SPECIAL GROWTH, U.S. GROWTH
BEST FOR RRSPs: DIVIDEND INCOME, MORTGAGE
BEST UNRATEDS: GLOBAL SCIENCE & TECHNOLOGY, U.S. VALUE

FUND RATINGS

CANADIAN EQUITY FUNDS

FIRST CANADIAN DIVIDEND INCOME FUND $$$ → G/FI No RSP INC

Manager: Michael Stanley (Jones Heward), since inception (1994)

MER: 1.64%

This is a first-rate choice for conservative investors seeking modest income flow. The fund invests primarily in blue-chip, dividend-paying common stocks such as banks, pipelines, and telecoms. The overall returns have been very good, as large-cap stocks have flourished in recent years. However, if your priority is steady income, this isn't the best place for your money. Cash return during 1997 was just 2.2%, according to a survey we did for the *Mutual Funds Update* newsletter. This fund is better suited as a low-risk equity holding in an RRSP.

FIRST CANADIAN EQUITY INDEX FUND $$ → G No RSP CE

Manager: Krista Clairmont (Jones Heward), since 1996

MER: 1.28%

Many of the First Canadian funds have experienced managerial changes in the past couple of years, as more of the portfolio responsibility has been shifted to wholly owned subsidiary Jones Heward Investment Counsel. This is one of the funds affected, although the impact of a managerial change should be minimal since the portfolio is designed to emulate the performance of the TSE 300 Index. As the index goes, so goes the fund. The manager only makes sure appropriate changes are made to reflect switches in the stocks that make up the Index. Since the TSE has been doing well in recent years, so has this fund. In fact, recent returns are better than average for Canadian equity funds as a group, which tells you that a majority of fund managers are not able to keep pace with hot markets. Generally, though, a fund managed by a good stock picker is a better bet — as demonstrated by the companion Canadian Growth Fund, which has produced better results over the past couple of years. Because this is an index fund, risk will mirror that of the TSE as a whole. Despite the good recent numbers, the $$ rating is maintained because (a) the fund is highly vulnerable in market corrections and (b) a good manager should be able to outperform an index fund.

FIRST CANADIAN GROWTH FUND $$$ → G No RSP CE

Manager: Michael Stanley (Jones Heward), since 1994

MER: 2.20%

The mandate of this fund is to invest in a limited portfolio (40–50 stocks) of high-growth potential Canadian companies. Results have been very good so far, with returns running above average for the Canadian equity category. The portfolio is well diversified with a lot of blue-chip companies and a strong weighting to the financial sector. Good safety rating. This is a strong candidate for your portfolio if you're a Bank of Montreal client.

FIRST CANADIAN RESOURCE FUND $ ↑ G No RSP SEC

Manager: Michael Stanley (Jones Heward), since 1998

MER: 2.22%

As you would expect from the name, the mandate here is to invest in Canada's natural resource sector. This is not one of your roll-the-dice equity funds, however; the management team at Jones Heward (a BofM subsidiary) places heavy emphasis on the blue-chip companies of this sector, such as Alcan, Noranda, and Inco. So the risk factor isn't quite as high as in some other resource funds that focus on junior companies. That said, no resource funds have done well recently and this one has taken a pounding along with all the rest. For very aggressive investors only who believe resource stocks are about to turn around. Note there was a managerial change in early '98, the second in two years, although Jones Heward is still in charge.

FIRST CANADIAN SPECIAL
GROWTH FUND $$$ → G No RSP CE

Manager: James Lawson (Jones Heward), since 1995

MER: 2.16%

This entry began slowly but has looked much better lately. In this case, the mandate is growth through investments in small- to medium-sized companies. As with many of the First Canadian funds, BofM-owned Jones Heward Investment Counsel runs the show. Their management style here is less risk-prone than in some of the more aggressive small-cap entries you can find. The returns have been impressive over the past few years; in a tough market for small-cap stocks this fund managed an average annual gain of better than 18.5% for the three years to June 30/98. A good choice for Bank of Montreal clients who want a more aggressive fund with strong growth potential for their account, and who are willing to accept more risk to achieve that goal.

U.S. AND INTERNATIONAL EQUITY FUNDS

FIRST CANADIAN EMERGING
MARKETS FUND $ ↑ G No £ EME

Manager: Richard Muckart (Edinburgh Fund Managers), since inception (1994)

MER: 2.10%

As emerging markets funds go, this one has a very low MER. It also has lost less money over the past three years than many of its competitors. There it is. That's the good news. The bad news is that, like most funds of this type, it has taken a beating and the bleeding still hadn't stopped through the first half of '98. The portfolio is reasonably balanced, with an emphasis on Latin America recently. But with investors fleeing to the quality of Wall Street and Europe, there really hasn't been anywhere for a manager to go to escape the pressure on developing countries. This one is strictly for bottom feeders.

FIRST CANADIAN EUROPEAN GROWTH FUND $$ → G No £ EE

Manager: Sharon Fay (Sanford C. Bernstein), since 1998

MER: 2.13%

This has been a decent performer, with a gain of 35.1% for the year to June 30/98 and an average annual compound rate of return of 22.8% over the past three years. However, that wasn't good enough to save the managerial job for Edinburgh Fund Manager PLC, who were dumped by the Bank of Montreal in January, 1998. Although the returns look impressive, they were below average for the European fund category and that appears to have been enough to pull the trigger. The fund's main focus is on large western European companies. Relatively low MER is an advantage. Best suited for Bank of Montreal clients who want to add European exposure to their First Canadian funds portfolio. However, this wouldn't be one of my top choices in the category, at least until such time as we get a better handle on the new management.

FIRST CANADIAN FAR EAST GROWTH FUND $ ↑ G No £ FEE

Manager: Patrick Cunningham (Edinburgh Fund Managers), since 1994

MER: 2.25%

There are worse Far East funds out there. That's about as much as I can say about a fund that has lost more than 40% in the past year. The mandate is to invest throughout Asia and Australasia, with the exception of Japan. Given the travails in the Far East, it may come as no surprise that more than a third of the portfolio was concentrated in Australia and New Zealand in the first half of '98. Hong Kong was the other major holding, at about 25%, with Singapore weighing in at 17%. That's about as low-risk a portfolio as you are likely to find in a Far East fund, but the reality is that nothing good will happen until an economic recovery sets in.

FIRST CANADIAN INTERNATIONAL GROWTH FUND $ → G No £ IE

Manager: Ian Rattray (Edinburgh Fund Managers), since 1992

MER: 2.00%

This fund invests in non-North American stocks of top-quality companies with good growth potential. Japan, which many managers see as a country full of bargains, has had a heavy weighting in the portfolio for the past few years. However, that market continued to languish through the first half of '98 and so did this fund. Returns haven't been terrible, by any means. But many international funds have done much better. Not one of the leading choices in this fund group.

FIRST CANADIAN JAPANESE GROWTH FUND $ ↑ G No £ FEE

Manager: Masata DeGaura (J.P. Morgan), since 1998

MER: 2.08%

The Bank of Montreal recently announced a managerial change for this underperforming fund. Investors hope the J.P. Morgan organization can do the job, because many other Japanese funds have managed to do much better over the past three years. This fund has suffered an average annual compound loss of 13.3% for the three years to June 30/98. By comparison, AGF Japan Class has managed to gain 1.4% per year during that time. The fund was still losing ground in the first half of '98, after the managerial switch, but the losses were not as bad as those incurred by some of the competition. Still, my advice is to steer clear of this one until there is evidence that Japan is back on track and that the new manager is able to consistently outperform the other funds in the peer group.

FIRST CANADIAN NAFTA ADVANTAGE FUND $$$ → G No £ AE

Managers: Jones Heward, Harris Investment, Grupo Bancomer, since inception (1994)

MER: 1.97%

As the name implies, this fund is designed to allow investors to participate in the growth of the NAFTA countries (Canada, Mexico, and the U.S.). The stocks are chosen on the basis of a company's ability to benefit from the North American Free Trade Agreement, and at least 20% of the assets will always be invested in each of the three countries. Results so far have been good if you measure them by international equity fund standards (some fund databases class this as a U.S. equity fund, which produces an unfair comparison). The risk factor here will be higher than in a pure U.S. or Canadian fund, because of the more volatile Mexican component, so keep that in mind when making your investment decision.

FIRST CANADIAN U.S. GROWTH FUND $$$ → G No £ USE

Manager: Donald Coxe (Harris Investment Management), since 1997

MER: 2.20%

You may be familiar with Donald Coxe, who took over this fund in '97, through his columns in *The Globe and Mail*. They're always on my must-read list — informative, sometimes witty, always insightful. So I'm delighted to be able to upgrade the rating on this fund based on its excellent performance since Coxe assumed control. As I said last year, anyone who can write that well has to be a good manager! The mandate here is to invest in large-cap U.S. companies, so you'll find a lot of familiar names in the lineup, from the trendy (Lucent Technologies) to the tried and true (Quaker Oats). Portfolio diversification is excellent, with financial services, technology stocks, and consumer goods heading the list in the first half of '98. This is a very good choice for investors seeking a position in blue-chip U.S. stocks.

BALANCED FUNDS

FIRST CANADIAN ASSET ALLOCATION FUND $ → FI/G No RSP CBAL

Manager: Jones Heward Investment Counsel

MER: 1.93%

This is a true balanced fund with a good mix of quality bonds, blue-chip Canadian stocks and foreign equities. However, its performance, while not terrible, has been below average for the balanced funds category. In the first half of '98, about half the portfolio was in equities, 37% in bonds, and the rest in cash. Results were showing some improvement, but not enough to warrant an upgrade. Historically, there's a 16% chance of loss over any given one-year period, putting this fund in the middle of the pack from a safety perspective.

FIXED INCOME AND MONEY MARKET FUNDS

FIRST CANADIAN BOND FUND $$ → FI No RSP CB

Manager: Mary Jane Yule (Jones Heward), since 1996

MER: 1.49%

Returns have slipped somewhat lately for this usually steady performer. As a result, three- and five-year returns are just about on average for the bond fund category as a whole. The portfolio is a mix of federal, provincial, and corporate issues, with Government of Canada bonds predominating. Nothing flashy or exciting here, just a sound, middle-of-the-road, no-surprises bond fund.

FIRST CANADIAN INTERNATIONAL
BOND FUND $ → FI No £ IB

Manager: Michael Turner (Edinburgh Fund Managers), since 1993

MER: 1.98%

You always have to be careful with international bond funds if you're considering them for an RRSP. This one is classed as foreign content because it invests directly in the debt securities of foreign governments and corporations, primarily in Europe. So it's not a good choice for your registered plan because it will chew up foreign content. On top of that, returns have been below average. If you want an international bond fund, there are much better choices available elsewhere.

FIRST CANADIAN MONEY
MARKET FUND $$ → C No RSP CMM

Manager: Dorothy Biggs (Jones Heward), since 1993

MER: 1.05%

So-so performer, nothing flashy but steady. About 40% of the portfolio is invested in corporate notes and bankers' acceptances, with the rest in government securities.

FIRST CANADIAN MORTGAGE FUND $$$ ↓ FI No RSP M

Manager: Mary Jane Yule (Jones Heward), since 1991

MER: 1.36%

Looked at over a 10-year span, this is the top-performing Canadian mortgage fund that's open to the general public. Its shorter term results also look pretty good when compared to its main competitors, the other big bank mortgage funds, although some of the smaller players like Hongkong Bank are generating better profits. The safety profile of this fund over the longer term is excellent; historically there is only a 1% chance of losing money in any one-year period, with the worst loss over any 12 months just 2.1%. Over a 10-year period, there's a 73% chance you'll receive an average annual return of better than 10%. Never had a losing calendar year prior to '94, when it dropped a fractional 0.5%. However, current returns will be below the long-term average because of the low interest rate environment. Also, there is a fair amount of short-term volatility in this fund, compared to the peer group. Recommended for conservative investors. AAA rated for safety by the Canadian Bond Rating Service. (This, of course, does not mean the fund can't lose money; the rating relates to the quality of the securities held in the portfolio.) As an added guarantee, the Bank of Montreal has undertaken to repurchase any defaulting mortgages from the fund, at no penalty to unitholders.

FIRST CANADIAN T-BILL FUND $$ ↓ C No RSP CMM

Manager: Dorothy Biggs (Jones Heward), since 1993

MER: 1.06%

A routine money market fund that invests in federal and provincial T-bills and government guaranteed notes. Nothing exciting; returns are about the same as for the companion Money Market Fund, which has a longer history. The essential difference is that this fund holds only government securities, while 40% of the Money Market Fund portfolio is in corporate notes.

BEUTEL GOODMAN MANAGED FUNDS

THE COMPANY

Beutel Goodman has been in the investment management business since 1967 but until fairly recently their activities were largely confined to pension fund management, pooled funds, and private client business. They now have a small family of mutual funds open to the general public, but their star performers are still only available to investors with a lot of money. One example: The regular Beutel Goodman Balanced Fund had a five-year average annual compound rate of return to June 30/98 of 11.6%. But the annual return on the company's high-end Private Balanced Fund over that time was 15.1% — a huge difference. Part of this is due to the lower management fees of the funds bearing the "Private" name, which accounts for slightly over one percentage point a year in the case of the two balanced funds. So if you have a lot of money to invest and you like Beutel Goodman's value style, you should check out the Private brands first. This company also manages funds for other organizations, such as Investors Group, which is an indication of their high reputation in the financial community. There's no sales commission if you buy directly from the manager, but you may have to pay up to 4% if you purchase units elsewhere. Note: All the funds are managed by a team concept, with no lead manager — at least that's the company's official position for public consumption.

THE DETAILS

NUMBER OF FUNDS:	7
ASSETS UNDER MANAGEMENT:	$416 MILLION
LOAD CHARGE:	NONE
SWITCHING CHARGE:	NONE
WHERE SOLD:	ACROSS CANADA
HOW SOLD:	DIRECTLY THROUGH THE MANAGER OR THROUGH BROKERS, DEALERS, AND FINANCIAL PLANNERS
PHONE NUMBER:	1-800-461-4551 OR (416) 932-6400
WEB SITE ADDRESS:	WWW.BEUTEL-CAN.COM
E-MAIL ADDRESS:	MARKETING@BEUTEL-CAN.COM

FUND SUMMARY

$$$$ - NONE
$$$ - INCOME, MONEY MARKET, SMALL CAP
$$ - AMERICAN EQUITY, BALANCED, CANADIAN EQUITY, INTERNATIONAL EQUITY
$ - NONE
NR - NONE

BEST CHOICES: INCOME, MONEY MARKET, SMALL CAP
BEST FOR RRSPS: INCOME
BEST UNRATEDS: N/A

FUND RATINGS

CANADIAN EQUITY FUNDS

BEUTEL GOODMAN CANADIAN EQUITY FUND $$ → G No RSP CE

Manager: Team

MER: 2.08%

The managers focus on medium- to large-size companies, although there is a small-cap holding as well. The emphasis is on strong fundamentals — firms with low debt, a low price/earnings ratio, and good profit potential. The number of holdings in the portfolio has expanded considerably in recent years. It used to be limited to about 40 stocks, but had about twice that many positions in the first half of 1998. Results have been fair but not great, although the five-year average annual return is slightly better than average for the Canadian equity fund category. Historically, there's a 17% chance of losing money in any one-year period, putting this fund at about the middle of the pack on the ATP risk scale.

BEUTEL GOODMAN SMALL CAP FUND $$$ → G No RSP CSC

Manager: Team

MER: 2.39%

This fund invests in stocks with a market capitalization of under $500 million (up from $300 million), and does a pretty good job of it. The portfolio is not as risky as you might expect for a small-cap fund, as it holds a number of real estate investment trusts and some financial institution stocks like Laurentian Bank. Returns tend to be above average for the small-cap category. All in all, a good choice for more aggressive investors. Debuts with a solid $$$ rating.

U.S. AND INTERNATIONAL EQUITY FUNDS

BEUTEL GOODMAN AMERICAN EQUITY FUND
$$ ↓ G No £ USE

Manager: Team

MER: 2.46%

The raw numbers on this fund look pretty good, but when you start to compare them to the competition, you'll quickly see that they are below average for the U.S. equity category. As with all BG funds, the managers use a disciplined stock selection approach, searching out companies with low debt, a reasonable stock price, and above-average growth potential. The portfolio is still small (less than $9 million at mid-year), but growing. Safety record is excellent; historically there is only a 4% chance of loss in any given 12-month period.

BEUTEL GOODMAN INTERNATIONAL EQUITY FUND
$$ → G No £ IE

Manager: Team

MER: 2.60%

The mandate is to invest in markets outside North America, using a fundamental, bottom-up approach. International funds tend to be more risky than global funds because they don't have the ability of investing in the U.S. during volatile periods. However, the risk profile of this fund has shown steady improvement in recent years, which is a good sign. Recent returns have tended to be below average, although five-year results are good. As of the first half of '98, about 50% of the portfolio was in Europe and 24% in Japan. This fund also includes some emerging markets stocks in its mix, which add to the profit potential, but also to the risk.

BALANCED FUNDS

BEUTEL GOODMAN BALANCED FUND $$ ↓ FI/G No RSP CBAL

Manager: Team

MER: 2.11%

This fund uses asset allocation principals, but within a limited range (60/40 stocks/bonds). The managers also make maximum use of the foreign content allowance. Canadian stocks tend towards the blue-chip variety, although there are some mid-caps and juniors in the mix. Foreign equities were concentrated in the U.S. and Europe in the first half of '98. Results have been showing improvement, with the five-year annual return now slightly better than average for the balanced fund category. Risk of loss in any one-year period is low at 4%. A respectable, well-managed fund.

FIXED INCOME AND MONEY MARKET FUNDS

BEUTEL GOODMAN INCOME FUND $$$ → FI No RSP CB

Manager: Team

MER: 0.66%

A good performer from the Beutel Goodman group, this fund maintains a mix of high-quality federal government and corporate bonds, in about a two-thirds/one-third ratio. All of the corporate issues are rated A or AA for safety, so there's little default risk here. The fund's duration (a measure of risk) tends to be close to that of the Scotia Capital Universe Bond Index, so you shouldn't have any unpleasant surprises. Returns are above average, helped in part by a low management expense ratio. A good choice for fixed-income investors.

BEUTEL GOODMAN MONEY MARKET FUND $$$ → C No RSP CMM

Manager: Team

MER: 0.58%

A sound entry. Returns have been well above average for the money market category, helped by the low management fee. Portfolio is very high quality, a combination of Treasury bills, short-term government strips, and corporate short-term notes and bonds. Recommended.

BISSETT & ASSOCIATES

THE COMPANY

In last year's edition I chose this as the Fund Company of the Year and referred to it as "one of the hidden treasures of the Canadian mutual fund industry". Well, it's hidden no longer. At the December, 1997 Mutual Funds Awards Gala in Toronto, a panel of experts endorsed my view and chose Bissett for their own Fund Company of the Year award, as well as naming the Bissett Canadian Equity Fund as the best in its category. High honours, which were prominently mentioned in the prospectus when the company made its first public offering early in 1998. The praise is all merited. This is a first-rate management house. The only problem may be that all the attention means they are growing more quickly than they would like!

The emphasis in their equity funds is on growth stocks, which means the managers search out companies that display above-average growth in earnings and dividends, and have a high return on equity. But they also look for good fundamentals — below average debt-to-equity ratio, a strong balance sheet, and a reasonable share price. The net result is good returns with no sales commissions — a rare and valuable combination.

For years this was strictly a regional company, open only to residents of Western Canada. But now residents of all provinces (Quebec registration was applied for in mid-'98) can order funds directly from the manager. But you'll need a fair amount of money. The minimum initial investment per fund is $10,000.

THE DETAILS

NUMBER OF FUNDS:	11
ASSETS UNDER MANAGEMENT:	$1.2 BILLION
LOAD CHARGE:	NONE IF PURCHASED DIRECTLY THROUGH MANAGER, OTHERWISE MAX. 2%
SWITCHING CHARGE:	NONE
WHERE SOLD:	EVERYWHERE EXCEPT QUEBEC
HOW SOLD:	DIRECTLY THROUGH THE MANAGER OR THROUGH BROKERS, DEALERS, AND FINANCIAL PLANNERS

PHONE NUMBER: 1-800-267-7388 (BIS-SETT)
WEB SITE ADDRESS: WWW.BISSETT.COM
E-MAIL ADDRESS: N/A

FUND SUMMARY

$$$$ - CANADIAN EQUITY, DIVIDEND INCOME, RETIREMENT
$$$ - BOND, MONEY MARKET, MULTINATIONAL GROWTH,
       SMALL CAP
$$ - AMERICAN EQUITY, INTERNATIONAL EQUITY
$ - NONE
NR - INCOME TRUST, MICROCAP
BEST CHOICES: CANADIAN EQUITY, DIVIDEND INCOME, RETIREMENT
BEST FOR RRSPS: BOND, CANADIAN EQUITY, DIVIDEND INCOME, RETIREMENT
BEST UNRATEDS: MICROCAP

FUND RATINGS

CANADIAN EQUITY FUNDS

BISSETT CANADIAN EQUITY FUND $$$$ ↓ G No RSP CE

Managers: Michael Quinn, since 1986; Fred Pynn, since 1994

MER: 1.29%

For some years I've been telling readers of this book how good this fund is. Now the excellence has been formally recognized with its selection as the 1997 Canadian Equity Fund of the Year. With the recognition has come lots of money. A year ago, this fund had about $100 million in assets. Now it's pushing five times that. I cannot recall seeing such a rapid growth spurt since Altamira Equity Fund first started to catch the eye of investors. Unfortunately, the result may be to dampen returns. As a small fund, the managers had a lot more flexibility, both in terms of where they invested the money (they had some microcaps in the fund for a while) and in their buy and sell decisions. The bigger a Canadian stock fund gets, the more it tends to buy large-cap issues and to perform closer to the market index. So we'll have to see what happens here. So far the performance is showing no signs of slackening, with returns that are well above average over all time frames, despite the fact the fund was holding large cash balances in the first half of '98. The portfolio is well diversified, including large-cap, mid-cap, and small-cap stocks. The managers use a bottom-up approach to stock selection, with emphasis on a company's fundamentals. The risk/return ratio of this fund is among the best in the Canadian equity funds category. Historically, the fund tends to outperform others in the category in both bull and bear markets. Expenses are low. This is a top-notch entry that's worthy of the $$$$ rating it proudly wears.

BISSETT DIVIDEND INCOME FUND $$$$ ↓ G/FI No RSP INC

Manager: Fred Pynn, since 1991

MER: 1.40%

Here's a dividend fund that manages to deliver both high total returns and good cash flow — a rare double. In the 1997 survey of dividend income funds done for my *Mutual Funds Update* newsletter, this fund showed up with one of the better cash flow returns for the year, at 5.1% based on the NAV at the start of '97. Of that, 57% was received as dividends and the rest as capital gains, all qualifying for a preferred tax rate. So this fund is well suited for the investor who wants a combination of income and growth (total gain for the year to June 30/98 was 17.2%). Better-than-average risk for a fund of this type, with only a 10% chance of loss in any one-year period. Formerly the Bissett Asset Allocation Fund and the Bissett Balanced Fund, which were folded together and given a new mandate in '93. This fund is now eligible for registered plans, and the company took steps over the summer to have it converted from a foreign-content fund to a domestic fund, making it 100% RRSP eligible. That was the one thing that held it back from $$$$ status in my mind, so the rating goes up as a result. A good choice for a RRIF.

BISSETT SMALL CAP FUND $$$ ↓ G No RSP CSC

Managers: David Bissett, since inception (1992), Gene Vollendorf, since 1998

MER: 1.82%

This fund specializes in small Canadian and U.S. companies. Originally, the focus was on Western Canada, but now it's a national portfolio and well diversified. David Bissett, the company's founder and the manager of this fund since its inception, took on a co-manager in early '98 — perhaps in preparation for retirement? Hopefully not, or at least not too soon, as this has been one of the country's premier small-cap funds under his direction. Returns are well above average for the small-cap category over all time frames. Plus the safety record is surprisingly good. Small-cap funds are expected to be more volatile than more broadly based port-folios, but this one has shown only a 12% chance of loss over any historic one-year period, and a zero chance of loss after a three-year hold. That puts it in the top rank in its cat-egory (A rating) from a safety perspective on the basis of Wilfred Vos's ATP analysis. The risk/reward ratio also comes in with an A. If you want to put some money into Canada's growing young companies, this is the place.

U.S. AND INTERNATIONAL EQUITY FUNDS

BISSETT AMERICAN EQUITY FUND $$ → G No £ USE

Manager: Jeff Morrison, since 1998

MER: 1.48%

This fund has a new face at the helm in the person of Jeff Morrison. He took over early in '98 from Fred Pynn as the company hired some new fund managers in response to a rapid growth in assets. Morrison has a tough act to follow as Pynn is a first-rate manager (he runs several other Bissett funds). However, the change may have come at the right time as this fund has started to lag a bit, due to under-weight positions in the technology and communications sectors. The emphasis is on mature, large-cap companies with strong fundamentals and good growth potential. The portfolio, which had been quite small, has now expanded to about 50 positions, providing wider diversification. Decent safety record, although there's historically a 6% chance you'll lose money over a three-year period. I said last year this fund was on the cusp of a rating cut if returns kept slipping. There hasn't been a notable improvement, and with a new person in charge it makes sense to cut this one back to $$ until we see where Morrison takes it.

BISSETT INTERNATIONAL EQUITY FUND $$ → G No £ IE

Manager: Fleming Investment Management, since inception (1994)

MER: 2.00%

This is the only Bissett fund that is not managed in-house and it is one of the weaker performers in the group. The mandate is to invest in non-North American countries. In the first half of '98, Japan was the largest single holding, with about a quarter of the portfolio. Despite the volatile Japanese market, the fund performed reasonably well over the past 12 months, however longer term results are below average. If you want to put some money into a Bissett fund that invests outside Canada, the Multinational Growth Fund is the better bet.

BISSETT MULTINATIONAL GROWTH FUND $$$ ↓ G No £ IE

Manager: Fred Pynn, since 1997

MER: 1.44%

The mandate of this fund is somewhat unusual. Manager Fred Pynn seeks out European and North American companies that operate on a multinational level and that offer a growing dividend stream. These aren't your traditional blue-chip stocks in most cases, but the next level down — major firms that are on the rise. Like just about every other fund from this company, results have been very good. One-year return to June 30/98 was 27.4%, while the three-year average annual compound gain was 29.2%. Risk is on the low side for the international equity category. This is shaping up to be an excellent fund, and if you're a Bissett client you should add it to your portfolio. Debut rating in the *Guide* is $$$.

BALANCED FUNDS

BISSETT RETIREMENT FUND $$$$ ↓ FI/G No RSP CBAL

Manager: Michael Quinn, since inception (1991)

MER: 0.37%

This is a fund of funds, investing in other Bissett funds. So its performance depends on Quinn's ability to assess market movements and decide how to weight the equity, bond, and cash components of this portfolio. So far, he's done very well, thanks in no small part to the excellent performance of most of the Bissett funds. Returns for this one are well above average for the balanced fund category right across the board. Since you're buying a portfolio of funds here, diversification is excellent. The weighting was slightly tilted to stocks in the first half of '98, with a 44% Bond Fund component. The safety record is outstanding. People are finally discovering this fund; last year there was just $26 million invested in it when this book was prepared. This year the fund is pushing $200 million in assets. About time!

FIXED INCOME AND MONEY MARKET FUNDS

BISSETT BOND FUND $$$ → FI No RSP CB

Manager: Michael Quinn, since inception (1986)

MER: 0.75%

Very sound entry. This fund has consistently turned in above-average results and that pattern continues to hold. The low management fee helps to improve investor profits. The portfolio is a mix of federal, provincial, and corporate issues. From a risk perspective, this fund shows worse than average month-to-month volatility, with about a one-third chance of being down in any given month. But over a year, the unit value changes tend to even out, and there is only an historic 4% chance of loss over any given 12-month period.

BISSETT MONEY MARKET FUND $$$ → C No RSP CMM

Manager: Michael Quinn, since 1993

MER: 0.50%

Steady performer. Returns have been consistently above average. Low management fees contribute significantly to that good result. Main holding is federal T-bills, but the fund also holds short-term corporate notes as well.

BNP (CANADA) MUTUAL FUNDS

THE COMPANY

Most mutual fund companies are willing to provide information to this *Guide*, understanding the importance of informing the public about their products. A few, however, have a different attitude. This is one example. After repeated attempts by our researcher to obtain answers to some basic questions, plus a copy of the latest prospectus and financial statements, she was told that everyone was too busy to provide any information. And anyway, her contact said: "If we give them to you this year, you'll just want all the same information again next year."

Whoops! We've been found out! We do indeed go back to all the fund companies every year for their latest information. How else does a book like this stay current? But obviously, BNP sees this as a great inconvenience to them, even though they only have three funds (we think).

BNP is the Canadian subsidiary of the large Banque Nationale de Paris. During the time I lived in France many years ago, I was struck by the arrogance with which the big banks in that country treated their customers. Apparently not only has nothing changed in the interim, but they are now exporting this haughty attitude to North America.

As a result of all this, some of the information below is based on last year's edition (when for some reason they were more co-operative) and is therefore out of date. Our apologies.

THE DETAILS

NUMBER OF FUNDS:	3
ASSETS UNDER MANAGEMENT:	$18.7 MILLION
LOAD CHARGE:	NONE
SWITCHING CHARGE:	NONE
WHERE SOLD:	QUEBEC ONLY
HOW SOLD:	DIRECTLY THROUGH BNP SECURITIES INC., THE PRINCIPAL DISTRIBUTOR, OR AT ANY BRANCH OF THE BANK.
PHONE NUMBER:	(514) 285-7597 OR 1-800-363-0415
WEB SITE ADDRESS:	N/A
E-MAIL ADDRESS:	N/A

FUND SUMMARY

$$$$ - NONE
$$$ - EQUITY, BOND
$$ - NONE
$ - MONEY MARKET
NR - NONE

BEST CHOICES: EQUITY
BEST FOR RRSPs: BOND, EQUITY
BEST UNRATEDS: N/A

FUND RATINGS

CANADIAN EQUITY FUNDS

BNP (CANADA) EQUITY FUND $$$ → G No RSP CE

Manager: Pierre Ouimet

MER: 2.35%

Small Montreal-based fund that puts the emphasis on blue-chip stocks, combined with some high-growth issues. Portfolio is well diversified and includes names like Alcan, Noranda, Petro-Canada, Bombardier, and Seagram. Good results, with above-average returns for all time periods. Worth a look.

FIXED INCOME AND MONEY MARKET FUNDS

BNP (CANADA) BOND FUND $$$ → FI No RSP CB

Manager: Maureen Stapleton

MER: 1.31%

A sound performer in the bond fund category, with above-average returns. Diversified portfolio offers a blend of federal, provincial, and corporate issues. Gain for the year to June 30/98 was 12.2%, extremely good for the bond fund category.

BNP (CANADA) MONEY MARKET FUND $ → C No RSP CMM

Manager: Maureen Stapleton

MER: 1.32%

This money market fund invests mainly in Government of Canada Treasury bills, with some short-term corporate notes and bankers' acceptances added to the mix. Returns have slipped to below average for the money market category, in part due to a high MER.

BPI MUTUAL FUNDS

THE COMPANY

This is a young and growing company with lots of energy and moxie, impressive managerial talent, and some very interesting funds on offer. The company has been around since 1987 but only hit the big leagues when it took over the much larger Bolton Tremblay funds in 1994 in a classic minnow swallows whale story. That meal took quite a while to digest and while that was happening the BPI board staged an executive suite coup d'état and deposed CEO and founder Mark Bonham (who has since resurfaced with his new Strategic Value Funds). The new managerial team started to post good results, investor dollars began to roll in, the stock price took off, and BPI established itself as a middle-tier player in the mutual fund marketplace.

The international funds, which are run from BPI's U.S. office in Orlando, Florida, have performed well. However, some of the company's key domestic equity funds have run into trouble recently, causing concern among investors. So you have to pick and choose carefully here.

BPI now offers a family of segregated funds under the name Legacy. These are regular BPI funds, but with added bells and whistles attached, such as creditor protection and capital guarantees. You pay a higher expense ratio for these extras but some folks seem to feel they're worth the price.

Good news: the MERs of many of the BPI funds are down from last year, in some cases considerably. This boosts investor returns.

THE DETAILS

NUMBER OF FUNDS:	27
ASSETS UNDER MANAGEMENT:	$3.8 BILLION
LOAD CHARGE:	FRONT: MAX. 5% FOR ALL FUNDS BUT MONEY MARKET WHERE MAX. IS 2%
	BACK: MAX. 6%
SWITCHING CHARGE:	2% MAXIMUM
WHERE SOLD:	ACROSS CANADA

HOW SOLD:	THROUGH LICENSED DEALERS
PHONE NUMBER:	1-800-937-5146 OR (416) 861-8191
WEB SITE ADDRESS:	WWW.BPIFUNDS.COM
E-MAIL ADDRESS:	BPI@BPIFUNDS.COM

FUND SUMMARY

$$$$ - DIVIDEND INCOME
$$$ - AMERICAN EQUITY VALUE, CANADIAN EQUITY VALUE , GLOBAL BALANCED RSP, GLOBAL EQUITY VALUE, GLOBAL RSP BOND, T-BILL
$$ - AMERICAN SMALL COMPANIES, GLOBAL SMALL COMPANIES, INCOME & GROWTH
$ - CANADIAN BOND, CANADIAN RESOURCE, CANADIAN SMALL COMPANIES
NR - ASIA PACIFIC, CANADIAN MID-CAP, CORPORATE BOND, DIVIDEND EQUITY, EMERGING MARKETS, HIGH INCOME, INTERNATIONAL EQUITY VALUE, U.S. MONEY MARKET

BEST CHOICES: AMERICAN EQUITY VALUE, DIVIDEND INCOME, GLOBAL EQUITY VALUE
BEST FOR RRSPS: CANADIAN EQUITY VALUE, GLOBAL BALANCED RSP
BEST UNRATEDS: HIGH INCOME

FUND RATINGS

CANADIAN EQUITY FUNDS

BPI CANADIAN EQUITY VALUE FUND $$$ → G #/* RSP CE

Manager: Steven Misener, since 1994

MER: 2.46%

This was one of the funds that got hit with a big write-down when YBM Magnex came under legal and regulatory scrutiny in early 1998 and trading was halted in the shares. The fund owned more than 380,000 shares entering the year, so the loss was significant. At the time of writing, the final fate of YBM Magnex is unknown, so a further write-down is possible. In part because of this, performance over the 12 months to June 30/98 came in below average for broadly diversified Canadian stock funds, with a gain of 8.9%. Large holdings in BCE and Nova Corp. helped to stem the bleeding. The portfolio was well diversified in the first half of '98, with a significant portion in foreign equities (14%). Manager Steven Misener uses a modified value investing approach, and the portfolio is a mix of large and small companies. Although it's not exactly shooting out the lights, this is the best choice among BPI's Canadian stock funds at this time. This fund was spawned from the merger of the old Bolton Tremblay Landmark Canadian Fund and the BPI Canadian Equity Fund.

BPI CANADIAN RESOURCE FUND $ ↑ G #/* RSP SEC

Manager: Fred Dalley, since 1994

MER: 2.99%

For resource fund managers, it's good news these days if your losses are less than those of the other guy. In this case, they're not. The net asset value is off more than 30% from a year ago, and the blood is still flowing. Resource stocks will come back some day but when, oh when? Manager Fred Dalley is betting on an early turnaround in the energy sector to boost this fund's fortunes, and had almost a third of the portfolio in oil and gas issues in mid-'98. Investors hope he's right. In the meantime, they can only hang on and hope for better days. The fund was originally known as the BT Landmark Resource Fund. It is best suited to more aggressive investors because of the high risk in resource stocks.

BPI CANADIAN SMALL COMPANIES FUND $ ↑ G #/* RSP CSC

Manager: Steven Misener, since 1994

MER: 2.83%

This fund specializes in small capitalization Canadian stocks, which makes it potentially more volatile than blue-chip funds. So it's not well suited for conservative investors. Steve Misener uses a modified value investing approach, which means he looks for special situations where good companies are underpriced. His focus is on what are known as "microcap" issues — ultra small companies. The fund did well immediately after Misener took it over in mid-'94, but it suddenly ran out of steam in '96 and has been slumping badly ever since, in part because microcaps have been out of favour. Misener feels the fortunes of these stocks will soon turn around, saying that "the weakness in this sector defies its powerful fundamentals". But so far, the market is stubbornly resisting and the losses continue. This fund is currently closed except to existing unitholders who may add to their positions. I can't think of any good reason why they should, at least until such time as we start to see some improvement in performance. Previously, this was the BPI Canadian Small Cap Fund and prior to that, the BT Landmark Small Cap Fund.

BPI DIVIDEND INCOME FUND $$$$ ↓ FI/G #/* RSP INC

Manager: Eric Bushell, since 1995

MER: 1.00%

This is a genuine "income" fund, in the true sense of that word. It offers a portfolio of preferred shares and dividend-paying common stocks that generates excellent cash flow for investors seeking steady income. In terms of cash-on-cash yield, this was one of the best performers in 1997 in the survey of dividend funds we did for *Mutual Funds Update* newsletter, as it had been the year previous. Total return has also been good, which is an unusual double in funds of this type. In mid-'98, manager Eric Bushell was extending the term of his preferred share portfolio to take advantage of a further expected decline in interest rates as a result of international deflationary trends. The safety record of this fund is very good; there is only a 10% chance of loss in any given year, and a zero chance that it will be more than 5% of NAV. This fund is a top-notch choice if you're looking for a combination of dividends and capital gains. Distributions are paid monthly. Rating moves up to $$$$ this year.

U.S. AND INTERNATIONAL EQUITY FUNDS

BPI AMERICAN EQUITY VALUE FUND $$$ → G #/* £ USE

Manager: Paul Holland, since 1997

MER: 2.37%

BPI set up its own international investment management company, based in Orlando, Florida, in March, '97. Responsibility for running this fund, which had been very capably managed for several years by Lazard Asset Management, was handed over to this new team. The mandate continues to be to invest in undervalued blue-chip stocks, such as American Express, Exxon, and General Electric. At the time of the managerial switch, I expressed concern as to whether the new people could live up to the Lazard record, but Paul Holland and his team have acquitted themselves nobly so far. Gain for the year to June 30/98 was an excellent 42.8%, well above average for the U.S. equity category. Rating moves up to $$$ on the strength of that performance. This was formerly the BT Landmark American Fund.

BPI AMERICAN SMALL COMPANIES FUND $$ → G #/* £ USSC

Manager: Thomas J. Sudyka Jr., since 1997

MER: 2.62%

The objective here is to invest in undervalued smaller American companies (market capitalization less than US$1 billion is "small" for these people!) with above-average growth potential. A new management team took over in early '97 and has done a credible job so far, although latest one-year results are slightly below average for small-cap U.S. funds. The small-cap market has been extremely volatile in recent years so no one is sure quite what to expect next. Manager Tom Sudyka is betting on a come-back that will favour consumer stocks and has positioned his portfolio to take advantage of that if it happens. Right now the companion American Equity Value Fund looks like a safer bet. Originally, this fund started life as the BPI Emerging Growth Fund, then was the BPI American Equity Growth Fund. It was renamed again a couple of years ago to more accurately reflect its mandate.

BPI GLOBAL EQUITY VALUE FUND $$$ ↓ G #/* £ IE

Manager: Daniel R. Jaworski, since 1997

MER: 2.42%

This fund has gone through a bunch of name changes and manager switches in the past couple of years. It was the BPI Global Equity Fund, and then the BPI International

Equity Fund was merged into it and responsibility for management turned over to BPI's new in-house international team, which has its headquarters in Orlando. Despite all this turmoil, the fund has performed very well for investors, especially since the management switch. Returns for all time periods have now improved to above average for the international fund category. As of mid-'98, manager Daniel Jaworski's portfolio was heavily weighted to North America (48%) and Europe (42%). Apart from a 3% weighting in Japan and 2% in Australia, the Far East was not represented in the mix, which contributed to the strong results. Good safety profile; ATP shows only a 6% chance of losing money in any one-year period, with the worst return a modest -3.4%. That's very good for an equity fund. Rating is boosted to $$$ on the strength of all this. Formerly the Walwyn International Fund.

BPI GLOBAL SMALL COMPANIES FUND $$ ↑ G #/* £ IE

Managers: Pablo Salas and Thomas J. Sudyka Jr., since 1997

MER: 2.59%

The fund invests in "small-cap" companies internationally — but small-cap in this case is defined as anything up to US$750 million in market capitalization! Some "big" Canadian companies are smaller. Europe and North America accounted for almost three quarters of the portfolio in the first half of '98 and this geographic concentration produced some decent returns for investors. The management team is part of BPI's international group, based in Orlando and so far they have done well. Rating is upgraded as a result.

BALANCED FUNDS

BPI INCOME & GROWTH FUND $$ → FI/G #/* RSP CBAL

Managers: Kevin Klassen and Eric Bushell, since inception (1997)

MER: 2.50%

Technically, this fund does not have a three-year record so should not be included in this book. However, in June/98, BPI received unitholder approval to merge the much older BPI Canadian Balanced Fund into this one. That fund did have a track record (not a good one, but improving) that qualified it for a rating, as well as the same manager on the equities side, Kevin Klassen. So on that basis, I decided to include the newer entry, which only started operation in June/97. Like the Canadian Balanced Fund, this one focuses on blue-chip stocks and high quality bonds. The portfolio is sound and well diversified, and I expect this merged entry to perform well over time. However, because of the merger and the newness of the surviving fund, we'll give it a middle-of-the-road $$ rating for now.

BPI GLOBAL BALANCED RSP FUND
$$$ → FI/G #/* RSP IBAL

Manager: Kevin Klassen, since 1996

MER: 2.24%

This is designed as a balanced fund for Canadians who want foreign exposure with 100% RRSP eligibility. Canadian stocks focus on corporations with strong international earnings, and there is a significant foreign equity component. Bonds are split between Canadian and foreign currency issues. I like the approach of this fund if you want to raise your RRSP/RRIF foreign content to above 20%. Returns are showing steady improvement under Kevin Klassen's direction. Rating is increased to $$$ as a result. The BPI North American Balanced RSP Fund was folded into this one in November, '96.

FIXED INCOME AND MONEY MARKET FUNDS

BPI CANADIAN BOND FUND
$ → FI #/* RSP CB

Manager: Ben Cheng, since 1997

MER: 1.50%

This has been a long-time underachiever, although it is now starting to look a bit better under the direction of new manager Ben Cheng, who took over in the fall of 1997. The portfolio is a mix of government and corporate issues. Not your best choice in the bond fund category, especially if you have to pay a load charge to get in. Originally formed out of the merger of the BPI Canadian Bond Fund, the BT Landmark Bond Fund and the Bolton Tremblay Bond Fund.

BPI GLOBAL RSP BOND FUND $$$ ↓ FI #/* RSP IB

Manager: Ben Cheng, since 1997

MER: 1.50%

This is a 100% RRSP-eligible international bond fund with above-average returns and a good safety record. That's an excellent combination, so if you're looking for this type of fund for your RRSP, this is worth considering. New manager Ben Cheng was maintaining a portfolio that was 63% exposed to the Canadian dollar and 29% to the U.S. dollar in mid-'98. Foreign-pay bonds represented only 3% of the mix, so Cheng was betting on the continued strength of North American currencies and on a revival of the loonie's fortunes. We'll start this off with a debut rating of $$$.

BPI T-BILL FUND $$$ → C #/* RSP CMM

Manager: Fred Dalley, since 1996

MER: 0.65%

This fund produces consistent above-average returns, thanks in part to a low expense ratio. Don't be misled by the name, however. This is not strictly a T-bill fund at all. In fact, corporate short-term notes make up the largest single holding in the portfolio. BPI should consider renaming the fund to reflect that reality. Caution: Don't buy this fund on a back-end load option; you may end up paying more in sales commissions than you earn in interest. This is one of the few money market funds that offers limited chequing privileges. It was formerly the BPI Money Market Fund and was beefed up by the addition of two funds from the now-dead Bolton Tremblay family: the BT Landmark Money Market Fund and the BT Landmark Short-Term Interest Fund.

CALDWELL INVESTMENT MANAGEMENT

THE COMPANY

Caldwell Securities is an investment dealer based in Toronto. The company has been in business since 1975, and offers a family of five funds. The company takes a highly disciplined, conservative approach to selecting the securities for its portfolios. Company founder Thomas Caldwell is the guru behind the funds, but the management of each is now designated by the company as a team.

THE DETAILS

NUMBER OF FUNDS:	5
ASSETS UNDER MANAGEMENT:	$135 MILLION
LOAD CHARGE:	FRONT: MAX. 5%; BACK: MAX. 4.5%
SWITCHING CHARGE:	2% MAXIMUM
WHERE SOLD:	ALL PROVINCES EXCEPT QUEBEC
HOW SOLD:	THROUGH LICENSED BROKERS, DEALERS, AND FINANCIAL PLANNERS
PHONE NUMBER:	(416) 593-4966 OR 1-800-256-2441
WEB SITE ADDRESS:	WWW.CALDWELLMUTUALFUNDS.COM
E-MAIL ADDRESS:	CALDWELL.SEC@SYMPATICO.CA

FUND SUMMARY

$$$$ - NONE
$$$ - NONE
$$ - ASSOCIATE
$ - INTERNATIONAL
NR - AMERICAN EQUITY, CANADIAN EQUITY, CANADIAN INCOME

BEST CHOICES: ASSOCIATE
BEST FOR RRSPS: ASSOCIATE
BEST UNRATEDS: AMERICAN EQUITY

FUND RATINGS
BALANCED FUNDS

CALDWELL ASSOCIATE FUND $$ → FI/G #/* RSP CBAL

Manager: Team

MER: 2.53%

The equities side of this fund is oriented towards blue-chip Canadian issues with strong growth potential, plus some top-grade U.S. shares. Past returns have been strong, but more recent results have slipped. In part, this was due to several underperforming resource stocks in the portfolio, such as Inco and Placer Dome, along with some troubled companies like Laidlaw, whose shares took a big hit after a U.S. court ruled they owed the IRS hundreds of millions in taxes. The fixed-income side of the portfolio (about 22% of the holdings in the first half of '98) was invested in medium-term CMHC and Ontario Hydro securities. The fund makes good use of the foreign content allowance with holdings in half a dozen blue-chip U.S. stocks (IBM, Motorola, etc.). Good stock-picking is the key to success as long as this fund remains heavily weighted to equities. Right now, the team is in a bit of a slump.

CALDWELL INTERNATIONAL FUND $ ↑ G/FI #/* £ IBAL

Manager: Team

MER: 3.56%

This small fund has struggled badly in the past couple of years and returns have slipped to well below average. This is somewhat surprising, given the emphasis on U.S. blue-chip stocks in the portfolio (Boeing, Hewlett Packard, Eastman Kodak). But because the portfolio held only 11 stocks in the first half of '98, it only took a couple of bad picks to knock down the results. About 20% of the portfolio was in U.S. government Treasury notes maturing in '02. Although this is technically a balanced fund, it does not hold fixed-income securities with maturities greater than five years, so the reliance is clearly on stocks to generate returns. That makes this fund somewhat higher risk than a normal balanced fund. High MER doesn't help matters. Rating drops a notch this year.

CAMAF

THE COMPANY

CAMAF is an acronym for Canadian Anaesthetists' Mutual Accumulating Fund Limited. Since no one wants to be burdened with that tongue-twister of a name, it was abbreviated to CAMAF a few years ago. Despite the name, this is not a restricted fund. Anyone may invest in it, anaesthetist or not.

THE DETAILS

NUMBER OF FUNDS:	1
ASSETS UNDER MANAGEMENT:	$42 MILLION
LOAD CHARGE:	NONE
SWITCHING CHARGE:	NONE
WHERE SOLD:	ACROSS CANADA
HOW SOLD:	DIRECTLY THROUGH THE MANAGER OR THROUGH BROKERS, DEALERS, AND FINANCIAL PLANNERS
PHONE NUMBER:	(416) 925-7331 OR 1-800-267-4713
WEB SITE ADDRESS:	N/A
E-MAIL ADDRESS:	N/A

FUND SUMMARY

$$$$ - NONE
$$$ -CANADIAN ANAESTHETISTS' MUTUAL ACCUMULATING
$$ - NONE
$ - NONE
NR - NONE

FUND RATINGS

CANADIAN EQUITY FUND

CANADIAN ANAESTHETISTS' MUTUAL ACCUMULATING FUND $$$ → G No RSP CE

Managers: Charles Wakefield (Canadian) and Peter Walter (Global), since 1994

MER: 1.47%

The Laketon Investment Management team that took over this underachiever in '94 has been doing a very good job with it. Over the past three years, investors have enjoyed an average annual compound rate of return of 19.6%, comfortably above average for Canadian equity funds as a group. The portfolio is well diversified, with a blue-chip tilt, and makes full use of the foreign content allocation. Main emphasis in the first half of '98 was on financial services and industrial products. The managers use a bottom-up investment style, focusing on fundamentals. This fund has improved greatly in recent years, and is worthy of a close look.

CANADA TRUST MUTUAL FUNDS

THE COMPANY

Canada Trust has developed a very successful line of mutual funds, and their entries have received good response from investors. The fund operation has moved into the top 10 in Canada in terms of assets under management, with more than $12 billion as of mid-1998. Of special note here are the international funds, which have been structured in such a way so as to provide full RRSP eligibility.

These funds used to bear the name Everest, but that designation was dropped at the beginning of 1997. They're now simply Canada Trust funds.

THE DETAILS

NUMBER OF FUNDS:	27
ASSETS UNDER MANAGEMENT:	$9.2 BILLION
LOAD CHARGE:	NONE
SWITCHING CHARGE:	NONE
WHERE SOLD:	ACROSS CANADA
HOW SOLD:	DIRECTLY THROUGH BRANCHES OF CANADA TRUST OR THROUGH BROKERS, DEALERS, AND FINANCIAL PLANNERS
PHONE NUMBER:	1-800-386-3757
WEB SITE ADDRESS:	WWW.CANADATRUST.COM
E-MAIL ADDRESS:	CTMAILBOX@CANADATRUST.COM

FUND SUMMARY

$$$$ - NONE

$$$ - AMERIGROWTH, BALANCED, BOND, EUROGROWTH, NORTH AMERICAN, STOCK

$$ - DIVIDEND INCOME, INTERNATIONAL EQUITY, MORTGAGE, SPECIAL EQUITY

$ - ASIAGROWTH, EMERGING MARKETS, INTERNATIONAL BOND, MONEY MARKET, U.S. EQUITY

NR - BALANCED INDEX, CANADIAN BOND INDEX, CANADIAN EQUITY INDEX, GLOBAL ASSET ALLOCATION, GLOBALGROWTH, HIGH YIELD INCOME, INTERNATIONAL

EQUITY INDEX, MONTHLY INCOME, PREMIUM MONEY
MARKET, RETIREMENT BALANCED, SHORT-TERM BOND,
U.S. EQUITY INDEX
BEST CHOICES: BALANCED, AMERIGROWTH, EUROGROWTH, STOCK
BEST FOR RRSPS: AMERIGROWTH, BALANCED, EUROGROWTH, MORTGAGE
BEST UNRATEDS: U.S. EQUITY INDEX

FUND RATINGS

CANADIAN EQUITY FUNDS

CANADA TRUST DIVIDEND INCOME FUND $$ → G No RSP INC

Manager: CT Investment Management Group, since inception (1994)

MER: 1.90%

This is Canada Trust's entry in the dividend fund area. The managers invest in a portfolio of common and preferred shares with good dividend payment records. Cash distributions are credited monthly, which theoretically makes this fund a good choice for income-oriented investors. However, things haven't worked out that way in practical terms. In 1997, for example, the cash yield on this fund (based on its NAV at the start of the year) was just 1.2%, according to a survey we did for *Mutual Funds Update* newsletter. That's a very weak cash flow from an income fund. Total returns have been slightly below average for the dividend category, with an average annual compound rate of return of 20.2% for the three years to June 30/98. This makes the fund better suited for the investor looking for a conservative blue-chip portfolio than for someone who needs steady income.

CANADA TRUST SPECIAL EQUITY FUND $$ → G No RSP CSC

Managers: Bissett & Associates, Guardian Capital, Warburg Pincus, since 1996

MER: 2.15%

This is an aggressive fund, specializing in small- and medium-sized Canadian companies with high growth potential. Its returns had been below average for Canadian small-cap funds so Canada Trust decided to shake things up in mid-'96 by bringing in new managers. Calgary-based Bissett & Associates is mainly responsible for small-cap selections, Toronto-based Guardian Capital focuses on mid-cap stocks, and New York-based Warburg Pincus looks after U.S. equities. Results over the past two years have improved to slightly better than average for small-cap funds of this type, with an average annual compound rate of return of 11.4% to June 30/98. Rating moves up a notch as a result.

CANADA TRUST STOCK FUND $$$ → G No RSP CE

Manager: CT Investment Management and Montgomery Asset Management, since 1996

MER: 1.87%

Canada Trust made several moves to improve fund performance in 1996. One of them was to bring this fund in-house after several years of below-average returns. It is more conservative in style than the Special Equity Fund, investing mainly in blue-chip Canadian stocks (Northern Telecom and Bank of Nova Scotia were among the major holdings in the first half of '98), and makes full use of foreign content. The management change continues to work well. The fund gained an average of 21.4% annually for the two years to June 30/98, well above average for the Canadian equity category. That's good enough to push the rating up another notch this year.

U.S. AND INTERNATIONAL EQUITY FUNDS

CANADA TRUST AMERIGROWTH FUND $$$ → G No RSP USE

Manager: State Street Global Advisors, since 1998

MER: 1.39%

Canada Trust offers several international funds that are fully RRSP eligible. This is one of them. Most of the portfolio is invested in Government of Canada T-bills to meet the 80% Canadian content requirement. The balance is in S&P 500 index futures. This fund was opened in 1993 so the S&P has been on the rise for most of its existence.

That explains the excellent returns to date — average annual gain of 20.4% for the five years to June 30/98. It also explains why this fund has chalked up such a good safety record so far — it hasn't had to contend with any bear markets, although that changed in August 1998. The managers warned investors of potential trouble ahead in their '96 and '97 annual reports, citing the Asian crisis and reduced corporate earnings in the U.S. as problem areas. When the U.S. market turns down, this fund follows right along — it's inevitable, given the nature of the portfolio. That's why rating a fund like this is so difficult — the historic numbers look great, but a correction knocks the stuffing out of it. A good manager in an actively run fund may be able to deal with that situation, but this is an index fund, with nowhere to hide. Still, this is one of the few funds that allows unlimited exposure to the U.S. market in an RRSP, and that's important to many people right now. So we'll bump up the rating to $$$.

CANADA TRUST ASIAGROWTH FUND $ ↑ G No RSP FEE

Manager: State Street Global Advisors, since 1998

MER: 2.48%

This is another fully RRSP-eligible fund. In this case, the focus is on the Far East, through investing in index futures on several key exchanges including Hong Kong and Tokyo. The past few years have not been kind to Asian markets, as everyone well knows, and this fund has been badly beaten up along with all the others, losing 35% last year. This is not a good time to be holding Asian funds in your RRSP, so give this one a pass until the situation in the Far East stabilizes.

CANADA TRUST EMERGING MARKETS FUND $ ↑ G No £ EME

Manager: Montgomery Asset Management

MER: 3.22%

Emerging markets funds have had their problems, but this one has been weaker than most. Over the three years to June 30/98, the average annual compound rate of return was -12.5%. Not good. There are better choices around.

CANADA TRUST EUROGROWTH FUND $$$ ↑ G No RSP EE

Manager: State Street Global Advisors, since 1998

MER: 2.20%

The target of this fund is to track the Morgan Stanley Europe Equity Index. The investing style is the same as for the other funds in CT's Growth series, thus allowing full RRSP eligibility. European markets have been on a fast track in recent years and the returns for this fund reflect that. Gain for the 12 months to June 30/98 was 32.3%. Three-year average annual gain was 26.7%, above average for the European fund category. The safety rating on this one is surprisingly weak, however.

CANADA TRUST INTERNATIONAL
EQUITY FUND $$ → G No £ IE

Manager: Montgomery Asset Management

MER: 2.62%

The mandate of this fund is to achieve long-term capital growth by investing primarily in companies outside North America. The San Francisco-based manager uses an active geographic switching policy in an effort to maximize gains. Portfolio is well diversified, and includes stocks from both developed nations and emerging markets. Emphasis was on Europe in the first half of '98. Results have started to perk up considerably. The fund gained 26% in the year to June 30/98, well above average for the category. That was good enough to pull the returns for all time periods to better than average as well. The risk level has shown improvement since last year. All this is enough for a rating boost to $$, with another one to come if results stay strong.

CANADA TRUST NORTH AMERICAN FUND $$$ → G No £ AE

Manager: CT Asset Management, since 1996

MER: 2.34%

Canada Trust switched the management of several of its funds in mid-'96. This was one that was affected, with responsibility for the portfolio brought in-house. The mandate of this fund is to invest in stocks listed on North

American exchanges, which really means the U.S. and Canada since Mexico has not been represented in the portfolio for the past few years. Results have improved since the management change, with the fund recording a good 19% average annual compound rate of return for the two years to June 30/98. Rating moves up another notch.

CANADA TRUST U.S. EQUITY FUND $ → G No £ USE

Manager: CT Asset Management, since 1996

MER: 2.34%

The portfolio of this fund leans strongly towards blue-chip stocks. However, it hasn't performed as well as might be expected, given the great run in the U.S. market in recent years. Gain for the year to June 30/98 was 22.3%, well below average for the U.S. fund category. That continues a sub-par pattern that has been evident in this fund for some time. The companion AmeriGrowth Fund, which is an index fund, continues to perform much better and is the preferred choice for now.

BALANCED FUNDS

CANADA TRUST BALANCED FUND $$$ ↓ FI/G No RSP CBAL

Managers: CT Investment Management, Montgomery Asset Management, State Street Global Advisors, Schroder Capital Management International

MER: 2.13%

This is another fund where Canada Trust has turned to a multi-manager approach in the hopes of boosting returns. Montgomery, based in San Francisco, does the international stock picking; Montreal-based State Street advises on index futures; New York-based Schroder handles the international bond side of things; and CT's in-house team looks after the rest. The fund offers a well-diversified portfolio of blue-chip stocks, high-grade bonds and T-bills, with some U.S. and international stocks and foreign-pay bonds added for good measure. It is suited for investors looking for a conservatively managed balanced fund. Returns continue to improve; gain for the year ending June

30/98 was above average at 10.7%. Longer-term results are pulling up as well. Safety rating is excellent. A good choice in the CT family, especially for an RRSP. Rating moves up to $$$.

FIXED INCOME AND MONEY MARKET FUNDS

CANADA TRUST BOND FUND $$$ → FI No RSP CB

Manager: James C. Dunlop, since 1994

MER: 1.35%

The portfolio of this fund consists mainly of federal and provincial bonds, with some corporate issues and mortgage-backed securities for variety. Returns have been improving in recent years and are now above average for the bond fund category. Gain for the 12 months to June 30/98 was 9.4%. James Dunlop is Canada Trust's Managing Director, North American Fixed Income, and works with a team on this and the company's other income funds.

CANADA TRUST INTERNATIONAL
BOND FUND $ ↑ FI No RSP IB

Manager: CT Investment Management, since 1994

MER: 2.07%

This fund is fully eligible for registered plans, so you can hold it in your RRSP without worrying about the foreign content implications. The question is, should you? From a safety perspective, the securities here are pure gold, only Canadian government and World Bank foreign currency issues. However, returns have left much to be desired. Average annual compound rate of return for the year to June 30/98 was only 5.5%, below average for the international bond category by a fair margin. Risk is worse than average. This would not be one of my top choices in the Canada Trust family.

CANADA TRUST MONEY MARKET FUND $ → C No RSP CMM

Manager: James C. Dunlop, since 1994

MER: 0.98%

This fund continues to produce below-average returns for its category and there is no obvious reason for this. The MER is competitive and the portfolio is a blend of government and corporate bonds. Not one of CT's better entries.

CANADA TRUST MORTGAGE FUND $$ ↓ FI No RSP M

Manager: James C. Dunlop, since 1994

MER: 1.59%

As financial institution mortgage funds go, this one is faring reasonably well. No mortgage fund is generating great returns these days, but the 4.4% advance here was more than any of the bank funds could do in the year to June 30/98. There's also a great safety record here; this is one of the few funds in the ATP analysis that has never experienced a loss in any 12-month period. A steady if unspectacular performer; worth considering for RRSPs and RRIFs.

CANSO INVESTMENT COUNSEL

THE COMPANY

Canso Investment Counsel is an investment counselling firm located in Richmond Hill, Ont. It specializes in corporate security selection by analyzing all present and future cash flows available to the investor. Only "cheap" securities, as determined by their methodology, are purchased. Overvalued securities are avoided as being too high risk. The company currently has two small funds available, a Canadian equity fund and a bond fund. Both are too new for a formal rating.

THE DETAILS

NUMBER OF FUNDS:	2
ASSETS UNDER MANAGEMENT:	$3 MILLION
LOAD CHARGE:	FRONT: MAX. 5%; BACK: MAX. 5%
SWITCHING CHARGE:	2% MAXIMUM
WHERE SOLD:	ACROSS CANADA
HOW SOLD:	THROUGH BROKERS
PHONE NUMBER:	(905) 339-3560 OR 1-888-601-2222
WEB SITE ADDRESS:	N/A
E-MAIL ADDRESS:	N/A

FUND SUMMARY

$$$$ - NONE
$$$ - NONE
$$ - NONE
$ - NONE
NR - CANADIAN EQUITY FUND, VALUE BOND FUND
BEST CHOICES: N/A
BEST FOR RRSPs: N/A
BEST UNRATEDS: VALUE BOND

FUND RATINGS

No fund has the three-year record required for a formal rating.

CAPSTONE FUNDS

THE COMPANY

This small fund group is operated by the Toronto-based firm of MMA Investment Managers Ltd. Although the funds have been around for more than a decade they are not well known and the asset base is very small. The funds are now under the direction of Michael A. Smedley, in the role of lead manager. He is executive vice-president and CEO of MMA.

THE DETAILS

NUMBER OF FUNDS:	3
ASSETS UNDER MANAGEMENT:	$12 MILLION
LOAD CHARGE:	NONE
SWITCHING CHARGE:	NONE
WHERE SOLD:	ALBERTA, B.C., AND ONTARIO
HOW SOLD:	THROUGH DEALERS AND CAPSTONE CONSULTANTS LTD.
PHONE NUMBER:	(416) 366-2931 OR 1-800-207-0067
WEB SITE ADDRESS:	WWW.MMA-INVESTMGR.COM
E-MAIL ADDRESS:	CAPSTONE@MMA-INVESTMGR.COM

FUND SUMMARY

$$$$ - NONE
$$$ - BALANCED TRUST
$$ - CASH MANAGEMENT, INTERNATIONAL TRUST
$ - NONE
NR - NONE
BEST CHOICES: BALANCED TRUST
BEST FOR RRSPs: BALANCED TRUST
BEST UNRATEDS: N/A

FUND RATINGS

U.S. AND INTERNATIONAL EQUITY FUNDS

CAPSTONE INTERNATIONAL TRUST $$ → G No £ IE

Manager: Michael A. Smedley, since 1997

MER: 2.00%

The mandate of this fund is to invest in international growth stocks. Although the emphasis is on the U.S., the portfolio also contains several Canadian, European, and South American issues. Last year I commented that, given the nature of the portfolio, it was puzzling to see that the fund managed to record a small loss. Things have now turned around under Michael Smedley's direction and this fund was hot, hot, hot in the first half of '98. The ripple effect from last year continues to drag down the longer term numbers, but this one looks like it may have turned a corner.

BALANCED FUNDS

CAPSTONE BALANCED TRUST $$$ → FI/G No RSP CBAL

Manager: Michael A. Smedley, since 1997

MER: 2.00%

This little fund (assets about $8 million) is starting to post some very impressive gains. It is coming off a good 12-month run that has boosted returns for all time periods to well above average for the balanced fund category. The stock portion of the portfolio favours blue-chips (e.g., banks, Bombardier, BCE) with a few small growth companies blended in. The bond side is composed entirely of federal government and CMHC notes. The portfolio weighting was about two thirds/one third in favour of equities in the first half of '98. Good safety record. Moves up to $$$ this year. Name changed in mid-'98 from Capstone Investment Trust.

FIXED INCOME AND MONEY MARKET FUNDS

CAPSTONE CASH MANAGEMENT FUND $$ → C No RSP CMM

Manager: Michael A. Smedley, since 1997

MER: 0.60%

This fund previously invested only in Government of Canada T-bills, however commercial short-term notes have now been added to the mix to boost returns. There's been another important change as well. In the past, the management fee was charged directly to the investor, which made the published returns on this fund appear unusually high. However, in mid-'98 the unitholders approved a proposal to charge a management fee of 0.6% directly against fund assets, which is the standard procedure in the industry. So future performance numbers will now accurately reflect how this fund is doing in relation to its peers. Good move.

CENTREPOST MUTUAL FUNDS

THE COMPANY

These used to be known as the OHA (Ontario Hospital Association) funds. The company recently changed the name to emphasize the fact their funds are open to the general public, not just hospital workers. The management style is conservative; in fact, they suggest you look elsewhere if razzle-dazzle growth is your goal. Major advantage: very low management fees.

THE DETAILS

NUMBER OF FUNDS:	5
ASSETS UNDER MANAGEMENT:	$290 MILLION
LOAD CHARGE:	NONE
SWITCHING CHARGE:	NONE
WHERE SOLD:	DIRECTLY THROUGH CENTREPOST: ONTARIO ONLY THROUGH BROKERS AND DEALERS: ACROSS CANADA EXCEPT QUEBEC AND THE TERRITORIES
HOW SOLD:	DIRECTLY BY THE MANAGER OR THROUGH BROKERS, DEALERS, AND FINANCIAL PLANNERS
PHONE NUMBER:	1-800-268-9597 OR (416) 205-1455
WEB SITE:	WWW.CENTREPOST.COM
E-MAIL:	THROUGH WEB SITE

FUND SUMMARY

$$$$ - NONE
$$$ - FOREIGN EQUITY, SHORT TERM
$$ - BOND
$ - BALANCED, CANADIAN EQUITY
NR - NONE
BEST CHOICE: FOREIGN EQUITY
BEST RRSP: BOND
BEST UNRATEDS: N/A

FUND RATINGS

CENTREPOST CANADIAN EQUITY FUND $ → G No RSP CE

Manager: Rick Hutcheon, since 1994

MER: 1.00%

The emphasis here is on mid- to large-cap companies. The small portfolio (about 25 stocks) includes well-known firms such as BCE, Barrick Gold, EdperBrascan, Nova, and TransCanada PipeLines. Results started to show improvement in the first half of '98, although longer term returns are still below average for the Canadian equity category. We'll have to see if the renewed momentum can be sustained before upgrading the rating. Formerly known as the OHA Canadian Equity Fund.

CENTREPOST FOREIGN EQUITY FUND $$$ → G No £ IE

Manager: Rick Hutcheon, since 1994

MER: 1.75%

Although the mandate of this fund allows it to invest around the world, the current emphasis is clearly on the U.S. with holdings in Disney, Gillette, Citicorp, and the like. This is a very small portfolio, with only about a dozen positions and less than $3 million in assets. Results have been good, with above-average returns across all time periods from one to five years. Respectable safety rating. Best bet in this group at the present time. Formerly known as the OHA Foreign Equity Fund.

CENTREPOST BALANCED FUND $ → FI/G No RSP CBAL

Managers: Rick Hutcheon (equities), since 1994, Fred Palik (fixed income), since 1996

MER: 1.00%

The equity side of this portfolio is a virtual clone of the holdings in the Centrepost Canadian Equity Fund. That fund has been doing better recently, but this one hasn't kept pace and is lagging the averages for the balanced fund category over all time frames, in spite of an MER that is way, way below the industry average. On the plus side, the fund is conservatively managed and the safety record is respectable. Still, some better results are needed before the rating can move up.

FIXED INCOME AND MONEY MARKET FUNDS

CENTREPOST BOND FUND $$ ↓ FI No RSP CB

Manager: Fred Palik, since 1996

MER: 1.00%

The focus here is on high-quality bonds, mainly Government of Canada issues with a few blue-chip corporates tossed in. Recently the portfolio has been quite defensive, with most of the issues maturing within five to six years. That provided an additional measure of safety for investors, but depressed returns relative to other bond funds. Gain for the 12 months to June 30/98 was just 7.2%. Longer term results are also below average. On the other side of the coin, as you might expect, the safety record is good. So it's a case of deciding whether you want to trade off some return potential for more safety. Given the current state of the bond market, my advice is to stay with more aggressive funds. Formerly the OHA Bond Fund.

CENTREPOST SHORT TERM FUND $$$ → C No RSP CMM

Manager: Fred Palik, since 1996

MER: 0.75%

This is a standard money market fund, with a mix of government and corporate notes. Results have consistently been above average, thanks in large measure to the low MER. A good short-term parking spot for your cash. Formerly the OHA Short Term Fund.

CHOU FUNDS

THE COMPANY

This is a small fund group that started out as an investment club. It's based in Toronto and run by investment counsellor Francis Chou, who is a very forthright person when it comes to communicating with his unitholders. For example, in his most recent annual report he looked at the high valuations in the market and candidly admitted that he had "no concrete idea of where to proceed from here." When was the last time you heard a manager say anything like that? However, he went on to add this: "But one thing is certain: I am not willing to overpay. I am willing to forego profit that is rooted in pure market timing and market speculation." That tells you just about all you need to know about the way in which these funds are managed. Note that the minimum investment for the Associates Fund is $25,000. However, you can get into the RRSP Fund for as little as $3,500.

THE DETAILS

NUMBER OF FUNDS:	2
ASSETS UNDER MANAGEMENT:	$13 MILLION
LOAD CHARGE:	FRONT: MAX. 9%
SWITCHING CHARGE:	NONE
WHERE SOLD:	ONTARIO
HOW SOLD:	THROUGH BROKERS
PHONE NUMBER:	(416) 299-6749
WEB SITE ADDRESS:	N/A
E-MAIL ADDRESS:	N/A

FUND SUMMARY

$$$$ - NONE
$$$ - ASSOCIATES, RRSP
$$ - NONE
$ - NONE
NR - NONE
BEST CHOICES: ASSOCIATES
BEST FOR RRSPS: RRSP
BEST UNRATEDS: N/A

FUND RATINGS

CHOU RRSP FUND $$$ ↓ G # RSP CE

Manager: Francis Chou, since inception (1986)

MER: 2.02%

This is a small fund, with about $2.2 million in assets. It deserves more attention and is starting to receive it since its latest numbers are popping out at close to the top of the list on various computer filters. Francis Chou seeks to minimize risk, selecting stocks on the basis of sound valuations. He is a unique person; when the fund was underperforming in '94 and '95, he waived the management fees, refusing to accept any payment for what he regarded as poor results. It was a matter of "fairness and honour" he told unitholders. That's the kind of approach this industry needs to see more of. Now that the fund is doing well, he's accepting the fees again, and on the basis of recent results they are well merited. This fund recorded a terrific 43.9% gain over the 12 months to June 30/98, which helped to pull up the longer-term results to well above average. He did this with a stock selection that was way off the beaten path of banks and utilities, recording big gains in companies like Astral Communications, Moffat Communications, Premier Choix, and Travelers Group. Safety record is very good, earning an A rating from Altamira's Wilfred Vos in his ATP analysis. A good show. Rating moves up to $$$ as a result.

U.S. AND INTERNATIONAL EQUITY FUNDS

CHOU ASSOCIATES FUND $$$ → G # £ USE

Manager: Francis Chou, since inception (1986)

MER: 1.86%

This fund concentrates on locating stocks trading at a deep discount to their underlying value. Manager Francis Chou professes to ignore exotic selection techniques, preferring the KISS (keep it simple, stupid) approach to choosing securities. His strategy is one of buy and hold. Results have shown continued improvement in recent years. Gain for the 12 months to June 30/98 was 22.9%, slightly below average for U.S. stock funds as a group. Five-year average annual compound rate of return to that date was 20.5%, well above average. Chou mainly invests in U.S. stocks, although he's not restricted to that country and recently he has had several Canadian stocks in the portfolio as well. Entering '98, there were only a baker's dozen securities in the small portfolio, with Travelers Group and Federal Home Loan Mortgage Corp. the largest holdings. Now eligible for RRSPs as foreign content. Excellent safety record. Originally started in '81 as an investment club, gained fund status in '86.

C.I. MUTUAL FUNDS

THE COMPANY

This is a very aggressive company that is constantly making changes in its lineup. Their major moves over the past year included the launch of a new line of segregated funds in partnership with Toronto Mutual Life Insurance and the termination of the underperforming Monarch fund line. We began to see the maturation of the company's new Harbour line, managed by Gerald Coleman who moved over from Mackenzie Financial in early 1997 in what was one of the biggest fund stories of that year.

The other C.I. (Canadian International) brand name worth noting is the Hansberger Value Series. These funds are managed by a bunch of ex-Templeton types, led by that company's former CEO, Thomas Hansberger (in fact, their offices are just across the street from Templeton's head office in Fort Lauderdale, Florida). Several of the Hansberger funds are clones of similar Templeton funds offered in Canada, but most have not performed as well in head-to-head competition.

Note: C.I. has several funds that include the word "sector" in their names. This ends up being confusing to investors, because there are actually two different types of funds involved here. One group is essentially identical to a parent fund with the same name (e.g., C.I. Global Sector Shares are the same as the C.I. Global Fund). However, the sector shares are grouped together under a single umbrella fund (C.I. Sector Fund Limited) so that assets can be transferred between the sectors without triggering capital gains liability. Returns tend to be lower than those of the parent funds, mainly due to the fact the sectors hold more cash to provide liquidity for the frequent switching. Since these sector funds are essentially the same as the parent funds, they are not reviewed separately.

The other funds with "sector" in the name invest in specific areas of the economy (this is the classic definition of a sector fund). So you'll find C.I. Global Technology Sector Shares, C.I. Global Health Sciences Sector Shares, etc. They are also part of the umbrella C.I. Sector Fund Ltd., but they have no corresponding stand-alone fund, so you can only buy them as part of the overall Sector Fund.

Confused? I'm not surprised. C.I. would do themselves a favour if they could somehow manage to simplify all this. It looks too clever by far.

THE DETAILS

NUMBER OF FUNDS:	59
ASSETS UNDER MANAGEMENT:	$8.7 BILLION
LOAD CHARGE:	FRONT: MAX. 5%; BACK: MAX. 5.5%
SWITCHING CHARGE:	2% MAXIMUM
WHERE SOLD:	ACROSS CANADA
HOW SOLD:	DIRECTLY THROUGH THE MANAGER OR THROUGH BROKERS, DEALERS, AND FINANCIAL PLANNERS
PHONE NUMBER:	1-800-563-5181
WEB SITE ADDRESS:	WWW.CIFUNDS.COM
E-MAIL ADDRESS:	WEBMASTER@CIFUNDS.COM

FUND SUMMARY

C.I. FUNDS

$$$$ - NONE

$$$ - CANADIAN BOND, CANADIAN INCOME, COVINGTON, GLOBAL, GLOBAL BOND RSP, INTERNATIONAL BALANCED, INTERNATIONAL BALANCED RSP, MONEY MARKET, U.S. MONEY MARKET

$$ - AMERICAN, CANADIAN BALANCED, CANADIAN GROWTH, GLOBAL EQUITY RSP, GLOBAL HIGH YIELD, WORLD BOND

$ - EMERGING MARKETS, LATIN AMERICAN, PACIFIC

NR - AMERICAN RSP, AMERICAN SECTOR SHARES, AMERICAN SEGREGATED, CANADIAN RESOURCE, CANADIAN SECTOR SHARES, DIVIDEND, EMERGING MARKETS SECTOR SHARES, GLOBAL CONSUMER PRODUCTS SECTOR SHARES, GLOBAL FINANCIAL SERVICES SECTOR SHARES, GLOBAL HEALTH SCIENCES SECTOR SHARES, GLOBAL RESOURCE SECTOR SHARES, GLOBAL SECTOR SHARES, GLOBAL SEGREGATED, GLOBAL TECHNOLOGY SECTOR SHARES, GLOBAL TELECOMMUNICATIONS SECTOR SHARES, LATIN AMERICAN SECTOR SHARES, MONEY MARKET SEGREGATED, PACIFIC SECTOR SHARES, SHORT-TERM SECTOR SHARES

HANSBERGER VALUE SERIES

$$$$ - NONE
$$$ - NONE
$$ - EUROPEAN
$ - ASIAN
NR - ASIAN SECTOR SHARES, DEVELOPING MARKETS,
DEVELOPING MARKETS SECTOR SHARES, EUROPEAN
SECTOR SHARES, GLOBAL SMALL-CAP, GLOBAL SMALL-CAP
SECTOR SHARES, INTERNATIONAL, INTERNATIONAL
SECTOR SHARES, VALUE, VALUE SECTOR SHARES, VALUE
SEGREGATED

HARBOUR FUNDS

$$$$ - NONE
$$$ - NONE
$$ - NONE
$ - NONE
NR - EXPLORER, EXPLORER SECTOR SHARES, GROWTH &
INCOME, GROWTH & INCOME SEGREGATED, HARBOUR
FUND HARBOUR SECTOR SHARES, HARBOUR SEGREGATED

BEST CHOICES: C.I. CANADIAN BOND, C.I. GLOBAL, C.I. INTERNATIONAL BALANCED
BEST FOR RRSPs: C.I. CANADIAN BOND, C.I. INTERNATIONAL BALANCED RSP
BEST UNRATEDS: C.I. AMERICAN RSP, C.I. DIVIDEND

FUND RATINGS

CANADIAN EQUITY FUNDS

C.I. CANADIAN GROWTH FUND $$ ↑ G #/* RSP CE

Manager: John Zechner, since inception (1993)

MER: 2.35%

The performance of this fund has improved recently after
manager John Zechner moved away from his heavy
weightings in the underachieving resource sector and
shifted his emphasis to areas like retailing, financial services, and consumer products. He was also carrying a
large cash component in the first half of '98 as a defence
against market volatility. The result was a 14.8% gain for
the year to June 30/98, which put this fund in the high

second quartile in its peer group. Longer term results are still weak, however. There's a lot of month-to-month volatility in this fund, with an historic 41% chance of the NAV dropping in any given month. However, the volatility tends to smooth out over longer periods. Still, the ATP analysis shows this fund ranks very low on the risk/reward scale.

C.I. COVINGTON FUND $$ ↑ G * RSP LAB

Managers: Grant Brown, since inception (1995) and Chip Vallis, since 1996

MER: 4.40%

This labour-sponsored venture capital fund is distributed through C.I. but operates on an independent basis. This has been one of my top labour fund recommendations from its inception. Grant Brown has established a sound reputation in the venture capital business over the years and Chip Vallis has a wealth of experience. The focus is on early-stage companies, and one of the big successes to date has been a $2.5-million stake in Playdium Entertainment Corporation. That company now operates a high-tech video games emporium in Mississauga, Ont. that is exceeding all revenue projections. This fund's 5.5% average annual compound rate of return for the three years to June 30/98 may look modest, but investors in labour-sponsored funds shouldn't expect big returns at this early stage. In fact, that result is better than average for the category. Labour funds have fallen out of favour since the federal and provincial governments cut their tax advantages. But if you're interested in acquiring some units, this is one of the better choices available.

U.S. AND INTERNATIONAL EQUITY FUNDS

C.I. AMERICAN FUND $$ ↓ G #/* £ USE

Manager: William Priest (BEA Associates), since inception (1992)

MER: 2.38%

This fund continues to churn out profits for C.I. investors, although it has slipped somewhat recently relative to other U.S. entries. Return for the year to June 30/98 was 24.7%, which looks pretty good until you learn that the average for the U.S. fund category was 27.5%, according to figures compiled by Southam. Manager Bill Priest was heavily into consumer products and communications stocks in the first half of '98, but had little in the hot technology sector. He uses a very disciplined stock selection process that focuses on cash flow and corporate commitment to enhancement of shareholder value. Despite the performance decline, the safety record of this fund remains unblemished. ATP analysis shows not a single 12-month period where you would have lost money here.

C.I. EMERGING MARKETS FUND $ ↑ G #/* £ EME

Manager: Nandu Narayana (BEA Associates), since 1997

MER: 2.71%

These are difficult times for emerging markets funds, what with all the turmoil in Asia and a flight to quality by investors. Manager Nandu Narayana has been attempting to deal with the problems by maintaining a very large cash position (37.4% of the portfolio in mid-'98) and by broad diversification (Mexico was the largest holding in mid-year, with 11.3% of the assets). There are also some unusual "emerging" countries represented. For example, Canadians might be surprised to learn we're considered an emerging market by some, but Canuck securities accounted for more than 5% of the portfolio in mid-'98. Other questionable emerging markets were Japan and the Netherlands. I guess when times are tough, anything goes. Certainly, these tactics mitigated the losses; the fund dropped 8.9% in the year ending June 30/98, which was a much better result than many similar funds managed to produce. Even so, you don't want to be here right now.

C.I. GLOBAL FUND $$$ ↓ G #/* £ IE

Manager: Bill Sterling (BEA Associates), since 1995

MER: 2.45%

Manager Bill Sterling is an intellectual (Ph.D. in economics from Harvard) who sees global investing as a three-dimensional chess game with the winners being those managers who can best simultaneously monitor the interest rates, exchange rates, and equity valuations that influence securities prices. Sounds like mind-boggling stuff, but the fund, which had been sliding, has turned around since he assumed control, with a three-year average annual compound rate of return of 19.3% to June 30/98. That was much better than average for the international fund category over that time frame. In mid-'98, the portfolio was heavily weighted to U.S. and European stocks (77% of the portfolio between them). The fund's mandate allows it to invest in emerging markets as well, but there were very few stocks from those nations represented. The risk profile of this fund is excellent and with the returns improving as well a boost in the rating to $$$ is more than warranted.

C.I. GLOBAL EQUITY RSP FUND $$ → G #/* RSP IE

Manager: Bill Sterling (BEA Associates), since 1995

MER: 2.43%

This is an RRSP-eligible international fund that uses a mix of equities and derivatives of various types to stay on the right side of the federal government's 20% foreign content rule. It should only be used by investors who have reached the foreign content limit in their registered plans but wish to add more international stock exposure. As of the end of June, '98, the portfolio was heavily focused on the U.S. (47.3%), and featured such blue-chip names as AT&T, Exxon, and General Electric. About a third of the portfolio was in Europe, with the rest sprinkled around the globe. The managers may invest in developing markets, but holdings there are insignificant at present. Returns have been about average for the global fund category, as reported by *The Financial Post*, but below those of the companion Global Fund, which is the better choice, unless you need the extra foreign content room.

C.I. LATIN AMERICAN FUND $ ↑ G #/* £ AE

Manager: Emily Alejos (BEA Associates), since 1997

MER: 2.75%

This fund was on a pretty good rebound after some tough years when, bang! It hit a brick wall in May/98, dropping 12.7% in a single month and followed that up with a 6.3%

loss in June. That's a huge decline by mutual fund standards. Most of the portfolio (more than 75%) was concentrated in Mexico and Brazil in mid-year, making this fund extremely vulnerable to any negative movements in either of those markets. In a climate of broad concern about emerging markets, this fund appears to be very high risk at present. Only investors with a strong stomach and a long time horizon should enter at this stage.

C.I. PACIFIC FUND $ ↑ G #/* £ FEE

Manager: Terry Mahoney, since 1996

MER: 2.50%

Terry Mahoney, who came on board at the end of '96 to work with long-time manager Shaun Chan, has now taken over complete responsibility for this portfolio. The "promotion" could hardly have come at a worse time, just as the Asian economic crisis was knocking the stuffing out of every Far East fund around, including this one. Loss for the year to June 30/98 was a mind-boggling 49.3%, and this despite a large cash position (27.1% of the portfolio at mid-year). Very few funds in the category did worse (although Hansberger Asian managed the trick). Mahoney was heavily concentrated in Hong Kong in the first half of '98 and was completely out of Japan, but there were no safe havens in Asia. Best to stand clear for now. Formerly known as Universal Pacific Fund.

HANSBERGER ASIAN FUND $ ↑ G #/* £ FEE

Manager: Thomas Hansberger, since 1996

MER: 2.75%

This has been a weak performer from the get-go. It was originally created as the C.I. Emerging Asian Fund in '93, and promptly proceeded to chalk up big losses for investors in its first two years. The troubled portfolio was handed to the Hansberger organization in '96, but they haven't been able to do any better. In fact, the loss for the year to June 30/98 was an almost unbelievable 59.8%. What more needs be said? Avoid this one.

HANSBERGER EUROPEAN FUND $$ → G #/* £ EE

Manager: Lauretta (Retz) Reeves, since 1996

MER: 2.43%

For some time, this fund was an embarrassment to the
C.I. Group, turning in below-average results. So when C.I.
made a deal with former Templeton International president Thomas Hansberger to set up a new line of value
funds bearing his name, this one was tossed into the hop-
per as well. With a new managerial team at the helm, none
of the history prior to '96 is relevant. The first two years
under the Hansberger banner have been okay but not
great — the fund returned 27.4% in the 12 months to the
end of June, '97 and added 25.2% over the next year, to
the end of June, '98. Those numbers were sub-par for the
hot-performing European fund category. The management style is value-oriented (many Hansberger employees were formerly with him at Templeton), so I expect
this fund to do reasonably well over time. However, the
rating holds at $$ for now.

BALANCED FUNDS

C.I. CANADIAN BALANCED FUND $$ → FI/G #/* RSP CBAL

Manager: John Zechner, since inception (1993)

MER: 2.30%

After an off-year last year, this fund has rallied somewhat,
thanks in large part to a different approach to the equities
section, which has de-emphasized the underperforming
resource stocks. Equities represented about half the holdings in mid-'98, with a relatively low cash position (8.2%)
compared to a year earlier. So at this stage, this is a well-
diversified balanced fund that's delivering reasonable
results. The fund is conservatively managed and historically has outperformed its peer group in down markets.
That's all fine, but long-term results are still below average. Rating holds at $$ for now.

C.I. CANADIAN INCOME FUND $$$ ↓ FI/G #/* RSP CBAL

Manager: John Zechner, since inception (1994)

MER: 1.82%

This balanced fund is designed for investors who don't want to take a lot of risk but want some exposure to the equity markets. Most of the portfolio is held in government and corporate bonds. But up to 30% may be in equities (as of June 30/98 the equity portion was actually 25.3%, including preferred shares). The stocks that are held tend to be of the ultra blue-chip variety, with the banks leading the list. Because of its defensive nature, the performance of this fund cannot be compared to the average balanced fund, which would normally hold a much higher percentage of stocks. Judged strictly on its own terms, this fund has performed quite well, with an average annual compound rate of return of 13% for the three years to June 30. That was actually better than the companion Canadian Balanced Fund, which has a larger proportion of stocks in its portfolio. If you're looking for a low-volatility balanced fund for your mix, this one is worth consideration.

C.I. INTERNATIONAL BALANCED FUND $$$ ↓ FI/G #/* £ IBAL

Manager: William Sterling (BEA Associates), since inception (1994)

MER: 2.40%

The mandate of this fund allows it to invest in both developed and emerging markets for maximum diversification. However, the emerging markets side does not figure very prominently in the picture these days. As of the beginning of July, '98, U.S. and European holdings dominated the portfolio (about one third each) and the manager had a huge cash position (more than a quarter of the assets). Asian holdings amounted to only about 3%, most of which was in Japan. The name of this fund is a bit misleading, since in mutual fund parlance the term "international" usually refers to a fund that doesn't invest in its home country or home continent. But this one is big in North America and even has a small Canadian holding (1.9%). But investors aren't quibbling because the performance has been very good. Average annual compound rate of return for the three years to June 30/98 was 17%, comfortably above average for the international balanced category. The safety record is also first-rate. This fund is very worthy of your consideration.

C.I. INTERNATIONAL BALANCED RSP FUND $$$ ↓ FI/G #/* RSP IBAL

Manager: William Sterling (BEA Associates), since inception (1994)

MER: 2.40%

This is yet another of the many mutual funds designed to circumvent the 20% foreign content rule for RRSPs (when is the finance minister going to wake up?). In this case, the fund invests in a diversified portfolio of stocks and bonds, along with the derivatives needed to keep these pseudo-Canadian funds on the right side of the rules. Although this is called an "international" fund, which in mutual fund parlance normally means it doesn't invest in North America, this one holds assets around the globe. As of the beginning of July, '98, the largest positions were in Europe (37.8%) and the U.S. (38.2%), with a smattering elsewhere. The balance was tilted towards equities, which made up 53.1% of the portfolio. Performance has been above average for its category, however the companion C.I. International Balanced Fund has done better. It should be used unless the foreign content restrictions prohibit that possibility.

FIXED INCOME AND MONEY MARKET FUNDS

C.I. CANADIAN BOND FUND $$$ → FI #/* RSP CB

Manager: John Zechner, since inception (1993)

MER: 1.65%

John Zechner is known more as an equity manager than a bond expert, but in relative terms this has been the most successful of the funds he runs for C.I. Average annual return for the three years ending June 30/98 was 12.2%. That makes it one of the top-performing bond funds in the country over that time. Zechner managed this despite a large cash weighting in recent months (over 20% in mid-'98), plus another 30% holding in short- to medium-term bonds with less than 10 years to maturity. Impressive. If you want to set up a diversified portfolio using C.I. funds, this one should be on your list.

C.I. GLOBAL BOND RSP FUND $$$ ↓ FI #/* RSP IB

Manager: Gregg Diliberto (BEA Associates), since inception (1993)

MER: 2.05%

This is a "pseudo-Canadian" fund that invests in international bonds but does so in such a way as to retain full RRSP eligibility. Okay performer in the international bond fund category, and it has actually done better than the companion World Bond Fund, also run by Diliberto. Three-year average annual compound rate of return to June 30/98 was 8.8%, better than average for the international bond fund category. Good safety record. A decent holding for an RRSP.

C.I. GLOBAL HIGH YIELD FUND $$ ↑ FI #/* £ IB

Manager: Gregg Diliberto (BEA Associates), since inception (1994)

MER: 2.15%

This is a global "junk bond" fund. It invests in bonds of governments and corporations in emerging countries and in high-yield bonds in developed countries like Canada and the U.S. The idea is to generate above-average returns, and the fund has been successful in achieving that objective over the past three years, with an average annual gain of 13.6% to June 30/98. However, latest results have been weak, in part due to the concern about emerging markets debt. This one is strictly for the adventurous.

C.I. MONEY MARKET FUND $$$ → C #/* RSP CMM

Manager: John Zechner, since 1994

MER: 0.75%

Good performer in the money market category. The mix has changed over the past year, however. The fund used to invest mainly in Government of Canada T-bills, but corporate notes and banker's acceptances now form the bulk of the portfolio. Useful as a temporary place to park cash while you're deciding which part of the world to invest in next. Tip: Don't buy this or any other money market fund on a back-end load basis. Try to get the front-end load waived as well.

C.I. U.S. MONEY MARKET FUND $$$ → C #/* £ IMM

Manager: John Zechner, since inception (1995)

MER: 0.51%

Very low-risk portfolio, with most of the money held in U.S. Government T-bills or Government of Canada U.S.-pay T-bills. The returns on this U.S.-dollar money market fund have been better than those of most of its competitors, thanks in part to a low MER. But that's before any sales commissions are calculated into the picture. If you can get this fund on a no-charge basis (front-end load option with zero commission), it's worth considering if it meets your needs. Note that you cannot hold this fund in a C.I. registered plan, but it is eligible as foreign content in a self-directed RRSP.

C.I. WORLD BOND FUND $$ → FI #/* £ IB

Manager: Gregg Diliberto (BEA Associates), since inception (1992)

MER: 2.05%

This is the foreign content companion to the Global RSP Bond Fund. Results have actually lagged behind the Global RSP Fund lately, so it's hard to see why you'd choose this one if you were in the market for an international bond fund at all. Certainly, it should not be used in registered plans under any circumstances because it will gobble up foreign content to no purpose. In mid-'98, the portfolio was heavily weighted towards the Canadian dollar, with very little U.S. currency exposure. The strategy wasn't working well at that point, as the loonie reached one new low after another!

CIBC MUTUAL FUNDS

THE COMPANY

CIBC has been playing an aggressive game of catch-up with the other big banks in terms of improving the performance of their mutual funds and adding to their product line. Within the past three years, 17 new funds have been launched, all of which are too new to be rated here. As well, there have been many managerial changes, and some of these are now starting to pay off with much better returns.

One area in which this group is assuming a leadership role is in its lineup of index funds. There are now a total of eight on offer, far more than you'll find with any other company. All have a very low management expense ratio of 0.90%. Index funds have become immensely popular in the U.S., and CIBC obviously feels that trend will take hold in Canada as well. So if you're an index fund fan, you'll want to take a close look at this organization.

From the one-time laggard of the big no-load fund groups, CIBC has now moved into a position of respectability with some very good offerings available.

THE DETAILS

NUMBER OF FUNDS:	34
ASSETS UNDER MANAGEMENT:	$13 BILLION
LOAD CHARGE:	NONE
SWITCHING CHARGE:	NONE
WHERE SOLD:	ACROSS CANADA
HOW SOLD:	DIRECTLY THROUGH ANY CIBC BRANCH, BY CIBC INVESTORS EDGE (DISCOUNT BROKERAGE), BY CIBC WOOD GUNDY (FULL SERVICE BROKERAGE), AND SOME OTHER DEALS AND DISCOUNT BROKERAGE SERVICES.
PHONE NUMBER:	1-800-465-3863 OR (416) 980-3863
WEB SITE ADDRESS:	WWW.CIBC.COM/MUTUAL FUNDS
E-MAIL ADDRESS:	N/A

FUND SUMMARY

$$$$ - NONE

$$$ - CANADIAN BALANCED, CANADIAN BOND, GLOBAL EQUITY, PREMIUM CANADIAN T-BILL, U.S. DOLLAR MONEY MARKET

$$ - CANADIAN EQUITY, CANADIAN SHORT-TERM BOND, CAPITAL
APPRECIATION, DIVIDEND, MORTGAGE, U.S. EQUITY

$ - CANADIAN T-BILL, FAR EAST PROSPERITY, GLOBAL
BOND, MONEY MARKET

NR - CANADIAN BOND INDEX, CANADIAN INDEX, CANADIAN
REAL ESTATE, CANADIAN RESOURCES, EMERGING
ECONOMIES, ENERGY, EUROPEAN, FINANCIAL COMPANIES,
GLOBAL BOND INDEX, GLOBAL TECHNOLOGY,
INTERNATIONAL INDEX, INTERNATIONAL INDEX RRSP,
INTERNATIONAL SMALL COMPANIES, JAPANESE, LATIN
AMERICAN, NORTH AMERICAN DEMOGRAPHICS, PRECIOUS
METALS, U.S. INDEX RRSP, U.S. SMALL COMPANIES

BEST CHOICES: CANADIAN BALANCED, CANADIAN BOND, GLOBAL EQUITY
BEST FOR RRSPS: CANADIAN BALANCED, CANADIAN BOND, U.S. MONEY MARKET
BEST UNRATED: EUROPEAN, NORTH AMERICAN DEMOGRAPHICS

FUND RATINGS

CANADIAN EQUITY FUNDS

CIBC CORE CANADIAN EQUITY FUND $$ → G No RSP CE

Manager: Réal Trépanier, since 1997

MER: 2.20%

Réal Trépanier, a former head of the Montreal Police
Pension Fund, took over responsibility for the portfolio
in February, '97. Since then this long-time underachiever
has started to look much more impressive. Gain for the
year to June 30/98 was 19.4%, which just missed making
the top decile in the Canadian equity fund category,
according to the Southam rankings. That performance
was also good enough to pull the three-year return to
above average. The portfolio emphasis is on lower risk,
large-cap stocks, and Trépanier intends to make more
aggressive use of foreign content than in the past, with a
focus on the U.S. The risk profile of this fund, historically
poor, is also starting to show improvement. Rating moves
up a notch this year, and if Trépanier can keep it up,
another upgrade will follow quickly.

CIBC CAPITAL APPRECIATION FUND $$ → G No RSP CSC

Manager: Virginia Wai-Ping, since 1997

MER: 2.40%

This fund has gone through three managerial changes in two years, with Virginia Wai-Ping assuming portfolio responsibility in late 1997. Despite the merry-go-round, the fund managed to turn in an above-average return of 12.7% for the year to June 30/98. This is CIBC's small-cap entry, although some of the companies in the portfolio hardly fit that bill (TD Bank and Bank of Montreal were among the top five holdings in the first half of '98!). So this would hardly qualify as a pure small-cap fund, although there are certainly plenty of stocks that fit that definition in the overall mix. As with the Canadian Equity Fund, more attention is being paid to the foreign content component of the portfolio, with 8.2% of the assets in U.S. growth stocks in the first half of '98. Like several other CIBC equity funds, this one looks like it has improved potential for more aggressive investors. Risk is about average for a small-cap fund.

CIBC DIVIDEND FUND $$ → G/FI No RSP INC

Manager: Réal Trépanier, since 1997

MER: 1.88%

Réal Trépanier, who also runs the Canadian Equity Fund, added this one to his string in late 1997, making him the third manager within a year. The portfolio composition favours blue-chip, dividend-paying common stocks, but there was a significant position in preferred shares (14.4%) and a large cash holding (20.2%) in the first half of '98. The result was a slightly better than average total return for the dividend fund peer group of 17% over the 12 months to June 30/98. However, cash flow to investors during calendar '97 was much lower than the previous year at just 2%, according to the annual survey done for the *Mutual Funds Update* newsletter. So don't choose this fund if steady income is your prime objective. Name changed from CIBC Equity Income Fund in August, '96.

U.S. AND INTERNATIONAL EQUITY FUNDS

CIBC FAR EAST PROSPERITY FUND $ ↑ G No £ FEE

Manager: Duncan Mount (CEF-TAL), since inception (1993)

MER: 2.69%

Like all Far East funds, this one took a licking last year, losing 35%. Is there more downside to come? No one knows at this stage, with Asia seemingly poised on the brink of a major depression. About the only thing that can be said is that the risks in that part of the world remain very high and only the most aggressive investors should consider taking new positions at this stage. This is one of the few Far East funds that can include Japanese stocks in its holdings, even though CIBC has another fund specifically designated for the Japan market. Manager Duncan Mount has a good reputation, but when the hurricane blows through, nothing is left standing.

CIBC GLOBAL EQUITY FUND $$$ ↓ G No £ IE

Manager: Gordon Fyfe, since 1996

MER: 2.50%

This fund is really starting to move under Gordon Fyfe's direction. The mandate is to invest in established growth companies in major markets around the world. The portfolio is huge — the list of holdings covers four-and-a-half pages in the annual report. The country diversification has a very distinct North American flavour to it, with almost half the assets in the U.S. and Canada in the first half of '98. Results are looking much better, with a gain of 27.5% for the year to June 30/98. As international funds go, this one has a pretty good historic risk profile, with just a 12% chance of being down in any one-year period. This one gets another rating upgrade this year.

CIBC U.S. EQUITY INDEX FUND $$ → G No £ USE

Manager: Mellon Capital Management, since 1998

MER: 0.90%

Big changes here! This fund has gone from being a run-of-the-mill large-cap U.S. equity fund to a pure index fund that tracks the Wilshire 5000. That's a little-known index that measures a broad range of large- and small-cap U.S. stocks, and this is the only fund in Canada that uses it as its benchmark. The move from an actively managed fund to a passive fund meant money in the pockets of investors, as CIBC dropped the MER all the way from 2.30% to 0.90%. That added up to a $5-million saving in fees. But will it pay off in terms of return? It's still too early to tell whether the new version of this fund will outperform the average for the U.S. equity fund category, but early results are impressive. Longer term results now mean nothing because of the mandate change. We'll hold the rating at $$ for now and see what happens.

BALANCED FUNDS

CIBC BALANCED FUND $$$ → FI/G No RSP CBAL

Manager: Jean-Guy Desjardins, since 1994

MER: 2.24%

This fund has been showing steady improvement in recent years, and returns have now moved to above average over all time periods. The fund invests in a wide variety of securities, including Canadian and U.S. equities, government bonds, corporate bonds, mort-gage-backed securities, and T-bills. You name it, and it's probably somewhere in the large portfolio. Gain for the 12 months to June 30/98 was a healthy 16.9%. This one looks good, especially for an RRSP investor seek-ing maximum diversification (it's a good RRSP starter fund). Name changed from CIBC Balanced Income and Growth Fund in August, '96.

FIXED INCOME AND MONEY MARKET FUNDS

CIBC CANADIAN BOND FUND $$$ → FI No RSP CB

Manager: John Braive, since 1994

MER: 1.55%

The portfolio of this fund is a well-diversified mix of fed-eral, provincial, and corporate bonds of varying maturities. Since John Braive of T.A.L. Investment Counsel (which is owned by CIBC) took over management responsibility in 1994, the returns have improved to well above average. Gain for the year to June 30/98 was 9.6%; three-year average annual compound rate of return was 10.5%. This is an attractive choice for the fixed-income segment of a CIBC mutual fund portfolio. Formerly known as the CIBC Fixed Income Fund.

CIBC CANADIAN SHORT-TERM BOND INDEX FUND
$$ ↓ FI No RSP CB

Manager: Freda Dong, since 1998

MER: 0.90%

This fund represents a compromise position for investors who want low risk but are unhappy with the tiny yields being paid by money market funds these days. The portfolio is designed to track the Scotia Capital Markets Short-Term Bond Index, so this is now a pure index fund. That makes it suitable for investors who want to reduce downside exposure in the event a rise in interest rates sparks a major bond market correction. The other side of this coin is that the return potential of this fund is much less than that of the regular CIBC Bond Fund. Greater safety, but less profit. That's the trade-off decision that has to be made here. Last year, for example, this fund gained only 4% compared to 9.6% for the CIBC Bond Fund. But if the option is this or a money market fund, put your money here. The shift in mandate to an index fund has resulting in a lower MER, which should help to boost the return a bit.

CIBC CANADIAN T-BILL FUND
$ ↓ C No RSP CMM

Manager: Steven Dubrovsky, since 1994

MER: 0.99%

Safe, solid performer from one of Canada's big banks. Nothing unusual, just steady return with little risk. Results are slightly below average for this category, although a reduced MER may help matters some.

CIBC GLOBAL BOND FUND $ → FI No RSP IB

Manager: Denis Senécal, since 1995

MER: 1.95%

This is a fully RRSP-eligible international bond fund that invests mainly in Canadian government securities denominated in foreign currencies. It's been a below average performer. There are better funds of this type around.

CIBC MONEY MARKET FUND $ → C No RSP CMM

Manager: Steven Dubrovsky, since 1994

MER: 0.99%

The Bank of Commerce has a large family of money market funds (four as of mid-'98). This is the original one. It's a steady performer, but results tend to be below average for this category. However, the MER was recently dropped to just below 1% (it was 1.20% at this time last year) so that should help. The fund is best suited to CIBC clients who want to get a better return on the money they've been holding in deposit accounts. The bank's Canadian T-Bill Fund offers slightly more safety and, oddly, its recent returns have been almost the same. But your best bet, if you have the minimum amount required, is the Premium Canadian T-Bill Fund.

CIBC MORTGAGE FUND $$ → FI No RSP M

Manager: Bert Pearsoll, since 1987

MER: 1.69%

Last year I noted this fund was turning in some impressive returns despite a management expense ratio that was higher than that of most of the other bank mortgage funds. Well, this year the MER is even higher but the results have fallen off considerably. The fund only gained 3.1% in the year to June 30/98. That was way below the average for the mortgage fund category and barely higher than the yield from the CIBC Money Market Fund. Not very good. CIBC has been reducing the MERs on several other funds; I suggest they may want to take a close look at this one as well. Otherwise, the returns are likely to languish as long as interest rates stay low. The safety record is good, however. Historically, there is only a 1% chance of a loss in any given 12-month period, although this fund tends to show more month-to-month volatility than the average mortgage fund. The portfolio is made up almost entirely of high-quality, NHA-insured mortgages. Best suited to ultra-conservative investors, but don't expect much in the way of returns right now. Rating drops back a notch this year.

CIBC PREMIUM CANADIAN T-BILL FUND $$$ ↓ C No RSP CMM

Manager: Steven Dubrovsky, since 1994

MER: 0.55%

This is the Bank of Commerce's money fund for the rich. Minimum investment is $250,000, in case you have the loose change around the house. Investment strategy is the same as for the Canadian T-Bill Fund, which you only need $500 to buy. The difference is that the management expense ratio on this fund is about half that of the regular T-bill fund, boosting your return accordingly.

CIBC U.S. DOLLAR MONEY MARKET FUND $$$ → C No RSP IMM

Manager: Steven Dubrovsky, since 1994

MER: 1.08%

The distinguishing feature of this U.S.-dollar fund is that it's fully RRSP eligible. The fund invests mainly in short-term Canadian securities, such as federal government T-bills, that are denominated in U.S. currency. This makes it especially useful if you want to increase U.S.-dollar assets in a registered plan, although if the Canadian dollar is expected to strengthen (it will happen someday!), that's not a great idea. Performance is above average.

CLARINGTON MUTUAL FUNDS

THE COMPANY

This is a new fund company under the direction of Terry Stone, who headed up the Bolton Tremblay funds prior to their purchase by BPI. It was launched with six funds in September, 1996, and now has a total of 11 offerings. Eventual goal is to have 20 funds available. Because this is a new firm, none of the funds has the necessary three-year track record to qualify for a formal rating.

THE DETAILS

NUMBER OF FUNDS:	11
ASSETS UNDER MANAGEMENT:	$283 MILLION
LOAD CHARGE:	FRONT: MAX. 5%; BACK: MAX. 5.75%
SWITCHING CHARGE:	2% MAXIMUM
WHERE SOLD:	ACROSS CANADA
HOW SOLD:	THROUGH INDEPENDENT BROKERS, DEALERS, AND FINANCIAL PLANNERS
PHONE NUMBER:	1-888-860-9888
WEB SITE ADDRESS:	N/A
E-MAIL ADDRESS:	FUNDS@CLARINGTON.CA

FUND SUMMARY

$$$$ - NONE
$$$ - NONE
$$ - NONE
$ - NONE
NR - ASIA PACIFIC, CANADIAN BALANCED, CANADIAN EQUITY, CANADIAN INCOME, CANADIAN MICRO-CAP, CANADIAN SMALL-CAP, GLOBAL COMMUNICATIONS, GLOBAL OPPORTUNITIES, MONEY MARKET, U.S. EQUITY, U.S. SMALLER COMPANY GROWTH

BEST CHOICES: N/A
BEST FOR RRSPs: N/A
BEST UNRATEDS: GLOBAL COMMUNICATIONS, GLOBAL OPPORTUNITIES, U.S. EQUITY, U.S. SMALLER COMPANY GROWTH

FUND RATINGS

No funds have been in existence long enough to qualify for a rating.

CLEAN ENVIRONMENT MUTUAL FUNDS

THE COMPANY

The name says it all. This company operates mutual funds that invest in environmentally friendly stocks, with a special emphasis on firms that are developing new technologies in the field. These include companies that have found new ways to reduce pollution, to recycle materials, and to use alternative energy sources. If you're a socially conscious investor, here's a way to put your money to work in a way that will allow you to sleep well at night, and make some profits too. The funds are all managed by Acuity Investment Management Inc.

THE DETAILS

NUMBER OF FUNDS:	4
ASSETS UNDER MANAGEMENT:	$466 MILLION
LOAD CHARGE:	FRONT: MAX. 5%; BACK: MAX. 5%
SWITCHING CHARGE:	2% MAXIMUM
WHERE SOLD:	ACROSS CANADA
HOW SOLD:	THROUGH BROKERS, DEALERS, AND FINANCIAL PLANNERS
PHONE NUMBER:	(416) 366-9933 OR 1-800-461-4570 (VANCOUVER: 1-888-903-7999)
WEB SITE ADDRESS:	WWW.CLEANENVIRONMENT.COM
E-MAIL ADDRESS:	MAIL@CLEANENVIRONMENT.COM

FUND SUMMARY

$$$$ - NONE
$$$ - BALANCED, EQUITY, INTERNATIONAL EQUITY
$$ - NONE
$ - INCOME
NR - NONE
BEST CHOICES: BALANCED, EQUITY
BEST FOR RRSPs: BALANCED
BEST UNRATED: N/A

FUND RATINGS

CANADIAN EQUITY FUNDS

CLEAN ENVIRONMENT EQUITY FUND $$$ → G #/* RSP CE

Manager: Ian Ihnatowycz, since inception (1991)

MER: 2.60%

If you're trying to find a socially responsible fund for your investment portfolio, look no further. This is it. Ihnatowycz has built a winner despite the self-imposed restriction to companies that have shown a strong environmental commitment and do not derive a significant portion of their earnings from products that may cause serious health problems. So who makes their list? High-tech companies like Geac and ATI, manufacturers like Cinram, and financial companies like Fairfax. Returns continue to be very good; average annual five-year rate of return to June 30/98 was 19%; one-year return was 29%. This is a very good stock fund by any standard of measurement, and you only need $500 for an initial investment.

U.S. AND INTERNATIONAL EQUITY FUNDS

CLEAN ENVIRONMENT INTERNATIONAL EQUITY FUND $$$ → G #/* £ IE

Manager: Ian Ihnatowycz, since inception (1993)

MER: 2.62%

This is supposed to be an international companion to the Canadian Equity Fund, investing mainly in non-Canadian companies. But there continues to be a lot of overlap between the two funds, a fact I have noted in previous years. Entering '98, all but three of the 29 securities in this fund are also in the Canadian equity fund. It's true that the percentage of holdings is different, but that's not the kind of diversification you'd expect between a Canadian and an international fund. Since they both hold many of the same stocks, both funds have done well — this one was ahead 43.2% for the year ending June 30/98. But until there is more differentiation between the two funds, there's little point in holding both in your portfolio.

BALANCED FUNDS

CLEAN ENVIRONMENT
BALANCED FUND $$$ ↑ G/FI #/* RSP CBAL

Manager: Ian Ihnatowycz, since inception (1991)

MER: 2.60%

Here's something a little offbeat — a balanced fund that doesn't own any bonds, at least not the conventional type. There were a couple of convertibles in the portfolio in the first half of '98, but most of the income investments were in royalty income trusts, which accounted for almost a quarter of the assets. Stocks made up almost half the portfolio and there was a large cash position, although that was being reduced. Despite the big cash holding, the fund continues to produce very good returns. Gain for the 12 months to June 30/98 was 23.4%, way above average for the balanced fund category. Longer term results are also very good, with a five-year average annual compound rate of return of 16.1%. Risk is on the high side as balanced funds go, however, because of the use of more volatile royalty trusts instead of bonds.

CLEAN ENVIRONMENT
INCOME FUND $ → G/FI #/* RSP INC

Manager: Ian Ihnatowycz, since inception (1991)

MER: 1.98%

The name of this fund may be confusing. When people see the words "income fund", they usually think of some type of bond portfolio, and that's where this fund appears in the mutual fund surveys in the business press. But it's not a bond fund, or anything like it. It's true the mandate of the fund allows it to invest in bonds and other types of fixed-income assets like mortgage-backed securities, and a few years ago these did indeed make up the bulk of the portfolio. But manager Ian Ihnatowycz has taken this fund in a different direction recently, bringing royalty income trusts, REITs, and high-yielding common stocks into the mix. He also holds a lot of cash, which is why recent returns have been relatively low (8.8% for the year to June 30/98). Last year I described this fund as a work in progress, and nothing much has changed since then. It's hard to know how to classify this fund, but it appears to be evolving towards becoming a dividend fund. The mandate is to deliver "a high level of current interest and dividend income within a prudent standard of risk".

COTE 100 FUNDS

THE COMPANY

This little but growing company is based in St. Bruno, Quebec, a leafy suburb of Montreal. It's the brainchild of Guy Le Blanc, who has developed his own unique computer program to identify undervalued stocks. The company specializes in Canadian and U.S. issues, and Le Blanc emulates the Warren Buffett approach — buy just a few good stocks, take large positions, and hold them for a long time. The results have been very successful. The versatile Le Blanc also publishes an investment advisory newsletter and is the author of two books on investing.

To show you how confident he and his staff are about their stock-picking technique, they actually reduce their management fee if they don't meet the level of certain benchmark indexes. In other words, if they don't perform well, they take less money. What a revolutionary idea! I doubt it will ever take hold on Bay Street.

THE DETAILS

NUMBER OF FUNDS:	6
ASSETS UNDER MANAGEMENT:	$159 MILLION
LOAD CHARGE:	NONE
SWITCHING CHARGE:	NONE
WHERE SOLD:	QUEBEC
HOW SOLD:	DIRECTLY THROUGH THE MANAGER
PHONE NUMBER:	1-800-454-COTE (2683)
WEB SITE ADDRESS:	WWW.COTE100.COM
E-MAIL ADDRESS:	COTE100@COTE100.COM

FUND SUMMARY

$$$$ - NONE
$$$ - EXP, RRSP
$$ - AMERIQUE
$ - NONE
NR - EXCEL, QSSP, U.S.
BEST CHOICES: RRSP (REER)
BEST FOR RRSPs: RRSP (REER)
BEST UNRATED: QSSP (REA-ACTION)

FUND RATINGS

CANADIAN EQUITY FUNDS

COTE 100 EXP $$$ → G No RSP CE

Manager: Guy Le Blanc, since inception (1994)

MER: 2.00%

The mandate of this fund differs from that of its older COTE 100 RRSP stablemate to the extent that the focus in this case is supposed to be on North American companies that derive much of their business from exporting. However, as of the first half of 1998 only three of the 27 securities in this portfolio were not held in the 100 RRSP portfolio as well. In other words, there was very little difference between the two funds. It should come as no big surprise, therefore, that their returns are similar, although this one didn't do quite as well last year, with a gain of 15%. There really isn't much to choose between these two funds as things currently stand.

COTE 100 RRSP (REER) $$$ → G No RSP CE

Manager: Guy Le Blanc, since inception (1992)

MER: 2.00%

This fund invests in growth companies, many of which you have probably never heard of. But some names will be familiar, such as Bombardier and Nike. The portfolio is small, about 25 securities, and Le Blanc makes full use of the 20% foreign content allowance. Returns have been excellent; the fund shows a five-year average annual compound rate of return of 17.2% to June 30/98, which is good enough to rank it as the 18th best in Canada out of 161, according to the Southam Mutual Fund SourceDisk. The management fee of this fund is reduced by up to 0.5% if the returns fail to at least match the TSE 300 Index in a given year.

U.S. AND INTERNATIONAL STOCK FUNDS

COTE 100 AMERIQUE $$ → G No £ AE

Manager: Guy Le Blanc, since inception (1992)

MER: 2.00%

This is a North American fund, with both Canadian and U.S. stocks in the mix. In the first half of '98, about 62% of the portfolio was in Canadian stocks, 31% in U.S. issues, and the balance in cash. Here again, there is significant overlap between this portfolio and that of the RRSP Fund. The mix is somewhat different because of the greater U.S. content here, but the company holdings are very much the same. So there is not a lot of differentiation between the funds from that perspective. The performance of the RRSP Fund has been much better, however, making it the preferred choice.

CSA MANAGEMENT ENTERPRISES

THE COMPANY

This Toronto-based company specializes in gold and precious metals investing. It was incorporated in 1994, with Goldcorp Inc., Dickenson Mines, and Goldquest Exploration. The key individual is Robert McEwen, who is chairman of the company and who manages the fund portfolios.

THE DETAILS

NUMBER OF FUNDS:	2
ASSETS UNDER MANAGEMENT:	$9 MILLION
LOAD CHARGE:	FRONT: MAX. 5%
SWITCHING CHARGE:	$25 PLUS GST
WHERE SOLD:	ACROSS CANADA
HOW SOLD:	THROUGH MUTUAL FUND BROKERS AND DEALERS
PHONE NUMBER:	(416) 865-0326
WEB SITE ADDRESS:	N/A
E-MAIL ADDRESS:	N/A

FUND SUMMARY

$$$$ - NONE
$$$ - NONE
$$ - NONE
$ - GOLDFUND, GOLDTRUST
NR - NONE
BEST CHOICES: NONE
BEST FOR RRSPS: NONE
BEST UNRATEDS: N/A

FUND RATINGS

CANADIAN EQUITY FUNDS

GOLDFUND $ ↑ G # £ PM

Manager: Robert McEwen, since 1986

MER: 2.18%

The bear market in gold and gold stocks continues to plague this and other precious metals funds. The numbers tell it all: a loss of 32.1% in the year to June 30/98; a three-year average annual loss of 18.4%; a five-year average annual loss of 8.2%. Even if you were in for the long haul, you'd still be suffering; over the past 10 years this fund lost an average of 2.1% a year in value. That may not seem like a lot, but it is very rare for a mutual fund to complete a decade and be in the red at the end of the day. It wasn't all the manager's fault, you can't fight a tumbling market if your mandate gives you nowhere to hide. But in the 1997 annual report, Robert McEwen formally apologized for "the frightful fall in our net asset value per share" and said he had been caught in a "bear trap". His only words of comfort, if they can be called that, were: "I believe that in the near future, the stock markets will experience a downturn of a similar magnitude and speed to that which we experienced recently in the gold market." Such an event, similar to what happened in Asia, would reinforce "gold's historic role as an unalterable store of value." Perhaps, but most people would regard that as a very tough lesson. My advice on funds like this is not to treat them as buy and hold investments. If you're a deft trader, you might try to get in at a low, wait until the fund takes off, and exit quickly with your profits. It can happen; this fund gained 115% in '93. But it's like a roulette wheel. If you keep playing after a big score, you'll eventually give it all back.

GOLDTRUST $ ↑ G # RSP PM

Manager: Robert McEwen, since 1986

MER: 1.81%

This is an RRSP/RRIF eligible sibling to Goldfund. The performance patterns of the two funds are similar, not surprisingly, since they're both run by the same manager. If you're going this route, I recommend Goldfund, held outside a registered plan. I think gold and gold funds are too speculative for retirement plans.

DESJARDINS FUNDS

THE COMPANY

Desjardins is a household name in Quebec, where the company is one of the dominant players in the financial services field through its omnipresent credit union and trust company network. Its mutual fund family has expanded greatly in the past few years, and the funds are now available in parts of Ontario as well. Some of them are very good performers, and worthy of your attention if you live in an area where they're sold. All the funds are managed by Canagex Inc.

THE DETAILS

NUMBER OF FUNDS:	16
ASSETS UNDER MANAGEMENT:	$3.7 BILLION
LOAD CHARGE:	NONE
SWITCHING CHARGE:	NONE
WHERE SOLD:	ONTARIO AND QUEBEC
HOW SOLD:	THROUGH DESJARDINS TRUST AND CREDIT UNION BRANCHES
PHONE NUMBER:	1-800-224-7737
WEB SITE ADDRESS:	WWW.DESJARDINS.COM
E-MAIL ADDRESS:	N/A

FUND SUMMARY

$$$$ - NONE
$$$ - DIVIDEND, ENVIRONMENT
$$ - BALANCED, BOND, EQUITY, GROWTH, INTERNATIONAL, MORTGAGE
$ - DIVERSIFIED AUDACIOUS, DIVERSIFIED MODERATE, DIVERSIFIED SECURE, MONEY MARKET
NR - AMERICAN MARKET, DIVERSIFIED AMBITIOUS, QUEBEC, WORLDWIDE BALANCED

BEST CHOICES: DIVIDEND, ENVIRONMENT
BEST FOR RRSPS: BALANCED, DIVIDEND
BEST UNRATEDS: AMERICAN MARKET

FUND RATINGS

CANADIAN EQUITY FUNDS

DESJARDINS DIVIDEND FUND $$$ → G No RSP INC

Manager: Deborah Frame, since 1997

MER: 1.94%

The objective of this fund is to generate above-average dividend income, eligible for the dividend tax credit. The portfolio is structured for that purpose, with a mixture of preferred shares and high-yielding common stocks. In the case of a dividend fund, your interest should not be in total return but in cash flow. On that count, this fund didn't do particularly well in calendar '97, generating about 32 cents a unit. That worked out to a yield of about 2.7% on the basis of the net asset value at the start of the year. Some dividend funds produced cash flow of more than double that amount. However, the fund has consistently produced above-average total returns. Average annual compound rate of return for the three years to June 30/98 was a shade over 20%. If you're looking for a fund that will generate consistently high tax-advantaged income, there are better choices. But as a conservatively managed stock fund for an RRSP, this is a decent selection. Rating moves up to $$$.

DESJARDINS ENVIRONMENT FUND $$$ → G No RSP CE

Manager: Deborah Frame, since 1997

MER: 2.12%

This is the Desjardins group's socially responsible fund. The assets are invested primarily in Canadian companies that make a contribution toward improving or maintaining the environment. It's always interesting to see what companies qualify for the portfolio of these funds. Some of the holdings at the start of '98 were Dofasco, Alcan, B.C. Gas, Northern Telecom, and several banks. This fund started off well, but ran into a bad patch for a time. However, it has looked very good for the past few years, with better-than-average returns. One-year gain to June 30/98 was 16.2%. Five-year average annual return stands at 14.5%, which places the fund in the second quartile among all Canadian equity funds over that time. Rating moves up as a result. A new manager was recently appointed, Deborah Frame of Canagex.

DESJARDINS EQUITY FUND $$ → G No RSP CE

Manager: Deborah Frame, since 1997

MER: 1.92%

This is one of the older mutual funds in Canada (launched in '56). Its mandate is growth through investment in larger companies, although there are a few small- and mid-cap stocks in the mix. Results had been showing improvement but have tailed off again; the fund gained just 9.9% in the year to June 30/98. A new manager was recently named.

DESJARDINS GROWTH FUND $$ → G No RSP CE

Manager: Deborah Frame, since 1997

MER: 1.95%

This is the mid-cap offering of this group, investing in medium-sized companies with good growth potential. Sometimes the manager stretches that mandate a bit, but generally the portfolio is quite faithful to the overall objective. Some winning stocks in the portfolio in early '98 included Ballard Power Systems, TLC, and Mitel. Recent returns have been very respectable, with a gain of 16.9% for the year to June 30/98. There's greater risk here because of the nature of the mandate, although volatility is not unusually high. The good performance merits an upgrade in the rating.

U.S. AND INTERNATIONAL EQUITY FUNDS

DESJARDINS INTERNATIONAL FUND $$ → G No £ IE

Manager: Canagex

MER: 2.29%

Returns have been slumping for this fund, which was once one of the stars of this group. The portfolio is well diversified internationally, and includes holdings in North

America, although the term "international" in this context usually refers to a fund that only invests outside of this continent. The drag on performance can be traced to an over-emphasis on Japan (almost 16% of the portfolio in early '98) and a relatively small weighting in Europe, where markets were hot. Return for the 12 months to June 30/98 was 12.2%, slightly below average for the international equity fund category. Three-year returns are also sub-par. Safety record is only so-so.

BALANCED FUNDS

DESJARDINS BALANCED FUND $$ → FI/G No RSP CBAL

Manager: Canagex

MER: 1.93%

This fund makes money for its investors on a consistent basis, but the returns are generally only about average for the balanced fund category. Gain for the year to June 30/98 was 9.7%, a bit sub-par compared to the peer group. The portfolio offers a little bit of everything, including a sizeable number of U.S. and international stocks. Bond holdings in early '98 accounted for just 27.1% of the mix. Worth considering as a starter fund for an RRSP.

DESJARDINS DIVERSIFIED
AUDACIOUS FUND $ → FI/G No RSP CBAL

Manager: Canagex

MER: 1.91%

Okay, so the name of this fund doesn't translate well from the French (Audacieux). In fact, it creates the impression of some kind of far-out fund that's suitable only for high-flyers. That's not the case, however. This is a balanced fund that will usually hold about half its assets in fixed-income securities. The result is a decent risk rating, but a low return by balanced fund standards. Average annual gain for the three years to June 30/98 was 10.9%. Still, that was better than the other funds in the Desjardins Diversified group, which are even more conservative in their portfolio mix.

DESJARDINS DIVERSIFIED MODERATE FUND

$ ↓ FI/G No RSP CBAL

Manager: Canagex

MER: 1.79%

The portfolio emphasis in this fund is on bonds, mortgages, and mortgage-backed securities, which will normally make up about 70% of the asset mix. That gives this fund a very good safety rating. But it's not going to make much money for you in today's climate. Average annual compound rate of return for the three years to June 30/98 was 8.9%.

DESJARDINS DIVERSIFIED SECURE FUND

$ ↓ FI/G No RSP CBAL

Manager: Canagex

MER: 1.70%

This fund is well named, no doubt about that. Your money will certainly be "secure" here. Half the portfolio is normally invested in the money market, with another 35% in bonds and mortgages. That leaves room for just 15% in equities. So there's a bit of growth potential but this is really a fund for super-ultra conservative investors who don't care about big returns. Average annual gain for the three years to June 30/98 was just 6.3%.

FIXED INCOME AND MONEY MARKET FUNDS

DESJARDINS BOND FUND

$$ → FI No RSP CB

Manager: Canagex

MER: 1.63%

A so-so performer, with returns that are generally average or slightly below. The portfolio was about half in Government of Canada bonds in the first half of '98, with 22.2% of the holdings in Quebec government and government-guaranteed issues. The percentage of corporate bonds has been increased since last year. Okay, but not a fund you'd cross the street for.

DESJARDINS MONEY MARKET FUND $ → C No RSP CMM

Manager: Canagex

MER: 1.11%

This portfolio offers a blend of Quebec government short-term notes and banker's acceptances, with a very small percentage of federal T-bills. Returns tend to be below average.

DESJARDINS MORTGAGE FUND $$ ↓ FI No RSP M

Manager: Canagex

MER: 1.61%

Returns for this usually steady mortgage fund have recovered recently after slipping for the past couple of years. The gain for the year to June 30/98 was 4.6%, which may not seem like a lot but was actually above average for the mortgage fund category. Although residential mortgages make up the bulk of the portfolio, a significant portion of the fund (31%) was invested in bonds in early '98. The big attraction here is a great safety record; this fund has never recorded a losing 12-month period in its history, and that goes all the way back to '65. That makes it an excellent core holding for a conservatively managed RRSP.

DOMINION EQUITY RESOURCE FUND

THE COMPANY

This is a one-fund company. Dominion Equity is a small, Calgary-based fund that specializes in the energy sector. Crescent Capital Corp. took over responsibility for managing this fund on Jan. 1, 1998. However, long-time manager R.B. Coleman continues to be associated with the fund, as chairman.

THE DETAILS

NUMBER OF FUNDS:	1
ASSETS UNDER MANAGEMENT:	$17.6 MILLION
LOAD CHARGE:	NONE
SWITCHING CHARGE:	NONE
WHERE SOLD:	ALBERTA, B.C., AND ONTARIO
HOW SOLD:	DIRECTLY THROUGH DOMINION EQUITY
PHONE NUMBER:	(403) 531-2657
WEB SITE ADDRESS:	WWW.SOFTOPTIONS.COM
E-MAIL ADDRESS:	DOMINION@SOFTOPTIONS.COM

FUND SUMMARY

$$$$ -	NONE
$$$ -	NONE
$$ -	NONE
$ -	RESOURCE
NR -	NONE

FUND RATINGS

DOMINION EQUITY RESOURCE FUND $ ↑ G No RSP SEC

Manager: Dean Prodan, since 1998

MER: 2.10%

This Calgary-based resource fund specializes (as you might expect) in oil and gas stocks. It has a spotty record, reflecting the ebb and flow of prosperity in the oil patch. Right now, it's coming off a poor year, with a loss of 18.9% for the 12 months to June 30/98, after two profitable years in a row. That pulled down the five-year average annual return to -5.2%. Over a decade, you'd have done slightly better, but your profit would only have been 2% annually. What this should tell you is that this is not a buy-and-hold fund. Get in when the energy sector is hot, make your money, and then exit and await the next opportunity. Highly volatile. Minimum initial investment is $20,000.

DUNDEE MUTUAL FUNDS

THE COMPANY

This is really the old Dynamic group, with a new look. In late July it was announced that a new fund family, Power, would join Dynamic as offerings under the Dundee label. This multi-family approach is becoming more common in the industry and is already being used by Mackenzie, AGF, C.I., and Investors Group, among others.

The Power Funds will use a growth strategy and will complement the original Dynamic Funds, which take more of a value approach. The key member of the Power team is Rohit Sehgal, who ran the London Life Canadian Equity Fund for 17 years. He is joined by Noah Blackstein, regarded as a rising star by the people at Goodman & Company, the advisors to all the funds, and Michael McHugh, who will look after the fixed income side.

Interestingly, the announcement of the launch of the Power Funds put a great deal of emphasis on Sehgal's credentials and track record. That's unusual because the company has been going to great lengths to disguise the names of the lead managers of the Dynamic Funds behind a bland "team" designation. Their standard line has become: "All Dynamic funds are managed on a team basis by Goodman & Company, Investment Counsel. There are 16 portfolio managers and analysts led by a core group of senior managers who have been together for more than a decade. The team's investment analysis is shared across all funds."

Regular readers know my views on this type of smoke-screen. Every fund has someone who is ultimately responsible for making the decisions, as Sehgal is acknowledged to be for the Power funds. I believe investors have a right to know who that person is and when a change is made. Hiding behind the "team" designation obscures that important piece of information.

On a more positive note, most of the MERs on the Dynamic funds are down this year. In many cases, the drop is significant, 20 basis points or more. That's going in the *right* direction.

THE DETAILS

NUMBER OF FUNDS:	26
ASSETS UNDER MANAGEMENT:	$6 BILLION
LOAD CHARGE:	FRONT: MAX. 5%; BACK: MAX. 6%
SWITCHING CHARGE:	2% MAXIMUM
WHERE SOLD:	ACROSS CANADA
HOW SOLD:	THROUGH BROKERS, DEALERS, AND FINANCIAL PLANNERS
PHONE NUMBER:	(416) 365-5100 OR 1-800-268-8186
WEB SITE ADDRESS:	WWW.DYNAMIC.CA
E-MAIL ADDRESS:	INVEST@DYNAMIC.CA

FUND SUMMARY

DYNAMIC FUNDS

$$$$ - NONE

$$$ - AMERICAS, DIVIDEND (CLOSED), EUROPE, INTERNATIONAL, REAL ESTATE EQUITY

$$ - DIVIDEND GROWTH, GLOBAL MILLENNIA, GLOBAL PARTNERS, GLOBAL RESOURCES, GOVERNMENT INCOME

$ - CANADIAN GROWTH, FAR EAST, FUND OF CANADA, GLOBAL BOND, INCOME, MONEY MARKET, PARTNERS, PRECIOUS METALS, TEAM

NR - CANADIAN REAL ESTATE, DOLLAR COST AVERAGING, GLOBAL INCOME & GROWTH, GLOBAL PRECIOUS METALS, ISRAEL GROWTH, LATIN AMERICA, QUEBEC, SMALL CAP

BEST CHOICES: AMERICAS, DIVIDEND, EUROPE, INTERNATIONAL, REAL ESTATE
BEST FOR RRSPS: GOVERNMENT INCOME
BEST UNRATEDS: QUEBEC, SMALL CAP

POWER FUNDS

$$$$ - NONE
$$$ - NONE
$$ - NONE
$ - NONE
NR - AMERICAN, BALANCED, BOND, CANADIAN

FUND RATINGS

Dynamic Funds

CANADIAN EQUITY FUNDS

DYNAMIC CANADIAN GROWTH FUND $ ↑ G #/* RSP CE

Manager: Team

MER: 2.31%

The mandate of this fund is to invest in Canadian companies with above-average growth potential. The portfolio is a mix of small-, medium-, and large-cap companies, and the managerial style is bottom-up stock selection. Recent results have been very weak, with the fund showing a loss of 5.8% for the year to June 30/98. Longer term returns out to five years are also below average, although if you go back a full decade this fund's numbers look very good (average annual compound rate of return of 13.3%). That tells you the trend line of this fund is on a downslope and that the strong 10-year results reflect good performance during the period prior to 1994. In fact, those numbers are really being carried by a sensational year in '93 when the fund doubled in value (that's right, a 100% gain). Since then, it hasn't been impressive. The historic record of this fund shows it to be of higher-than-average risk, with a 22% chance of being in the red after a five-year hold. Take that into account in your investment decision. This fund started out as part of the Allied group, which was taken over by Dynamic in the early '90s.

DYNAMIC DIVIDEND FUND $$$ ↓ FI/G #/* RSP INC

Manager: Team

MER: 1.51%

Good news. Dynamic reopened this classic dividend fund for new business on Jan. 2, '98. It had been closed for a year because of a shortage of preferred shares, but the supply has now increased to the point where the company felt it could accept new investments while retaining the character and objective of the fund. This is one of the best funds around for investors looking for steady cash flow. A survey published in the March, '98 issue of *Mutual Funds Update* shows that during calendar '97, this was the most efficient dividend fund in Canada in terms of delivering tax-advantaged cash flow to investors. Based on the unit value at the start of '97, investors enjoyed a cash return of 9.1%, an outstanding result in a low interest rate climate. About half (51%) of the payments were received as dividends, the rest as capital gains. Don't be misled by the total return numbers, which are much lower than for many other dividend funds (10.9% for the year to June 30/98). If cash flow is your need, this is a great place to be.

DYNAMIC DIVIDEND
GROWTH FUND $$ → G/FI #/* RSP INC

Manager: Team

MER: 1.57%

This fund holds a higher percentage of common stock in its portfolio than the companion Dividend Fund, so it is suited to those looking for a combination of dividend income and capital gains. Total returns are generally higher than those of the Dividend Fund, although this was not the case in the year to June 30/98 when this fund gained just 6.1%. Cash flow is less than you'll get from the Dividend Fund, although it was a very respectable 5.8% in '97. The fund maintains a diversified portfolio that includes Canadian and foreign common stocks, preferred shares, a small holding in bonds, and lots of cash and short-term notes. Safety record is average for the dividend fund category. As things stand right now, if you're looking for a dividend fund, I recommend Dynamic Dividend over this one. Formerly the Allied Dividend Fund; name changed in April, '93.

DYNAMIC FUND OF CANADA $ → G #/* RSP CE

Manager: Team

MER: 2.24%

This long-running fund (it's been around more than 40 years) is more conservatively managed than the companion Canadian Growth Fund. That gives it a somewhat better safety record and its returns have certainly been much stronger in recent years. That doesn't mean you should rush right out and buy it, however. Compared to other funds in the Canadian equity category, performance is well below average, with a five-year average annual compound rate of return of just 7% to June 30/98. The portfolio is well diversified, but recent performance was held back by an extremely small weighting in the hot financial services sector.

DYNAMIC PRECIOUS METALS FUND $ ↑ G #/* RSP PM

Manager: Team

MER: 2.47%

How's this for a statistic: over the past 10 years, this was the number-two pure precious metals fund in Canada in terms of return. And how much money would you have made had you invested a decade ago? Exactly 1% a year! That tells you all you need to know about the ups and downs of precious metals funds. There's nothing at all wrong with the management of this fund. Jonathan Goodman (who is a key member of this fund behind that "team" facade) is a trained geologist and a CFA, so he knows the business. This fund also avoids the highly promoted junior issues and sticks to sound companies. But when the whole market is plunging, not even the best manager in the world can stand up to it. I've come to the conclusion that the only way to make decent money on precious metals funds is to trade in and out of them, like stocks. Buy when gold markets are down, wait for a big year, such as these funds experienced in '93, and then scoop your profits and run. For speculators only.

U.S. AND INTERNATIONAL EQUITY FUNDS

DYNAMIC AMERICAS FUND $$$ → G #/* £ AE

Manager: Team

MER: 2.37%

This fund has really taken off since lead responsibility was handed to Anne McLean (she's hiding behind the "team" designation), who took charge in early '95 after moving to Dynamic from Gluskin, Sheff & Associates. She overhauled the portfolio from top to bottom, dumping the resource stocks that had dominated the lineup and replacing them with issues focusing on retailing, manufacturing, and financial services. She also added some Latin American stocks to the mix, about 9% of the portfolio in the first half of '98. You can't argue with the results; in the three years to June 30/98 this fund shows an average annual compound rate of return of 32.7%. That's first rate, even given the fact markets were strong during that time. MacLean runs a tight portfolio, and clearly knows her stuff. Good safety record. One of Dynamic's strongest entries.

DYNAMIC EUROPE FUND $$$ → G #/* £ EE

Manager: Team

MER: 2.50%

When this fund was launched in late '89, it was with the idea of enabling Canadian investors to profit from the bright new future that was to unfold in Europe when trade barriers were eliminated in '92. Unfortunately, the European dream got derailed along the way, amid political and currency turmoil. This fund lost money for investors in each of the first three years of its existence. I maintained its rating, however, with the comment that I thought Europe might be about to turn the corner, and suggested that if you wanted to take a flyer, this might be worth a little money. Europe did indeed turn the corner, and the fund shows an average annual return of 24.8% for the five years ending June 30/98. The latest one-year result was particularly impressive, up 39%. The portfolio is not your usual mix of big European nations; during the first half of '98 the major holdings were in Sweden (17.3%), the U.K. (12.1%), and Finland (10.9%). So the managers aren't afraid to place big bets on smaller countries. So far, it's worked. Name changed from Dynamic Europe 1992 Fund in March, '93.

DYNAMIC FAR EAST FUND $ ↑ G #/* £ FEE

Manager: Team

MER: 2.78%

This fund continues to be one of the better performers in the Far East category, but that only means it has lost less ground than many of its competitors. Things are pretty bad when a drop of 28.9% in a single year is considered to be an above-average result, but that's the case here. The mandate allows the managers to invest anywhere in the region, including Japan, India, Russia (which does extend to the Pacific, remember), and Australia. The portfolio is well diversified; in the early part of '98, China, Hong Kong, and India were the main areas of focus. When the Far East comes back, this fund will be worth looking at. But stand aside until then.

DYNAMIC GLOBAL MILLENNIA FUND $$ → G #/* £ IE

Manager: Team

MER: 2.41%

This fund has gone through so many manifestations that even I'm starting to lose track. First it was the Dynamic Global Fund. Then the company tried to cash in on environmental enthusiasm by dressing it in a green suit and naming it Dynamic Global Green. When that approach stalled, the company shifted gears again, changing the name Global Millennia. Even more important, Dynamic chairman Ned Goodman took over responsibility for the portfolio in December, '95 to see if he could work some magic. This fund did very well for the next two years, but is now in a slump, having dropped 9% in the 12 months to June 30/98. However, the three-year average annual compound rate of return is still above par at 16.3%. The portfolio specializes in corporate turnarounds, restructurings, and other situations in which a company appears to be undervalued by the marketplace. Sounds good, but the recent weak returns suggest we should ease back on the rating of this one for the time being.

DYNAMIC GLOBAL RESOURCE FUND $$ ↑ G #/* £ SEC

Manager: Team

MER: 5.19%

Resource funds have had a tough slog in recent years, but if you have been in this one for a while, you've done all right. Although there was a loss of 17.8% for the year to June 30/98, the three-year average annual compound rate of return to that date was an impressive 14.1%, best among all resource funds in Canada. However, all of that was thanks to a huge year in 1996; otherwise, the fund hasn't looked particularly great. There's also a very high MER to consider, which looks out of line in weak years. The fund's mandate allows it to invest internationally in resource stocks of all types, from gold to forests. However, don't be misled. This is not a true international fund, at least at the present time. Canadian stocks accounted for almost 70% of the portfolio entering 1998, with foreign stocks only representing 23% of the assets. So this is really more like a Canadian resource fund with a slightly higher-than-usual international exposure. The managers use a bottom-up approach to stock analysis, choosing their holdings on the basis of the outlook for an individual company, rather than industry sectors or geographic regions. As of early '98, the portfolio was heavily weighted towards oil and gas stocks (44%) and gold (25%). Despite the great results in '96, I'm uncomfortable with an "international" resource fund that is so heavily concentrated in Canada. The managers should look to add more geographic diversification.

DYNAMIC INTERNATIONAL FUND $$$ → G #/* £ IE

Manager: Team

MER: 2.57%

This is Dynamic's broad-based international fund, with a mandate to roam the world. Unlike most international funds, it's managed out of Toronto, but Goodman & Company have excellent foreign contacts and know how to sniff out value. Results are good; return for the year to June 30/98 was 11.1%. Over the past three years, this fund has averaged 18.1% a year, a very good performance. More than half the portfolio was in North America and Europe in the first half of '98. The fund also has some Far East holdings and emerging markets in the mix, which kept returns from being even better. Previously the Allied International Fund; name changed in April, '93.

DYNAMIC REAL ESTATE EQUITY FUND $$$ ↑ G #/* £ SEC

Manager: Team

MER: 2.72%

Dynamic was the first fund company to respond to the rebound in real estate prices, with the launch of this fund in May, 1995. Unlike traditional real estate funds, which invested in bricks and mortar, this one puts its money into stocks and real estate investment trusts. The majority of the holdings are in the U.S., which is why this fund is classed as foreign content for registered plans. The company also has a Canadian Real Estate Fund, but it is still too new for a rating. However, if you want a real estate fund in your portfolio, I recommend this one because the Canadian market does not have the growth potential you'll get in the U.S. or overseas. If you got into this fund at the outset, you've had a very good run. Average annual gain for the three years to June 30/98 was an impressive 31.4%. Momentum has slowed lately, as the bargains that were available after the real estate meltdown of the early '90s have now largely been snapped up. However, there still should be room for more profits in the current real estate cycle and manager Anne MacLean has a target average annual return of 15%, which she believes is attainable. Just remember that real estate is very cyclical. Don't be holding units in this fund when the next big slide comes along.

BALANCED FUNDS

DYNAMIC GLOBAL PARTNERS FUND $$ → FI/G #/* £ IBAL

Manager: Team

MER: 2.47%

This international balanced fund has tailed off in performance recently, with a return of just 2.9% for the year to June 30/98. That's disappointing because it had been doing quite well to that point. The portfolio has been revamped since last year to put more emphasis on North American securities. That improved matters in the first half of '98 when the fund gained 9.1% in six months (it was a net loser in the last half of '97). The bond side of the portfolio is mainly Canadian issues denominated in foreign currencies and represented about 30% of the assets in early '98. Rating drops a notch while we await a return to former glories.

DYNAMIC PARTNERS FUND $ → FI/G #/* RSP CBAL

Manager: Team

MER: 2.30%

This is a conservatively managed fund that will always hold at least 35% of its portfolio in fixed-income securities. The person who calls the shots for that side of the fund is Norm Bengough, who is known for his cautious approach and his emphasis on capital preservation. So it should come as no surprise that in early '98 almost 36% of this fund was in cash, with another 24% in bonds. That mix certainly reduced the risk, but it also suppressed returns. The fund gained just 5.1% for the year to June 30/98, well below average for the balanced category. The equities side of the portfolio (39% in early '98) is a selection of stocks from a broad range of sectors. The fund also makes good use of the foreign content allowance. If you're a very conservative investor take a look, but it would not be one of my top choices from Dynamic.

DYNAMIC TEAM FUND $$ → FI/G #/* RSP CBAL

Manager: Team

MER: 0.52%

This is a fund of funds, investing in units of other mutual funds managed by Dynamic. It's a way to buy a piece of the entire Dynamic group, rather than buying funds individually. In theory, when other Dynamic funds are going well, so will this one; when they're experiencing problems, this one will too. But it doesn't always work out that way. This fund actually lost a small amount of money (0.8%) over the year to June 30/98. That was well below average for a balanced fund and worse than the companion Partners Fund, which at least showed a profit, if not a big one. Reason: Because this fund is fully RRSP eligible, it is limited in its foreign content. So it had only limited exposure to some of the best-performing Dynamic funds (e.g., Americas, Europe) and heavy exposure to funds that performed poorly (e.g., Global Bond, Canadian Growth). Name changed in May, '96 from Dynamic Managed Portfolio.

FIXED INCOME AND MONEY MARKET FUNDS

DYNAMIC GLOBAL BOND FUND $ ↑ FI #/* RSP IB

Manager: Team

MER: 1.78%

This fund invests mainly in bonds issued by Canadian governments and corporations and by eligible supranational organizations like the World Bank, which are denominated in foreign currencies. This gives it full RRSP/RRIF eligibility. The fund will also hold debt securities issued directly by foreign governments, within the foreign content limit. It had been a steady performer but it slipped badly last year with a loss of 4.3% over the 12 months to June 30/98. That pulled the results for all time periods to below average. Main reason: a very small exposure to the U.S. dollar entering '98 and a heavy weighting towards currencies that took a big hit, including the Australian dollar and our own loonie. Risk is at the high end of the scale for a fund of this type.

DYNAMIC GOVERNMENT INCOME FUND $$ ↓ FI # RSP CB

Manager: Team

MER: 0.85%

This is a short-term bond fund that invests exclusively in federal and provincial government securities with maturities of no more than five years. It offers better returns than a money market fund with just slightly more risk. Useful for a conservative portfolio or in an RRSP or RRIF. Surprisingly, returns have been much better recently than those of the companion Income Fund, which has a more flexible investment mandate. Excellent safety record. This fund is not available with a deferred sales charge option.

DYNAMIC INCOME FUND $ → FI #/* RSP CB

Manager: Team

MER: 1.55%

This was one of the few bond funds that made money when the bond market experienced its worst meltdown in decades back in '94, and historically it outperforms other funds in the bond category in down markets by a wide margin. Reason: The managers put the emphasis on safety over profits. If they smell trouble ahead as a result of antic-ipated higher interest rates, they will shorten maturities to keep the risk to a minimum. This approach often results in below-average returns, especially when the bond market is strong. That has been the case in recent years. But what was really surprising was to see that this conservatively managed fund actually lost money over the year to June 30/98. The amount wasn't large, just 0.6%. But for any bond fund to lose ground in that period was very unusual. The main reason was currency exchange. The fund was very heavily exposed to Canadian and New Zealand cur-rencies, and had very little U.S. dollar weighting. We all know what happened to the U.S. dollar over the first half of '98! If you're looking for a conservative fixed-income fund from Dynamic, the Government Income Fund is a better choice.

DYNAMIC MONEY MARKET FUND $ ↓ C #/* RSP CMM

Manager: Team

MER: 0.80%

This fund invests primarily in Government of Canada T-bills. Optional front-end load of up to 4% or back-end load starting at 6%. Those rates are too heavy for a fund that's only returning about 3% these days. If you can't get the commissions waived, pass.

POWER FUNDS

The Power Funds were launched in July, 1998 so none has been in existence long enough to qualify for a rating.

ELLIOTT & PAGE MUTUAL FUNDS

THE COMPANY

This is one of those mutual fund companies that's not well known by the general public but commands a lot of respect among investment professionals. It is owned by Manulife, and manages some of their segregated funds, as well as offering its own independent product line. If you like these funds, you have to give careful consideration to how you buy them, because there are several purchase options available. I've been critical of their complex structure in years past but, so far, nothing has changed.

Here's an overview. Elliott & Page has a negotiable back-end load structure that bases the sales person's commission on how high a redemption schedule he/she can persuade you to accept. If you agree to a schedule starting at 6% in year one and declining to 3.5% in year six, the broker gets a 5% pay-out from E&P. If you negotiate a schedule starting at 2% in year one, the broker only gets a 1% commission. Clearly, *you* want the lowest schedule possible and the broker wants you to accept the highest. Buying a mutual fund is getting to be almost as bad as buying a car! Also, if you go for the back-end load, you may be charged a switching fee of up to 2% if you want to move some assets to another E&P fund. If you're going to invest here, I recommend avoiding the back-end load option, unless you can negotiate the lowest schedule. But the front-end load isn't straightforward either. There's a standard option, where you can be charged from 2% to 5%. But there is also a low-load option, which carries a maximum commission of 2%. That's clearly your best bet. However, units in the T-Bill Fund can only be purchased through the deferred sales charge (back-end load) option. That fund returned 2.2% in the year to June 30/98. If you cashed out in the first year, you would have barely broken even, assuming you had negotiated the lowest redemption schedule available.

Then there's the E&P Money Fund. It has the advantage of being the company's only no-load entry, which is nice. But the management fee is a problem — it is charged directly to the unitholder rather than deducted from the fund's asset before valuation. This makes it appear that performance is much better than it actually is.

I ask again: Why do they have to make it all so complicated? Surely it isn't because sales reps are demanding all these wrinkles. If they were, everyone would be doing it.

THE DETAILS

NUMBER OF FUNDS:	14
ASSETS UNDER MANAGEMENT:	$1.9 BILLION
LOAD CHARGE:	FRONT: MAX. 5%; BACK: MAX. 6% (LOW-LOAD OPTIONS ALSO AVAILABLE)
SWITCHING CHARGE:	2% MAXIMUM
WHERE SOLD:	ACROSS CANADA
HOW SOLD:	THROUGH BROKERS, DEALERS, AND DISCOUNT BROKERAGE FIRMS
PHONE NUMBER:	1-888-588-7999
WEB SITE ADDRESS:	N/A
E-MAIL ADDRESS:	N/A

FUND SUMMARY

$$$$ - NONE
$$$ - AMERICAN GROWTH, GLOBAL EQUITY, MONEY
$$ - BALANCED
$ - ASIAN GROWTH, BOND, EMERGING MARKETS, EQUITY, GLOBAL BALANCED, GLOBAL BOND, T-BILL
NR - MONTHLY HIGH INCOME, U.S. MID-CAP, VALUE EQUITY
BEST CHOICES: AMERICAN GROWTH, GLOBAL EQUITY
BEST FOR RRSPS: BALANCED
BEST UNRATEDS: U.S. MID-CAP

FUND RATINGS

CANADIAN EQUITY FUNDS

ELLIOTT & PAGE EQUITY FUND $ → G #/* RSP CE

Manager: Nereo Piticco (PCJ Investment Counsel), since 1993

MER: 1.94%

This was one of the better performing equity funds in Canada for some time, but performance has been slipping in recent years. During the year to June 30/98, the return was a paltry 3.6%, way below average for Canadian stock funds as a group. The 10-year returns still look good but this is a case of "What have you done for me lately?" The managers use a sector rotation approach to stock selection, overweighting the portfolio in areas of the economy they think will produce above-average returns. If you want clues as to why they underperformed, look at the weightings at the start of '98 — a quarter of the portfolio was in the weak resource sector. By mid-year, that situation had changed, with industrial products stocks as the core sector holding. But the move came too late to salvage the returns. As you can see, the problem with a sector rotation approach is that if you get the sectors wrong, you're toast. Rating drops a notch.

U.S. AND INTERNATIONAL EQUITY FUNDS

ELLIOTT & PAGE AMERICAN
GROWTH FUND $$$ ↓ G #/* £ USE

Manager: Robert Jones (Goldman Sachs), since 1997

MER: 1.41%

Robert Jones assumed the responsibility as lead manager on this fund in '97 but the Goldman Sachs organization has been at the helm since '93. They use a value-oriented style combined with a quantitative approach to search out stocks that are underpriced. They have put together a well-structured portfolio of about 90 stocks. There are a lot of big company names on the list (AT&T, Procter & Gamble) but also a good representation of smaller growth companies as well. Results have been very good recently, with a big 35.6% gain over the year to June 30/98. Five-year returns, covering the time period the fund has been handled by Goldman Sachs, are also well above average, at 21.2% annually. Safety rating has improved to A under the Vos ranking system. Formerly the Metropolitan American Growth Fund, taken over by E&P in April/93.

ELLIOTT & PAGE ASIAN GROWTH FUND $ ↑ G #/* £ FEE

Manager: Jonathan Lowe (Jardine Fleming), since 1994

MER: 3.76%

No manager, no matter how nimble, has been able to stand up against the Asian juggernaut. Jonathan Lowe is no exception, but the fund's 31% loss in the year to June 30/98 wasn't as bad as the damage incurred by some of the competitors. Still, this is one to stay clear of for now.

ELLIOTT & PAGE EMERGING MARKETS FUND $ ↑ G #/* £ EME

Manager: Steven Bates (Flemings London), since 1994

MER: 4.69%

Here's another case where the manager has done better than many competitors but doesn't get much credit for it. After all, a loss of 27.3% in the year to June 30/98 isn't a great reason to stand up and cheer. High MER on top of that too. This one may be worth looking at when the developing world finds its feet again, but not now.

ELLIOTT & PAGE GLOBAL EQUITY FUND $$$ → G #/* £ IE

Manager: Ian Henderson (Flemings London), since 1994

MER: 2.00%

This fund can invest around the world and has recently been heavily weighted in the U.S. (about half the portfolio). That has helped it to produce better-than-average returns, with a gain of 17% in the year to June 30/98. The managers use a top-down approach, meaning they identify those countries they believe will outperform and then overweight the portfolio with stocks from those nations. So far, it's working here. We'll give this one a $$$ rating for its premiere appearance.

BALANCED FUNDS

ELLIOTT & PAGE BALANCED FUND $$ ↑ FI/G #/* RSP CBAL

Manager: Gord Higgins and Gary Stewart, since 1998

MER: 1.80%

E&P made some changes here at the beginning of '98 following several years of indifferent performance. The management of the equity side of the fund was brought in-house and handed to Gord Higgins. As well, the stock side of the portfolio was scaled back to 50% (from 59% entering '98) and the bond component was strengthened. The moves showed an immediate pay-off as the fund gained 6.5% in the first half of '98, above average for the balanced category. Still, it's too soon to consider a rating increase. We'll watch and see what happens in the coming months. This fund is quite a bit more volatile than the average balanced fund, hence the higher risk rating.

ELLIOTT & PAGE GLOBAL BALANCED FUND $ ↑ G/FI #/* £ IBAL

Manager: David Boardman and Ian Henderson (Flemings London), since 1994

MER: 2.74%

Although this is a balanced fund, it will normally be weighted towards equities. That was the case in the first half of '98 when stocks accounted for 63% of the portfolio while bonds made up just 33% and cash the balance. You would think that, given those ratios and a heavy preference for U.S. stocks, this fund would be doing well. However, returns have actually been quite mediocre. Three-year average annual compound rate of return to June 30/98 was 9.4%, well below the 14.4% average for the global balanced category as reported by *The Financial Post*. Risk factor is also high, at least thus far in this fund's young life. We'll start it off at the bottom with a $ rating and hope the managers can work their way up the ladder.

FIXED INCOME AND MONEY MARKET FUNDS

ELLIOTT & PAGE BOND FUND $ → FI #/* RSP CB

Manager: Gary Stewart, since 1997

MER: 1.94%

This fund has gone through a couple of managerial changes in recent years and now appears to be heading in the right direction. Lead manager Gary Stewart and his team use an interest rate anticipation approach to building the portfolio. This involves making a decision on where rates are likely to move over the next three to six months and acting accordingly. Entering '98, the duration of the total fund (a measure of risk) was 5.3 years, but by Spring it had been lengthened to 6.5 years, a more aggressive position. Gain for the year to June 30/98 was 10.6%, the first above-average return we have seen from this fund for some time. If the pattern continues, the rating will improve next year. The portfolio is a mix of federal and provincial government securities, with a few corporates added for spice.

ELLIOTT & PAGE GLOBAL BOND FUND $ → FI #/* £ IB

Manager: David Boardman (Flemings London), since 1994

MER: 1.97%

As with other E&P funds managed by Flemings London, the managers take a top-down approach here. That means identifying those countries whose bond markets are expected to outperform and overweighting the portfolio towards them. The U.S. and Japan topped the list in the first half of '98. Results have been below average, with an annual gain of just 3.4% for the three years to June 30/98.

ELLIOTT & PAGE MONEY FUND $$ ↓ C No RSP CMM

Manager: Maralyn Kobayashi, since inception (1984)

MER: 0.27%

The nominal returns of this fund have been well above average (but with a caveat, see below). Well-diversified portfolio is another plus. And, as a bonus, the company has made this into a no-load fund, the only one they offer. However, the actual return to you may be less than what you see in the newspapers. That's because there's a negotiable annual management fee of up to 1%, which Elliott & Page splits with the sales person (which is why the MER appears low at first glance). Only half of that is taken into account in calculating the published return. So if you're paying more than 0.5%, you have to reduce the published return by the amount of your fee over and above 0.5% to determine the actual yield to you. (In other words, if you're paying 1%, knock off 0.5% from the published rate.) If you're in that situation, you'll quickly see your return drops to below average for the money fund category. One other wrinkle to watch for if you move cash in and out of money funds frequently: E&P allows two free redemptions a month from this fund but reserves the right to charge a $10 fee for each transaction beyond that.

ELLIOTT & PAGE T-BILL FUND $ ↓ C No RSP CMM

Manager: Maralyn Kobayashi, since inception (1994)

MER: 1.75%

Unlike the companion Money Fund, this operates as a conventional money market fund, with the management fee charged directly to the assets before valuation. Problem is the management fee is way too high, at 1.75%. In times of low interest rates, no manager can turn in even an average performance on this type of fund with a handicap like that. Not a good choice.

ETHICAL FUNDS

THE COMPANY

The flagship of this group it the Ethical Growth Fund, which has the honour of being the first socially responsible fund ever created in this country, back in 1986. The initiative was taken by the Vancouver City Savings Credit Union, which perceived a nascent demand for this type of investment vehicle. In the years since, the family has grown to eight funds and is now run by the Credit Unions of Canada. The funds were once considered fringe players in the market but the strong showing of Ethical Growth (which was the Fund of the Year in the *1998 Buyer's Guide*) has propelled them into the mainstream.

THE DETAILS

NUMBER OF FUNDS:	8
ASSETS UNDER MANAGEMENT:	$1.2 BILLION
LOAD CHARGE:	NONE
SWITCHING CHARGE:	NONE
WHERE SOLD:	ALL PROVINCES EXCEPT QUEBEC
HOW SOLD:	THROUGH CREDIT UNIONS AND THEIR REPRESENTATIVES
PHONE NUMBER:	1-800-267-5019
WEB SITE ADDRESS:	WWW.ETHICALFUNDS.COM
E-MAIL ADDRESS:	SAME - "CLIENT RELATIONS"

FUND SUMMARY

$$$$ - GROWTH
$$$ - BALANCED, INCOME, NORTH AMERICAN EQUITY
$$ - MONEY MARKET
$ - NONE
NR - GLOBAL BOND, PACIFIC RIM, SPECIAL EQUITY

BEST CHOICES: GROWTH
BEST FOR RRSPs: BALANCED, GROWTH, INCOME
BEST UNRATEDS: N/A

FUND RATINGS

CANADIAN EQUITY FUNDS

ETHICAL GROWTH FUND $$$$ → G No RSP CE

Manager: Larry Lunn (Connor, Clark & Lunn), since 1992

MER: 2.10%

This was the first mutual fund in Canada to combine conscience with profits by investing in companies that meet specific standards of practice. It was taken over by the Credit Union Central of Canada in late '92 to form the cornerstone of a new Ethical Funds family. The manager is Larry Lunn of Connor, Clark & Lunn. He brings a conservative style to the fund, moving heavily into cash at times of above-average risk to protect capital. For that reason, this fund has historically outperformed its peers in bear market situations by more than nine percentage points, according to Altamira's ATP analysis. Ethical screens exclude firms involved in military contracts, the tobacco industry, nuclear power, or unfriendly environmental activities. The performance numbers are very good — you don't have to sacrifice returns for the sake of conscience here. The fund was ahead 13.7% for the year to June 30/98, another better-than-average result. Over the past decade, the fund generated an average annual compound rate of return of 11.8%. Very few funds did better. This was last year's Fund of the Year, and it retains its $$$$ status once again.

ETHICAL SPECIAL EQUITY FUND $$ → G No RSP CSC

Manager: Leigh Pullen (QVDG Investors Inc.), since 1997

MER: 2.71

A few years ago, the Ethical group added several new funds to flesh out its lineup. This was one of them, a small-cap entry that offered higher return potential with enhanced risk. The fund has now reached its third birthday and so qualifies for inclusion here. It has been an okay performer so far — nowhere near as impressive as Ethical Growth, but better than many others in the small-cap category. Average annual compound rate of return for the three years to June 30/98 was 14.4%. Safety record is pretty good for a fund of this type. We'll start it off with a $$ rating.

ETHICAL NORTH AMERICAN EQUITY FUND $$$ → G No £ USE

Manager: Cynthia Frick (Alliance Capital Management), since 1992

MER: 2.47%

Although this is billed as a North American Fund, the portfolio is invested only in U.S. stocks. There hasn't been a single Canadian or Mexican equity in the fund for several years. That could change, of course, but if you're considering an investment this should be viewed as a U.S. fund rather than a North American one. Returns have gone from very good to outstanding. Gain for the year to June 30/98 was an amazing 55.9%. Over the past five years, the fund has averaged 26.3% a year, which places it second only to AIC Value Fund in the U.S. equity category among funds open to the general public. The only real negative with this fund, and the reason it does not qualify for a top $$$$ rating, is its safety record. There's a 5% chance you could be in the red after a three-year hold, and the performance in bear markets is worse than average for its category. But if it keeps churning out these huge returns, it won't be possible to deny it that top ranking much longer. Started out as the Co-operative Trust Growth Fund; purchased from Co-operative Trust Company in September, '92 by the Credit Union Central of Canada to become part of the Ethical Funds family.

ETHICAL PACIFIC RIM FUND $ ↑ G No £ FEE

Manager: Royce Brennan (Guinness Flight Hambro Asia), since inception (1995)

MER: 3.15%

Every chain has its weak link and here it is. No one is making any money in the Far East these days but this one has lost more than most. For the year ending June

30/98, the decline was a staggering 57.9%. My sympathies to those who rode it down. The portfolio was heavily focused on Hong Kong entering '98, but there was nowhere to hide when all the markets went south. Stand clear of this one for now.

BALANCED FUNDS

ETHICAL BALANCED FUND $$$ → FI/G No RSP CBAL

Manager: Jim MacDonald (Co-operators Investment Counselling), since 1992

MER: 2.08%

This fund just keeps looking better. It offers investors a well-diversified portfolio, which includes a mix of blue-chip Canadian and U.S. stocks, some smaller growth companies, and a bond component that blends government and corporate issues. Results are now consistently above average for the balanced fund category. The fund gained 19.9% in the year to June 30/98, and three-year results show annual gains of 17.3% — way better than the norm for this category. A good starter fund for an RRSP. Formerly known as the Classic I-Plan Balanced Fund.

FIXED INCOME AND MONEY MARKET FUNDS

ETHICAL GLOBAL BOND FUND $$ → FI No RSP IB

Manager: Andrew Martin Smith (Guinness Flight Hambro), since inception (1995)

MER: 2.56%

If you're looking for an international bond fund for your RRSP that won't eat up your precious foreign content, here it is. The fund invests mainly in federal and provincial bonds, but also includes some foreign government issues and some foreign exchange contracts. Emphasis in the first half of '98 was on North American currencies, which worked out well when the U.S. dollar took off. Returns are slightly above average for the category, with an average annual gain of 7.2% for the three years to June 30/98. The fund debuts with a $$ rating.

ETHICAL INCOME FUND $$$ → FI No RSP CB

Manager: Jim MacDonald (Co-operators Investment Counselling), since 1992

MER: 1.63%

Another strong entry from the Ethical group. Gain for the past year was again well above average for the bond fund category at 10.4%. In fact, all time periods out to five years show superior results. The portfolio is heavily weighted to provincial and federal government bonds, with some corporate issues also in the mix.

ETHICAL MONEY MARKET FUND $ → C No RSP CMM

Manager: Jim MacDonald (Co-operators Investment Counselling), since 1992

MER: 1.25%

This fund started out as the Co-operative Trust Interest Fund and is now part of the Ethical Funds group offered by the credit unions of Canada. The portfolio is a mix of federal government T-bills, provincial short-term notes, bankers' acceptances, and corporate notes. Returns tend to be average to slightly below, in part due to a high MER. The Ethical people should consider reducing it. It's too high to be, well, ethical.

EXCEL FUND MANAGEMENT INC.

THE COMPANY

This is a small firm based in Mississauga, Ont. So far, it has just one fund on offer, the Excel India Fund, which, as the name tells you, invests primarily in the Indian sub-continent. The fund was launched early in 1998 and is managed by Birla Capital International AMC, a leading investment house in India.

THE DETAILS

NUMBER OF FUNDS:	1
ASSETS UNDER MANAGEMENT:	$350,000
LOAD CHARGE:	FRONT: MAX. 5%; BACK: MAX. 5.75%
SWITCHING CHARGE:	N/A
WHERE SOLD:	ONTARIO, B.C., ALBERTA
HOW SOLD:	THROUGH FINANCIAL ADVISORS
PHONE NUMBER:	N/A
WEB SITE ADDRESS:	WWW.EXCELFUNDS.COM
E-MAIL ADDRESS:	RAJ@EXCELFUNDS.COM

FUND SUMMARY

There is only one fund in this group and it is too new to qualify for a rating.

FICADRE FUNDS

THE COMPANY

This is a small Quebec City-based group. The funds are available only in Quebec and are distributed through Sogefonds MFQ representatives.

THE DETAILS

NUMBER OF FUNDS:	5
ASSETS UNDER MANAGEMENT:	$106 MILLION
LOAD CHARGE:	BACK: MAX. 5%
SWITCHING CHARGE:	NONE
WHERE SOLD:	QUEBEC
HOW SOLD:	DIRECTLY THROUGH THE MANAGER OR THROUGH REPRESENTATIVES OF MFQ LIFE AND OTHER LICENSED DEALERS
PHONE NUMBER:	(418) 692-1221
WEB SITE ADDRESS:	WWW.MFQ.QC.CA
E-MAIL ADDRESS:	JPTREMBLAY@MFQ.QC.CA

FUND SUMMARY

$$$$ - NONE

$$$ - NONE

$$ - BOND

$ - BALANCED, EQUITY, MONEY MARKET, MORTGAGE

NR - NONE

BEST CHOICES: BOND

BEST FOR RRSPS: BOND

BEST UNRATEDS: N/A

FUND RATINGS

CANADIAN EQUITY FUNDS

FICADRE EQUITY FUND $ → G * RSP CE

Manager: Ubald Cloutier

MER: 2.04%

This fund had been looking better, but slipped badly last year, gaining just 4.8% over the 12 months to June 30/98. That pulled the results for all time periods to below average. A heavy weighting in the resource sector was part of the problem. The portfolio is a smorgasbord of stocks, from blue-chips to small growth situations. Formerly the SNF Stock Fund.

BALANCED FUNDS

FICADRE BALANCED FUND $ → FI/G * RSP CBAL

Manager: Ubald Cloutier

MER: 1.97%

Performance continues to slip relative to other funds in the balanced category. The stock portion of the portfolio is a mix of blue-chip, mid-size companies and small-caps — a real cross-section of the Canadian markets, with a small percentage of foreign stocks as well. It's extremely large in terms of total securities held, with some very small positions — as few as 50 shares in some cases. The bond segment is well-diversified, including some Quebec-based issues, Canada bonds, corporate notes, and international securities. Formerly known as the SNF Balanced Fund.

FIXED INCOME AND MONEY MARKET FUNDS

FICADRE BOND FUND $$ → FI * RSP CB

Manager: Jean Duguay

MER: 1.54%

This fund holds a mix of federal, provincial, municipal, and corporate bonds. Recent returns have been average for the bond fund category, with a one-year gain of 8.6% to

June 30/98. A sound, middle-of-the-road performer, nothing exciting. Formerly the SNF Bond Fund.

FICADRE MONEY MARKET FUND $\rightarrow$ C * RSP CMM

Manager: Jean Duguay

MER: 1.35%

The holdings here are mainly Government of Canada T-bills, but there are some corporate and Quebec notes in the mix as well. Returns have fallen back to below average, due in part to a higher MER.

FICADRE MORTGAGE FUND $\rightarrow$ FI * RSP M

Manager: Jean Duguay

MER: 1.62%

This is supposed to be a mortgage fund but most of the assets were in bonds entering 1998. Unimpressive results so far; gain for the year to June 30/98 was 4%.

FIDELITY INVESTMENTS

THE COMPANY

Fidelity Investments Canada is part of the international Fidelity organization, which has its headquarters in Boston. The Canadian operation was set up in 1987 and since that time it has grown into one of the largest load fund groups in this country. The parent organization has been in business since 1946 and is huge, with more than 300 researchers. However, the company still has not built any Canadian-based money management expertise, running all its Canadian funds out of the U.S. They are starting to have more success with this strategy, especially with any funds involving Alan Radlo, who seems to have a good feel for the Canadian market. The Fidelity Focus funds are sector plays, but are too new to be rated since all were created in June, 1997.

THE DETAILS

NUMBER OF FUNDS:	24
ASSETS UNDER MANAGEMENT:	$15.5 BILLION
LOAD CHARGE:	FRONT: MAX. 5%; BACK MAX. 4.9%
SWITCHING CHARGE:	2% MAXIMUM
WHERE SOLD:	ACROSS CANADA
HOW SOLD:	THROUGH REGISTERED BROKERS, FINANCIAL ADVISORS, OR INSURANCE AGENTS
PHONE NUMBER:	1-888-203-4778 (ENGLISH) OR 1-888-203-5483 (FRENCH) OR 1-800-983-8389 (CHINESE)
WEB SITE ADDRESS:	WWW.FIDELITY.CA
E-MAIL ADDRESS:	CS.ENGLISH@FMR.COM (ENGLISH) OR SC.FRANCAIS@FMR.COM (FRENCH)

FUND SUMMARY

$$$$ - INTERNATIONAL PORTFOLIO

$$$ - CANADIAN ASSET ALLOCATION, CANADIAN GROWTH COMPANY, EUROPEAN GROWTH, GLOBAL ASSET ALLOCATION, GROWTH AMERICA, SMALL CAP AMERICA

$$ - Canadian Bond, Canadian Income, U.S. Money
         Market
 $ - Canadian Short Term Asset, Capital Builder,
         Emerging Markets Bond, Emerging Markets
         Portfolio, Far East, Japanese Growth, Latin
         American Growth, North American Income
NR - Focus Consumer Industries, Focus Financial
         Services, Focus Health Care, Focus Natural
         Resources, Focus Technology, True North

Best choices: European Growth, Growth America, International
Portfolio

Best for RRSPs: Canadian Asset Allocation

Best unrateds: True North

FUND RATINGS

CANADIAN EQUITY FUNDS

FIDELITY CANADIAN GROWTH
COMPANY FUND $$$ ↑ G #/* RSP CSC

Manager: Alan Radlo, since inception (1994)

MER: 2.48%

It's either been a feast or a famine for Canadian small-cap
funds in recent years. Some have floundered while others,
such as this one, have performed extremely well.
However, there is some smoke and mirrors here. Although
this is officially classed as a small-cap fund, many of the
stocks in the portfolio are anything but that. Examples: the
mega-conglomerate Power Corporation of Canada and the
telecommunications giant Teleglobe. They presumably
qualify because they are "growth" companies, but they
certainly don't fit the mandate of "smaller or lesser-
known" firms that this fund is supposed to focus on. Still,
investors aren't quibbling over semantics given the fact the
fund generated an average annual return of 23.8% over the
three years ending June 30/98. That's good enough to
make anyone smile and earns this fund a $$$ rating in its
debut.

FIDELITY CAPITAL BUILDER FUND $ → G #/* RSP CE

Managers: Robert Haber and Stephen Binder, since 1998

MER: 2.45%

The Fidelity organization is really struggling with this chronic underachiever. In July 1998, the company made its second managerial change in two years, bringing in the team of Robert Haber and Stephen Binder to replace Tom Sweeney. Haber is the chief investment officer for Fidelity Investments Canada and is clearly the senior person on the team. He's been with the organization since 1985 and has managed several funds that were available only in the U.S. Fidelity also announced a change in the mandate of this fund, moving it more towards a large-cap bias. Among the first moves of the new team was a decision to "modestly" reduce the resource segment of the portfolio, which represented about 50% of the total assets. On the other side of the ledger, they have increased the fund's position in interest-sensitive stocks, such as the telecoms. The management style is bottom-up, with an emphasis on out-of-favour stocks. Obviously, it is way too soon to get any clear read on how the new managers will perform, but just about anything would be an improvement over what we have seen. The fund lost 23.1% over the 12 months to Aug. 31/98 and has barely managed to break even over the past three years. Not impressive! It appears the goal now is to transform this into Fidelity's core Canadian equity fund, with a large-cap mandate and a lower-risk approach. We'll see if it works, but the rating won't move up until the performance does. The companion True North Fund still looks like the better bet right now, although it's still too new to get a formal rating.

U.S. AND INTERNATIONAL FUNDS

FIDELITY EMERGING MARKETS PORTFOLIO FUND $ ↑ G #/* £ EME

Manager: David Stewart, since 1997

MER: 3.55%

Here's a fund that's hard to like. For starters, it has a really bad track record. Over the three years to June 30/98, investors lost an average of 15.8% annually, making this the worst performer in the emerging markets category among funds available to the general public. Then, to make bad matters worse, Fidelity has the nerve to charge through the nose for the privilege of investing in this dog. Look at the management expense ratio. It's not the highest in the peer group, but it's not far off. In mid-'98, the portfolio was weighted towards Latin America, with Brazil and Mexico the two largest country holdings, followed by South Africa. Steer clear of this one.

FIDELITY EUROPEAN GROWTH FUND $$$ ↓ G #/* £ EE

Manager: Sally Walden, since inception (1992)

MER: 2.73%

After a bit of a slump relative to other European funds last year, this one has come roaring back with a huge 45.4% gain for the year to June 30/98. That re-establishes its position as one of the best European funds around. Plus, there's a great safety record: ATP analysis shows no 12-month period since inception that this fund produced a loss. British-based manager Sally Walden uses a bottom-up investing style and searches out companies with strong balance sheets and a clear focus on cash generation. Companies with heavy debt loads are avoided. Walden maintains a well-diversified portfolio, which was most heavily weighted to the U.K. (about 30% of the portfolio) in mid-'98. One of the better choices from the Fidelity group.

FIDELITY FAR EAST FUND $ ↑ G #/* £ FEE

Manager: K.C. Lee, since inception (1991)

MER: 2.80%

Nobody, but nobody, can salvage anything out of the Far East these days, not even a fine veteran manager like K.C. Lee. This fund lost 38.7% in the year to June 30/98 and about all that can be said on the good side is that some others lost more. Five-year returns are still above average for the Far East fund category, but your average annual compound rate of return over that time was just 3.3%. A money market fund would have been more productive, without the aggravation. There is a hidden danger in this fund that is not readily apparent. Because of losses in many Asian stocks and Lee's policy of maintaining key positions that may have substantial gains, two securities, HSBC and Hutchison Whampoa, accounted for 42% of the portfolio in the first half of '98. That's an enormous weighting for just two stocks. If either should go into a deep tailspin, unitholders might think the headaches they've experienced in the past year are a picnic. Be wary.

FIDELITY GROWTH AMERICA FUND $$$ ↓ G #/* £ USE

Managers: Brad Lewis, since inception (1990), Steve Snider, since 1998

MER: 2.33%

The goal of this fund is to consistently outperform the S&P 500 index. Brad Lewis and his new co-manager, Steve Snider, use a highly complex computer screening system to choose stocks, monitoring over 2,000 issues a day. They also consider certain key economic factors, such as yield curves, changes in money supply, and interests rates when making decisions. The system obviously works. This has been one of the better performing funds in the U.S. equity category over the past five years, with an average annual compound rate of return of more than 22%. Gain for the 12 months to June 30/98 was 34.5%. This was achieved despite the fact the portfolio was overweighted in the weak-performing energy sector and underweighted in technology issues. There's a fine safety record to go along with the good returns. Historically, there is only a 2% chance of loss in any given 12-month period. For the long term, this is one of the better choices in the Fidelity lineup.

FIDELITY INTERNATIONAL PORTFOLIO FUND $$$$ ↓ G #/* £ IE

Manager: Dick Habermann, since 1993

MER: 2.69%

This is a broadly diversified international fund that continues to churn out consistently good returns for investors. Gained 24.1% in the 12 months to June 30/98. Five-year average annual return is a very good 18.2%. In mid-'98, the portfolio emphasis was heavily on U.S. stocks, which comprised almost half the portfolio. That weighting was about the same as the previous year, meaning manager Dick Habermann was employing a very different strategy than that being used by Mark Holowesko at Templeton Growth Fund, who had cut U.S. holdings in half. So far, Habermann's approach has worked better. He uses a classic bottom-up style, which is a hallmark of Fidelity, selecting stocks on the basis of the prospects for each individual company. Excellent safety rating. The fine track record over a decade (the fund dates back to 1987) warrants an upgrade this year to $$$$ status, making this the first Fidelity fund to earn that honour.

FIDELITY JAPANESE GROWTH FUND $ ↑ G #/* £ FEE

Manager: Yoko Tilley, since inception (1993)

MER: 3.01%

Most Japanese funds are in the red these days, and this one is no exception. Over the three years to June 30/98, investors lost an average of 5% annually. To keep that in perspective, however, many other Japan funds did worse — in some cases, much worse. Manager Yoko Tilley supposedly focuses on small- to mid-cap Japanese stocks, with special emphasis on those that stand to benefit most from growth in southeast Asian markets. Of course, when those markets are stagnant, that strategy doesn't work very well! That may explain why the current portfolio doesn't look much like the style she's supposed to be following. Instead, the list of top 10 holdings is studded with the names of such giants as Toyota, Honda, Sony, Fuji, and Canon. It appears this fund has moved away from its basic philosophy in an effort to cut losses. I always worry when I see situations like that. Not recommended at this time.

FIDELITY LATIN AMERICAN GROWTH FUND $ ↑ G #/* £ AE

Manager: Patti Satterthwaite, since inception (1994)

MER: 3.13%

Latin funds had been sailing along quite nicely until the Asian contagion spread across the South Pacific. The malaise really began to bite in the second quarter of 1998; this fund dropped 16.4% from April 1 to the end of June. Unless you're a born speculator, you may want to stand clear for a while until the situation improves. Manager Patti Satterthwaite does her best to mitigate risk by selecting companies that are relatively immune to serious economic difficulties and that have strong export potential. As a result you'll find a lot of utilities in the portfolio, especially telecoms and power generating firms. The fund had the misfortune to be launched in early '94, within a few weeks of the collapse of the Mexican peso, and so it took a battering initially. But it bounced back very well and turned in an excellent gain of 43.3% over the 12 months to June 30/97. Unfortunately, investors have now given some of that back. This is a volatile part of the world so you can never be sure what to expect next. Don't put this one in your RRSP.

FIDELITY SMALL CAP AMERICA FUND $$$ ↑ G #/* £ USSC

Managers: Brad Lewis, since inception (1994) and Tim Krochuk, since 1998

MER: 2.51%

As the name suggests, this fund focuses on the small-cap sector in the U.S. That's defined as companies with market capitalization up to $1 billion. Brad Lewis, who also runs Growth America, applies his complex stock selection techniques here as well, to generally good effect. He has a new co-manager to assist him, Tim Krochuk, but Lewis remains responsible for overall direction. This has been the top performing U.S. small-cap fund available in this country over the past three years according to data published by *The Financial Post*, with an average annual compound rate of return of 20.8% to June 30/98. This fund is best suited for more aggressive investors who can handle the additional risk involved in small-caps.

BALANCED FUNDS

FIDELITY CANADIAN ASSET ALLOCATION FUND $$$ → FI/G #/* RSP CBAL

Manager: Dick Habermann, since inception (1994)

MER: 2.47%

Question: What do you do with a fund that's turning in lousy results? Answer: You fold it into another fund and pretend it never existed. That's what's happened here. The Fidelity Growth and Income Fund was turning into something of an embarrassment for the company (it earned a $ rating in the 1996 edition). So in November, '95 it was merged into this new fund and its record expunged from the history books. Perhaps that's fair in a way, since this fund is under the direction of a different managerial team (lead manager Dick Habermann is assisted by Alan Radlo on the equities side and Ford O'Neil, who looks after fixed-income). But the mandate is more or less the same, so there is some continuity here. So how has it done since the merger? Very well, actually. Gain for the 12 months to June 30/98 was 20%, well above average for the balanced fund category. Three-year average annual compound rate of return over the same period was 21.4%, also much better than average. That period slops back into the old Growth and Income Fund, but it's a pretty fair measure of the high standard the revised team has established. The good performance was helped by the fact the fund was weighted towards equities in the first six months of '98 (about half the assets), with bonds accounting for about a third of the portfolio. Rating moves up again this year in recognition of the continued good results.

FIDELITY GLOBAL ASSET ALLOCATION FUND $$$ → FI/G #/* £ IBAL

Manager: Dick Habermann, since 1996

MER: 2.70%

This fund applies asset allocation principles on an international scale to minimize risk and generate above-average returns. It got off to a slow start but has looked very good over the past three years, with an average annual compound rate of return of 19.7%. The fund continues to be heavily overweighted in the U.S. (39% of the portfolio in U.S. stocks), with a 9% equity weighting in Japan and 8% in the U.K. Bonds represented less than 20% of the assets in mid-'98. A respectable addition if you have a Fidelity portfolio.

FIXED INCOME AND MONEY MARKET FUNDS

FIDELITY CANADIAN BOND FUND $$ → FI #/* RSP CB

Manager: Ford O'Neil, since 1992

MER: 1.35%

This fund started out as a balanced fund, under the name Fidelity Capital Conservation Fund, then was called Fidelity Government Bond Fund for a while. It still invests mainly in government bonds but the percentage of corporate issues is on the rise and this appears to be giving the results some juice. Return for the year to June 30/98 was a respectable 9.3%. The five-year average annual compound rate of return was 8.1%, just a touch below the average for the Canadian bond fund category. The Fidelity RSP Global Bond Fund was folded into this one in mid-1998.

FIDELITY CANADIAN INCOME FUND $$ ↓ FI #/* RSP CB

Manager: Ford O'Neil, since inception (1995)

MER: 1.25%

This is Fidelity's defensive bond fund, designed to preserve capital by investing mainly in short- and mid-term bonds. That means less risk, but also lower returns when bond markets are strong. Over the three years to June 30/98, the fund gained 7.6% annually. That was about two percentage points below the average for Canadian bond funds as a group, but not bad considering the nature of the portfolio. If you have some short-term money to park, you'll get a better return here than from a money market fund.

FIDELITY CANADIAN SHORT TERM ASSET FUND $ → C #/* RSP CMM

Manager: Robert Duby, since inception (1991)

MER: 1.25%

This fund currently invests exclusively in short-term corporate notes. You'd expect that to produce above-average returns, but that's not the case. Results are consistently below the standards set by competitors. Gain for the year to June 30/98 was just 2.9%. Part of the reason is the relatively high management expense ratio, which bites deeply into yields when interest rates are low. Not a good money market alternative. If you do buy, try to acquire this one without any load fee. The return is weak enough without paying a sales commission too.

FIDELITY EMERGING MARKETS BOND FUND $ ↑ FI #/* £ IB

Manager: John Carlson, since 1995

MER: 2.24%

The goal of this fund is to produce higher returns than the average fixed-income fund by investing in the debt securities of developing countries. If the idea of holding bonds and debentures from such countries as Russia, Bulgaria, and Kazakstan doesn't bother you, then take a look. Over the past three years, the returns have been exceptional by international bond fund standards, with an average annual gain of 22.2% to June 30/98. However, momentum has slowed recently with the flight to quality that has resulted from the Asian crisis and the near-collapse of Russia's finances. The fund was virtually flat in the first half of '98. Although we could see a comeback in third-world bonds, I don't like the risk/return equation right now. Use caution.

FIDELITY NORTH AMERICAN INCOME FUND $ ↑ FI #/* £ IB

Manager: Ford O'Neil, since inception (1993)

MER: 1.75%

The idea sounds great — earn better returns by investing in North American bonds that include issues from high-yield countries like Mexico. Just one slight problem. This fund was hardly up and running when the Mexican peso collapsed. Disaster! This fund lost 12.4% in '94, and is still trying to recover. As a result, the five-year return is atrocious — worst in the international bond fund category at just 2.9% annually. Gain for the 12 months to June 30/98 was 4.9%, modestly better, but still not impressive.

FIDELITY U.S. MONEY MARKET FUND $$ → C #/* £ IMM

Manager: Robert Duby, since inception (1994)

MER: 1.25%

Unlike the U.S. money funds of some competitors, this one is considered foreign content in an RRSP, so it is not recommended for that purpose (why waste valuable foreign content room on a money fund?). Distributions are paid monthly, if steady U.S.-dollar cash flow is important. Returns are slightly above average for the peer group, with a three-year average annual compound rate of return of 4.4% (exclusive of currency gains) to June 30/98. The portfolio is entirely invested in commercial notes.

FIRST HERITAGE FUND

THE COMPANY

This is a one-fund operation, based in Toronto. Focus is on natural resources.

THE DETAILS

NUMBER OF FUNDS:	1
ASSETS UNDER MANAGEMENT:	$5 MILLION
LOAD CHARGE:	FRONT: MAX. 5% BACK: MAX. 5%
SWITCHING CHARGE:	N/A
WHERE SOLD:	ONTARIO
HOW SOLD:	REGISTERED SECURITIES DEALERS
PHONE NUMBER:	1-800-268-9165
WEB SITE ADDRESS:	N/A
E-MAIL ADDRESS:	N/A

FUND SUMMARY

$$$$ - NONE
$$$ - NONE
$$ - NONE
$ - FIRST HERITAGE
NR - N/A

BEST CHOICES: NONE
BEST FOR RRSPS: NONE
BEST UNRATEDS: N/A

FUND RATINGS

CANADIAN EQUITY FUNDS

FIRST HERITAGE FUND $ ↑ G #/* RSP SEC

Manager: First Grenadier Fund Management

MER: 4.10%

This is a small natural resource fund so, as you might expect, it's been going though rough times. Loss over the year to June 30/98 was a tad under 26%. If you'd held this fund over a decade, you would be ahead, but only by 1.2% a year. High risk factor here, as there is in most resource funds. ATP analysis shows a 39% historical chance you'll be in the red after three years in this fund, and a 26% chance you'd be down after five years. Name changed from Canadian Natural Resource Fund in June, '94.

FIRST HORIZON CAPITAL CORP.

THE COMPANY

This Vancouver-based company specializes in using derivatives to invest in international markets. Their objective is to reduce overall portfolio volatility, while adding to diversification and growth potential.

THE DETAILS

NUMBER OF FUNDS:	2
ASSETS UNDER MANAGEMENT:	$27.5 MILLION
LOAD CHARGE:	FRONT: MAX. 6%; BACK: MAX. 6%
SWITCHING CHARGE:	NONE
WHERE SOLD:	RRSP HEDGE FUND - ALBERTA, B.C., AND YUKON MULTI-ASSET FUND - ALBERTA, B.C., ONTARIO, AND YUKON
HOW SOLD:	THROUGH BROKERS AND FINANCIAL PLANNERS
PHONE NUMBER:	(604) 688-7333
WEB SITE ADDRESS:	WWW.FIRSTHORIZON.COM
E-MAIL ADDRESS:	CLIENTINFO@FIRSTHORIZON.COM

FUND SUMMARY

$$$$ - NONE
$$$ - NONE
$$ - NONE
$ - HORIZONS MULTI-ASSET
NR - HORIZONS RRSP HEDGE

BEST CHOICES: NONE
BEST FOR RRSPS: NONE
BEST UNRATEDS: HORIZONS RRSP HEDGE

FUND RATINGS

U.S. AND INTERNATIONAL EQUITY FUNDS

HORIZONS MULTI-ASSET FUND $ ↑ G #/* D

Manager: Fred Purvis (First Horizon Management), since 1994

MER: 2.00%

This is an offshore fund, headquartered in Barbados. It is available only to "sophisticated" investors, which means you need a minimum of $25,000 to $150,000 to get in, depending on your province of residence. The fund invests in derivatives (futures, options, etc.) on various indexes throughout the world. In their literature, the company says that Canadian residents receive a tax break through this fund. No tax is payable until an investor redeems units, and then all gains are taxed as a dividend, eligible for the federal dividend tax credit. The offering memorandum contains a detailed explanation of all this, which you should read carefully before investing. Returns have been unimpressive; the fund gained just 1.1% in the year to June 30/98.

FRIEDBERG MERCANTILE GROUP

THE COMPANY

The Friedberg Mercantile Group is a well-respected Toronto-based currency and commodities trading firm and is considered one of Canada's leading experts in these specialized fields. Their funds, most of which are relatively new, are designed to make this expertise available to a wider range of investors who understand the risks involved. They have recently launched a new series of funds that are sold only by offering memorandum, with a minimum investment of $150,000. The Friedberg Currency Fund, which has a good track record, is no longer accepting new investments.

THE DETAILS

NUMBER OF FUNDS:	6
ASSETS UNDER MANAGEMENT:	$123 MILLION
LOAD CHARGE:	NONE
SWITCHING CHARGE:	NONE
WHERE SOLD:	ACROSS CANADA, EXCEPT QUEBEC
HOW SOLD:	DIRECTLY THROUGH FRIEDBERG MERCANTILE GROUP AND OTHER AUTHORIZED DEALERS
PHONE NUMBER:	(416) 364-1171
WEB SITE ADDRESS:	WWW.FRIEDBERG.COM
E-MAIL ADDRESS:	FMGTOR@INFORAMP.NET

FUND SUMMARY

$$$$ - NONE
$$$ - NONE
$$ - NONE
$ - DOUBLE GOLD PLUS
NR - CURRENCY, DIVERSIFIED, FOREIGN BOND, FUTURES, TORONTO TRUST EQUITY - HEDGE, TORONTO TRUST INTERNATIONAL SECURITIES

BEST CHOICES: NONE
BEST FOR RRSPs: NONE
BEST UNRATEDS: CURRENCY

FUND RATINGS

CANADIAN EQUITY FUNDS

FRIEDBERG DOUBLE GOLD PLUS FUND $ ↑ G # RSP PM

Manager: Albert D. Friedberg, since inception (1987)

MER: 0.00%

This fund is in the process of closing.

GBC ASSET MANAGEMENT

THE COMPANY

GBC Asset Management is the marketing division of Pembroke Management Ltd., which was set up in 1968. The company's focus is on high net worth individuals and special institutional situations, which helps explain why this group of funds requires a minimum of $100,000 to open an account with them. The company has special expertise in North American small- to mid-cap equities, and the funds they manage in-house are on a team basis. Mutual funds requiring detailed knowledge of other markets (e.g., international equities, bonds) are run by outside firms.

THE DETAILS

NUMBER OF FUNDS:	5
ASSETS UNDER MANAGEMENT:	$433 MILLION
LOAD CHARGE:	NONE, IF PURCHASED DIRECTLY THROUGH GBC, OTHERWISE FRONT: MAX. 3%
SWITCHING CHARGE:	NONE
WHERE SOLD:	THROUGH GBC: ONTARIO, QUEBEC, AND B.C. THROUGH BROKERS AND DEALERS: ELSEWHERE
HOW SOLD:	DIRECTLY THROUGH GBC, OR THROUGH REGISTERED BROKERS, DEALERS, AND FINANCIAL PLANNERS
PHONE NUMBER:	(416) 366-2550 OR 1-800-668-7383
WEB SITE ADDRESS:	WWW.GBC.CA
E-MAIL ADDRESS:	INFO@GBC.CA

FUND SUMMARY

$$$$ - NONE
$$$ - CANADIAN BOND, CANADIAN GROWTH, NORTH AMERICAN GROWTH
$$ - MONEY MARKET
$ - INTERNATIONAL GROWTH
NR - NONE

BEST CHOICES: CANADIAN GROWTH
BEST FOR RRSPS: CANADIAN BOND, CANADIAN GROWTH
BEST UNRATED: N/A

FUND RATINGS

CANADIAN EQUITY FUNDS

GBC CANADIAN GROWTH FUND $$$ → G No RSP CSC

Manager: Pembroke Management Ltd., since inception (1988)

MER: 1.92%

The mandate of this fund is to invest primarily "in common shares of small and medium sized Canadian corporations" and shares of companies "the fund initially invested in when they were small and medium sized and has continued to hold as the corporations maintain above-average growth". That helps explain why you'll find names like MDS Inc. and Geac in the portfolio, companies that have grown quite large in recent years. However, the main focus is still on smaller firms, and the managers have done very well in their selection process. This fund consistently turns in above-average returns and is coming off another good year with a profit of 18.3% for the 12 months to June 30/98. Five-year average annual compound rate of return is a healthy 15.2%. Well worth a look, if you have the price of admission.

U.S. AND INTERNATIONAL EQUITY FUNDS

GBC INTERNATIONAL GROWTH FUND $ ↑ G No £ IE

Manager: Babson-Stewart Ivory Ltd., since 1995

MER: 1.84%

This continues to be the weak link in the otherwise excellent GBC family, although it is starting to show some signs of life with a 14.1% gain in the first half of '98. Longer term performance is still below average for the international fund category, however. The managers, who are based in Edinburgh, Scotland, use a bottom-up stock selection approach with an emphasis on financially strong companies with proven track records. Note that this fund is excluded from investing in Canada and the U.S., which is one of the reasons returns are sub-par when compared to the full range of global funds. Historically, the risk factor here is high. This fund has a 35% chance of losing money over any one-year period according to ATP analysis. Over three years, there's still a 19% chance you'll be down. This risk is not offset by a strong potential for big gains; over any five-year period the historic likelihood of earning an annual return of better than 10% is zero. However, if the new momentum the fund seems to be showing can be maintained, those numbers will start to look better in a couple of years.

GBC NORTH AMERICAN GROWTH FUND $$$ ↑ G No £ AE

Manager: Pembroke Management Ltd., since inception (1988)

MER: 1.93%

Although the majority of the holdings are in U.S. equities, this fund also holds some Canadian stocks, such as Hummingbird and Franco-Nevada. They represent about 10% of the portfolio. The focus is on high-growth companies in which management has a large ownership position. This fund has been a good performer for a long time. However, it has to be compared to the correct peer group for that fact to show up. *The Globe and Mail* compares its returns to U.S. equity funds, which make the results appear to be below average. *The Financial Post*, by contrast, has a separate category for North American funds. There, the fund's results are better than average for all time frames out to 10 years. The risk profile of this fund is somewhat higher than normal for this category. The ATP analysis shows an historic 27% chance of a loss over any one-year period (including a 4% chance that loss could exceed 20%). Even after a three-year hold, there's a small chance (2%) you could still be down.

FIXED INCOME AND MONEY MARKET FUNDS

GBC CANADIAN BOND FUND $$$ → FI No RSP CB

Managers: Greydanus Boeckh and Associates, since inception (1984)

MER: 1.09%

This is a consistently above-average performer, in part due to a relatively low MER. Ten-year average annual rate of return to June 30/98 was 10.6%, well above the 9.7% average for the Canadian bond fund category as reported by *The Globe and Mail*. The fund invests mainly in government securities; there were no corporate bonds in the portfolio in mid-'98. The risk profile of this fund shows that historically there is only a 5% chance of a loss over any given one-year period according to ATP analysis; however, some shorter term volatility is noted.

GBC MONEY MARKET FUND $$ → C No RSP CMM

Managers: Greydanus Boeckh and Associates, since inception (1988)

MER: 0.75%

Despite a relatively low management fee, returns for this fund are just average. The fund invests all its assets in federal government T-bills.

GLOBAL STRATEGY FUNDS

THE COMPANY

This company recently announced another major overhaul of its fund lineup, merging seven small funds into larger ones (pending unitholder approval) in a move designed to streamline the entire operation and cut costs. Funds getting the axe are to include the Asia Fund, Japan Fund, and Latin America Fund, all of which are to be folded into World Companies Fund. Also going are the Diversified Asia Fund, Diversified Japan Plus Fund, and Diversified Latin America Fund, all of which will move into the Diversified World Equity Fund; and the Diversified Foreign Bond Fund, which becomes part of the Diversified Bond Fund. The sweetener for investors is a reduction of 25 basis points in the management fee charged against the continuing funds after the merger. In the case of the World Companies Fund and the Diversified World Equity Fund, which between them will absorb six of the merged funds, this amounts to a 10% fee reduction. That money will go straight into unitholders' pockets. Several other Global Strategy funds have also enjoyed a reduction in MERs in the past year.

As a bonus, several of the funds are now posting good returns. This continues to be a turnaround situation, and investors who have shunned Global Strategy funds in the past might take a fresh look. However, be selective. Some funds in this group are still chronic underachievers, and some potentially good ones haven't been around long enough to qualify for a formal rating (e.g., the Canadian Opportunities Fund). Cherry-picking is definitely the order of the day here.

THE DETAILS

NUMBER OF FUNDS:	15
ASSETS UNDER MANAGEMENT:	$4.3 BILLION
LOAD CHARGE:	FRONT: MAX. 9%; BACK: MAX. 5.8% (EQUITY FUNDS), 4.7% (INCOME FUNDS)
SWITCHING CHARGE:	2% MAXIMUM

WHERE SOLD:	ACROSS CANADA
HOW SOLD:	THROUGH REGISTERED BROKERS AND DEALERS
PHONE NUMBER:	(416) 966-8667 OR 1-800-387-1229
WEB SITE ADDRESS:	WWW.GLOBALSTRATEGYFUNDS.COM
E-MAIL ADDRESS:	SERVICE@GLOBALSTAT.COM

FUND SUMMARY

$$$$ - INCOME PLUS
$$$ - DIVERSIFIED EUROPE, DIVERSIFIED WORLD EQUITY, U.S. EQUITY, WORLD COMPANIES, WORLD EQUITY
$$ - CANADIAN SMALL CAP, DIVERSIFIED BOND, EUROPE PLUS, WORLD BOND
$ - BOND, CANADA GROWTH, GOLD PLUS, MONEY MARKET
NR - CANADIAN OPPORTUNITIES

BEST CHOICES: DIVERSIFIED EUROPE, DIVERSIFIED WORLD EQUITY, INCOME PLUS
BEST FOR RRSPs: DIVERSIFIED WORLD EQUITY, INCOME PLUS
BEST UNRATED: CANADIAN OPPORTUNITIES

FUND RATINGS

CANADIAN EQUITY FUNDS

GLOBAL STRATEGY CANADA GROWTH FUND $ → G #/* RSP CE

Manager: Tony Massie, since inception (1992)

MER: 2.57%

There was a lot of publicity and anticipation when high-profile fund manager Tony Massie left the Vancouver-based Sagit organization a few years ago and hooked up with Global Strategy to launch this fund. Massie had enjoyed great success with Sagit and much was expected of his new entry. But, except for a flash of excitement last year when the fund gained 26.4%, returns have tended to be below average. The latest one-year figures, to June 30/98, show a disappointing advance of just 7%. A contributing factor appears to have been a heavy weighting in resource stocks, particularly the oil and gas sector, which has now been trimmed back. Massie uses a value investing approach, looking for good fundamentals and has a commitment to maximizing shareholder returns. So far, we still haven't seen sustained evidence that the "maximizing" part of the mandate is working.

GLOBAL STRATEGY CANADIAN
SMALL CAP FUND $$ ↑ G #/* RSP CSC

Manager: John Sartz, since inception (1994)

MER: 2.71%

John Sartz is one of the country's true small-cap gurus. He has a well-established style of investing, which he sticks to through thick and thin, and usually makes good returns for investors. The past 12 months have been an exception, however; this fund dropped 1% over the year to June 30/98. However, longer term results are well above average for the small-cap category, with a 16.7% average annual compound rate of return for the three years to June 30/98. Sartz only selects growth companies for his fund; you won't find any gold mines here. Despite the recent weak returns, I expect this fund to be an above-average performer over the long haul. However, we'll start it off with $$ until there is evidence it's back in a profitable mode.

GLOBAL STRATEGY GOLD PLUS FUND $ ↑ G #/* RSP PM

Manager: Tony Massie, since inception (1993)

MER: 2.75%

Global Strategy publishes a twice-monthly magazine for mutual fund sales reps called *Stratagems*. One of the features is a review of every fund in the group, which includes a risk/return rating. This fund gets the highest rank for risk (I strongly agree) but also the highest rank for return potential (I definitely do not agree). If you accept the high potential return idea, you have to believe that gold bullion is going to make a roaring comeback sometime soon. Maybe it will happen, but I wouldn't want to bet a lot of money on it. So far, anyone who has put dollars into this fund has seen a lot of them vanish. Average annual loss for the three years to June 30/98 was 15.3%. I suggest you look elsewhere in this group. And even though this fund is RRSP eligible, don't even consider it for that purpose.

U.S. AND INTERNATIONAL EQUITY FUNDS

GLOBAL STRATEGY DIVERSIFIED
EUROPE FUND $$$ ↓ G #/* RSP EE

Manager: Richard Robinson (Rothschild Asset Management Ltd.),
since 1998

MER: 2.51%

This is Global Strategy's Europe fund for RRSP investors who don't want to use their foreign content to get exposure to those markets. Index futures are used to provide exposure to several European exchanges. Recently, this fund has outperformed the more conventional Europe Plus Fund. Gain for the year to June 30/98 was above average for the European fund category at 39.6%. Three-year returns are slightly above average, at 26.9% annually. Good safety record.

GLOBAL STRATEGY DIVERSIFIED
WORLD EQUITY FUND $$$ → G #/* RSP IE

Manager: Rupert Robinson, Rothschild Asset Management Ltd,
since 1994

MER: 2.37%

This is one of the GS funds that has experienced a major overhaul recently. It used to be a balanced fund but has been renamed and given an equities-only mandate. It also was one of the key funds in the September, 1998 mergers, with three smaller funds folded into it. As with all GS funds that bear the "Diversified" name, this one is fully RRSP eligible. It invests in index futures on a variety of international stock exchanges, including the U.S. Results since the changeover are steadily improving; the fund is coming off its second good year in a row with an 18.6% gain. Average annual compound rate of return for the three years to June 30/98 was 17.6%, very good for the international equity category. Rating moves up a notch in recognition. This is a good way to get more international exposure into your RRSP without eating up foreign content room.

GLOBAL STRATEGY EUROPE PLUS FUND $$ → G #/* £ EE

Managers: Gartmore Capital Management, Rothschild Asset
Management Ltd., since 1994; Schroder Capital Management, since 1997

MER: 2.79%

The name of this fund was changed from Global Strategy
Europe in early '95 and it was given a new team of managers. As a result, GS is presenting this as a brand-new
fund — you'll find only short-term performance results in
the business press. That's understandable, since the predecessor fund had never been very impressive. The new
version has done okay, with a 33.9% advance in the year to
June 30/98. However, for the second year in a row the
return was well below the performance recorded by the
companion Diversified Europe Fund, which is an index
fund. Given the heavyweight nature of the three companies responsible for this portfolio, we should expect better.
Some of the portfolio is invested in the emerging markets
of Eastern Europe, but the major concentration is in the
U.K., France, and Germany. Each manager brings a different investing style and each is responsible for a specific
portion of the fund.

GLOBAL STRATEGY U.S. EQUITY FUND $$$ → G #/* £ USE

Managers: AIM Capital Management, Rothschild Asset Management
Ltd., Schroder Capital Management, since 1994

MER: 2.59%

This fund invests in a wide range of U.S. stocks, with a
number of Dow holdings on the top 15 list, such as
American Express and Wal-Mart. Each manager is responsible for part of the portfolio, with AIM looking for growth
companies, Rothschild focusing on large-caps, and
Schroder specializing in small-cap issues. Returns have
been quite good; the fund averaged 25.3% a year for the
three years to June 30/98. We'll start it off with a $$$ rating
to reflect that.

GLOBAL STRATEGY WORLD COMPANIES FUND $$$ → G #/* £ IE

Managers: Montgomery Asset Management, Rothschild Asset Management Ltd., Perpetual Portfolio Management, since 1994

MER: 2.79%

The objective of this fund is to seek out companies with significant growth potential in all parts of the world. These may include small-cap stocks in developed nations as well as larger companies in emerging markets. Results have been quite good, with a three-year average annual compound rate of return of 22.1% to June 30/98. The three managers each bring a different approach to their portion of the portfolio. The fund was originally named World Emerging Companies but this was changed to clarify the fact it is not an emerging markets fund. Debuts with a $$$ rating.

GLOBAL STRATEGY WORLD EQUITY FUND $$$ → G #/* £ IE

Managers: Capital International Ltd., Rothschild Asset Management Ltd., Schroder Capital Management, since 1994

MER: 2.79%

In January, '95, GS folded their underachieving Global Strategy Fund into this new creation, using a multi-manager approach with each company responsible for a third of the portfolio. Each manager brings a different discipline: Capital International takes a value investing approach, Rothschild Asset Management uses a top-down system that allocates assets among different countries, while Schroder Capital specializes in small- and mid-cap stocks. One result of the change was to expunge the returns of the old Global Strategy Fund from the records; the business press mutual fund listings only show returns for this fund from the start of '95. That's fair in one sense, but it makes it appear as though this fund has no prior history — which it does, and not a good one. Returns since the change are better, with a three-year average annual compound rate of return of 17.8% to June 30/98. That's better than the norm for the international category. The difference between this and the Diversified World Equity Fund is that these managers invest directly in equities rather than indirectly through derivatives. As a result, this fund counts as foreign content in an RRSP. Since the three-year returns are about the same, choose the Diversified fund if you're investing inside a retirement plan.

BALANCED FUNDS

GLOBAL STRATEGY INCOME PLUS FUND $$$$ ↓ FI/G #/* RSP CBAL

Manager: Tony Massie, since inception (1992)

MER: 2.40%

When Tony Massie moved to Global Strategy from Sagit, he launched two new funds (a third, Gold Plus, has since been added to his stable). His Canadian equity fund has disappointed, but this balanced fund has been on target with returns that are consistently at or above average. The portfolio is a mix of high-quality bonds, income trusts, T-bills, common stocks, and preferred shares. In the past year, the weighting of common shares was trimmed back from 62% of the portfolio to just under 50%, thereby reducing the fund's exposure to the summer market correction. Return for the 12 months to June 30/98 was 16.2%. Five-year average annual compound rate of return was 15.1%, making this one of the best performers in the Canadian balanced fund category over that time. Very good safety record too. This continues to be one of Global Strategy's stronger entries, and would make an excellent addition to a well-balanced RRSP. Rating moves up to the top $$$$ level this year, making this the first Global Strategy Fund to achieve that rank.

FIXED INCOME AND MONEY MARKET FUNDS

GLOBAL STRATEGY BOND FUND $ ↓ C #/* RSP CB

Manager: Scott Elphinstone (Five Continents Financial), since 1994

MER: 1.50%

GS offers several bond funds. This is the domestic Canadian version. It invests mainly in federal, provincial, and Crown corporation issues, but there may also be some foreign bonds in the mix, within the 20% limit. Manager

Scott Elphinstone has taken a very defensive position with this fund lately. The portfolio duration in the first half of '98 was just 2.4 years. (Duration is a measure of risk in a bond fund; the shorter the duration, the less the risk.) As a result, recent returns have been low, only 3.7% for the year to June 30/98. The trade-off is a high degree of safety. You have to decide where you want to place your priority.

GLOBAL STRATEGY DIVERSIFIED
BOND FUND $$ → FI #/* RSP IB

Manager: Ceris Williams (Rothschild Asset Management), since 1992

MER: 2.40%

This is a fully RRSP-eligible bond fund, for those wishing to increase the foreign exposure in their registered plans. Invests directly in RRSP-eligible bonds from Canadian and approved international institutions (e.g., the World Bank), as well as in bond futures and foreign issues within the 20% foreign content limit. Long-term bonds are limited to those with a AA rating or better, for added safety. This used to be the largest international bond fund in Canada, but has now dropped to number three. Results are so-so. Gain for the year to June 30/98 was 8.1%, a little below average for the international bond fund category. However, three-year returns are above average for the peer group. The Diversified Foreign Bond Fund was to be folded into this one in the fall of 1998.

GLOBAL STRATEGY MONEY
MARKET FUND $ → C #/* RSP CMM

Manager: Scott Elphinstone (Five Continents Financial), since 1987

MER: 0.84%

This fund invests in higher yielding provincial and municipal short-term notes, as well as corporate issues. Returns are below average for the money market category. The load charges on this fund could be unrealistically high if you're not careful; negotiate with your advisor. Formerly called the T-Bill Savings Fund.

GLOBAL STRATEGY WORLD BOND FUND $$ → FI #/* £ IB

Manager: Ceris Williams (Rothschild Asset Management), since 1992

MER: 2.10%

This fund differs from the companion Diversified Bond Fund in that it is only eligible for RRSPs as foreign content. That means the managers can invest directly in debt securities issued by foreign governments, whereas the Diversified Fund is restricted in that respect by the 20% rule. The fund is overseen by the Fixed Income and Currency team of the London-based N.M. Rothschild organization, which should know something about this business, having nearly 200 years of experience (although not with this particular fund, of course). Returns are similar to those of the Diversified Bond Fund, average to slightly below.

THE GOODWOOD FUND

THE COMPANY

This is a small, family-run operation located in Goodwood, Ontario (hence the name). There is just one fund, a Canadian equity fund that opened in 1996 and is therefore too new to be rated. Manager is Peter Puccetti of Puccetti Funds Management. The fund is sold under offering memorandum, so the minimum purchase ranges from a low of $25,000 to as high as $150,000, depending on your province of residence. Returns so far have been good.

THE DETAILS

NUMBER OF FUNDS:	1
ASSETS UNDER MANAGEMENT:	$2 MILLION
LOAD CHARGE:	BACK: MAX. 5%
SWITCHING CHARGE:	NONE
WHERE SOLD:	ONTARIO, NOVA SCOTIA, ALBERTA, B.C., AND THE YUKON TERRITORY
HOW SOLD:	DIRECTLY THROUGH THE MANAGER OR THROUGH BROKERS, DEALERS, AND FINANCIAL PLANNERS
PHONE NUMBER:	(905) 649-5588
WEB SITE ADDRESS:	N/A
E-MAIL ADDRESS:	N/A

FUND SUMMARY

$$$$ - NONE
$$$ - NONE
$$ - NONE
$ - NONE
NR - THE GOODWOOD FUND

FUND RATINGS

This fund is too new to qualify for a rating.

GREEN LINE FUNDS (TORONTO DOMINION BANK)

THE COMPANY

In terms of size, TD's Green Line Funds are second only to the giant Royal Bank entry among the major banks. In terms of quality, they also rank high on the list. This is a well-balanced, highly diversified fund group that is aggressively expanding on all fronts. There are lots of good choices in the lineup, but some weak spots as well. Some of the new go-go funds are of special interest to growth-oriented investors, such as the Science & Technology and Health Sciences Funds. There's also a good selection of fixed-income offerings. Among the bank fund groups, this continues to be one of the best bets.

THE DETAILS

NUMBER OF FUNDS:	33
ASSETS UNDER MANAGEMENT:	$14.8 BILLION
LOAD CHARGE:	NONE
SWITCHING CHARGE:	NONE
WHERE SOLD:	ACROSS CANADA
HOW SOLD:	THROUGH BRANCHES OF TD BANKS OR THROUGH BROKERS, DEALERS, AND FINANCIAL PLANNERS
PHONE NUMBER:	1-800-268-8166 OR (416) 982-6432
WEB SITE ADDRESS:	WWW.GREENLINEFUNDS.COM
E-MAIL ADDRESS:	FUNDERMAN@TDBANK.CA

FUND SUMMARY

$$$$ - NONE

$$$ - BALANCED GROWTH, BALANCED INCOME, CANADIAN BOND, CANADIAN EQUITY, CANADIAN MONEY MARKET, CANADIAN T-BILL, DIVIDEND, EUROPEAN GROWTH, GLOBAL SELECT, SCIENCE & TECHNOLOGY, U.S. MID-CAP GROWTH, U.S. MONEY MARKET, VALUE

$$ - BLUE CHIP EQUITY, CANADIAN GOVERNMENT BOND INDEX, CANADIAN INDEX, GLOBAL GOVERNMENT BOND,

> GLOBAL RSP BOND, MORTGAGE BACKED, REAL RETURN
> BOND, SHORT TERM INCOME, U.S. INDEX
>
> $ - ASIAN GROWTH, EMERGING MARKETS, ENERGY,
> INTERNATIONAL EQUITY, JAPANESE GROWTH, LATIN
> AMERICAN GROWTH, MORTGAGE, PRECIOUS METALS,
> RESOURCE
>
> NR - CANADIAN SMALL CAP EQUITY, DOW JONES INDUSTRIAL
> AVERAGE INDEX, ENTERTAINMENT & COMMUNICATIONS,
> EUROPEAN INDEX FUND, HEALTH SCIENCES,
> INTERNATIONAL RSP INDEX, JAPANESE INDEX, MONTHLY
> INCOME, PREMIUM MONEY MARKET, U.S. BLUE CHIP
> EQUITY, U.S. RSP INDEX, U.S. SMALL CAP EQUITY

BEST CHOICES: BALANCED GROWTH, BALANCED INCOME, CANADIAN BOND, GLOBAL SELECT

BEST FOR RRSPs: BALANCED GROWTH, BALANCED INCOME, CANADIAN BOND, U.S. MONEY MARKET

BEST UNRATED: ENTERTAINMENT & COMMUNICATIONS, HEALTH SCIENCES, U.S. BLUE CHIP EQUITY

FUND RATINGS

CANADIAN EQUITY FUNDS

GREEN LINE BLUE CHIP EQUITY FUND $$ → G No RSP CE

Manager: Douglas Simmons (Sceptre Investment Counsel), since 1997

MER: 2.25%

Green Line now offers six Canadian stock funds, so you have to be very careful to match your selection to your goals. The objective of this fund is to invest in blue-chip stocks with good growth potential. Performance had improved significantly in recent years, however the gain for the 12 months to June 30/98 was below average for the Canadian equity category at 10.2%. Three- and five-year results are still above average, although not quite as good as some of your other alternatives in this group. The manager is Sceptre Investment Counsel, a Toronto-based company with an excellent reputation in the industry. Originally called the FuturLink Canadian Growth Fund; taken over by TD Bank and Green Line as part of the purchase of Central Guaranty Trust several years ago.

GREEN LINE CANADIAN EQUITY FUND $$$ → G No RSP CE

Managers: John Weatherall, since 1997

MER: 2.10%

Manager John Weatherall was formerly chairman of TD Asset Management. He retired in 1995, but continues to keep a hand in running this fund, using value investment principles. He's a long-term investor who uses a complex stock screening method to make his decisions. The fund has been responding well to his direction and now shows above-average returns over all time frames. Gain for the 12 months to June 30/98 was 11.2%. The portfolio is a blend of small, medium, and large companies and was weighted towards financial service stocks and industrial products in the first half of '98. Weatherall also makes full use of the foreign content allotment. A good choice for a fully managed fund in the Green Line stable.

GREEN LINE CANADIAN INDEX FUND $$ → G No RSP CE

Managers: Tim Thompson, since 1996; Enrique Cuyegkeng, since 1992

MER: 0.80%

This fund is designed to mirror the stocks that make up the TSE 300 Index. It never quite achieves that goal, however, because of the management fee involved (even though it's relatively low and was taken down again recently). This fund had the best return of the four broadly based Green Line Canadian equity entries last year, with a gain of 15.4%, but the previous year it trailed the others. Over 10 years, it has done slightly better than the Blue Chip Fund, slightly worse than the Canadian Equity Fund. However, in a down market I would prefer to be in a fully managed fund.

GREEN LINE DIVIDEND FUND $$$ → G No RSP INC

Managers: Doug Warwick, since 1993; Paul Harris, since 1996

MER: 2.00%

This fund has recently been recast in a more traditional dividend mode, with the emphasis supposedly on after-tax income. The portfolio has been moved into high-yielding common stock and preferred shares, mainly floating-rate issues. This theoretically makes this fund more suitable for income-oriented investors. But the reality is somewhat different. Total returns continue to be excellent, with a nice gain of 23.5% for the year to June 30/98. However, tax-advantaged cash flow continues to be very weak. Our annual survey of dividend funds in *Mutual Funds Update* found only a 1% cash-on-cash return in 1997. So if income is your objective, this isn't your fund. But if you'd like a conservatively managed stock fund for your portfolio, this one will fit just fine; in fact, it has outperformed all the other Green Line Canadian equity funds by a considerable margin in recent years.

GREEN LINE ENERGY FUND $ ↑ G No RSP SEC

Manager: Rob Cassels, since inception (1994)

MER: 2.10%

There are not many pure energy funds around and they are a risky play at the best of times because of the volatility of oil prices in recent years. This one has fared much worse than the others to date because of its specific focus: medium-size exploration companies, especially those with good international prospects. While that approach may work out in the long term, it has hurt short-term results because exploration companies tend to get whacked much harder in a downturn than the big integrated firms like Imperial and Petrocan, neither of which figure prominently in this fund's holdings. Unitholders have been paying the price. The fund took a huge hit over the 12 months to June 30/98, losing 38.5% during that period. Compare that to the Royal Energy Fund (-14.6%) and the CIBC Energy Fund (-16.6%) and you can see the impact the particular style of the Green Line fund has had. I do not recommend putting any money here until we start to see a recovery in oil prices and that could be some time in coming, given the Asian situation.

GREEN LINE PRECIOUS METALS FUND $ ↑ G No RSP PM

Manager: Margot Naudie, since 1998

MER: 2.12%

Precious metals funds continue to wallow and that is unlikely to change until the price of bullion starts to move. It's not clear what it will take to trigger that since even a major economic crisis in Asia — the type of catalyst that has worked in the past — has failed to have any impact. In the meantime, fund managers are scrambling to find value anywhere they can. In this case, new manager Margot Naudie, who took over in March, '98, is maintaining the fund's significant exposure to silver through Royal Bank silver certificates, the largest single holding (11.4% of the portfolio in the first half of the year). The investment strategy on the gold side is shifting away from diversified mining companies and towards selected gold producers. Still, it will be a long haul before this one starts to recover.

GREEN LINE RESOURCE FUND $ ↑ G No RSP SEC

Managers: Rob Cassels, since 1993

MER: 2.12%

As you can tell from the name, the mandate of this fund is to invest in the natural resource sector. Resource stocks are cyclical in nature, which means they are subject to big up and down swings, depending on general economic conditions, commodity prices, and a number of other factors. As I result, I generally suggest not investing in funds like this on a buy-and-hold basis. Rather, buy them as a short-term hold and be prepared to switch after you've had some good gains. As far as broadly based resource funds go, this one is coming off a rough year, with a big loss of 35.5%. That was worse than average for the category. Don't put this one in your RRSP.

GREEN LINE VALUE FUND $$$ → G No RSP CE

Managers: Rob Cassels and Bonnie Bloomberg, since 1994

MER: 2.09%

This fund had been the shining star in Green Line's Canadian equity lineup since its launch at the end of '93, but it ran into some tough sledding last year, with a gain of just 4.5%. In a commentary to investors, the managers suggested it was because their style was somewhat out of favour (although several other value funds did well) but said they would stick to their game plan of choosing undervalued companies with strong business franchises and good management. The portfolio cuts across all sectors and includes all types of companies, big and small. Despite the weak short-term returns, the fund's three-year average annual compound rate of return is a solid 21.3%, well above par for the Canadian equity category. We'll write off last year as an aberration and leave the rating intact for now.

U.S. AND INTERNATIONAL EQUITY FUNDS

GREEN LINE ASIAN GROWTH FUND $ ↑ G No £ FEE

Manager: Bruce Seton (Darier, Hentsch), since 1993

MER: 2.60%

This fund invests through Asia, with the exception of Japan. Far East markets have been tough on managers in recent years, but this fund held its ground reasonably well until last year when it took the gas pipe, dropping a breathtaking 49.9%. There's not much more to say. Stand clear until Asia makes a comeback.

GREEN LINE EMERGING MARKETS FUND $ ↑ G No £ EME

Managers: Madhav Dhar (Morgan Stanley), since 1992

MER: 2.69%

This fund is under the direction of Morgan Stanley Asset Management, one of the pioneers in emerging markets investing. The portfolio is broadly diversified, with no disproportionate bets on any one country, although South Africa has been a recent favourite. However, that didn't help to shield the fund from a big loss when emerging markets tumbled around the world in the past year. The drop to June 30/98 was 31.3%. Stand aside for now.

GREEN LINE EUROPEAN GROWTH FUND $$$ → G No £ EE

Manager: Patricia Maxwell-Arnot (Credit Suisse), since 1994

MER: 2.58%

This is a very traditional European fund, with an emphasis on large companies and a bottom-up approach to stock selection, which looks first and foremost at the fundamentals of a company. It's the type of fund that is unlikely to deliver any major surprises; as long as the European markets are doing well, this fund will also. As with most funds of this type, the U.K. is the number-one geographic holding at about a third of the portfolio. Other significant positions are in countries like Germany, France, Switzerland, and the Netherlands. Returns have been above average for the European equity category. Average annual compound rate of return for the three years to June 30/98 was 29.4%. If you have a non-registered Green Line account, this fund should be part of your mix.

GREEN LINE GLOBAL SELECT FUND $$$ → G No £ IE

Managers: Bob Yerbury (Perpetual Portfolio Management), since 1993

MER: 2.34%

This is Green Line's flagship global investment fund. The mandate allows the manager to invest anywhere in the world, including the U.S. and Canada. In fact, U.S. stocks accounted for more than 35% of the portfolio in the first half of 1998, which is one of the main reasons why this fund has continued to outperform the companion International Fund by quite a wide margin. Average annual compound rate of return over the three years to June 30/98 was above average, at 16.8%. This is the best bet in this group if you want a well-diversified international fund.

GREEN LINE INTERNATIONAL EQUITY FUND $ ↑ G No £ IE

Manager: Jan Kees van Heusde (Schroder Capital Management), since 1995

MER: 2.32%

The mandate in this case is to invest in non-North American companies. Without a U.S. component, the manager has been forced to look mainly at Europe for gains, with Far East markets floundering. Judged against other funds with the same limitations, this fund hasn't done particularly well, although it was starting to show signs of life in the first half of '98. But we need more than a six-month spurt to boost the rating here. The safety rating also leaves much to be desired.

GREEN LINE JAPANESE GROWTH FUND $ ↑ G No £ FEE

Manager: Donald Farquharson (Schroder Capital Management), since inception (1994)

MER: 2.59%

These have been hard times for investors who have been betting on a turnaround in Japan. Instead of the expected recovery, conditions in that country have gone from bad to worse, to the point where there are serious fears that the world's second largest economy is on the brink of a depression. All the Japan-specific mutual funds have suffered as a result. About the only good thing that can be said about this one is that others have fared worse. Over the three years to the end of June/98, unitholders lost an average of 7% annually. If that makes you blue, just be thankful you didn't own shares in InvesNat Japanese Equity. Those units dropped 13.1% annually on average over the same period.

GREEN LINE LATIN AMERICAN GROWTH FUND $ ↑ G No £ AE

Managers: Andy Scov and Robert Meyer (Morgan Stanley), since 1997

MER: 2.66%

This has been a decent performer in the Latin American category over the past three years (average annual return of 10.2% to June 30/98). However, the ongoing economic crisis in Asia has hurt investor confidence in all developing markets, and Latin America hasn't escaped. The fund went into a deep slide in the late spring of 1998 and these doldrums could continue for some time. As with most Latin funds, Brazil and Mexico are the lynchpins of the portfolio. Not a good place for your money in the current conditions.

GREEN LINE SCIENCE AND TECHNOLOGY FUND $$$ → G No £ IE

Manager: Charles A. Morris (T. Rowe Price), since 1993

MER: 2.58%

This was one of the first sector funds to open up in Canada. It got off to a terrific start, riding the high-tech wave to huge gains in the first year. Then it faltered a bit, not surprisingly perhaps. Recent gains have been better; the fund was ahead 22.1% in the year to June 30/98. Most of the companies in the portfolio are U.S. based, which may reflect the fact that Morris is a vice president of U.S. investment house T. Rowe Price. There are a few Canadian entries, however. If you take the long view, high tech is going to be the place to be for decades to come. Add some to your non-registered portfolio and let it sit.

GREEN LINE U.S. INDEX FUND $$ → G No £ USE

Managers: Tim Thompson, since 1996; Enrique Cuyegkeng, since 1992

MER: 0.66%

For several years, I complained that Green Line only offered one U.S. equity fund. They must have been paying attention, because now they have six. This was the original one and even though I've never been a great fan of index funds I have to admit it has done well for investors over the years. Average annual compound rate of return over the decade to June 30/98 was 16.8%. Only four funds did better. Index funds, by definition, will track the average of the index to which they're tied — in this case, the Standard & Poor's 500. When the market is strong, as it has been in recent years, you'll do well. When it tumbles, there is no place to hide. The low management fee really helps here. I'm uncomfortable giving an index fund better than $$ because by definition it should always be an average performer. However, the reality is that many managed funds can not do as well. This is one of the better index funds available in this country and they are becoming more popular, so if that sort of investing approach appeals to you, put this one on your list.

GREEN LINE U.S. MID-CAP GROWTH FUND $$$ → G No £ USE

Manager: Brian W.H. Berghuis (T. Rowe Price), since 1993

MER: 2.33%

The name of this fund was recently changed from North American Growth Fund to better reflect the investment mandate, which is to focus on medium-size U.S. companies. Brian Berghuis is a vice president with the well-known U.S. investment house of T. Rowe Price. He uses a fundamental, bottom-up stock selection approach. The fund is coming off a very good year, with a gain of 37.3% to June 30/98. That was the best result among Green Line's six (count 'em!) U.S. stock funds last year. It's a good choice, but only if you have room for a specific market niche fund in your portfolio.

BALANCED FUNDS

GREEN LINE BALANCED
GROWTH FUND $$$ → G/FI No RSP CBAL

Managers: Mary Hallward (McLean Budden), since 1993

MER: 1.95%

The main difference between this and the companion Balanced Income Fund is a greater emphasis on stocks for enhanced growth potential. This fund also makes more use of foreign content, with almost 20% of the portfolio in U.S. and foreign equities. The fund has shown significant improvement since McLean Budden, one of Canada's top pension fund managers, took over portfolio responsibility. Average gain for the five years to June 30/98 is above average for the balanced fund category, at 11.6%. The portfolio was about 45% in bonds and cash in the first half of '98, with the rest in equities. A good RRSP choice. Formerly the FuturLink Select Fund.

GREEN LINE BALANCED
INCOME FUND $$$ → FI/G No RSP CBAL

Managers: Douglas Simmons, since 1998; William Malouin, since 1993

MER: 1.95%

The mandate here is to generate income through a combination of high-quality fixed-income securities, money market instruments, and stocks. That means there will usually be a higher proportion of bonds and other debt securities in this portfolio than you'll find in the Balanced Growth Fund. As a result, over a longer time frame the Balanced Growth Fund should outperform in strong markets, although this could be the better defensive fund. The returns bear this out; this fund has averaged 10.8% annually over the past five years while the Balanced Growth Fund has done slightly better, at 11.6%. The managers are with Sceptre Investment Counsel. Formerly known as the Green Line Canadian Balanced Fund.

FIXED INCOME AND MONEY MARKET FUNDS

GREEN LINE CANADIAN BOND FUND $$$ → FI No RSP CB

Manager: Satish Rai, since inception (1988)

MER: 0.94%

A very steady performer; generally turns in above-average profits for its investors. Gain for the year ending June 30/98 was 11.3%, well above average. This is the best long-term performer among the five Green Line Canadian bond entries (one is too young to be rated here). The portfolio emphasis is heavily on corporate bonds. Low management expense ratio is a big plus. If you're only adding one Green Line bond fund to your portfolio, make it this one.

GREEN LINE CANADIAN GOVERNMENT
BOND INDEX FUND $$ → FI No RSP CB

Managers: Lori MacKay, since 1996; Kevin LeBlanc, since 1993

MER: 0.80%

This was the first bond index fund to be offered in Canada, although others have appeared recently. The portfolio is structured to track the Canadian government bond portion of the Scotia Capital Markets Universe Bond Index. The holdings will consist of federal, provincial, and municipal bonds of varying terms. Results have not been as good as the more aggressively managed Canadian Bond Fund, but they have tended to be above average for the bond fund category. Gained 9.7% last year; average annual compound rate of return for the five years to June 30/98 was 8.9%. The Canadian Bond Fund is the better choice. Formerly the FuturLink Government Bond Fund.

GREEN LINE CANADIAN MONEY MARKET FUND
$$$ → C No RSP CMM

Manager: Satish Rai, since inception (1988)

MER: 0.84%

Excellent performance since '88 launch, with consistently above-average returns. Invests mainly in commercial paper and short-term (less than one year) government bonds. Low MER helps boost investor returns.

GREEN LINE CANADIAN T-BILL FUND
$$$ ↓ C No RSP CMM

Manager: Satish Rai, since inception (1991)

MER: 0.86%

Another Green Line money market offering. The only difference is that this one invests solely in Government of Canada Treasury bills, giving you a slightly higher level of safety. Returns tend to be a bit less than for the Canadian Money Market Fund, although they're still better than average for the money market category.

GREEN LINE GLOBAL GOVERNMENT BOND FUND
$$ → FI No £ IB

Managers: Harritt Richmond, since 1992, Brian Morris, since 1996

MER: 2.07%

This is a true international bond fund, investing in government and corporate issues from around the world. The portfolio is run by J.P. Morgan Investment Management. The fund is broadly diversified geographically and the currency risk is actively managed to protect investors from declines in the value of the Canadian dollar. It was doing just that in the first half of '98, with large U.S. bond holdings that contributed to an 11.9% advance for the year to June 30. Longer term results still look weak, but are improving.

GREEN LINE GLOBAL RSP BOND FUND $$ → FI No RSP IB

Manager: Satish Rai, since inception (1993)

MER: 2.00%

This is one of the many international bond funds that retains full RRSP eligibility by investing in Canadian debt securities denominated in foreign currencies and in bonds issued by Finance Department-approved supranational organizations like the World Bank. This has been much the better performer of the two Green Line international bond funds over the longer term, with an average annual gain of 8.1% in the three years to June 30/98. If you want this type of fund in your portfolio, this is still the best choice in the Green Line group.

GREEN LINE MORTGAGE FUND $ ↓ FI No RSP M

Manager: Satish Rai, since 1991

MER: 1.59%

The returns on this fund have fallen to below average all the way out to five years, and considering what funds of this type are yielding these days, that's not very good. The companion Mortgage-Backed Fund is now doing better, but only slightly. Somewhat offsetting the weak profit is a great safety record; the only losing calendar year since the fund was launched in '73 was a fractional 0.7% drop in '94. ATP analysis shows only a 1% chance of loss over any given 12-month period. The managers use computer models to create the optimal mortgage fund portfolio, taking into account such variables as interest rates, prepayment risk, penalty interest, and average maturity schedules. Still, we'd like to see slightly better yields.

GREEN LINE MORTGAGE-BACKED FUND $$ ↓ FI No RSP M

Manager: Satish Rai, since 1993

MER: 1.55%

One of the benefits to investors of the integration of the old Central-Guaranty FuturLink funds into Green Line was the creation of the most diversified range of fixed-income funds within any single group. This one was formerly the FuturLink Mortgage Fund. It now specializes in mortgage-backed securities, which are guaranteed for both principal and interest by CMHC (in effect, by the federal government). As well, the fund also invests in pooled mortgages and short-term notes. Historic results had been lower than those of the companion Mortgage Fund, but this fund has now crept ahead. Risk is about the same for both funds. This is now the better choice of the two. Both mortgage funds pay income distributions quarterly.

GREEN LINE REAL RETURN BOND FUND $$ ↑ FI No RSP CB

Manager: Satish Rai, since 1994

MER: 1.53%

There aren't many bond funds of this type around, and it's worth a look for specific types of investors. The emphasis here is on "real returns" — that's the payout you receive from your bonds, after accounting for inflation. The federal government has issued a number of real return bonds, which guarantee inflation-adjusted rates of return of 4.25%, and these form the core of the portfolio. As well, the fund holds some long-term strips. The manager can also add international bonds, within the foreign-content limit, but as of June/98 there were no such holdings in the portfolio. This fund has generated above-average returns recently because of the long average term to maturity of the portfolio (25 years). Long-term bonds appreciate in market value when interest rates are declining, as they have been in recent years. However, the long maturities of the securities add to the risk element of this fund. This fund is suited to investors who need regular income and who want to protect the fixed-income section of their portfolio against a possible comeback by inflation (unlikely in the present environment but possible longer term). Quarterly cash distributions make it a good candidate for a RRIF.

GREEN LINE SHORT TERM INCOME FUND $$ ↓ C No RSP CB

Manager: Satish Rai, since 1993

MER: 1.10%

This is a short-term bond fund that can invest in securities with a maturity of up to three years. In a time of low interest rates, this should result in a higher return than you'll receive from a money market fund, but at slightly more risk because unit values may fluctuate. When rates are rising, this fund is safer than a regular bond fund because of the short maturities. This was proven in the first half of '94 when the loss here was less than half that of Green Line's other bond funds. However, predictably, this fund did not perform as well when the bond market snapped back. Long-term results are below average by bond fund standards, but well above average when compared to money market fund returns. That's not surprising, since this fund is really a hybrid of the two. Use it for defensive purposes, where interest rates appear about to rise.

GREEN LINE U.S. MONEY MARKET FUND $$$ → C No RSP IMM

Manager: Satish Rai, since inception (1988)

MER: 1.24%

This fund invests in short-term securities denominated in U.S. dollars but issued by Canadian governments and corporations. This makes it fully RRSP/RRIF eligible, which is useful if you want to reduce Canadian currency risk in a retirement plan. On the surface, returns don't look great — the fund was ahead 4.6% for the year to June 30/98. But that figure did not include the big gain on currency exchange. Add that on and investors were up more than 12% on the year. Not bad for a money fund.

GREYSTONE CAPITAL MANAGEMENT INC.

THE COMPANY

This Regina-based investment counselling firm manages more than $7.5 billion worth of assets, including pension plans, trusteed funds, pooled funds, and individual accounts. They currently offer just two mutual funds to the general public, which are managed using a team approach. Initial minium investment is $10,000.

THE DETAILS

NUMBER OF FUNDS:	2
ASSETS UNDER MANAGEMENT:	$50 MILLION
LOAD CHARGE:	NONE
SWITCHING CHARGE:	NONE
WHERE SOLD:	ACROSS CANADA
HOW SOLD:	DIRECTLY THROUGH THE MANAGER
PHONE NUMBER:	(403) 423-3544 OR 1-800-287-5211 OR 1-800-213-4286
WEB SITE ADDRESS:	N/A
E-MAIL ADDRESS:	BJTHOMAS@SK.SYMPATICO.CA

FUND SUMMARY

$$$$ - NONE
$$$ - MANAGED GLOBAL, MANAGED WEALTH
$$ - NONE
$ - NONE
NR - NONE
BEST CHOICES: MANAGED GLOBAL
BEST FOR RRSPs: MANAGED WEALTH
BEST UNRATEDS: N/A

FUND RATINGS

U.S. AND INTERNATIONAL EQUITY FUNDS

GREYSTONE MANAGED GLOBAL FUND $$$ ↓ G No £ IE

Manager: Team

MER: 2.37%

This is an international equity fund that may invest anywhere in the world except Canada. In the first half of '98,
the portfolio was heavily concentrated in Europe (45%)
and the U.S. (29%). Stocks tend towards the blue-chip
variety, with large holdings including Knight-Ridder,
McDonald's Corp., Chubb, and the like. This fund is performing very well for its investors. Gain for the year ending June 30/98 was 31%, one of the best results in the
international fund category. Three-year average was
25.4%. Good safety record to date, although this is still a
young fund ('94). A very sound choice.

BALANCED FUNDS

GREYSTONE MANAGED WEALTH FUND $$$ → G No RSP CE

Manager: Team

MER: 2.87%

This fund offers a mix of Canadian, U.S., and international
stocks, as well as fixed-income securities. The return has
been improving and this fund gained a tidy 17.7% for the
year to June 30/98. Three-year average annual compound
rate of return is 15.1%, above average for the balanced
fund category. In the first half of '98, about 40% of the portfolio was in bonds, with 37% in Canadian stocks, most of
which were of the blue-chip variety. The fund was also
holding about 16% foreign content. Rating moves up to
$$$ on the strength of improving returns.

GUARDIAN GROUP

THE COMPANY

This is one of those companies that often gets lost in the mutual fund shuffle. It shouldn't. Guardian offers a conservative approach to investing and some very good funds. They use what they call a "GARP" approach to investing, which means Growth at Reasonable Prices. Not for these folks the expensive high-flyers. This is a company that focuses on good value — even at the risk of being out of sync with the markets at times. Over the long term the results speak for themselves, but there have been periods, including recently, when their funds get caught on the wrong side of the market. History suggests they will right themselves fairly quickly, however.

The main problem with Guardian is they can't seem to figure out the best way to sell their product. Not long ago they set up two classes for each fund, A units and B units, each with a different purchase option and management fee. But they decided that wasn't working so they have changed the system again. New investors have the following choices:

1) Classic units: These are the old A units. They are now subject to a minimum investment of $50,000 (not applicable to existing unitholders). These units will carry a management fee that is at least 0.6% lower (and often much more) than that of the corresponding Mutual Fund B units. They are sold on a front-end load basis.

2) Mutual Fund units: These are the old B units. They are optional front- or back-end load units, with a higher management fee. Minimum investment is $500.

THE DETAILS

NUMBER OF FUNDS:	17
ASSETS UNDER MANAGEMENT:	$2.5 BILLION
LOAD CHARGE:	FRONT: MAX. 9%; BACK: MAX. 6%
SWITCHING CHARGE:	2% MAXIMUM
WHERE SOLD:	ACROSS CANADA
HOW SOLD:	THROUGH REGISTERED BROKERS, DEALERS, AND FINANCIAL PLANNERS

Phone number:	1-800-668-7327 (English) or
	1-800-304-7151 (French)
Web site address:	www.guardianfunds.com
E-mail address:	ggofcomments@guardianfunds.com

FUND SUMMARY

$$$$ - None

$$$ - Enterprise, Foreign Income Class A, Growth Equity, International Income, Monthly Dividend, U.S. Money Market

$$ - American Equity, Canadian Income, Global Equity

$ - Asia Pacific, Canadian Balanced, Canadian Money Market, Emerging Markets, International Balanced

NR - Growth & Income, Large Cap American Equity, Monthly High Income

Best Choices: Enterprise, Growth Equity
Best for RRSPs: Growth Equity, U.S. Money Market
Best unrateds: Monthly High Income

FUND RATINGS

CANADIAN EQUITY FUNDS

GUARDIAN ENTERPRISE FUND $$$ → G #/* RSP CSC

Manager: Gary Chapman, since 1994

MER: Classic units 2.07%/Mutual Fund units 2.75%

The mandate of this fund is to concentrate on small- and medium-sized companies with a strong entrepreneurial bent. This fund has generally done well since Gary Chapman rejoined Guardian Capital after a sabbatical and took over the portfolio, although he's in a bit of a slump right now. Chapman's style is to look for companies with strong growth prospects and then hold them while they expand. His approach worked well in 1995–96, when this fund gained 45.8%. Chapman followed that up with a 32% gain over the next 12 months, to June 30/97. But recent returns have fallen off considerably, so while long-term results are still impressive, short-term numbers look weak. Major reasons for the

problem: an underweighting in the utilities and communications and media sectors — two strong areas in the first
half of '98 — and an overweighting in oil and gas issues.
Guardian believes their unusual portfolio strategy will start to
pay off soon, so we'll give them the benefit of a doubt and
leave the rating at $$$ for now. Note: Funds like this carry
inherently more risk than regular equity funds, but the safety
record of this one has been quite good.

GUARDIAN GROWTH EQUITY FUND $$$ → G #/* RSP CE

Manager: John Priestman, since inception (1989)

MER: Classic units 2.09%/Mutual Fund units 2.75%

The main difference between this and the Enterprise Fund
is that here the mandate is to invest in medium to large companies. However, in recent months, manager John
Priestman has been shaping his portfolio more along the
lines of Enterprise, with a bias towards smaller companies
(although he does continue to own all the big banks). The
portfolio is restrained, with just 25–35 stocks. Recent results
have been sub-par because Priestman has almost eliminated
utilities from the portfolio, believing that stocks like BCE
Inc. were way overpriced. Instead, he's placed a big bet on
energy companies that have extensive natural gas holdings.
There are three reasons for this: an anticipated price rise;
increased pipeline capacity, which will allow more Canadian
exports to the U.S.; and growing merger and acquisition
activity. If he's right, this fund should be performing well as
we enter '99. If the numbers are still soft at that point,
Priestman has a big problem. Note that this fund is a pure
Canadian play — there is no foreign content whatsoever.
Rating stays intact for now, but I'll be watching closely.
Previously known as the Guardian Vantage Fund.

GUARDIAN MONTHLY DIVIDEND FUND $$$ → FI #/* RSP INC

Manager: John Priestman, since 1990

MER: Classic units 1.25%/Mutual Fund units 1.85%

This is one of the best dividend funds around in terms of
cash flow (not total return). The portfolio is almost entirely

held in preferred shares. Monthly payout is 3.5 cents a unit. Unfortunately, it was closed to new investors in October, '96. Try the Monthly High Income Fund instead (not rated).

U.S. AND INTERNATIONAL EQUITY FUNDS

GUARDIAN AMERICAN EQUITY FUND $$ → G #/* £ USE

Manager: Michael Rome (Lazard Asset Management), since 1998

MER: Classic units 2.20%/Mutual Fund units 2.79%

There's a new management team at the head of this underachiever. Michael Rome of the highly respected New York house of Lazard Asset Management took control of the portfolio in January, 1998 and immediately set out to reposition it. He is targeting three types of stocks: takeover candidates, companies that are out of favour with investors for some reason, and what Lazard calls "undercovered" opportunities — mid-cap stocks that have been inadequately covered by Wall Street analysts. It's still too early to get a handle on what all this will eventually mean for investors. However, if you want a clue check out what happened to BPI's U.S. equity funds, which were run by Lazard until 1997. Their results were better than average. For now, however, we'll set the rating at $$ while we wait for Rome to complete his rebuilding work.

GUARDIAN ASIA PACIFIC FUND $ ↑ G #/* £ FEE

Manager: Sian Jenkins (Dresdner RCM Global Investors), since inception (1994)

MER: Classic units 1.68%/Mutual Fund units 2.96%

The best thing I can say about this fund is that it has not performed as badly as some of the others that focus on the Far East. Still, you were better off out of it than in it. Manager Sian Jenkins can invest anywhere throughout the Pacific Rim, including Japan, Australia, and New Zealand, which provides maximum flexibility. The fund also has some built-in rules to help reduce risk, such as no more than 15% of the portfolio in any one industry and no more than 10% in any one country that is classed as an "emerging market" (Hong Kong and Japan are among those that are exempt). The portfolio is well diversified, normally holding between 100 and 150 stocks, with an emphasis on larger companies. In the first half of 1998 about 36% of the portfolio was in Japan, 34% in "mature" markets of Asia (Hong Kong, Australia, Singapore, Malaysia) and about 26% in various emerging markets (e.g., China, Taiwan, Korea). I have the feeling this could be a pretty good performer once the Asian economies start to recover, but that may take some time. Until then, best to stay on the sidelines.

GUARDIAN EMERGING MARKETS FUND $ ↑ G #/* £ EME

Manager: Mark Phelps (Dresdner RCM Global Investors), since inception (1994)

MER: Classic units 0.80%/Mutual Fund units 2.93%

It's been tough to make a buck in the emerging markets in recent years, and this fund has struggled along with most of the others. The portfolio is well diversified, normally holding between 100 and 150 stocks covering at least 10 industry sectors. The geographic mix is also well dispersed. As of the first half of 1998, Latin America and the Far East each accounted for about a quarter of the portfolio. Europe and Africa (mainly South Africa) comprised 46% of the mix with a small cash balance. Based on the evidence to date, this is not one of the leaders in the emerging markets category so I would not recommend going out of your way to acquire it. If you must have some, try to acquire the Classic units, which have a much lower MER.

GUARDIAN GLOBAL EQUITY FUND $$ → G #/* £ IE

Manager: Juliet Cohn (Dresdner RCM Global Investors), since 1990

MER: Classic units 1.80%/Mutual Fund units 2.85%

This fund has consistently made money for Guardian investors, which is the good news. The bad news is that its returns tend to be below average for the international category. The emphasis is on growth stocks with relatively low risk. The portfolio offers broad international diversification, including North American issues (U.S. stocks were about a fifth of the weighting in the first half of '98). A small percentage of the portfolio is in emerging markets.

Results have been spotty, although the fund looked quite strong in the first half of '98, thanks to a heavy Europe component. Far East exposure is minimal at this time. This one is okay, but there are better around.

BALANCED FUNDS

GUARDIAN CANADIAN BALANCED FUND $ ↓ FI/G #/* RSP CBAL

Manager: Larry Kennedy, since inception (1976)

MER: Classic units 1.70%/Mutual Fund units 2.67%

This fund has a unique record: it is the only major Canadian balanced fund to have gone for more than a decade without losing money in a single calendar year ('81 was the last time it suffered a loss, and then only a small one). That earns it a top safety rating from the ATP analysis. But, but, but — performance has fallen to the mediocre level. Recent results are so weak that they have pulled longer term numbers to below average across the board. If you want to know why, read the reviews for Guardian Enterprise and Guardian Growth and then add in the fact that this fund was way underweighted in financial service stocks in the first half of '98 — not one bank appears in the list of their 20 largest holdings. Veteran manager Larry Kennedy believes in sticking to fundamentals and avoiding higher risk situations, but it looks like he went out too far on this particular limb. Rating is reduced to $ until we see evidence of an improvement.

GUARDIAN INTERNATIONAL BALANCED FUND $ → FI/G #/* RSP IBAL

Manager: Laurence Linklater (Dresdner RCM Global Investors), since inception (1993)

MER: Classic units 2.12%/Mutual Fund units 2.93%

This balanced fund roams the world for investments, but retains full RRSP eligibility in the process. This is achieved through the use of derivatives (e.g., stock index options) and by purchasing foreign-currency denominated Canadian bonds as well as issues of supranational corporations. In the first half of 1998, the portfolio was evenly balanced between equities and bonds (all bonds are AAA rated), with good geographic diversification. However, a heavy weighting in Far East and emerging market equities (almost a quarter of the total portfolio) hurt recent results. As a result, the fund's returns are now showing as below average for its peer group across the board. This is one of those funds that, on paper, looks much better than its track record — sort of like a sports team full of high-paid stars that isn't performing to expectation. Its main attraction right now is the fact you can put it into your retirement plan without eating up precious foreign content.

FIXED INCOME AND MONEY MARKET FUNDS

GUARDIAN CANADIAN INCOME FUND $$ ↓ FI #/* RSP CB

Manager: Larry Kennedy, since 1987

MER: Classic units 1.11%/Mutual Fund units 1.92%

This is a short-term bond fund, with an emphasis on safety and regular monthly payments. Most of the portfolio is in short-term corporate notes with a maximum of five years to maturity (usually less). This is one of those funds that will create a misleading impression for investors who judge strictly by numbers. If you compare the total returns to the universe of Canadian bond funds, they look pretty weak. But you have to look at other factors. Cash flow is one. For the first five months of 1998, the Classic units of the fund paid out about 21 cents a unit. Based on the net asset value at the start of the year, that put the fund on a pace to generate a cash yield of almost 5% over a 12-month period. That's a very good cash return on a low-risk fund such as this and makes it a worthy candidate for inclusion in a RRIF (for that specific use, the rating would rise to $$$). Note that the Mutual Fund units don't perform as well, in large part because of the much higher MER, so stick to the Classic units if you can afford them. This sort of fund is especially valuable when interest rates may be on the rise and you don't want to run the risk of having your money in a regular bond fund. But just remember that it will not generate great total return numbers when bond markets are strong. Previously known as Guardian Canada Bond Fund.

GUARDIAN CANADIAN MONEY MARKET FUND

$ → C #/* RSP CMM

Manager: Larry Kennedy, since 1987

MER: Classic units 0.84%/Mutual Fund units 1.55%

This fund invests entirely in short-term, high-grade corporate notes. That should produce above-average returns for this category, and indeed that's been the case in the past. But recent yields have been unimpressive, with the Mutual Fund units especially hard-hit because of the high management fee. Don't buy this fund on a back-end load basis, whatever you do! Previously called Guardian Short Term Money Fund.

GUARDIAN FOREIGN INCOME FUND

$$$ ↓ FI #/* RSP IB

Manager: Laurence Linklater (Dresdner RCM Global Investors) , since inception (1994)

MER: Classic units 1.69%/Mutual Fund units 2.66%

This small fund (less than $10 million in assets) is a kissing cousin to the better known Guardian International Income Fund, and has the same management team. The main difference is that this fund has no Canadian dollar exposure at all. Assets are denominated in U.S. currency, which means this is the place to be if the loonie is sliding but not such a great holding if our dollar is on the rise. Since the Canuck buck has been weak recently, this fund has looked better than International Income. Gain for the 12 months to June 30/98 was a strong 15.3% or 16.1%, depending on which type of units you held (the Classic units always give the higher return because of the lower MER). But if the loonie should ever turn around, this fund won't look as good. Of course, the way things are going that's a big if. This is a useful fund for those who want to stash some of their RRSP/RRIF assets into U.S. dollars without taking up foreign content room.

GUARDIAN INTERNATIONAL INCOME FUND $$$ ↓ FI #/* RSP IB

Manager: Laurence Linklater (Dresdner RCM Global Investors) , since 1990

MER: Classic units 2.04%/Mutual Fund units 2.73%

This international bond fund is fully RRSP/RRIF eligible. It achieves this by investing mainly in the securities of international financial institutions, such as the World Bank, that have been granted special RRSP/RRIF eligibility status by the Canadian government. As well, the portfolio holds bonds issued directly by foreign governments and banks and invests in forward and option currency contracts. It does not invest in Canadian government bond issues. The fund employs a conservative management style and actively uses currency hedging (in the first half of 1998, the portfolio was hedged back into Canadian and U.S. dollars). Since it's fully RRSP eligible, owning it won't infringe on your foreign content. Results have improved to above average. Very good safety record.

GUARDIAN U.S. MONEY MARKET FUND $$$ → C #/* RSP IMM

Manager: Larry Kennedy, since 1987

MER: Classic units 0.89%/Mutual Fund units 1.53%

U.S. dollar money market funds have been outperforming their Canadian cousins over the past two years because, for the first time in anyone's memory, our short-term interest rates have been lower than theirs. This fund gained 4.9% in the year to June 30/98 (Classic units), a much better return than the Canadian MMF. However, only the Classic units are recommended; the high MER that's charged against the Mutual Fund units makes them only a so-so investment. A major attraction of this fund is that it's fully RRSP/RRIF eligible, because it invests mainly in Canadian corporate notes denominated in U.S. dollars. So you can stash some of your retirement savings away in greenbacks if you're concerned about the future direction of our dollar. Don't buy this one on a back-end load basis though; the high management fees will kill you.

GUARDIAN TIMING SERVICES

THE COMPANY

Guardian Timing Services was started in 1984 to implement the investment philosophies and techniques developed by its president, Jean-Pierre Fruchet. His emphasis is on asset protection, so the funds in this group are of special interest to investors who are willing to sacrifice higher returns for a greater degree of safety. The company is 100% owned by InterUnion, an investment bank that specializes in the financial sector. The funds are sold through offering memorandum only, which means they are for "sophisticated investors". Minimums to get in are $150,000 for Ontario and Quebec residents; $100,000 for Alberta, New Brunswick, Manitoba, Newfoundland, and Nova Scotia; and $25,000 in B.C. Not sold in the other provinces.

THE DETAILS

NUMBER OF FUNDS:	3
ASSETS UNDER MANAGEMENT:	$14.9 MILLION
LOAD CHARGE:	DIFFERS FOR EACH FUND
SWITCHING CHARGE:	NOT PERMITTED
WHERE SOLD:	ONTARIO, QUEBEC, ALBERTA, MANITOBA, NOVA SCOTIA, BRITISH COLUMBIA
HOW SOLD:	BY OFFERING MEMORANDUM DIRECTLY THROUGH GUARDIAN TIMING SERVICES INC.
PHONE NUMBER:	(416) 960-4890
WEB SITE ADDRESS:	N/A
E-MAIL ADDRESS:	N/A

FUND SUMMARY

$$$$ - NONE
$$$ - NONE
$$ - NONE
$ - CANADIAN PROTECTED FUND, FIRST AMERICAN FUND, PROTECTED AMERICAN FUND
NR - NONE

BEST CHOICES: NONE
BEST FOR RRSPs: NONE
BEST UNRATEDS: N/A

FUND RATINGS

CANADIAN EQUITY FUNDS

CANADIAN PROTECTED FUND $ ↓ G #/* RSP CE

Manager: Jean-Pierre Fruchet, since inception (1984)

MER: 2.40%

Manager Jean-Pierre Fruchet uses portfolio insurance and market timing techniques to limit risk. His objective is to avoid any down years and to outperform the TSE over two full market cycles. His system worked well during the market crash year of '87 and kept the fund in the black during the rough markets of '89 and '90. In fact, this was the number-one performing Canadian equity fund in '90, a year when most equity funds lost ground. The fund suffered a small loss of 1.5% in '94, the first down year in its history — but even that was better than the average Canadian equity fund, which fell 2.7%. The problem is that when markets are strong, as they have been for several years, the system has tended to deliver below-average results. For example, during the year ending June 30/98, this fund gained 9.6% — not terrible by any means but below the average of 10.3% for diversified Canadian stock funds as reported by *The Financial Post*. Results for longer time periods are also below average. However, Fruchet has been working hard to refine his market timing models and told investors in his 1997 year-end report: "We are confident that the benefits of our investment methodology will allow the fund to significantly outperform the market in both absolute and relative terms over the years." We'll watch and see, but it's a good sign that returns in the first half of '98 showed improvement. You can buy Class A units on a front-end load basis (maximum commission is 5%) or Class B units on a back-end load option (maximum 5%).

U.S. AND INTERNATIONAL EQUITY FUNDS

FIRST AMERICAN FUND $ → G * RSP USE

Manager: Jean-Pierre Fruchet, since inception (1991)

MER: 2.80%

This fund was launched after some of his investors told manager Jean-Pierre Fruchet they wanted something more exciting. This fund certainly has the potential to be just that. It can be 100% long, or 100% short, it can use leveraging — in other words, it can do all the things that frighten most ordinary investors. So far, however, results have been sub-par. Average annual return for the five years to June 30/98 was just 0.5%, and the fund recorded a loss over the 12 months to June 30/97 at a time when U.S. markets were red hot. I said in the past this fund was in need of a fix and Fruchet has responded by revamping his models so as to better capture market up trends. This change appears to be bearing fruit; the fund gained 8.4% in the first half of '98, a very good performance by previous standards. At that point, about 70% of the assets were in S&P 500 futures contracts. No rating increase yet, but this one may have turned the corner.

PROTECTED AMERICAN FUND $ → G #/* RSP D

Manager: Jean-Pierre Fruchet, since inception (1985)

MER: 2.30%

This fund invests mainly in U.S. stock index futures and Treasury bills. Manager Jean-Pierre Fruchet employs timing systems and portfolio insurance techniques to avoid losses. This is one of the few mutual funds in Canada that will take short positions. Objective is to outperform the Standard & Poor's 500 Index by at least 6% annually in U.S. dollar terms over a three-year period, while avoiding any down years. Results have tended to be above average during bear market periods but well below average when markets are running strong. For example, the fund gained 10.7% in '90, while the S&P dropped 6.6%. But over the 12 months to June 30/97, it actually lost 3.5%, while the S&P was posting big gains. As with his other funds, Fruchet has been fine-tuning the system and we were starting to see some better returns in the first half of '98. Began life as the Protected Bond Fund in '85. Mandate was changed in January, '90.

HEMISPHERE CAPITAL CORP.

THE COMPANY

A small independent Calgary-based firm established in 1991, Hemisphere's main business is in providing private portfolio management services to individuals, families, foundations, and small institutions. They also offer one balanced mutual fund to the general public.

THE DETAILS

NUMBER OF FUNDS:	1
ASSETS UNDER MANAGEMENT:	$1.75 MILLION
LOAD CHARGE:	NONE
SWITCHING CHARGE:	NONE
WHERE SOLD:	ALBERTA, SASKATCHEWAN
HOW SOLD:	THROUGH REGISTERED BROKERS AND DEALERS
PHONE NUMBER:	(403) 205-3588 OR 1-800-471-7853
WEB SITE ADDRESS:	N/A
E-MAIL ADDRESS:	HEMISPHERE@SPRINT.CA

FUND SUMMARY

$$$$ - NONE
$$$ - NONE
$$ - NONE
$ - VALUE
NR - NONE

BEST CHOICES: VALUE
BEST FOR RRSPS: VALUE
BEST UNRATEDS: N/A

FUND RATINGS

BALANCED FUNDS

HEMISPHERE VALUE FUND $ → FI/G No RSP CBAL

Manager: Jim Aronitz, since inception (1994)

MER: 1.80%

The equity side of this balanced portfolio is comprised mainly of large, well-established companies. This is not a fund that engages in speculative investments. The bond side (about 36% of assets in the first half of '98) is a mix of corporate securities with some provincial and federal issues. Performance so far has been below average when compared to the balanced fund category as a whole. Average annual compound rate of return for the three years to June 30/98 was 10%. The recent weakness on the equities side was caused in part by a large holding in resource issues in the first half of '98, including Noranda, Petro Canada, and TVX Gold. All are good companies but were out of favour, thereby pulling down the returns.

HILLSDALE INVESTMENT MANAGEMENT

THE COMPANY

A number of micro fund companies have sprung up in the past few years, and this is one of them. The Hillsdale name is drawn from the Toronto street where manager A. Christopher Guthrie has his office. His single fund is intended for wealthy investors who want a more aggressive style that employs both long and short positions, as well as leveraging. Minimum initial subscription is US$150,000.

THE DETAILS

NUMBER OF FUNDS:	1
ASSETS UNDER MANAGEMENT:	$6.8 MILLION
LOAD CHARGE:	NONE
SWITCHING CHARGE:	NONE
WHERE SOLD:	ACROSS CANADA
HOW SOLD:	THROUGH PRIVATE PLACEMENT
PHONE NUMBER:	(416) 422-4144
WEB SITE ADDRESS:	N/A
E-MAIL ADDRESS:	AKAUL@HILLSDALEINV.COM

FUND SUMMARY

$$$$ - NONE
$$$ - NONE
$$ - NONE
$ - NONE
NR - LONG/SHORT AMERICAN EQUITY

FUND RATINGS

There is just one fund here and it is too new to have a formal rating.

HIRSCH ASSET MANAGEMENT CORP.

THE COMPANY

If you've been following mutual funds at all, you know the name of Veronika Hirsch. She was the high-profile manager who made very large waves in 1996 when she left AGF, which had promoted her heavily on television, to join Fidelity as manager of their new True North Fund. Shortly thereafter she ran into some problems with securities regulators and she and Fidelity parted ways.

She has since reached a settlement with the Ontario and B.C. Securities Commissions and is now back doing what she does best — running mutual funds. This time it's with her own fund group under the name Hirsch Asset Management. Originally, there was just one fund, the Hirsch Canadian Growth Fund, but three more were launched in June, 1998 to bring the total to four.

Although she made her reputation wheeling and dealing in the volatile resource sector, the Canadian Growth Fund takes a very different slant. The focus is on stocks that are involved in consolidation plays, either through acquisitions, divestitures, or as targets. Companies like Clublink and Yogen Früz fit the bill, as does a firm like Noranda, which is in the process of getting rid of its non-core businesses and turning itself into a pure mining company.

"This kind of action is what's driving the market right now," she says. "You'll find it in virtually every sector. I expect this will be an ongoing theme of the fund for at least the next five years."

The three newcomers include a natural resource entry and the traditional balanced and fixed-income funds.

THE DETAILS

NUMBER OF FUNDS:	4
ASSETS UNDER MANAGEMENT:	$11 MILLION
LOAD CHARGE:	FRONT: MAX. 5%
	BACK: MAX. 5.75%
SWITCHING CHARGE:	2% MAXIMUM
WHERE SOLD:	ACROSS CANADA

How sold:	Through brokers and financial planners
Phone number:	(416) 360-1906
Web site address:	WWW.HIRSCHFUNDS.COM
E-mail address:	INFO@HIRSCHFUNDS.COM

FUND SUMMARY

$$$$ - None
$$$ - None
$$ - None
$ - None
NR - Balanced, Canadian Growth, Fixed Income,
Natural Resource

Best choices: N/A
Best for RRSPs: N/A
Best unrateds: Canadian Growth

FUND RATINGS

No fund has the three-year record needed for a rating.

HONGKONG BANK MUTUAL FUNDS

THE COMPANY

Hongkong Bank of Canada has branches across the country. They now have 14 funds in their lineup, including the recently launched Global Equity Fund and U.S. Dollar Money Market Fund. They are overseen by Hongkong Bank Securities Inc. All the funds are managed by HSBC Asset Management, a Hongkong Bank subsidiary. The domestic funds are under the direction of HSBC Asset Management Canada, which was formerly M.K. Wong & Associates. The firm has part of the HSBC group since 1996, but the name was only changed in mid-1998.

The Lotus Group of Funds, which were previously distributed through M.K. Wong, have now been incorporated into the Hongkong Bank family, although they retain their own identity, at least for now. There are four funds currently active in this group.

This company offers a large number of high-quality funds, including 13 that earn $$$ ratings this year. It's an organization that deserves careful consideration from any fund investor.

THE DETAILS

NUMBER OF FUNDS:	18
ASSETS UNDER MANAGEMENT:	$2.3 BILLION
LOAD CHARGE:	NONE
SWITCHING CHARGE:	2% MAXIMUM
WHERE SOLD:	ALBERTA, B.C., MANITOBA, ONTARIO, QUEBEC, NEW BRUNSWICK, NEWFOUNDLAND, NOVA SCOTIA, SASKATCHEWAN
HOW SOLD:	DIRECTLY THROUGH BRANCHES OF HONGKONG BANK AND THROUGH REGISTERED BROKERS AND INVESTMENT DEALERS
PHONE NUMBER:	(604) 517-2215 OR 1-800-830-8888
WEB SITE ADDRESS:	WWW.HKSI.COM
E-MAIL ADDRESS:	INFO@HKBC.COM

FUND SUMMARY

Hongkong Bank Funds

$$$$ - None
$$$ - Balanced, Canadian Bond, Dividend Income, Equity, European Growth, Money Market, Mortgage, Small Cap Growth, U.S. Equity
$$ - Global Bond
$ - Asian Growth, Emerging Markets
NR - Global Equity, U.S. Dollar Money Market

Best choices: Balanced, Dividend Income, Equity, European Growth, Small Cap
Best for RRSPs: Balanced, Canadian Bond, Equity, Mortgage
Best unrateds: Global Equity

Lotus Funds

$$$$ - None
$$$ - Balanced, Bond, Canadian Equity, Income
$$ - None
$ - None
NR - None

Best Choices: Bond, Canadian Equity
Best for RRSPs: Balanced
Best unrateds: N/A

FUND RATINGS

Hongkong Bank Funds

CANADIAN EQUITY FUNDS

HONGKONG BANK DIVIDEND INCOME FUND $$$ ↓ G/FI No RSP INC

Manager: Team, led by Robert DeHart (HSBC Asset Management Canada), since 1994

MER: 1.88%

This fund is designed to produce a combination of long-term capital gains plus dividend income, using a mix of preferred shares and high-yielding common stocks. It's doing well on both counts. The annual dividend fund survey published in *Mutual Funds Update* showed a healthy 4% cash flow from this fund in 1997. Meantime, total return for the three years to June 30/98 averaged out to 22.4% annually. That's an excellent one-two punch, and it's good enough to earn this fund a $$$ rating in its debut appearance here. Good safety record too.

HONGKONG BANK EQUITY FUND $$$ → G No RSP CE

Manager: Team, led by Robert DeHart (HSBC Asset Management Canada), since 1988

MER: 1.89%

This was an index fund until the fall of '92. At that time, the mandate was changed to make it a fully-managed equity fund. Performance continues to be good, with a gain of 12.8% for the year ending June 30/98. Three-year results are also above average, at 19.4% annually. The portfolio favours large-cap issues, with some smaller growth stocks mixed in for extra "oomph". There is also a significant U.S. equity position. A very respectable choice.

HONGKONG BANK SMALL
CAP GROWTH FUND $$$ → G No RSP CSC

Manager: Team, led by Robert DeHart (HSBC Asset Management Canada), since 1994

MER: 2.19%

This fund invests in a well-diversified portfolio of smaller Canadian companies. The small-cap market has been a minefield for managers in recent years, but this fund has more than held its ground, especially in 1995 and 1996 when it scored good gains of 40.3% and 15.5%. Average annual compound rate of return for the three years to June 30/98 works out to 19.6%, very good for the small-cap category. A good choice for a more aggressive investor who understands the risks involved in this type of fund. Debuts at $$$.

U.S. AND INTERNATIONAL EQUITY FUNDS

HONGKONG BANK ASIAN GROWTH FUND $ ↑ G No £ FEE

Manager: Team, led by Ian Burden (HSBC Asset Management Hong Kong), since 1993

MER: 2.26%

This fund invests throughout the Far East and Australia, with the exception of Japan. The portfolio is well diversified, with an unusually large Australian component (over 25% in early '98). But, like all other Far East funds, it was clobbered by events in Asia and suffered a 47% loss for the year to June 30/98. Best to steer clear of this one until the Asian economy starts to recover.

HONGKONG BANK EMERGING MARKETS FUND $ ↑ G No £ EME

Manager: Team, led by Ian Burden (HSBC Asset Management Hong Kong), since 1994

MER: 2.56%

No emerging markets fund has fared well recently. This one has taken its lumps along with the others. It dropped 32.8% in the year to June 30/98 and there is no sign of things improving any time soon.

HONGKONG BANK EUROPEAN GROWTH FUND $$$ → G No £ EE

Manager: Team, led by Dean Buckley (HSBC Asset Management Europe), since 1994

MER: 2.22%

This is a traditional European fund that focuses on EEC member states. So you'll find lots of stocks from the U.K., Germany, France, and Switzerland but nothing at all from Eastern Europe. This fund has been one of the better performers in the European Equity category, with a 28.9% average annual compound rate of return for the three years to June 30/98. Makes its first appearance here with a healthy $$$ rating. Hongkong Bank clients should certainly include this one in their mix; non-clients may find it is worth a visit to add it.

HONGKONG BANK U.S. EQUITY FUND $$$ → G No £ AE

Manager: Team, led by Paul Guidone and Petra Kettler-Rheim (HSBC Asset Management Americas), since 1994

MER: 2.24%

Technically, this fund can invest in a mix of U.S. and Latin American stocks. So far, however, the Latins haven't made the cut and this fund has focused almost exclusively on the States. Investors don't mind since the returns have been great. The fund gained 33% in the year to June 30/98. Three-year average annual compound rate of return to that date was an impressive 27.8%. The portfolio is mainly large-cap stocks with many familiar names: American Express, Boeing, Bristol Myers Squibb, Coca-Cola, Exxon, GE, and the rest. If it's on the Dow, it's probably here. Very good safety record to go along with the impressive returns. We'll start it off with a well-earned $$$.

BALANCED FUNDS

HONGKONG BANK
BALANCED FUND $$$ → FI/G No RSP CBAL

Manager: Team, led by Robert DeHart (HSBC Asset Management Canada), since 1992

MER: 1.82%

This fund is now turning in consistently good results following a strategy change on the equity side that placed greater emphasis on larger, more stable companies to reduce volatility. As a result, you'll find lots of banks and utilities here. Return for the year to June 30/98 was better than average for the balanced fund category at 10.4%. The portfolio was slightly weighted towards equities in the first half of '98, but with a healthy bond component. This fund is a good choice for a conservative investor and would make a fine starter fund for an RRSP.

FIXED INCOME AND MONEY MARKET FUNDS

HONGKONG BANK CANADIAN BOND FUND $$$ → FI No RSP CB

Manager: Team, led by Robert DeHart (HSBC Asset Management Canada), since 1994

MER: 1.16%

This portfolio favours government bonds, mainly federal and Ontario. However, about one quarter of the assets were in corporate securities in the first half of '98. Most of the bonds at that time were short- to medium-term, with a few longer term issues for extra profit potential. Performance has been better than average. Rate of return for the three years to June 30/98 worked out to 10.5% annually. A good choice for conservative investors. Would be a very comfortable fit for an RRSP.

HONGKONG BANK GLOBAL BOND FUND $$ → FI No £ IB

Manager: Team, led by Dean Buckley (HSBC Asset Management Europe) since 1994

MER: 2.05%

This fund invests mainly in debt securities issued by foreign governments, but also holds some corporate issues as well. About a third of the portfolio was in U.S. Treasury bonds in the first half of '98, which helped the fund to an 11% gain over the 12 months ending June 30/98. Results prior to that were soft, however. We'll start it off at $$.

HONGKONG BANK MONEY MARKET FUND $$$ → C No RSP CMM

Manager: Team, led by Robert DeHart (HSBC Asset Management Canada), since 1988

MER: 0.90%

This used to be primarily a T-bill fund but now almost half of the holdings are in corporate short-term notes. Returns are slightly above average for the money market category.

HONGKONG BANK MORTGAGE FUND $$$ → FI No RSP M

Manager: Team, led by Robert DeHart (HSBC Asset Management Canada), since 1992

MER: 1.45%

This fund should be one of your core holdings if you're a conservative investor who does business with Hongkong Bank. It offers relatively low risk and decent returns for this low-paying fund category. Average annual compound rate of return for the five years to June 30/98 was 8%, well above average for the peer group. More recent results have slipped somewhat, but this is still a useful fund to hold in the fixed-income section of an RRSP.

LOTUS FUNDS

CANADIAN EQUITY FUNDS

LOTUS CANADIAN EQUITY FUND $$$ ↑ G No RSP CSC

Manager: Team, led by Robert DeHart (HSBC Asset Management Canada), since 1988

MER: 2.05%

Although the prospectus does not limit this fund's mandate, the portfolio emphasis is on small- and medium-sized companies. It has had several good years, and proudly displays a three-year average annual compound rate of return of 22.5% for the period to June 30/98 — very good for this type of fund. The most recent 12 months were less impressive, however, with an advance of just 5.4%. Still, that was above average for the Canadian small-cap fund category. There is a lot of overlap between this fund and the Hongkong Bank Small Cap Growth Fund, so don't buy both. And don't be surprised if the two funds merge eventually. Also, there's a fair amount of volatility here, so be careful not to overload a retirement plan with it.

BALANCED FUNDS

LOTUS BALANCED FUND $$$ → FI/G No RSP CBAL

Manager: Team, led by Robert DeHart (HSBC Asset Management Canada), since 1984

MER: 2.07%

This entry has been around for a decade, with largely indifferent results. But the past few years have produced better-than-average profits, with a gain of over 13% for the 12 months to June 30/98. That comes on top of a 20%+ gain last year. The bond section of the portfolio is conservatively managed, with a mix of Government of Canada, provincial, and high-grade corporate bonds, along with some mortgage-backed securities. The stock section is more aggressive, with many of the same holdings as the companion Canadian Equity Fund, although in this case a few more blue-chips like BCE are tossed in. Improving returns merit a boost in the rating this time around. Name changed from Lotus Fund in April, '94.

FIXED INCOME AND MONEY MARKET FUNDS

LOTUS BOND FUND $$$ → FI No RSP CB

Manager: Team, led by Robert DeHart (HSBC Asset Management Canada), since 1993

MER: 0.77%

Good-looking bond fund with a nice mix of government and corporate issues. Gained 10.1% in the year to June 30/98 and sports an excellent three-year average annual compound rate of return of 11%. However, there really isn't much to distinguish this fund from the Hongkong Bank Canadian Bond Fund, except for the fact this one is extremely small. I expect it to be absorbed into the larger fund before too long. With only $1.3 million in assets, it's uneconomical.

LOTUS INCOME FUND

$$$ ↓ C No RSP CMM

Manager: Team, led by Robert DeHart (HSBC Asset Management Canada), since 1984

MER: 0.76%

It's hard to know where to put this fund. Its mandate suggests it's a short-term bond fund — the portfolio may have an average term to maturity of not more than five years, and may hold securities with maturities up to seven years out. In practice, however, the managers have been running it as a money market fund, investing primarily in Canada T-bills, with some corporate notes also in the mix. Before you invest any money, you may wish to obtain clarification from them as to their future plans. Good results; average annual five-year rate of return is slightly above average at 4.4%. However, this fund may not be long for this world because of its small size. It's an obvious candidate for a merger into the Hongkong Bank Money Market Fund. Name changed from MKW Income Fund in April, '94.

INFINITY GROUP OF FUNDS

THE COMPANY

This is a new fund group that has managed to generate a fair amount of controversy in its relatively short existence, including a legal battle with the AIC Funds that was still going on as this was written. Their investment philosophy is stated as: "Buying great businesses that are domiciled in strong, long-term growth industries, managed by capable shareholder oriented management." The funds in this group are too new for a formal rating but some made impressive debuts.

THE DETAILS

NUMBER OF FUNDS:	5
ASSETS UNDER MANAGEMENT:	$788 MILLION
LOAD CHARGE:	FRONT: MAX. 5% BACK: MAX. 5.5%
SWITCHING CHARGE:	2% MAXIMUM
WHERE SOLD:	ACROSS CANADA
HOW SOLD:	THROUGH BROKERS, DEALERS, AND FINANCIAL PLANNERS
PHONE NUMBER:	1-800-835-7131
WEB SITE ADDRESS:	WWW.INFINITYFUNDS.COM
E-MAIL ADDRESS:	INFORMATION@INFINITYFUNDS.COM

FUND SUMMARY

$$$$ - NONE
$$$ - NONE
$$ - NONE
$ - NONE
NR - CANADIAN, INCOME & GROWTH, INTERNATIONAL, T-BILL, WEALTH MANAGEMENT

BEST CHOICES: N/A
BEST FOR RRSPs: N/A
BEST UNRATEDS: CANADIAN, INTERNATIONAL, WEALTH MANAGEMENT

FUND RATINGS

The Infinity Funds are all too new for a formal rating.

INTEGRA CAPITAL MANAGEMENT

THE COMPANY

The main business of this company, which is a joint venture of Gryphon Investment Counsel and Lincluden Management, is to provide financial services to pension plans, endowment funds, foundations, and individuals. It currently has about $5 billion under management. The five mutual funds are a relatively small part of the business, but growing. The minimum investment for funds in this group is $10,000. Note that investors are charged management fees directly, so the MERs on these funds will appear unusually low. As a result, the returns are somewhat inflated because most other funds deduct expenses before performance numbers are calculated.

THE DETAILS

NUMBER OF FUNDS:	5
ASSETS UNDER MANAGEMENT:	$290 MILLION
LOAD CHARGE:	NONE
SWITCHING CHARGE:	NONE
WHERE SOLD:	ACROSS CANADA
HOW SOLD:	DIRECTLY THROUGH INTEGRA CAPITAL FINANCIAL CORPORATION
PHONE NUMBER:	(416) 367-0404
WEB SITE ADDRESS:	WWW.INTEGRA.COM
E-MAIL ADDRESS:	INVEST@INTEGRA.COM

FUND SUMMARY

$$$$ - NONE
$$$ - SHORT TERM INVESTMENT
$$ - BALANCED, BOND, INTERNATIONAL EQUITY
$ - EQUITY
NR - NONE

BEST CHOICES: SHORT-TERM INVESTMENT
BEST FOR RRSPs: BALANCED
BEST UNRATEDS: N/A

FUND RATINGS

CANADIAN EQUITY FUNDS

ICM EQUITY FUND $ → G No RSP CE

Managers: Gryphon Investment Counsel and Lincluden Management

MER: 0.09%

There are two managerial teams involved in running this fund and each employs a different style for their own half of the assets. Gryphon uses a top-down investing approach, which involves identifying key sectors of the economy that are expected to do well and selecting large-cap stocks that will profit as a result. Lincluden takes a value-oriented, bottom-up approach, selecting stocks on the basis of their intrinsic value without reference to overall trends. This interesting combination has produced a fund with below-average returns over all time periods out to five years. However, the results certainly are not terrible. Average annual compound rate of return for the five years to June 30/98 was 12.2%. The average Canadian equity fund returned 12.4%, according to figures published by *The Globe and Mail*. However, once management fees are taken into account (which can run as high as 1.75%), the gap widens. I cannot provide any portfolio details about the current holdings of this or any other ICM fund since the information was not given to us by the company and is not offered on their web site.

U.S. AND INTERNATIONAL EQUITY FUNDS

ICM INTERNATIONAL EQUITY FUND $$ → G No £ IE

Managers: Brinson Partners, Inc. and UBS International Investment London Ltd.

MER: 0.40%

The mandate of this fund is to invest in non-North American companies, with a focus on Europe, the Far East, and Australia. The portfolio is well diversified and is concentrated in more developed countries. Results had been good but the return slipped to just 7.9% over the year to June 30/98. That was even less once you subtracted the annual management fee you'll be assessed (1.95% maximum). Five-year results are better, however.

BALANCED FUNDS

ICM BALANCED FUND $$ → FI/G #/No RSP CBAL

Managers: Gryphon Investment Counsel and Lincluden Management, since inception (1987)

MER: 0.17%

Here again we have a fund that is run using two different management styles. Short-term results are below average. Longer term returns are better than average, but that's before the management fee is calculated into the equation. In April, '96 Integra Capital began charging a maximum 1.75% annual management fee directly to investors rather than paying it from fund assets as most other mutual funds do. Historical results have been adjusted to eliminate the effect of the management fee over all time periods, which brings a measure of consistency to the performance figures.

FIXED INCOME AND MONEY MARKET FUNDS

ICM BOND FUND $$ ↓ No RSP CB

Managers: Gryphon Investment Counsel and Lincluden Management, since inception (1992)

MER: 0.16%

This fund invests mainly in Government of Canada issues, with a few provincial and corporate bonds tossed in as well. The management style is conservative. Returns are about average once the annual management fee of up to 1.3% is factored in. Very good safety profile.

ICM SHORT TERM INVESTMENT FUND $$$ ↓ No RSP CMM

Managers: Gryphon Investment Counsel and Lincluden Management, since inception (1992)

MER: 0.07%

Pick up the newspaper and check the monthly mutual fund performance numbers. This fund will stand out. Its average annual return is either right at the top of the list or close to it. That's because they don't deduct the management fee before calculating the returns and submitting them to the media. The effect is to make the fund appear to be doing better in relation to competitors who deduct the fee directly from fund assets. In this case, if you're a retail investor you'll be assessed a management fee of 1% a year of the value of your assets (institutions and group RRSPs get a reduction). So to find your actual return, subtract the management fee from the published result. For the year ending June 30/98, for example, the paper says you earned 4% in this fund — one of the better results in the money market fund category. But knock a percentage point off that and you're down to 3%. That's just below the average for money market funds. The same process produces slightly better than average returns over three years, but not as good as you'd first think by the fund survey reports. So take that into account before you invest.

INVESTORS GROUP

THE COMPANY

This Winnipeg-based company is one of the giants of the mutual funds industry. In terms of assets under management, it has been number one for years (almost $36 billion at the end of June, 1998). The 52 funds offered by the company are the most of any single organization (some might argue there are too many and that selection becomes confusing). Several of these funds are run by outside firms (Sceptre, Beutel Goodman, Merrill Lynch, Rothschild/Global Strategy) in an effort to provide clients with more diversity in management styles.

Investors Group funds are sold only by their own representatives and are not available through any outside third party. Note the unusual commission structure. There is no front end load for equity or balanced funds if your total investment in all funds exceeds $10,000 (it's 2.5% if your holdings are less than that). A redemption charge will apply if you sell before seven years (maximum 3%). This means that if you invest less than $10,000, you'll potentially face both a front-end and back-end load. Equity funds are also assessed an annual "service fee" of 0.5% on the market value of your investments (this is over and above the normal management fee). If your total assets are between $35,000 and $150,000, you'll receive a partial rebate of this amount. Over $150,000, you get it all back. The rules are somewhat different for fixed-income and money market funds. Investors Group representatives (there are 3,600 sales reps) can give you more details of this rather complex payment structure.

This company is to be commended for the quality of its communications with clients, and for being up-front about the lead managers on all funds and their tenure in that position.

THE DETAILS

NUMBER OF FUNDS: 52
ASSETS UNDER MANAGEMENT: $36 BILLION
LOAD CHARGE: FRONT: MAX. 2.5%; BACK: MAX. 3%

SWITCHING CHARGE:	NONE
WHERE SOLD:	ACROSS CANADA
HOW SOLD:	EXCLUSIVELY THROUGH INVESTORS GROUP REPRESENTATIVES
PHONE NUMBER:	1-888-PHONE IG OR 1-888-746-6344
WEB SITE ADDRESS:	WWW.INVESTORSGROUP.COM
E-MAIL ADDRESS:	THROUGH WEB PAGE

FUND SUMMARY

$$$$ - NONE

$$$ - ASSET ALLOCATION, DIVIDEND, CORPORATE BOND, GLOBAL, GOVERNMENT BOND, GROWTH PLUS PORTFOLIO, GROWTH PORTFOLIO, MUTUAL OF CANADA, NORTH AMERICAN GROWTH, SPECIAL, SUMMA, U.S. GROWTH

$$ - EUROPEAN GROWTH, REAL PROPERTY, RETIREMENT GROWTH PORTFOLIO, RETIREMENT MUTUAL

$ - CANADIAN EQUITY, GLOBAL BOND, INCOME PORTFOLIO, INCOME PLUS PORTFOLIO, JAPANESE GROWTH, MONEY MARKET, MORTGAGE, PACIFIC INTERNATIONAL, RETIREMENT PLUS PORTFOLIO, WORLD GROWTH PORTFOLIO

NR - CANADIAN BALANCED, CANADIAN ENTERPRISE, CANADIAN NATURAL RESOURCE, CANADIAN SMALL CAP II, GLOBAL SCIENCE AND TECHNOLOGY, IG BEUTEL GOODMAN CANADIAN BALANCED, IG BEUTEL GOODMAN CANADIAN EQUITY, IG BEUTEL GOODMAN CANADIAN SMALL CAP, IG SCEPTRE CANADIAN BALANCED, IG SCEPTRE CANADIAN BOND, IG SCEPTRE CANADIAN EQUITY, LATIN AMERICAN GROWTH, MERRILL LYNCH CANADIAN EQUITY, MERRILL LYNCH CAPITAL ASSET, MERRILL LYNCH EMERGING MARKETS, MERRILL LYNCH WORLD ALLOCATION, MERRILL LYNCH WORLD BOND, NORTH AMERICAN HIGH YIELD BOND, ROTHSCHILD SELECT: GS AMERICAN EQUITY, ROTHSCHILD SELECT: GS CANADIAN BALANCED, ROTHSCHILD SELECT: GS CANADIAN EQUITY, ROTHSCHILD SELECT: GS INTERNATIONAL BOND, ROTHSCHILD SELECT: GS INTERNATIONAL EQUITY, U.S. MONEY MARKET, U.S. OPPORTUNITIES

BEST CHOICES: GLOBAL, SUMMA, U.S. GROWTH

BEST FOR RRSPS: CORPORATE BOND, GOVERNMENT BOND, MUTUAL OF CANADA, SUMMA
BEST UNRATEDS: ROTHSCHILD SELECT: GS AMERICAN EQUITY, ROTHSCHILD SELECT: GS CANADIAN BALANCED, ROTHSCHILD SELECT: GS INTERNATIONAL EQUITY, IG SCEPTRE CANADIAN BOND, MERRILL LYNCH CAPITAL ASSET

FUND RATINGS

CANADIAN EQUITY FUNDS

INVESTORS CANADIAN EQUITY FUND $ → G * RSP CE

Manager: Scott Penman, since 1985

MER: 2.46%

Investors Group offers a dozen options for those interested in Canadian equity funds. Of these, seven are broad-based equity funds with varying mandates and different managers. This fund focuses on long-term growth with some income, through holdings in medium to large Canadian companies. It offers a well-diversified portfolio and a conservative management style under the capable direction of Scott Penman, an in-house manager who has been at the helm for more than a decade. There's not a lot that's exciting in this huge, $4-billion fund. The performance numbers have tailed off recently and the fund gained only 3.6% in the year to June 30/98, in part because of a heavy portfolio weighting of resource stocks and cyclicals. Ten-year results are above average but if you ask "What have you done for me lately?", the answer is "Not very much." There are better choices in this group.

INVESTORS DIVIDEND FUND $$$ → G/FI * RSP INC

Manager: Tighe A. McManus, since 1985

MER: 2.36%

This fund invests mainly in high-yielding common stocks (e.g., banks, utilities, pipelines). As of the end of June/98, these made up 53% of the total portfolio. Preferred share holdings are relatively small (16%) and the fund holds an unusually high percentage of bonds and cash (31%). As a result, the dividend cash flow is not as high as with many other dividend funds. In a survey done for my *Mutual Funds Update* newsletter, we found that this fund generated a cash return of 2.9% in 1997, which is on the low side. Total return has been reasonably good, however, with a 21.5% advance in the year to June 30/98. Still, if high cash flow is your goal this fund won't work as well as some others. Treat it as a balanced fund with a blue-chip stock propensity and you'll be more on the mark here.

INVESTORS REAL PROPERTY FUND $$ → G * RSP RE

Manager: Murray Mitchell, since 1989

MER: 2.39%

Real estate mutual funds have been a wasteland for investors in recent years. This one has held up better than most, but it certainly hasn't been a top performer, with an average annual return over the three years to June 30/98 of just 5.8%. But before you write it off entirely, it's important to understand how these funds work. You don't (or shouldn't) invest in them for capital gains, but rather for tax-advantaged income. In other words, judge the performance of these funds on the basis of cash flow, not total profit. By that standard, this one didn't do badly in '97. Based on distributions of 20.7 cents per unit, the income flow to investors during the year was 4.9%, using a unit valuation of $4.25 at the start of '97. A good chunk of that revenue was tax sheltered. In these times of low interest rates, that's not a bad performance if you're an income-oriented investor (better than a GIC, after all), hence the $$ rating. RRSP/RRIF eligible, but you'll lose the tax breaks if you hold units in registered plans.

INVESTORS RETIREMENT
GROWTH PORTFOLIO $$ → G * RSP CE

Manager: I.G. Investment Management

MER: 2.62%

Investors Group offers a number of "portfolio" funds. These invest in units of several Investors funds to provide more diversification. The composition of this one is 30% in units in the Canadian Equity Fund, 20% Global Fund, and

50% Retirement Mutual Fund. Whether you'd be better off putting your money here or investing directly in the Retirement Mutual Fund is questionable and depends on year-over-year results. Right now, this one appears to be a slightly better bet, but both funds are below average for the Canadian equity category.

INVESTORS RETIREMENT MUTUAL FUND $$ → G * RSP CE

Manager: Scott Penman, since 1993

MER: 2.42%

This huge $3.4-billion fund has the same manager as the companion Canadian Equity Fund. Not surprisingly, the portfolios of the two are similar, although not quite the same. This fund supposedly places more emphasis on blue-chip stocks, although there are a few smaller companies in the portfolio. There hasn't been a lot to choose from between this and the Canadian Equity Fund, but recently this one has been a slightly better performer.

INVESTORS SUMMA FUND $$$ ↓ G * RSP CE

Manager: Allan Brown, since 1997

MER: 2.48%

This is a "socially responsible" fund: investment policies preclude companies involved in tobacco, alcohol, munitions, pornography, and gambling. Returns have been the best of any fund Investors Group offers in the Canadian equity category, over all time frames. For the year to June 30/98, the fund turned in an excellent 24.3% gain. The three-year average was exactly the same, which shows the consistency this fund has displayed in recent years. ATP analysis shows this fund rates very highly from a safety perspective, making it the best choice right now on a risk/return basis of all the Canadian equity options available from Investors. The only point of concern, and the reason why this fund doesn't move up to $$$$ status, is that there is a new manager at the helm. We'll want to be sure Allan Brown can live up to the same standard as his predecessor, Quinn Bamford, before moving this one into the top rank.

U.S. AND INTERNATIONAL EQUITY FUNDS

INVESTORS EUROPEAN GROWTH FUND $$ → G * £ EE

Manager: Derek M. Smith, since inception (1990)

MER: 2.45%

This fund had not performed up to the standards of its peer group until recently. But it has put on a spurt and now boasts a one-year return to June 30/98 of 38.3%, slightly better than average for the European category. Longer term results are just about average. As of the end of June, 31% of the portfolio was in the U.K., with other significant holdings in Germany, the Netherlands, France, and Switzerland. A small corner has been reserved for some of the emerging markets in the east (e.g., Croatia, Hungary, Poland). Still, this is very much a middle-of-the-road portfolio; you won't find a lot of risk here. If you're an Investors Group client, having a little money in this one isn't a bad idea. Remember, the $$ rating is compared to competitive European funds; when you look at this one in the context of the Investors Group internal universe, it looks great.

INVESTORS GLOBAL FUND $$$ ↓ G * £ IE

Manager: Martin Fahey, since 1995

MER: 2.36%

Investors Group offers a wide range of international funds for its clients. The mandate of this one is far-reaching; the fund can invest anywhere the manager sees opportunities, with a focus on large, well-managed companies. Results have been very strong recently, thanks to a heavy weighting in the record-setting U.S. market (44% at the beginning of July/98). Gain for the year ending June 30/98 was 22.9%, making this the hottest of Investors' broadly based international funds over that time. Five-year average annual compound rate of return was 16.6%. That was also above average. The safety rating of this one is very good in comparison to the peer group. All in all, a very sound choice.

INVESTORS GROWTH PORTFOLIO $$$ ↓ G * £ IE

Manager: I.G. Investment Management

MER: 2.61%

This is a fund of funds, holding units in several Investor
Group growth funds for greater diversification, with an
emphasis on foreign stocks. As of early July, 1998, holdings
were the Global Fund (40%), Canadian Equity Fund
(20%), U.S. Growth Fund (20%), Special Fund (10%), and
North American Growth Fund (10%), unchanged from the
previous year. Results have been above average for this
category, and over time about the same as those of the
companion Global Fund. Five-year average annual compound rate of return to June 30/98 was 16.6%, exactly the
same as for Investors Global. This is a useful choice for
those who prefer a more diversified approach, which also
helps give this fund a better-than-average safety record.

INVESTORS JAPANESE GROWTH FUND $ ↑ G * £ FEE

Manager: Colin Abraham, since 1994

MER: 2.47%

Japanese equity funds have gone through hard times in
recent years, but this one has fared worse than most. It lost
29.6% in the year to June 30/98, and the average annual compound rate of return over the past five years is minus 5.6%.
That's not good. The Far East is not one of this company's
strengths so if you want to invest there you should look elsewhere. However, I recommend you hold off directing new
money to that part of the world until we have a clear signal
that the economy is on the road to recovery.

INVESTORS NORTH AMERICAN GROWTH FUND $$$ ↓ G * £ AE

Manager: William D. Chornous, since 1995

MER: 2.38%

Invests mainly in Canadian and U.S. stocks. Until recently,
American shares formed the bulk of the portfolio, but as of
July/98 the fund was fairly evenly balanced between

Canadian (40%) and U.S. (50%) equities. A reliable long-term performer, however, the one-year gain to June 30/98 showed some slippage, to a below-average 8.9%. That's not bad enough to consider a downgrade in the rating after so many good years, but be warned. The rating will drop if performance does not improve.

INVESTORS PACIFIC INTERNATIONAL FUND $ ↑ G * £ FEE

Manager: Jeremy Higgs, since 1993

MER: 2.50%

Most Far East funds have taken a beating recently, but this has been one of the hardest hit. Loss over the 12 months to June 30/98 was a terrible 51.3%, much worse than average for the Far East category. The portfolio focuses on the Pacific Rim, excluding Japan. It is well diversified, with Hong Kong the largest single component at 29% of the assets at the beginning of July. Right now, this is a fund for speculators only. Do not put it into an RRSP.

INVESTORS SPECIAL FUND $$$ → G * £ AE

Manager: William G. Chornous, since 1994

MER: 2.39%

Like the Investors North American Growth Fund, this fund also invests in North American stocks, mainly U.S. and Canada, but with an occasional Mexican entry tossed in. The main difference from North American Growth is an emphasis on small- and medium-sized companies with high growth potential. As well, this fund had a higher proportion of Canadian content (47%) in July/98. This has been a solid long-term performer, with a 10-year average annual return of 14.3%. Recent results have been weak when compared to pure U.S. funds, but above the average for Canadian stock funds. In recent years it has been a better performer than its North American Growth stablemate. Risk has improved to about average.

INVESTORS U.S. GROWTH FUND $$$ ↓ G * £ USE

Manager: Terry Wong, since 1998

MER: 2.41%

The big news here is the departure of long-time manager Larry Sarbit, who had been running this top-notch fund since 1987. He has moved to the Berkshire Investment Group, so we'll watch for news of his responsibilities there. Terry Wong, who worked on this fund as a portfolio assistant since 1987, assumed lead manager responsibility on June 1. Sarbit's departure casts a shadow over the terrific performance of this fund — gain for the year ending June 30/98 was a sparkling 44%. This has been one of the star performers for Investors Group for many years, combining a conservative style with consistency and steady results. Under Sarbit, the portfolio emphasized stocks with good growth potential and was managed on a highly disciplined basis, never holding more than about 20–25 companies. Sarbit didn't do a lot of trading, preferring to find good companies and hold them for the long term. Average annual rate of return for the decade was 19.6%, best in the U.S. equity category among funds available to the general public. With his departure, the future outlook becomes somewhat uncertain. As a result, I am downgrading the rating to $$$ until we have an opportunity to assess the performance of the new manager.

INVESTORS WORLD GROWTH PORTFOLIO $ ↑ G * £ IE

Manager: I.G. Investment Management

MER: 2.62%

This fund of funds offers a somewhat different mix than the Growth Portfolio. The Canadian component drops out and the focus is more tightly on the U.S., Europe, and Asia. Composition in mid-'98 was 30% European Growth Fund, 20% Japanese Growth Fund, 20% North American Growth Fund, 15% Pacific International Fund, and 15% Special Fund, unchanged from a year ago. Recent returns have been below average, pulled down by the weak performance of the Far East component. The fund recorded a loss of 2.7% for the year to June 30/98. As long as the

Asia components remain a significant part of this portfolio and the economy in that part of the world is weak, I suggest you choose a different option.

BALANCED FUNDS

INVESTORS ASSET ALLOCATION FUND $$$ ↑ G/FI * RSP CBAL

Manager: Eric Innes (Yield Management Group), since inception (1994)

MER: 2.73%

Investors offers several choices in the balanced fund category and the selection isn't always simple. This fund uses asset allocation techniques to vary the portfolio weighting between Canadian stocks, foreign equities, and bonds. Manager Eric Innes is given free rein to heavily overload the portfolio in favour of one category or another, so this fund doesn't operate under the usual parameters of a balanced fund. For example, this fund may hold a disproportionately high percentage of stocks during bull market periods, as has been the case recently. That's a higher risk approach than you'll find in a fund that confines the manager to, for example, a 60% maximum in any single asset class. Plus, the make-up of this fund is unlike anything else Investors offers. The portfolio includes index futures as well as common stocks, including futures on several international markets. All this adds up to more return potential, so it should come as no surprise that this was the best performer among Investors' balanced funds and portfolios over the past three years, with an average annual compound rate of return of 16.9% to June 30/98. However, as you might also expect, the safety rating of this fund is very poor for the balanced category, according to ATP analysis. So be prepared for some ups and downs with this one.

INVESTORS GROWTH PLUS PORTFOLIO $$$ ↓ G/FI * £ IBAL

Manager: I.G. Asset Management

MER: 2.45%

Investors Group offers three balanced portfolio funds, which invest in units of other funds for more diversification. This has been one of the most successful. It holds units in six Investors funds: Government Bond, Corporate Bond, Canadian Equity, Global, Real Property, and U.S. Growth Fund. If you want a balanced fund that really covers the investment horizon, this is it. Good results too; average annual rate of return for the five years ending June 30/98 was a very respectable 13%. ATP analysis reveals a good safety record here, with only a 7% chance of loss over any one-year period. This is the best choice among the balanced portfolio funds if foreign content in an RRSP or RRIF is not a factor in your decision.

INVESTORS INCOME PLUS PORTFOLIO $ ↓ FI/G * RSP CBAL

Manager: I.G. Asset Management

MER: 2.29%

This is another of the seven "funds of funds" from Investors Group. The emphasis in this case is on income, with some growth potential thrown in. Units in six Investors Group funds are held, with the main weighting being the Dividend Fund and the Government Bond Fund, each with 25% of the total portfolio. Long-term results have been mediocre, although they have been better lately. The safety record is good. If cash flow is your goal, the Dividend Fund is a better bet. If it's a balanced investment approach you're looking for, Investors Mutual produces higher returns.

INVESTORS MUTUAL OF CANADA $$$ → FI/G * RSP CBAL

Manager: Geoff Barth, since 1996

MER: 2.37%

This was the fund that got Investors Group started in the mutual fund business back in 1950, so it has a proud history attached to it. Returns have shown improvement since Geoff Barth took charge, with a 13.2% gain for the year to June 30/98. That was better than average for the balanced fund category. Portfolio is well diversified, with 40% in bonds, preferreds, and cash at the beginning of July and the balance in common stocks. The stocks tend toward the blue-chip variety, with lots of banks in the mix, but there are enough growth companies included to make things interesting. There is also a healthy sprinkling of U.S. stocks in the portfolio. If you're an Investors client seeking a balanced fund for your portfolio, here it is. Rating moves up to $$$.

INVESTORS RETIREMENT PLUS PORTFOLIO $ → FI/G * RSP CBAL

Manager: I.G. Asset Management

MER: 2.41%

This "fund of funds" is more diversified than the Income Plus Portfolio. It holds units in eight Investors Group funds, with no single fund having more than a 20% weighting. Returns are below average in relation to the balanced fund category as a whole. Investors Mutual of Canada is a better bet in the balanced class. The historical risk is slightly higher here than for the Income Plus Portfolio, according to ATP analysis.

FIXED INCOME AND MONEY MARKET FUNDS

INVESTORS CORPORATE BOND FUND $$$ ↓ FI * RSP CB

Manager: Paul Hancock, since inception (1994)

MER: 1.89%

The mandate of this fund is to invest primarily in corporate bonds, although there were some government issues (about 26%) in the portfolio at the beginning of July/98. You'd expect a corporate bond fund to generate a better return than a government bond fund, so it may come as a surprise that the Investors Government Bond Fund did as well as this one over the three years to June 30/98, with an average annual compound rate of return of 10.3%. Also surprising is the fact that the risk profile of this fund is better. That's because it has a shorter average duration (5.4 years versus 6.6 years in the Government Bond Fund). Duration is a measure of risk; the shorter the duration the less vulnerable a bond fund is to big losses in the event of an interest rate jump. There's really not a lot of difference between the two funds at this stage. So take your pick. They're both good.

INVESTORS GLOBAL BOND FUND $ → FI * £ IB

Manager: Chris P. McGinty, since inception (1992)

MER: 2.18%

This is not one of Investors more impressive offerings. The fund's three-year performance record is well below average for the international bond fund category (just 3.5% for the period ending June 30/98). However, more recent results have been better. The portfolio is well diversified, with European and Canadian bonds currently the dominant holdings. One of the reasons this fund hasn't been stronger is that U.S. bonds have only been a small part of the overall mix.

INVESTORS GOVERNMENT BOND FUND $$$ → FI * RSP CB

Manager: Alan Brownridge, since 1984

MER: 1.90%

Solid performer, with above average returns over all time periods. Despite the name change (it was previously the Investors Bond Fund), there are still some corporate issues in the portfolio, totalling about 9% of the holdings as of mid-'98. However, most of the assets conform to the fund's mandate to stick to government issues only — federal, provincial, and municipal. Return for the 12 months to June 30/98 was 9.6%. Ten-year results are almost bang on the average for the Canadian bond category, at 9.8%.

INVESTORS INCOME PORTFOLIO FUND $ → FI * RSP B/M

Manager: I.G. Investment Management

MER: 2.06%

This is a "fund of funds" that invests one third of its assets in the Investors Government Bond Fund, one third in the Mortgage Fund, and one third in the Corporate Bond Fund. Returns are not as good as those of the Government Bond Fund, although the safety record is better. Right now, investing directly in the Government Bond Fund and/or the Corporate Bond Fund is wiser.

INVESTORS MONEY MARKET FUND $ → C No RSP CMM

Manager: Alan Brownridge, since inception (1985)

MER: 1.07%

Below-average performer that is heavily weighted towards corporate short-term notes, a departure from the past when the fund showed more balance between government and corporate issues. The only no-load fund offered by Investors Group.

INVESTORS MORTGAGE FUND $ ↓ FI * RSP M

Manager: Rick Fourneaux, since 1986

MER: 1.90%

For many years, this was the largest mutual fund in Canada. It has now lost that title, but it's still a biggie, with assets of about $2.3 billion, although the base is gradually declining. Results have been sub-par as mortgage funds go. Gain for the year to June 30/98 was just 2.9%. The Money Market Fund, which is no great shakes itself, did better. A high MER is the problem here. The safety record is very good, though. ATP analysis shows this to be one of those classic invest-it-and-forget-it funds, where you won't lose a moment's sleep wondering what's happening to your money. There's only a 3% chance of loss over any 12-month period, and then the maximum drop has been 3.1%. A small portion of the assets is held in industrial and commercial mortgages but most of the fund is in residential mortgages.

IRIS GROUP OF FUNDS

THE COMPANY

The Laurentian Bank of Canada recently acquired two fund groups in the purchase of other financial institutions. Six Cornerstone funds were added when the Bank purchased North American Trust (they were North American's house line). Another nine funds came in when Laurentian acquired Savings and Investment Trust.

In June, 1998, unitholders approved a plan merging these funds into a new group called IRIS. The reorganization took effect on July 31. Nine funds were created from the merged Cornerstone/Savings and Investment Trust groups, and four new ones were added, making a total of 13 IRIS entries.

The funds rated below are those that previously existed and are continuing under the IRIS name. The four newly created IRIS funds are not rated. They are the Strategic Income Option Balanced, Strategic Growth Option Balanced, Tactical Option Balanced, and Small Cap Canadian Equity funds.

THE DETAILS

NUMBER OF FUNDS:	13
ASSETS UNDER MANAGEMENT:	$300 MILLION
LOAD CHARGE:	NONE
SWITCHING CHARGE:	NONE
WHERE SOLD:	ACROSS CANADA
HOW SOLD:	THROUGH BRANCHES OF LAURENTIAN BANK OR LAURENTIAN TRUST OR THROUGH REGISTERED DEALERS
PHONE NUMBER:	1-800-565-6513
WEB SITE ADDRESS:	WWW.LAURENTIANBANK.COM
E-MAIL ADDRESS:	N/A

FUND SUMMARY

$$$$ - NONE
$$$ - BOND, GLOBAL EQUITY
$$ - BALANCED, CANADIAN EQUITY, DIVIDEND

$ - Money Market, Mortgage, North American High
Yield Bond, U.S. Equity

NR - Small Cap Canadian Equity, Strategic Income
Option Balanced, Strategic Growth Option
Balanced, Tactical Option Balanced

Best choices: Bond, Global Equity

Best for RRSPs: Bond

Best unrateds: None - new funds too recent to assess

FUND RATINGS

CANADIAN EQUITY FUNDS

IRIS CANADIAN EQUITY FUND $$ → G No RSP CE

Manager: TPR Investment Management

MER: 1.93%

Primary mandate is to invest in shares of TSE 300 corporations, but smaller companies with high growth potential are also included in the portfolio. Foreign content consists mainly of S&P 500 stocks. The continuing fund here is the old Savings and Investment Trust Canadian Fund, with the Cornerstone Growth Fund merged into it. The S&I fund is coming off a mediocre year, with a gain of 8.5% to June 30/98. We'll start off the merged entity at $$ and see where it goes.

IRIS DIVIDEND FUND $$ → G No RSP INC

Manager: TPR Investment Management

MER: 1.62%

The objective of this fund is to generate tax-advantaged income, eligible for the dividend tax credit. The managers may invest in common stock, preferred shares, income trusts, or fixed-income securities. This was previously the Savings and Investment Trust Dividend Fund. Returns under that name were generally above average, although the gain over the most recent 12 months, to June 30/98, was just 11.1%, sub-par for the dividend category.

U.S. AND INTERNATIONAL EQUITY FUNDS

IRIS GLOBAL EQUITY FUND $$$ → G No £ IE

Manager: TPR Investment Management

MER: 2.37%

The mandate of this fund allows it to invest around the world, including the United States. A portion of the portfolio may also be placed in emerging markets. The continuing fund in this case is the Savings and Investment Trust International Fund, which has been putting up some pretty good numbers. Gain for the year to June 30/98 was 16.1%, almost the same as the three-year average annual compound rate of return of 16%. The Cornerstone Global Fund was folded into this one; it was formerly the Metropolitan Speculators Fund.

IRIS U.S. EQUITY FUND $ → G No £ USE

Manager: TPR Investment Management

MER: 2.23%

This fund invests mainly in S&P 500 companies, although the managers are not limited to that list. The continuing fund is the Savings and Investment Trust American Fund, with the Cornerstone U.S. Fund merged into it. The S&I fund received a $ rating in last year's edition and is coming off another sub-par year (it gained 18% to June 30/98 but that was well below average for U.S. equity funds as a group). By contrast, the Cornerstone Fund, which was run by Wellington Management of Boston, gained 34.2% over the same 12-month period, which would have been more than enough to maintain last year's $$$ rating. A very questionable decision by Laurentian here. The merged entry starts with just $.

BALANCED FUNDS

IRIS BALANCED FUND $$ → FI/G No RSP CBAL

Manager: TPR Investment Management

MER: 1.95%

The continuing fund here is the Cornerstone Balanced Fund, with the Savings and Investment Trust Retirement Fund merged into it. The investment mandate is typical for a balanced fund, nothing unusual about it. There is no stipulation that requires minimum percentages of stocks or bonds in the portfolio at any given time. The track record of Cornerstone Balanced was not exciting, and the S&I fund hasn't been much better recently. The $$ rating is therefore a bit generous. Be guided accordingly.

FIXED INCOME AND MONEY MARKET FUNDS

IRIS BOND FUND $$$ → FI No RSP CB

Manager: TPR Investment Management

MER: 1.58%

The continuing fund is Cornerstone Bond Fund, which TPR had been running, so there is continuity here. The mandate is to invest in high-quality bonds, both government and corporate. Returns for the Cornerstone fund are above average, with a gain of 10.1% for the year to June 30/98. This looks like one of the better choices in the new group, at least at this early stage.

IRIS MONEY MARKET FUND $ → C No RSP CMM

Manager: TPR Investment Management

MER: 1.14%

The Cornerstone Government Money Fund is the continuing fund here. In the past, the fund invested exclusively in Canada T-bills, but there is no restriction in the mandate of the new fund that limits the managers in this regard. Results of both predecessor funds tended to be below average for the money market category.

IRIS MORTGAGE FUND $ → FI No RSP M

Manager: TPR Investment Management

MER: 1.68%

This is just a name change, not a merger of two funds. The Savings and Investment Trust Mortgage Fund, which is the predecessor to this one, tended to be an underperformer, especially in recent years. There is no reason to expect a different name will help.

IRIS NORTH AMERICAN HIGH YIELD
BOND FUND $ ↑ FI No RSP CB

Manager: TPR Investment Management

MER: 1.88%

The goal here is to generate above-average returns by investing in a portfolio of Canadian and U.S. corporate bonds, which may include unrated securities or even those that are in default at the time of purchase. Obviously, there is more risk here than in an ordinary bond fund, but the potential returns are higher as well. This was previously the Savings and Investment Trust Global Bond Fund. Returns in that guise were below average and the $ rating is based on that. But the mandate is somewhat different now so we'll have to see what happens.

JONES HEWARD GROUP

THE COMPANY

This is an investment counselling firm that is now owned by Bank of Montreal, but continues to operate its own independent fund group as well as handling the management duties for several of the Bank's First Canadian Funds. The small family of five funds has a long history, but has undergone many changes in recent years, so past results don't mean a great deal.

Of special note is the recent move to cut the management fee of the Money Market Fund in half, to 0.5%. This will provide a significant boost to returns during this time of low interest rates.

THE DETAILS

NUMBER OF FUNDS:	5
ASSETS UNDER MANAGEMENT:	$165 MILLION
LOAD CHARGE:	FRONT: MAX. 9% (EXCEPT MONEY MARKET, MAX. 2%); BACK: MAX. 5%
SWITCHING CHARGE:	2% MAXIMUM
WHERE SOLD:	ACROSS CANADA
HOW SOLD:	THROUGH BROKERS, DEALERS, AND FINANCIAL PLANNERS
PHONE NUMBER:	1-800-361-1392
WEB SITE ADDRESS:	WWW.JONESHEWARD.COM
E-MAIL ADDRESS:	N/A

FUND SUMMARY

$$$$ - NONE
$$$ - AMERICAN, MONEY MARKET
$$ - BOND, JONES HEWARD FUND LTD.
$ - CANADIAN BALANCED
NR - NONE

BEST CHOICES: AMERICAN, MONEY MARKET
BEST FOR RRSPS: BALANCED, JONES HEWARD FUND
BEST UNRATEDS: N/A

FUND RATINGS

CANADIAN EQUITY FUNDS

JONES HEWARD FUND $$ → G #/* RSP CE

Manager: James Lawson, since 1997

MER: 2.50%

Manager James Lawson has been at the helm of this long-established fund for a little more than a year. He takes a fundamental, bottom-up approach to stock selection. During the first half of '98, he took the portfolio in a very conservative direction, holding very few highly priced stocks and limiting exposure in sectors that could suffer the greatest fall-out from the Far East. However, that defensive stance was undermined to a degree by the fund's mandate to hold approximately a third of the portfolio in small-cap stocks. These stocks tend to be hit hardest in turbulent markets and much of 1998 fell into that category. Still, Lawson managed to provide investors with an above-average gain of 13.2% over the 12 months to June 30/98, a good performance under the circumstances. Since he hasn't been in charge very long, it's too soon to raise the rating. But the debut was impressive. This fund was founded in '39 as Group Investment Ltd., making it one of the oldest continuous funds in Canada.

U.S. AND INTERNATIONAL EQUITY FUNDS

JONES HEWARD AMERICAN FUND $$$ → G #/* £ USE

Manager: Harris Bretall Sullivan & Smith, since 1995

MER: 2.50%

This long-time underperformer had a managerial change in '95, with portfolio responsibility handed over to Harris Bretall Sullivan & Smith Inc. of San Francisco. They got off to a slow start, but now they seem to be rolling. Gain for the 12 months to June 30/98 was a very good 35.9%, well above average for the U.S. equity category. Three-year average annual compound rate of return had improved to 24.6%, also better than average. In the first half of '98, the portfolio was heavily weighted to consumer stocks (33%) and technology issues (23%). Fine performance warrants a rating upgrade.

BALANCED FUNDS

JONES HEWARD CANADIAN
BALANCED FUND $ → FI/G #/* RSP CBAL

Managers: Mary Jane Yule and Michael Stanley, since 1997

MER: 2.40%

This fund has gone through two managerial changes in the past three years, and is finally starting to look a little better. The managers took a defensive posture in the first half of '98 in both the stock and bond holdings. On the equities side, Michael Stanley limited exposure to the resource sector, which served investors well. Meanwhile, Mary Jane Yule, who runs the fixed-income side of the portfolio, was also defensively positioned, reflecting her concerns about low bond yields and a flattening of the yield curve. All this technical stuff boiled down to a slightly better-than-average gain of 10.4% for the year to June 30/98. It's too soon to raise the rating on the strength of that, but the direction is good. Formerly the Burns Fry Canadian Fund.

FIXED INCOME AND MONEY MARKET FUNDS

JONES HEWARD BOND FUND $$ → FI #/* RSP CB

Manager: Mary Jane Yule, since 1996

MER: 1.75%

As with the fixed-income section of the companion Canadian Balanced Fund, manager Mary Jane Yule was in a defensive mode in the first half of '98. As a result, this fund didn't participate in the strong bond market to the same degree as some of its peers. Gain for the year to June 30/98 was 7.8%, below average for the bond fund category. The portfolio offers a diversified mix of federal, provincial, and corporate issues. Formerly the Burns Fry Bond Fund.

JONES HEWARD MONEY MARKET FUND

$$$ → C # RSP CB

Manager: Dorothy Biggs, since 1994

MER: 0.50%

The recent cut in the MER of this fund from 1% to 0.5% should provide a nice boost to returns, which were already average to slightly above. Had the change been in effect for the year to June 30/98, this fund would have yielded 3.5%, well in excess of the 3.1% average for Canadian money funds as a group. Only a few funds of this type offer as low an MER and most of them require very high minimum investments. You can get into this one for as little as $1,000. The fund is only sold on a front-end load basis, with a maximum commission of 2%. If you can get that waived, you've got a real bargain here. The portfolio is a mix of government and corporate notes.

LEITH WHEELER INVESTMENT COUNSEL

THE COMPANY

This is a Vancouver-based, employee-owned company, founded by Murray Leith and Bill Wheeler. It is working hard to establish a foothold in the crowded mutual funds marketplace. The firm was started in 1982 and currently manages more than $2.6 billion worth of assets for individuals, foundations, charitable organizations, and pension funds. The mutual fund line is just a small part of their total business. Their managerial style is a value-oriented, conservative approach. The funds were only available in B.C. and Alberta for many years but can now also be purchased by residents of Ontario, Manitoba, and Saskatchewan. Minimum investment is $50,000, although it can be waived.

THE DETAILS

NUMBER OF FUNDS:	5
ASSETS UNDER MANAGEMENT:	$150 MILLION
LOAD CHARGE:	NONE
SWITCHING CHARGE:	NONE
WHERE SOLD:	ALBERTA, B.C., MANITOBA, ONTARIO, AND SASKATCHEWAN
HOW SOLD:	DIRECTLY THROUGH LEITH WHEELER
PHONE NUMBER:	(604) 683-3391 OR 1-888-292-1122
WEB SITE ADDRESS:	WWW.LEITHWHEELER.COM
E-MAIL ADDRESS:	LWIC@DIRECT.CA

FUND SUMMARY

$$$$ - NONE
$$$ - BALANCED, CANADIAN EQUITY, FIXED INCOME, MONEY MARKET,
$$ - NONE
$ - U.S. EQUITY
NR - NONE
BEST CHOICES: BALANCED, CANADIAN EQUITY
BEST FOR RRSPs: BALANCED
BEST UNRATEDS: N/A

FUND RATINGS

CANADIAN EQUITY FUNDS

LEITH WHEELER CANADIAN
EQUITY FUND $$$ ↓ G No RSP CE

Manager: Leith Wheeler Investment Committee, since inception (1994)

MER: 1.40%

This is essentially a buy-and-hold fund. All securities are purchased with the intention of retaining them for two to four years, so there isn't a lot of active trading going on. The portfolio is a mix of large-cap and medium-sized companies. In the first half of '98 it was most heavily weighted towards the financial services sector. The heavy resource weighting of a year earlier had been cut way back. Returns continue to be very good. The fund gained almost 20% in the year ending June 30/98. Three-year average annual compound rate of return was 23.6%. Although the fund is still new, the risk factor so far is better than average. I've been saying for a couple of years that this is one of those good little funds that too few people know about (it has only $12 million in assets). It deserves more attention.

U.S. AND INTERNATIONAL EQUITY FUNDS

LEITH WHEELER U.S. EQUITY FUND $ → G No £ USE

Manager: Leith Wheeler Investment Committee, since inception (1994)

MER: 1.25%

As with the other Leith Wheeler funds, a value-oriented approach is the order of the day here. Companies selected for the portfolio are leaders in their respective fields, with good management, strong competitive positions, and sound growth prospects — all at a reasonable price, of course. There are a lot of household names in the portfolio (Pepsico, McDonald's, Toys R Us) but also several companies you're probably unfamiliar with. The results have been mediocre — average annual compound rate of return for the three years to June 30/98 was 18.4%. That may not look bad at first glance but it was actually well below the average for U.S. equity funds as a group. Not the strongest entry from this group.

BALANCED FUNDS

LEITH WHEELER BALANCED FUND $$$ ↓ G/FI No RSP CBAL

Manager: Leith Wheeler Investment Committee, since inception (1987)

MER: 1.10%

The portfolio of this fund is well constructed and makes good use of U.S. stocks to add foreign content and boost returns. The mandate allows the managers a fairly wide latitude in determining their asset allocation; the fund can hold between 25% and 75% in equities. In the first half of '98, the balance was 57% stocks (of which 40% were Canadian) and the rest in bonds and cash. Returns for all time periods are above average. Gain for the year to June 30/98 was 15.4%. Five-year annual average is 13.5%, while the 10-year average was 11.1%. Excellent safety record. This is a very fine fund for an investor seeking conservative management and above-average returns. Name changed from Leith Wheeler All-Value Balanced Fund in '94.

FIXED INCOME AND MONEY MARKET FUNDS

LEITH WHEELER FIXED INCOME FUND $$$ ↓ FI No RSP CB

Manager: Leith Wheeler Investment Committee, since inception (1994)

MER: 0.75%

This portfolio invests mainly in Government of Canada issues, with a few foreign pay bonds and provincials added. Returns are better than the norm, with an average annual compound rate of return of 9.8% over the three years to June 30/98. The safety record of this fund is also very good. Rating moves up a notch.

LEITH WHEELER MONEY
MARKET FUND $$$ ↓ C No RSP CMM

Manager: Leith Wheeler Investment Committee, since inception (1994)

MER: 0.60%

Although this fund can invest in corporate notes, the holdings have been entirely in federal T-bills for the past few years. Returns have been above average, thanks to the low management fee.

LION FUNDS MANAGEMENT

THE COMPANY

The organization is new although one of its funds is not. Lion Funds is the result of an agreement between Pacific Capital Management of Vancouver and Yorkton Securities of Toronto that was reached in late 1997. Under the arrangement, Lion Fund Management was created and received the right to operate the Pacific Special Equity Fund, which was reviewed under that name in last year's *Buyer's Guide.* The fund's name was changed to Lion Knowledge Industries Fund and a second fund was added, Lion Natural Resources Fund. Both funds focus on small- and mid-cap companies and both are run by Graham Henderson, who managed the Pacific Special Equity Fund.

THE DETAILS

NUMBER OF FUNDS:	2
ASSETS UNDER MANAGEMENT:	$16.4 MILLION
LOAD CHARGE:	FRONT: MAX. 5%; BACK: MAX. 6%
SWITCHING CHARGE:	2% MAXIMUM
WHERE SOLD:	ACROSS CANADA
HOW SOLD:	THROUGH BROKERS, DEALERS, AND FINANCIAL PLANNERS
PHONE NUMBER:	1-800-250-3303
WEB SITE ADDRESS:	N/A
E-MAIL ADDRESS:	N/A

FUND SUMMARY

$$$$ - NONE
$$$ - NONE
$$ - NONE
$ - KNOWLEDGE INDUSTRIES FUND
NR -NONE
BEST CHOICES: NONE
BEST FOR RRSPs: NONE
BEST UNRATEDS: NONE

FUND RATINGS

CANADIAN EQUITY FUNDS

LION KNOWLEDGE INDUSTRIES FUND $ ↑ G #/* RSP CSC

Manager: Graham Henderson, since inception (1993)

MER: 2.90%

This was previously known as the Pacific Special Equity Fund. The revised goal is to focus on Canadian knowledge-based companies, which can include technology companies, communications firms, biotechnology companies, media and entertainment ventures, plus a lot more. All in all, it's quite a broad mandate. Results haven't been impressive recently, either in the old guise or the new one. The fund lost 8.7% in the year to June 30/98 and seems to be having problems finding a winning direction. Risk is on the high side. The concept is good but you may wish to bide your time until there is evidence the manager can make it work effectively.

MACKENZIE FINANCIAL CORPORATION

THE COMPANY

This is one of the largest organizations in the country in terms of the total number of funds offered, as well as assets under management. As of mid-1998, the company had 42 funds available to the public through its four lines: Industrial, Ivy, Universal, and, brand new to the list, Cundill. The latter is Mackenzie's latest acquisition, in a deal reached shortly before this edition was put to bed. As a result, the Cundill funds have been moved to this listing, instead of being shown as an independent group.

Since Mackenzie now offers four families, it's important to differentiate between them when making your investment decisions. Here's a summary of each one's approach, as I interpret it:

Cundill: Deep value bias, stocks at 50 cents on the dollar is the goal. Contrarian in approach; Peter Cundill was buying up Japan in early 1998 when no one else would touch it. Requires patience from investors.

Industrial: Mackenzie's roots. Funds here still place a big emphasis on the resource sector, although Bill Procter is trying to steer away from that. Traditional approach.

Ivy: Growth with reasonable risk. No big chances here. A conservative, straightforward style that most investors will feel comfortable with.

Universal: The go-go family. Higher risk, higher reward potential. Best suited to more aggressive investors.

Mackenzie also offers 17 STAR portfolios, managed by Garmaise Investment Technologies. These provide an asset allocation approach to investing suitable for a range of needs and objectives. The portfolios went through a major overhaul in July, 1998, clearing out some deadwood and adding new funds to the mix.

There are four different classes of portfolios:

Registered: Eligible for registered plans; contain foreign content up to the 20% limit.

Canadian: Eligible for registered plans; contain no foreign content funds but do provide foreign exposure through derivatives.

Investment: Blend of Canadian and foreign funds; not intended for registered plans.

Foreign: Completely foreign content; no Canadian exposure.

The portfolio approach has recently been expanded to a new product line, Keystone. It offers a blend of Mackenzie funds with those from other companies, including AGF, BPI, Beutel Goodman, Saxon, Sceptre, and Spectrum United. Garmaise Investment Technologies also takes care of the management for these.

THE DETAILS

NUMBER OF FUNDS:	41
ASSETS UNDER MANAGEMENT:	$24.9 BILLION
LOAD CHARGE:	FRONT: MAX. 5%; BACK: MAX. 5.5%
SWITCHING CHARGE:	2% MAXIMUM
WHERE SOLD:	ACROSS CANADA
HOW SOLD:	THROUGH BROKERS, DEALERS, AND FINANCIAL PLANNERS
PHONE NUMBER:	(416) 922-5322 OR 1-888-653-7070
WEB SITE ADDRESS:	WWW.MACKENZIEFINANCIAL.COM
E-MAIL ADDRESS:	INVEST@MACKENZIEFINANCIAL.COM

FUND SUMMARY

CUNDILL FUNDS

$$$$ - NONE
$$$ - SECURITY
$$ - VALUE
$ - NONE
NR - NONE

BEST CHOICES: SECURITY
BEST FOR RRSPs: SECURITY
BEST UNRATEDS: N/A

THE INDUSTRIAL GROUP OF FUNDS

$$$$ - CASH MANAGEMENT
$$$ - BOND, DIVIDEND GROWTH, HORIZON, PENSION
$$ - AMERICAN, BALANCED, INCOME, MORTGAGE SECURITIES
$ - EQUITY, GROWTH, SHORT-TERM
NR - NONE

BEST CHOICES: CASH MANAGEMENT, DIVIDEND GROWTH, HORIZON
BEST FOR RRSPs: CASH MANAGEMENT, HORIZON, PENSION
BEST UNRATEDS: N/A

IVY FUNDS

$$$$ - CANADIAN
$$$ - ENTERPRISE, GROWTH AND INCOME, MORTGAGE
$$ - FOREIGN EQUITY
$ - NONE
NR - NONE

BEST CHOICES: CANADIAN
BEST FOR RRSPS: CANADIAN, GROWTH AND INCOME
BEST UNRATEDS: N/A

THE UNIVERSAL FUNDS

$$$$ - NONE
$$$ - CANADIAN GROWTH, EUROPEAN OPPORTUNITIES, FUTURE
$$ - AMERICAS, INTERNATIONAL STOCK, U.S. EMERGING
GROWTH, WORLD BALANCED RRSP, WORLD INCOME
RRSP, WORLD TACTICAL BOND
$ - CANADIAN RESOURCE, FAR EAST, JAPAN, PRECIOUS
METALS, U.S. MONEY MARKET, WORLD ASSET
ALLOCATION, WORLD EMERGING GROWTH, WORLD
GROWTH RRSP
NR - CANADIAN BALANCED, WORLD HIGH YIELD, WORLD REAL
ESTATE, WORLD SCIENCE & TECHNOLOGY, WORLD VALUE

BEST CHOICES: CANADIAN GROWTH, EUROPEAN OPPORTUNITIES, FUTURE
BEST FOR RRSPS: CANADIAN GROWTH
BEST UNRATEDS: WORLD SCIENCE & TECHNOLOGY

FUND RATINGS

CUNDILL FUNDS

CANADIAN EQUITY FUNDS

CUNDILL SECURITY FUND $$$ ↓ G # RSP CE

Manager: Tim McElvaine, since 1992

MER: 2.39%

This fund has been around since '79 but it never did much
of anything until McElvaine joined the Cundill organiza-
tion in '92. Since then it has blossomed as McElvaine has
successfully implemented the value investing principles of
Dr. Benjamin Graham. However, he's been having diffi-

culty finding bargains in the high markets we've been experiencing. As a result, the fund has been holding unusually high levels of cash. Performance is still good, however; return for the year to June 30/98 was 17.8%. Five-year average annual compound rate of return (which roughly corresponds with McElvaine's tenure) is well above average, at 17.5%. Portfolio is kept small and easily manageable. One word of caution, however. Most of the foreign component of this fund is held in potentially volatile Japanese stocks (Japan is the new happy hunting ground for the bargain-driven Cundill organization). That could help boost returns if things go well, but it could also have the opposite effect.

U.S. AND INTERNATIONAL EQUITY FUNDS

CUNDILL VALUE FUND $$ ↓ G # £ IE

Manager: Peter Cundill, since 1974

MER: 2.36%

Peter Cundill told unitholders at the May annual meeting in Toronto that his fund has experienced two major problems over the years: "in too early and out too early". By that he meant he acquired large positions in unloved companies long before anyone else discovered them, and then sold them before they had maxxed out their profits. This type of approach reduces portfolio risk (one of the long-term advantages of this fund). But it can also suppress returns. Right now, we're seeing yet another replay. Last year, the fund began selling off its winning positions in Europe, which continued to stay hot. Instead, bargain-hunter Cundill and his associates turned their sights on Japan, where they are discovering one company after another that is trading at well below break-up value. The portfolio was a third in Japanese stocks at the start of '98, and the managers were adding more. Now, this bet will likely pay off at some point. As Cundill says, all you need to invest in his fund is "patience, patience, patience". But there is no way of knowing how long that will be. In the meantime, returns are slumping; the fund actually lost 6.2% in the year to June 30/98. All the long-term results have also fallen to below average. That leaves me no choice but to drop the rating back to $$, until we see evidence that this latest move is going to start producing better returns. Don't put any new money here until there are signs the Japanese market has turned around.

INDUSTRIAL GROUP OF FUNDS

CANADIAN EQUITY FUNDS

INDUSTRIAL DIVIDEND GROWTH FUND $$$ → G/FI #/* RSP INC

Manager: Bill Procter, since 1994

MER: 2.38%

Over the past year, this fund has moved a lot closer to being a true dividend fund. The portfolio composition is now heavily weighted towards dividend-paying equities, with names like Bank of Montreal and EdperBrascan among the largest holdings. The pure growth segment of the portfolio was at just 5% in the first half of '98. This is a good choice for cash flow, in that it pays a monthly distribution of 5 cents per share. That works out to a 3.8% yield based on the net asset value in mid-'98. But be aware that a large part of that payout is really a return of capital. In fact, in calendar 1997, more than two thirds of the distribution fell into this category. This is a non-taxable payment that really amounts to getting some of your own money back because the fund is not generating enough internal cash flow to fulfill the promised payment. That's why it is better to hold this fund outside a registered plan. Such payments made within a RRIF or RRSP would be taxable if withdrawn, but are received tax-free outside. Total returns have been very good; in fact, this has been the best Canadian equity performer in the Industrial group over the past several years. Gain for the 12 months to June 30/98 was 21.7%, and the five-year average annual compound rate of return is almost 17%. This is a good choice for a conservative portfolio held outside an RRSP/RRIF.

INDUSTRIAL EQUITY FUND $ ↑ G #/* RSP CSC

Manager: Ian Osler, since 1997

MER: 2.42%

The big news here is that Fred Sturm, who headed up this disappointing fund for a decade, has handed over the reins to a successor, Ian Osler. Sturm will continue to manage other Mackenzie funds that focus on the resource sector. Investors can only hope the changeover signals better times ahead, as happened with Industrial Horizon when a managerial change was made there. Certainly, this fund has been a disaster in recent years. If you had been in it for five years up to the end of June, you would have lost an average of 5.9% annually. The only other funds in the small- to mid-cap category that have fared worse are those run by the highly aggressive Sagit company of Vancouver. Main reason for the poor results was a heavy emphasis on the weak resource sector. The new manager has trimmed that back some, but more than a third of the assets were still in resources in the first half of 1998. Osler is increasing the fund's exposure to mid-cap companies and has adopted a rigorous value approach to the selection of stocks. This should improve returns over time but I suggest you put your money elsewhere until we see clear evidence that a turnaround has started.

INDUSTRIAL GROWTH FUND $ → G #/* RSP CE

Manager: Alex Christ, since inception (1967)

MER: 2.37%

"But how," sighed a Mackenzie employee, who for the sake of his job shall be nameless here, "do we tell the chairman that we're taking this fund away from him?" Not easily. But someone should suck up their gut and break the news. Alex Christ is one of the founders of Mackenzie Financial. He is a legend in the mutual fund business and one of the pioneers of the hugely successful Canadian fund industry. At one time, he was a brilliant manager — Industrial Growth was one of the great funds of the '80s. But let's be blunt. He doesn't appear to have it any more and it's time to pass the reins. Returns, which have been poor for some time, are deteriorating still more. The fund lost 6.2% for the year to June 30/98, during a period when the average Canadian equity fund was generating double-digit gains. Meantime, the companion Industrial Horizon Fund, which was handed to Bill Procter in late '96, was chalking up a nice 15.4% advance. Assets have been bleeding away as the performance has weakened. This was once the largest equity fund in Canada; it is now down to just over $800 million in size. The portfolio continues to be heavily weighted to the natural resource sector, with more than half the assets in that area in the first half of '98. When resources stage a rally, this fund will look great. But who knows how long that will be. The safety record is as weak as the performance. Not recommended.

INDUSTRIAL HORIZON FUND $$$ → G #/* RSP CE

Manager: Bill Procter, since 1996

MER: 2.37%

Bill Procter assumed responsibility for the portfolio of this long-time laggard in November, '96 and immediately started to implement changes. The natural resource component of this fund was pared down (it was 23% of the portfolio in the first half of '98). The financial services and industrial products sectors have been boosted. The number of stocks held has been cut in half, from 80 to about 40. The mandate was clearly defined to focus on large-cap companies in established industries. Procter is a bottom-up manager who chooses stocks on the basis of fundamentals. His predecessor, Neil Lovatt, took a top-down sector approach, similar to that still being employed by Industrial Growth. The improved results speak for themselves. The fund gained 15.4% in the year to June 30/98, and showed a two-year average annual compound rate of return of 18.6%. If you're looking for a sound, middle-of-the-road fund from Mackenzie, this one is respectable again. Rating moves up to $$$.

U.S. AND INTERNATIONAL EQUITY FUNDS

INDUSTRIAL AMERICAN FUND $$ → G #/* £ USE

Manager: Veronica Onyskiw, since 1996

MER: 2.38%

This fund invests in a diversified portfolio of U.S. stocks, with an emphasis on blue-chip issues, especially multinational corporations. The manager's style is a combination of value and growth. In the first half of '98, the portfolio focus was on the consumer products, interest sensitive, and technology categories, much the same as the year previous. Although the fund has been profitable in recent years (gain of 21% in the 12 months to June 30/98), results continue to lag behind the competition in the U.S. equity category, both short and long term.

BALANCED FUNDS

INDUSTRIAL BALANCED FUND $$ → FI/G #/* RSP CBAL

Manager: Tim Gleeson, since 1991

MER: 2.37%

Mackenzie Financial offers four balanced funds, each with a different investment emphasis. This one comes the closest to a true balanced fund, with equity and fixed-income securities each representing 40% to 60% of the portfolio at any given time. The equity side of the portfolio invests in mid- to large-cap stocks. The bonds are mainly Government of Canada issues with a small amount of corporate holdings. Foreign content is at the 20% maximum allowable. Recent returns have been spotty. After a poor result in the year to June 30/96, the fund rebounded with a gain of 24.3% over the next 12 months. But just when it seemed things were going well, performance slackened off again and the gain for the year to June 30/98 was a miserly 3.2%. This fund needs to show more consistency before any further rating increase will be considered.

INDUSTRIAL INCOME FUND $$ → FI/G #/* RSP CBAL

Manager: Tim Gleeson, since 1992

MER: 1.86%

This is not a true fixed-income fund, despite the name, hence its inclusion in the balanced section. Federal government bonds are the core holding, but the manager may also invest up to 30% of the fund's assets in stocks. The fund's portfolio was 77% in fixed-income securities and cash in the first half of '98, and 23% in equities. Despite that, this fund actually generated a better return over the year to June 30/98 than the companion Balanced Fund, even though the latter has a much heavier stock allocation. There are now two classes of this fund available. The A units are the original ones, and pay an annual distribution of $1 each, a portion of which is a non-taxable return of capital (which means the portfolio is not generating enough cash to make up the whole amount so they give you some of your money back). The B units pay an annual distribution of 40 cents each. Both the A and B units are otherwise the same. You would choose the A units if cash flow is important to you. If they are your choice, the fund is better held outside a registered plan. If you choose the B units, more money will be left in the fund and the value of your units will be worth more over time.

INDUSTRIAL MORTGAGE
SECURITIES FUND $$ ↓ FI/G #/* RSP CBAL

Managers: Tim Gleeson and Chris Kresic, since 1997

MER: 1.86%

This is a fixed-income fund with some equity exposure (maximum 25%) to provide extra growth potential. Mackenzie Financial ranks this as the most conservative of their four balanced funds. At least half the portfolio is in mortgage-backed securities, which are guaranteed for principal and interest by Canada Mortgage and Housing Corporation (so, in effect, by the federal government). Another 25% will normally be in Government of Canada bonds. In the first half of '98, the fund was even more conservatively positioned than these target ratios would suggest, with 60% in mortgage-backed securities and only 15% in stocks. They must have picked the wrong stocks, however, because the gain for the year to June 30/98 was a very weak 0.6%. Even given the reduced risk, that is not a very good show. Rating is dropped a notch as a result. Name changed from Mackenzie Income Fund in December, '92.

INDUSTRIAL PENSION FUND $$$ → G/FI #/* RSP CBAL

Manager: Bill Procter, since 1995

MER: 2.40%

I hope Mackenzie is paying Bill Procter well. He's propping up their Industrial group of funds almost single-handedly. Horizon, Dividend Growth, and this one are the only decent equity/balanced performers in this lineup. Maybe they should turn all the rest over to him as well. This fund invests mainly in stocks, with a small bond component tossed in (21% in the first half of '98 plus a large 16% cash position). So this is the fund to choose if you're looking for a Mackenzie entry that emphasizes stocks but offers some fixed-income exposure as well. It's been by far the best performer of the Mackenzie four-horse balanced entry in recent years. Gain for the 12 months to June 30/98 was 14.6%. Three-year average annual compound rate of return (which corresponds to the period Procter has been in charge) was 19.5%, well above average for the balanced category. Because of the higher equity content the risk factor will be greater here than you'll find in the other Industrial balanced funds. But the long-term growth potential is also better. Don't choose this one if cash distributions are important to you; there are none to speak of. I like this one for an RRSP.

FIXED INCOME AND MONEY MARKET FUNDS

INDUSTRIAL BOND FUND $$$ ↑ FI #/* RSP CB

Managers: Tim Gleeson, since 1996, and Chris Kresic, since 1997

MER: 1.87%

The portfolio of this fund consists mainly of Government of Canada issues, although some high-quality corporates may also be included. In the first half of '98, the portfolio weighting was tilted towards longer term issues, which contributed to above-average returns. This is consistent with the more aggressive management style we've seen in this fund recently. That approach will continue to work well as long as interest rates stay weak, but poses dangers if rates go back up. Nonetheless, the numbers are good, with a 10% return for the year to June 30/98 and an average annual three-year compound rate of return of 11.5%.

INDUSTRIAL CASH MANAGEMENT FUND $$$$ ↓ C # RSP CMM

Manager: Mackenzie Team, since 1986

MER: 0.50%

One of the better money market funds in the country. Combines above-average returns with a high degree of safety (the entire portfolio is normally invested in

Government of Canada T-bills). Returns are well above average, thanks in part to a very low management expense ratio. (Compare this fund's MER to that of the companion Short-Term Fund and you can immediately see why this one consistently outperforms it.) As a bonus, this fund offers good chequing privileges for non-registered accounts over $3,000. Try to get it without paying any load fee. Minimum investment is $1,500. Available to investors who buy Mackenzie funds on a front-end load basis.

INDUSTRIAL SHORT-TERM FUND $ ↓ C * RSP CMM

Manager: Mackenzie Team, since 1991

MER: 1.25%

Investment objectives and portfolio are similar to companion Cash Management Fund. However, there are three big differences: 1) this fund has no chequing privileges; 2) sales charge is on a back-end load basis; and 3) management fee is much higher, reducing return accordingly. The Cash Management Fund is by far the better choice if you are eligible for it.

IVY FUNDS

CANADIAN EQUITY FUNDS

IVY CANADIAN FUND $$$$ ↓ G #/* RSP CE

Manager: Jerry Javasky, since 1997

MER: 2.38%

Former manager Gerald Coleman made the headlines in early '97 when he walked away from this top-performing fund to join the C.I. group. His place was taken by Jerry Javasky, who worked with Coleman at the United Funds and came over to Mackenzie with him in '92. The Ivy group was specifically created for their value-investing style, which is a much different approach to stock selection than you'll find in the Industrial or Universal groups. Javasky is his own man, however, and one of his first moves was to dump out several of the stocks in the portfolio. His target is a core of about 25 positions, each representing about 4% of the total assets. So the fund under his tenure is not being run in exactly the same way, although the underlying approach to stock selection remains constant. So is the objective, which is to provide above-average returns at below-average risk. Thus far, this fund has been very successful at that. Returns are above average for all time periods and the fund has shown no signs of faltering since Javasky took over. Gain for the year to June 30/98 was 17.4%, well above the norm for the Canadian equity category. And this was despite the fact that the fund was in a very high cash position for much of that time. The safety record remains unblemished — not a single 12-month period in which an investor would have lost money, according to ATP analysis. That earns the fund an A rating in the risk category from Altamira's Wilfred Vos. Safety as well as returns — the combination every investor is looking for. If you're interested in building a Mackenzie portfolio, this fund should certainly be part of it. It's the best one in their stable and the rating goes up to $$$$ to underline the point.

IVY ENTERPRISE FUND $$$ → G #/* RSP CSC

Manager: Chuck Roth, since 1997

MER: 2.39%

Jerry Javasky had been running this small- to mid-cap fund, but his expanded responsibilities elsewhere in the Mackenzie organization necessitated a change and Chuck Roth assumed the manager's role in late 1997 after moving to Mackenzie from Ultravest. If his name doesn't ring a bell, check out the entry for the Colonia funds in the *1998 Buyer's Guide*, particularly the Colonia Special Growth Fund, which has a similar mandate to Ivy Enterprise. Roth did a terrific job with that one, bringing it in as the top-performing fund in its category over the three-year period to June 30/97. There is no reason to believe that the move over to Mackenzie will cause him to lose his touch, and in fact Ivy Enterprise posted a better-than-average return for the small-cap category in the first half of '98. The portfolio is small (about 30 companies) and is not heavily weighted towards any particular sector. Roth has been sitting on a large cash position (20% in the first half of '98), waiting for good values to emerge. The risk here is higher because of the nature of the mandate, but aggressive investors who go in for the longer term should be well rewarded. Formerly called Mackenzie Equity Fund.

U.S. AND INTERNATIONAL EQUITY FUNDS

IVY FOREIGN EQUITY FUND $$ ↓ G #/* £ IE

Manager: Bill Kanko, since 1997

MER: 2.39%

Bill Kanko assumed responsibility for this portfolio in mid-'97, taking over from Jerry Javasky. He brings a somewhat different style to the table, although his overall bottom-up method of stock selection is fully consistent with the Ivy mandate. This fund invests mainly in U.S. stocks, with some non-North American companies added for diversity. But don't be misled — basically what you are buying here is a U.S. stock fund with an emphasis on multinational firms. A big chunk of the portfolio (24%) was in cash in the first half of '98, but the fund still managed a tidy profit. It's difficult to know how to measure it, though. For the 12 months to June 30/98, the gain was 21.5%. That was above average for the international equity category but below par if you compare this to U.S. equity funds as a group. Take your pick, but the heavy emphasis on U.S. issues leads me to the opinion that the more accurate comparison is there. Very good safety profile so far, with no losing 12-month periods. The Universal Growth Fund was merged into this one in mid-1998.

BALANCED FUNDS

IVY GROWTH AND INCOME FUND $$$ ↓ FI/G #/* RSP CBAL

Manager: Jerry Javasky, since 1997

MER: 2.12%

Last year I commented that this wasn't a true balanced fund, since bond holdings were minimal. That situation has since been rectified and this fund now fits more comfortably into its classification. As of the first half of '98, bonds represented about 30% of the mix, cash was another 22% and the rest was in Canadian and foreign stocks.

However, this fund has no set asset allocation parameters, so the ratios could swing dramatically in any direction at any time. The changeover from Gerald Coleman to Jerry Javasky has been smooth and this fund continues to produce very decent returns for investors. Gain for the year to June 30/98 was 16.6%, well above average for the Canadian balanced category. Excellent safety record. If you're looking for a sound balanced fund with growth potential for your RRSP, your choice in the Mackenzie lineup should come down to this one or Industrial Pension Fund.

FIXED INCOME AND MONEY MARKET FUNDS

IVY MORTGAGE FUND $$$ ↓ FI #/* RSP M

Manager: MRS Trust, since 1994

MER: 1.89%

This fund invests mainly in CMHC-insured residential first mortgages, of varying maturities. As of mid-1998, the mortgage component was comprised of approximately 20% five-year mortgages, 28% four-year, 16% three-year, 10% two-year, and the remainder with one year or less until maturity. The average rate on the mortgages held by the Fund is 6.88%. Returns had been better than average for the mortgage fund category, but slumped to just 4% in the year to June 30/98. Longer term results are still above par, however. The fund pays distributions on a monthly basis, which makes it useful for cash-flow purposes. To the end of July 1998, year-to-date payments totalled 5.6 cents a unit (about 8/10 of a cent a month). Based on a unit price of about $2, that works out to an annual cash-on-cash yield of about 4.8%, which is pretty good for a fund of this type. The combination of income and safety makes this fund a decent choice for a RRIF.

CANADIAN EQUITY FUNDS

UNIVERSAL CANADIAN GROWTH FUND $$$ → G #/* RSP CE

Managers: Dina DeGeer, since 1995; Dennis Starritt, since 1996

MER: 2.39%

The performance results published in the media show only recent results, making it appear that this fund has no history, but it does. It was managed by Mackenzie Financial for many years for the old Universal Group (now Canadian International), under the name of Universal Canadian Equity. Mackenzie bought this and four other Universal funds early in '93 and this fund's future was in limbo for some time. But now it has been resurrected, with two former Trimark managers overseeing operations. They maintain a relatively small portfolio of about 20–25 Canadian companies and 5–8 international stocks. The fund posted an above-average return for the year to June 30/98, gaining 12.7%. Despite this, at mid-year the managers reported that they were not happy with their results. However, a strong cash position (about 30%) provided a cushion against the slumping market, and gave the managers some serious buying power to snap up bargains as they emerged. This fund has shown a great deal of improvement in the past couple of years, warranting a promotion to $$$.

UNIVERSAL CANADIAN RESOURCE FUND $ ↑ G #/* RSP SEC

Manager: Fred Sturm, since 1991

MER: 2.39%

It has been a terrible time for resource funds, and this one didn't escape the carnage, with a loss of 25.7% for the 12 months to June 30/98. But then what could you expect, with world commodity prices at 12-year lows. Not even the greatest fund manager can turn water into wine. Despite the tough times, manager Fred Sturm remains fully invested, with only 5% cash, believing we will soon see a rebound in the resource sector. It would be nice if he's right, but I'm skeptical. Then there's the risk factor to consider: ATP figures show almost an even chance of a gain or a loss over any 12-month period. Worse, there's a 15% chance you still could be down after five years in this one. In my view, the short-term prospects are not encouraging and I don't recommend committing new dollars at this stage. When resource stocks do recover, the ride up may be very fast. I advise you to step off after chalking up a good gain because of the cyclical nature of these funds.

UNIVERSAL FUTURE FUND $$$ → G #/* RSP CE

Manager: John Rohr, since 1993

MER: 2.38%

The mandate of this fund is to focus on technology companies, with about half the portfolio committed to this sector. The balance is supposed to be invested in other growth-oriented stocks, although 17% of the portfolio was in cash in the first half of '98, and another 17% was in Mackenzie's beloved resource sector, which, on the surface at least, hardly seems to qualify for a future-oriented portfolio. Although this is perceived as a small-cap fund by some people, the portfolio contains many large companies such as BCE, Magna, Petro-Canada, and Northern Telecom. So don't be misled. Foreign content is kept near the maximum 20% limit to allow significant investment in the U.S. technology market. Recent results have been good; the fund gained 12.7% over the year to June 30/98, which was above average for Canadian stock funds as a group. Note that the name was changed from Industrial Future Fund in January, '98.

UNIVERSAL PRECIOUS METALS FUND $ ↑ G #/* RSP PM

Manager: Fred Sturm, since inception (1994)

MER: 2.42%

This fund has a widely diversified portfolio across the precious metals sector including both senior and junior companies and a small position (in mid-'98) in gold and silver bullion. Manager Fred Sturm sees the cheap prices in the industry as a buying opportunity and has been maintaining a very low cash position. That means the fund was pounded hard as the price of gold stocks sank. Loss for the year to June 30/98 was a whopping 33%. For speculators only.

U.S. AND INTERNATIONAL EQUITY FUNDS

UNIVERSAL AMERICAS FUND $$ ↑ G #/* £ AE

Manager: Paul Baran, since 1998

MER: 2.55%

The name of this fund was changed from Universal American Fund in April, '94 to reflect the inclusion of Latin American and Canadian issues in the portfolio. As of mid-'98, U.S. issues dominated, representing almost half the portfolio. Canadian stocks were 10% of the holdings with Latin America accounting for the rest except for a small amount of cash. New manager Paul Baran was in the process of taking advantage of the weakness in Latin markets to build positions there, with a target of 40% of the portfolio. That may pay off down the road, but right now the fund is in a slump with a gain of just 3% for the 12 months to June 30/98. The advantage of this fund is that it offers a more balanced way to obtain exposure to the up-and-down Latin markets while laying off some of the risk. Still, you have to expect some volatility if you go this route.

UNIVERSAL EUROPEAN OPPORTUNITIES FUND $$$ ↑ G #/* £ EE

Manager: Steven Peak (Henderson Investors of London), since inception (1994)

MER: 2.48%

This isn't your typical, run-of-the-mill European entry. It's a higher risk way to approach the European market, with above-average return potential and above-average risk. The fund concentrates on three areas: small companies in mature economies (e.g., Britain and Germany); European emerging markets (Poland, Hungary, and the like); and special situations such as government privatizations. As of the beginning of August, 1998, most of the portfolio was concentrated in the traditional markets of western Europe, with only 1% of the assets in the old Iron Curtain countries. Results have been very good, with a three-year average annual compound rate of return of 35.8% to June 30/98. But don't lose sight of the higher risk involved. A good choice for the more aggressive investor.

UNIVERSAL FAR EAST FUND $ ↑ G #/* £ FEE

Manager: Diahann Brown, since inception (1993)

MER: 2.58%

Wow! All Far East funds have had their problems, but this one lost more than half its value in just a year (-50.7% to June 30/98). A few others were worse, but not many. Manager Diahann Brown told unitholders in mid-'98 that she isn't convinced the worst is over and remains cautious. Cash has been raised and she's focusing on companies with strong balance sheets that are in a good position to ride out the crisis. But it's going to take a while. I suggest you put your money elsewhere for now.

UNIVERSAL INTERNATIONAL STOCK FUND $$ ↑ G #/* £ IE

Manager: Iain Clark (Henderson Investors of London), since 1992

MER: 2.45%

This fund does not invest in Canada or the U.S. As of mid-'98, the main focus was on Europe, with small positions in Latin America and the Far East. That balance helped the fund to a big 26.7% gain in the first half of '98, as European markets took off. Longer term results are fair. The portfolio includes both developed and emerging markets, and manager Iain Clark seeks to exploit the timing of stock market cycles to maximize returns. Historically high risk factor remains a negative. Name changed in January, '98 from Universal World Equity Fund. Prior to that, it was known as the Industrial Global Fund.

UNIVERSAL JAPAN FUND $ ↑ G #/* £ FEE

Manager: Campbell Gunn (Thornton Management), since 1996

MER: 2.54%

This fund invests across the full spectrum of Japanese stocks, from the giant multinationals to small, emerging companies. Like most other Japan funds, it was hit hard in the year to June 30/98, with a loss of just under 24%. Your only solace if you own units is that many other Japanese funds did worse. There's no way of knowing when the

Japanese economy is going to turn around and head off into a new boom period, so unless you're a speculative investor you may wish to stay on the sidelines for now.

UNIVERSAL U.S. EMERGING
GROWTH FUND $$ ↑ G #/* £ USSC

Manager: James Broadfoot, since inception (1992)

MER: 2.40%

This fund was sailing along as nicely as you please when, whump! A flat tire! The U.S. small-cap market went soft, and this fund took a tumble. It dropped almost 7% in value over the year to June 30/97. However, it bounced back in the next 12 months with a gain of 20.2%, slightly better than average for the U.S. small-cap category according to numbers published by *The Financial Post*. The focus is on smaller U.S. companies with high growth potential. Manager James Broadfoot operates out of Mackenzie's Boca Raton, Florida office. His style is not to do a lot of on-site company inspections, but rather to gather information from a variety of sources, including the brokerage community and industry conferences. His portfolio is well diversi-fied, with business services the largest asset class in mid-'98. For more aggressive investors only.

UNIVERSAL WORLD
EMERGING GROWTH FUND $ ↑ G #/* £ IE

Manager: Peter Bassett (Henderson Investors of London), since incep-tion (1993)

MER: 2.54%

The mandate of this fund is somewhat unusual. It invests in a combination of larger companies in emerging markets and smaller companies in developed markets (except Canada and the U.S.). That is supposed to give the manager the best of both worlds to choose from, but a counter-argument might be made to the effect that this fund ends up trying to straddle the fence with an unclear direction. Recent results are weak; return for the year to June 30/98 showed a loss of 24.1% as emerging markets tanked. However, the fund's three-year record is marginally profitable, which is something of a feat in these times. Still, this is a volatile area right now, and only suited to brave investors.

UNIVERSAL WORLD GROWTH RRSP FUND $ → G #/* RSP IE

Managers: Barbara Trebbi and Michael Landry, since inception (1994)

MER: 2.44%

This is one of those pseudo-Canadian funds that has been created to get around the foreign content rules that govern registered plans. In this case, the managers invest mainly in futures contracts on various international exchanges in order to keep the fund RRSP eligible. These may include plays on both developed and emerging markets. As of the beginning of August, '98 about 46% of the portfolio was in Europe (including the U.K.), with 15% in the U.S. Three-year returns are about average (annual gain of 15% for the period to June 30/98). But more recent results have been weak. Strictly for those who want to go beyond 20% foreign content in their RRSPs.

BALANCED FUNDS

UNIVERSAL WORLD ASSET
ALLOCATION FUND $ ↑ G/FI #/* £ IBAL

Managers: Charles Gave and John Ricciardi (Cursitor-Eaton Asset Management), since inception (1993)

MER: 2.47%

This fund invests primarily in six economies: the U.S., the U.K., Germany, Japan, France, and Switzerland; however, other countries do sneak into the mix on occasion, such as Spain and Italy in mid-1998. The portfolio may hold stocks, bonds, short-term notes, and gold. This is not a balanced fund in the usual sense. Asset allocation decisions are made on the basis of economic conditions and market outlook, and the fund could be entirely in a single asset class at any time. Returns were very weak up to the first half of 1998 when the fund suddenly caught fire and added 22.5% in just six months. Main reason was zero exposure to the Far East and a strong weighting in Europe, where stocks took off. But six months does not a track record make, especially after several years of indifferent results. We'll hold off upping the rating for a while and see what happens.

UNIVERSAL WORLD
BALANCED RRSP FUND $$ → FI/G #/* RSP IBAL

Managers: Michael Landry and Barbara Trebbi, since inception (1994)

MER: 2.41%

This is a pseudo-Canadian fund that uses market index futures to provide investors with international exposure while retaining full RRSP/RRIF eligibility. The portfolio is broadly diversified, with the emphasis on Europe in the first half of '98. You'd expect the fund to have produced good returns as a result of that, but the gain for the 12 months to June 30/98 was a meagre 5.7%. That was very disappointing compared to the strong showing in previous years. Part of the reason was the fund's exposure to Asia and emerging markets (the latter comprised 13% of the portfolio in mid-'98). Worth considering if you're at the 20% foreign content limit and want more international weighting in your retirement plan, but not as strongly recommended as previously. Not recommended outside an RRSP or RRIF.

FIXED INCOME AND MONEY MARKET FUNDS

UNIVERSAL U.S. MONEY MARKET FUND $ ↓ C #/* £ IMM

Manager: Mackenzie team, since inception (1994)

MER: 1.25%

This is a rather undistinguished U.S.-dollar money fund. Returns have been below the level of many others in its category (gain of 3.7% for the year to June 30/98, plus currency profit). Plus it is not eligible for registered plans, even as foreign content. There's a maximum front-end load of 2% or you can buy on a back-end load basis, which I would not advise. Conclusion: If you want a U.S. money fund, this is not the best choice.

UNIVERSAL WORLD INCOME RRSP FUND $$ ↓ FI #/* RSP IB

Managers: Michael Borowsky and Brian Barrett, since 1998

MER: 2.15%

Formerly the Universal Canadian Bond Fund, this Mackenzie Financial entry has been converted into an RRSP-eligible international bond fund, investing in foreign bonds and bond index futures. The fund also acquired a new management team in the spring of 1998. All that makes the long-term track record of the old fund obsolete. Recent results, which is all you can really judge by, have been above average, with a return of 5.2% for the six months to June 30/98. Very good safety rating.

UNIVERSAL WORLD TACTICAL BOND FUND $$ ↑ FI #/* £ IB

Managers: Charles Gave and John Ricciardi (Cursitor-Eaton Asset Management), since inception (1994)

MER: 2.32%

The goal of this fund is to invest in the world's safest bond markets, with the idea of appealing to investors who want to minimize risk. As of the beginning of August, '98 only three countries were represented in the portfolio: Germany (33%), the U.S. (24%), and the U.K. (7%). The balance (36%) was in cash. There's no doubt that from a credit perspective, you won't get much better quality than that and performance has started to pick up, with a gain of 8.9% in the first half of '98. Surprisingly, however, the risk rating is not good; the Vos analysis gives this fund an E for safety (the lowest rating) in the international bond category (that can result from other factors besides the quality of the bonds in the portfolio; for example, duration). The Universal World Income RRSP Fund has been the stronger performer over time and has a better safety record, so it would be the preferred choice, especially for registered plans.

STAR PORTFOLIOS

BALANCED FUNDS

STAR FOREIGN BALANCED
GROWTH AND INCOME PORTFOLIO $$ → FI/G #/* £ IBAL

Manager: Garmaise Investment Technologies, since inception (1995)

MER: 0.10%

All STAR portfolios are funds of funds. They invest exclusively in other Mackenzie funds, with the mix varying depending on the investor's objective. This portfolio takes a balanced approach with an emphasis on international investing. It has been one of the better STAR performers recently with a gain of 13.7% for the year to June 30/98, but longer term results are still below average. This, along with most other STAR portfolios, underwent a major overhaul in mid-'98. The Universal World Science and Technology Fund and the Universal European Opportunities Fund were added to the mix, while Universal Precious Metals and Universal World Asset Allocation were eliminated and Industrial American reduced. Other funds include Ivy Foreign Equity, Universal International Stock, and Universal World Tactical Bond. Recent weighting has been heavily towards stocks.

STAR FOREIGN MAXIMUM
LONG-TERM GROWTH PORTFOLIO $ ↑ G/FI #/* £ IBAL

Manager: Garmaise Investment Technologies, since inception (1995)

MER: 0.10%

As the name suggests, this portfolio aims at generating above-average, long-term returns, but the price is more risk. Previous components included the Universal Precious Metals Fund and the Universal Far East Fund, which have been big drags on performance. Gain for the year to June 30/98 was a mere 1.4%. This was another fund that went through a major revamp in mid-'98 with the Precious Metals Fund dropped, along with the Universal World Asset Allocation Fund. Two fixed-income funds were added, Universal World Income RRSP and Universal

World Tactical Bond. These changes should reduce volatility and provide better long-term balance. However, the rating stays low until we see some results.

STAR INVESTMENT BALANCED
GROWTH AND INCOME PORTFOLIO $$ → FI/G #/* IBAL

Manager: Garmaise Investment Technologies, since inception (1995)

MER: 0.10%

There are so many STAR portfolios that after a while it becomes difficult to understand the nuances between each one. This one places a dual emphasis on capital growth and income flow. The funds held run the spectrum from the conservative Ivy Mortgage Fund to the much higher risk Universal World Emerging Growth Fund. Some of these combinations make me uncomfortable! This fund has had okay returns, but nothing to get excited about. Three-year average annual compound rate of return to June 30/98 was 12%. The July overhaul saw the removal of the Universal World Asset Allocation Fund from the mix and a reduction of the equity weight to 55%. The result should be less volatility.

STAR INVESTMENT CONSERVATIVE
INCOME AND GROWTH PORTFOLIO $$ → FI/G #/* IBAL

Manager: Garmaise Investment Technologies, since inception (1995)

MER: 0.10%

The goal of this portfolio is predictable cash flow, with preservation of capital. You would expect that to mean a mix of bond and mortgage funds, and they are present. But, until July, so were highly volatile funds like Universal Precious Metals and Universal European Opportunities, which don't seem to fit the mandate. Precious Metals is now gone, and European Opportunities has been reduced. In their place we now have the more conservative Ivy Foreign Equity Fund and Industrial Dividend Growth. Results prior to the shakeup weren't bad, however; the fund gained 13.9% for the year to June 30/98, which was better than average for the international balanced category. Longer term results are about average.

STAR INVESTMENT
LONG-TERM GROWTH PORTFOLIO $$ → G/FI #/* IBAL

Manager: Garmaise Investment Technologies, since inception (1995)

MER: 0.10%

The goal here is, of course, long-term growth. The portfolio is heavily weighted towards stock funds, including good performers like Ivy Canadian and Industrial Dividend Growth. But there were also some dogs in the mix, like Industrial Growth. Fortunately, it was dropped from the mix in the July, '98 overhaul. The overall result is about average for the international balanced category, with an annual return of 13.7% for the three years to June 30/98. Of course, because of the reallocation that took place in mid-'98, past performance is not a good indicator of what may happen going forward.

STAR INVESTMENT MAXIMUM
LONG-TERM GROWTH PORTFOLIO $ ↑ G/FI #/* IBAL

Manager: Garmaise Investment Technologies, since inception (1995)

MER: 0.10%

This portfolio tries to maximize long-term capital gains and uses several aggressive Universal funds to achieve that goal, along with Ivy Canadian and, for some strange reason, Industrial Equity (until July, that is; it was bumped in the shakeup that took place at that time). Results have been weak compared to several other STAR portfolios. This fund gained just 6.5% in the year to June 30/98. Other mixes have worked better, although the recent addition of Ivy Enterprise may help in the future.

STAR REGISTERED BALANCED
GROWTH AND INCOME PORTFOLIO $ → FI/G #/* RSP CBAL

Manager: Garmaise Investment Technologies, since inception (1995)

MER: 0.10%

This portfolio is designed for conservative investors who want decent growth potential without a lot of volatility. Seven funds are included in the mix, ranging from the ultra-conservative Ivy Mortgage Fund to more aggressive funds like Universal Americas. Blending funds like that together in one nest can be tricky, and the results here are not exciting. Average annual compound rate of return for the three years to June 30/98 was 12.1%. That wasn't awful but it was below average for the balanced fund category. The July, '98 overhaul added Ivy Foreign Equity to the mix and eliminated Universal Emerging Growth.

STAR REGISTERED CONSERVATIVE INCOME AND GROWTH PORTFOLIO $ → FI/G #/* RSP CBAL

Manager: Garmaise Investment Technologies, since inception (1995)

MER: 0.10%

This is the most conservative of the STAR balanced portfolios, at least in theory. However, one wonders what the Universal Precious Metals Fund and Industrial Growth Fund were doing in a so-called conservative portfolio. They certainly didn't do much to help returns. The folks at Garmaise and Mackenzie must have felt the same way because those two funds went bye-bye in July, replaced by Ivy Enterprise and Industrial Dividend Growth. Three-year results averaged 11.3% annually to June 30/98, not very impressive at first glance. However, the risk inherent in this portfolio is supposed to be lower, as a compensation.

STAR REGISTERED LONG-TERM GROWTH PORTFOLIO $ → G/FI #/* RSP CBAL

Manager: Garmaise Investment Technologies, since inception (1995)

MER: 0.10%

This fund offers a larger equity component than the Balanced or Conservative entries but it hasn't done much better, despite the bull market of the late '90s. Average annual compound rate of return for the three years to June 30/98 was just 12.3%, below average for the balanced category. Funds include Ivy Canadian, Industrial American, and Industrial Bond. Industrial Growth was also here, pulling down returns, but it was replaced in July by Universal Canadian Growth.

STAR REGISTERED MAXIMUM
LONG-TERM GROWTH PORTFOLIO $$ → G/FI #/* RSP CBAL

Manager: Garmaise Investment Technologies, since inception (1995)

MER: 0.10%

This fund portfolio is intended to maximize your long-term RRSP returns, and so far it has done better than the other registered offerings. Average annual return for the three years to June 30/98 was 13.2%. That was below average for the Canadian equity category, but not by a lot. Universal World Growth RRSP, one of the largest holdings, was reduced in July and Universal European Opportunities was added. Universal World Income RRSP and Ivy Canadian are other large holdings.

MANULIFE CABOT FUNDS

THE COMPANY

Some insurance companies now offer two distinct fund product lines — one that is tied directly to insurance contracts (so-called "segregated funds") and one that is a regular mutual fund line, available to everyone. The Cabot group is Manulife's non-segregated offering, launched in 1994. Altamira was involved in managing most of the funds but that relationship has been cut back following a high-profile takeover battle last year. Manulife-owned Elliott & Page replaced Altamira on two of the funds in 1998 — the Money Market Fund and the Diversified Bond Fund.

THE DETAILS

NUMBER OF FUNDS:	7
ASSETS UNDER MANAGEMENT:	$180 MILLION
LOAD CHARGE:	NO LOAD EXCEPT FOR A REDEMPTION FEE OF UP TO 2% FOR SALES OR TRANSFERS WITHIN 90 DAYS OF PURCHASE
SWITCHING CHARGE:	NONE, EXCEPT FOR THE ABOVE RESTRICTION
WHERE SOLD:	ACROSS CANADA
HOW SOLD:	THROUGH MUTUAL FUND REPRESENTATIVES LICENSED WITH MANULIFE SECURITIES
PHONE NUMBER:	1-888-MANULIFE
WEB SITE ADDRESS:	WWW.MANULIFE.COM
E-MAIL ADDRESS:	N/A

FUND SUMMARY

$$$$ - NONE
$$$ - BLUE CHIP, CANADIAN EQUITY, CANADIAN GROWTH
$$ - DIVERSIFIED BOND, EMERGING GROWTH, GLOBAL EQUITY
$ - MONEY MARKET
NR - NONE

BEST CHOICES: BLUE CHIP, CANADIAN EQUITY, CANADIAN GROWTH
BEST FOR RRSPs: CANADIAN EQUITY
BEST UNRATEDS: N/A

FUND RATINGS

CANADIAN EQUITY FUNDS

MANULIFE CABOT BLUE-CHIP FUND $$$ → G No RSP CE

Managers: Alex Sasso (Altamira), since 1998 and Richard Crook (Manulife International), since inception (1994)

MER: 2.50%

This fund invests primarily in units of the companion Canadian Equity Fund. The difference is that, in this case, allowable foreign content is maximized so investors receive exposure to international securities as well, without sacrificing RRSP eligibility. So the portfolio is spiced by a well-diversified mix of blue-chip stocks from around the world, names like British Telecom, Sony Corp., Unilever, Nestlé, and the like. You'd think this would mean better returns than those from the Canadian Equity Fund. You'd be wrong. Average annual compound rate of return for the three years to June 30/98 was 18.3%. The Canadian Equity Fund averaged 18.8%. Still, both were well above average for the peer group. But you have to wonder why the foreign content hasn't seemed to help this one.

MANULIFE CABOT CANADIAN EQUITY FUND $$$ → G No RSP CE

Manager: Alex Sasso (Altamira), since 1998

MER: 2.50%

This fund was managed by Altamira's Frank Mersch until his abrupt departure from the company. Alex Sasso picked up the pieces in May, 1998. This fund doesn't have the overseas component of the Blue-Chip Fund, confining itself to Canadian stocks with the emphasis on large corporations. The performance has been slightly better than that of the Blue-Chip Fund, with a one-year gain of 16.8% to June 30/98, and a three-year average annual compound rate of return of 18.8%. A good choice, but tends to be overlooked by investors.

MANULIFE CABOT CANADIAN GROWTH FUND $$$ ↑ G No RSP CE

Manager: Sue Coleman (Altamira), since inception (1994)

MER: 2.50%

This is the small-mid-cap entry in the Cabot lineup. It is designed for more aggressive investors, seeking above-average growth potential. Many of the companies are quite small, but you might recognize some of the names in the portfolio, such as Chapters and Sun Media. This fund had been doing quite well, but ran into tough sledding last year with a fractional loss. Three-year results are above average, however, at 18.9% a year to June 30/98.

MANULIFE CABOT EMERGING GROWTH FUND $$ ↑ G No RSP CE

Managers: Sue Coleman (Altamira) and Richard Crook (Manulife International), since inception (1994)

MER: 2.50%

The only difference between this and the Canadian Growth Fund is foreign content. In fact, the domestic section of this fund's portfolio consists only of units in the Canadian Growth Fund. The international section zeros in on small- and mid-size growth companies from around the world. That should give this fund a performance edge but so far it hasn't worked out that way as the Canadian Growth Fund has consistently done better. Stick with it for now.

U.S. AND INTERNATIONAL EQUITY FUNDS

MANULIFE CABOT GLOBAL EQUITY FUND $$ ↓ G No £ IE

Manager: Richard Crook (Manulife International), since inception (1994)

MER: 2.50%

As the name suggests, this fund can invest around the world, except for Canada, with no limitation on the size of companies that can be held. In the first part of '98, about a third of the portfolio was in the U.S., with other extensive holdings in Britain and Japan — much the same pattern as the previous year. Returns have been fair, but not exciting. Three-year average annual compound rate of return to June 30/98 was 14.7%, slightly below average for the international equity category. The safety rating so far is very good, with only a 3% chance of loss in any 12-month period.

FIXED INCOME AND MONEY MARKET FUNDS

MANULIFE CABOT DIVERSIFIED BOND FUND
$$ → FI No RSP CB

Manager: Malcolm Benn (Elliott & Page), since 1998

MER: 2.00%

This is not your standard, run-of-the-mill bond fund. The portfolio offers a blend of Canadian-dollar domestic securities, foreign-currency Canadian government and corporate bonds, foreign currency contracts, bond futures contracts, and notes issued by offshore governments and banks. Results have finally started to show some improvement with a one-year gain of 8.9% to June 30/98. However, a new manager took over in Spring, 1998 so we'll have to see if this results in any major changes in the investing style.

MANULIFE CABOT MONEY MARKET FUND
$ → C No RSP CMM

Manager: Maralyn Kobayashi (Elliott & Page), since 1998

MER: 1.25%

The portfolio of this fund is mainly invested in Treasury bills, with some bankers' acceptances and corporate notes blended in. Results have been below average for the money market fund category. New manager took over in Spring, 1998.

MARATHON FUNDS

THE COMPANY

The Marathon Funds are the creation of First Marathon Capital Corp. Two have been around for some time, and several more have recently been added under the Performance name. They are too new to qualify for a rating.

THE DETAILS

NUMBER OF FUNDS:	7
ASSETS UNDER MANAGEMENT:	$181.5 MILLION
LOAD CHARGE:	FRONT: MAX. 5%; BACK: MAX. 5%
SWITCHING CHARGE:	2% MAXIMUM
WHERE SOLD:	ALL PROVINCES, EXCEPT PEI FOR MARATHON EQUITY
HOW SOLD:	THROUGH BROKERS, DEALERS, AND FINANCIAL PLANNERS
PHONE NUMBER:	1-888-731-3676 (PERFORM)
WEB SITE ADDRESS:	WWW.FMARATHON.COM
E-MAIL ADDRESS:	HSLIWOWI@FMARATHON.COM

FUND SUMMARY

$$$$ - NONE
$$$ - NONE
$$ - NONE
$ - EQUITY
NR - PERFORMANCE CANADIAN BALANCED, PERFORMANCE CANADIAN CASH MANAGER, PERFORMANCE LARGE-CAP CANADIAN, PERFORMANCE LARGE-CAP U.S., PERFORMANCE NORTH AMERICAN LONG SHORT, RESOURCE

BEST CHOICES: NONE
BEST FOR RRSPs: NONE
BEST UNRATEDS: PERFORMANCE LARGE-CAP U.S.

FUND RATINGS

CANADIAN EQUITY FUNDS

MARATHON EQUITY FUND $ ↑ G No RSP CSC

Manager: Wayne Deans, since 1994

MER: 2.51%

This fund experienced such rapid growth that the company was forced to close it to new investors in May, '96. It is now accepting clients again but not many people are rushing to get in because returns have fallen off dramatically. Over the 12 months to June 30/98, the fund went into a deep slump, losing 23.6%. Nervous investors who wonder what's going on won't get much help from the company's web site. In mid-August, the most recent information offered was a reassuring letter written in November, 1997. Since then, the fund has dropped another 15%+. Manager Wayne Deans was honoured as Fund Manager of the Year at the 1996 Mutual Funds Award Gala. That award is now looking like a curse, similar to what athletes experience when they hit the cover of *Sports Illustrated*. Let's hope it's lifted soon.

MARGIN OF SAFETY FUND

THE COMPANY

This is a small, one-fund operation managed by John D. Hillery of Toronto.

THE DETAILS

NUMBER OF FUNDS:	1
ASSETS UNDER MANAGEMENT:	$5.8 MILLION
LOAD CHARGE:	NONE
SWITCHING CHARGE:	N/A
WHERE SOLD:	ONTARIO
HOW SOLD:	DIRECTLY THROUGH THE MANAGER
PHONE NUMBER:	(416) 234-0846
WEB SITE ADDRESS:	N/A
E-MAIL ADDRESS:	JDHICI@PATHCOM.COM

FUND SUMMARY

$$$$ - NONE
$$$ - NONE
$$ - MARGIN OF SAFETY FUND
$ - NONE
NR - NONE

BEST CHOICES: MARGIN OF SAFETY
BEST FOR RRSPs: N/A
BEST UNRATEDS: N/A

FUND RATINGS

U.S. AND INTERNATIONAL EQUITY FUNDS

MARGIN OF SAFETY FUND   **$$ ↓ G No USE**

Manager: John Hillery, since inception (1988)

MER: 1.88%

This small fund specializes in value investing by seeking out U.S. stocks trading at a discount to the underlying worth of the business (the "margin of safety"). Got off to a good start in '89, but then performance slipped — largely, manager John D. Hillery later admitted, because of a too-conservative investing approach. But he continues to refuse to overpay for a stock and said in his 1997 annual report that he was having trouble finding good value in the markets. As a result, the fund was sitting on a lot of cash (almost 40% of the assets) going into '98. That acted as a drag on returns, with the fund gaining just 17.8% for the year to June 30/98. That wasn't terrible, but it was well below what the S&P 500 was doing in the U.S. Still, you won't expose yourself to a lot of risk with this kind of approach. As Hillery commented in his '97 year-end report to investors: "My relatively risk-averse investment approach may at times like the present seem out of touch, out of date, and out of fashion. But it is the only approach I feel I know how to execute and feel comfortable with." ATP analysis confirms the safety aspect, with less than a one in 10 chance of a loss in any given one-year period. The minimum investment is $150,000. Not eligible for RRSPs/RRIFs.

MAWER INVESTMENT MANAGEMENT

THE COMPANY

This Calgary-based company has been in business since 1974. Originally, it confined itself to investment management for individuals, pension plans, and foundations, but in 1987 the company launched a family of five no-load mutual funds (now grown to 10) which are open to the general public. The funds are now registered for sale in all provinces, and are available through third party distributors as well as directly from the company in Alberta and Saskatchewan. There's an initial minimum of $25,000 per account if you buy directly from Mawer, although the company has the discretion to waive that. If you buy through a dealer, the minimum is $5,000 per fund (note the distinction between "per fund" and "per account").

THE DETAILS

NUMBER OF FUNDS:	10
ASSETS UNDER MANAGEMENT:	$371.5 MILLION
LOAD CHARGE:	NONE
SWITCHING CHARGE:	NONE
WHERE SOLD:	ACROSS CANADA
HOW SOLD:	THROUGH INVESTMENT DEALERS OR DIRECTLY THROUGH THE MANAGER (THE LATTER OPTION ONLY AVAILABLE IN ALBERTA OR SASKATCHEWAN)
PHONE NUMBER:	1-888-549-6248
WEB SITE ADDRESS:	WWW.MAWER.COM
E-MAIL ADDRESS:	WEBMASTER@MAWER.COM

FUND SUMMARY

$$$$ - CANADIAN BALANCED RETIREMENT SAVINGS

$$$ - CANADIAN BOND, CANADIAN DIVERSIFIED INVESTMENT, CANADIAN EQUITY, CANADIAN INCOME, CANADIAN MONEY MARKET, NEW CANADA, U.S. EQUITY, WORLD INVESTMENT

$$ - NONE

$ - NONE

NR - HIGH YIELD BOND

Best Choices: Canadian Balanced Retirement Savings, U.S. Equity, World Investment
Best for RRSPs: Canadian Balanced Retirement Savings, Canadian Bond
Best unrateds: High Yield Bond

FUND RATINGS

CANADIAN EQUITY FUNDS

MAWER CANADIAN EQUITY FUND $$$ → G No RSP CE

Manager: Bill MacLachlan, since 1993

MER: 1.27%

This small entry specializes in shares of medium to large Canadian corporations. The company describes this fund as best suited to investors seeking long-term growth, who are prepared to accept a moderate to high degree of risk compared to other funds offered by the company (not the total fund universe; risk here is about average compared to other Canadian stock funds). The investment strategy is primarily bottom-up. The portfolio in mid-'98 had a strong blue chip look to it, with heavy weighting in the financial services and industrial sectors. Results have been improving. The fund recorded a very good 17.8% gain for the year to June 30/98. Three-year average annual compound rate of return has moved to above average at 17.2%. That's good enough for a rating boost to $$$.

MAWER NEW CANADA FUND $$$ → G No RSP CSC

Manager: Bill MacLachlan, since 1996

MER: 1.47%

This fund zeros in on small-cap stocks with good growth potential. These may include start-up situations. The strategy is to buy and hold for the long term to maximize growth potential. Recent results have fallen off somewhat, but are still above average for the small-cap category. The fund gained 6.2% last year. Three-year average annual compound rate of return was a very good 17.8%. Original mandate was to invest in all North American issues, but the fund now focuses on Canada. Safety record is relatively good for the small-cap category. Name changed from Mawer North American Shares Fund in January, '94.

U.S. AND INTERNATIONAL EQUITY FUNDS

MAWER U.S. EQUITY FUND $$$ ↓ G No £ USE

Manager: Darrell Anderson, since 1994

MER: 1.32%

This U.S. stock fund seeks to generate a combination of capital gains and dividends for investors, and it is very successful at its job, thank you. Lots of big names in the portfolio (Chase Manhattan, Wendy's) but there's a smattering of smaller growth stocks and medium-size companies as well. As with all Mawer equity funds, the investment style is mainly bottom-up. Gain for the year to June 30/98 was a very good 34.3%. Five-year average annual compound rate of return was 20.6%, among the best in this category. The safety record is perfect — not a single 12-month period shows a loss, according to ATP analysis. That's outstanding, and so is this fund. More people should discover it.

MAWER WORLD INVESTMENT FUND $$$ → G No £ IE

Manager: Gerald Cooper-Key, since inception (1987)

MER: 1.40%

This fund invests in equities outside of North America, specifically Europe, the Pacific Basin, and Latin America. The fund went into a bit of a tailspin in late '97 as a result of the Asian mess but rebounded well in the first half of '98 thanks to a heavy weighting in the hot European market. As of mid-'98, Europe was still the big favourite, with a 70% portfolio weighting. Long-term results are above average for the international category, with an annual return of 16.2% for the five years to June 30/98.

BALANCED FUNDS

MAWER CANADIAN BALANCED
RETIREMENT SAVINGS FUND $$$$ ↓ FI/G No RSP CBAL

Manager: Donald Ferris, since inception (1988)

MER: 1.00%

This fund is fully RRSP eligible while the companion Canadian Diversified Investment Fund is not. This is a high-quality balanced fund, investing in short-term notes, bonds, and Canadian and foreign equities, within the content limit. It also holds positions in other Mawer funds, including the New Canada Fund, World Investment Fund, and U.S. Equity Fund. Performance has been very good, with above-average returns over all time frames. Gain for the year to June 30/98 was 13.7%. The safety record is top-notch, with only a 7% chance of loss in any given 12-month period. The manager has been around for more than a decade, so there's real stability at the top. You can't ask for much more than this from a fund, so the rating moves up to $$$$ this time around. An excellent candidate for your RRSP.

MAWER CANADIAN
DIVERSIFIED INVESTMENT FUND $$$ ↓ FI/G No £ CBAL

Manager: Donald Ferris, since inception (1988)

MER: 0.95%

Mawer plans to increase the foreign content holdings of this portfolio to provide broader diversification, but as of mid-'98 it only stood at 19%. The main emphasis will be on U.S. securities, but international holdings will be built up as well. That should help to distinguish this fund from the companion Balanced Retirement Savings Fund, which it has resembled until now. So it will probably come as no surprise that the returns have been similar as well. That has meant above-average performance, although not quite to the same level as that achieved by the Balanced Retirement Savings Fund. The results and the excellent safety record merit an increase in the rating to $$$, but I'd feel more comfortable in giving it if I had a better handle on where this fund will be a year from now. If you're considering it for your portfolio, ask some hard questions about that before you make a decision.

MAWER CANADIAN INCOME FUND $$$ ↓ FI/G No RSP CBAL

Manager: Gary Feltham, since 1993

MER: 1.01%

This fund differs from the other balanced funds in this group in that it places more emphasis on current income. Most of the portfolio is in government and corporate bonds, but 16% of the assets consist of preferred shares and high-yielding common stocks (mid-'98). You can arrange for regular distributions from this fund on a monthly or quarterly basis, which is useful for retirees. Risk is relatively low, which makes this a good holding for a RRIF. Recent returns have slumped somewhat (7.9% for the year to June 30/98). Longer term results are above average for the bond category but sub-par if you measure this against other balanced funds. Safety rating is first rate. This is a special situation fund, but if used correctly it can be quite valuable.

FIXED INCOME AND MONEY MARKET FUNDS

MAWER CANADIAN BOND FUND $$$ ↓ FI No RSP CB

Manager: Gary Feltham, since 1993

MER: 1.01%

Here's a bond fund that continues to improve. It had been somewhat ho-hum, but over the past three years it has emerged as a winner. The portfolio is a mix of government and corporate bonds and the manager's style is what is technically known as "interest rate anticipation". That means the portfolio is adjusted depending on the outlook for rates. Gain for the year to June 30/98 was 9.5%, and the fund's numbers are above average for all time periods out to five years. Safety rating is very good.

MAWER CANADIAN
MONEY MARKET FUND

$$$ → C No RSP CMM

Manager: Bill MacLachlan, since 1993

MER: 0.69%

This fund invests mainly in corporate notes, with a few government T-bills tossed in. Returns have improved to above average, thanks in part to the low management fee.

MAXXUM GROUP OF FUNDS

THE COMPANY

This was formerly the Prudential Fund organization. The family was purchased by London Life in early 1996, and the name changed to Maxxum. Many of the original managers were retained, however. Although these funds are owned by an insurance firm, they are not "segregated" funds and their purchase is not tied to any type of insurance contract or annuity. Note that the money market fund can be purchased on a no-load basis, but you may be charged a commission if you move assets out of it into another fund in the group.

THE DETAILS

NUMBER OF FUNDS:	9
ASSETS UNDER MANAGEMENT:	$812 MILLION
LOAD CHARGE:	FRONT: MAX. 5%; BACK: MAX. 5%
SWITCHING CHARGE:	2% MAXIMUM
WHERE SOLD:	ACROSS CANADA
HOW SOLD:	THROUGH BROKERS, DEALERS, FINANCIAL PLANNERS, AND LONDON LIFE INSURANCE AGENTS
PHONE NUMBER:	1-888-4MAXXUM (462-9986)
WEB SITE ADDRESS:	WWW.MAXXUMFUND.COM
E-MAIL ADDRESS:	N/A

FUND SUMMARY

$$$$ - NONE

$$$ - AMERICAN EQUITY, DIVIDEND, GLOBAL EQUITY, INCOME, MONEY MARKET

$$ - CANADIAN BALANCED

$ - CANADIAN EQUITY GROWTH, NATURAL RESOURCE, PRECIOUS METALS

NR - NONE

BEST CHOICES: CANADIAN BALANCED, DIVIDEND, INCOME

BEST FOR RRSPs: CANADIAN BALANCED, INCOME, MONEY MARKET

BEST UNRATEDS: N/A

FUND RATINGS

CANADIAN EQUITY FUNDS

MAXXUM DIVIDEND FUND $$$ → G/FI #/* RSP INC

Manager: Jackee Pratt, since 1995

MER: 1.73%

This is a fund that works much more effectively for investors looking for long-term capital gains than for those who are seeking above-average cash flow. The portfolio mainly invests in blue-chip stocks, including some U.S. issues, which wouldn't normally be expected in a true Canadian dividend fund. There is also a small amount of preferreds, royalty trusts, and convertibles in the mix. The result is a fund that's been producing some terrific total returns in recent years. Average annual compound rate of return for the three years to June 30/98, which roughly coincides with manager Jackee Pratt's tenure, is almost 23%. But cash flow has been relatively poor. The annual dividend fund survey prepared for my *Mutual Funds Update* newsletter shows this fund returned just 1.7% in the way of distributions in 1997, most of it in the form of capital gains. So if cash is the goal, look elsewhere. But if you want a good portfolio with a combination of modest income and decent capital gains potential (sounds like RRSP material to me!), this fund will work very nicely. Formerly known as the Prudential Dividend Fund.

MAXXUM CANADIAN EQUITY GROWTH FUND $ → G #/* RSP CE

Manager: Jackee Pratt, since 1995

MER: 2.13%

This fund invests across the full spectrum of Canadian industry and so includes small, mid-sized, and large companies in the mix. Manager Jackee Pratt favours a bottom-up investment style (choosing stocks on the basis of a company's fundamentals regardless of what the economy is doing). Initial returns after she took charge were good, but this fund has been in a slump over the past couple of years. One-year gain to June 30/98 was just 6.5%, in part due to underweight positions in financial services and communications issues. The fact that over 20% of the portfolio was in the resource sector in mid-'98 also didn't help matters. The Dividend Fund, also managed by Pratt, is a better choice in this group. Formerly the Prudential Growth Fund of Canada.

MAXXUM NATURAL RESOURCE FUND $ ↑ G #/* RSP SEC

Manager: Jackee Pratt, since 1995

MER: 2.23%

This fund had an outstanding record for several years under the direction of Veronika Hirsch, when she and it were part of the Prudential organization. When she jumped to AGF in the fall of 1995, her mantle fell to Pratt, a veteran of the business who had previously had stints with Investors Group and T.A.L. Investment Counsel. Her initial results were good, but then came a bear market that took commodity prices to their lowest levels in more than a decade. No fund manager could hold back that tidal wave. Loss for the year to June 30/98 was 31.2%, a painful reminder to investors of the volatility of the resource sector. In mid-'98, Pratt had the portfolio heavily weighted towards energy (38%) and gold (26%). If one or both of those sectors bounce back, look for this fund to perform well. But only aggressive investors should take the bet.

MAXXUM PRECIOUS METALS FUND $ ↑ G #/* RSP PM

Manager: Martin Anstee, since 1995

MER: 2.23%

For the third consecutive year, my observation of this fund is that it's a wild and woolly ride. Unfortunately, it's a ride that only goes in one direction these days — straight down. It started with Bre-X. This fund had a big position in the ill-fated stock and was beaten up as a result. But it didn't stop there. The whole gold sector went into a deep funk, from which it still has to emerge. Loss has piled on loss; in the 12 months to June 30/98 this fund dropped 34.1%. Veteran manager Martin Anstee is responding about the only way he can given his limited mandate here: by focusing his portfolio on top-quality companies (Barrick, Euro-Nevada, Kinross) and toughing it out. You can make lots of money on funds like this in the good times, but you'd better keep your heart pills handy. It's a risky play. Historically there's a 23% chance you could suffer a loss over a three-year period according to ATP analysis. This was formerly the Prudential Precious Metals Fund.

U.S. AND INTERNATIONAL EQUITY FUNDS

MAXXUM AMERICAN EQUITY FUND $$$ → G #/* £ USE

Manager: Warren Lammert (Janus Capital) since 1997

MER: 2.48%

The primary mandate of this fund is to invest in large U.S. corporations, but the manager may also place up to 30% of the portfolio in international companies when conditions warrant. In the first half of '98, the emphasis here was on technology issues, which made up about a third of the holdings. Some of the better-known names included Microsoft and America Online. Manager Warren Lammert also runs the Janus Mercury Fund in the States. He is a believer in the importance of getting out and meeting the management of the companies in which he is interested, rather than sitting at a computer terminal and talking to other Wall Street types. His results with this fund since taking charge have been impressive; the gain for the first six months of '98 was a big-time 33.8%. That earns it a $$$ rating in its debut here.

MAXXUM GLOBAL EQUITY FUND $$$ → G #/* £ IE

Manager: Helen Young Hayes (Janus Capital) since 1997

MER: 2.48%

This fund can invest anywhere in the world and the manager has taken full advantage of that to build a well diversified portfolio that currently emphasizes U.S. and European issues. Helen Young Hayes and her staff rack up the frequent flyer points by travelling all over the world to look for investment opportunities. She brings an aggressive style to this fund, as shown by the fact that she tends to be fully invested at all times, with small cash holdings. Results have been very good; this fund has consistently been in the top quartile of the international category since it was launched in early 1995. In the first half of '98, after Young assumed control, it gained almost 27%. A sound choice for your portfolio.

BALANCED FUNDS

MAXXUM CANADIAN
BALANCED FUND $$ → FI #/* RSP CBAL

Managers: Gerald Boychuk, Doug Crawford, and Martin Anstee, since 1995

MER: 2.13%

The portfolio of this fund offers a good mix of blue-chip stocks, government and corporate bonds, and first mortgages. The balance between fixed-income securities and equities was almost 50/50 in mid '98, so you're getting the straight goods here. Returns tend to flirt with the averages. Gain for the 12 months to June 30/98 was 9.2%, below par for the balanced category. But some longer term results are above average. The historic risk rating is not great, and this fund tends to underperform in bear markets. The rating of this one tends to flip-flop between $$ and $$$; this year it is $$. This was formerly the Prudential Diversified Investment Fund of Canada.

FIXED INCOME AND MONEY MARKET FUNDS

MAXXUM INCOME FUND $$$ → FI #/* RSP CB

Manager: Gerald Boychuk, since 1987

MER: 1.73%

This portfolio is a blend of government and corporate bonds, about equally divided. Manager Gerry Boychuk has been weighting the mix towards longer term bonds and that decision has paid off for investors over the past couple of years. The fund gained 16% in the year to June 30/98, one of the best performances in the bond category. All longer term results are also above average. The only problem with placing a big bet on long bonds is that if interest rates turn up, a fund can be badly hurt if the manager isn't nimble. As you might expect, ATP analysis shows this fund with unusually high month-to-month volatility compared to its peers. However, over the longer term, the risk factor tends to smooth out. Formerly the Prudential Income Fund.

MAXXUM MONEY MARKET FUND $$$ → C No RSP CMM

Manager: Doug Crawford, since 1992

MER: 0.84%

A solid performer, consistently among the leaders in this field. Composition of the portfolio is a mixture of short-term corporate notes and Canadian T-bills. The only no-load fund in the Maxxum family; however, if you switch to another fund in the group a commission will be assessed. Formerly the Prudential Money Market Fund.

McDONALD INVESTMENT MANAGEMENT

THE COMPANY

This Toronto-based investment advisory firm was founded in 1989 and is 100% employee-owned by the four portfolio managers. The company provides investment management services to high net worth individuals, foundations, companies, etc. They employ highly sophisticated research techniques, and the managers travel extensively throughout the globe, looking for reasonably priced growth stocks. Each mutual fund in the family has its performance measured against a specific benchmark to determine how well it is doing. For example, the return of the McDonald New Japan Fund is matched against the Nikkei 225 Index. Most of these funds are still too new to qualify for a rating.

The company also offers six "fund of funds" portfolios, designed for various investment needs. These are sold under the Ambassador name.

THE DETAILS

NUMBER OF FUNDS:	14
ASSETS UNDER MANAGEMENT:	$10.8 MILLION
LOAD CHARGE:	MCDONALD FUNDS - FRONT: MAX. 5%
	AMBASSADOR FUNDS - FRONT: MAX. 7%
SWITCHING CHARGE:	2% MAXIMUM
WHERE SOLD:	ONTARIO AND NEW BRUNSWICK
HOW SOLD:	THROUGH MCDONALD FINANCIAL CORPORATION AND REGISTERED MUTUAL FUND DEALERS
PHONE NUMBER:	(416) 594-1979
WEB SITE ADDRESS:	WWW.MCDONALDFUNDS.COM
E-MAIL ADDRESS:	N/A

FUND SUMMARY

$$$$ - NONE
$$$ - NONE
$$ - NONE
$ - CANADA PLUS
NR - AMBASSADOR - AGGRESSIVE GLOBAL RRSP PORTFOLIO, AGGRESSIVE PORTFOLIO, BALANCED GLOBAL RRSP

PORTFOLIO, BALANCED PORTFOLIO, CONSERVATIVE
GLOBAL RRSP PORTFOLIO, CONSERVATIVE PORTFOLIO;
MCDONALD - ASIA PLUS, EMERGING ECONOMIES,
ENHANCED BOND, ENHANCED GLOBAL, EURO PLUS, NEW
AMERICA, NEW JAPAN

BEST CHOICES: NONE
BEST FOR RRSPS: CANADA PLUS
BEST UNRATEDS: EURO PLUS

FUND RATINGS

BALANCED FUNDS

MCDONALD CANADA PLUS FUND $ ↑ FI/G # RSP CBAL

Manager: Team

MER: 2.88%

This fund invests in a combination of Canadian stocks and
bonds, plus international securities. The company uses
what they call a "play it safe" formula in selecting securities and managing the fund. In the first half of '98, the
portfolio was heavily weighted towards stocks, with
Canadian equities accounting for 58% of the assets. There
was a broad range of international securities from countries
as diverse as Germany and Venezuela. Bond assets were
just 14% of the mix. The fund has been profitable for
investors, but returns have been below average when compared to the universe of Canadian balanced funds. Three-
year average annual compound rate of return to June 30/98
was 9.4%. ATP historical analysis shows this fund to have
a very high degree of volatility for the balanced category,
hence the high risk rating.

McLEAN BUDDEN FUNDS

THE COMPANY

This company is mainly a pension fund manager, which offers some small mutual funds almost as a sideline (total assets under management exceed $6 billion, of which the mutual funds account for only $72 million). Their investment style is growth-oriented and they are one of the best at that type of money management, even though the firm isn't well known. The company is owned by Sun Life Assurance, with the management team holding a 40% stake.

In mid-1998, the company added its first new fund in several years, the McLean Budden International Equity Fund, marking the first time they have ventured outside North America.

At the same time, the company announced reductions in the MERs of three funds: Balanced Growth, Fixed-Income, and Money Market.

THE DETAILS

NUMBER OF FUNDS:	6
ASSETS UNDER MANAGEMENT:	$95.8 MILLION
LOAD CHARGE:	NONE
SWITCHING CHARGE:	NONE
WHERE SOLD:	ACROSS CANADA
HOW SOLD:	THROUGH REGISTERED DEALERS, WITH A COMMISSION. NO LOAD, IN ONTARIO AND QUEBEC DIRECTLY THROUGH THE MANAGER. ELSEWHERE, THROUGH SUN LIFE SECURITIES (1-800-457-8343)
PHONE NUMBER:	(416) 862-9800 OR 1-800-884-0436
WEB SITE ADDRESS:	WWW.MCLEANBUDDEN.COM
E-MAIL ADDRESS:	N/A

FUND SUMMARY

$$$$ - NONE
$$$ - AMERICAN GROWTH, BALANCED, EQUITY GROWTH, FIXED-INCOME, MONEY MARKET
$$ - NONE
$ - NONE
NR - INTERNATIONAL EQUITY

BEST CHOICES: ALL
BEST FOR RRSPS: BALANCED, EQUITY GROWTH, FIXED-INCOME
BEST UNRATED: INTERNATIONAL EQUITY

FUND RATINGS

CANADIAN EQUITY FUNDS

McLEAN BUDDEN EQUITY GROWTH FUND $$$ → G No RSP CE

Manager: Team

MER: 1.75%

McLean Budden is one of Canada's few pure growth managers, and all their funds reflect this style. This fund specializes in shares of mid- to large-size Canadian companies, although up to 10% of the portfolio may be in foreign stocks. Heavy weightings in industrial products and financial services helped returns in the past year, but a fairly sizeable position in oil stocks and small holdings in metals and gold kept the fund's overall return for the year to June 30/98 to 9.9%, slightly below average for the Canadian equity category. Longer term results continue to be comfortably above average, however. A very good choice.

U.S. AND INTERNATIONAL EQUITY FUNDS

McLEAN BUDDEN AMERICAN GROWTH FUND $$$ ↓ G No £ USE

Manager: Team

MER: 1.75%

The goal of this fund is long-term growth by investing in a diversified portfolio of U.S. stocks. Emphasis is on large companies, although you will find a few unfamiliar names in the mix. As you might expect, this fund chalked up some very impressive returns in recent years, with a five-year average annual gain of 22% to June 30/98. Latest one-year results were below average for the U.S. equity category, however, at 27.3%. Very impressive safety record for a fund of this type, with ATP showing only a 1% probability of loss over any 12-month period and a strong tendency to outperform in bear market conditions.

BALANCED FUNDS

McLEAN BUDDEN
BALANCED GROWTH FUND $$$ → FI/G No RSP CBAL

Manager: Team

MER: 1.25%

This fund employs a conservative investment strategy, combining stocks of large companies with bonds and debentures with at least an A safety rating. Maintains a truly balanced portfolio with equity component between 40% and 60%. Results have been very good in recent years; gain for the 12 months to June 30/98 was 11.6%, above average for the balanced category. Longer term performance is also above average. Worthy of your attention.

FIXED INCOME AND MONEY MARKET FUNDS

McLEAN BUDDEN
FIXED-INCOME FUND $$$ → FI No RSP CB

Manager: Team

MER: 0.80%

This small fund specializes in high-quality government and corporate bonds. It generally produces very good results. Example: a 10.9% gain for the year to June 30/98, well above the average return of 8.6% for the Canadian bond fund category. Five-year average annual return was 9.4%, also well above average. Another good choice in this sound family.

McLEAN BUDDEN
MONEY MARKET FUND $$$ → C No RSP CMM

Manager: Team

MER: 0.60%

This fund invests mainly in Canadian T-bills, with some banker's acceptances and corporate short-term notes added to the mix to boost returns. Results are above average and should improve thanks to a 15-basis-point cut in the MER in mid-'98.

MIDDLEFIELD GROUP

THE COMPANY

The Middlefield organization offers a range of financial products, from resource limited partnerships to venture capital funds. Their mutual funds group, with the exception of Middlefield Growth, the original fund, is new and expanding.

THE DETAILS

NUMBER OF FUNDS:	4
ASSETS UNDER MANAGEMENT:	$50 MILLION
LOAD CHARGE:	NONE
SWITCHING CHARGE:	NONE
WHERE SOLD:	ALBERTA, BRITISH COLUMBIA, MANITOBA, ONTARIO, SASKATCHEWAN
HOW SOLD:	DIRECTLY THROUGH MIDDLEFIELD OR THROUGH BROKERS, DEALERS, AND FINANCIAL PLANNERS
PHONE NUMBER:	(416) 362-0714
WEB SITE ADDRESS:	WWW.MIDDLEFIELD.COM
E-MAIL ADDRESS:	INVEST@MIDDLEFIELD.COM

FUND SUMMARY

$$$$ - NONE
$$$ - NONE
$$ - NONE
$ - GROWTH
NR - CANADIAN REALTY, ENHANCED YIELD, MONEY MARKET
BEST CHOICES: NONE
BEST FOR RRSPS: NONE
BEST UNRATEDS: MONEY MARKET

FUND RATINGS

CANADIAN EQUITY FUNDS

MIDDLEFIELD GROWTH FUND $ ↑ G RSP SEC

Manager: Garth J. Jestley, since 1993

MER: 2.55%

This fund focuses primarily on the oil and gas sector, which accounted for over 60% of the portfolio in the first half of '98. The mix includes both small- and mid-sized companies as well as one giant, Petro-Can. The fund also had a large cash position, at more than 35% of assets. Given the heavy weighting towards the energy sector, it's clear that results will reflect whatever is happening there. A year ago returns were good. This time around they're not so good, although the 9.5% drop in the year to June 30/98 was a lot better than most other resource-based funds could manage. When the price of oil and/or gas rebounds, as it will, this fund will do well. But it's a gamble.

MILLENNIUM FAMILY OF MUTUAL FUNDS

THE COMPANY

The Millennium Funds are operated by Morrison & Williams Investment Management Ltd., a Toronto-based firm founded in 1992. The company provides services to pension funds, institutional investors, and private clients, as well as running this small, three-fund family.

THE DETAILS

NUMBER OF FUNDS:	3
ASSETS UNDER MANAGEMENT:	$75.5 MILLION
LOAD CHARGE:	FRONT: MAX. 4%
SWITCHING CHARGE:	NONE
WHERE SOLD:	ALL PROVINCES EXCEPT QUEBEC
HOW SOLD:	THROUGH BROKERS, DEALERS, AND FINANCIAL PLANNERS
PHONE NUMBER:	1-888-647-3611
WEB SITE ADDRESS:	N/A
E-MAIL ADDRESS:	INFO@MILLENNIUM-FUNDS.COM

FUND SUMMARY

$$$$ - NONE
$$$ - DIVERSIFIED, NEXT GENERATION
$$ - NONE
$ - NONE
NR - INCOME

BEST CHOICES: DIVERSIFIED, NEXT GENERATION
BEST FOR RRSPs: DIVERSIFIED
BEST UNRATEDS: INCOME

FUND RATINGS

CANADIAN EQUITY FUNDS

MILLENNIUM NEXT GENERATION FUND $$$ → G # RSP CSC

Manager: K. Leslie Williams, since inception (1993)

MER: 2.50%

This is a small-cap fund that seeks out stocks that are expected to show strong growth potential in the coming years. The investment approach uses a bottom-up style of stock picking and aims at minimizing risk (not easy with a small-cap fund) and generating "exceptional returns". In the first half of '98, this meant avoiding commodity-based stocks and focusing on industrials, consumer products, and "soft cyclicals" — companies that do not rely on inflation but are propelled by a strong economy. Turnaround situations and speculative issues are avoided. The approach has paid off. The year ending June 30/98 was a difficult period for many small-cap managers but this fund gained 13.3%, better than average for the category. Three-year average annual compound rate of return to that date was an excellent 28.8%. Despite the good results, this is still an undiscovered fund, with less than $20 million in assets. Aggressive investors should take a look.

BALANCED FUNDS

MILLENNIUM DIVERSIFIED FUND $$$ → FI/G # RSP CBAL

Managers: K. Leslie Williams and Barry A. Morrison, since inception (1993)

MER: 2.50%

This is a conservatively run fund that uses an active asset mix approach, which means the stock/bond ratio will vary depending on conditions. The managers are especially interested in undervalued situations. The stock sector focuses on the TSE 100, with a few smaller issues added in, so it's essentially blue-chip quality. Foreign content is usually in the form of S&P Depositary Receipts. The bonds are all Government of Canada issues. As of Spring, '98, about 37% of the portfolio was in fixed-income securities, with the balance in equities. Very good results to date. The fund gained 15.6% for the year to June 30/98 and the three-year average annual return was 17.4%, well above the norm for Canadian balanced funds as a group.

MOF FUNDS

THE COMPANY

These two funds are run more or less out of his back pocket by C. Channing Buckland, a Vancouver-based broker with a sharp eye for up-and-coming junior stocks and a wealth of contacts in that turbulent marketplace. They're for speculators only.

THE DETAILS

NUMBER OF FUNDS:	2
ASSETS UNDER MANAGEMENT:	$20 MILLION
LOAD CHARGE:	FRONT: MAX. 6%
SWITCHING CHARGE:	NONE
WHERE SOLD:	MULTIPLE OPPORTUNITIES IN B.C. ONLY. SPECIAL OPPORTUNITIES IN ALL PROVINCES EXCEPT QUEBEC AND NOVA SCOTIA.
HOW SOLD:	DIRECTLY THROUGH THE MANAGER OR THROUGH BROKERS, DEALERS, AND FINANCIAL PLANNERS
PHONE NUMBER:	(604) 643-7416 OR 1-800-663-6370
WEB SITE ADDRESS:	N/A
E-MAIL ADDRESS:	N/A

FUND SUMMARY

$$$$ - NONE
$$$ - NONE
$$ - MULTIPLE OPPORTUNITIES
$ - SPECIAL OPPORTUNITIES
NR - NONE
BEST CHOICES: MULTIPLE OPPORTUNITIES
BEST FOR RRSPs: NONE
BEST UNRATEDS: N/A

FUND RATINGS

CANADIAN EQUITY FUNDS

MULTIPLE OPPORTUNITIES FUND $$ ↑ G # RSP CSC

Manager: C. Channing Buckland, since inception (1985)

MER: 2.50%

A small, roller-coaster fund for stout-hearted B.C. residents only. Invests mainly in junior companies traded on the Vancouver Stock Exchange. Extremely volatile, so expect big gains and big losses. Over the past couple of years the fund has been in a slump; it dropped 8.4% for the 12 months to June 30/98. But longer term investors have done well. Even with the recent losses, the five-year average annual compound gain is an impressive 18.6%. But the recent weakness, the high volatility, the small size of the fund (only $10 million in assets), the speculative nature of the investments, and the fact it's only available to B.C. residents are serious negatives. We'll drop the rating back to $$ for now until manager Channing Buckland goes off on another hot streak. Don't put this one in your RRSP, even though it's eligible. This is for high-rollers only.

U.S. AND INTERNATIONAL EQUITY FUNDS

SPECIAL OPPORTUNITIES FUND $ ↑ G # £ IE

Manager: C. Channing Buckland, since inception (1987)

MER: 2.14%

This was originally intended as the international stablemate of the companion Multiple Opportunities Fund. It still retains international status for registered plans, but Buckland is running it more along the lines of Multiple Opportunities these days. The fund invests in ultra-small companies, with market capitalization of less than $25 million. This quote from the prospectus will give you the flavour: "These companies typically will have no history of earnings and will include natural resource companies in the exploration and development stage and industrial companies in the start-up stage." This fund trailed way behind Multiple Opportunities in performance for years, but started a turnaround under Buckland's new approach last year, gaining almost 27%. On the basis of that, I raised the rating. But, oh woe, it's now back to its losing ways, dropping a big 21.7% last year. The poor market for junior mines was a prime reason for the falloff, and there aren't bright prospects for a quick improvement. So the rating is being slashed back to $ while we await better times. This fund is available in most parts of Canada, but many brokers and investment dealers may not offer it. In that case, call the company directly if you're a high-roller type.

MONTRUSCO ASSOCIATES INC.

THE COMPANY

Montrusco Associates is a prominent Montreal-based money management firm that manages assets for pension plans, high-net worth clients, and mutual fund companies such as the Scotia Funds. The firm offers one fund that is available to all investors: the successful Quebec Growth Fund. It also has a lineup of "Select" funds that require an initial investment of $150,000. These are sold on a front-end load basis only and the management fee is charged directly to the investor rather than to the fund itself.

THE DETAILS

NUMBER OF FUNDS:	15
ASSETS UNDER MANAGEMENT:	$2 BILLION
LOAD CHARGE:	FRONT: MAX. 6%
SWITCHING CHARGE:	NONE
WHERE SOLD:	ACROSS CANADA
HOW SOLD:	THROUGH SALES REPRESENTATIVES
PHONE NUMBER:	(514) 842-6464 - NICOLE CHARLAND
WEB SITE ADDRESS:	WWW.MONTRUSCO.COM
E-MAIL ADDRESS:	INVFMS@MONTRUSCO.COM

FUND SUMMARY

$$$$ - NONE

$$$ - QUEBEC GROWTH, SELECT BALANCED+, SELECT INCOME, SELECT NON-TAXABLE U.S. EQUITY, SELECT T-MAX

$$ - SELECT BALANCED, SELECT CANADIAN EQUITY, SELECT E.A.F.E, SELECT GROWTH, SELECT TAXABLE U.S. EQUITY

$ - NONE

NR - SELECT BOND INDEX+, SELECT CONTINENTAL EUROPE EQUITY, SELECT HIGH YIELD BONDS, SELECT STRATEGIC U.S. EQUITY, SELECT UNITED KINGDOM EQUITY

BEST CHOICES: BALANCED+, NON-TAXABLE U.S. EQUITY, QUEBEC GROWTH

BEST FOR RRSPs: BALANCED+, QUEBEC GROWTH

BEST UNRATEDS: CONTINENTAL EUROPE EQUITY

FUND RATINGS

CANADIAN EQUITY FUNDS

MONTRUSCO SELECT
CANADIAN EQUITY FUND $$ → G # RSP CE

Manager: Peter Harrison, since 1997

MER: 0.08%

This has been a decent performer over the years. The return for the year to June 30/98 was slightly below average at 10.3%, but longer term results are much stronger. Five-year average annual compound rate of return was 14.9% compared to an average of 12.4% for the Canadian equity category, as reported by *The Globe and Mail.* However, remember that the annual management charge needs to be deducted from the reported Montrusco figure to get an accurate comparison. Safety record is so-so, but the fund has shown an historic tendency to do better than its peer group in bear markets.

MONTRUSCO SELECT GROWTH FUND $$ ↑ G # RSP CSC

Manager: Mark Wait, since 1987

MER: 0.07%

This is the company's small-cap offering. It has struggled recently, losing 1.9% for the year to June 30/98. But longer term results are more impressive. The fund's 10-year average annual compound rate of return of 17% is among the best in the small-cap category. Risk level is on the high side, however, according to ATP analysis. The fund has the added attraction of long-term stability of management, with Mark Wait having been on the job for more than a decade.

QUEBEC GROWTH FUND $$$ ↑ G No RSP CE

Manager: Christine Décarie, since 1993

MER: 2.00%

This is one of the few funds in the country that focuses entirely on Quebec stocks and it is only available to residents of that province. (Anyone living in the rest of the country that wants a pure Quebec fund should consider Dynamic Quebec.) If you do live in Quebec and want to invest in your home province, then this fund is certainly worth a look. It seeks out companies that manager Christine Décarie believes offer significant growth potential. That exposes it to some obvious political risk, but for investors who have been prepared to accept that fact the rewards have been good. Gain for the year to June 30/98 was a sterling 38%. Five-year average annual compound rate of return (the time frame that covers the period since Décarie assumed control of the portfolio) was 19%. You can't argue with those results, but don't overlook the risk. Rating moves up this year.

U.S. AND INTERNATIONAL FUNDS

MONTRUSCO SELECT E.A.F.E. FUND $$ → G # £ IE

Manager: Michel Bastien, since 1987

MER: 0.15%

The mandate of this fund allows it to invest in E.A.F.E. countries, which excludes North America. So manager Michel Bastien can't boost returns by loading up on U.S. stocks. The results have been average to slightly below for funds that face this type of investment restriction, according to figures published by *The Financial Post*. Gain for the year to June 30/98 was 9%. Safety rating is average.

MONTRUSCO SELECT
NON-TAXABLE U.S. EQUITY FUND $$$ ↓ G # £ USE

Manager: Michel Bastien, since 1987

MER: 1.00%

This U.S. equity fund is designed to be used in registered plans, as foreign content, or by tax-exempt investors. That's the background to the unusual name, otherwise it is a fairly standard U.S. stock fund. Returns have been extremely good. Gain for the year to June 30/98 was 30%, and returns over all time periods are above average. Safety record is also better than average. A good choice from this group.

MONTRUSCO SELECT
TAXABLE U.S. EQUITY FUND $$ → G # £ USE

Manager: Michel Bastien, since 1987

MER: 0.47%

The objective of this fund is to achieve long-term capital appreciation by investing in a portfolio of U.S. common shares. Returns have lagged well behind those of the companion Non-Taxable U.S. Equity Fund. Gain for the year to June 30/98 was 18.1%, compared to 30% for the stablemate. The portfolio is heavily concentrated in a few companies, so one or two major reverses can drag down the total return. Ten-year results are above average, however.

BALANCED FUNDS

MONTRUSCO SELECT
BALANCED FUND $$ → FI/G # RSP CBAL

Manager: André Marsan, since 1987

MER: 0.14%

The portfolio of this fund is highly diversified and ranges from government bonds to Canadian and foreign stocks to REITs. Long-term results are good, but the latest returns are below average for the balanced category, in part due to the resource holdings in the equity side of the portfolio. Taking the long view, however, the fund shows an average annual compound rate of return of 11.7% over the decade to June 30/98, which is above the norm for the category, even after allowing for the deduction of management fees.

MONTRUSCO SELECT
BALANCED+ FUND $$$ → FI/G # RSP CBAL

Manager: André Marsan, since 1993

MER: 0.09%

Montrusco offers two balanced funds to investors. This one is more aggressively run and manager André Marsan, a well-known and highly-respected Montreal money guru, may use such derivatives as options and index futures to add to the potential return. That suggests somewhat higher risk than the companion Balanced Fund but, interestingly, historical performance results compiled by the ATP system show that has not materialized to date. Profits have certainly been much better here than in the regular Balanced Fund. This one advanced 12.5% in the year to June 30/98, and the five-year average annual compound rate of return to that date was a very healthy 17.3%. If you're selecting one of Montrusco's balanced entries, this is your best bet.

FIXED INCOME AND MONEY MARKET FUNDS

MONTRUSCO SELECT INCOME FUND $$$ ↓ FI # RSP CB

Manager: Yves Paquette, since 1993

MER: 0.12%

This is an impressive fixed-income fund that has done very well for investors over the years. Returns are above average for all time frames. The 11.5% average annual compound rate of return for the decade to June 30/98 is among the best in the bond fund category, even after allowance is made for the annual management fee. The safety record is outstanding. All in all, a very fine package.

MONTRUSCO SELECT T-MAX FUND $$$ ↓ C # RSP CMM

Manager: Yves Paquette, since 1995

MER: 0.05%

Good money market entry with above-average returns and a fine safety record.

THE MUTUAL GROUP OF FUNDS

THE COMPANY

Mutual Life owns these funds through subsidiary companies, but they are not segregated funds and are not tied to any kind of insurance contract. However, in January, 1998 the company responded to the growing public interest in seg funds by launching a new product called the Mutual Investment Portfolio (MIP). The idea is similar to that being used by a number of other mutual fund companies: to create seg fund clones of their regular funds for those investors who want that specific product. The MIP invests directly in the underlying Mutual Group funds and offers a 75% return on capital guarantee (which means you will get no less than 75% of your money back at maturity) and a 100% death benefit. All MIP investment options are no load. The seg funds are not reviewed separately since they are essentially the same as the regular mutual funds except for the purchase option.

Most of the Mutual funds are available on a no-load basis with the exception of those in their Leader series: Mutual Bond, Mutual Diversifund 40, Mutual Equifund, and Mutual Amerifund. These are sold with a front-end load of up to 3.75%.

Mutual is a large fund group, with more than 175,000 accounts and assets under management in excess of $3.6 billion. The company recently took over the Strata funds, merging them into their existing lineup. Most of their funds are managed by Perigee Private Management, a spinoff company that went public in early 1998. However, the Summit line is run by Mackenzie Financial, and Alpine funds are under the direction of AGF.

The company lost one of its key managers late in 1997, when Suzann Pennington left to join the new Synergy funds. When information was supplied to us for this year's edition, we noted with interest that individual fund managers were no longer named — only a management company. So Mutual has joined the unfortunately growing number of fund companies who no longer provide investors with important information about managerial changes.

THE DETAILS

NUMBER OF FUNDS:	20
ASSETS UNDER MANAGEMENT:	$4.2 BILLION
LOAD CHARGE:	FRONT: MAX. 3.75% (ONLY FOR BOND, DIVERSIFUND 40, EQUIFUND, AND AMERIFUND). NO LOAD FOR THE REMAINING FUNDS IN GROUP
SWITCHING CHARGE:	NONE
WHERE SOLD:	ACROSS CANADA
HOW SOLD:	THROUGH LICENSED MUTUAL INVESTCO AGENTS AND ALLSTATE AGENTS
PHONE NUMBER:	1-888-864-5463
WEB SITE ADDRESS:	WWW.THEMUTUALGROUP.COM
E-MAIL ADDRESS:	THROUGH SITE

FUND SUMMARY

$$$$ - NONE

$$$ - AMERIFUND, DIVERSIFUND 40, EQUIFUND, PREMIER BLUE CHIP, PREMIER AMERICAN, PREMIER INTERNATIONAL

$$ - MONEY MARKET, PREMIER BOND, PREMIER DIVERSIFIED, PREMIER GROWTH

$ - BOND, PREMIER MORTGAGE

NR - ALPINE ASIAN, ALPINE EQUITY, ALPINE RESOURCES, PREMIER EMERGING MARKETS, SUMMIT EQUITY, SUMMIT FOREIGN EQUITY, SUMMIT DIVIDEND GROWTH, SUMMIT GROWTH & INCOME

BEST CHOICES: AMERIFUND, EQUIFUND, PREMIER INTERNATIONAL, PREMIER BLUE CHIP

BEST FOR RRSPS: DIVERSIFUND 40

BEST UNRATEDS: ANY OF THE SUMMIT SERIES

FUND RATINGS

CANADIAN EQUITY FUNDS

MUTUAL EQUIFUND $$$ → G # RSP CE

Manager: Perigee Private Management

MER: 1.78%

This fund had been doing nicely under the direction of Suzann Pennington, who had been running the show since '93. However, in December, '97 she left Mutual to join Joe Canavan's new Synergy Funds. Obviously, any time there is a major managerial change a fund has to be watched carefully. This fund had generated above-average returns over the three years prior to Pennington's departure, but we'll have to see if the new team can keep up the pace. Initial results are encouraging; the fund gained 7.4% in the first half of 1998, above average for the Canadian equity category for that time frame. The fund invests primarily in Canadian common stocks but also holds some American issues. I'll maintain the rating for now but if you're considering making an investment, remember that the manager responsible for the good-looking historical returns is gone. The Canadian Indexfund and the Strata Growth Fund were both merged into this fund.

MUTUAL PREMIER BLUE CHIP FUND $$$ ↓ G No RSP CE

Manager: Perigee Private Management

MER: 2.27%

This fund has a mandate to invest in large companies. It was also run by Suzann Pennington, who left the company in late 1997, handing over responsibility to a new team. The portfolios of this fund and Mutual Equifund are very similar. In fact, there's not a lot of difference between the two, apart from the purchase option, the higher management fee this one charges, and the fact that Equifund may hold small- to mid-cap stocks as well as blue-chips, which makes it a little more aggressive. Recent returns for this fund have been somewhat higher than for Equifund, with an advance of 10.8% for the first six months of '98 (the period the new team has been in place). That's a reflection of the relative strength of large-cap stocks during that period, compared to the rest of the market. Very good safety record. The Strata Canadian Fund became part of this one.

MUTUAL PREMIER GROWTH FUND $$ → G No RSP CSC

Manager: Perigee Private Management

MER: 2.26%

Here the objective is above-average growth through investments in small- to medium-size companies. Many funds of this type struggled last year, and this was one of them, posting a small loss of 1.8% for the 12 months to June 30/98. That didn't help the fund's previously very good safety rating, which lost some of its glitter. Rating drops back a notch while we await a return to better times.

U.S. AND INTERNATIONAL EQUITY FUNDS

MUTUAL AMERIFUND $$$ → G # £ USE

Manager: Perigee Private Management

MER: 2.03%

This is a small fund that invests mainly in U.S. blue-chip stocks, although some smaller growth companies are held as well. Results are very good. The fund gained 30.1% in the year to June 30/98, and longer term results out to five years are also impressive. The five-year average annual compound rate of return stood at better than 20% in mid-'98. Recent portfolio weighting was towards consumer products and capital goods and technology.

MUTUAL PREMIER AMERICAN FUND $$$ → G No USE

Manager: Perigee Private Management

MER: 2.31%

The no-load brother of the Amerifund, this fund has the same manager and a similar portfolio. The main difference is the purchase option and the slightly higher management fee. Returns have tended to be a bit less than those of the Amerifund, in part due to the MER differential. Last year's gain, for example, was 28.4% (to June 30/98) for this one compared to 30.1% for Amerifund. The same pattern shows up over the longer term. However, the Amerifund published returns aren't discounted to reflect the sales commission. Over time, the higher management fee will end up costing more, but in this case the difference is only 28 basis points (0.28%). So it will take over 13 years to make up the difference if you pay a 3.75% commission for Amerifund. It's hard to plan that far ahead so take the no-load option in this case.

MUTUAL PREMIER INTERNATIONAL FUND $$$ → G No £ IE

Manager: Perigee Private Management

MER: 2.36%

The mandate of this fund is to invest outside Canada and the U.S. Early in '98, the portfolio was heavily concentrated in Europe, with very little money invested in other parts of the globe (Japan and the Far East were only 16% of the mix, fortunately). Predictably, that resulted in an above-average return compared to the international equity category of 16.3% for the year to June 30/98. That helped to pull the five-year average number up to 14.3%, also above par for the peer group. A respectable choice. Rating moves up to $$$.

BALANCED FUNDS

MUTUAL DIVERSIFUND 40 $$$ ↓ FI/G # RSP CBAL

Manager: Perigee Private Management

MER: 1.77%

Until 1996, the Mutual Group offered three "Diversifunds", the only difference being the percentage of stocks in each portfolio. The three have now become one with this, the most balanced of the options, as the sole survivor. Stocks may make up between 25% and 55% of the portfolio, depending on conditions, while bonds and other fixed-income securities will account for at least 45% of the holdings at any time. That means this fund is managed more conservatively than the companion Premier Diversified Fund, which may hold a much higher percentage of stocks. The performance continues to be very good, with a 12.3% gain in the year to June 30/98. Returns out to five years are all above average for the balanced category. Decent safety record. A good choice, especially for a balanced RRSP portfolio.

MUTUAL PREMIER DIVERSIFIED FUND $$ → G/FI No RSP CBAL

Manager: Perigee Private Management

MER: 2.28%

This fund tends to be managed somewhat more aggressively than the companion Diversifund 40 fund, with a heavier emphasis on equities. For example, entering 1998 the bond component of this fund was just 41%, compared to 55% for the Diversifund. You would have expected that to result in a better return here over the last 12 months, but that was not the case. The gain to June 30/98 was 10.2%, more than two percentage points below that of Diversifund 40. The managers put the blame on the negative impact of the Asian crisis on Canadian stocks. Despite this aberration, expect this fund to normally perform better than Diversifund when stock markets are strong, but to be more exposed to risk in downturns. That shows up in the ATP safety ratings, which rank this one much lower than Diversifund.

FIXED INCOME AND MONEY MARKET FUNDS

MUTUAL BOND FUND $ → FI # RSP CB

Manager: Perigee Private Management

MER: 1.86%

The Mutual Group has two bond funds on offer. This is a front-end load option, with, in theory, a lower management fee. However, the MER of this fund has tended to be almost exactly the same as that of the no-load Premier fund. That makes Premier Bond the better choice, plus it has better returns lately. This fund invests in a mix of government and corporate issues with some mortgage-backed securities. The fund's mandate calls for it to be more income-oriented than the Premier fund, so if cash flow is important to you, check out that aspect in detail before making a decision. Returns over time have been below average. The Strata Income Fund was merged into this fund.

MUTUAL PREMIER BOND FUND $$ → FI No RSP CB

Manager: Perigee Private Management

MER: 1.88%

This is the no-load companion to Mutual's older Bond Fund. In this case, the manager places more emphasis on capital growth. Results have been better than those of the Bond Fund, with an 8.8% gain last year compared to 7.9% for the Bond Fund. Of the two, this is the better choice at present, unless cash flow is your prime objective.

MUTUAL MONEY MARKET FUND $$ → C No RSP CMM

Manager: Perigee Private Management

MER: 1.02%

Routine performer. Portfolio is heavily weighted to corporate notes, with about a third of the holdings in federal and provincial T-bills.

MUTUAL PREMIER MORTGAGE FUND $ → FI No RSP M

Manager: Perigee Private Management

MER: 1.77%

This is a middle-of-the-road mortgage fund with the objective of earning a high level of income consistent with reasonable safety. Returns have been below average for the mortgage category. Gain for the 12 months to June 30/98 was 3.9%.

NATIONAL BANK MUTUAL FUNDS

THE COMPANY

National Bank doesn't register very highly on the radar scopes of investors outside Quebec, but it is the sixth-largest bank in the country after the Big Five. The InvesNat Funds are their in-house line. As well, the General Trust Funds come under their aegis, as that company is now part of the National Bank organization.

In January, 1998, National Bank launched a line of segregated funds called the InvesNat Protected Mutual Funds. These are not clones of existing InvesNat funds; although they will have the same managers, their portfolios will be somewhat different. See the separate listing in the Segregated Funds chapter for more information.

THE DETAILS

NUMBER OF FUNDS:	20
ASSETS UNDER MANAGEMENT:	$3.1 BILLION
LOAD CHARGE:	NONE
SWITCHING CHARGE:	NONE
WHERE SOLD:	QUEBEC, ONTARIO, AND NEW BRUNSWICK
HOW SOLD:	THROUGH BRANCHES OF NATIONAL BANK
PHONE NUMBER:	1-888-270-3941
WEB SITE ADDRESS:	N/A
E-MAIL ADDRESS:	N/A

FUND SUMMARY

$$$$ - NONE

$$$ - BOND, CORPORATE CASH MANAGEMENT, EUROPEAN EQUITY, INTERNATIONAL RSP BOND, MORTGAGE, SMALL CAPITALIZATION, TREASURY BILL PLUS, U.S. MONEY MARKET

$$ - AGGRESSIVE DIVERSIFIED, DIVIDEND, GENERAL TRUST CANADIAN EQUITY, GENERAL TRUST MONEY MARKET, GENERAL TRUST MORTGAGE, MONEY MARKET, PRESUMED SOUND INVESTMENTS, SHORT-TERM GOVERNMENT BOND

$ - CANADIAN EQUITY, FAR EAST EQUITY, JAPANESE EQUITY,
RETIREMENT BALANCED,
NR - AMERICAN INDEX PLUS, CANADIAN INDEX PLUS,
TREASURY MANAGEMENT
BEST CHOICES: BOND, EUROPEAN EQUITY, INTERNATIONAL RSP BOND,
MORTGAGE
BEST FOR RRSPs: BOND, INTERNATIONAL RSP BOND
BEST UNRATEDS: AMERICAN INDEX PLUS

FUND RATINGS

INVESTNAT FUNDS

CANADIAN EQUITY FUNDS

INVESNAT CANADIAN EQUITY FUND $ → G No RSP CE

Manager: Sylvain Bélanger (Natcan Investment Management), since 1997

MER: 2.11%

This is a middle-of-the-road fund with a well-balanced portfolio and a blue-chip orientation. It had a great year over the 12 months to June 30/97, but results since then have been weak. Gain for the year to June 30/98 was a very modest 0.5%. The problem was basically a high percentage of resource stocks in the portfolio, which dragged down the return. As a result, the numbers over all time periods have slipped to below par. This leaves me with no choice but to cut back the rating a notch.

INVESNAT DIVIDEND FUND $$ → FI No RSP INC

Manager: Jacques Chartrand (Natcan Investment Management), since 1992

MER: 1.63%

This small fund from National Bank has a portfolio that is in keeping with a true dividend fund, with the majority of the investments in preferred shares (about two thirds of the total in early '98). Overall performance has lagged behind other dividend funds recently because of the high percentage of preferreds, which are more stable in price than the blue-chip common stocks held by many other dividend funds. But the distribution pattern is decent, with a cash yield of 3.2% in calendar '97, based on the net asset value at the start of that year. A good choice for National Bank customers looking for tax-advantaged income.

INVESNAT SMALL CAPITALIZATION FUND

$$$ → G No RSP CSC

Manager: Benoit Durand (Natcan Investment Management), since 1988

MER: 2.16%

This is one of the old General Trust funds that was brought into the InvesNat lineup in August, 1998. The mandate is to invest in growth-oriented stocks, with an emphasis on small- to mid-cap companies. Although the name changed, the manager stays the same so there is continuity here. Results have been consistently above average for the small-cap category, with an average annual compound rate of return of 12% for the decade to June 30/98. Latest one-year gain was 11.8%. A good choice for more aggressive investors.

U.S. AND INTERNATIONAL EQUITY FUNDS

INVESNAT EUROPEAN EQUITY FUND

$$$ → G No £ EE

Managers: Caspar Rock and Christopher Murphy (Framlington Investment Management), since 1995

MER: 2.21%

This is a fairly straightforward fund that focuses on western Europe and avoids the high-risk emerging growth markets of the old Communist hegemony. It got off to a strong start, slumped a bit, but came back last year with a strong gain of 45.9% over the 12 months to June 30/98. About a third of the portfolio was in the U.K. entering '98.

INVESNAT FAR EAST EQUITY FUND

$ ↑ G No £ FEE

Manager: Gerard Smith (Baillie Gifford Overseas Ltd.), since 1995

MER: 2.47%

All Far East funds have been slaughtered recently and this one was no exception with a loss of 42.2% for the year to June 30/98. The fund can invest throughout the region, except in Japan, but there was nowhere to hide from the devastation. Stand clear for now.

INVESNAT JAPANESE EQUITY FUND $ ↑ G No £ FEE

Manager: Angus McLeod (Baillie Gifford Overseas Ltd.), since 1996

MER: 2.46%

There are lots of bargains in Japan these days and at some point they will assert themselves. But in the meantime, investors are suffering huge losses. This fund fell more than 30% in value during the year to June 30/98. Wait for the recovery to begin before taking a position.

BALANCED FUNDS

INVESNAT AGGRESSIVE DIVERSIFIED FUND $$ → G/FI No RSP CBAL

Manager: Marc St. Pierre (Natcan Investment Management), since 1994; Simon Key (Framlington Investment Management), since 1995

MER: 1.75%

This was formerly the General Trust Balanced Fund. It has now been brought into the InvesNat family and given a new name, which suggests the management style will be more aggressive than that of the companion Retirement Balanced Fund. However, all this happened in August, just as this edition was being finalized, so we don't yet have a clear picture of where this fund is going. In its previous guise it was no better than an average performer. We'll leave the rating at $$ for now until we see how it all shakes out.

INVESNAT RETIREMENT BALANCED FUND $ → FI/G No RSP CBAL

Managers: Simon Key (Framlington Investment Management), since 1995 and Michel Tremblay (Natcan Investment Management), since 1998

MER: 2.10%

This is a well-diversified entry, with a portfolio that includes a sprinkling of just about everything: federal government bonds, Quebec bonds, municipal debentures, corporate bonds, T-bills, Canadian common stocks, warrants, U.S. stocks, and a wide range of international equities. Whew! That's a lot to keep track of. The results of this stew haven't been very exciting. Gain for the year to June 30/98 was just 5.9%. That was especially disappointing because of the very strong performance recorded the previous year, which gave the appearance the fund was starting to move up. Rating drops back as a result.

FIXED INCOME AND MONEY MARKET FUNDS

INVESNAT BOND FUND $$$ → FI No RSP CB

Manager: Gilles Chouinard (Natcan Investment Management), since 1994

MER: 1.25%

This was the old General Trust Bond Fund. It was renamed in August, 1998, but the manager and the mandate are the same. The portfolio is a blend of Government of Canada bonds, Quebec government issues, and some corporate and municipal bonds. Returns have generally been above average. Over the three years to June 30/98, the fund generated an annual gain of 10.3%.

INVESNAT CORPORATE
CASH MANAGEMENT FUND $$$ → C No RSP CMM

Manager: Richard Lévesque (Natcan Investment Management), since 1995

MER: 0.52%

The emphasis here, as you might guess by the name, is on corporate short-term notes. However, about a third of the portfolio is invested in federal T-bills, so this is not a pure corporate play. This is the best performer among the bevy of money market entries on offer from National Bank, but you'll need $250,000 to get in. That's the minimum initial investment requirement.

INVESNAT INTERNATIONAL
RSP BOND FUND $$$ → FI No RSP IB

Manager: Gilles Chouinard (Natcan Investment Management), since 1995

MER: 1.94%

This is a 100% RRSP-eligible fund that invests mainly in Canadian bonds denominated in foreign currencies. Part of the mandate is to protect investors against a falling

Canadian dollar, and it has succeeded in doing that quite effectively. Returns have been above average for the international bond category, with a gain of 9.6% for the year to June 30/98. Debuts at $$$.

INVESNAT MONEY MARKET FUND $$ → C No RSP CMM

Manager: Richard Lévesque (Natcan Investment Management), since 1995

MER: 1.05%

This is one of six money market funds offered by National Bank. It invests mainly in federal T-bills (about two thirds of the portfolio) with the rest in provincial and corporate notes. Returns are about average for the money market category.

INVESNAT MORTGAGE FUND $$$ ↓ FI No RSP M

Manager: Gilles Tremblay (Natcan Investment Management), since inception (1991)

MER: 1.55%

This fund is a decent choice in the mortgage category, although recent returns have dipped to below average. Longer term results are above average, however (five-year average annual gain of 6.6% to June 30/98). Plus, the safety record is unblemished. ATP analysis shows this fund has never gone through a 12-month period with a loss. It even managed to stay in the black in '94, when many mortgage funds recorded small losses. A worthwhile option if you're looking for a low-risk fund.

INVESNAT PRESUMED SOUND INVESTMENTS FUND $$ → FI No RSP CMM

Manager: Richard Lévesque (Natcan Investment Management), since 1997

MER: 1.10%

This oddly named fund was previously the InvesNat Canadian Bond Fund. The new name reflects the fact the fund meets the Quebec Civil Code requirements for a "presumed sound investment", which carries a certain degree of credibility in the province. The new objective of the fund is "maximum protection of capital while providing competitive short-term income". Translation: This is a cross between a money market fund and a short-term bond fund that will hold securities that mature in no more than 25 months. As a result, all previous returns are meaningless, since in the past this was a middle-of-the-road bond fund. InvesNat already has a bunch of other money market funds plus a Short-Term Government Bond Fund, so it's not clear why they felt the need to add this one to their mix, but here it is. Prior to its latest name change, this was the Natcan Canadian Bond Fund, so it has gone through more metamorphoses than a butterfly.

INVESNAT SHORT-TERM GOVERNMENT BOND FUND $$ ↓ FI No RSP CB

Manager: Gilles Chouinard (Natcan Investment Management), since 1994

MER: 1.32%

This used to be a regular bond fund but now it operates as a low-risk, short-term fund. That makes it a good choice for defensive investors during periods of rising rates. However, the fund will tend to underperform when rates are declining. That's what happened over the 12 months to June 30/98 when the fund returned only 4%. About three quarters of the portfolio is in Canada short-term bonds and T-bills. There are also investments in Quebec government bonds and short-term notes issued by Quebec municipalities, hospitals, and community colleges.

INVESNAT TREASURY BILL PLUS FUND $$$ ↓ C No RSP CMM

Manager: Richard Lévesque (Natcan Investment Management), since 1995

MER: 0.77%

You need a $50,000 minimum to get into this fund. For that, you get a fund that invests heavily in federal and Quebec T-bills, and has a lower management fee than the companion Money Market Fund. The returns have improved to above average. You can expect to receive an annual yield here that's about 30 basis points (0.3 percentage points) higher than that of the Money Market Fund — which, not coincidentally, is about the difference in the two management fees. Formerly the Natcan Treasury Bill Fund.

INVESNAT U.S. MONEY MARKET FUND $$$ ↓ C No RSP IMM

Manager: Richard Lévesque (Natcan Investment Management), since 1995

MER: 1.10%

This is a fully RRSP-eligible fund that invests in Canadian securities (mainly Government of Canada T-bills) that are denominated in U.S. dollars. Good quality portfolio, with above-average returns. A good hedge against a further decline in the Canadian dollar (heaven forbid!).

GENERAL TRUST FUNDS

CANADIAN EQUITY FUNDS

GENERAL TRUST CANADIAN EQUITY FUND $$ → G No RSP CE

Manager: Sylvain Bélanger (Natcan Investment Management), since 1997

MER: 2.15%

The mandate of this fund is to invest in large Canadian companies, and the portfolio reflects that direction, with lots of banks, big manufacturing companies, and conglomerates in the mix. However, there are still a few smaller companies as well. This fund had been doing well, but came up flat over the 12 months to June 30/98, recording a zero gain. Also, there's a new manager in charge who may shake things up. We'll cut the rating a notch until we get a better handle on where this one is going.

FIXED INCOME AND MONEY MARKET FUNDS

GENERAL TRUST MONEY MARKET FUND $$ → C No RSP CMM

Manager: Gilles Chouinard (Natcan Investment Management), since 1994

MER: 1.15%

The portfolio is invested primarily in federal government T-bills, with about a quarter of the assets in Quebec government notes. Results are about average to slightly below. Nothing special.

GENERAL TRUST MORTGAGE FUND $$ ↓ FI No RSP M

Manager: Gilles Chouinard (Natcan Investment Management), since 1994

MER: 1.57%

This is a decent mortgage fund with average returns. The good news is the fine safety record — this was one of the few mortgage funds to stay in the black during the rough times of '94, with a gain of 3%. That was enough to make this the number-two-performing mortgage fund in the country that year, according to Southam's *Mutual Fund SourceBook*. But I suspect this fund is not long for this world. InvesNat already has a decent mortgage fund and there doesn't seem to be any valid reason for the two to co-exist. Watch for news of a merger soon.

NAVIGATOR FUND COMPANY LTD.

THE COMPANY

The Navigator fund group is a Vancouver-based organization. Control of the company was acquired in mid-1998 by Nova Bancorp Group, a privately owned firm also based in Vancouver.

THE DETAILS

NUMBER OF FUNDS:	8
ASSETS UNDER MANAGEMENT:	$83 MILLION
LOAD CHARGE:	FRONT: MAX. 5% BACK: MAX. 5%
SWITCHING CHARGE:	2% MAXIMUM
WHERE SOLD:	ALBERTA, B.C., MANITOBA, ONTARIO, SASKATCHEWAN
HOW SOLD:	THROUGH REGISTERED BROKERS AND DEALERS
PHONE NUMBER:	1-800-665-1667
WEB SITE ADDRESS:	WWW.NAVIGATOR.CA
E-MAIL ADDRESS:	INFO@NAVIGATOR.CA

FUND SUMMARY

$$$$ - NONE

$$$ - CANADIAN INCOME, AMERICAN VALUE INVESTMENT RETIREMENT

$$ - ASIA PACIFIC

$ - VALUE INVESTMENT RETIREMENT

NR - AMERICAN GROWTH, CANADIAN GROWTH, CANADIAN GROWTH & INCOME, CANADIAN TECHNOLOGY

BEST CHOICES: AMERICAN VALUE INVESTMENT RETIREMENT, CANADIAN INCOME

BEST FOR RRSPs: CANADIAN INCOME

BEST UNRATEDS: AMERICAN GROWTH

FUND RATINGS

CANADIAN EQUITY FUNDS

NAVIGATOR VALUE
INVESTMENT RETIREMENT FUND $ ↑ G #/* RSP CSC

Manager: Wayne Deans, since 1994

MER: 2.94%

This is one of those funds with a name that definitely does not tell all. The words "retirement" and "value" seem to imply a conservative investment style, but that is not at all the case. The mandate is to invest in small to mid-size companies, which is what manager Wayne Deans specializes in. So this is much more of a go-go fund than a sleepy, put-some-money-aside-for-the-future entry. It is really best suited to aggressive investors, who can stand the volatility, not to folks dutifully saving for their retirement years. Returns have been extremely volatile. The fund lost 21.9% over the year to June 30/98. But despite that tumble, the five-year average annual compound rate of return remains firmly in positive territory, at 14.4%. Deans has been stung twice by corporate meltdowns in the past couple of years. In 1997 it was Bre-X, in which the fund had a large position. In 1998 it was YBM Magnex. Bad news for investors! This fund offers a wild ride, with potential for big swings in either direction. Be sure you understand the risks before you commit any money.

U.S. AND INTERNATIONAL EQUITY FUNDS

NAVIGATOR AMERICAN
VALUE INVESTMENT FUND $$$ → G #/* £ USE

Manager: Anthony Browne (Roxbury Capital Management), since 1997

MER: 2.99%

This is a large-cap fund that focuses on blue-chip stocks. So you'll find lots of familiar names in the portfolio, like Coca Cola, General Electric, and Walt Disney. That was where the big growth was in U.S. markets in recent years so it should not be a surprise that this fund performed well. One-year gain to June 30/98 was 28.4%. Three-year average annual compound rate of return was 23.9%, well above average. Blue-chip U.S. stocks are always a good place to be so we'll give this fund a $$$ rating in its first appearance here.

NAVIGATOR ASIA-PACIFIC FUND $$ ↑ G #/* £ FEE

Managers: Cheah Cheng Hye and V-Nee Yeh (Value Partners), since 1997

MER: 3.01%

This fund may invest throughout Asia, with the exception of Japan. Like all other Far East funds, it was hit by the Asian flu, but the loss was not as bad as some others experienced. The fund dropped 26.9% in the year to June 30/98, but the three-year average annual compound rate of return stayed in the black, at 8.4%. That was the best result of any Far East fund over that time frame. The portfolio was heavily concentrated in Hong Kong and China in the first half of '98, with Singapore the only other large position. The Far East is a turbulent place right now but if you must have money there, this fund is a better bet than most.

FIXED INCOME AND MONEY MARKET FUNDS

NAVIGATOR CANADIAN INCOME FUND $$$ ↑ FI #/* RSP CB

Manager: Doug Knight, since 1994

MER: 2.45%

The mandate of this fund is to invest in corporate bonds with the twin goals of providing maximum yield with minimum volatility. Although this isn't officially called a high-yield bond fund, the portfolio consists mainly of lower-grade issues. There are no BCE or big bank bonds here; instead you're investing in issues of companies like Domtar, Stelco, Avenor, and Rogers, which have lower safety ratings and higher yields. The three-year returns are well above average for the Canadian bond fund category (an average of 11.5% for the period to June 30/98). However, the latest results are slightly sub-par. A good choice for more aggressive bond fund investors, as long as you understand the nature of the portfolio you're buying into.

NORTHWEST MUTUAL FUNDS

THE COMPANY

The Northwest funds is a new name but the funds themselves are not. This was formerly the Concorde fund group. It was purchased by a new organization headed by mutual fund marketing expert Michael Butler and now does business under this new banner. Don't confuse these funds with the segregated funds offered by Northwest Life. This is a completely separate group.

The company supplied us with minimal information and their web site is not very helpful, so some of the details below are drawn from last year's edition when the funds still operated under the Concorde name.

THE DETAILS

NUMBER OF FUNDS:	7
ASSETS UNDER MANAGEMENT:	$135 MILLION
LOAD CHARGE:	FRONT: MAX. 6% BACK: MAX. 5%
SWITCHING CHARGE:	NONE
WHERE SOLD:	ACROSS CANADA
HOW SOLD:	THROUGH FINANCIAL ADVISORS
PHONE NUMBER:	(416) 922-6633 OR 1-888-809-3333
WEB SITE ADDRESS:	WWW.NORTHWESTFUNDS.COM
E-MAIL ADDRESS:	TEVESON@NORTHWESTFUNDS.COM

FUND SUMMARY

$$$$ - NONE

$$$ - NONE

$$ - BALANCED, DIVIDEND, GROWTH, INTERNATIONAL, MONEY MARKET

$ - INCOME, MORTGAGE

NR - NONE

BEST CHOICES: DIVIDEND, GROWTH, INTERNATIONAL
BEST FOR RRSPs: GROWTH
BEST UNRATEDS: N/A

FUND RATINGS

CANADIAN EQUITY FUNDS

NORTHWEST GROWTH FUND $$ → G #/* RSP CE

Manager: Richard Fogler (Kingwest and Company), since 1997

MER: 2.00%

In its previous guise as the Concorde Growth Fund, this entry offered a well-diversified portfolio that focused on medium and larger size companies. A new manager was brought on board in late 1997, so we don't have a clear idea at this stage where the fund is heading from here. The revamped fund showed well in the first half of '98, gaining 12% in six months. But with all this change, we'll drop the rating from the old Concorde fund by a notch until a clearer picture emerges.

NORTHWEST DIVIDEND FUND $$ → FI/G #/* RSP INC

Manager: Ubald Cloutier (TPR Investment Management), since inception (1994)

MER: 1.75%

This fund invests in a portfolio of preferred and common shares with a view to generating a combination of dividends and capital gains. Results have been slightly above average for the balanced category, with an average annual compound rate of return of 22.9% for the three years to June 30/98. Debuts at $$. Formerly the Concorde Dividend Fund.

U.S. AND INTERNATIONAL EQUITY FUNDS

NORTHWEST INTERNATIONAL FUND $$ → G #/* £ IE

Manager: Pierre Dauron (OpCap Advisors), since 1998

MER: 2.25%

The new owners changed the manager of this fund early in 1998. We'll see if that was a good idea, because this had been one of the best performers in the Concorde stable. Average annual compound rate of return for the three years to June 30/98 was 16.1%, slightly above average for the international fund category. Because of the manager change, we'll start this one off at $$ in its debut here.

BALANCED FUNDS

NORTHWEST BALANCED FUND $$ → FI/G #/* RSP CBAL

Manager: Richard Fogler (Kingwest and Company), since 1997

MER: 2.00%

So-so performer. Gain for the year to June 30/98 was above average at 11.2%. Longer term results are a bit below the norm. Nothing to get excited about. Formerly the Concorde Balanced Fund.

FIXED INCOME AND MONEY MARKET FUNDS

NORTHWEST INCOME FUND $ → FI #/* RSP CB

Manager: Jean Duguay (TPR Investment Management), since inception (1992)

MER: 1.75%

As the Concorde Income Fund, this was an unimpressive entry. The management firm is still the same but returns have strengthened recently. The portfolio has become more balanced with a significant holding of Government of Canada issues as well as bonds issued by other provinces. One-year return to June 30/98 was 9.1%, above average for the bond category. Longer term results are still sub-par, however.

NORTHWEST MONEY MARKET FUND $$ → C #/* RSP CMM

Manager: Jean Duguay (TPR Investment Management), since inception (1992)

MER: 1.00%

Routine money market fund. The portfolio is a mix of government and corporate notes. Returns are average to slightly above.

NORTHWEST MORTGAGE FUND $ → FI #/* RSP M

Manager: Jean Duguay (TPR Investment Management), since inception (1991)

MER: 1.75%

This was not a strong performer as the Concorde Mortgage Fund and the new name hasn't done much to help. Gain for the year to June 30/98 was a piddling 1.9% — even the money market fund did better. Moreover, you have to pay a load fee to acquire it. There are many better no-load options available. Pass.

THE O'DONNELL GROUP OF FUNDS

THE COMPANY

This fund group was launched at the beginning of the 1996 RRSP season, so it is now entering its third year. The organization is headed by industry veteran James O'Donnell, who is regarded as one of the leading innovators in the fund business. The company was an instant success story, pulling in more than $1 billion in assets faster than any other startup. A public stock offering in mid-1997 was hugely oversubscribed and the stock quickly rose to well above its initial price. However, the past year has been more difficult. Many of the original funds that got off to a fast start slowed down and all but O'Donnell High Income were underperforming the two-year average in their respective categories as of June 30/98. Several of the funds created since the launch were also struggling, although O'Donnell Select, run by ex-Trimark manager Wally Kusters, was a pleasant exception.

Predictably, the growth pace of the company slowed considerably (they had $1.4 billion in assets under management at the end of July/98), and the value of the shares tumbled.

The next year will be a testing time for this young firm. It's important that more of the funds start to perform well or financial advisors who went out of their way to recommend them initially may start to move assets out.

THE DETAILS

NUMBER OF FUNDS:	13
ASSETS UNDER MANAGEMENT:	$1.8 BILLION
LOAD CHARGE:	FRONT: MAX. 5%; BACK: MAX. 5.75%
SWITCHING CHARGE:	NONE
WHERE SOLD:	ACROSS CANADA
HOW SOLD:	THROUGH BROKERS, DEALERS, AND FINANCIAL PLANNERS
PHONE NUMBER:	1-800-292-5658 OR (416) 221-2800
WEB SITE ADDRESS:	WWW.ODONNELLFUNDS.COM/ADVISOR
E-MAIL ADDRESS:	INVEST@ODONNELLFUNDS.COM

FUND SUMMARY

$$$$ - None
$$$ - None
$$ - None
$ - None
NR - American Sector Growth, Balanced, Canadian, Canadian Emerging Growth, Growth, High Income, Money Market, U.S. Mid-Cap, Select, Short Term, U.S. High Income, World Equity, World Precious Metals

Best Choices: N/A
Best for RRSPs: N/A
Best unrateds: High Income, Select, U.S. Mid-Cap

FUND RATINGS

All the funds in this group have been in existence less than three years, so do not qualify for a rating.

OPTIMA STRATEGY FUNDS

THE COMPANY

This is a Winnipeg-based fund group, managed by Loring Ward Investment Counsel. The company, founded in 1987, offers a wide range of investment management services and has developed a reputation for creating innovative new financial products. For four consecutive years (1994–97) the firm was named one of the 50 Best Managed Private Companies in Canada by *The Financial Post*. It is a member of the Assante Group.

You'll see that the management expense ratio for each fund seems very low. That's because management fees are charged directly to investors, an unusual practice in the industry. So you may be charged as much as 2.5% a year, depending on the fund. These fees are not reflected in the performance records of the funds published in the business media, so you would have to subtract the costs to arrive at a net return. One other point: Optima operates two "umbrella" funds that allow for switches without triggering capital gains tax liability. This is similar to the programs offered by AGF, C.I., AIM GT, and a few other firms.

These funds are intended for individuals and families with $100,000 or more to invest, so they are strictly for the high-end market.

THE DETAILS

NUMBER OF FUNDS:	8
ASSETS UNDER MANAGEMENT:	$2.2 BILLION
LOAD CHARGE:	FRONT: MAX. 4%; BACK: MAX. 5.5%
SWITCHING CHARGE:	2% MAXIMUM
WHERE SOLD:	NS, NB, QC, ON, MB, SK, AB, BC, YK
HOW SOLD:	THROUGH THE ASSANTE DEALER DISTRIBUTION NETWORK AND OTHER SELECT FINANCIAL PLANNERS
PHONE NUMBER:	1-800-267-1730 EXT. 348 (ADVISOR SERVICES)
WEB SITE ADDRESS:	N/A
E-MAIL ADDRESS:	INFO@LORINGWARD.CA

FUND SUMMARY

$$$$ - NONE
$$$ - CANADIAN EQUITY, CANADIAN FIXED INCOME, U.S. EQUITY
$$ - INTERNATIONAL EQUITY, GLOBAL FIXED INCOME
$ - SHORT TERM INVESTMENT
NR - CASH MANAGEMENT, REAL ESTATE INVESTMENT

BEST CHOICES: CANADIAN EQUITY, U.S. EQUITY
BEST FOR RRSPs: CANADIAN EQUITY, CANADIAN FIXED INCOME
BEST UNRATEDS: REAL ESTATE INVESTMENT

FUND RATINGS

CANADIAN EQUITY FUNDS

OPTIMA STRATEGY
CANADIAN EQUITY SECTION $$$ → G #/* RSP CE

Manager: Daniel Bubis, since 1993

MER: 0.40%

This fund uses a disciplined value investing approach to its stock selection, looking for out-of-favour companies that trade at a low price/earnings multiple. The portfolio is small and makes good use of foreign content, with some U.S. and Mexican holdings. For the past couple of years, the portfolio has been weighted towards financial services and industrial products, with very little exposure to the troubled resource sector. This helped propel the fund to an above-average 15.8% gain in the year ending June 30/98. Five-year average annual rate of return was 19.9%, well above-average for the Canadian equity category. The maximum annual management fee for this fund is 2.5%, so even after deducting that payment we have a winner here.

OPTIMA STRATEGY INTERNATIONAL
EQUITY SECTION $$ → G #/* £ IE

Manager: Glenn Wellman (Credit Suisse), since inception (1994)

MER: 0.47%

This fund offers a very large, highly diversified portfolio, which includes stocks from both developed countries and emerging markets (e.g., Hungary, Croatia). Teams of specialists make recommendations for various regions around the world, which are then screened for the right portfolio balance. Returns have slumped in the past two years. Gain for the 12 months to June 30/98 was just 4.5%, well below average for the international fund category. Three-year average annual compound rate of return was 15.9%, before management fees. These may be up to 2.5% a year; if you're paying that much your net average annual return for three years drops to 13.4%. That's okay, but not great.

OPTIMA STRATEGY U.S.
EQUITY SECTION $$$ ↓ G #/* £ USE

Manager: Thomas F. Sassi (Scudder Kemper Investments), since 1997

MER: 0.41%

Like the Canadian Equity Section, this portfolio is value-driven. The advisor is New York-based Scudder Kemper Investments, which was formed from a complex corporate arrangement that absorbed Dreman Value Advisors, who had been handling the chores. The manager uses a contrarian approach to stock selection, focusing on stocks with very low price/earnings ratios. The goal is not only to produce good returns, but also to provide good downside protection in bad markets. Results have been very good, even after deducting management fees. Gain for the year to June 30/98 was 38.5%, while the three-year average annual compound rate of return was an excellent 36.2%. To date, there hasn't been a single 12-month period when this fund has shown a loss, so the risk rating is excellent. Maximum management fee is 2.5%.

FIXED INCOME AND MONEY MARKET FUNDS

OPTIMA STRATEGY CANADIAN
FIXED INCOME SECTION $$$ → FI #/* RSP CB

Manager: Daniel Bubis, since inception (1993)

MER: 0.39%

The fund invests mainly in Government of Canada bonds with varying maturities, as well as some provincial issues and a few corporates. Returns have been above average. The fund gained 13.6% in the year to June 30/98, thanks mainly to strength in the long bond market. However, a management fee of up to 2% applies; deduct that and the net return is 11.6%. That was still considerably better than the average for Canadian bond funds as a group, however.

OPTIMA STRATEGY GLOBAL
FIXED-INCOME SECTION $$ → FI #/* £ IB

Manager: Leslie J. Nanberg (MFS Institutional Advisors), since inception (1994)

MER: 0.48%

This international bond fund invests in government issues from around the globe. The manager looks for undervalued bonds and currencies. Results have started to pick up, with the fund recording an 11.4% gain before management fees for the year to June 30/98. The outlook for international bonds is much improved so the rating moves up a notch.

OPTIMA STRATEGY SHORT-TERM
INVESTMENT SECTION $ ↓ FI #/* RSP CB

Manager: Daniel Bubis, since inception (1993)

MER: 0.27%

This fund is designed for investors who want less risk in their bond fund holdings. The portfolio holds government and corporate issues with maturity dates of no more than five years. In fact, the average duration of the portfolio (a measure of risk) is much less than that; it was 1.37 years entering 1998. This type of fund will typically underperform when bond markets are strong, but will protect your asset base when bonds hit the skids. However, the returns here have been weaker than those of other defensive bond funds, especially when you take the management fee of up to 1.5% into account. Average annual compound rate of return for the three years to June 30/98 was just 6.3%, before fees. By way of comparison, the comparable Phillips, Hager & North fund averaged 8.1% for the same period, net of all management fees. If you're an Optima Strategy client, this isn't the best place to be spending your money.

OPTIMUM FUNDS

THE COMPANY

This group of funds is based in Montreal, and is only available to residents of the Province of Quebec. The sponsor, Optimum Placements Inc., is a wholly owned subsidiary of Groupe Optimum Inc. Management is by Les Conseillers Financiers du St.-Laurent.

THE DETAILS

NUMBER OF FUNDS:	6
ASSETS UNDER MANAGEMENT:	$49 MILLION
LOAD CHARGE:	NONE
SWITCHING CHARGE:	NONE
WHERE SOLD:	QUEBEC
HOW SOLD:	DIRECTLY THROUGH THE MANAGER OR THROUGH BROKERS AND DEALERS
PHONE NUMBER:	1-888-OPTIMUM (678-4686)
WEB SITE ADDRESS:	WWW.FONDSOPTIMUM.COM
E-MAIL ADDRESS:	OPI@GROUPE-OPTIMUM.COM

FUND SUMMARY

$$$$ - NONE
$$$ - BOND, EQUITY, INTERNATIONAL, SAVINGS
$$ - BALANCED
$ - NONE
NR - GROWTH AND INCOME
BEST CHOICES: BOND, EQUITY, INTERNATIONAL
BEST FOR RRSPs: BOND, EQUITY
BEST UNRATEDS: GROWTH AND INCOME

FUND RATINGS

CANADIAN EQUITY FUNDS

OPTIMUM EQUITY FUND $$$ → G No RSP CE

Manager: Les Conseillers Financiers du St-Laurent, since 1994

MER: 1.62%

The approach here is top-down, with the managers identifying sectors of the economy they believe will outperform. The portfolio favours large corporations, with names like BCE, Royal Bank, Manitoba Tel, etc. dominating the list. This is a very small fund, with only $4.3 million in assets. However, results have been good. The fund gained 13.3% in the year to June 30/98, and the three-year average annual compound rate of return is above average at 18.9%.

U.S. AND INTERNATIONAL EQUITY FUNDS

OPTIMUM INTERNATIONAL FUND $$$ → G No £ IE

Manager: Les Conseillers Financiers du St-Laurent, since 1994

MER: 1.96%

This fund's mandate allows the managers to invest anywhere in the world, and to take currency positions as well. As a result, the fund was heavily exposed to the U.S. in the first half of '98, with 50% of the portfolio in U.S. stocks and a 69% exposure to the rising U.S. dollar. This contributed to another year of very good returns for this small entry. Gain for the 12 months to June 30/98 was 25.4%. Three-year average annual compound rate of return was a very good 17.5%. We'll give this one $$$ in its first appearance here.

BALANCED FUNDS

OPTIMUM BALANCED FUND $$ → FI/G No RSP CBAL

Manager: Les Conseillers Financiers du St-Laurent, since inception (1986)

MER: 1.46%

This fund has been weighted towards bonds for the past couple of years, unlike most other balanced funds in Canada, which have favoured stocks. Still, the return for the year to June 30/98 was slightly above average for the balanced category at 10.8% and the fund was better positioned to cope with the mid-summer downturn in the stock market. The stock portion of the portfolio is a mix of blue-chip, mid-cap, and small-cap issues. The bond section is comprised mainly of federal government and Quebec provincial issues. Formerly known as St. Laurent Optimum Balanced Fund.

FIXED INCOME AND MONEY MARKET FUNDS

OPTIMUM BOND FUND $$$ → FI No RSP CB

Manager: Les Conseillers Financiers du St-Laurent, since inception (1986)

MER: 1.39%

This is a small fund with some decent returns. Average annual 10-year gain to June 30/98 was 10.8% percent, making this little-known fund one of the better performers in the country over that time. The portfolio used to be almost exclusively comprised of Quebec government issues, but it has been switched to almost two thirds federal government T-bills and bonds. Formerly St. Laurent Optimum Bond Fund.

OPTIMUM SAVINGS FUND $$$ → C No RSP CMM

Manager: Les Conseillers Financiers du St-Laurent, since inception (1985)

MER: 0.71%

Decent results from this small fund. Invests in a mix of Government of Canada T-bills and corporate notes. Formerly known as St. Laurent Optimum Savings Fund.

ORBIT MUTUAL FUNDS

THE COMPANY

The two Orbit funds are operated by Orbit Mutual Fund Management, a Montreal-based company. Each fund has a separate investment advisor, so the strategy is quite different. The newer North American Equity Fund, run by Magna Vista Capital Management of Montreal, is too young to qualify for a rating, but has looked good so far.

THE DETAILS

NUMBER OF FUNDS:	2
ASSETS UNDER MANAGEMENT:	$12 MILLION
LOAD CHARGE:	FRONT: MAX. 5%
SWITCHING CHARGE:	2% MAXIMUM
WHERE SOLD:	QUEBEC AND ONTARIO
HOW SOLD:	THROUGH BROKERS, DEALERS, AND FINANCIAL PLANNERS
PHONE NUMBER:	(514) 932-3000
WEB SITE ADDRESS:	N/A
E-MAIL ADDRESS:	N/A

FUND SUMMARY

$$$$ - NONE
$$$ - WORLD
$$ - NONE
$ - NONE
NR - NORTH AMERICAN EQUITY
BEST CHOICES: WORLD
BEST FOR RRSPs: WORLD (FOREIGN CONTENT)
BEST UNRATEDS: NORTH AMERICAN

FUND RATINGS

U.S. AND INTERNATIONAL EQUITY FUNDS

ORBIT WORLD FUND $$$ → G # £ IE

Managers: David Marvin and Stanley Palmer (Marvin & Palmer Associates), since 1995

MER: 2.65%

After a long struggle, we've seen a real turnaround here and this is now a fund worth your attention. It gained a very respectable 34% last year, and has an average annual compound rate of return of 18.7% for the three years to June 30/98. That's an important number, because it more or less coincides with the period that Marvin & Palmer Associates have been in charge. Prior to that, the fund was something of an orphan. It was launched in '88, under the direction of Dr. Richard Coghlan, then chief economist for Swiss Bank Julies Baer. When he was no longer able to continue, management was shifted to Union Bank of Switzerland, Philips & Drew in London. After a few years, it was felt the fund wasn't getting enough attention, so responsibility was moved again. However, the new manager's trading strategy was deemed to be too risky, so in late '95 there was yet another change, to Marvin & Palmer of Wilmington, Delaware. They have focused on the U.S. and Europe and that strategy has paid off well. The managers use a complex method of stock selection that involves an initial screening approach covering thousands of funds, followed by fundamental analysis of individual stocks, countries, and currencies. Obviously, it works.

PERIGEE INVESTMENT COUNSEL

THE COMPANY

This is a new mutual fund group but the parent company, Perigee, is not. It has been in business since 1972, providing investment advice to leading corporations. Their new fund line features no-load charges and very low management fees. The dozen mutual funds provide broad diversification, with money market, U.S. equity, international equity, fixed-income, and four Canadian equity offerings. Minimum initial investment is $5,000 unless you open a monthly investment plan, in which case $2,500 will get you started.

THE DETAILS

NUMBER OF FUNDS:	12
ASSETS UNDER MANAGEMENT:	$3.8 MILLION
LOAD CHARGE:	NONE
SWITCHING CHARGE:	NONE
WHERE SOLD:	ALBERTA, B.C., AND ONTARIO
HOW SOLD:	DIRECTLY THROUGH PERIGEE INVESTMENT COUNSEL
PHONE NUMBER:	1-888-437-3333
WEB SITE ADDRESS:	WWW.PERIGEEMUTUALFUNDS.COM
E-MAIL ADDRESS:	FUNDS@PERIGEEMUTUALFUNDS.COM

FUND SUMMARY

$$$$ - NONE
$$$ - NONE
$$ - NONE
$ - NONE
NR - ACCUFUNDS, ACTIVE BOND, CANADIAN AGGRESSIVE GROWTH EQUITY, CANADIAN SECTOR EQUITY, CANADIAN VALUE EQUITY, DIVERSIFUND, INDEX PLUS BOND, INTERNATIONAL EQUITY, NORTH AMERICAN EQUITY, SYMMETRY BALANCED, T-PLUS, U.S. EQUITY

BEST CHOICES: N/A
BEST FOR RRSPs: N/A
BEST UNRATEDS: ALL THE FUNDS ARE TOO NEW FOR AN OPINION TO BE FORMED.

FUND RATINGS

None of the funds in this group has been in existence long enough to qualify for a rating.

PHILLIPS, HAGER & NORTH INVESTMENT MANAGEMENT

THE COMPANY

This is a highly respected Vancouver-based investment house with some outstanding performers in its stable. The firm has been in business since 1965 and manages money for pension plans, individuals, foundations, and the like as well as operating its family of mutual funds. Management fees are among the lowest in the industry. The funds in this group are best suited to conservative, long-term investors. Minimum initial investment is a hefty $25,000 per account, with subsequent minimum purchases of $5,000. RRSP accounts can be opened with $10,000 if the RRSP is held by PH&N (minimum of $1,000 in any single fund). New RRIF accounts require a $50,000 minimum.

THE DETAILS

Number of funds:	12
Assets under management:	$6.75 billion
Load charge:	None
Switching charge:	None
Where sold:	Across Canada
How sold:	Directly through PH&N or through brokers, dealers, and financial planners
Phone number:	(604) 408-6100 or 1-800-661-6141
Web site address:	www.phn.ca
E-mail address:	info@phn.ca

FUND SUMMARY

$$$$ - Bond, Canadian Money Market, Dividend Income, U.S. Equity, $U.S. Money Market

$$$ - Balanced, North American Equity, Canadian Equity, Canadian Equity Plus, Short Term Bond and Mortgage, Vintage

$$ - None

$ - International Equity

NR - None

BEST CHOICES: BOND, DIVIDEND INCOME, U.S. EQUITY

BEST FOR RRSPs: BOND, BALANCED, DIVIDEND INCOME, SHORT TERM BOND AND MORTGAGE

BEST UNRATEDS: N/A

FUND RATINGS

CANADIAN EQUITY FUNDS

PHILLIPS, HAGER & NORTH
CANADIAN EQUITY FUND
$$$ → G No RSP CE

Manager: Team

MER: 1.10%

This is a pure Canadian stock fund with no foreign content (the companion Canadian Equity Plus Fund holds foreign stocks as well). It is a growth-oriented fund, with the main holdings in medium- to large-size companies. This fund ran into some tough times in the mid to early '90s, but has now righted itself and is producing excellent returns again. Results for the year to June 30/98 were modestly above average, with an 11.5% gain. Coincidentally, that was exactly the same as the average annual return over the past decade, which gives you an idea of the consistency at work here. The latest returns probably would have been better were it not for the fact that almost a quarter of the portfolio was in the troubled resource sector in the first half of '98. But let's not quibble. This doesn't rank in the top echelon of Canadian stock funds, but it is most respectable.

PHILLIPS, HAGER & NORTH
CANADIAN EQUITY PLUS FUND
$$$ → G No RSP CE

Manager: Team

MER: 1.16%

The performance pattern here is similar to the company's Canadian Equity Fund, so the same broad comments apply. The portfolios are also similar; the main difference is that a chunk of this fund's holdings are in foreign securities (14.6% as of mid-'98), thus providing international diversification. Somewhat surprisingly, returns were significantly lower than those of the companion Canadian Equity Fund over the 12 months to June 30/98, at 9.7%. Longer term results are just about the same, however. This was formerly known as the Phillips, Hager & North RSP/RIF Equity Fund.

PHILLIPS, HAGER & NORTH
DIVIDEND INCOME FUND $$$$ ↓ G/FI No RSP INC

Manager: Team

MER: 1.16%

The portfolio concentrates on high-yielding common stocks, rather than preferreds (in fact, preferred shares make up less than 1% of the portfolio). This produces less dividend income than some competitor funds offer, but higher capital gains potential. In calendar '97, an analysis done for my *Mutual Funds Update* newsletter showed a dividend yield of 2% based on net asset value at the start of the year, down considerably from the year before. A number of other dividend funds produced better cash flow, so if income is essential this isn't the best choice. However, on a total return basis this fund is one of the consistent leaders in this category. In fact, it's been doing better than the regular PH&N stock funds lately. Last year's gain (to June 30/98) was 36.6% and that came on top of a spectacular 47.9% advance the year before. Those results helped to boost the 10-year average annual compound rate of return to 15.6%, best in the dividend fund category. Just remember, this is not a conventional dividend fund. It's really a blue-chip stock fund and it will be especially vulnerable to developments like a big pull-back in bank share prices, such as we saw in August, 1998. Still, for a long-term investor, you won't do much better.

PHILLIPS, HAGER & NORTH
VINTAGE FUND $$$ → G No RSP CE

Manager: Ian Mottershead, since inception (1986)

MER: 1.75%

This is the most aggressive fund in the Phillips, Hager & North family, specializing in growth stocks. It is not a small-cap fund as such, however — many of the holdings are large corporations that manager Ian Mottershead feels have above-average potential (e.g., CIBC, Mackenzie Financial, Royal Bank). A portion of the assets (10.3% in the first half of '98) are invested in international securities. Both short- and long-term results have been very good. This fund gained over 11.5% last year and has one of the top 10-year records in this category. The fund was closed to new subscribers in March, '93, but current unitholders who hold the fund directly in a PH&N RRSP are allowed to add to their holdings. If you're in that position, do so.

U.S. AND INTERNATIONAL EQUITY FUNDS

PHILLIPS, HAGER & NORTH
INTERNATIONAL EQUITY FUND $ → G No £ IE

Manager: Team

MER: 1.49%

This continues to be the weak link in the PH&N chain, despite the fact I've been told they are trying to improve matters. It's an international fund that invests throughout the world outside North America. The approach is top-down, which involves identifying the seven to 12 countries with the best prospects and then buying a basket of stocks that reflect the leading index of the nations selected. Sounds good in theory, but results have been well below average for the international equity fund category, mainly because the screening process keeps zeroing in on nations like Japan (almost 20% of the portfolio in mid-'98) and some other Far East countries. This fund is clearly not one of the company's strengths. I've been making that point for several years, but nothing changes. Let me be more blunt: Get a new screening system, folks — this one doesn't work. In the meantime, investors should look elsewhere for their international funds.

PH&N NORTH AMERICAN EQUITY FUND $$$ → G No £ AE

Manager: Team

MER: 1.12%

The mandate of this fund is long-term growth through investments in Canadian, U.S., and Mexican stocks. It got off to a strong start but then suffered a major setback in '94, in part due to the unexpected devaluation of the peso. It bounced back strongly in the mid-'90s; however, the last results are disappointing. The fund gained just 7.8% over the year to June 30/98, compared to an average of 15.3% for all entries in the North American equity category of *The Financial Post*. However, three-year results are well above average at 20.3%. As a result, we'll maintain the $$$ rating for now and hope to see some improvement in returns.

PHILLIPS, HAGER & NORTH
U.S. EQUITY FUND $$$$ ↓ G No £ USE

Manager: Team

MER: 1.09%

This fund is an excellent long-term performer, and it continues to generate decent results. Average annual return over the past decade is 18.3%, making it one of the top performers in the U.S. equity category. Latest one-year return was a bit disappointing, at 24.8% (to June 30/98). I say disappointing because that was actually below average for U.S. stock funds as a group. However, all longer term results are still above par. The portfolio is weighted towards blue-chip issues. Altamira's ATP analysis shows this fund to have one of the best risk profiles in the U.S. equity fund category. It also tends to outperform its peers in bear markets, because of the conservative management style. With all those positives going for it, we'll maintain the $$$$ rating, although I'd like to see a return to at least second quartile results next year.

BALANCED FUNDS

PHILLIPS, HAGER & NORTH
BALANCED FUND $$$ ↓ FI/G No RSP CBAL

Manager: Team

MER: 0.89%

This is a well-diversified fund, with a portfolio made up of a carefully chosen mix of Canadian stocks, federal, provincial, and corporate bonds, and units of the U.S. and International funds for foreign content. (I'd be happier if the latter were left out; they've been a drag on returns here.) The portfolio was weighted towards equities in mid-'98. Good results. Five-year average annual return to June 30/98 was 12.6%, comfortably above average. Good risk profile. This one won't shoot the lights out, but you won't toss and turn at night worrying about your money either.

FIXED INCOME AND MONEY MARKET FUNDS

PHILLIPS, HAGER & NORTH
BOND FUND $$$$ ↓ FI No RSP CB

Manager: Team

MER: 0.57%

This is quite simply one of the best bond funds you can buy. Both short- and long-term results are well above average. Gain last year was 10%. The 10-year annual average compound rate of return to June 30/98 was 11.2%, the same number as last year (how's that for consistency?). Among funds open to the general public, only Altamira Income and Altamira Bond were better over that time. The portfolio is weighted to government securities, with some corporate issues and mortgages also in the mix. An extra benefit is the very low management expense ratio, which makes this one of the best values you'll find in bond funds from that point of view. The risk rating is excellent. What more do you want?

PHILLIPS, HAGER & NORTH
CANADIAN MONEY MARKET FUND $$$$ → C No RSP CMM

Manager: Team

MER: 0.44%

The portfolio invests mainly in high-grade corporate notes, which enhances return with slightly more risk. Major advantage: one of the lowest management fees in the business. Consistently good returns, timeliness, and no-load status earn it a top rating.

PHILLIPS, HAGER & NORTH SHORT
TERM BOND AND MORTGAGE FUND $$$ ↓ FI No RSP B/M

Manager: Team

MER: 0.63%

This is a half-way house between the company's successful Bond Fund and their money market funds. The idea is to generate a better return than you'll get from low-interest money funds these days, but with less risk than a conventional bond fund would carry. To achieve that, the fund invests in bonds that mature within five years as well as conventional mortgages. The result is just what you might expect: a very good safety record but lower returns than a conventional bond fund would produce. However, results are substantially higher than the average mortgage fund (average annual compound rate of return of 8.1% over the three years to June 30/98). If you're looking for a defensive fund with decent returns, this one will work.

PHILLIPS, HAGER & NORTH
$U.S. MONEY MARKET FUND $$$$ → C No RSP IMM

Manager: Team

MER: 0.52%

Solid U.S. money fund with full RRSP eligibility. Invests in short-term notes issued by Canadian governments and corporations but denominated in U.S. currency. Offers one of the lowest management fees in this category. A good choice, especially for those who want to hold U.S. dollars in their RRSPs or RRIFs.

PRIMUS CAPITAL ADVISORS

THE COMPANY

This is yet another new player on the mutual fund stage, but with a somewhat different approach. The company selects the top money managers in Canada and abroad and engages them to manage a portion of the various portfolios they offer. Some of the managers are not available to most fund investors because of the high minimums they charge for their own funds, or because they mainly operate in the pension field. One example: Irwin Michael. His ABC funds cost a minimum of $150,000 to buy but you can acquire his services for a portion of the PRIMUS Canadian Equity Fund for an initial investment of just $1,000. Of course, you're getting five other managers as well. All the PRIMUS funds use a multi-manager approach.

So far, the results look pretty good. Of the six funds the company currently offers, five scored above-average returns in their respective categories in their first year. That's too soon to draw any meaningful judgments, but it's a good start.

PRIMUS is the Canadian subsidiary of SEI Investments of Oaks, Pennsylvania. The parent firm trades on NASDAQ and also has offices in Zurich, Switzerland.

THE DETAILS

NUMBER OF FUNDS:	6
ASSETS UNDER MANAGEMENT:	$600 MILLION
LOAD CHARGE:	NONE
SWITCHING CHARGE:	NONE
WHERE SOLD:	ACROSS CANADA
HOW SOLD:	THROUGH THE NESBITT BURNS QUADRANT PROGRAM OR THROUGH SELECT FINANCIAL ADVISORS
PHONE NUMBER:	(416) 368-0533 EXT. 539
WEB SITE ADDRESS:	WWW.SEIC.COM
E-MAIL ADDRESS:	JPIKE@SEIC.COM

FUND SUMMARY

$$$$ - NONE

$$$ - NONE

$$ - NONE

$ - NONE

NR - CANADIAN EQUITY, CANADIAN FIXED INCOME, EAFE EQUITY, EMERGING MARKETS, PRIME CREDIT MONEY MARKET, U.S. EQUITY

BEST CHOICES: N/A

BEST FOR RRSPs: N/A

BEST UNRATEDS: CANADIAN EQUITY, U.S. EQUITY

FUND RATINGS

None of the funds in this group have been in existence long enough to qualify for a rating.

PURSUIT GROUP OF FUNDS

THE COMPANY

This small fund group is owned and managed by Nigel Stephens Counsel of Toronto, a company that handles portfolio management for pension plans, foundations, individuals, etc. There's a purchase wrinkle to note with these funds: in addition to the initial sales commission, you may be charged an annual "service fee" of up to 1% a year. The fee is negotiable with the sales representative at the time of purchase. Obviously, any such fee will reduce your net return accordingly.

THE DETAILS

NUMBER OF FUNDS:	6
ASSETS UNDER MANAGEMENT:	$58.3 MILLION
LOAD CHARGE:	FRONT: MAX. 5%
SWITCHING CHARGE:	2% MAXIMUM
WHERE SOLD:	ONTARIO
HOW SOLD:	DIRECTLY THROUGH THE MANAGER OR THROUGH BROKERS, DEALERS, AND FINANCIAL PLANNERS
PHONE NUMBER:	(416) 502-9300 OR 1-800-253-9619
WEB SITE ADDRESS:	N/A
E-MAIL ADDRESS:	PURSUIT@NIGEL.COM

FUND SUMMARY

$$$$ - NONE
$$$ - CANADIAN EQUITY, MONEY MARKET
$$ - CANADIAN BOND, GROWTH
$ - NONE
NR - GLOBAL BOND, GLOBAL EQUITY
BEST CHOICES: CANADIAN EQUITY, MONEY MARKET
BEST FOR RRSPs: CANADIAN EQUITY, MONEY MARKET
BEST UNRATEDS: GLOBAL EQUITY

FUND RATINGS

CANADIAN EQUITY FUNDS

PURSUIT CANADIAN EQUITY FUND $$$ → G # RSP CE

Manager: Nigel Stephens Counsel, since 1990

MER: 1.50%

This fund invests in a combination of blue-chip and mid-size growth companies — no junior issues. There used to be a strong foreign component, but now the portfolio is strictly Canadian. The emphasis is on firms that are globally competitive (e.g., CAE Inc., Bombardier) and the portfolio is kept small — about 10 to 15 stocks. Results since have been in and out, but recent returns have shown steady improvement. The fund gained 20.3% over the 12 months to June 30/98, well above average. Five-year average annual compound rate of return is 15.6%, also very good. This has become a very respectable little fund, worthy of your attention.

U.S. AND INTERNATIONAL EQUITY FUNDS

PURSUIT GROWTH FUND $$ → G # £ IE

Manager: Nigel Stephens Counsel, since 1996

MER: 1.75%

This used to be the Pursuit American Growth Fund. The name was changed in '96 and the fund was given a new mandate that allows the managers to invest around the world and shifts the focus from small-cap to larger companies. The core holdings are still U.S. (about two thirds of the stocks in the first half of '98), with a sprinkling of other countries such as the U.K. and Sweden in the portfolio. Gain for the year to June 30/98 was 25.5%. That was way above average by international equity fund standards, but this isn't a true international fund because of its very heavy U.S. weighting. Compared to U.S. stock fund performance, that result was sub-par. This is one of those funds whose portfolio doesn't really reflect its mandate, so make sure you understand how it operates before you invest.

FIXED INCOME AND MONEY MARKET FUNDS

PURSUIT CANADIAN BOND FUND $$ → FI # RSP CB

Manager: Nigel Stephens Counsel, since 1990

MER: 0.80%

There has been a change of direction here. Previously, this fund was managed defensively to protect capital. For example, entering '97 the fund was entirely in short-term notes because of concerns on the part of the managers about an interest rate increase. However, over the subsequent 12 months, the managers extended the term of the portfolio considerably, going out as far as 2023. When interest rates declined, those long bonds gained in value and the fund recorded a 13.9% increase over the year to June 30/98, well above average for the Canadian bond category. All the assets are held in Government of Canada issues, so the quality of the portfolio is good. Rating moves up a notch this year. Formerly the Realgrowth Active Income Fund.

PURSUIT MONEY MARKET FUND $$$ ↓ C No RSP CMM

Manager: Nigel Stephens Counsel, since 1990

MER: 0.50%

Good results plus safety from a portfolio made up entirely of federal government T-bills. The high returns (for this category) are made possible by the low management fee. The only totally no-load entry from Pursuit. But try to avoid the annual service fee on this one, otherwise your returns will look pretty anaemic.

RESOLUTE GROWTH FUND

THE COMPANY

This small fund is managed by Toronto-based Deacon Capital Corporation.

THE DETAILS

NUMBER OF FUNDS:	1
ASSETS UNDER MANAGEMENT:	$5.5 MILLION
LOAD CHARGE:	FRONT: MAX. 5% BACK: MAX. 5%
SWITCHING CHARGE:	N/A
WHERE SOLD:	ALBERTA, B.C., AND ONTARIO
HOW SOLD:	DIRECTLY THROUGH THE MANAGER OR THROUGH BROKERS, DEALERS, AND FINANCIAL PLANNERS
PHONE NUMBER:	1-888-332-2661 OR (416) 350-3232
WEB SITE ADDRESS:	N/A
E-MAIL ADDRESS:	N/A

FUND RATINGS

CANADIAN EQUITY FUNDS

RESOLUTE GROWTH FUND   **$$ ↑ G #/* RSP CE**

Manager: Tom Stanley, since inception (1993)

MER: 2.00%

This fund specializes in small-cap stocks, with heavy weightings in a limited number of positions. This makes for potentially high volatility, and the results bear that out. The fund gained 66% in the first six months of '96, a terrific result. But then the balloon burst. Over the next 12 months, the unit value fell 17.5%. However, it has since rebounded and finished the year to June 30/98 with a gain of 14.8%, above average for the small-cap category. We'll move the rating up a notch on the strength of that, but don't lose sight of the volatility here.

ROYAL MUTUAL FUNDS

THE COMPANY

This is the mutual fund family of the Royal Bank and its subsidiary, Royal Trust. It is the largest no-load fund group in the country, with well over $28 billion in assets under management. The lengthy merger of the old RoyFund and Royal Trust groups is now complete and the revamped Royal Funds line is available at all financial institutions under the Royal umbrella, with the exception of the three Advantage balanced funds, which continue to be sold only by Royal Trust. The primary manager of the funds is Royal Bank Investment Management (RBIM), which contracts sub-advisors for some of the foreign funds.

THE DETAILS

NUMBER OF FUNDS:	32
ASSETS UNDER MANAGEMENT:	$30 BILLION
LOAD CHARGE:	NONE
SWITCHING CHARGE:	NONE
WHERE SOLD:	ACROSS CANADA
HOW SOLD:	DIRECTLY THROUGH ANY ROYAL BANK OR ROYAL TRUST BRANCH OR THROUGH BROKERS, DEALERS, AND FINANCIAL PLANNERS
PHONE NUMBER:	1-800-463-FUND (3863) - ENGLISH 1-800-668-FOND (3663) - FRENCH
WEB SITE ADDRESS:	WWW.ROYALBANK.COM/ENGLISH/RMF (ENGLISH) OR WWW.ROYALBANK.COM/FRENCH/RMF (FRENCH)
E-MAIL ADDRESS:	FUNDS@ROYALBANK.COM

FUND SUMMARY

$$$$ - DIVIDEND

$$$ - BOND, ROYAL TRUST ADVANTAGE BALANCED, ROYAL TRUST ADVANTAGE INCOME, U.S. EQUITY, $U.S. MONEY MARKET, ZWEIG STRATEGIC GROWTH

$$ - BALANCED, CANADIAN EQUITY, CANADIAN MONEY MARKET, CANADIAN T-BILL, ENERGY, GLOBAL BOND, INTERNATIONAL EQUITY, MORTGAGE

$ - ASIAN GROWTH, CANADIAN GROWTH, CANADIAN SMALL
     CAP, EUROPEAN GROWTH, JAPANESE STOCK, PRECIOUS
     METALS, ROYAL TRUST ADVANTAGE GROWTH

NR - BALANCED GROWTH, CANADIAN STRATEGIC INDEX,
     CANADIAN VALUE, LATIN AMERICAN, LIFE SCIENCE AND
     TECHNOLOGY, MONTHLY INCOME, PREMIUM MONEY
     MARKET, U.S. GROWTH STRATEGIC INDEX, U.S. VALUE
     STRATEGIC INDEX, ZWEIG GLOBAL MANAGED ASSETS

BEST CHOICES: BOND, DIVIDEND, ZWEIG STRATEGIC GROWTH

BEST FOR RRSPS: BOND, DIVIDEND

BEST UNRATEDS: CANADIAN STRATEGIC INDEX, LIFE SCIENCE AND TECHNOLOGY,
U.S. GROWTH STRATEGIC INDEX, ZWEIG GLOBAL MANAGED
ASSETS

FUND RATINGS

CANADIAN EQUITY FUNDS

ROYAL CANADIAN EQUITY FUND $$ → G No RSP CE

Manager: John Embry, since 1991

MER: 1.95%

This fund offers a large, diverse portfolio that favours blue-chip holdings. It is designed for growth-oriented investors who take a long-term view. In mid-'98, the largest portfolio holdings were in the banks (all but the Royal, which the fund can't buy because of potential conflict of interest), BCE, Bombardier, and the like. The portfolio was oriented toward the financial services sector, and had a 13.4% foreign content. Results have been spotty. One-year return to June 30/98 was above average at 13.2%. But longer term results (really of the predecessor funds) are in and out. An okay entry, but not one of the Bank's best. The fund was formed from the merger of the Royal Trust Canadian Stock Fund and the RoyFund Canadian Equity Fund.

ROYAL CANADIAN GROWTH FUND $ → G No RSP CE

Manager: John Embry, since 1993

MER: 2.23%

This and the companion Small Cap Fund have similar mandates, and the same manager. In both cases, the focus is on growth stocks. The difference is that this fund can also invest in medium- and large-sized companies, while the Small Cap Fund is generally limited to firms with a market capitalization that does not exceed 0.1% of the total capitalization of the TSE 300 Index. Both funds are coming off sub-par years in comparison to others in their peer group. Of the two, this has emerged as the better choice (although that honour can switch from year to year). Last year's return (to June 30/98) was a very modest 0.5%; however that was a lot better than the 5.7% loss turned in by the Small Cap Fund. The investment mandate makes it somewhat less risky than the Small Cap Fund, which is another good reason for choosing this one if you must have one of the two for some reason. But there are better small-cap choices around than either of these entries.

ROYAL CANADIAN SMALL CAP FUND $ ↑ G No RSP CSC

Manager: Elizabeth Cheung, since 1997

MER: 2.23%

Many small-cap funds have been having a tough time lately, and this is one of them. Except for a decent run in '95–'96, this fund really hasn't done much to get excited about. It lost 5.7% over the 12 months to June 30/98 and the longer term results are anaemic. Elizabeth Cheung took charge in late 1997 to try to get things turned around. We'll see what happens.

ROYAL DIVIDEND FUND $$$$ → G/FI No RSP INC

Manager: John Kellett, since 1993

MER: 1.77%

The goal here is to maximize tax-advantaged income through the use of the dividend tax credit, as well as to generate capital gains. It does both jobs very nicely. The dividend payout in calendar '97 was 4.2% according to a survey done by *Mutual Funds Update* newsletter. So if cash flow is high on your priority list, this fund delivers it. But that's not the whole story. Total return (dividends plus capital gains) has also been excellent. The fund gained 31.5% for the year to June 30/98, way above the average for dividend funds as a group. Longer term results from the predecessor funds, which John Kellett also ran, were very good as well. This is one of the best choices in the Royal stable — and to illustrate how much it is respected, rival CIBC selected it for their Choice Funds program. Rating moves up to $$$$ this year in recognition of Kellett's fine work. The fund was created by the merger of the Royal Trust Growth and Income Fund and the RoyFund Dividend Fund.

ROYAL ENERGY FUND $$ ↑ G No RSP SEC

Manager: Gordon Zive, since 1994

MER: 2.28%

This fund's performance waxes and wanes with the fortunes of Canadian energy stocks. It was hot in '96–'97, with a big 37.6% advance. But then the price of oil collapsed and the fund dropped 14.6% over the 12 months to June 30/98. Still, some other energy funds did a lot worse (Green Line was down 38.5%). The volatility of this sector makes it higher risk than regular equity funds — it's definitely not for retired people. Manager Gordon Zive is focusing on large producers and integrated oil companies at the present time in an effort to minimize risk. Still, this fund is for aggressive investors only.

ROYAL PRECIOUS METALS FUND $ ↑ G No RSP PM

Manager: John Embry, since 1994

MER: 2.41%

This was one of the screamingly hot funds that came crashing to earth in the wake of the Bre-X scandal. Investors enjoyed a dizzying one-year return of almost 80% in the 12 months to June 30/96. But the Bre-X collapse and the collateral damage it caused to the rest of the gold sector resulted in a steep 19.4% plunge over the next

12 months. And that was just a warmup for the 30.4% decline for the year to June 30/98. Hold on to your hat! Manager John Embry had more than a quarter of the portfolio in gold and silver bullion in mid-'98 and was forecasting a strengthening in the gold price when the Asian economies start to recover. But who knows when that will be? How quickly this fund recovers will depend on a restoration of investor confidence in the gold sector, plus an improvement in the price of bullion. It could take some time. This is a speculative fund, definitely not for retirement plans.

U.S. AND INTERNATIONAL EQUITY FUNDS

ROYAL ASIAN GROWTH FUND $ ↑ G No £ FEE

Manager: Philip Chiu, since 1997

MER: 2.97%

Wow! All Far East funds have taken a terrible beating lately, but not many lost more than half their value in a year. But this one did, dropping 50.5% in the 12 months to June 30/98. As of mid-'98, the portfolio was heavily weighted towards Hong Kong, Singapore, and Taiwan in hopes of a recovery in those markets. But you're best to put your money elsewhere until we start to see clear signs that Asia is on the mend.

ROYAL EUROPEAN GROWTH FUND $$ ↑ G No £ EE

Manager: Ross Youngman (BT Funds Management), since 1996

MER: 2.51%

This fund has been managed by BT (Banker's Trust) since its inception in '87, but Ross Youngman was given portfolio responsibility only in '96. After slipping a bit relative to the competition, returns recovered nicely in the year to June 30/98, with the fund posting a gain of almost 42%. The portfolio was heavily focused on western Europe in mid-'98, with the U.K., France, Germany, and Switzerland the largest national holdings. The risk profile of this fund is not particularly good; historically there's a 25% chance that you could be on the losing end even after a three-year hold, according to ATP figures. Still, the strong recent results are a plus. Another year of above-average returns will see a rating increase.

ROYAL INTERNATIONAL EQUITY FUND $$ → G No £ IE

Manager: Tim Sanderson (Delaware International Advisors), since inception (1993)

MER: 2.68%

The mandate here is to invest in countries outside North America. Manager Tim Sanderson takes a value approach to stock selection, looking for bargains around the world. As of mid-'98, the portfolio was heavily weighted to Europe, although Australia/New Zealand represented almost 14% of the assets and Japan about 12%. That mix generated a below-average return of 10.7% for the year to June 30/98. Risk is pretty good for a fund of this type; historically there is just an 8% chance of loss in any 12-month period. However, take that with a grain of salt until the fund experiences a real bear market.

ROYAL JAPANESE STOCK FUND $ ↑ G No £ FEE

Manager: Yoji Takeda, since 1997

MER: 2.82%

This was the worst-performing pure Japan fund in Canada over the three years to June 30/97, with an annualized loss of 9.2%. So Royal made a managerial change last year. The initial result was good. No Japanese fund managed to make a profit over the 12 months to June 30/98, but this one lost less than most of the others, at 17.5%. That doesn't mean you should rush to put your money in, but value investors are claiming to find great bargains in Japan these days. This one will be worth a flyer once the recession in that country ends and a recovery starts to take hold.

ROYAL U.S. EQUITY FUND $$$ ↓ G No £ USE

Manager: Jim Young, since 1991

MER: 2.11%

This fund was created by combining the RoyFund U.S. Equity Fund and the Royal Trust American Stock Fund. Manager Jim Young had been running both previously, so continuity has been maintained into the new entity. The Royal Trust version had been one of the oldest of the financial institution U.S. stock funds, dating back to 1966. The mandate is to invest in "major" U.S. companies, and the portfolio is a mix of big blue-chips and mid-size firms, with a heavy emphasis on consumer goods in mid-'98. Return for the 12 months to June 30/98 was 20.7%, which looks pretty good but was actually well below average for the U.S. equity fund category. That had the effect of pulling down all the returns out to five years to below average as well. On the bright side, the risk rating is very good for a fund of this type. This fund is hovering on the brink of a drop back to $$, but the good safety record saves it for now. Young needs to pull up his socks, however.

ZWEIG STRATEGIC GROWTH FUND $$$ ↓ G No £ USSC

Manager: David Katzen (Zweig/Glaser Advisors), since inception (1992)

MER: 2.49%

This fund is overseen by U.S. investment guru Martin Zweig, although one of his aides handles the day-to-day management chores. It invests mainly in smaller U.S. companies with above-average growth potential, which may sound like high-risk stuff at first blush. But the Zweig organization puts a conservative spin on the theme, battening down the hatches and reducing risk if troubles loom on the stock market horizon. The fund's mandate allows it to invest up to 35% of the portfolio in top 500 U.S. firms, as well as to hold non-U.S. small-caps, so there is lots of flexibility here. The technique works; this fund has one of the best safety records in the U.S. small-cap category since inception, with only a 2% chance of loss over any 12-month period according to ATP analysis. The trade-off is slightly below-average returns. Over the five years to June 30/98, average annual gain was 17.3%. The average for U.S. equity funds as a group was 19.1%. So you give up a bit for the enhanced safety. That makes this fund an appropriate choice for investors who want exposure to the U.S. small-cap market without the increased degree of risk normally associated with such funds.

BALANCED FUNDS

ROYAL BALANCED FUND $$ → FI/G No RSP CBAL

Manager: Team

MER: 2.25%

This is a conservatively managed portfolio, focusing on high-grade fixed-income securities and stocks of large companies with a proven track record. Results have generally been below average for the balanced fund category; however, the latest numbers show some improvement with a gain of 11.9% for the year to June 30/98. In mid-'98, slightly over half the portfolio was in stocks, with the rest in bonds and cash, a much less aggressive mix than a year earlier. Formerly the RoyFund Balanced Fund.

ROYAL TRUST ADVANTAGE BALANCED FUND $$$ → FI/G No RSP CBAL

Manager: John Kellett, since 1995

MER: 1.78%

This fund of funds invests in other Royal mutual funds using asset mix principles. Each of the three Advantage funds has a different orientation, with this being the most balanced one. Equity holdings normally represent 40% to 60% of fund assets. So this fund strikes a middle ground between the conservative Advantage Income Fund and the more aggressive Advantage Growth Fund. Over a 10-year period, there's not a lot to choose between this and the Income Fund in terms of total return, but the Growth Fund has lagged behind. This fund averaged 10% a year over the decade to June 30/98, the Income Fund averaged 9.8% a year, and the Growth Fund averaged 9.3%. Which you choose depends on your goals. Note that the three

Advantage funds are only available through Royal Trust and are not sold in Royal Bank branches.

ROYAL TRUST ADVANTAGE GROWTH FUND $ → G/FI No RSP CBAL

Manager: John Kellett, since 1995

MER: 1.90%

This fund uses the same techniques as the other RT Advantage funds but puts a greater emphasis on stocks (usually 60% to 80% of the portfolio). This makes it slightly higher risk than the other two entries. This fund should do best when stock markets are strong, but its recent returns are below average for the balanced fund category, despite the fact Canadian and U.S. markets were hot through the mid-'90s. In fact, both of the other Advantage funds outperformed it over the 12 months to June 30/98.

ROYAL TRUST ADVANTAGE INCOME FUND $$$ ↓ FI/G No RSP CBAL

Manager: John Kellett, since 1995

MER: 1.63%

The emphasis here is on fixed-income investments, with stocks normally limited to 15% to 30% of the portfolio. As a result, this fund holds up better when stock markets are weak, but in theory should underperform when they're strong. It doesn't always work out that way, however; this fund gained 10.2% in the year to June 30/98, which was right on average for the balanced fund category, outdoing the companion Advantage Growth Fund in the process, even though the latter had a much heavier stock weighting. The safety record is also far superior. ATP analysis shows only a 4% chance of loss in any 12-month period, compared to 13% for the Balanced Fund and 15% for the Growth Fund. If safety and a decent return are a useful combo for you, try this one.

FIXED INCOME AND MONEY MARKET FUNDS

ROYAL BOND FUND $$$ → FI No RSP CB

Manager: Tom Czitron, since 1994

MER: 1.39%

This fund invests mainly in Government of Canada bonds with some provincial and U.S. issues tossed in. Manager Tom Czitron has done very well with this one, extending the duration of the portfolio over the past year to capitalize on declining interest rates. Gain for the 12 months to June 30/98 was a fine 11.7% and returns for all time periods are above average. The RoyFund Bond Fund and the Royal Trust Bond Fund were combined to form this new entry on July 1, '97.

ROYAL CANADIAN
MONEY MARKET FUND $$ → C No RSP CMM

Manager: Barry Edwards, since 1986

MER: 0.95%

Last year I said a lower MER would really be helpful here. The Royal Funds graciously complied, reducing the expense ratio by 33 basis points. That helped to boost the return to above average for the first time in memory (3.2% for the year to June 30/98). Most of the assets are in corporate notes and bankers' acceptances, which will help keep returns up. Rating moves up a notch this year. The Royal Trust and RoyFund money market funds were combined to create this one.

ROYAL CANADIAN T-BILL FUND $$ ↓ C No RSP CMM

Manager: Barry Edwards, since 1991

MER: 0.92%

As the name suggests, the fund invests only in Government of Canada T-bills. That provides a small additional measure of safety. Recent returns have been slightly less than those of the Money Market Fund. However, this fund has slightly less risk because of the nature of the portfolio. The old Royal Trust and RoyFund T-bill funds were merged to create this new fund.

ROYAL GLOBAL BOND FUND $$ → FI No RSP IB

Manager: Jim Davis, since 1993

MER: 1.87%

This fund maintains full RRSP eligibility by investing in foreign currency bonds issued by Canadian governments and by international agencies like the World Bank. After slipping a bit, it staged a comeback last year with a good 9.1% advance. U.S.-dollar securities dominated the portfolio in mid-'98. The Royal Trust International Bond Fund and the RoyFund International Income Fund were merged in mid-'97 to create this new entry.

ROYAL MORTGAGE FUND $$ → FI No RSP M

Managers: Barry Edwards and Jim Davis, since 1992

MER: 1.56%

This fund was something of an underachiever in the year to June 30/98, gaining just 4%. In an effort to boost returns, the managers extended the average term of the portfolio to 4.2 years in the second quarter of 1998, which is quite an aggressive stance by mortgage fund standards. That means if interest rates decline in the next 12 months this fund will do well by the standards of its peer group. If they rise, be careful. The damage won't be great, but the fund will underperform. The old Royal Trust and RoyFund mortgage funds were folded into this one in mid-'97.

ROYAL $U.S. MONEY MARKET FUND $$$ → C No RSP IMM

Manager: Barry Edwards, since 1991

MER: 1.12%

This is another Royal entry that was formed from the merger of a RoyFund and Royal Trust fund, in this case their U.S. money market entries. The fund invests in short-term notes issued by Canadian corporations and governments. Returns have been above average.

SAGIT INVESTMENT MANAGEMENT

THE COMPANY

Sagit is a Vancouver-based operation that is characterized by an aggressive investment style that won't be to all tastes. The company was formed in 1982 and the principal owner is Raoul Tsakok, who has almost 25 years of investment experience. He and senior vice-president Ted Ohashi manage all the funds. The main focus is on small-cap companies and the investment style is bottom-up, which means placing the emphasis on corporate fundamentals. There are two fund groups within this organization, Cambridge and Trans-Canada. The Trans-Canada funds tend to be more sedate. Note that the back-end load redemption fee schedule is negotiable; ask for the best rate.

The expense ratios on most Sagit funds are very high because the funds are small. This means you are paying a relatively higher price for management services than with most other companies.

THE DETAILS

NUMBER OF FUNDS:	15
ASSETS UNDER MANAGEMENT:	$64.5 MILLION
LOAD CHARGE:	FRONT: MAX. 8.75%; BACK: MAX. 7%
SWITCHING CHARGE:	2% MAXIMUM
WHERE SOLD:	ACROSS CANADA
HOW SOLD:	THROUGH BROKERS, DEALERS, AND FINANCIAL PLANNERS
PHONE NUMBER:	(604) 685-3193 OR 1-800-663-1003
WEB SITE ADDRESS:	WWW.SAGIT.COM/FUNDS
E-MAIL ADDRESS:	CLIENT@SAGIT.COM

FUND SUMMARY

CAMBRIDGE FUNDS

$$$$ - NONE
$$$ - NONE
$$ - AMERICAN GROWTH, AMERICAS
$ - BALANCED, CHINA, GLOBAL, GROWTH, PACIFIC, RESOURCE, SPECIAL EQUITY
NR - PRECIOUS METALS

Best Choices: Americas
Best for RRSPs: Americas (as foreign content)
Best unrateds: None

Trans-Canada Funds

$$$$ - None
$$$ - Money Market
$$ - None
$ - Bond, Dividend, Pension, Value
NR - None

Best Choices: Money Market
Best for RRSPs: Money Market
Best unrateds: N/A

FUND RATINGS

Cambridge Funds

CANADIAN EQUITY FUNDS

CAMBRIDGE GROWTH FUND $ ↑ G #/* RSP CE

Manager: Raoul Tsakok, since 1992, and Ted Ohashi, since 1995

MER: 3.46%

Investing in this fund is not for the faint of heart. Like many of the other funds in this group, it is subject to big gains and losses. Lately, unfortunately, it's mostly been losses. The fund lost 29% in the year to June 30/98 and its five-year average annual compound rate of return is -12.5%. Think of this fund as a baseball power hitter. It's either out of the park or a strike out. There's not much middle ground. This isn't my kind of investing, which is why the low rating. But I recognize that the home runs will come, and if you can live with the slumps, you might want to have some money in this company when the periodic breakouts occur, as happened in '93 when the fund gained more than 60% in 12 months. But if you do invest here, plan to be an active trader. This is not a buy-and-hold fund. Over the past decade, the average annual compound rate of return was zero. That's right, zero. GICs did much better, with less risk of a heart attack.

CAMBRIDGE RESOURCE FUND $ ↑ G #/* RSP SEC

Managers: Raoul Tsakok, since 1987, and Ted Ohashi, since 1995

MER: 3.42%

If there is one point of consistency in the Cambridge equity funds, it is volatility. Like the others in the family, this one is subject to huge losses — it fell more than 45% in the year ending June 30/98, thanks to weakness in the resource sector. But it also can record huge gains — the fund was up almost 85% in the 12 months to June 30/96. Overall, however, the results are not good. The fund shows a loss of 1.8% a year over the past decade and is in the red for all time periods. I really don't like these wild swings and personally would not buy this fund for my own portfolio. The ATP analysis tells you why. Historically, this fund has a 44% chance of loss over any given 12-month period. There is a 20% chance you'll be in the red after five years. And, despite the occasional big gain, there's only a 41% chance that you'll end up with an average annual profit of over 10% after five years, and just a 20% chance after a decade. I don't like the odds. You might luck out and score big, but don't invest here unless you can handle the action. And don't put your money in if you're the type to panic and sell out at the first big drop. You'll be gone before you ever make a penny.

CAMBRIDGE SPECIAL EQUITY FUND $ ↑ G #/* RSP CSC

Manager: Raoul Tsakok, since 1989, and Ted Ohashi, since 1995

MER: 3.46%

The performance history of this fund is absolutely mind-boggling. After three years of losses in a row, including a 26.6% drop in '92, investors in this one suddenly won the lottery. The fund gained 146.9% in '93. Some of the technology and oil and gas issues took off and bingo! In a small fund, the effect of a few big gainers can be dramatic. Predictably, new investors flooded in — and got hit. The fund dropped 20.3% in '94. But then it did an about-face and soared to a 22.1% gain in '95. In the first half of '96, it gained another 28% — an amazing result considering that it plummeted more than 20% in June alone. But that freefall was just the beginning. Over the next 12 months, to June 30/97, the value of this fund dropped by a heart-stopping 47.1%! Last year, to June 30/98, it dipped another 22.5%. I give you this lengthy performance history so you'll have a clearer idea of the volatility here. The net result over the long term is one of the few funds in Canada to be in the red after a decade. The average annual return for the 10 years to June 30/98 was -3%. Ouch!

U.S. AND INTERNATIONAL EQUITY FUNDS

CAMBRIDGE AMERICAN GROWTH FUND $$ → G #/* £ USE

Managers: Raoul Tsakok, since inception (1992) and Ted Ohashi, since 1995

MER: 3.50%

This fund has undergone a transformation in the past couple of years. It has moved from being a free-wheeling, small-cap operation, similar to the Cambridge Growth Fund, to become a respectable blue-chip entry made up almost exclusively of Dow stocks like Merck, Motorola, Proctor & Gamble, McDonalds, and the like. The result has been a great improvement in results, especially in comparison to other Cambridge entries. Still, the returns aren't as good as you might expect, given the portfolio composition. Gain for the year to June 30/98 was 14.2%, well below average for the U.S. equity category. However, the portfolio is solid and should fare relatively well in any market downturn, so we'll leave the $$ rating intact for now. Sagit clients who are concerned about the volatility of other funds might want to shift some assets here as a safer haven.

CAMBRIDGE AMERICAS FUND $$ → G #/* £ AE

Managers: Raoul Tsakok, since 1989, and Ted Ohashi, since 1995

MER: 3.50%

This used to be strictly a U.S. equity fund but the mandate has been changed to allow it to invest in Latin America as well. Stocks are chosen on the basis of a company's ability to profit from the relaxation of tariff barriers in the Americas, and the portfolio is a mix of big U.S. blue-chips and single country funds, such as the Mexico Fund,

Chile Fund, and Argentina Fund. It's been the star performer in the Sagit group recently, with a big advance of 44.1% in the first six months of 1998. That helped to pull all the returns out to three years to above average; however, a dazzling six months isn't enough for a rating boost. We'll see what happens over the next year. This fund doesn't have the gunslinger aura of so many of the other entries in this group, so if you're a Sagit investor you might want some in your portfolio.

CAMBRIDGE CHINA FUND $ ↑ G #/* £ FEE

Managers: Raoul Tsakok, since inception (1994), and Ted Ohashi, since 1995

MER: 3.51%

The mandate of this fund is simple: to invest in growth companies in China. That country hasn't suffered as badly as others in the Asian meltdown, so this fund fared better than most Far East entries last year, losing only 16.7%. ("Only" is a relative term in this context, but when you have some funds losing over 40%, this one looks pretty good.) I believe it is still too soon to go bargain hunting in Asia, but when that time comes this fund may do well.

CAMBRIDGE GLOBAL FUND $ ↑ G #/* £ IE

Managers: Raoul Tsakok, since 1987, and Ted Ohashi, since 1995

MER: 3.54%

This fund has travelled a long road to its current position. It started as a Canadian equity fund (called Trans-Canada Shares Series B) and then, more recently, it was known as Cambridge Diversified Fund. Now it's a global fund, at least in theory. In fact, most of the assets are in U.S. and Canadian companies, with only a sprinkling from elsewhere. The small portfolio is a strange mix, to say the least. It ranges from speculative junior mining companies to huge corporations like Microsoft, McDonalds, and DuPont. I'm not sure just what to make of all this; it's almost like two conflicting forces are at work. The net result has not been pleasant for investors; the fund lost almost 40% in the year to June 30/98. I suggest you stand well clear of this one until the folks at Sagit decide exactly where it is going.

CAMBRIDGE PACIFIC FUND $ ↑ G #/* £ FEE

Managers: Raoul Tsakok, since inception (1989), and Ted Ohashi, since 1995

MER: 3.68%

Like most Far East funds, this one was badly rocked in the past year, losing more than 45% for the period to June 30/98. Five-year average annual compound rate of return is -15.3%. There's not much else to say.

BALANCED FUNDS

CAMBRIDGE BALANCED FUND $ ↑ G/FI #/* RSP CBAL

Managers: Raoul Tsakok, since 1992, and Ted Ohashi, since 1995

MER: 3.48%

Normally, we think of balanced funds as being conservatively managed, but not in this case. Last year there were a few blue-chip names on the stock list, like CIBC. But there isn't even that safety net now; virtually all the equities held are junior growth companies. And stocks made up more than three quarters of the portfolio in the first half of '98, so the small bond section wasn't a big help. Result: a loss of 28.9% for the year to June 30/98, the worst performance in the Canadian balanced category. Five-year average annual compound rate of return was -9.9%, also the worst, so the one-year result was no fluke. Ironically, Sagit lists this among the "conservative" funds on their web site. Maybe by their standards. Not by mine. This is not a fund I think most balanced investors would be comfortable with.

TRANS-CANADA FUNDS

CANADIAN EQUITY FUNDS

TRANS-CANADA DIVIDEND FUND $ → FI/G #/* RSP INC

Manager: Raoul Tsakok, since 1987, and Ted Ohashi, since 1995

MER: 3.51%

The emphasis here is on high-yielding common stocks. However, some of the companies in the mix don't fit the mandate and there is an 8% holding of U.S. stocks, which aren't eligible for the dividend tax credit. In terms of performance, the fund hasn't shown anything like the powerful returns of most dividend entries over the past couple of years. Gain for the 12 months to June 30/98 was just 4.5%. That was well below the average of 15.9% for the dividend fund group. This is one of the more conservative of the Sagit stock funds, but there are many better dividend funds around. Formerly known as Trans-Canada Shares Series C and more recently as Trans-Canada Income Fund.

TRANS-CANADA VALUE FUND $ → G #/* RSP CE

Manager: Raoul Tsakok, since 1987, and Ted Ohashi, since 1995

MER: 3.52%

This is one of the company's more conservative portfolios. It's a much smaller fund than the companion Cambridge Growth, and there are more recognizable blue-chip names, from Royal Bank to McDonalds. But there are also some small growth companies in the mix, such as GHP Exploration Corp. So this fund is a strange blend of big blue-chips and tiny growth firms. Sagit should decide which way it wants to go here. Loss for the year to June 30/98 was 18.8%, not good, especially after the fund had done well the year before. Formerly known as Trans-Canada Equity Fund.

BALANCED FUNDS

TRANS-CANADA PENSION FUND $ → G #/* RSP CBAL

Manager: Raoul Tsakok, since 1989, and Ted Ohashi, since 1995

MER: 3.48%

This is supposed to be a balanced fund, but it's primarily a stock fund with no long-term bonds in the mix at all in the first half of '98. This fund is specifically intended for pension plans, so the portfolio is more conservative than you'll find in most other Sagit funds, but there are a few off-beat entries as well. The lower risk approach made this the top performer in the Sagit stable by far in the year to June 30/98, with a fat gain of almost 43%, but the return tailed off dramatically in the subsequent 12 months and the fund ended up losing a small 0.4% in the period to June 30/98. I hope it wasn't a one-year wonder, but I'm taking away one $ until we see. Formerly MER Equity Fund, taken over by Sagit Management in '89.

FIXED INCOME AND MONEY MARKET FUNDS

TRANS-CANADA BOND FUND $ ↓ FI #/* RSP CB

Managers: Raoul Tsakok, since 1989, and Ted Ohashi, since 1995

MER: 2.92%

This fund invests exclusively in bonds and T-bills issued or guaranteed by the Government of Canada. This gives it a high degree of safety in terms of investment quality, which is the fund's main advantage. But returns tend to be below average for this category, in part because the managers concentrate their holdings in short- to mid-term bonds. The extremely high management fee doesn't help either. Gain for the 12 months to June 30/98 was just 3.4%. That was only slightly better than the companion Money Market Fund. If you're looking for a defensive short-term bond fund, there are better ones out there.

TRANS-CANADA MONEY MARKET FUND $$$ ↓ C #/* RSP CMM

Managers: Raoul Tsakok, since 1989, and Ted Ohashi, since 1995

MER: 0.65%

A steady performer from Sagit Management, with a high degree of safety — all the assets are normally held in Government of Canada Treasury bills. Don't bother if you can't get the sales commission waived, however; there are no-load entries that are just as good.

SAXON FUNDS

THE COMPANY

The Saxon Funds are owned and managed by Howson Tattersall Investment Counsel of Toronto. The firm is known for its expertise in the small-cap sector, and manages portfolios or portions of portfolios for institutional and individual clients. The five mutual funds are managed by the company's principals, Richard Howson and Robert Tattersall.

THE DETAILS

NUMBER OF FUNDS:	5
ASSETS UNDER MANAGEMENT:	$123 MILLION
LOAD CHARGE:	NONE IF PURCHASED DIRECTLY THROUGH THE MANAGER, OTHERWISE 2% MAXIMUM
SWITCHING CHARGE:	NONE
WHERE SOLD:	ALBERTA, B.C., ONTARIO
HOW SOLD:	DIRECTLY THROUGH THE MANAGER OR THROUGH BROKERS, DEALERS, AND FINANCIAL PLANNERS OR DIRECTLY THROUGH THE MANAGER IN ONTARIO
PHONE NUMBER:	(416) 979-1818 OR 1-888-287-2966
WEB SITE ADDRESS:	WWW.SAXONFUNDS.COM/~SAXON
E-MAIL ADDRESS:	SAXON@SAXONFUNDS.COM

FUND SUMMARY

$$$$ - NONE
$$$ - SMALL CAP, STOCK
$$ - BALANCED, WORLD GROWTH
$ - NONE
NR - HIGH INCOME
BEST CHOICES: SMALL CAP, STOCK
BEST FOR RRSPs: STOCK
BEST UNRATEDS: HIGH INCOME

FUND RATINGS

CANADIAN EQUITY FUNDS

SAXON SMALL CAP FUND $$$ ↓ G No RSP CSC

Manager: Robert Tattersall, since inception (1985)

MER: 1.75%

This fund specializes in small Canadian companies, with a market capitalization of less than $150 million. Theoretically, this fund should be higher risk than the companion Stock Fund because of its small size ($23.7 million) and type of investments. In fact, that has not proven to be the case. ATP analysis reveals that this fund is actually slightly safer and ranks as one of the lowest risk funds in the Canadian small-cap category. One reason is that the investment approach here is value oriented, which is somewhat less risky than the growth style used in most small-cap entries. This fund has also been putting up better numbers than the Stock Fund in recent years. Over the 12 months to June 30/98 it gained an impressive 21%. Three-year average annual compound rate of return was 23.9%, among the best in the peer group. Manager Robert Tattersall looks for stocks that are out of favour and especially likes micro-caps — the smallest of the small-caps. He maintains a fairly large portfolio (50 or more names), given the size of the fund, in order to reduce risk. He does not trade actively; typically a stock will be held three to five years. This fund is a good choice for the investor who wants to add a quality small-cap entry to a portfolio for diversification.

SAXON STOCK FUND $$$ → G No RSP CE

Manager: Richard Howson, since 1989

MER: 1.75%

This fund is something of an in-and-outer. It had good years in '92 and '93, slipped badly relative to the competition in '94, and then came back very strongly in '95 to rank in the top 10% of all Canadian stock funds, according to Southam's *Mutual Fund SourceBook*. Gain for the year to June 30/97 was 25.8%, and manager Richard Howson followed that up with a 13.4% advance for the period to June 30/98. Longer term results for all time periods are above average for the Canadian equity category. The portfolio contains more large company stocks than you'll find in the Small Cap Fund, although mid-size and smaller companies are also represented. Howson employs a combination of top-down (sector selection) and bottom-up (corporate fundamentals) techniques in making his picks. A good choice among the smaller fund groups.

U.S. AND INTERNATIONAL EQUITY FUNDS

SAXON WORLD GROWTH FUND $$ → G No £ IE

Manager: Robert Tattersall, since inception (1985)

MER: 1.75%

This fund was rolling along very nicely when suddenly someone seems to have slammed on the brakes. Last year at this time it was the best performer in the broadly based international equities category over the previous five years with an average annual return of 22.3%. That was better than Trimark, better than Templeton, better than Fidelity. But it is coming off a very weak year, in which the return was just 5.9%. Reason: This is basically a small-cap international fund, and small-cap stocks were having a tough time in the U.S. and overseas, hit by the "flight to quality" phenomenon. So while longer time numbers continue to look good, this fund's performance is in a temporary hiatus. The portfolio is well balanced internationally, with just over half of the holdings in the U.S. Manager Robert Tattersall uses the same value investing approach here as with the Small Cap Fund, and trades infrequently to minimize taxable distributions.

BALANCED FUNDS

SAXON BALANCED FUND $$ ↑ FI/G No RSP CBAL

Manager: Richard Howson, since 1989

MER: 1.75%

There's a lot more volatility here than you would normally expect to find in a balanced fund. Since people looking for a balanced fund tend to be more conservative in their investment approach, that could be an important factor in deciding whether or not to put some money here. ATP analysis shows that, historically, there's a 24% chance that you could be on the losing side after being in this fund for a full five years. On the reward side, there's just a 43% chance you'll come away with an average annual gain of better than 10% over that time, and a 17% chance over a decade (those are better numbers than a year ago, but still not great). On the positive side, this fund has been looking good recently, with a gain of 10.7% for the year to June 30/98, and returns over most time periods are above average. As of mid-'98, the portfolio was heavily weighted to equities (64%), with a mix of blue-chips (C.P., Thomson Corp., banks), and small growth stocks. Bonds were only 32% of the holdings, with the rest in cash.

SCEPTRE INVESTMENT COUNSEL

THE COMPANY

Sceptre is one of the country's largest investment counselling firms, with over $17 billion in assets under management. The company has been in business since 1955, and its clients include pension funds, institutions, other fund companies, and individuals.

In July, 1998 the company announced its first new funds in several years. They are the Canadian Equity Fund, which will focus on large and mid-size companies, and the U.S. Equity Fund, which will invest in a diversified portfolio of American stocks.

Minimum investment for opening an account is $5,000.

THE DETAILS

NUMBER OF FUNDS:	8
ASSETS UNDER MANAGEMENT:	$1 BILLION
LOAD CHARGE:	NONE IF PURCHASED DIRECTLY FROM MANAGER, OTHERWISE FRONT: MAX. 2%
SWITCHING CHARGE:	NONE
WHERE SOLD:	ACROSS CANADA
HOW SOLD:	THROUGH BROKERS, DEALERS, AND FINANCIAL PLANNERS OR DIRECTLY THROUGH THE MANAGER IN ONTARIO AND B.C.
PHONE NUMBER:	(416) 360-4826 OR (604) 899-6002 OR 1-800-265-1888
WEB SITE ADDRESS:	WWW.SCEPTRE.CA
E-MAIL ADDRESS:	MAIL@SCEPTRE.CA

FUND SUMMARY

$$$$ - BALANCED GROWTH, MONEY MARKET
$$$ - BOND
$$ - EQUITY GROWTH, INTERNATIONAL
$ - ASIAN GROWTH
NR - CANADIAN EQUITY, U.S. EQUITY

BEST CHOICES: BALANCED GROWTH
BEST FOR RRSPS: BALANCED GROWTH
BEST UNRATEDS: U.S. EQUITY

FUND RATINGS

CANADIAN EQUITY FUNDS

SCEPTRE EQUITY GROWTH FUND $$ → G No RSP CE

Manager: Allan Jacobs, since 1993

MER: 1.42%

Oh, what a stumble here. Last year I classified this as one of the premier Canadian equity funds in the country. Then what happens? It goes into a tailspin and finishes the 12 months to June 30/98 with a gain so tiny you'd need a magnifying glass to see it (0.3%). How did the mighty fall so fast? Well, it didn't help that the fund's largest single holding going into April was YBM Magnex, the company whose shares went from more than $20 to who knows what (zero?) after a stunning series of events (including an FBI raid on their corporate headquarters in the U.S.) led to an indefinite suspension in the trading of the shares. All the longer term averages are still above par, but this stunning one-year reversal, which became worse in July/98, is definitely a cause for concern. The fund's main emphasis is on small to medium-size companies, but large-cap stocks are also included in the portfolio to add value and reduce risk. Recent examples: CIBC, Royal Bank, BCE. Manager Allan Jacobs employs a bottom-up, value-investing approach to his stock selections, and holds a minimum of 50 issues in the portfolio. The historic safety record of this fund had been among the best in the industry, but that too has been shaken by the recent developments. I'm cutting this rating all the way back to $$ as a result of what has happened. That's a huge drop for a $$$$ fund, but the recent performance here has made me quite nervous. Let's hope Jacobs engineers a fast turnaround here and that the fund quickly regains its previous form.

U.S. AND INTERNATIONAL EQUITY FUNDS

SCEPTRE ASIAN GROWTH FUND $ → G No £ FEE

Manager: Tariq Ahmad, since 1995

MER: 2.45%

Manager Tariq Ahmad's mandate extends throughout the Far East, including Japan. He selects his preferred countries on the basis of those with the best economic prospects, and then uses fundamental analysis to choose individual stocks. Unfortunately, the market meltdown in the Far East devastated this fund; it lost 54.4% in the year to June 30/98. I hope you weren't on board for that ride! This is the weakest link in the Sceptre family.

SCEPTRE INTERNATIONAL FUND $$ → G No £ IE

Manager: Lennox McNeely, since inception (1986)

MER: 2.07%

This has not been a good year for Sceptre. Not only did their Equity Growth Fund stumble badly, but so did this one. Previously, it had been one of the better choices among international equity funds, with very good long-term returns (average annual gain of 13.9% over the decade to June 30/98). But things turned sour last year and the fund dropped 5% in value over 12 months. The main reason appears to have been an overweighting towards the Far East in 1997, which was maintained for too long. Even with those markets being mangled, almost a quarter of the portfolio was invested in that part of the world entering '98. Manager Lennox McNeely has since pared back those holdings and strengthened the U.S. and European positions, and the result was an 8% advance in the first six months of '98. But too much damage had been done to save the year. McNeely uses a top-down approach to identify regions and countries that are likely to outperform, and then employs a bottom-up fundamental style to select individual stocks. The portfolio is well diversified, with over 200 stocks in 30 countries. Rating drops back a notch this year.

BALANCED FUNDS

SCEPTRE BALANCED GROWTH FUND
$$$$ ↓ FI/G No RSP CBAL

Manager: Lyle Stein, since 1993

MER: 1.44%

This is a very good balanced fund but, like most other Sceptre entries, it is coming off an indifferent year. Investors did record a profit of 8.2%, but that was below average for the balanced category. Manager Lyle Stein runs a well-structured portfolio that takes good advantage of the foreign content allowance. Stock holdings tend to be of the blue-chip variety (Bombardier, CIBC, Telus, BCE). Longer term returns are very good. The average annual gain over the past decade is 11.5%, so this fund has legs. No other publicly available balanced fund did better except ABC Fully-Managed, and it costs $150,000 to get into. The safety record is good, with just a 9% chance of loss over any one-year period, reducing to zero over three years, according to ATP figures. Still a very good choice and the recent performance was not bad enough to warrant stripping it of its $$$$ rating. However, I'll be looking for better things at the next review.

FIXED INCOME AND MONEY MARKET FUNDS

SCEPTRE BOND FUND
$$$ → FI No RSP CB

Manager: Ian Lee, since 1996

MER: 0.98%

The portfolio of this fund is divided into three distinct components. Government securities form the core of the holdings, providing security and liquidity. Corporate and municipal bonds make up about a third of the assets, providing higher yields. Finally, foreign currency bonds may be used when appropriate. The result is a fund that performs very well. Gain for the year to June 30/98 was 13.3%, and the returns for all time periods out to 10 years are above average for the bond fund category. Returns will be further helped by Sceptre's decision to cap the MER on this fund at 0.95%, effective Dec. 1/97. Risk is about average. A good pick from this group.

SCEPTRE MONEY MARKET FUND $$$$ ↓ C No RSP CMM

Manager: Ian Lee, since 1997

MER: 0.75%

Very good, consistent performer. Safety-oriented portfolio; invests primarily in government or government-guaranteed notes. Returns are consistently above average.

SCOTIA FUNDS

THE COMPANY

This is the house line of the Bank of Nova Scotia and related companies. The group was strengthened immensely by the merger of the Scotia and Montreal Trust funds in mid-'95 and again in mid-1998 by bringing in the National Trust funds. As a result, this lineup now contains several very strong entries and ranks as one of the top bank fund groups in the country.

The management team handling these funds has also had a shakeup. The money management firm of Cassels Blaikie, which has been running the National Trust funds, has been merged with Scotia Investment Management Ltd. to form Scotia Cassels Investment Counsel Ltd. The new organization has taken over the management of some of the funds from Montreal-based Montrusco & Associates, although the latter company still remains in charge of the Total Return, International, and Canadian Growth funds.

As well, the "Excelsior" name has been dropped from this family. They're now simply the Scotia Funds.

All clear?

THE DETAILS

NUMBER OF FUNDS:	21
ASSETS UNDER MANAGEMENT:	$7.7 BILLION
LOAD CHARGE:	NONE
SWITCHING CHARGE:	NONE
WHERE SOLD:	ACROSS CANADA
HOW SOLD:	THROUGH BRANCHES OF THE BANK OF NOVA SCOTIA, SCOTIA DISCOUNT BROKERAGE, AND SCOTIA MCLEOD
PHONE NUMBER:	(416) 750-3863 OR 1-800-268-9269 (ENGLISH) OR 1-800-387-5004 (FRENCH)
WEB SITE ADDRESS:	WWW.SCOTIABANK.CA
E-MAIL ADDRESS:	THROUGH WEB SITE

FUND SUMMARY

$$$$ - NONE

$$$ - CANAM U.S. $ INCOME, CANADIAN BALANCED, CANADIAN INCOME, CANGLOBAL INCOME, CANADIAN DIVIDEND, CANADIAN MID-LARGE CAP, MORTGAGE INCOME, PREMIUM T-BILL, TOTAL RETURN

$$ - AMERICAN GROWTH, CANAM STOCK INDEX, CANADIAN SHORT-TERM INCOME, CANADIAN SMALL CAP, GLOBAL INCOME, INTERNATIONAL GROWTH, MONEY MARKET

$ - CANADIAN BLUE CHIP, CANADIAN GROWTH, EMERGING MARKETS, LATIN AMERICAN GROWTH, PACIFIC RIM GROWTH, PRECIOUS METALS, T-BILL

NR - AMERICAN STOCK INDEX, CANAM U.S. $ MONEY MARKET, CANADIAN STOCK INDEX, EUROPEAN GROWTH

BEST CHOICES: CANADIAN BALANCED, CANADIAN INCOME, CANAM U.S. $ INCOME, DIVIDEND

BEST FOR RRSPs: CANADIAN BALANCED, CANADIAN INCOME

BEST UNRATEDS: CANAM U.S. $ MONEY MARKET, EUROPEAN GROWTH

FUND RATINGS

CANADIAN EQUITY FUNDS

SCOTIA CANADIAN BLUE CHIP FUND $ → G No RSP CE

Manager: Scotia Cassels

MER: 1.93%

The emphasis is on large-cap stocks, a section of the market that has generally performed quite well recently. The portfolio is well diversified and includes many familiar names like BCE, Canadian Pacific, and a lot of banks. It should be doing just fine, given this makeup, but the results continue to disappoint. Gain for the year to June 30/98 was just 7.4%, well below average for the Canadian equity category. All longer term results are also sub-par. This one simply isn't cutting the mustard. Something needs to be done, since this should be one of the group's flagship funds. Formerly known as the Scotia Canadian Equity Growth Fund.

SCOTIA CANADIAN GROWTH FUND $ → G No RSP CE

Manager: Montrusco

MER: 2.09%

This fund had been doing well until the former manager, Denis Ouellet, left for rival CIBC. Since then, it has been just so-so. Gain for the year to June 30/98 was 8.2%, better than the companion Blue Chip Fund but below average for the Canadian equity category. The portfolio is a diversified mixture of small-, medium-, and large-cap companies. Many of the largest holdings are the same as those of the Blue Chip Fund. Although the management team is different, there is not much else to distinguish between the two funds at this time. Formerly the Montreal Trust Excelsior Equity Fund.

SCOTIA CANADIAN DIVIDEND FUND $$$ → FI/G No RSP INC

Manager: Scotia Cassels

MER: 1.07%

This is a case of two good funds getting together. Both the National Trust Dividend Fund (which is the continuing fund here) and the Scotia Excelsior Dividend Fund were first-rate performers. The combination is a solid dividend fund with a portfolio that's well designed to take advantage of the dividend tax credit. As of mid-'98, just over 70% of the holdings were in high-yielding common stocks, with the balance in preferred shares and cash. As you might expect, the portfolio included a lot of banks, utilities, and telecoms. Cash yield for the old Scotia Fund in calendar '97 was a high 4.9% according to the annual survey done for the *Mutual Funds Update* newsletter. The National Trust entry didn't do as well on that score, but had a much higher total return for the year to June 30/98, at 35.1%. This is a good choice in the dividend fund category, and it would also work in a RRIF, although you would lose the benefit of the tax credit. Farther back, it was the Montreal Trust Dividend Fund.

SCOTIA CANADIAN MID-LARGE CAP FUND
$$$ → G No RSP CE

Manager: Scotia Cassels

MER: 1.55%

This was formerly the National Trust Canadian Equity Fund and it had been doing quite well in that incarnation under the guidance of the Cassels Blaikie organization. Average annual compound rate of return over the three years to June 30/98 was a healthy 18.1%. The portfolio will focus on mid- to large-cap stocks, which makes it look very similar to the Blue Chip Fund and the Canadian Growth Fund. Why all three are needed is unclear, but perhaps everything will unfold in the course of time. In the meantime, this fund has the best record of the three, although now that the Blue Chip Fund is under the same direction, that could change.

SCOTIA CANADIAN SMALL CAP FUND
$$ ↑ G No RSP CSC

Manager: Scotia Cassels

MER: 2.50%

This was formerly the National Trust Special Equity Fund. In that role, it specialized in small to medium-size growth companies. It got off to a great start in '93, with a gain of more than 44% but then languished for a time before turning in a 20% plus return in the 12 months to June 30/97. The most recent year wasn't as productive, with a gain of 6.1% to June 30/98, but that was better than average for the small-cap category. The new name suggests the mid-cap part of the portfolio will be de-emphasized and the future focus will be more tightly on small-caps.

SCOTIA PRECIOUS METALS FUND
$ ↑ G No RSP PM

Manager: Scotia Cassels

MER: 2.19%

Like most precious metals funds, this one has taken its lumps over the past couple of years. Loss for the 12 months to June 30/98 was an ugly 36.1%. Gold will recover at some point. I just don't know when. Stay clear for now.

U.S. AND INTERNATIONAL EQUITY FUNDS

SCOTIA AMERICAN GROWTH FUND $$ → G No £ USE

Manager: Scotia Cassels

MER: 2.19%

This fund can invest in the full range of U.S. equities, although the emphasis these days is on large-cap stocks like Chase Manhattan, Pitney Bowes, Ralston Purina, etc. The portfolio is kept relatively small, about 25–30 stocks. Results had been somewhat weak relative to the competition, but showed a nice pickup in the year to June 30/98 with a gain of better than 30%. Average annual rate of return for all other time periods remains below average, but that result is encouraging enough to warrant a rating boost back to $$. The National Trust American Equity Fund became part of this one in mid-'98.

SCOTIA CANAM STOCK INDEX FUND $$ → G No RSP USE

Manager: Scotia Cassels

MER: 1.34%

This is a pseudo-Canadian fund, designed to bolster exposure to the U.S. stock market in an RRSP or RRIF without encroaching on your precious 20% foreign content allowance. This is achieved by loading up the portfolio with Canadian T-bills, which are used to secure the purchase of S&P 500 futures contracts. As you might expect, the returns in recent years have been good because of the strength of the U.S. markets in the mid-'90s. Average annual compound rate of return for the three years to June 30/98 was a sparkling 262%. But of course when New York goes into the tank, which it inevitably will, this fund will fall in value as well. Still, it's a good way to have more U.S. content in a registered plan, and if you hang in for the long term you'll do okay. The $$ rating is intended to reflect the fact this is an index fund, which will always return close to the market average. Name changed from Scotia CanAm Growth Fund in mid-'98.

SCOTIA EMERGING MARKETS FUND $ ↑ G No £ EME

Manager: Scotia Cassels

MER: 2.72%

This was formerly the National Trust Emerging Markets Fund, now renamed to reflect its entry into the Scotia family. Like most other emerging markets funds, it has suffered cruel treatment at the hands of the international markets in recent years, with a 37.6% drop over the year to June 30/98. Best to stay out of the path of the truck for now.

SCOTIA INTERNATIONAL GROWTH FUND $$ → G No £ IE

Manager: Montrusco

MER: 2.23%

This fund was originally formed from the merger in August, '95 of the Montreal Trust Excelsior International Fund and the Scotia Global Growth Fund. In mid-'98, the National Trust International Equity Fund was folded into it as well so, in effect, you're getting a three-for-one deal here. And, lately, it's been a pretty good deal. The fund's mandate allows it to invest anywhere in the world except Canada. Emphasis is on large companies (Intel, Disney, Mattel). In mid-'98, about half the portfolio was in U.S. stocks, with most of the rest in Europe. That paid off with a healthy 16.5% return in the first six months of '98, which pulled what had been a losing 12-month period well into the black. This fund is now looking much better. Another above-average year will see a rating rise. Formerly the Scotia Excelsior International Fund.

SCOTIA LATIN AMERICAN GROWTH FUND $ ↑ G No £ AE

Manager: Scotia Cassels

MER: 2.39%

Latin American funds have had their ups and downs in recent years, but this one fared better than most. In fact, over the three years to June 30/98, this was the top-performing Latin fund in the country, averaging an annual return of 13.6%. However, hard times flowed across the Pacific from Asia in the spring of '98, and the fund took a nosedive, losing 18.8% over the three months from April to the end of June. Mexico and South America will continue to be high risk areas as long as the market turmoils continue, so conservative investors should exercise extreme caution here. The portfolio is somewhat more diversified than in many Latin funds, although Brazil and Mexico are the lynchpins, as they usually are. More exposure to Argentina and Chile is what makes this one a bit different. The managers try to hedge foreign exchange risk by holding assets in several currencies, but the fact remains that this fund is likely to be quite volatile. It should not account for more than 1%–2% of your portfolio at most, and is not suitable for registered plans. The rating is downgraded to $ for now; however, this is no reflection on the management of the fund, which has done quite well. It is simply a signal to be wary at this time.

SCOTIA PACIFIC RIM GROWTH FUND $ ↑ G No £ FEE

Manager: Scotia Cassels

MER: 2.13%

I'll say this much about this fund: others have done a whole lot worse. While the average Far East fund dropped 12.6% annually over the three years to June 30/98, this one only gave up 4.5% a year. So if you were in it, be consoled! That said, it looks like there is still more turbulence to come in Asia before those countries reach a new level of economic stability, so I would avoid this one for now. Certainly keep it well away from your RRSP.

BALANCED FUNDS

SCOTIA CANADIAN BALANCED FUND $$$ ↓ FI/G No RSP CBAL

Manager: Scotia Cassels

MER: 1.74%

This is the old National Trust Balanced Fund with a new name. The equity portion of this portfolio has a strong blue-chip flavour, with a healthy dose of U.S. stocks in the mix. The bond portion invests only in issues with a safety rating of A or higher. The result is an impressive fund that has been performing well. Gain for the year to June 30/98 was 15.5%, and that came on top of a healthy 24% return over the previous 12 months. Three- and five-year results are also above average. Good safety record enhances the picture. Rating advances to $$$ on the strength of all this. The Scotia Excelsior Balanced Fund was folded into this one.

SCOTIA TOTAL RETURN FUND $$$ → G/FI No RSP CBAL

Manager: Montrusco

MER: 2.27%

Scotiabank offers two balanced entries. This one adopts a more aggressive investment approach. That means pursuing capital gains more vigorously, with a potentially higher degree of risk. Results have generally been quite good, although the return over the year to June 30/98 was below average for the balanced category, at 8.1%. All longer term returns are strong, however, so hopefully this slight slump is an aberration. As of mid-'98, the portfolio was just about evenly divided between bonds and cash (52%) and stocks (48%). The managers use foreign content effectively, adding both U.S. and international equities to the mix. Over the past few years the National Trust Balanced Fund (now the Scotia Canadian Balanced Fund) has done somewhat better, however both are good choices. Formerly the Montreal Trust Total Return Section; renamed in August, '95 as part of the merger of the Scotia and Montreal Trust funds.

FIXED INCOME AND MONEY MARKET FUNDS

SCOTIA CANADIAN INCOME FUND $$$ → FI No RSP CB

Manager: Scotia Cassels

MER: 1.21%

This is the old National Trust Canadian Bond Fund, which dates back to 1957, with the Scotia Income Fund merged into it. The National Trust entry had been the stronger performer of the two, so this is a positive move for Scotia Income Fund investors. Portfolio composition is mainly federal and provincial bonds, with a small holding of corporate issues. Returns for the National Trust entry have been above average over all time frames. Most recent results show a one-year gain of 9.5% to June 30/98. This merger has produced a strengthened fund and it is a good choice for Scotia fixed-income investors. Formerly the Scotia Excelsior Income Fund.

SCOTIA CANADIAN
SHORT-TERM INCOME FUND $$ ↓ FI No RSP CB

Manager: Scotia Cassels

MER: 1.37%

Invests in high-grade bonds and notes, primarily government or government-guaranteed, with relatively short maturities (maximum five years). The fund has a longer time horizon than a money market fund, but a shorter one than most bond funds, thus reducing its volatility during times of sharp interest rate movements (hence the word "defensive" in the name). During a period of falling interest rates, a fund like this will underperform most conventional bond funds. But when rates are rising, it will do much better. That's exactly what's happened recently. When interest rates rose in the first half of '94, this fund held its ground better than most. But last year, returns here were lower than you'd expect from a bond fund —3.8% for the 12 months to June 30/98. This is a fund to move your money into if you're a cautious investor and/or it looks like rates are heading up. Formerly the Scotia Excelsior Defensive Income Fund.

SCOTIA CANAM U.S. $ INCOME FUND $$$ → FI No RSP IB

Manager: Scotia Cassels

MER: 1.60%

The portfolio of this fund is made up mainly of fixed-income securities issued by Canadian governments and corporations that are denominated in U.S. dollars. As a result, it offers RRSP/RRIF investors full U.S. dollar exposure, while still retaining 100% registered plan status. The unit value is expressed in U.S. dollars, so when the Canadian dollar is falling, as it did like a stone in the summer of 1998, this fund will do extremely well, and vice-versa. As you might expect, the latest numbers are very good. The fund gained 14.6% for the year to June 30/98, and tagged an additional 3% on to that in July. Five-year average annual return to June 30 was a more modest 7.7%, but that was above average for the international bond fund category. This is a useful fund for investors who want more U.S. dollar exposure in their retirement plans without sacrificing foreign content room. Formerly known as the Scotia CanAm Income Fund.

SCOTIA CANGLOBAL INCOME FUND $$$ → FI No RSP IB

Manager: Scotia Cassels

MER: 1.76%

This was formerly the National Trust International RSP Bond Fund. As the old name suggests (you wouldn't know from the new one) this is a 100% RRSP-eligible international bond fund, which differentiates it from the companion Global Income Fund, which is classified as foreign content. Performance has been above average for the international bond category, with an average annual compound rate of return of 9.6% for the three years to June 30/98.

SCOTIA GLOBAL INCOME FUND $$ → FI No £ IB

Manager: Scotia Cassels

MER: 1.99%

The fund invests in an international selection of government and corporate bonds denominated in a range of currencies for diversification. It classifies as foreign content, so is not a good choice for an RRSP. Started off slowly, so three-year performance is well below average. However, it has looked better recently with a one-year return of 9.7% to June 30/98. More than half the portfolio was in U.S. dollars in mid-'98, with only a 10% exposure to the loonie. Formerly the Scotia Excelsior Global Bond Fund.

SCOTIA MONEY MARKET FUND $$ → C No RSP CMM

Manager: Scotia Cassels

MER: 1.14%

The National Trust Money Market Fund is the continuing fund in this recent merger, with the Scotia Excelsior Money Market Fund folded into it. Both were routine performers and there is no reason to expect the merged entity to be any different. Portfolio holds a combination of T-bills and corporate notes.

SCOTIA MORTGAGE INCOME FUND $$$ ↓ FI No RSP M

Manager: Scotia Cassels

MER: 1.59%

This merged fund is a combination of the National Trust Mortgage Fund (the continuing fund) and the Scotia Excelsior Mortgage Fund. There hasn't been much to choose between them in terms of performance in recent years and the safety records of both have been good. Net result: a decent, low-risk choice for fixed-income investors.

SCOTIA PREMIUM T-BILL FUND $$$ ↓ C No RSP CMM

Manager: Scotia Cassels

MER: 0.52%

The only difference between this and the regular T-bill Fund is a lower management fee and a minimum initial purchase requirement, in this case of $100,000. The lower MER accounts for the better returns this one generates.

SCOTIA T-BILL FUND $ ↓ C No RSP CMM

Manager: Scotia Cassels

MER: 1.00%

Invests exclusively in federal T-bills, giving it a slight safety edge over the companion Money Market Fund. However, the returns of the Money Market Fund tend to be slightly higher. You'll have to decide if the small extra margin of safety here is worth it.

SCUDDER FUNDS OF CANADA

THE COMPANY

This big U.S. company is making inroads into the Canadian market with a line of no-load, low management fee funds, several of which have generated good returns. The firm has been carrying on business south of the border since 1919, and currently manages over CDN $275 billion in assets, invested in more than 45 countries around the world. The invasion of Canada started in 1995 and was met with little enthusiasm initially. However, an intensive marketing campaign and impressive results have spurred investor interest recently.

THE DETAILS

NUMBER OF FUNDS:	10
ASSETS UNDER MANAGEMENT:	$600 MILLION
LOAD CHARGE:	NONE
SWITCHING CHARGE:	NONE
WHERE SOLD:	ACROSS CANADA
HOW SOLD:	DIRECTLY THROUGH SCUDDER IN ALBERTA, B.C., ONTARIO, AND SASKATCHEWAN. THROUGH BROKERS, DEALERS, AND FINANCIAL PLANNERS IN ALL PROVINCES AND TERRITORIES.
PHONE NUMBER:	1-800-850-FUND (3863)
WEB SITE ADDRESS:	WWW.SCUDDER.CA
E-MAIL ADDRESS:	CANADA_MAIL@SCUDDER.COM

FUND SUMMARY

$$$$ - NONE
$$$ - NONE
$$ - NONE
$ - NONE
NR - CANADIAN BOND, CANADIAN EQUITY, CANADIAN MONEY MARKET, CANADIAN SHORT TERM BOND, CANADIAN SMALL COMPANY, EMERGING MARKETS, GLOBAL, GREATER EUROPE, PACIFIC, U.S. GROWTH & INCOME
BEST CHOICES: N/A
BEST FOR RRSPS: N/A
BEST UNRATEDS: CANADIAN EQUITY, GLOBAL, GREATER EUROPE

FUND RATINGS

None of the funds in this group has been in existence long enough to qualify for a rating.

SPECTRUM UNITED MUTUAL FUNDS

THE COMPANY

Spectrum United is wholly owned by one of Canada's largest insurance companies, Sun Life. The Spectrum funds have been in existence since 1987 and over the past decade have absorbed two other major families, the Calvin Bullock Funds (1990) and the United Funds (1995). The company now has over $7 billion under management.

THE DETAILS

NUMBER OF FUNDS:	32
ASSETS UNDER MANAGEMENT:	$7.7 BILLION
LOAD CHARGE:	FRONT: MAX. 6%; BACK: MAX. 4.5% (ONLY ON SELECTED FUNDS)
SWITCHING CHARGE:	2% MAXIMUM
WHERE SOLD:	ACROSS CANADA
HOW SOLD:	THROUGH FINANCIAL ADVISORS
PHONE NUMBER:	1-800-404-2227 OR (416) 352-3050
WEB SITE ADDRESS:	WWW.SPECTRUMUNITED.CA
E-MAIL ADDRESS:	INFO@SPECTRUMUNITED.CA

FUND SUMMARY

$$$$ - NONE

$$$ - AMERICAN EQUITY, AMERICAN GROWTH, CANADIAN EQUITY, CANADIAN INVESTMENT, DIVIDEND, DIVERSIFIED, EUROPEAN GROWTH, GLOBAL EQUITY, GLOBAL TELECOMMUNICATIONS, LONG-TERM BOND, U.S. DOLLAR MONEY MARKET

$$ - ASSET ALLOCATION, BALANCED PORTFOLIO, CANADIAN GROWTH, CANADIAN STOCK, GLOBAL DIVERSIFIED, MID-TERM BOND, MONEY MARKET, OPTIMAX USA

$ - ASIAN DYNASTY, EMERGING MARKETS, GLOBAL BOND, GLOBAL GROWTH, RRSP INTERNATIONAL BOND, SHORT TERM BOND

NR - CANADIAN CONSERVATIVE PORTFOLIO, CANADIAN GROWTH PORTFOLIO, CANADIAN INCOME PORTFOLIO, CANADIAN MAXIMUM GROWTH PORTFOLIO, CANADIAN

RESOURCE, CANADIAN SMALL MID-CAP, GLOBAL
GROWTH PORTFOLIO

BEST CHOICES: AMERICAN EQUITY, CANADIAN EQUITY, DIVERSIFIED, LONG-
TERM BOND

BEST FOR RRSPs: CANADIAN EQUITY, DIVERSIFIED

BEST UNRATEDS: CANADIAN CONSERVATIVE PORTFOLIO

FUND RATINGS

CANADIAN EQUITY FUNDS

SPECTRUM UNITED
CANADIAN EQUITY FUND $$$ → G #/* RSP CE

Manager: Catherine (Kiki) Delaney (C.A. Delaney Capital Management),
since 1992

MER: 2.35%

Kiki Delaney is one of Canada's high-profile fund managers with good reason: she does a consistently fine job for
her investors. She's managed this fund since 1992 and has
done such a good job with it that Spectrum insisted on having her signed to a long-term deal before they went ahead
with the purchase of the United Funds back in '95.
Delaney uses a bottom-up stock selection approach with
an emphasis on value. "The most growth for the least
price" is this fund's motto. The fund will normally hold a
larger proportion of blue-chip stocks than the companion
Growth Fund. In August, 1998 for example, the largest
holdings were in BCE, National Bank, Teleglobe, and
Sears Canada. Returns are above average for all time periods. The fund gained 12.4% over the year to June 30/98
and posted an average annual compound rate of return of
13.9% over five years. This is a very sound choice for any
equity fund investor. Formerly called the United Canadian
Equity Fund.

SPECTRUM UNITED
CANADIAN GROWTH FUND $$ → G #/* RSP CSC

Manager: Lynn Miller (C.A. Delaney Capital Management), since 1992

MER: 2.35%

This small-cap entry was closed to new investors in April, '96 "to preserve the purity of its Canadian small- and mid-cap mandate and its performance potential". Performance then proceeded to tail off. The fund gained 18.2% for the year to June 30/97, but that was slightly below average for the small-cap category. Over the subsequent 12 months, to June 30/98, things got worse and the fund lost 6.1%. So you probably wouldn't want to invest right now, even if the fund were reopened. Rating drops a notch with this review. Management was taken over by Kiki Delaney's company in '92, with Lynn Miller handling the day-to-day responsibilities. Previously known as the United Venture Retirement Fund and the United Canadian Growth Fund.

SPECTRUM UNITED
CANADIAN INVESTMENT FUND $$$ → G #/* RSP CE

Manager: Kim Shannon (AMI Partners), since 1996

MER: 2.33%

This is the oldest continuously operated fund in Canada, operating under the name Canadian Investment Fund since 1932. It had become almost moribund until Kim Shannon of AMI Partners grabbed hold of it in '96 and turned it around. Her investment style is a conservative buy-and-hold, with a focus on blue-chip stocks within the TSE 100 Index. Many of the companies in the portfolio are household names, like BCE, Imasco, and a bunch of banks. That kind of combination was a surefire winner last year, and the fund racked up an 18.6% gain over the 12 months to June 30/98. That came on top of a 34.5% advance over the previous year and helped to boost all returns out to five years to above average. Safety record continues to improve, reflecting the low-risk approach that Shannon takes. This fund is an excellent choice for the conservative investor and would fit well in an RRSP or RRIF.

SPECTRUM UNITED
CANADIAN STOCK FUND
$$ → G #/* RSP CE

Managers: Brian Dawson and Susan Shuter (McLean Budden), since 1997

MER: 2.33%

In its previous incarnation as the Spectrum Canadian Equity Fund, this was a blue-chip, value-oriented fund with a sub-par track record and a poor historical risk rating. However, management responsibility was shifted to McLean Budden in late '97, and the fund has been given a new growth focus, consistent with that company's strengths. This looks like a good move for this long-time underachiever, and the initial results under the new direction are promising with the fund advancing 8.3% in the first half of '98. I'm moving the rating up to $$ on the strength of the McLean Budden reputation and those initial good results.

SPECTRUM UNITED DIVIDEND FUND $$$ → FI #/* RSP INC

Manager: Stuart Pomphrey (McLean Budden), since 1994

MER: 1.61%

The focus of this fund is on high-quality preferred shares (about two thirds of the assets in mid-'98). The manager avoids the more cyclical sectors of the market and concentrates on stable businesses like pipelines, utilities, and banks. Total returns tend to be below average for the dividend fund category, although the 16.6% gain for the year to June 30/98 was slightly above par. Cash flow is very good, however. During calendar 1997, unitholders received distributions amounting to 5.2% of the fund's value on the first of that year, all of which was tax-advantaged. This fund is a good choice for income-oriented investors seeking to make use of the dividend tax credit, and would also fit into a RRIF.

U.S. AND INTERNATIONAL EQUITY FUNDS

SPECTRUM UNITED ASIAN DYNASTY FUND $ ↑ G #/* £ FEE

Manager: Graham Bamping (Morgan Grenfall), since 1993

MER: 2.58%

This fund may invest throughout the Far East, including Japan. The focus is on mid- to large-size companies, although some small-cap Japanese stocks may be included. This hasn't been a good time for Far East funds (to put it mildly) and this fund lost a whopping 49.1% in the year to June 30/98. 'Nuf said. Originally the Bullock Asian Dynasty Fund.

SPECTRUM UNITED AMERICAN EQUITY FUND $$$ → G #/* £ USE

Manager: Kevin Parke (MFS Institutional Advisors), since 1995

MER: 2.30%

This fund offers a highly diversified portfolio of small-, medium-, and large-cap stocks, so you're getting the entire U.S. spectrum here. The investment style is a mix of growth and value, using a bottom-up, fundamental stock selection approach. That simply means choosing companies on the basis of their strengths and prospects as opposed to which section of the economy they happen to operate in. Manager Kevin Parke has been at the helm only since December, '95, after the Spectrum organization decided to shift portfolio responsibility to an affiliated company in the Sun Life empire, MFS Asset Management of Boston. I expressed concern at the time about the management shift and for a period the fund's return sank into the third quartile — below average for its peer group. However, things are now back on a winning track. The fund gained 31.7% over the year to June 30/98 and that was good enough to pull the numbers for all time periods to above average. As a result, the former $$$ status is now being restored. Formerly known as the United American Equity Fund and before that as the United Accumulative Fund.

SPECTRUM UNITED
AMERICAN GROWTH FUND $$$ ↑ G #/* £ USSC

Manager: John Ballen (MFS Institutional Advisors), since 1995

MER: 2.35%

This fund is Spectrum United's U.S. small- to mid-cap entry, so will carry somewhat more risk than the companion American Equity Fund. That makes it more suitable for aggressive investors who are looking for potential higher returns. The fund delivered exactly that in the 12 months to June 30/98, gaining an impressive 40.4%. A heavy emphasis on the high-tech system with large holdings in companies like Microsoft and Oracle helped to fuel the advance. This fund was created in late 1995 out of a merger between the Bullock American Fund and the United American Growth Fund. Both had been doing very well prior to the merger but neither manager survived the changeover. Portfolio responsibility was handed over to MFS Asset Management of Boston, which, like Spectrum United, is part of the Sun Life organization. MFS got off to a slow start and the return for the year to June 30/97 was a disappointing 11.2%. But last year's impressive performance warrants a return to $$$ status.

SPECTRUM UNITED
EMERGING MARKETS FUND $ ↑ G #/* £ EME

Manager: Ewen Cameron-Watt (Mercury Asset Management), since 1996

MER: 2.66%

This had been one of the best emerging markets funds in the country, but like all other funds of this type it has been hammered unmercifully lately. Loss for the year to June 30/98 was 31.1%, and the bleeding continued on through the summer. In mid-'98, the portfolio focus was heavily on Latin America and Europe, but even those markets, which had been doing well, got smashed. Best to stay clear of this one for now. Originally the Bullock Emerging Markets Fund.

SPECTRUM UNITED
EUROPEAN GROWTH FUND $$$ ↑ G #/* £ EE

Manager: Edoardo Mercandante (Mercury Asset Management), since 1997

MER: 2.60%

This is a European small-cap fund, one of the few around. As such, it has a higher risk profile than the more traditional European funds, but also offers greater return potential as well. The focus is on the bigger western Europe markets but the manager may also invest up to 15% of the portfolio in emerging east European countries (only 10% in small-caps, though). Major holdings in mid-'98 were in the U.K. (24% of the portfolio), Switzerland (13%), and France (12%). Good results; three-year average annual compound rate of return to June 30/98 was an above-average 31.1%. Formerly known as the Bullock European Enterprise Fund. It merits a $$$ rating on the basis of performance, but remember the higher risk level.

SPECTRUM UNITED GLOBAL EQUITY FUND $$$ → G #/* £ IE

Manager: Patrick Deane (Morgan Grenfell), since 1998

MER: 2.30%

This fund can invest around the world, but it was heavily concentrated in the U.S. and Europe in mid-'98 (more than 90% of the portfolio). That geographic focus helped to propel it to a gain of 18.3% over the year to June 30/98, well above average for the international equity category. The portfolio emphasis is distinctly blue-chip, with the largest holdings including familiar names like General Electric, Microsoft, Coca-Cola, and Nestlé. Stocks are chosen 70% on the basis of corporate fundamentals and 30% regional allocation. The mandate is to focus on developed economies but the manager has the discretion to invest up to 15% of the portfolio in emerging markets. Of course, that's not being done at present. The improved returns merit a boost in the rating to $$$ this time around. This fund was originally formed from a merger of the Spectrum International Equity and United Global Equity.

SPECTRUM UNITED GLOBAL GROWTH FUND $ ↑ G #/* £ IE

Manager: James Skinner (Mercury Asset Management), since 1997

MER: 2.30%

This is the small- to mid-cap international entry in the Spectrum United lineup. Stocks are selected on the basis of corporate fundamentals and growth potential and the portfolio was heavily concentrated in the U.S. (50%) and Europe (32.5%) in mid-'98. Results had been mediocre, but perked up recently with a gain of 13.8% in the first half of '98. Longer term results continue to be sub-par, however. Note that this fund will be higher risk by nature than the companion Global Equity Fund because of the focus here on small-cap stocks. Previously known as the United Venture Fund.

SPECTRUM UNITED GLOBAL TELECOMMUNICATIONS FUND $$$ → G #/* £ SEC

Manager: Maura Shaughnessy (MFS Institutional Advisors), since 1997

MER: 2.55%

Great idea for the 21st century. This fund will make money for you by investing in telecommunications companies around the world. The mandate lets the manager buy just about anything: small, medium, and large companies and stocks from emerging markets as well (should those markets ever come back!). Should be a world-beater and indeed it started off strongly. But then it went into a slump, with a gain of just 2.6% in the year to June 30/97. A managerial change late in that year seems to have turned things around, however; the fund surged ahead by 32.4% in the first half of '98. That pulled all the results out to three years back above average. Rating moves up a notch as a result. Formerly the United Global Telecommunications Fund.

SPECTRUM UNITED OPTIMAX USA FUND $$ → G #/* £ USE

Manager: Daniel Cardell (Weiss, Peck & Greer), since 1997

MER: 2.35%

This fund uses a computer program to select stocks from the S&P 500 Index, using the principles of portfolio theory developed by Nobel Prize-winning economist Dr. Harry

Markowitz. Sounds impressive but the returns were nowhere close to matching the Index and in fact were well below average for the U.S. equity fund category. However, there was a managerial change in April, '97 and things have looked better since. The fund gained 30.3% over the 12 months to June 30/98, a very good result. Longer term performance is still sub-par, but this one now seems to be on track.

BALANCED FUNDS

SPECTRUM UNITED ASSET ALLOCATION FUND $$ → FI/G #/* RSP CBAL

Manager: David DeGrasse (AMI Partners), since 1998

MER: 2.22%

The fund employs an aggressive asset allocation management strategy. New manager David DeGrasse of Montreal-based AMI Partners (who had been handling the portfolio previously) maximizes the allowable foreign content holdings and may invest up to 15% of the assets in foreign pay bonds. Derivatives, such as TIPs, may also be used. The parameters allow for wide leeway in asset class allocation. Up to 60% of the portfolio may be in cash at any time, up to 70% in bonds, and up to 90% in stocks. So if you're looking for a middle-of-the-road balanced fund, this may not be it. As of mid-'98, the portfolio was 59% in stocks, 37% in stocks, and the rest in cash. Results have been improving. The fund gained 13.3% over the year to June 30/98, well above average for the balanced category. Three-year average annual compound rate of return was 13.8%, just a shade above average. We'll move the rating up a notch on the strength of this. This previously was the Bullock Asset Strategy Fund and prior to that, the Bullock Balanced Fund.

SPECTRUM UNITED BALANCED PORTFOLIO $$ → FI/G #/* RSP CBAL

Manager: Committee chaired by Karen Bleasby, since 1996

MER: 2.00%

Spectrum United offers several funds of funds. These are portfolios made up of a mix of their other funds, designed to meet specific investor needs. As the name suggests, this fund takes a balanced investing approach. Largest holdings in mid-'98 were in the Canadian Equity Fund (30.2%) and the Mid-Term Bond Fund (29.7%), with a sprinkling of eight other funds in the mix. This is the only portfolio fund that has been in existence long enough to have a rating (it was formerly known as the Spectrum United Canadian Portfolio of Funds). Results have been average to slightly below when compared to Canadian balanced funds as a group. Both the Asset Allocation Fund and the Diversified Fund have produced better returns over the past three years. Either looks like a better choice at this time.

SPECTRUM UNITED
DIVERSIFIED FUND $$$ → FI/G #/* RSP CBAL

Manager: Brian Dawson (McLean Budden), since 1997

MER: 2.08%

This is a conservatively managed fund that invests mainly in blue-chip stocks and government bonds. It is now being run by McLean Budden, a top-notch money management company that is partly owned by Sun Life, which is also the parent of Spectrum United. This fund is a good choice for risk-averse investors who want some growth potential but don't like a lot of risk or big asset class bets. That makes it a sound choice for RRSPs. As of mid-'98, the portfolio was almost evenly divided between stocks (50.5%) and bonds/cash. Foreign content maximum is 15%. Performance improved to above average in recent years, with a gain of 12.6% over the 12 months to June 30/98. Rating moves ahead to $$$.

SPECTRUM UNITED GLOBAL
DIVERSIFIED FUND $$ → FI/G #/* £ IBAL

Manager: Charles Prideaux (Mercury Asset Management), since 1996

MER: 2.30%

This is a global balanced fund that invests in stocks and bonds from around the world. Direction is by Mercury Asset Management of London, who use an active asset allocation approach. Equities accounted for about 60% of the portfolio in mid-'98, with the U.S. and Europe dominating. Bonds were 35% of the mix. Gain for the 12 months to June 30/98 was 15.2%, above average for the international balanced fund category. However, longer term results aren't so hot. Formerly the United Global Portfolio of Funds.

FIXED INCOME AND MONEY MARKET FUNDS

SPECTRUM UNITED CANADIAN MONEY MARKET FUND $$ → C No RSP CMM

Manager: Cort Conover (McLean Budden), since 1996

MER: 1.01%

This is a standard money market fund, investing in a mix of government T-bills, corporate short-term notes, and bankers' acceptances. Performance is average. Note that although there is no sales charge for buying units in this fund, you will be subject to normal commissions if you transfer into another fund later. Formerly the Spectrum United Canadian T-Bill Fund.

SPECTRUM UNITED GLOBAL BOND FUND $ → FI #/* £ IB

Manager: Ken Yoshida (Mercury Asset Management), since 1995

MER: 2.03%

This fund invests in bonds from around the world, mainly government bonds rated AA or AAA for quality. Currencies are actively hedged to protect the asset base. About the best that can be said of it are that the returns are better than those of the companion RRSP International Bond Fund. Both are below average, however. Formerly the Bullock Global Bond Fund.

SPECTRUM UNITED LONG-TERM BOND FUND $$$ ↑ FI #/* RSP CB

Manager: Stuart Pomphrey (McLean Budden), since 1989

MER: 1.66%

The Spectrum United Canadian bond fund lineup contains three distinct offerings. All have the same manager, the difference is the term to maturity of the portfolio. This fund will be the most volatile of the three, as long-term bonds are more sensitive to interest rate movements, up or down. Over time, returns from this fund should be higher than from its two companions. But expect some unit value fluctuation along the way. Over the year to June 30/98, when the bond market was strong, this fund returned 16.7%, compared to 8.8% for the Mid-Term Fund and 3.2% for the Short-Term Fund. This fund is best suited to patient investors with a long-time horizon, or to high-rollers who want to take advantage of rising bond prices and then switch out when interest rate directions change. The trick with that is to get it right! The United Canadian Bond Fund and the Spectrum Government Bond Fund were folded together to create this entity.

SPECTRUM UNITED MID-TERM
BOND FUND $$ → FI #/* RSP CB

Manager: Stuart Pomphrey (McLean Budden), since 1987

MER: 1.59%

This fund's mandate is to focus on mid-term issues, which means bonds maturing in five to 10 years. That places it squarely in the middle of the Spectrum United bond fund grouping, both in terms of risk and potential return. So it's for investors who want some fixed-income exposure without undue risk. That would make it most suitable to those about to retire, or for use in a RRIF. Formerly known as the Spectrum Interest Fund.

SPECTRUM UNITED RRSP
INTERNATIONAL BOND FUND $ → FI #/* RSP IB

Manager: Stuart Pomphrey (McLean Budden), since 1993

MER: 1.98%

This fully RRSP-eligible fund invests mainly in Canadian securities denominated in foreign currencies. The portfolio must be confined to high-grade issues to protect the fund's AAA rating from the Canadian Bond Rating Service. Started off well, but recent results have been unimpressive. Gain for the year to June 30/98 was just 5.3%. Neither of Spectrum United's international bond funds are performing well at this time; look elsewhere if this is an area that interests you. Formerly the Spectrum International Bond Fund.

SPECTRUM UNITED
SHORT-TERM BOND FUND $ ↓ FI #/* RSP CB

Manager: Stuart Pomphrey (McLean Budden), since 1996

MER: 1.45%

This is the most defensive of the three Spectrum Canadian bond offerings, and therefore the fund that combines the lowest risk with the lowest potential returns. This was previously the United Canadian Mortgage Fund. The mandate was amended in August, '96 to allow investment in bonds and other debt securities that mature in five years or less, as well as in conventional first mortgages. It's only one step removed from a money market fund, and recent returns have been about on that level.

SPECTRUM UNITED U.S. DOLLAR
MONEY MARKET FUND $$$ → C No IMM

Manager: Cort Conover (McLean Budden), since 1996

MER: 1.19%

Invests in U.S. dollar denominated short-term securities, which sure was a great place to be in the summer of '98. Results have generally been above average, but remember the numbers you see in the paper don't reflect your currency exchange profits. Use this fund as a hedge if you're worried about a further decline in the value of the Canadian dollar. Formerly the United U.S. $ Money Market Fund. Not eligible for registered plans.

STANDARD LIFE MUTUAL FUNDS

THE COMPANY

The Standard Life organization offers two distinct types of funds. The family described here is a regular mutual funds group. They are all directed by Standard Life Portfolio Management, a subsidiary company of Standard Life. No individual manager names are made available.

The company also sells several segregated funds that can only be purchased as part of an insurance contract under the name "Ideal". You'll find details about those in the Segregated Funds section of this book.

THE DETAILS

NUMBER OF FUNDS:	10
ASSETS UNDER MANAGEMENT:	$131.8 MILLION
LOAD CHARGE:	FRONT: MAX. 5%; BACK: MAX. 5%
SWITCHING CHARGE:	NONE
WHERE SOLD:	ACROSS CANADA
HOW SOLD:	THROUGH PERFORMA REPRESENTATIVES
PHONE NUMBER:	1-800-665-6237
WEB SITE ADDRESS:	WWW.STANDARDLIFE.CA
E-MAIL ADDRESS:	INFORMATION@WEB.STANDARDLIFE

FUND SUMMARY

$$$$ - NONE

$$$ - BALANCED, BOND, CANADIAN DIVIDEND, EQUITY, GROWTH EQUITY, INTERNATIONAL BOND, MONEY MARKET, U.S. EQUITY

$$ - INTERNATIONAL EQUITY

$ - NATURAL RESOURCES

NR - NONE

BEST CHOICES: ALL EXCEPT NATURAL RESOURCE AND INTERNATIONAL EQUITY
BEST FOR RRSPs: BALANCED, BOND, CANADIAN DIVIDEND, INTERNATIONAL BOND
BEST UNRATED: N/A

FUND RATINGS

CANADIAN EQUITY FUNDS

STANDARD LIFE CANADIAN DIVIDEND MUTUAL FUND $$$ → G #/* RSP CE

Manager: Standard Life Portfolio Management

MER: 1.50%

This is really more of a blue-chip stock fund than a dividend income fund, and I have classified it accordingly. The small portfolio is invested almost exclusively in common shares, with no preferreds, royalty trusts, and the like. As a result, total returns have been very good but cash flow will tend to be less than you can expect from a dividend fund with a stronger income focus. But if you want a conservative stock fund for your portfolio, here it is. The fund averaged 32.5% a year for the three years to June 30/98, the best result in the dividend fund category. Of course, it was hit in the late summer market correction, but investors could afford to give something back after gains like that. Debuts with a $$$ rating.

STANDARD LIFE EQUITY MUTUAL FUND $$$ ↓ G #/* RSP CE

Manager: Standard Life Portfolio Management

MER: 2.00%

This fund offers a large portfolio that includes a mix of small, medium, and large companies. It has been producing some very good returns for its investors, with a 12-month gain of 19.5% for the year to June 30/98. That was way above average for Canadian stock funds as a group. Three-year and five-year average annual returns are also superior, at 20.4% and 16% respectively. The safety record is excellent, with only a 4% chance of loss in any given 12-month period, according to Altamira's ATP analysis. This often-overlooked fund is a first-rate choice for investors and should be given serious consideration.

STANDARD LIFE GROWTH
EQUITY MUTUAL FUND $$$ ↑ G #/* RSP CSC

Manager: Standard Life Portfolio Management

MER: 2.00%

This is Standard Life's small-cap entry and a good one at that. The portfolio focuses on Canadian stocks but there is enough U.S. representation within the foreign content limit to keep things interesting. Returns have been very good in the tough small-cap category. The fund gained 18.1% over the year to June 30/98 and averaged 18.8% annually for the three years to that date. Like many other of the fine funds in this group, this one is often lost in the shuffle. More aggressive investors who can accept the added risk of a small-cap fund should investigate this one.

STANDARD LIFE NATURAL
RESOURCE MUTUAL FUND $ ↑ G #/* RSP SEC

Manager: Standard Life Portfolio Management

MER: 2.00%

As the name implies, this fund invests in the resource sector, which has been badly downtrodden recently. About the best thing that can be said of this one right now is that it lost less than many of the others in its category over the year to June 30/98, dropping 20.1%. The resource sector will recover at some point and when it does this will be a good place to be. But the risk is high and the outlook uncertain.

U.S. AND INTERNATIONAL EQUITY FUNDS

STANDARD LIFE INTERNATIONAL
EQUITY MUTUAL FUND $$ → G #/* £ IE

Manager: Standard Life Portfolio Management

MER: 2.00%

The mandate of this fund is to invest in countries outside North America, so you won't find any Canadian or U.S. stocks in the portfolio. However, the foreign securities are obtained by purchasing American Depositary

Receipts (ADRs), which trade on U.S. exchanges. These represent shares in major foreign companies so the portfolio will focus on large corporations, such as Volkswagen and British Telecom. The geographic mix heavily favoured Europe in the first half of '98, pushing the fund to an 18.2% gain for the six months to June 30. However, previous results had been sub-par. We'll open the bidding at $$ for this one as it makes its first appearance here.

STANDARD LIFE U.S.
EQUITY MUTUAL FUND $$$ → G #/* £ USE

Manager: Standard Life Portfolio Management

MER: 2.00%

This fund can invest across the entire spectrum of U.S. stocks, although the portfolio was more focused on large companies, especially in the consumer goods field, in the first half of 1998. It has been a consistently above-average performer, with a gain of 30.7% over the year to June 30/98 and a three-year average annual compound rate of return of 26.2%. This is its first appearance here, and it merits the $$$ rating it has received.

BALANCED FUNDS

STANDARD LIFE
BALANCED MUTUAL FUND $$$ → FI/G #/* RSP CBAL

Manager: Standard Life Portfolio Management

MER: 2.00%

This fund offers a diversified portfolio that includes a large holding in federal and provincial bonds, a large representation of Canadian stocks, and some U.S. equities. Returns have been nicely above average for the balanced fund category. The fund was ahead 14.5% for the year ending June 30/98. Five-year average annual compound rate of return was 12.3%, also above the norm. The safety record is pretty good too, not right at the top of the category but close to it. An especially good choice for an RRSP.

FIXED INCOME AND MONEY MARKET FUNDS

STANDARD LIFE BOND MUTUAL FUND $$$ ↑ FI #/* RSP CB

Manager: Standard Life Portfolio Management

MER: 1.50%

Another fine entry from this underrated group. This fund invests almost entirely in government issues. The bulk of the portfolio is in federal government bonds, but there are also some top-rated provincial securities (Alberta, Ontario). So the quality of the assets is excellent. Returns have been modestly above average for the bond fund category, with an average annual compound rate of return of 8.4% for the five years to June 30/98. The only negative is the safety record; there's a 16% chance you could be in the red after a 12-month hold, which is high for the bond fund category. After three years, the odds on a loss drop to zero, however.

STANDARD LIFE INTERNATIONAL BOND MUTUAL FUND $$$ → FI #/* RSP IB

Manager: Standard Life Portfolio Management

MER: 1.50%

This fully RRSP-eligible fund offers international diversification by investing in bonds issued by the federal and provincial governments that are denominated in foreign currencies. Some bonds issued by international agencies like the World Bank are also held. This was a good place to be during the dollar crisis of mid-1998. The fund gained 17.6% over the year to July 31, a very healthy advance for a portfolio of this type. International bonds will do well if stock markets continue to struggle, so you might want to have some assets here.

STANDARD LIFE MONEY MARKET MUTUAL FUND $$$ → C * RSP CMM

Manager: Standard Life Portfolio Management

MER: 0.90%

Useful entry that invests in a mix of corporate notes and T-bills. Returns have been above average. Don't pay a sales commission to acquire it, however.

STONE & CO.

THE COMPANY

This fledgling fund group is the brainchild of Richard Stone, an energetic go-getter who has been involved on the marketing side of the mutual funds industry for a number of years. The company's funds are managed by McLean Budden, one of the top investment houses in Canada. All are too new for a formal rating but the flagship Stock Fund Canada has been a very strong performer to date.

THE DETAILS

NUMBER OF FUNDS:	3
ASSETS UNDER MANAGEMENT:	$155 MILLION
LOAD CHARGE:	FRONT: MAX. 5%; BACK: MAX. 5%
SWITCHING CHARGE:	NONE
WHERE SOLD:	ACROSS CANADA
HOW SOLD:	THROUGH BROKERS, DEALERS, AND FINANCIAL PLANNERS
PHONE NUMBER:	1-800-336-9528
WEB SITE ADDRESS:	WWW.STONECO.COM
E-MAIL ADDRESS:	INFO@STONECO.COM

FUND SUMMARY

$$$$ - NONE
$$$ - NONE
$$ - NONE
$ - NONE
NR - GROWTH AND INCOME, MONEY MARKET, STOCK FUND CANADA
BEST CHOICES: N/A
BEST FOR RRSPs: N/A
BEST UNRATEDS: STOCK FUND CANADA

FUND RATINGS

All the funds in this group are too new for a formal rating.

STRATEGIC VALUE FUNDS

THE COMPANY

Mark Bonham was one of the founders of the BPI group. He left that company in the fall of 1995 and founded this new firm the following year. In 1997, Strategic Value acquired the moribund Laurentian Mutual Funds, bringing in about $2 billion in assets in the process. Since then, Bonham and his team have been working hard to revitalize the Laurentian funds, which have all been renamed, and to raise the profile of Strategic Value in the crowded fund marketplace. They're making progress; some funds in this group now look very attractive.

THE DETAILS

NUMBER OF FUNDS:	18
ASSETS UNDER MANAGEMENT:	$2.2 BILLION
LOAD CHARGE:	FRONT: MAX. 9%; BACK: MAX. 10%
SWITCHING CHARGE:	2% MAXIMUM
WHERE SOLD:	ACROSS CANADA
HOW SOLD:	THROUGH BROKERS, DEALERS, AND FINANCIAL PLANNERS
PHONE NUMBER:	1-800-408-2311
WEB SITE ADDRESS:	N/A
E-MAIL ADDRESS:	STRATEGICVALUE.FUNDS@SYMPATICO.COM

FUND SUMMARY

$$$$ - NONE

$$$ - DIVIDEND, EUROPE, INCOME

$$ - AMERICAN EQUITY, CANADIAN BALANCED, CANADIAN EQUITY, CANADIAN SMALL COMPANIES, COMMONWEALTH, GLOBAL BALANCED, GOVERNMENT BOND, INTERNATIONAL

$ - ASIA PACIFIC, EMERGING MARKETS, MONEY MARKET

NR - CANADIAN EQUITY VALUE, GLOBAL BALANCED RSP, RSP, STRATEGIC VALUE FUND

BEST CHOICES: DIVIDEND, INCOME

BEST FOR RRSPS: CANADIAN BALANCED, GOVERNMENT BOND, INCOME

BEST UNRATEDS: GLOBAL BALANCED RSP

FUND RATINGS

CANADIAN EQUITY FUNDS

STRATEGIC VALUE CANADIAN EQUITY FUND

$$ → G #/* RSP CE

Manager: Ian Nakamoto, since 1997

MER: 2.68%

The mandate of this fund is to invest primarily in medium to large companies. Under the old management, the results left much to be desired. It has looked better under the new bosses, although the heavy portfolio weighting in banks and other interest-sensitive stocks hit it hard during the summer stock market slide. The relatively small cash position at that time (6% at the end of July) contributed to the big drop. Prior to then, things had been going well, with a gain of 13.3% for the year to June 30/98. But a 5.1% loss in July and a further big 18.1% drop in August cost investors all that gain and then some. When blue-chip funds come back into fashion, this will be a good place to be. But wait for the markets to turn before taking new positions. Don't confuse this (and it's easy to do) with the similarly named Strategic Value Canadian Equity Value Fund, which is run by company president Mark Bonham. This one was formerly the Laurentian Canadian Equity Fund and prior to that the Viking Canadian Fund.

STRATEGIC VALUE CANADIAN SMALL COMPANIES FUND

$$ → G #/* RSP CSC

Manager: Christine Hughes, since 1997

MER: 2.69%

This is the old Laurentian Special Equity Fund with a new name that more accurately focuses on the small-cap bias of the portfolio, although medium-size firms are also part of this mix. Under the Laurentian banner, it was an historic underachiever but new manager Christine Hughes turned it around in a hurry. Gain for the year to June 30/98, which roughly corresponds with her tenure, was a very good 15%. Unfortunately, the fund gave back all those gains and then some, dropping more than 19% during July and August. We'll wait and see how she makes out in a recovery phase before changing the rating. Formerly called the Endurance Canadian Equity Fund.

STRATEGIC VALUE DIVIDEND FUND $$$ → FI/G #/* RSP INC

Manager: Mark Bonham, since 1997

MER: 2.68%

This isn't a flashy dividend fund, but historically it was steady and dependable under the Laurentian banner. Bonham's twin objectives are capital growth and dividend income, and he is making a concerted effort to enhance the cash yield of the fund. The goal is to produce a fixed pay-out of between 4% and 5% annually, with distributions on a monthly basis. These were set at 5 cents a month in 1998. The portfolio is made up mainly of high-yielding common stocks and preferreds, with a sizeable chunk of bonds as well. This portfolio mix helped to shield the fund from the worst ravages of the summer market tumble. It lost about 12.5% over July and August, much less than many other dividend funds that were more heavily concentrated in common shares. A good choice for an income-oriented investor. Originally known as the Viking Dividend Fund.

U.S. AND INTERNATIONAL EQUITY FUNDS

STRATEGIC VALUE AMERICAN EQUITY FUND $$ → G #/* £ USE

Manager: Anthony McGarel Groves (Guinness Flight Hambro), since 1997

MER: 2.68%

The mandate of this fund is to invest mainly in large U.S. corporations. You'll recognize a lot of the names immediately: General Electric, Travelers, etc. Like many other funds in this group, it had been cruising along nicely under the new direction, with a gain of 29.1% to June 30/98. Then came the summer market crash, and investors gave back almost 14% over July and August. It could have been worse, however — and in the case of many other funds, it was. This one looks like a good choice under the new manager. Previously known as the Laurentian American Equity Fund and prior to that as the Viking Growth Fund.

STRATEGIC VALUE ASIA PACIFIC FUND $ ↑ G #/* £ FEE

Manager: Richard Farrell (Guinness Flight Hambro), since 1997

MER: 2.57%

This fund can invest throughout the Far East, including Japan, India, and Australia, but there was no escape from the ravages in that part of the world. The fund lost 40% in the year to June 30/98, and the unit value dropped another 9%+ through July and August. The Far East must be getting close to the bottom, but don't jump in until a clear turnaround has begun.

STRATEGIC VALUE EMERGING
MARKETS FUND $ ↑ G #/* £ EME

Manager: James Hancocks (Guinness Flight Hambro), since 1997

MER: 2.94%

Emerging markets funds have been slaughtered recently. Sorry, but there's no other word for it. This one lost 35.1% over the year to June 30/98, but that was just a warmup. Over the next two months, it crash-dived another 19%. Look elsewhere for now, although when emerging markets do recover there could be some big gains here.

STRATEGIC VALUE EUROPE FUND $$$ → G #/* £ EE

Manager: Maureen Taylor (Guinness Flight Hambro), since 1997

MER: 2.68%

This fund invests primarily in medium and large companies, with the emphasis on western Europe. It was originally part of the Laurentian family, with Strategic Value assuming control in May, '97. Since then, performance has shown improvement (gain of 39.2% in the year to Feb. 28/98). And it hung in well over the terrible summer of '98, giving back just over 6% in July and August. This one is emerging as a good choice in the European category.

STRATEGIC VALUE
INTERNATIONAL FUND

$$ → G #/* £ IE

Manager: Julian Chillingworth (Guinness Flight Hambro), since 1997

MER: 2.69%

The focus here is on growth stocks, with an emphasis on large corporations. North American and European issues made up 85% of the portfolio at the end of July/98 but there was no safe haven when markets tumbled over the summer. The fund gained 16.3% in the first six months of '98, but gave back almost 9 percentage points of that in July and August. The portfolio is very large and highly diversified, with a weighting towards consumer goods and financial services. Despite the summer pullback, results are looking better than in the past when this was known as the Laurentian International Fund and, prior to that, the Viking International Fund.

BALANCED FUNDS

STRATEGIC VALUE
CANADIAN BALANCED FUND

$$ → FI/G #/* RSP CBAL

Manager: Mark Bonham, since 1997

MER: 2.69%

The mandate is to invest in a mix of shares of medium to large companies and high quality government and corporate bonds. The fund has also added REITs and royalty income trust units to the portfolio. Manager Mark Bonham is a traditional value manager, concentrating on 50–75 good companies and looking for bargains in the marketplace. Performance over the 12 months to June 30/98 was slightly below average, with a gain of 9.2%. But the fund gave all that back in July and August, retreating more than 13% in the market slump. Weighting in mid-'98 was 54% stocks, 40% bonds, and the rest in cash. Designed for conservative investors. Originally called Endurance Canadian Balanced Fund and more recently the Laurentian Canadian Balanced Fund.

STRATEGIC VALUE
COMMONWEALTH FUND $$ → G/FI #/* £ IBAL

Manager: Julian Chillingworth (Guinness Flight Hambro), since 1997

MER: 2.69%

This started life as a balanced fund, became a primarily international stock fund, and now has been reclassified as a global balanced fund again. The emphasis is still very heavily on stocks, however (80% at the beginning of August) so this is not a true balanced entry. However, it stood its ground reasonably well in the summer market slide, losing less than 9% over July and August. This fund is not confined to Commonwealth countries (Strategic Value would have done investors a service by changing that misleading name after they took it over from Laurentian). Rather, the manager roams the world, with a special focus on large-cap companies. The portfolio in mid-'98 was weighted towards North America and Europe, which together represented 86% of the geographic mix. This long-time non-achiever is starting to look better with a new team at the helm. We'll see how it does when markets recover. Formerly known as the Viking Commonwealth Fund.

STRATEGIC VALUE GLOBAL
BALANCED FUND $$ → FI/G #/* £ IBAL

Manager: Julian Chillingworth (Guinness Flight Hambro), since 1997

MER: 2.65%

This fund invests in a portfolio of large international companies and high-quality foreign currency bonds. It has been a chronic underperformer in recent years, but started to come on strong in the first half of '98 with a gain of 13.4%. Impressively, it held most of those gains through the dog days of July and August, losing only 3% during that time despite a 61% stock weighting entering August. That performance alone is enough to merit a rating increase to $$. Formerly the Laurentian Global Balanced Fund and before that the Endurance Global Equity Fund.

FIXED INCOME AND MONEY MARKET FUNDS

STRATEGIC VALUE GOVERNMENT
BOND FUND $$ ↓ FI #/* RSP CB
Manager: Michael Labanowich, since 1997

MER: 2.18%

This bond fund invests primarily in short- to medium-term
securities (not exceeding five years) issued or guaranteed by
various levels of government. This strategy will make the
portfolio less vulnerable to losses when interest rates rise,
but returns in good bond years will tend to be lower. Gain
for the 12 months to June 30/98 was 4.5%. Conservative
investors may like the extra safety this fund offers. Main
negative: the MER is too high for a fund of this type.
Formerly the Laurentian Government Bond Fund and prior
to that the Endurance Government Bond Fund.

STRATEGIC VALUE INCOME FUND $$$ → FI #/* RSP CB

Manager: Michael Labanowich, since 1997

MER: 2.18%

A more conventional bond fund than the companion
Government Bond Fund. Invests in a range of debt issues,
with the emphasis on medium to longer term securities.
This is exactly the type of bond fund that has thrived
under recent conditions. Gain for the year to June 30/98
was 15% and the fund held on to almost all that through
July and August. A good place for your money right now;
would be even better with a reduced MER. Rating moves
ahead to $$$. Previously known as the Laurentian Income
Fund and before that as the Viking Income Fund.

STRATEGIC VALUE MONEY
MARKET FUND $ ↓ C #/* RSP CMM
Manager: Michael Labanowich, since 1997

MER: 1.19%

Results are well below average, due in part to a high
MER. Most of the assets are held in federal and provincial
government T-bills. Formerly known as the Laurentian
Money Market Fund and prior to that as the Viking
Money Market Fund.

SYNERGY ASSET MANAGEMENT

THE COMPANY

This is one of the newest entries into the mutual funds arena. The company was launched at the beginning of 1998, just in time for the RRSP season. It's the brainchild of Joe Canavan, a high-profile fund marketer and administrator who piloted the GT Global family to instant success before unexpectedly resigning as president in mid-1997 (GT has since merged into the AIM Group).

Now he's back with a six-fund group built on management style. You can buy a value fund, a growth fund, a momentum fund, a small-cap fund, or all of the above rolled into one. He has plans to expand his lineup going forward but the first challenge is to get the Synergy name established in the crowded funds marketplace.

All the funds are too new for a rating. The Momentum and Growth entries got off to the fastest start, but the market correction of July and August left them down on the year compared to the original NAV. However, it's very early days and this looks like a family worth keeping an eye on.

THE DETAILS

NUMBER OF FUNDS:	6
ASSETS UNDER MANAGEMENT:	$35 MILLION
LOAD CHARGE:	FRONT: MAX. 5%; BACK: MAX. 5%
SWITCHING CHARGE:	2% MAXIMUM
WHERE SOLD:	ACROSS CANADA
HOW SOLD:	THROUGH FINANCIAL ADVISORS
PHONE NUMBER:	1-888-664-4784
WEB SITE ADDRESS:	WWW.SYNERGYASSET.COM
E-MAIL ADDRESS:	INFO@SYNERGYASSET.COM

FUND SUMMARY

$$$$ - NONE
$$$ - NONE
$$ - NONE
$ - NONE
NR - CANADIAN GROWTH, CANADIAN MOMENTUM, CANADIAN

Short-Term Income, Canadian Small Cap, Canadian Style Management, Canadian Value

Best Choices: N/A
Best for RRSPs: N/A
Best Unrateds: Growth, Momentum

FUND RATINGS

No fund in this group has been in existence for the three years needed to acquire a rating.

TALVEST/HYPERION FUNDS

THE COMPANY

The Talvest/Hyperion Funds are overseen by T.A.L. Investment Counsel, a Montreal-based portfolio management firm, founded in 1972. It is owned by CIBC, but maintains independent management. The mutual fund operation was established in 1985. Two groups have been combined to form this lineup, the original Talvest funds and the Hyperion funds, which were taken over from CIBC a few years ago.

One comment: In these days of high-speed communication, this company needs to be more attentive to its web site. In early September, after a summer of stock market turmoil, it was still featuring fund reports dating all the way back to March 31. Ancient history!

THE DETAILS

NUMBER OF FUNDS:	24
ASSETS UNDER MANAGEMENT:	$2 BILLION
LOAD CHARGE:	FRONT: MAX. 1%; BACK: MAX. 0.5%
SWITCHING CHARGE:	2% MAXIMUM
WHERE SOLD:	ACROSS CANADA
HOW SOLD:	THROUGH BROKERS, DEALERS, AND FINANCIAL PLANNERS
PHONE NUMBER:	1-800-268-8258
WEB SITE ADDRESS:	WWW.TALVEST.COM
E-MAIL ADDRESS:	MARKETING@TALVEST.COM

FUND SUMMARY

$$$$ - NONE

$$$ - BOND, EUROPEAN, FOREIGN PAY CANADIAN BOND, HIGH YIELD BOND, INCOME, MONEY, SMALL CAP CANADIAN EQUITY, VALUE LINE U.S. EQUITY

$$ - CANADIAN ASSET ALLOCATION, CANADIAN EQUITY VALUE, CANADIAN MEDICAL DISCOVERIES, GLOBAL ASSET ALLOCATION, GLOBAL RRSP, GLOBAL SCIENCE AND TECHNOLOGY

$ - ASIAN, NEW ECONOMY

NR - CANADIAN EQUITY GROWTH, CANADIAN RESOURCE,
CANADIAN SCIENCE AND TECHNOLOGY GROWTH, CHINA PLUS,
DIVIDEND, GLOBAL HEALTH CARE, GLOBAL SMALL CAP
BEST CHOICES: BOND, EUROPEAN, FOREIGN PAY CDN. BOND, INCOME, VALUE LINE
BEST FOR RRSPS: BOND, FOREIGN PAY CDN. BOND, INCOME
BEST UNRATEDS: DIVIDEND

FUND RATINGS

TALVEST FUNDS

CANADIAN EQUITY FUNDS

CANADIAN MEDICAL DISCOVERIES FUND $$ ↑ G * RSP LAB

Manager: Dr. Calvin Stiller, since inception (1995)

MER: 5.80%

This is a labour-sponsored venture capital fund that is distributed through Talvest. Check the section on labour-sponsored funds for a detailed writeup.

TALVEST CDN. EQUITY VALUE FUND $$ → G #/* RSP CE

Manager: Monique Malo, since 1997

MER: 2.40%

This fund focuses on finding undervalued stocks, mostly of the blue-chip variety. The portfolio normally contains about 45–50 issues. Past results are spotty; however, the fund gained an above-average 11.2% in the 12 months to June 30/98 under the direction of new manager Monique Malo. Sadly, it gave all of that back and a lot more in July and August, tumbling more than 22% in those two bad months. The rating is maintained for now, but we'll be looking for a better performance when the market turns back up.

TALVEST NEW ECONOMY FUND $ ↑ G #/* RSP CE

Manager: Pierre Bernard, since 1994

MER: 2.50%

The mandate of this fund is to focus on so-called "New Economy" companies, the type that will supposedly be the big money makers in the next century. So you'd expect to find a lot of technology and health care stocks in this fund, and you do. What you won't find are "Old Economy" stocks, such as steel companies. They're limited to a maximum of 15% of the portfolio. All this has yet to jell, however. The fund gained just 8.2% in the year to June 30/98, and three-year returns to that point were well below average. Summer was a disaster, with the fund losing 6.6% in July and another 22.1% in August. To make matters worse, the volatility is quite high. Plus, Talvest and economist Nuala Beck, on whose book the concept of the fund was based, ended their relationship in mid-1998. This one is drifting. Avoid.

TALVEST/HYPERION SMALL CAP CDN. EQUITY FUND $$$ ↑ G #/* RSP CSC

Manager: J. Sebastian van Berkom (Van Berkom and Associates), since inception (1993)

MER: 2.50%

As you would assume from the name, the focus of this fund is on small-cap Canadian growth stocks. Sebastian van Berkom is regarded as one of the country's top managers in this field and the fund's previous results showed that. Gain for the year to June 30/98 was 10.2%, well above average for the Canadian small-cap category. Three-year average annual compound rate of return was an excellent 21.5% at that point. But summer was a killer; the fund lost 4.6% in July and then plummeted more than 19% in August. Not a pretty picture. Still, van Berkom has a good record and this should recover in time. I won't knock back the rating because of one bad month, but be a little cautious here for now. Formerly known as the Aurora Fund.

U.S. AND INTERNATIONAL EQUITY FUNDS

TALVEST/HYPERION ASIAN FUND $ ↑ G #/* £ FEE

Manager: Duncan Mount, since inception (1990)

MER: 3.25%

I said in last year's edition that Asia was heading into turbulent times and warned readers to be cautious of this fund. Sadly, I was right. Loss for the year to June 30/98 was 34.4%. That wasn't as bad as some other Far East funds, so technically this one came in above average. But it was not an average most investors would aspire to. Wait for the recovery.

TALVEST/HYPERION EUROPEAN FUND $$$ → G #/* £ EE

Manager: Sarah Caygill, since 1997

MER: 3.00%

This fund had been managed from London by Baring International Investment Ltd., but responsibility was recently passed to Sarah Caygill, who is based in Geneva with T.A.L. Europe. Results had been sub-par for the European fund category, but they have been improving under her watch. The fund gained 39.4% over the year to June 30/98 and only gave back about 6% in July and August. The focus is on mid- to large-cap stocks, but the fund may also invest in new public offerings and special situations. The portfolio is mainly in western European stocks. Rating moves up this year.

TALVEST GLOBAL RRSP FUND $$ → G #/* RSP IE

Manager: Guy Normandin, since 1997

MER: 2.50%

This is one of the pseudo-Canadian funds that uses futures contracts and other derivatives to allow RRSP investors to increase their international exposure beyond the normal 20% limit. Returns were below average, but the fund has shown significant improvement recently, with a 26.6% gain in the year to June 30/98. Summer was bad but not horrible, with the NAV dropping about 6.5% over July and August. Compared to some of the carnage elsewhere, that was a pretty good performance. Rating moves up a notch as a result of all this.

TALVEST/HYPERION GLOBAL
SCIENCE AND TECHNOLOGY FUND $$ → G #/* £ IE

Manager: Stephen Kahn, since 1996

MER: 2.25%

It's really hard to know what to say about this fund. It was actually started way back in '70 as the NW Equity Fund. It was acquired by Talvest in mid-'92 and renamed the Talvest U.S. Growth Fund. Then in late '96, it was renamed again and given a totally new mandate to focus on science and technology stocks around the world. However, about 90% of the global market for such stocks is in the U.S., so the portfolio will be heavily weighted there and manager Stephen Kahn is actually T.A.L.'s vice-president, U.S. equities. All the changes mean that past results are totally meaningless, so only short-term numbers count. They were pretty impressive for the year to June 30/98, with a big gain of 44.6%. But summer was a nightmare, with the fund losing almost 20% in July and August as high-tech stocks were battered on NASDAQ. You have to expect that kind of volatility with a high-tech fund like this. We need more time to get a handle on how this one will develop in more stable markets so we'll leave the rating alone for now.

TALVEST/HYPERION VALUE
LINE U.S. EQUITY FUND $$$ → G #/* £ USE

Manager: Nancy L. Bendig, since 1991

MER: 3.00%

This fund takes a unique investing approach; in fact, you won't find another like it in Canada. The portfolio advisor is Value Line Inc. of New York, whose analyses of stocks are among the most widely followed in the industry. Shares for the fund are selected on the basis of a high timeliness ranking under the Value Line system. This ranking takes into account a number of measures, such as earnings, price, and momentum. With this kind of blue-ribbon direction you'd expect results that would be near the top of this category. Initially, they weren't, but the fund has improved and shown staying power. Five-year average annual compound rate of return to June 30/98 was 19.6%, slightly better than average for the U.S. equity category. Summer was rough, however, with the fund giving back more than 15% in July and August. But no one escaped, so I'm not about to change the rating on the basis of two bad months.

BALANCED FUNDS

TALVEST CDN. ASSET ALLOCATION FUND $$ ↑ G/FI #/* RSP CBAL

Manager: Jean-Guy Desjardins, since inception (1986)

MER: 2.42%

This fund is allowed to hold up to 75% of its portfolio in stocks, which makes it somewhat higher risk than the average balanced fund. In the first half of '98, about two thirds of the portfolio was in equities, with the rest in bonds, mortgage-backed securities, and cash. The bond side of the portfolio leans towards government issues, with some corporates mixed in. Returns to the end of June/98 had improved to above average over all time frames for the balanced category. One-year gain was 16.1% while the 10-year average annual compound rate of return was bang on 10%. As with most funds, the summer was rough but this one hung in reasonably well in tough conditions. No change in the rating for now, but if this one continues to fare well in a difficult market setting it will be a candidate for an upgrade next time around.

TALVEST GLOBAL ASSET ALLOCATION FUND $$ → FI/G #/* £ IBAL

Manager: Gordon J. Fyfe, since 1987

MER: 2.75%

This is a highly diversified international balanced fund, holding stocks and bonds from both developed countries and emerging markets. Manager Gordon Fyfe uses a number of criteria in his management style, seeking to identify the countries with the best growth prospects, balancing off currency movements, watching international interest rate trends, and more. The results have been sub-par, with gains well below average for the international balanced fund category. But this fund held up extremely well in the market downturn of July and August, '98. It actually gained 1.5% in July and only gave up about 5% in August. Given what was happening to world markets at that point, most investors would be delighted to escape with such light damage!

FIXED INCOME AND MONEY MARKET FUNDS

TALVEST BOND FUND $$$ → FI #/* RSP CB

Manager: John W. Braive, since 1973

MER: 1.99%

Good performer over both the short and long term with above-average numbers across the board. Gain for the year to June 30/98 was 8.9%. The portfolio favours government bonds with some corporate issues and mortgages. This is a sound, well-managed fund. A good choice for an RRSP or RRIF.

TALVEST FOREIGN PAY
CDN. BOND FUND $$$ → FI #/* RSP IB

Manager: Denis Senécal, since 1997

MER: 2.15%

This is an RRSP-eligible international bond fund that invests in foreign currency denominated debt securities issued by Canadian governments and corporations and international agencies like the World Bank. Results have improved to above average, with a 10.9% gain for the year to June 30/98. This was where you wanted to be during the summer market turmoil; the fund gained 2.5% in July and another 4.6% in August. Now you see the virtue of a balanced portfolio! Rating jumps to $$$.

TALVEST/HYPERION
HIGH-YIELD BOND FUND $$$ ↑ FI #/* RSP CB

Manager: Chris Currie, since 1998

MER: 2.10%

This fund was originally known as the Hyperion Fixed Income Trust. The name was changed in late '96 and the fund was given a new mandate to invest in the high-yield bond market (sometimes known as "junk bonds"). It took a while, but by the start of '98 the changeover was complete. The fund is mainly in corporate issues, with a large foreign-pay component. That helped to propel it to an 11% gain over the 12 months to June 30/98 and the fund tacked on another 2% in July while holding its ground in August. There's a new manager at the helm; Chris Currie took over in early '98.

TALVEST INCOME FUND $$$ ↓ FI #/* RSP CB

Manager: John W. Braive, since 1974

MER: 1.50%

This fund invests in a mixture of short- to mid-term bonds, with a very small percentage of the portfolio in mortgages. This makes it more appropriate for defensive investors, because the shorter term of the securities means it is less vulnerable to interest rate movements. But it will not do well in a strong bond market. Example: Over the year to June 30/98, this fund gained just 3.9% while the companion Bond Fund was advancing 8.9% and the Talvest/Hyperion High Yield Bond Fund jumped 11%. It's the old issue of risk versus return. This one is low risk, low return. Great safety record, as you might expect. There's only a tiny 3% chance of loss in any 12-month period, and then the maximum drop has been just 3.8%. A good choice if reducing risk is an objective, (for example, in a RRIF), but you will sacrifice some return when bond markets are strong.

TALVEST MONEY FUND $$$ → C #/* RSP CMM

Manager: Steven Dubrovsky, since 1994

MER: 0.75%

Quality portfolio made up of a good mix of government securities and corporate notes. Results have been comfortably above average in recent years. Try to get it with no load charge.

TEMPLETON FUNDS

THE COMPANY

Templeton Management Limited is the Canadian subsidiary of one of the world's largest investment firms, the Franklin Templeton Group of San Mateo, California. The organization's guru and guiding philosophical force is Sir John Templeton, who now lives in retirement in the Bahamas. He no longer manages any of the company's mutual funds, but his pronouncements on investing and the course of the markets still command international attention. The company's oldest fund is the venerable Templeton Growth Fund, which still retains the honour of being one of the best international funds available to Canadians.

THE DETAILS

NUMBER OF FUNDS:	14
ASSETS UNDER MANAGEMENT:	$19.6 BILLION
LOAD CHARGE:	FRONT: MAX. 6%; BACK: MAX. 6%
SWITCHING CHARGE:	2% MAXIMUM
WHERE SOLD:	ACROSS CANADA
HOW SOLD:	THROUGH BROKERS, DEALERS, FINANCIAL PLANNERS, TD BANK, SUNETCO, CT SECURITIES, AND LONDON LIFE
PHONE NUMBER:	(416) 364-4672 OR 1-800-387-0830 (ENGLISH) OR 1-800-897-7281 (FRENCH) OR 1-800-661-3339 (CHINESE)
WEB SITE ADDRESS:	WWW.TEMPLETON.CA
E-MAIL ADDRESS:	TOR-WEBMASTER@TEMPLETON.CA

FUND SUMMARY

$$$$ - GROWTH, INTERNATIONAL STOCK

$$$ - BALANCED

$$ - CANADIAN ASSET ALLOCATION, CANADIAN STOCK, GLOBAL BALANCED, INTERNATIONAL BALANCED, TREASURY BILL

$ - CANADIAN BOND, EMERGING MARKETS, GLOBAL BOND, GLOBAL SMALLER COMPANIES

NR - FRANKLIN U.S. SMALL CAP GROWTH, MUTUAL BEACON

BEST CHOICES: GROWTH, INTERNATIONAL STOCK
BEST FOR RRSPS: BALANCED, GROWTH
BEST UNRATEDS: MUTUAL BEACON

FUND RATINGS

CANADIAN EQUITY FUNDS

TEMPLETON CANADIAN STOCK FUND $$ → G #/* RSP CE

Manager: Norman Boersma, since 1992

MER: 2.44%

This is the Templeton group's only dedicated Canadian equity fund. It was a very poor performer in its early years, gave a brief spurt in the mid-'90s, but has been looking tired again recently. A glance down the portfolio of this fund may surprise you. Most Canadian equity funds use U.S. stocks for the foreign content portion. Not here. You'll find companies like Banco Popular Espanol, Banque Nationale de Paris, Deutsche Bank, Telecom Italia, Volkswagen, Air New Zealand, and many more. Templeton is obviously using its worldwide expertise to make the most of the fund's foreign content allowance. It's a unique approach among Canadian equity funds, but the total package hasn't been inspiring lately. The fund gained a below-average 8.5% for the year to June 30/98. Three-year average annual compound rate of return of 15.8% was also slightly below par. Summer was a shock, with the fund losing about 16% from July 1 to Aug. 31. We'll give manager Norm Boersma some time to regroup before changing the rating, however. Name changed from Templeton Heritage Retirement Fund.

U.S. AND INTERNATIONAL FUNDS

TEMPLETON EMERGING MARKETS FUND $ ↑ G #/* £ EME

Manager: Mark Mobius, since inception (1991)

MER: 3.24%

Mobius is a colourful globe-trotter who brings Templeton's traditional eye for value to the management of this fund. He's always upbeat, and that's probably what's helped pull him through this very hard period for emerging markets. He told the Templeton annual meeting in July/98 that the Asian situation appeared to be nearing bottom and that a combination of undervalued stocks and increasing exports resulting from devalued currencies should begin to pull the region back fairly soon. As this is written, we're still waiting. The portfolio of this fund is broadly diversified, with about 30 countries represented, from China to South Africa. No one country dominates, although the fund had fairly large holdings in Latin America in the first half of '98. Countries not often found in portfolios like this include Israel, Botswana, Jordan, and Ghana. That Mobius fellow sure gets around! As with all emerging markets funds, this one is a roller-coaster ride. It suffered small losses in both '92 and '94, but more than made up for those with a gain of almost 83% in '93. Profit for the year to June 30/97 was 31.4% but in the subsequent 12 months the fund gave most of it back, losing 30.9%. Then came the big slide of July and August, 1998 and investors dropped another 20%. All that reminded us yet again that emerging markets are only for investors who are prepared to take risks and stick with their convictions through the down times.

TEMPLETON GLOBAL
SMALLER COMPANIES FUND $ → G #/* £ IE

Manager: Norman Boersma, since 1997

MER: 2.61%

This fund underwent a major managerial change in mid-'97 when the colourful Marc Joseph parted company with the Templeton organization. During the two years he had been at the helm the fund gained an average of 16.8% annually, slightly above the norm for the international equity fund category. The mandate is to invest in small companies around the world. The original emphasis was on developing nations but that has changed; the portfolio now includes both industrialized nations and emerging markets. Recent results have not been impressive. Gain for the year to June 30/98 was only 4.7% and the fund took some heavy losses over the summer. Rating is cut back to $. Formerly the Templeton Developing Growth Stock Fund.

TEMPLETON GROWTH FUND $$$$ → G #/* £ IE

Manager: Mark Holowesko, since 1987

MER: 2.00%

One of the granddaddies of the mutual fund industry, this giant has become the largest fund in Canada with assets of more than $10 billion in mid-'98 — a number once thought unachievable in this country. Investors are attracted by the Templeton organization's sound reputation, the fund's stability, and, of course, the many years of above-average returns. Over the decade to June 30/98, you'd have earned 14.5% a year in this fund. A few have done better, but not many. The fund employs a highly disciplined stock selection process, with the strong value orientation that's the trademark of the Templeton organization. Stocks are chosen from both developed and emerging countries, to provide a broad mix. Over the past year, the fund has pared back its U.S. stock holdings and has focused more on Europe and, somewhat surprisingly, emerging markets where the Templeton researchers were purporting to find great values. Those profits are obviously still to come, however. The fund gained an uncharacteristically low 8.9% for the year to June 30/98. It held its own in July but took a big dive in August. None of this is good news for investors, but if you've been in this fund for any length of time you've made a lot of money. One bad year doesn't translate into a rating drop for a fund with the history this one brings to the table. But I'll be watching it closely to see how the unusual portfolio moves develop over the next few months.

TEMPLETON INTERNATIONAL STOCK FUND $$$$ → G #/* £ IE

Manager: Donald Reed, since 1989

MER: 2.49%

The mandate of this fund restricts it from North American investments so European stocks have figured very heavily in the portfolio recently (about two thirds of the portfolio in mid-'98). Despite the fact the fund is shut out of the U.S. market, it has been the best performer of the Templeton stock entries over the past five years, with an average annual gain of 19.3% to June 30/98. The fund even managed to gain ground in July (2.3%) before slipping back in the August correction. This fund is an excellent choice for investors looking for diversification outside North America and merits a boost into the $$$$ category this year. Name changed from Templeton Heritage Growth Fund in April, '93.

BALANCED FUNDS

TEMPLETON BALANCED FUND $$$ → FI/G #/* RSP CBAL

Managers: Neil Devlin, since 1990, and George Morgan, since 1996

MER: 2.44%

This is a balanced entry with a strong foreign component. Returns have been above average, but slipped a bit in the year to June 30/98 with a gain of just 8.8%. Longer term results were still above the norm for the balanced category, however. The portfolio was heavily weighted towards stocks in mid-'98 (63% of the portfolio), which didn't help matters during the slide of July and August. This isn't the top Canadian balanced fund available but it's not bad, and is a better choice than the companion Templeton Asset Allocation Fund. This was originally a pure stock fund under the name Templeton Canadian Fund.

TEMPLETON CANADIAN ASSET ALLOCATION FUND $$ → FI/G #/* RSP CBAL

Managers: George Morgan and Thomas Dickson, since 1996

MER: 2.15%

This fund differs from the companion Balanced Fund in that it takes an asset allocation approach to portfolio management. The target is 65% equities, and 35% fixed-income, although this can vary somewhat. In mid-'98, the equity segment was down to 52%, with 35% in bonds and the balance in cash. That was a somewhat more conservative posture than the Balanced Fund, and it paid off during the market slide in August when the losses here were lower. Historically, this entry has shown less volatility than the Balanced Fund, but the results are lower as well.

Three-year average annual compound rate of return to June 30/98 was 12.5%, compared to 14.8% for the Balanced Fund. If you want potentially higher returns, the Balanced Fund is the choice. However, if safety is the major concern this is the better pick.

TEMPLETON GLOBAL BALANCED FUND $$ → FI/G #/* £ IBAL

Managers: George Morgan and Thomas Dickson, since 1996

MER: 2.55%

The difference between this and the companion International Balanced Fund is that in this portfolio the managers can invest anywhere in the world, including North America. However, the managers cut back on their Canadian and U.S. equity positions in the first half of '98, reducing them to about 10% of the portfolio by the first of August. The rest of the stock mix was widely diversified internationally. Equities made up about half the portfolio at that stage, with bonds and cash making up the other half. Average annual compound rate of return for the three years to June 30/98 was 13.2%, a bit under the average for the global balanced category.

TEMPLETON INTERNATIONAL BALANCED FUND $$ → FI/G #/*£ IBAL

Managers: Thomas Dickson, since 1994, and Heather Arnold, since 1998

MER: 2.55%

The mandate of this fund is to maintain a balanced portfolio of equities and fixed-income securities, with a target weighting of 65%/35%. The managers may invest anywhere with the exception of Canada and the U.S. That was a significant handicap at a time when North American markets were strong and the results show that. The fund has earned below average returns for the past three years (average annual gain of 11.7% to June 30/98). The companion Global Balanced Fund, which faces no such constraints, didn't shoot the lights out, but it did better. In mid-'98 the portfolio was heavily concentrated in Europe, however the managers were scouting out bargains in the troubled Asian markets. About 57% of the holdings were in stocks, with the balance in bonds and cash.

FIXED INCOME AND MONEY MARKET FUNDS

TEMPLETON CANADIAN BOND FUND $ → FI #/* RSP CB

Manager: Thomas Dickson, since 1996

MER: 1.65%

This is a very unusual fund. Most Canadian bond funds invest only in domestic issues. But this one maximizes the foreign content allowance of 20% to bring in a wide range of international debt securities from countries as diverse as Belgium and New Zealand. Despite the imaginative portfolio, returns have been weak. Gain for the year to June 30/98 was just 5%, compared to an average of 8.6% for Canadian bond funds as a group. Not your best choice in bond funds. Formerly called Templeton Heritage Bond Fund.

TEMPLETON GLOBAL BOND FUND $ → FI #/* £ IB

Manager: Neil Devlin, since inception (1988)

MER: 2.25%

This is a true global bond fund, investing primarily in securities issued by foreign governments and corporations, although some Canadian issues may also be held in the portfolio. As a result, it may only be held in RRSPs and RRIFs as foreign content. Manager Neil Devlin has built a broadly based portfolio, including bonds and T-bills from some emerging market countries like Brazil, India, and Panama as well as from major nations like the U.S. and the U.K. He may hedge currencies to reduce the risk of volatile price movements. Recent results have slipped in comparison to other international bond funds. Return for the year to June 30/98 was just 2.1%. You'd have done better in a money market fund. Rating drops back to $. Formerly known as the Templeton Global Income Fund.

TEMPLETON TREASURY BILL FUND $$ ↓ C No RSP CMM

Manager: Donald Reed, since 1989

MER: 0.75%

A so-so performer. The name could be misleading, however; the manager is allowed to invest up to 30% of the assets in short-term corporate notes and bankers' acceptances. So far, however, the portfolio has been entirely in federal government T-bills. Templeton's only no-load entry.

TRIMARK MUTUAL FUNDS

THE COMPANY

The Trimark organization has grown into one of the top fund groups in Canada since its creation in the early 1980s, but it has being going through a difficult period. The weak performance of many of the company's equity funds in recent years has resulted in large-scale redemptions and stalled the firm's drive to replace Investors Group as the largest fund manager in the country. In fact, Trimark has now fallen back to the number-three spot, replaced by the onrushing Royal Funds with their awesome marketing reach.

In an effort to deal with the outflow of money, Trimark has brought in some new managers and launched three new funds, as well as a line of segregated funds. They have continued to maintain their top-quality, back office service, and excellent client communications. However, the bottom line is that only a turnaround in performance can restore this company's former status as the darling of the industry. The coming year will be a critical one for Trimark's future.

THE DETAILS

NUMBER OF FUNDS:	30
ASSETS UNDER MANAGEMENT:	$28.2 BILLION
LOAD CHARGE:	FRONT: MAX. 9%; BACK: MAX. 4.5%
SWITCHING CHARGE:	2% MAXIMUM
WHERE SOLD:	ACROSS CANADA
HOW SOLD:	THROUGH LICENSED FULL-SERVICE FINANCIAL ADVISORS
PHONE NUMBER:	1-800-387-9845
WEB SITE ADDRESS:	WWW.TRIMARK.COM
E-MAIL ADDRESS:	SERVICE@TRIMARK.COM

FUND SUMMARY

$$$$ - TRIMARK FUND

$$$ - ADVANTAGE BOND, CANADIAN BOND, INTEREST, SELECT GROWTH

$$ - AMERICAS FUND, GOVERNMENT INCOME, INCOME GROWTH, SELECT BALANCED

$ - Canadian, Indo-Pacific, RSP Equity, Select Canadian Growth

NR - Discovery, Europlus, Resources, Small Companies (Also not rated are 13 segregated funds that are clones of the mutual funds listed here)

Best Choices: Advantage Bond, Canadian Bond, Trimark Fund

Best for RRSPs: Canadian Bond, Trimark Fund

Best unrateds: Europlus

FUND RATINGS

CANADIAN EQUITY FUNDS

TRIMARK CANADIAN FUND $ → G # RSP CE

Manager: Vito Maida, since 1995

MER: 1.53%

In the *1998 Buyer's Guide to Mutual Funds* I expressed concern about the deteriorating performance of this and the other Trimark Canadian stock funds. At the time I pointed out that although the long-term record still looked impressive, results in recent years had slipped to below average. Unfortunately, the situation has not improved. This fund returned a fractional 0.9% over the year to June 30/98, way below average for the Canadian equity category. And that was before stock markets hit the wall in July and August. All the Trimark Canadian stock portfolios have heavy weightings in resource companies, which look like real bargains at today's price. Perhaps at some point that value will emerge, but it has been a long, painful time coming. Many investors and brokers have called for the company to make a managerial change to attempt to shake things up, but it hasn't happened here — yet. On the plus side, some Trimark funds do not saddle investors with the administration expenses; except for brokerage charges, these are paid for directly by the company instead of from fund assets. This is one such fund, which is why the management expense ratio is relatively low. The fund also has a good safety record. Over the past decade, there has been just one losing calendar year, 1990, although 1998 could end up in the red if the fund doesn't rally in the Fall. The main difference between this and the other two Trimark Canadian equity funds are the purchase options; this one is strictly front-end load.

TRIMARK RSP EQUITY FUND $ → G * RSP CE

Managers: Keith Graham and Geoff MacDonald, since 1998

MER: 2.00%

After a great deal of pressure, Trimark made a managerial change on this underperforming fund in late August, 1998. Keith Graham and Geoff MacDonald, who were originally brought in to run the new Small Companies Fund and Resource Fund, were given the huge task of turning around this laggard. It will be a challenge. This fund actually lost money (2%) over the 12 months to June 30/98, and that was before the markets tumbled in July and August. By the time that slide was over, unitholders were out of pocket another 20%! It's too early to know whether the new team will make a significant difference, but investors have their fingers crossed. At least with different leadership at the top there is now something that will allow investors to distinguish between Trimark's three Canadian stock funds beyond the purchase option. This one is a back-end load entry. You pay a higher management fee for the privilege of avoiding up-front sales commissions.

TRIMARK SELECT CANADIAN
GROWTH FUND $ → G #/* RSP CE

Manager: Vito Maida, since 1995

MER: 2.32%

This is another struggling Trimark entry. Returns have been slumping for the past few years, and there isn't any sign of a turnaround on the immediate horizon. Gain for the 12 months to June 30/98 was a very weak 0.9%, and investors took a big hit during the summer stock market slide. The company is sticking with manager Vito Maida, however, in the hope that his deep-value picks will eventually turn out okay. Many of them are concentrated in the resource sector (Renaissance, Fletcher Challenge, Alcan), so it's unlikely we'll see significant improvement until that sector of the economy comes back. The purchase option of this fund differs from its two Canadian stablemates. This one can be bought on either a front- or back-end load basis. It also has the highest management fee of the three. This is the largest of the three Canadian entries, but the asset base, which had topped $5 billion, is slipping.

U.S. AND INTERNATIONAL EQUITY FUNDS

TRIMARK FUND $$$$ ↓ G # £ IE

Manager: Robert Krembil, since inception (1981)

MER: 1.52%

It's hard to explain why, but I've seen it again and again. One group of funds within a company starts to deteriorate, and the disease spreads. There's no obvious reason why the performance of this fund should be infected with the virus that has plagued the Canadian equity entries. This is an international fund with a different manager (company co-founder Robert Krembil) and a sparkling long-term track record (10-year average annual compound rate of return of 15.9% to June 30/98). But something has gone wrong. After posting an excellent 22.9% gain for the year to June 30/97, this fund fell back to a mediocre 7.4% advance over the next 12 months. Then it gave back all that and more in the summer slide, dropping almost 12% from July 1 to Aug. 31. Many funds did a lot worse, but if things don't turn around this one could end up in the red for calendar 1998. That hasn't happened since 1990. However, the long-term safety record of this fund continues to be very good. Although this is an international fund, it has historically concentrated its holdings in the U.S. The portfolio in mid-'98 was 53% in American issues. Japan was the next largest holding at 16.5%, a significant increase from the previous year and one of the reasons for the recent underperformance. Investors in this front-end load fund benefit from a low management expense ratio compared to most of the competition. I'm maintaining this fund's $$$$ rating for now because of its long-term high standards and Krembil's proven acumen. But it is on watch.

TRIMARK INDO-PACIFIC FUND $ ↑ G #/* £ FEE

Manager: Pamela Chan, since inception (1994)

MER: 2.95%

Trimark's move into the Far East began well enough but, like just about every other fund in this category, things got very rough in the autumn of 1997 and have remained that way. Over the 12-month period to June 30/98 this fund, which had been comfortably in the black before then, gave back almost half of its value. That brought the average annual compound rate of return for the three-year period into negative territory, with an average annual loss of 10.5%. If you don't have money here now, best to stay on the sidelines until the situation in Asia clarifies.

TRIMARK SELECT GROWTH FUND $$$ ↓ G * £ IE

Manager: Robert Krembil, since inception (1989)

MER: 2.32%

This is a back-end load companion to the front-end Trimark Fund. It features the same manager, same style, and a similar, but not identical, portfolio. Nominal returns will generally be slightly below those of the Trimark Fund because this one has a higher management expense ratio. It has grown more rapidly because of the public's preference for back-end load funds, but it may not be the better choice because of the expenses charged against it. Example: Over the five years to June 30/98, the Trimark Fund had an average annual return of 17.7%. If you paid a 3% front-end load, your actual adjusted annual return would be 17%. The average annual return for this fund over the same period was 15.4%. I've been doing this calculation for several years now, and the result always comes out in favour of the Trimark Fund. Be guided accordingly.

TRIMARK - THE AMERICAS FUND $$ → G #/* £ AE

Manager: Richard Whiting, since inception (1993)

MER: 2.65%

The mandate of this fund is to offer investors exposure to Latin America, but with a healthy dose of U.S. stocks added for stability. Like so many other Trimark stock funds, it has been in a slump lately. It was showing very well, with a good 21.5% in the year to June 30/97, almost exactly the same as in the 12 months prior to that. But then it went into a nosedive. Latin stocks hit the skids in the spring of 1998 and the 50% U.S. component wasn't enough to keep this one out of the red. It lost 4.4% over the year to June 30/98, and slid another 21% in the next two months as Latin stocks kept diving and Wall Street joined them. The concept of this fund is still a good one for more aggressive investors, but it may take a while for it to bounce back.

BALANCED FUNDS

TRIMARK INCOME GROWTH FUND $$ → FI/G # RSP CBAL

Managers: Vito Maida and Patrick Farmer, since 1997

MER: 1.56%

Former manager Wally Kusters left this fund in August, '97 and now manages money for the O'Donnell group. At the time, I expressed the view that his departure wouldn't have a major impact. I was wrong. This fund's performance has tailed off badly. In the year to July 31/98 (almost a full 12 months since Kusters left), this fund lost 5.8%. Balanced funds as a group weren't great over that period, gaining just 3% on average. But that's a lot better than a loss. And this is a fund that had been rolling along at an above-average clip. It's not the fault of the fixed-income side, managed by Patrick Farmer. In fact, Trimark's fixed-income funds have been the company's only bright spot in these troubled times. The damage was inflicted from the equities side, which represented about half the portfolio in mid-'98. As with so many of Trimark's other funds, there's a lot of repair work needed here. The main difference between this and the companion Select Balanced Fund is the purchase option. This one is strictly front-end load. Rating drops a notch this year.

TRIMARK SELECT
BALANCED FUND $$ → FI/G #/* RSP CBAL

Managers: Vito Maida and Patrick Farmer, since 1997

MER: 2.24%

This is an optional front- or back-end load companion to the Income Growth Fund. It features the same management team and a similar portfolio. You'd expect the returns to be a little lower due to the higher management fees, but that hasn't been the case in recent years. For the 12 months ending July 31/98, this one lost 3.2%, compared to 5.8% for Income Growth. Over five years, the published results are about the same, but this one has actually done better because investors in the Income Growth Fund had to pay a front-end load, which isn't factored into the performance figures. Also, the safety record of this fund is somewhat better than that of Income Growth. This is likely due to the fact that this fund usually maintains larger cash holdings, because most of the new money is flowing in here (this fund is now about six times larger than Income Growth). Of the two, this is the preferred choice, although both are currently struggling.

FIXED INCOME AND MONEY MARKET FUNDS

TRIMARK ADVANTAGE BOND FUND $$$ → FI #/* RSP CB

Manager: Patrick Farmer, since inception (1994)

MER: 1.25%

You know things aren't going well within the Trimark organization when a bond fund is one of their top performers, but that was the case for the year to June 30/98. This fund's 10.2% return over that period was among the best the company could muster, beating all the equity funds except the new Discovery Fund, which weighed in at 12.8%. This is a somewhat unusual bond fund in terms of its portfolio structure. Manager Patrick Farmer holds a core of federal government bonds for stability and then blends in some high-yield issues to boost returns. His results have been impressive. Average annual compound rate of return for the three years to June 30 was 12.2%, comfortably above average for the bond fund category. That warrants a $$$ rating as this fund makes its debut here. If you're a Trimark client, be sure you have some of this one in your asset mix.

TRIMARK CANADIAN BOND FUND $$$ → FI #/* RSP CB

Manager: Patrick Farmer, since inception (1994)

MER: 1.25%

This fund hasn't had as impressive returns as its companion, the Advantage Bond Fund, but it has been a very respectable fixed-income addition for Trimark nonetheless. Patrick Farmer also runs Advantage Bond but this fund's mandate doesn't include the high-yield component that drives its stablemate. That makes for somewhat less risk in the portfolio, but also somewhat lower returns. Over the three years to June 30/98, this fund gained an average of 10.6% annually, about two percentage points a year less than Advantage Bond. Still, those results are quite acceptable. The portfolio is a mix of federal and provincial bonds plus some corporate issues. We'll assign it a debut rating of $$$.

TRIMARK GOVERNMENT INCOME FUND $$ ↓ FI #/* RSP CB

Manager: Patrick Farmer, since inception (1993)

MER: 1.25%

This is a defensive bond fund. The securities are all government or government-guaranteed issues, and all have relatively short maturities, not exceeding five years. Some mortgage-backed securities are included in the mix. A portfolio such as this will produce below-average returns in strong markets, but will preserve capital when bond markets weaken. The published returns will appear to be below average when compared to the total bond fund universe. However, when you look at them in the context of other defensive funds, they aren't that bad. For example, over the three years to June 30/98, the average annual compound rate of return for this fund was 6.5%. The comparable Scotia fund gained 6% on average while the Green Line fund weighed in at 5.9%. However, the Phillips, Hager & North entry gained an annual average of 8.1% over that time and the CIBC fund was close behind at 7.5%. So this fund falls in the middle of this particular pack, hence the $$ rating.

TRIMARK INTEREST FUND $$$ → C # RSP CMM

Manager: Patrick Farmer, since 1993

MER: 0.75%

This fund invests entirely in commercial paper (no government T-bills). This boosts returns, but adds a slightly higher degree of risk. Average annual return over the five years to June 30/98 was 4.3%. The average fund in the money market category returned a shade less, at 4.1%. You may be charged a front-end load of up to 2% or, alternatively, a semi-annual commission of 0.25% (half a percent annually). Try to obtain the fund without any of these charges; otherwise you may want to check out other options. There are plenty to choose from.

UNIVERSITY AVENUE FUNDS

THE COMPANY

This is a small, Toronto-based firm founded in 1992 that operates a growing family of seven mutual funds. Originally, the funds were offered on a no-load basis but are now sold with an optional front- or back-end load charge. In 1997, the company formed an alliance with Goodreid Investment Counsel Inc., which provides management services to some of the funds. As well, it went public with a share issue on the Alberta Stock Exchange.

There have been some changes in the lineup, including one that may be a bit confusing: the University Avenue Bond Fund, which had a $$ rating in last year's edition, has been renamed the University Avenue Balanced Fund and given a new mandate.

THE DETAILS

NUMBER OF FUNDS:	7
ASSETS UNDER MANAGEMENT:	$20 MILLION
LOAD CHARGE:	FRONT: MAX. 3%; BACK: MAX. 5%
SWITCHING CHARGE:	NONE
WHERE SOLD:	ACROSS CANADA
HOW SOLD:	THROUGH BROKERS, DEALERS, AND FINANCIAL PLANNERS
PHONE NUMBER:	(416) 351-1617 OR 1-800-465-1812
WEB SITE ADDRESS:	WWW.UNIVERSITYAVENUE.COM
E-MAIL ADDRESS:	INFO@UNIVERSITYAVENUE.COM

FUND SUMMARY

$$$$ - NONE
$$$ - NONE
$$ - U.S. GROWTH
$ - BALANCED, CANADIAN
NR - CANADIAN SMALL CAP, MONEY, U.S. SMALL CAP, WORLD
BEST CHOICES: U.S. GROWTH
BEST FOR RRSPs: BALANCED
BEST UNRATEDS: U.S. SMALL CAP

FUND RATINGS

CANADIAN EQUITY FUNDS

UNIVERSITY AVENUE CANADIAN FUND $ ↑ G #/* RSP CE

Manager: Judy Cameron (AlphaQuest Capital Management), since 1997

MER: 2.40%

This diversified fund has gone through a number of management changes in recent years. Judy Cameron, who uses a classic value approach to stock selection, took over in '97, but after a year at the helm this fund is still struggling, losing a fractional 0.3% in the 12 months to June 30/98. Another negative here is a high risk ranking, according to the ATP analysis. We need to see some progress before any change is made to the rating.

U.S. AND INTERNATIONAL EQUITY FUNDS

UNIVERSITY AVENUE U.S. GROWTH FUND $$ ↑ G #/* £ USE

Manager: Gordon Reid (Goodreid Investment Counsel), since 1997

MER: 2.40%

The original mandate of this fund was to invest in Canadian, U.S., and British issues, but the emphasis is now on American stocks and the name has been changed to reflect that by adding "U.S.". Returns have shown significant improvement since Gordon Reid assumed managerial responsibility in January, 1997. Gain for the 12-month period to June 30/98 was a sparkling 33%, well above average for the U.S. equity category. The fund took a hit during the summer and longer term results are still sub-par, but there's progress here. We'll boost the rating a notch as a result.

UNIVERSITY AVENUE BALANCED FUND

$$ → FI/G #/* RSP CBAL

Manager: Robert Boaz, since 1998

MER: 1.75%

This was the University Avenue Bond Fund but now it has been given an equity component and a new manager. So previous history is meaningless, even though technically this is an ongoing fund. We'll leave the rating at $$ (the old Bond Fund ranking) until we can get a better handle on where this one is going.

VALOREM FUNDS

THE COMPANY

This Quebec-based firm started out as the investment division of SSQ VIE, a life insurance company. It became an independent corporation in 1994, although SSQ remains the controlling shareholder. The company offers a range of money management services to institutions and high net worth individuals, as well as a line of seven mutual funds. All funds are too new for a rating.

THE DETAILS

NUMBER OF FUNDS:	7
ASSETS UNDER MANAGEMENT:	$22.3 MILLION
LOAD CHARGE:	FRONT: MAX. 5%
SWITCHING CHARGE:	2% MAXIMUM
WHERE SOLD:	QUEBEC
HOW SOLD:	THROUGH BROKERS, DEALERS, AND FINANCIAL PLANNERS
PHONE NUMBER:	(418) 527-2880 OR 1-888-922-5622
WEB SITE ADDRESS:	N/A
E-MAIL ADDRESS:	N/A

FUND SUMMARY

$$$$ - NONE

$$$ - NONE

$$ - NONE

$ - NONE

NR - CANADIAN BOND-VALUE, CANADIAN EQUITY-VALUE, DEMOGRAPHIC TRENDS, DIVERSIFIED, GLOBAL EQUITY-VALUE, GOVERNMENT SHORT-TERM, U.S. EQUITY-VALUE

BEST CHOICES: N/A

BEST FOR RRSPS: N/A

BEST UNRATEDS: CANADIAN BOND-VALUE, DEMOGRAPHIC TRENDS

FUND RATINGS

All the funds in this group are too new to be eligible for a formal rating.

VISION EUROPE FUND

THE COMPANY

This small fund is operated by General Trust, but is not part of that company's in-house fund line, which is no-load. This is a back-end load fund, distributed through the brokerage firm of Lévesque Beaubien Geoffrion.

THE DETAILS

NUMBER OF FUNDS:	1
ASSETS UNDER MANAGEMENT:	$43.6 MILLION
LOAD CHARGE:	BACK: MAX. 5%
SWITCHING CHARGE:	NONE
WHERE SOLD:	QUEBEC, ONTARIO, B.C., ALBERTA, NEW BRUNSWICK, AND NOVA SCOTIA
HOW SOLD:	THROUGH REGISTERED BROKERS AND DEALERS
PHONE NUMBER:	(514) 871-7470
WEB SITE ADDRESS:	N/A
E-MAIL ADDRESS:	N/A

FUND SUMMARY

$$$$ - NONE
$$$ - VISION EUROPE
$$ - NONE
$ - NONE
NR - NONE
BEST CHOICES: VISION EUROPE
BEST FOR RRSPs: NONE
BEST UNRATEDS: N/A

FUND RATINGS

U.S. AND INTERNATIONAL EQUITY FUNDS

VISION EUROPE FUND $$$ → G * £ EE

Manager: Didier Le Conte, Indosuez Asset Management, since inception (1987)

MER: 2.38%

This is a European equity fund that places special emphasis on privatization issues of previously public companies. The portfolio favours major developed nations (U.K., Germany) but also includes smaller countries like Portugal and Ireland. There are a lot of telecoms and banks in the mix, as well as international giants like Unilever. Gain for the year to June 30/98 was well above average for the European stock fund category, at 41.5%. Longer term results are also good. Formerly known as European Investment and Privatization Fund.

YIELD MANAGEMENT GROUP

THE COMPANY

This company has been in business since the early '80s and was one of the first to actively use hedging strategies in this country. The core of their YMG fund lineup is the old Hodgson Roberton Laing (HRL) group of funds. They were sold to the Yield Management Group of Toronto in 1997, and the names changed. As well, a number of other funds have recently been added to the mix, for a current total of 12, including two that are only offered as private placements (Hedge Fund and Emerging Companies Fund).

THE DETAILS

NUMBER OF FUNDS:	12
ASSETS UNDER MANAGEMENT:	$144 MILLION
LOAD CHARGE:	FRONT: MAX. 5%; BACK: MAX. 6%
SWITCHING CHARGE:	2% MAXIMUM
WHERE SOLD:	ACROSS CANADA
HOW SOLD:	THROUGH BROKERS, DEALERS, AND FINANCIAL PLANNERS
PHONE NUMBER:	(416) 955-4883 OR 1-888-964-3533
WEB SITE ADDRESS:	WWW.YMG.CA
E-MAIL ADDRESS:	FUNDS@YMG.CA

FUND SUMMARY

$$$$ - NONE
$$$ - MONEY MARKET
$$ - GROWTH, INCOME
$ - BALANCED, INTERNATIONAL
NR - AMERICAN GROWTH, BOND, CANADIAN VALUE, ENTERPRISE, EMERGING COMPANIES, HEDGE, STRATEGIC FIXED INCOME

BEST CHOICES: MONEY MARKET
BEST FOR RRSPs: MONEY MARKET
BEST UNRATEDS: HEDGE

FUND RATINGS

CANADIAN EQUITY FUNDS

YMG GROWTH FUND $$ → G #/* RSP CSC

Manager: Malvin Spooner, since 1996

MER: 2.25%

The revised mandate of this former HRL fund is to invest in small companies with good growth potential, so it should be compared with other funds in the small-cap category. However, you'll still find it listed among broadly based Canadian stock funds in some of the monthly fund surveys in the media. The distinction is very important. Manager Malvin Spooner administered a large dose of adrenalin to this fund in his first year at the helm, gaining an impressive 41.9% for the 12 months to June 30/97. But over the subsequent year, to June 30/98, the return fell off to 4.4%. Compared to the diversified Canadian equity fund universe, that was a poor performance. But by the standard of small-cap funds, many of which had a tough slog over that time, it was above average. The fund might have done even better had it not been for a heavy weighting in the resource sector (about 40% of the portfolio in the first half of '98). Looks like this one could develop into an impressive entry over time. Formerly known as the HRL Canadian Fund and prior to that the Waltaine Canadian Fund.

U.S. AND INTERNATIONAL EQUITY FUNDS

YMG INTERNATIONAL FUND $ ↑ G #/* £ IE

Manager: Michael Doran, since 1997

MER: 2.00%

The fund invests in non-U.S./Canada stocks, and includes both developed countries and emerging markets in the portfolio. The managers may also use derivatives such as equity futures contracts and forward foreign currency exchange contracts, which may add to the risk. In the first half of '98, the largest single country holding was in Japan

(15.6%). From a continental perspective, however, Europe dominated with 62.5% of the total portfolio. Returns have been below average, although the fund put on a strong spurt in the first six months of '98, gaining 15.1%. We'll have to see more evidence of a turnaround before raising the rating, however. Formerly the HRL Overseas Growth Fund.

BALANCED FUNDS

YMG BALANCED FUND $ ↑ FI/G #/* RSP CBAL

Manager: Eric A.T. Innis, since 1996

MER: 1.75%

The old HRL group had a lot of funds that were steady but unimpressive performers. This fund fit right into the mould. Unfortunately, the new folks in charge haven't been able to break out of that pattern so far. This was one of the few Canadian balanced funds to lose money over the 12 months to June 30/98, dropping 1.7%. The strategy of this fund is to focus on mid-cap stocks on the equity side while augmenting returns on the fixed-income side by adding REITs and royalty income trusts to the mix, as well as more traditional bonds. Therein lies the reason for the recent poor performance: royalty trusts were hard hit in the past year as commodity prices tumbled. I think conceptually this new approach will work over time, but the rating stays at $ until we see some evidence of that. Formerly the HRL Balanced Fund and before that the Waltaine Balanced Fund.

FIXED INCOME AND MONEY MARKET FUNDS

YMG INCOME FUND $$ ↑ FI #/* RSP INC

Manager: Greg Edwards, since 1997

MER: 1.50%

This used to be a conventional, middle-of-the-road bond fund. No more! YMG has reshaped it into a high-income fund that can invest in a wide range of securities, including bonds, preferreds, high-yield common stocks, bond futures contracts, REITs, and royalty trusts. Manager Greg Edwards also uses a covered call option writing strategy to further enhance returns. This adds up to a very unusual portfolio mix that should produce good tax-advantaged cash flow, but which also incorporates more risk than is usually associated with a fund of this type. That's reflected in recent returns, which show a 5.3% loss for the year to June 30/98. A heavy concentration in royalty trusts (45% of the portfolio in mid-'98) was the reason. Offsetting that is a good income stream; the fund paid out 42 cents a unit in distributions in the first half of the year. Despite the loss last year, this fund is worth a look from investors who want above-average, tax-advantaged income and are prepared to accept some risk to achieve that goal. Formerly the HRL Bond Fund and before that the Waltaine Bond Fund.

YMG MONEY MARKET FUND $$$ → C # RSP CMM

Manager: Jane-Marie Rocca, since 1996

MER: 0.50%

This money fund invests in a mixed portfolio of T-bills, bankers' acceptances, and commercial notes. Results since the management change continue to be above average, with a gain of 3.4% over the year to June 30/98. Available only on a front-end load basis, with a maximum commission of 2%. Formerly known as the HRL Instant $$ Fund and before that as the Waltaine Instant $$ Fund.

SEGREGATED FUNDS

Talk about a rapidly changing marketplace! This is it!

For years, segregated funds ("seg" funds for short) were sleepy products offered as a kind of after thought by the insurance industry. But then the folks at Manulife came up with a marketing idea that turned everything upside down. They decided to take a bunch of regular mutual funds and dress them up in seg fund clothes. The result was to add an array of bells and whistles that made the whole package look a lot more attractive. These include:

1) Guarantees. All seg funds come with some type of guarantee, which limits potential investor loss. Typically, this will be a commitment on the part of the insurance company to repay at least 75% of the invested money at maturity or death. However, many companies extend the guarantee to 100% of the amount invested in certain circumstances. The death guarantee is especially attractive to older people who want to protect the value of their estate from big losses in stock market tumbles such as we saw in the summer of 1998.

2) Creditor protection. Because they are insurance products (usually sold as deferred annuities), seg funds enjoy a high degree of protection from creditors. This isn't absolute (the courts have denied protection in a few cases), but it will be effective in many situations.

3) Estate planning. If the policy to which the fund is tied has a specific, named beneficiary (not the estate), the assets in the fund will pass directly to that person on death, without probate delays or creditor claims.

Until now, most people knew little or nothing about the advantages of seg funds. However, all that is changing. Manulife's highly successful experiment has prompted several mainstream fund companies to bring out seg fund versions of their most popular products. Already on board are C.I., National Bank, BPI, Trimark, Templeton, and Talvest, with more to come.

If you buy one of these brand-name offerings, you'll pay a premium price in the form of higher management fees. You may consider that the cost is worth the added benefits, but be sure you look at all the options carefully before you act. Often, traditional insurance company seg funds will be less expensive and offer performance potential that's every bit as good. Scan through the ratings in this section before you make a final decision.

APEX FUNDS

(SEABOARD LIFE)

THE COMPANY

This is the segregated fund line of Seaboard Life Insurance Company. Some of the equity and balanced funds are managed by AGF. The maturity and death guarantees offered here are 75% of the total amount invested, which puts a floor under any losses. However, some other segregated funds carry 100% guarantees. Seaboard says they are looking at this carefully and there may be more news by the time you read this, so ask the sales representative.

THE DETAILS

NUMBER OF FUNDS:	12
ASSETS UNDER MANAGEMENT:	$1.5 BILLION
LOAD CHARGE:	FRONT: MAX. 4%; BACK: MAX. 6%
SWITCHING CHARGE:	FOUR FREE SWITCHES PER YEAR, SERVICE CHARGE THEREAFTER
WHERE SOLD:	ALL PROVINCES EXCEPT QUEBEC AND NEW BRUNSWICK
HOW SOLD:	THROUGH INDEPENDENT INSURANCE AGENTS
PHONE NUMBER:	1-800-363-2166
WEB SITE ADDRESS:	WWW.SEABOARDLIFE.COM
E-MAIL ADDRESS:	INFO@SEABOARDLIFE.COM

FUND SUMMARY

$$$$ - NONE
$$$ - NONE
$$ - FIXED INCOME
$ - ASIAN PACIFIC, BALANCED (AGF), CANADIAN GROWTH (AGF), MONEY MARKET, MORTGAGE
NR - BALANCED (DYNAMIC), CANADIAN STOCK, CANADIAN VALUE (DYNAMIC), GLOBAL EQUITY, GROWTH AND INCOME, U.S. EQUITY

BEST CHOICES: FIXED INCOME
BEST FOR RRSPs: FIXED INCOME
BEST UNRATED: GLOBAL EQUITY, U.S. EQUITY

FUND RATINGS

CANADIAN EQUITY FUNDS

APEX CANADIAN GROWTH FUND (AGF) $ → G #/* RSP S CE

Manager: Martin Hubbes (AGF), since 1998

MER: 3.00%

This fund actually has quite a long history. It was originally established as the Century Growth Fund in 1969 by Fidelity Life Assurance. The name was changed to Fidelity Growth Fund (no relation to the existing Fidelity group) in 1976. Fidelity and Seaboard Life amalgamated in 1986, and this fund acquired the name of APEX Equity Growth Fund in 1993. It was changed again in mid-'98 to better reflect the fact that it is run by AGF. Martin Hubbes of AGF now calls the shots, having taken over from Laura Wallace in early '98. The reason, to put it bluntly, was that the folks at Seaboard were unhappy with the fund's performance, disturbed by the high redemption rate, and wanted a better quality portfolio that was more suited to their clientele. Hubbes has set out to achieve that by reconstructing the portfolio as a more traditional large-cap mutual fund. That has involved such moves as a big reduction in the oil and gas holdings and a corresponding increase in the financial sector, which became the heaviest weighting in the fund after his arrival. These changes should improve performance considerably, and fairly quickly, so the rating here may well go up the next time we look at it. One other observation: the MER on this fund is extremely high for a Canadian equity entry. That, Seaboard explains, is because of the additional costs involved in hiring outside managers like AGF.

U.S. AND INTERNATIONAL EQUITY FUNDS

APEX ASIAN PACIFIC FUND $ ↑ G #/* £ S FEE

Managers: Tim Moorehouse and Claire Gibbs (FP Asset Managers), since 1994

MER: 2.80%

Like most other Asian funds, this one has been going through a rough period. The managers are allowed to invest across the entire Pacific Rim, including Japan, and the fund was heavily weighted towards Japanese stocks in the first half of '98, with 36% of the portfolio in that country. Hong Kong was next at 26%, Australia at 13%, and Singapore at 5%. As you might expect, you're looking at very high volatility here. The fund historically has a 63% chance of being in a loss position over any given three-year period, according to ATP analysis. That is uncomfortably high and suggests you may wish to look elsewhere.

BALANCED FUNDS

APEX BALANCED FUND   (AGF) $ → FI/G #/* RSP S CBAL

Managers: Clive Coombs, since 1994, Martin Hubbes, since 1998

MER: 3.00%

This is another AGF-managed fund and, like the Canadian Growth Fund, it is undergoing a radical transformation. Originally, the portfolio of this fund was modelled on the AGF asset allocation service. As the Seaboard people now put it: "It seemed like a good idea at the time, but it didn't work." The AGF asset mix model turned out to be way too conservative for the strong stock markets of the mid-'90s and this fund underperformed as a result. Example: Entering '98, more than half the portfolio was in cash, which was hardly a way to earn big returns. Meantime, less than 20% of the assets were in equities. Seaboard instructed AGF to raise the quality of the management and to drop the model. Martin Hubbes was brought in to run the equity side and by the start of the second quarter of '98 the equity side of the portfolio was up to 44% while the cash component was down to 26%.

The changes are likely for the best and this fund should look better in time.

FIXED INCOME AND MONEY MARKET FUNDS

APEX FIXED INCOME FUND $$ → FI #/* RSP S CB

Manager: Brad Bondy, since 1997

MER: 2.30%

This is another fund that has a much longer history than you might think, having been originally established in 1970 as the Seaboard Accumulation Fund #2. It now has a new name and a new manager, but it's still a fairly standard bond fund. The emphasis is on Government of Canada issues, although there are some corporate bonds in the mix. Returns tend to be slightly below average.

APEX MONEY MARKET FUND $ → C #/* RSP S CMM

Manager: Brad Bondy, since 1997

MER: 1.55%

Routine money market fund that invests in Government of Canada T-bills and short-term commercial notes. Relatively high MER makes it difficult for Bondy to achieve even average returns in a low interest rate environment.

APEX MORTGAGE FUND $ → FI #/* RSP S M

Managers: Rob Mitchell and Brad Bondy, since 1997

MER: 2.00%

This is kind of interesting. It's a mortgage fund that doesn't hold any mortgages. Now there's an original approach! The portfolio of this fund was about two thirds in federal government bonds in the first half of '98. Another 19% was in corporate bonds and 10% in CMHC bonds, the closest thing to a mortgage in the portfolio. So, despite the name, this is really a short-term bond fund. That makes it useful for defensive purposes, but Seaboard should either change the name or revamp the portfolio.

ASTRA FUNDS

THE COMPANY

This is a new family of segregated funds offered in Quebec only under the sponsorship of the SSQ Vie of Ste. Foy. There are nine funds in the group but none have been around long enough to qualify for a formal rating.

THE DETAILS

NUMBER OF FUNDS:	9
ASSETS UNDER MANAGEMENT:	$58 MILLION
LOAD CHARGE:	FRONT: MAX. 5%; BACK: MAX. 5%
SWITCHING CHARGE:	NONE
WHERE SOLD:	QUEBEC ONLY
HOW SOLD:	THROUGH BROKERS AND LICENSED INSURANCE REPRESENTATIVES
PHONE NUMBER:	1-800-320-4887
WEB SITE ADDRESS:	N/A
E-MAIL ADDRESS	RENTES-MARK@SSQ.QC.CA

FUND SUMMARY

$$$$ - N/A
$$$ - N/A
$$ - N/A
$ - N/A
NR - ACTIONS AMÉRICAINES (U.S. EQUITY), ACTIONS CANADIENNES (CANADIAN EQUITY), ACTIONS INTERNATIONALES (INTERNATIONAL EQUITY), DIVIDENDES (DIVIDEND), ÉQUILIBRÉ (BALANCED), MARCHÉ MONÉTAIRE (MONEY MARKET), OBLIGATIONS (BOND), 110, TENDANCES DÉMOGRAPHIQUES (DEMOGRAPHIC TRENDS)

BEST CHOICES: N/A
BEST FOR RRSPS: N/A
BEST UNRATEDS: TENDANCES DÉMOGRAPHIQUES (DEMOGRAPHIC TRENDS)

FUND RATINGS

None of the funds in this group has a three-year record, so no formal ratings are included.

BPI LEGACY FUNDS

Segregated funds have attracted so much attention as a result of the Manulife GIF initiative that a number of mainstream companies now offer seg versions of their regular mutual funds. BPI entered this arena in February, 1998 with a line of 11 funds. They're sold in conjunction with Transamerica Life Insurance Company of Canada under the trade name "Legacy". These are not separate funds, however, since they invest exclusively in units of the underlying BPI fund of the same name. The only difference is in the packaging and the cost. The Legacy funds will not be reviewed separately. You can find ratings for the underlying mutual funds in the BPI section.

CANADA LIFE ASSURANCE CO.

THE COMPANY

Canada Life is one of the country's oldest life insurance companies, with a history dating back to 1847. Their family of funds includes one of the top offerings available from the insurance industry, the high-performance U.S. & International Equity Fund, which became the first segregated fund to earn a $$$$ rating. Redemption fees on all funds are payable if you cash in within seven years of purchase. You'll get a return of at least 75% of your contributions at maturity if you hold your units for 10 years. If you die, your estate will receive no less than the full value of your contributions. If the units have gained in value in the meantime, the payouts will, of course, reflect that.

All the fund managers are with INDAGO Capital Management.

THE DETAILS

NUMBER OF FUNDS:	9
ASSETS UNDER MANAGEMENT:	$3.5 BILLION
LOAD CHARGE:	BACK: MAX. 4.5%
SWITCHING CHARGE:	EIGHT FREE SWITCHES PER YEAR
WHERE SOLD:	ACROSS CANADA
HOW SOLD:	THROUGH LICENSED INSURANCE REPRESENTATIVES
PHONE NUMBER:	(416) 597-6981 OR 1-888-CLA-1847
WEB SITE ADDRESS:	WWW.CANADALIFE.COM/INDIVIDUAL
E-MAIL ADDRESS:	CANINDSERV@CANADALIFE.COM

FUND SUMMARY

$$$$ - U.S. AND INTERNATIONAL EQUITY
$$$ - NONE
$$ - CANADIAN EQUITY, FIXED INCOME, INTERNATIONAL BOND, MANAGED
$ - MONEY MARKET
NR - ASIAN PACIFIC, ENHANCED DIVIDEND, EUROPEAN EQUITY

BEST CHOICES: U.S. AND INTERNATIONAL EQUITY
BEST FOR RRSPs: CANADIAN EQUITY, MANAGED
BEST UNRATEDS: ENHANCED DIVIDEND, EUROPEAN EQUITY

FUND RATINGS

CANADIAN EQUITY FUNDS

CANADA LIFE CANADIAN EQUITY (S-9) $$ → G * RSP S CE

Manager: John M. Vipond, since 1996

MER: 2.25%

This is a broadly diversified fund that invests in everything from blue-chip stocks to small-cap companies, with some international equities tossed in. Had been showing improvement but recent results have slipped to below average, in part due to a recent slight overweighting in the gold sector. Rating drops back a notch as a result.

U.S. AND INTERNATIONAL EQUITY FUNDS

CANADA LIFE U.S. AND INTERNATIONAL EQUITY (S-34) $$$$ ↓ G * £ S IE

Managers: Gary Kondrat, since 1994, Thomas Tibbles and Diane Haflidson, since 1996

MER: 2.40%

This top-performing fund underwent a managerial shake-up in mid-'96, but it continues to do extremely well. Since the shake-up, the fund has generated an average annual compound rate of return of 23.4% over the two years to June 30/98. That's way better than the average for the international fund category. So this continues to be the best performer in the Canada Life stable. It offers a well-diversified portfolio, with broad international representation. In other words, it's not just a U.S. fund with some token foreign holdings. In the first half of '98, 46% of the portfolio was in U.S. stocks, 30% in European equities, and 17% in the Far East and emerging markets, with the balance in cash. The safety record is very good and the fund has a history of outperforming its peers in bear market situations, which is comforting to know in times like these. Top rating is maintained for another year.

BALANCED FUNDS

CANADA LIFE
MANAGED FUND (S-35) $$ → FI/G * RSP S CBAL

Manager: John M. Vipond, since 1996

MER: 2.25%

This fund invests in a combination of bonds and Canadian and international stocks. Over the years, it has produced respectable returns, hovering just below or above the average for the balanced category. The fund makes good use of foreign content, with international equities accounting for 18% of the portfolio in the first half of '98. Canadian stocks are of the blue-chip variety. Average risk.

FIXED INCOME AND MONEY MARKET FUNDS

CANADA LIFE FIXED
INCOME FUND (S-19) $$ → FI * RSP S CB

Manager: Gary Morris, since 1993

MER: 2.00%

This had been one of the few weaker performers in the Canada Life group, but results have shown definite improvement over the past couple of years, to the point where a rating upgrade is in order. The fund is managed conservatively, to minimize risk. Portfolio is a mix of government and corporate issues. One negative is the MER, which is high by bond fund standards.

CANADA LIFE INTERNATIONAL
BOND FUND (S-36) $$ → FI * RSP S IB

Managers: Bill Harer and Gary Morris, since inception (1994)

MER: 2.00%

This international bond fund is fully eligible for registered plans, investing in foreign-currency denominated securities issued by Canadian governments and their agencies as well as by such supranational organizations as the World Bank. Returns, which had been quite weak, have strengthened greatly in the past year, in large part due to the portfolio emphasis on U.S. dollar issues. Rating goes up a notch to reflect this.

CANADA LIFE
MONEY MARKET FUND (S-29) $\$ \rightarrow$ C * RSP S CMM

Manager: Andrew G. Osterback, since 1994

MER: 1.25%

This fund tends to be a below-average performer in the money market category. As with the Fixed Income Fund, the relatively high management fee contributes to this, especially at a time of low interest rates. Another drawback is the fact that redemption fees of up to 4.5% apply for seven years if you cash in. Money market funds should be viewed as short-term investments; you shouldn't have to pay a fee to withdraw cash. The good news is that transfers to other Canada Life funds are exempt from this charge, as long as you don't switch your money more than eight times a year. Portfolio is high-grade, consisting mainly of T-bills and bankers' acceptances.

C.I. SEGREGATED FUNDS

C.I. was the first mainstream mutual fund company to jump on the seg funds bandwagon by creating clones of some of their products for this specific marketplace. Working in concert with Toronto Mutual Life Insurance Company, they offer six seg funds that are clones of regular C.I. funds: Harbour, Harbour Growth & Income, Hansberger Value, Global, American, and Money Market. We will not review these seg funds separately in this *Buyer's Guide* because they are not truly independent funds. See the writeups on the underlying funds in the C.I. Mutual Funds section.

COLONIA INVESTMENT FUNDS

THE COMPANY

In September, 1997 it was announced that Empire Life had acquired the assets of Colonia, including this fund family. However, the group still continues to operate on an independent basis and no merger plans with the Empire funds have been announced, although Empire has assumed management responsibility for all the funds. Note that the Mortgage Fund was closed as of August, 1998.

THE DETAILS

NUMBER OF FUNDS:	5
ASSETS UNDER MANAGEMENT:	$91 MILLION
LOAD CHARGE:	BACK: MAX. 6%
SWITCHING CHARGE:	TWO FREE TRANSFERS PER YEAR, $50 THEREAFTER
WHERE SOLD:	ACROSS CANADA
HOW SOLD:	THROUGH LICENSED INSURANCE AGENTS
PHONE NUMBER:	1-800-461-1086 OR 1-800-465-8686 (QUEBEC)
WEB SITE ADDRESS:	WWW.COLONIALIFE.COM
E-MAIL ADDRESS:	JMCCARTNEY@COLONIALIFE.COM

FUND SUMMARY

$$$$ - NONE
$$$ - SPECIAL GROWTH
$$ - EQUITY, MONEY MARKET
$ - BOND
NR - STRATEGIC BALANCED

BEST CHOICES: SPECIAL GROWTH
BEST FOR RRSPS: EQUITY, MONEY MARKET
BEST UNRATEDS: STRATEGIC BALANCED

FUND RATINGS

CANADIAN EQUITY FUNDS

COLONIA EQUITY FUND $$ → G * RSP S CE

Manager: Empire Financial Group, since 1998

MER: 2.27%

The mandate of this fund is to invest in large companies with strong growth potential. As a result, the portfolio has a decidedly blue-chip look, with lots of banks and big industrial firms. However, there are also a number of cyclical growth stocks in the mix, to provide extra profit potential. After some years of indifferent results, this fund started to get its act together over the past two years. However, management responsibilities were taken over by Empire Life at the beginning of 1998 and the recent track record of their Canadian stock funds has not been as good as this one's. So we'll have to wait and see what happens here.

COLONIA SPECIAL GROWTH FUND $$$ → G * RSP S CSC

Manager: Empire Financial Group, since 1998

MER: 2.27%

This is the small-cap companion to the equity fund. As such, it offers greater growth potential, but with the trade-off of higher risk. Some of the companies in the portfolio are really more mid-cap than small-cap, but investors won't quibble because results have been excellent. Whether that will continue now that the management responsibilities have passed to Empire is a question mark, however.

FIXED INCOME AND MONEY MARKET FUNDS

COLONIA BOND FUND $ → FI * RSP S CB

Manager: Empire Financial Group, since 1998

MER: 1.63%

The look of this fund's portfolio has changed in the past year. It is no longer invested exclusively in government of Canada issues, but now has a significant corporate component as well. The fund is being defensively managed right now because of concern about a possible interest rate rise. This has contributed to below average returns across all time frames.

COLONIA MONEY MARKET FUND $$ → C No RSP S CMM

Manager: Empire Financial Group, since 1998

MER: 1.00%

Very small fund from this life insurance group. The nature of the portfolio has changed over the past year and it is now mainly invested in corporate notes and short-term bonds. Recent returns have slipped to below average.

COMMERCIAL UNION LIFE ASSURANCE CO.

THE COMPANY

This is a new player on the segregated fund scene, with a lineup of six funds all launched at the beginning of 1998. But while the fund line may be new, Commercial Union has been around for a long time. The parent Commercial Union Group was founded in 1861 and has grown to become one of the biggest companies in the U.K. and among the top 20 in the world based on managed assets. The funds carry a 100% guarantee that you will at least recover your principal at maturity or death, no matter what the markets do. Sales are on a back-end load basis. None of the funds has been around long enough to qualify for a rating.

THE DETAILS

NUMBER OF FUNDS:	6
ASSETS UNDER MANAGEMENT:	$21.4 MILLION
LOAD CHARGE:	BACK: MAX. 6%
SWITCHING CHARGE:	FIVE FREE TRANSFERS PER YEAR, $75 THEREAFTER
WHERE SOLD:	ACROSS CANADA
HOW SOLD:	THROUGH LICENSED LIFE INSURANCE AGENTS
PHONE NUMBER:	1-888-249-7920
WEB SITE ADDRESS:	N/A
E-MAIL ADDRESS:	N/A

FUND SUMMARY

$$$$ - NONE
$$$ - NONE
$$ - NONE
$ - NONE
NR - ASSET ALLOCATION, CANADIAN BOND INDEX, CANADIAN MONEY MARKET, CANADIAN TSE 35 TOTAL RETURN INDEX, INTERNATIONAL G7, U.S. EQUITY

BEST CHOICES: N/A
BEST FOR RRSPS: N/A
BEST UNRATEDS: CANADIAN TSE 35 TOTAL RETURN INDEX

FUND RATINGS

No funds have the three-year record needed to qualify for a rating.

COMMON SENSE FUNDS

(PRIMERICA LIFE)

THE COMPANY

This fund group represents an imaginative approach to retirement investing from Primerica Life. The five Asset Builder funds are all balanced funds, each with a different asset mix based on the maturity date. The closer you are to retirement, the higher the percentage of fixed-income securities. For example, Asset Builder I is designed for people who will need their money in 2009 and 2010, so it will normally have the lowest percentage of stocks in its portfolio (the maturity date must be at least 10 years after the issue date of the contract). At the other extreme, Asset Builder V is for young people who won't retire until 2041 to 2050, so its stock holdings will be much higher. All the funds are run by Jerry Javasky of Mackenzie Financial's Ivy family. His former co-manager Gerald Coleman withdrew from these funds in mid-1997 when he left Mackenzie to move over to C.I. Funds.

These funds represent an excellent way to build a retirement account over the long term and are worthy of serious consideration by investors.

THE DETAILS

NUMBER OF FUNDS:	6
ASSETS UNDER MANAGEMENT:	$260 MILLION
LOAD CHARGE:	BACK: MAX. 5%
SWITCHING CHARGE:	NONE
WHERE SOLD:	ACROSS CANADA
HOW SOLD:	THROUGH PRIMERICA LIFE INSURANCE LICENSED REPRESENTATIVE
PHONE NUMBER:	1-800-463-9997 (ENGLISH)
	1-800-463-7774 (FRENCH)
WEB SITE ADDRESS:	N/A
E-MAIL ADDRESS:	N/A

FUND SUMMARY

$$$$ - Asset Builder I, Asset Builder II, Asset Builder
III, Asset Builder IV, Asset Builder V

$$$ - None

$$ - Cash Management

$ - None

NR - N/A

Best choices: All, depending on age
Best for RRSPs: All, depending on age
Best unrateds: N/A

FUND RATINGS

BALANCED FUNDS

COMMON SENSE ASSET BUILDER FUND I

$$$$ ↓ FI/G * RSP S CBAL

Manager: Jerry Javasky, since 1997

MER: 2.28%

This fund is designed for people who will retire in 2009–2010. The stocks held in this fund are the same as in all the other Common Sense funds, the only difference being the percentage of total equities in the overall portfolio. For this fund, stocks accounted for not quite half the fund in the first half of '98 with bonds, T-bills, and cash making up the rest. The equity portfolio is mainly composed of well-known blue-chips, such as Royal Bank and Northern Telecom, with a few small growth companies added. All these funds have done very well, although, as you might expect, those with the highest percentage of stocks have generated the best returns over the past three years. This one gained 17.4% for the 12 months to June 30/98. Three-year average annual compound rate of return was 17.2%. All the Common Sense funds score very highly on the ATP safety scale, which is not surprising when you consider that manager Jerry Javasky is a conservative value manager. This family is a good choice for a long-term investor who wants to use seg funds, and represents a sound method of investing. As a result, I am hiking the ratings of all these funds to the top $$$$ level.

COMMON SENSE ASSET
BUILDER FUND II $$$$ ↓ G/FI * RSP S CBAL

Manager: Jerry Javasky, since 1997

MER: 2.28%

The target group for this fund is people who expect to retire between the years 2011 and 2020. Equities made up two thirds of the portfolio in the first half of '98. Return for the 12 months to June 30/98 was 22.8%; three-year average annual return was 20.9%.

COMMON SENSE ASSET
BUILDER FUND III $$$$ ↓ G/FI * RSP S CBAL

Manager: Jerry Javasky, since 1997

MER: 2.31%

Here we move to a target retirement period of 2021–2030, so this fund is intended for people who are roughly in the 35–45 age group at present. The equity component here at the start of '98 was just over 66%, about the same as Asset Builder II. One-year return was 24.3%; three-year average was 22.4%.

COMMON SENSE ASSET
BUILDER FUND IV $$$$ ↓ G/FI * RSP S CBAL

Manager: Jerry Javasky, since 1997

MER: 2.32%

Target retirement years are now out to 2031 to 2040. The equity portion of the portfolio increases to 72%. One-year return was 23.5%; three-year annual average was 22.2%.

COMMON SENSE ASSET
BUILDER FUND V $$$$ ↓ G/FI * RSP S CBAL

Manager: Jerry Javasky, since 1997

MER: 2.36%

Retirement years here are 2041 to 2050, which makes this a fund for young people who are just starting out. Equities made up about 70% of the portfolio entering '98. However, this fund had a large cash position, which pulled down returns a bit. One-year gain was 22.6%; three-year average annual return was 22.1%.

FIXED INCOME AND MONEY MARKET FUNDS

COMMON SENSE CASH MANAGEMENT FUND $$ ↓ C No RSP S CMM

Manager: Jerry Javasky, since 1997

MER: 0.76%

This fund is a place to hold short-term cash, although there doesn't seem to be much reason to use it in this family, given its investment strategies. The portfolio is invested mainly in Government of Canada T-bills.

THE CO-OPERATORS GROUP

THE COMPANY

Co-operators General Insurance Company is a Regina-based firm that's owned by such grassroots organizations as credit unions, agricultural co-operatives, and the like. So its roots are deep in the Prairies, and a long way from Bay Street. That's why it's refreshing to report they've put together a small but very respectable lineup of segregated funds that are worthy of your attention.

THE DETAILS

NUMBER OF FUNDS:	6
ASSETS UNDER MANAGEMENT:	$7.1 BILLION
LOAD CHARGE:	NONE
SWITCHING CHARGE:	FOUR FREE TRANSFERS PER YEAR, $20 THEREAFTER
WHERE SOLD:	ALL PROVINCES EXCEPT QUEBEC
HOW SOLD:	THROUGH LICENSED CO-OPERATORS INSURANCE AGENTS
PHONE NUMBER:	CONTACT YOUR LOCAL CO-OPERATORS OFFICE
WEB SITE ADDRESS:	WWW.COOPERATORS.CA/YOURNEED/RRSP.HTM
E-MAIL ADDRESS:	N/A

FUND SUMMARY

$$$$ - NONE
$$$ - BALANCED, CANADIAN EQUITY, FIXED INCOME, U.S. EQUITY
$$ - NONE
$ - NONE
NR - MONEY MARKET, U.S. DIVERSIFIED
BEST CHOICES: U.S. EQUITY
BEST FOR RRSPS: BALANCED, FIXED INCOME
BEST UNRATEDS: U.S. DIVERSIFIED

FUND RATINGS

CANADIAN EQUITY FUNDS

CO-OPERATORS CANADIAN EQUITY FUND
$$$ → G No RSP S CE

Manager: James Blake, since 1996

MER: 2.06%

The management strategy used for this fund is sector rotation, which involves identifying those areas of the economy that are expected to outperform and overweighting the portfolio towards them. Individual stocks within the chosen sectors are selected on the basis of careful fundamental analysis of over 460 Canadian companies. Returns had been below average, but a managerial change in '96 has sparked this fund to above-average gains for two years running. Return for the year to June 30/98 was a healthy 20.1%. That's good enough for a boost to a $$$ rating this time around.

U.S. AND INTERNATIONAL EQUITY FUNDS

CO-OPERATORS U.S. EQUITY FUND
$$$ → G No £ S USE

Manager: Milton Burns, since inception (1994)

MER: 2.12%

In last year's edition, I reported the shocking news that, of all the great U.S. stock funds available in this country, this little entry from the Prairies was the number-one performer over the previous three years. Well, I'm sorry to say that's no longer the case. The 30.1% return over the year to June 30/98 wasn't good enough to allow this fund to retain the honour. But, hey, it's still number 11 in the Southam rankings, with an average annual compound rate of return of 30.9% over the past three years. As they say, that ain't exactly chopped liver! Unfortunately, there still aren't enough people taking advantage of this good run. Although the fund has almost tripled in size since a year ago, it still has only $14 million in assets. Stocks are chosen by a fundamental analysis, bottom-up approach. So, unlike the Canadian Equity Fund, the industry weightings in this portfolio are determined first and foremost by where the managers find the best share value, not by identifying industry sectors that are expected to outperform and then finding stocks that fit. A good selection.

BALANCED FUNDS

CO-OPERATORS
BALANCED FUND $$$ → FI/G No RSP S CBAL

Manager: James MacDonald, since 1997

MER: 2.06%

This is a fund of funds, which uses holdings in Co-operators Canadian Equity, U.S. Equity, and Fixed-Income funds, changing the asset mix as appropriate. This fund scores in the top 10% of all Canadian balanced funds over the past five years, with an average annual compound rate of return of 14.3% to June 30/98.

FIXED INCOME AND MONEY MARKET FUNDS

CO-OPERATORS FIXED INCOME FUND $$$ ↑ FI No RSP S CB

Manager: James Lorimer, since inception (1992)

MER: 2.06%

Securities for this fund are selected on the basis of economic and market forecasts, using a top-down approach. Interest rate anticipation, spread treading, and analysis of credit ratings are all tools that are used by the manager to enhance returns. The objective is to beat the Scotia McLeod Universe Bond Index over time. Results continue to be very good. The fund gained 11.8% in the year to June 30/98 and ranks in the top 10 bond funds in Canada in five-year performance according to the Southam Mutual Fund SourceDisk. However, there's more volatility here than you might normally expect in a fixed-income fund, hence the higher risk rating.

EMPIRE FINANCIAL GROUP

THE COMPANY

Empire Financial Group is the marketing arm of The Empire Life Insurance Company, which is based in Kingston, Ontario. Empire Life has been in business since 1923 and is one of Canada's larger insurance firms. It is also one of the most strongly capitalized companies in the insurance business today, so you don't need to worry about the safety of your investments. As with all segregated funds, these offer death and maturity guarantees. Check with an Empire Life representative for details.

THE DETAILS

NUMBER OF FUNDS:	11
ASSETS UNDER MANAGEMENT:	$1.7 BILLION
LOAD CHARGE:	PREMIER EQUITY - FRONT: MAX. 5%
	ALL OTHERS - BACK: MAX. 5%
SWITCHING CHARGE:	FOUR FREE TRANSFERS PER YEAR, $50 THEREAFTER
WHERE SOLD:	ACROSS CANADA
HOW SOLD:	THROUGH EMPIRE LIFE AGENTS AND LICENSED BROKERS
PHONE NUMBER:	(613) 548-1881
WEB SITE ADDRESS:	WWW.EMPIRE.CA
E-MAIL ADDRESS:	N/A

FUND SUMMARY

$$$$ - NONE

$$$ - NONE

$$ - ASSET ALLOCATION, BALANCED, ELITE EQUITY, INTERNATIONAL GROWTH, PREMIER EQUITY

$ - BOND, MONEY MARKET, FOREIGN CURRENCY CANADIAN BOND

NR - DIVIDEND GROWTH, SMALL CAP, S&P 500 INDEX

BEST CHOICES: PREMIER EQUITY

BEST FOR RRSPs: ASSET ALLOCATION, PREMIER EQUITY

BEST UNRATEDS: DIVIDEND GROWTH, S&P 500 INDEX

FUND RATINGS

CANADIAN EQUITY FUNDS

EMPIRE ELITE EQUITY FUND $$ ↓ G * RSP S CE

Manager: Jill Pepall, since 1996

MER: 2.43%

The objective here is capital growth, with income secondary. Large, diversified portfolio mixes both small- and large-cap companies. This fund did very well from 1993-96 under the direction of Catharina van Berkel. However, she has since moved on and the latest one-year returns have slipped to below average, with a gain of 8.1% over the 12 months to June 30/98. Two- and three-year returns are still well above pay for the Canadian equity category, but the falloff since the managerial change has to cause some concern. Safety rating continues to be good, which is a big plus. Still, I'm dropping the rating back a notch until the new team shows evidence they can bring this one back up to at least the second quartile. Note: Although the portfolios aren't exactly the same, there is a great deal of similarity between the holdings of this fund and the companion Empire Premier Fund, and both have the same manager. The difference is in the purchase option and management fee. The Elite funds are back-end load, with a 2.4% base annual management charge, plus expenses. The Premier fund is front-end load (5% for the first $100,000, declining after that), but has a much lower management fee. If you're investing for the long term, the Premier fund may be the better choice.

EMPIRE PREMIER EQUITY FUND $$ → G # RSP S CE

Manager: Jill Pepall, since 1996

MER: 1.44%

Main investment goal is capital appreciation. Portfolio is similar to other Empire equity funds, but a lower management fee gives it an edge over the Elite Fund. For example, this one gained 10% for the year to June 30/98, while the Elite Fund was ahead only 8.1%. About one percentage point of that difference was in the management fees and expenses. Of course, the published return on this fund doesn't take into account the 5% sales commission, so you have to be in for several years to profit from the lower management fee. Name changed from Equity Growth Fund #1 in January, '92.

U.S. AND INTERNATIONAL EQUITY FUNDS

EMPIRE INTERNATIONAL GROWTH FUND $$ → G * £ S IE

Manager: Jill Pepall, since 1996

MER: 2.45%

As with several of the other Empire equity funds, there has been a slippage in returns since a managerial change in '96. Gain for the year to June 30/98 was 11.5%. That wasn't terrible, but it was below average for the international fund category and not up to the standard investors had been enjoying. The portfolio is relatively small and was about equally divided between North American stocks and those from other parts of the world in early '98. Rating drops a notch.

BALANCED FUNDS

EMPIRE ASSET ALLOCATION FUND $$ → G/FI * RSP S CBAL

Managers: Jill Pepall, since 1996, and Paul Pathak, since 1997

MER: 2.46%

The difference between this fund and the companion Balanced Fund is that this one is more aggressively managed and could theoretically be entirely in one asset class (stocks, bonds, or cash) at any given time, depending on the circumstances. However, in practice, the two funds track each other quite closely. Entering '98, about 45% of the portfolio was in stocks, about the same as the Balanced Fund. Returns here have been slightly better recently, but not enough to make any great difference. I suggested last year that Empire should try to differentiate more between these funds, or merge them. So far nothing has happened. Both funds are on the verge of a rating drop if results don't pick up.

EMPIRE BALANCED FUND $$ → FI/G * RSP S CBAL

Managers: Jill Pepall, since 1996 and Paul Pathak, since 1997

MER: 2.44%

This fund aims for a balance between long-term growth and preservation of capital with a portfolio that invests in stocks, bonds, mortgages, and short-term notes. Returns have slipped to below average. There is very little to distinguish this from the companion Asset Allocation Fund.

FIXED INCOME AND MONEY MARKET FUNDS

EMPIRE BOND FUND $ → FI * RSP S CB

Manager: Paul Pathak, since 1997

MER: 2.05%

Returns have started to perk up here, following Paul Pathak's insertion as the new manager in 1997. Gain for the 12 months to June 30/98 was a touch above average for the Canadian bond fund category, although longer term results are still sub-par. The portfolio is heavily weighted to federal and provincial government issues. Another good year will produce a rating upgrade.

EMPIRE FOREIGN CURRENCY CANADIAN BOND FUND $ → FI * RSP S IB

Manager: Paul Pathak, since 1997

MER: 2.11%

This is an RRSP-eligible international bond fund that invests in debt securities issued by Canadian governments and corporations that are denominated in foreign currencies. It's a very small fund, with sub-par returns. Average annual compound rate of return for the three years to June 30/98 was just 2.2%. Debuts at $.

EMPIRE MONEY MARKET FUND $ → C No RSP S CMM

Manager: Paul Pathak, since 1997

MER: 1.43%

Steady money fund from Empire Life, but returns are somewhat below average, due in part to the high management fee. Invests primarily in corporate notes. New manager took over in '97, but he won't be able to do much to improve returns unless the MER is reduced considerably.

EQUITABLE LIFE GROUP

THE COMPANY

Equitable Life has been in business in Canada since 1920. Head office is in Waterloo, Ontario, where 340 people are employed. Assets under management are in the $1-billion range. The company has seven segregated funds but only five are currently available to the general public so they are the only ones included in this edition.

THE DETAILS

NUMBER OF FUNDS:	5
ASSETS UNDER MANAGEMENT:	$271 MILLION
LOAD CHARGE:	BACK: MAX. 6%
SWITCHING CHARGE:	NONE
WHERE SOLD:	ACROSS CANADA
HOW SOLD:	THROUGH INDEPENDENT LIFE INSURANCE BROKERS
PHONE NUMBER:	1-800-668-4095
WEB SITE ADDRESS:	WWW.EQUITABLE.CA
E-MAIL ADDRESS:	CUSTOMER-SERVICE@EQUITABLE.CA

FUND SUMMARY

$$$$ - NONE
$$$ - CANADIAN BOND, INTERNATIONAL
$$ - ASSET ALLOCATION, CANADIAN STOCK
$ - MONEY MARKET
NR - NONE

BEST CHOICES: CANADIAN BOND, INTERNATIONAL
BEST FOR RRSPs: CANADIAN BOND, INTERNATIONAL
BEST UNRATEDS: N/A

FUND RATINGS

CANADIAN EQUITY FUNDS

EQUITABLE LIFE CANADIAN STOCK FUND $$ → G * RSP S CE

Manager: Bob Hammill (Guardian Capital), since 1997

MER: 2.25%

The goal of this fund is to provide a combination of moderate growth plus good dividend income. That gives it a decidedly blue-chip tilt. This fund had been doing quite well under the direction of Phillips, Hager & North, with above-average results. However, in May, '97 the management responsibility moved over to Guardian Capital. Guardian is a fine company, but their own stock funds have struggled recently and the effect was catching. Return on this fund was just 6.4% for the year to June 30/98, due in part to a heavy resource sector weighting entering '98 (about one quarter of the portfolio). That concerns me, and it's enough to warrant dropping the rating a notch. All Equitable funds carry a guarantee that the death benefit will not be less than 100% of the value of your contributions. The floor on maturity value is 75%.

U.S. AND INTERNATIONAL EQUITY FUNDS

EQUITABLE LIFE INTERNATIONAL FUND $$$ → G * RSP S IE

Managers: Kim Moore and Robert Head, since 1995

MER: 2.75%

This international fund retains 100% RRSP eligibility by using derivatives, mainly index futures. So what you are really buying here is a portfolio that offers a range of international equity indexes, such as the S&P 500 in the U.S. That's not a bad way to approach global investing and this fund has performed very well, with an average annual compound rate of return of 20.1% for the three years to June 30/98. The safety record is pretty good too. We'll give it a $$$ rating in its debut here.

BALANCED FUNDS

EQUITABLE LIFE ASSET
ALLOCATION FUND $$ → FI/G * RSP S CBAL

Managers: Kim Moore and Robert Head, since 1995

MER: 2.25%

This is a middle-of-the-road balanced fund that invests in a mix of stocks, bonds, and short-term notes. Returns have tended to be slightly below average. Nothing special but okay if you're a client of the company. Don't become one just to buy it, however.

FIXED INCOME AND MONEY MARKET FUNDS

EQUITABLE LIFE
CANADIAN BOND FUND $$$ → FI * RSP S CB

Manager: Robert Head, since 1995

MER: 2.00%

This fund continues to produce above-average returns for investors. The portfolio is well diversified and includes a mix of federal, provincial, and high-grade corporate bonds. Gain for the 12 months to June 30/98 was an above-average 9.4%. Three-year results have also improved to better than average, at 11.7%. A very respectable entry.

EQUITABLE LIFE MONEY MARKET FUND $ → C * RSP S CMM

Manager: Kim Moore, since 1994

MER: 1.75%

Ms. Moore may be a great manager but she hasn't a hope of producing decent returns with this fund during a time of low interest rates. If you want to know why, just look at the MER. It's way out of line. The portfolio is a nice blend of federal and provincial T-bills and corporate short-term notes, but this is one to avoid until the company decides to get real with its fee structure.

GREAT-WEST LIFE ASSURANCE

THE COMPANY

Winnipeg-based Great-West Life is one of Canada's largest insurance companies. They've been in business more than 100 years (since 1891 to be exact) and are considered to be a solid, stable, well-financed organization. Their line of segregated funds is huge, by far the largest offered by any insurance company. A total of 16 new funds came into being on January 1, 1996, more than doubling the size of this group, and another eight were launched in the fall of 1997. This brings the total size of this group to 42 funds.

Several outside managers have been engaged to run the new entries, including Mackenzie, AGF, Sceptre, and Beutel Goodman. The problem for investors will be to figure out which funds to buy; for example, there are now eight balanced funds to choose from, each with slight variations in mandate and style. Great-West has created some software to help the process, a Windows-based asset allocation program called Discovery that is designed to help people determine which funds best meet their needs. If you're interested in this company's funds, you should ask a representative to lead you through it.

For reference, if you want to know which outside manager is running a given fund, check the initial in brackets after the name. "G" indicates the fund is managed in-house.

A = AGF
B = Beutel Goodman
M = Mackenzie Financial
P = Putnam
S = Sceptre

Unfortunately, Great-West Life is no longer providing the names of the lead managers for individual funds, only a corporate designation. This is a growing trend in the industry, one I deplore as it deprives investors of a key piece of information.

There are two purchase options for all GWL funds. You can choose to pay a no-load charge up front but be assessed a higher annual management fee. Or you can buy on a back-end load basis (maximum 4.5% declining to zero after seven years) and pay a slightly lower management charge. The difference is small: about a quarter of a percent a year. But if you're going to invest in a segregated fund it should be for the long haul, so you may as well realize the saving and choose the back-end load.

Over the years, I have commented many times on the high management expense ratios (MERs) of some of this company's funds. So I'm pleased to report that they have been reduced in many cases, by anywhere from .06% to .24%.

The folks at Great-West have expressed concern about my comments on their MERs, saying they feel they are being unfairly compared to a universe that includes direct-sale no-load funds, funds with high minimums, funds with varying objective mandates, etc. They also make the point there are no charges for fund transfers and no trustee fees. Some of this is correct; however, MER comparisons are only made with other funds of the same type. It is also true that segregated funds have higher MERs to cover the cost of the various guarantees they offer. But at the end of the day, investors need to understand that high MERs can have a major impact on returns, especially in fixed-income and money market funds. Great-West's Money Market Fund, for example, has consistently been a sub-par performer over the years. It's not the manager's fault; the high MERs made this result inevitable. Thankfully, it's one of the funds that has received the largest cut.

THE DETAILS

NUMBER OF FUNDS:	42
ASSETS UNDER MANAGEMENT:	$3.5 BILLION
LOAD CHARGE:	BACK: MAX. 4.5%
SWITCHING CHARGE:	NONE
WHERE SOLD:	ACROSS CANADA
HOW SOLD:	THROUGH INSURANCE REPRESENTATIVES
PHONE NUMBER:	1-800-665-5758
WEB SITE ADDRESS:	WWW.GWL.CA
E-MAIL ADDRESS:	THROUGH WEB SITE

FUND SUMMARY

$$$$ - NONE

$$$ - INCOME (G), INTERNATIONAL EQUITY (P), MORTGAGE (G)

$$ - CANADIAN BOND (G), EQUITY INDEX (G), GOVERNMENT BOND (G), INTERNATIONAL BOND (P), REAL ESTATE (G), US EQUITY (G)

$ - CANADIAN EQUITY (G), DIVERSIFIED RS (G), EQUITY BOND (G), MONEY MARKET (G)

NR - ADVANCED PORTFOLIO RS (G), AGGRESSIVE PORTFOLIO RS (G), AMERICAN GROWTH (A), ASIAN GROWTH (A), BALANCED (B), BALANCED (M), BALANCED (S), BALANCED PORTFOLIO RS (G), BOND (B), BOND (S), CANADIAN OPPORTUNITY (M), CANADIAN RESOURCES (A), CONSERVATIVE PORTFOLIO RS (G), DIVIDEND (G), DIVIDEND GROWTH (M), EQUITY (M), EQUITY (S), EUROPEAN EQUITY (S), GLOBAL INCOME (A), GROWTH AND INCOME (A), GROWTH AND INCOME (M), GROWTH EQUITY (A), INCOME (M), INTERNATIONAL OPPORTUNITY (P), LARGER COMPANY (M), MID CAP CANADA (G), MODERATE PORTFOLIO RS (G), NORTH AMERICAN EQUITY (B), SMALLER COMPANY (M)

BEST CHOICES: INCOME (G), INTERNATIONAL EQUITY (P)

BEST FOR RRSPs: INCOME (G)

BEST UNRATEDS: AMERICAN GROWTH (A), EQUITY (S), GROWTH & INCOME (M), INTERNATIONAL OPPORTUNITY (P), MID CAP CANADA (G)

FUND RATINGS

CANADIAN EQUITY FUNDS

GREAT-WEST LIFE CANADIAN EQUITY FUND (G) $ → G */No RSP S CE

Manager: GWL Investment Management

MER: A - 2.64% B - 2.40%

This is the original Canadian equity fund in this group, managed in-house. It has been around since '87 and focuses on big companies, although the mandate allows up to 25% of the portfolio to be in small-cap stocks. Generally, it's been an uninspiring performer. At times, it has managed to do better than the companion Equity Index Fund, but over the past five years the Index Fund has been much stronger and is the better choice. Gain for this one over the 12 months to June 30/98 was 7.9% for the load version, well below average for its peer group. I expect that some of the new Canadian equity funds will be better long-term bets than either of the older ones, and initial results are confirming that. However, none of the newcomers yet qualifies for a rating, so we'll have to wait and see.

GREAT-WEST LIFE EQUITY INDEX FUND (G) $$ → G */No RSP S CE

Manager: GWL Investment Management

MER: A - 2.57% B - 2.33%

This fund is designed to mirror the performance of the TSE 300 Index. When the stock market is strong, it will do well. For example, the fund gained 13.3% (load units) for the year to June 30/98. That was slightly better than average for the Canadian equity category, but below the return of the TSE 300 because of the management fee, which is high for a fund of this type, although it has been reduced slightly.

GREAT-WEST LIFE REAL ESTATE FUND (G) $$ ↑ G */No RSP S RE

Manager: GWL Investment Management

MER: A - 2.94% B - 2.70%

Great-West Life has finally seen the light and is again publishing the returns of this fund in the business press (a practice they had suspended for several years when it was doing poorly). An upswing in the return may have helped change their minds; the load units gained 14.3% over the year to June 30/98. Five-year results are still bad (average annual gain of just 2.6%) but at least the trend is improving. This is one of the largest industrial and commercial real estate funds in Canada.

U.S. AND INTERNATIONAL EQUITY FUNDS

GREAT-WEST LIFE INTERNATIONAL
EQUITY FUND (P)
$$$ → G */No £ S IE

Manager: Putnam Advisory Company

MER: A - 2.93% B - 2.69%

This fund's mandate is to invest in countries outside North America, so it has not participated in the U.S. bull market. Nonetheless, it has produced some good results, with an average annual compound rate of return of 18.5% (load units) for the three years to June 30/98. Putnam Advisory is based in Boston and is one of the oldest and largest money management firms in the States. This fund will normally hold between 90 and 120 positions and will be invested in at least 10 different countries at any given time. It looks good, and we'll start it off with a $$$ rating.

GREAT-WEST LIFE U.S.
EQUITY FUND (G)
$$ → G */No £ S USE

Manager: GWL Investment Management

MER: A - 2.79% B - 2.55%

The mandate of this fund is to invest in mid- to large-cap U.S. stocks, although up to 25% of the assets may be in small-cap issues. The portfolio will normally hold between 30 and 70 securities. The fund started slowly but more recent results have been much better. Gain for the year to June 30/98 was 31.1% for the load units. Three-year results are below average, however.

BALANCED FUNDS

GREAT-WEST LIFE
DIVERSIFIED RS FUND (G)
$$ → FI/G */No RSP S CBAL

Manager: GWL Investment Management

MER: A - 2.64% B - 2.40%

This long-time underperformer is starting to look better. Return on the load units over the year to June 30/98 was 12.6%, better than average for the balanced fund category.

Longer term results (three years plus) are still below par but hopefully this fund has started an upward trend line that will lead to a better rating. One reason for the mediocre results: the fund invests in a portfolio of other Great-West Life mutual funds. They need to do well if this one is to pay off.

GREAT-WEST LIFE
EQUITY/BOND FUND (G) $ → G/FI */No RSP S CBAL

Manager: GWL Investment Management

MER: A - 2.64% B - 2.40%

This is another balanced entry from Great-West Life. The difference is that this one invests independently, rather than being a fund of funds. Ten-year results are marginally better than those of the Diversified RS Fund, but it has done better recently. Gain for the year to June 30/98 was a below-average 9.6% (load units). Recent portfolio mix was about two thirds stocks, one third bonds. Neither of these old entries is very inspiring, but some of the new balanced funds from other managers are showing better over the short term. Best over the past two years: Mackenzie's Growth & Income (M) Fund, with an average annual compound rate of return of 18.1%.

GREAT-WEST LIFE INCOME
FUND (G) $$$ → FI/G */No RSP S CBAL

Manager: GWL Investment Management

MER: A - 2.17% B - 1.93%

This is a conservatively managed balanced fund that puts a heavy emphasis on bonds while blending in some stocks for growth potential to a maximum of 20% of the portfolio. So it will generally underperform other balanced funds but will do better than most bond funds. Perhaps the best description for it is a "near-bond" fund. The load units produced an average annual compound rate of return of 12.6% over the three years to June 30/98, very good for a low-risk fund of this type. Debuts with a $$$ rating.

GREAT-WEST LIFE CANADIAN
BOND FUND (G) $$ → FI */No RSP S CB

Manager: GWL Investment Management

MER: A - 2.07% B - 1.82%

This fund invests mainly in high-quality bonds with an emphasis on government issues, although some corporates are also included in the portfolio to a maximum of 30% of the holdings. At least half the issues in the fund will have a credit rating of AA or higher. Past results have been below average but the fund has been showing improvement over the past couple of years. Gain to the end of June/98 was 9.1% for one year, 10.8% annually over two years. That was better than average for the bond fund category, and the best result turned in by one of GWL's pure bond funds.

GREAT-WEST LIFE
GOVERNMENT BOND FUND (G) $$ ↓ FI */No RSP S CB

Manager: GWL Investment Management

MER: A - 2.09% B - 1.84%

This is a defensively managed bond fund, designed to minimize risk. It will normally hold at least 25% of the portfolio in federal government bonds and may invest up to 25% of the assets in mortgage-backed securities. The average term of the portfolio will range from two to five years, so this is a short-term bond fund that will underperform in strong markets but protect your money when bond prices fall. Expect returns to be higher than those from a money market fund, but less than you'll normally receive from a regular bond fund.

GREAT-WEST LIFE
INTERNATIONAL BOND FUND (P) $ → FI */No £ S IB

Manager: Putnam Advisory Company

MER: A - 3.06% B - 2.80%

The goal of this fund is to invest in high-quality government and government-agency bonds from around the world. The portfolio will normally hold a minimum of 25 to 30 issues from five to 15 countries. At least 85% of assets will have a credit rating of A or higher. Currency hedges may be used to reduce the exchange risk. Returns thus far have not been good; the load units gained only 2% in the year to June 30/98. Not recommended at this time. Note that this fund is considered as foreign content for RRSPs.

GREAT-WEST LIFE MONEY
MARKET FUND (G) $ → C */No RSP S CMM

Manager: GWL Investment Management

MER: A - 1.64% B - 1.38%

Portfolio is a mix of Canada T-bills, bankers' acceptances, high-quality corporate notes, and short-term bank bonds. The management fee on this fund has been reduced but is still on the high side. Results are below average.

GREAT-WEST LIFE
MORTGAGE FUND (G) $$$ ↑ FI */No RSP S M

Manager: GWL Investment Management

MER: A - 2.40% B - 2.16%

This fund invests mainly in apartment building and commercial mortgages, unlike most mortgage funds, which concentrate on single-family residential first mortgages. Commercial mortgages typically have a longer term than residential mortgages, which makes them vulnerable to bigger losses when interest rates rise. Conversely, when rates are declining a fund like this should outperform others in the mortgage category. That's what has been happening recently. The load units of this fund gained 7.5% in the year to June 30/98. That was the best result in the mortgage category for the second year running and it was achieved despite the high MER. Results for all time periods are now above average. We'll raise the rating again to reflect that, but be aware that this fund has a much higher risk factor than you'd normally associate with a mortgage fund.

GROW*SAFE* FUNDS

(TRANSAMERICA LIFE)

THE COMPANY

The Transamerica Life Insurance Company of Canada is the Canadian subsidiary of the U.S. giant of the same name. Grow*safe* is their line of segregated funds. Several of the funds are managed by Guardian Capital Limited, a company with a reputation for a conservative style and good results. Note that these funds can be purchased either on a back-end load option or a no-load option. The latter doesn't get much promotion and it may not even be mentioned to you because the sales person will receive less commission if you choose it. But it is there if you insist.

THE DETAILS

NUMBER OF FUNDS:	10
ASSETS UNDER MANAGEMENT:	$203 MILLION
LOAD CHARGE:	BACK: MAX. 6%
SWITCHING CHARGE:	NONE
WHERE SOLD:	ACROSS CANADA
HOW SOLD:	THROUGH INDEPENDENT FINANCIAL ADVISORS
PHONE NUMBER:	1-800-268-8814
WEB SITE ADDRESS:	WWW.TRANSAMERICA.COM/CANADA
E-MAIL ADDRESS:	THROUGH WEB SITE

FUND SUMMARY

$$$$ - NONE
$$$ - NONE
$$ - CANADIAN MONEY MARKET
$ - CANADIAN BALANCED, CANADIAN BOND, CANADIAN EQUITY, INTERNATIONAL BALANCED
NR - CANADIAN DIVIDEND & INCOME, EUROPEAN 100 INDEX, JAPANESE 225 INDEX, U.S. 500 INDEX, U.S. 21ST CENTURY INDEX

BEST CHOICES: CANADIAN MONEY MARKET
BEST FOR RRSPs: CANADIAN BALANCED
BEST UNRATEDS: EUROPEAN 100 INDEX, U.S. 500 INDEX, U.S. 21ST CENTURY INDEX

FUND RATINGS

CANADIAN EQUITY FUNDS

GROW*SAFE* CANADIAN EQUITY FUND $ → G */No RSP S CE

Managers: John Priestman and Gary Chapman (Guardian Capital), since inception (1993)

MER: 2.45%

The mandate of this fund is to invest mainly in large Canadian corporations, although some small and medium-sized companies may be included in the mix (up to 20% of the total assets). The portfolio is kept relatively small (35–45 stocks) and is well diversified with no heavy over-weighting to a single industry sector. The fund slumped badly last year, gaining just 3% in the 12 months to June 30/98, in part because of the managers' aversion to the hot banking sector. Three-year results are also below average as a result.

BALANCED FUNDS

GROW*SAFE* CANADIAN BALANCED FUND $ → FI/G */No RSP S CBAL

Managers: John Priestman, Peter Hargrove, and Gary Chapman (Guardian Capital), since inception (1993)

MER: 2.46%

This is a classic balanced fund, with a mandate to invest across a broad spectrum of securities. The managers may shift their asset weightings but may not exceed 70% equities or 70% bonds at any time. Bond holdings must be rated at least BBB or higher. Returns have been below average; this fund gained 7% in the year ending June 30/98. The average Canadian balanced fund gained 10.2%, according to figures published by *The Globe and Mail*.

GROW*SAFE* INTERNATIONAL BALANCED FUND $ → FI/G */No RSP S IBAL

Managers: Guardian Capital Management, Kleinwort Benson
Investment Management, since inception (1993)

MER: 2.79%

Although this is an international fund, it is structured in such a way as to maintain full RRSP eligibility. It achieves this by investing in stock index futures, bonds of supra-national financial institutions like the World Bank, and directly in foreign bonds and stocks within the 20% foreign content limit. Sounds like a good idea, but returns have been consistently below average for the international balanced category. Average annual compound rate of return for the three years to June 30/98 was 12.6%, compared to an industry average of 13.8%.

FIXED INCOME AND MONEY MARKET FUNDS

GROW*SAFE* CANADIAN BOND FUND $ → FI */No RSP S CB

Manager: Peter Hargrove (Guardian Capital), since 1995

MER: 2.25%

This is a well-diversified bond fund that holds a mix of government and corporate bonds, mortgage-backed securities, and AAA-rated supranational bonds. Returns have been below average in comparison to its peer group, but latest results look better with a gain of 8.8% for the year to June 30/98. High MER hurts here.

GROW*SAFE* CANADIAN MONEY MARKET FUND $$ → C */No RSP S CMM

Manager: Mark Jackson, since 1995

MER: 0.96%

This fund invests mainly in high-grade corporate notes, with a small percentage of Treasury bills added to the mix. Returns have improved to above average over the short term but three-year results are still a bit sub-par.

HARTFORD LIFE INSURANCE CO. OF CANADA

THE COMPANY

Hartford Life is a large U.S. insurance firm that has been operating in Canada since 1994. They recently launched a family of eight segregated funds, all of which are too new to qualify for a rating.

THE DETAILS

NUMBER OF FUNDS:	8
ASSETS UNDER MANAGEMENT:	$11.6 MILLION
LOAD CHARGE:	BACK: MAX. 6%
SWITCHING CHARGE:	TWO FREE TRANSFERS PER YEAR, $50 THEREAFTER
WHERE SOLD:	ACROSS CANADA
HOW SOLD:	THROUGH INSURANCE BROKERS
PHONE NUMBER:	1-888-249-9903
WEB SITE ADDRESS:	N/A
E-MAIL ADDRESS:	KELLYO@HARTFORDLIFE.CA

FUND SUMMARY

$$$$ - N/A
$$$ - N/A
$$ - N/A
$ - N/A
NR -ASSET ALLOCATION, AGGRESSIVE GROWTH, CANADIAN ADVANCED TECHNOLOGY, CANADIAN EQUITY, CANADIAN INCOME, MONEY MARKET, REAL ESTATE INCOME, SELECT WORLD ECONOMICS

BEST CHOICES: N/A
BEST FOR RRSPs: N/A
BEST UNRATEDS: CANADIAN INCOME

FUND RATINGS

None of the funds have been in existence the requisite three years to qualify for a rating.

IMPERIAL LIFE

THE COMPANY

Imperial Life is a long-established Canadian firm, with roots going way back to the 19th century (1896 to be exact), a time when the average life expectancy in this country was just 47. They are now part of the Desjardins-Laurentian Life Group. Their segregated funds are managed by a sister company within that group, Canagex. The original Imperial funds were closed to new investors in late 1995, although existing unitholders can add to their positions. The company's new fund line, known as Millennia III, offers a choice between back-end load and no-load purchase options, with the latter carrying a higher management fee. All the funds in this line are too new for a formal rating.

THE DETAILS

NUMBER OF FUNDS:	8
ASSETS UNDER MANAGEMENT:	$592 MILLION
LOAD CHARGE:	CHOICE OF NO-LOAD OPTION OR BACK: MAX. 5.5% OPTION
SWITCHING CHARGE:	NONE
WHERE SOLD:	ACROSS CANADA
HOW SOLD:	THROUGH REPRESENTATIVES OF IMPERIAL LIFE FINANCIAL, IMPERIAL LIFE FINANCIAL SERVICES, REPRESENTATIVES OF DESJARDINS IN QUEBEC, AND CERTAIN BROKERS.
PHONE NUMBER:	(416) 926-2700 EXTENSION 7952
WEB SITE ADDRESS:	WWW.IMPERIAL-LIFE.CA
E-MAIL ADDRESS:	N/A

FUND SUMMARY

$$$$ -	N/A
$$$ -	N/A
$$ -	N/A
$ -	N/A
NR -	MILLENNIA III FUNDS: AMERICAN EQUITY, CANADIAN BALANCED, CANADIAN DIVIDEND, CANADIAN EQUITY, INCOME, INTERNATIONAL EQUITY, MONEY MARKET, NORTH AMERICAN SMALL COMPANY

BEST CHOICES: N/A
BEST FOR RRSPs: N/A
BEST UNRATEDS: MILLENNIA III: AMERICAN EQUITY, INTERNATIONAL EQUITY

FUND RATINGS

All Millennia III funds are too new for a formal rating. The older Imperial Growth funds have been closed to new investors so will no longer be reviewed here.

INDUSTRIAL ALLIANCE

THE COMPANY

Industrial Alliance is a Quebec-based company that offers a variety of funds. However, only the "Ecoflex" line is available to individual investors. All others are sold through group pension plans and group RRSPs.

The Ecoflex funds are also sold by North West Life Assurance Company of Canada, which is a West Coast clone of Industrial Alliance. The funds, managers, and terms are exactly the same in both cases.

Note: These funds are available either by back-end load purchase or through a no-load option. The no-load choice is not publicized or promoted and is used only in "exceptional" cases, at the request of a sales rep. But it is available, so if you're considering doing business with either Industrial Alliance or North West Life, you should ask about it.

THE DETAILS

NUMBER OF FUNDS:	17
ASSETS UNDER MANAGEMENT:	$40 MILLION
LOAD CHARGE:	BACK: MAX. 5%, OR NO-LOAD ON A SELECTIVE BASIS
SWITCHING CHARGE:	NONE
WHERE SOLD:	ACROSS CANADA
HOW SOLD:	THROUGH LIFE INSURANCE AGENTS
PHONE NUMBER:	1-800-463-6236 OR (418) 463-6236
WEB SITE ADDRESS:	WWW.INALCO.COM
E-MAIL ADDRESS:	CLIENTELE@QUE.INALCO.COM

FUND SUMMARY

$$$$ - NONE

$$$ - NONE

$$ - ECOFLEX A (STOCKS)

$ - ECOFLEX B (BONDS), ECOFLEX D (DIVERSIFIED), ECOFLEX M (MONEY MARKET), ECOFLEX H (MORTGAGE)

NR - ECOFLEX ANL (STOCKS), ECOFLEX BNL (BOND), ECOFLEX DNL (DIVERSIFIED), ECOFLEX E (EMERGING MARKETS),

ECOFLEX G (GLOBAL BONDS), ECOFLEX I (INTERNATIONAL STOCK), ECOFLEX N (CANADIAN ADVANTAGE), ECOFLEX R (INCOME), ECOFLEX S (AMERICAN STOCKS), ECOFLEX T (SELECT CANADIAN), ECOFLEX U (U.S. ADVANTAGE), ECOFLEX V (DIVERSIFIED)

BEST CHOICES: ECOFLEX A (STOCKS)
BEST FOR RRSPs: ECOFLEX D (DIVERSIFIED)
BEST UNRATEDS: ECOFLEX I (INTERNATIONAL)
ECOFLEX S (U.S. STOCKS)

FUND RATINGS

CANADIAN EQUITY FUNDS

INDUSTRIAL ALLIANCE ECOFLEX "A" STOCKS FUND

$$ → G */No RSP S CE

Manager: Industrial Alliance

MER: 2.48%

The mandate of this fund is to focus primarily on large-cap Canadian stocks. So that makes it difficult to understand, at least at first glance, why this fund has performed so poorly recently after compiling a very respectable track record until now. The gain for the year to June 30/98 was just 2.2%, well below average for the Canadian equity fund category. Once you take a closer look at the portfolio, you begin to understand, however. Going into 1998, more than a third of the assets were in the underperforming resource sector. With such a high weighting in stocks that were generally tumbling, the manager was lucky to make any profit at all! Unfortunately, the bad year has pulled results for all time periods to below average. Rating drops a notch as a result.

BALANCED FUNDS

INDUSTRIAL ALLIANCE ECOFLEX "D" DIVERSIFIED FUND

$ → FI/G */No RSP S CBAL

Manager: Industrial Alliance

MER: 2.48%

This is a broadly diversified fund that includes stocks, bonds, and mortgage-backed securities in the mix. The portfolio was fairly evenly balanced between equities and bonds in the first half of '98. Returns have slipped to below average, with a gain of 7.8% for the year to June 30/98. Longer term performance is also sub-par.

FIXED INCOME AND MONEY MARKET FUNDS

INDUSTRIAL ALLIANCE ECOFLEX "B" BOND FUND $ → FI */No RSP S CB

Manager: Industrial Alliance

MER: 1.86%

The diversified portfolio includes federal and Quebec government bonds as well as issues from corporations, municipalities, hospitals, school boards, universities, etc. Returns have been below average, with an annual five-year compound rate of return of 7.2% to June 30/98, about a percentage point below the norm.

INDUSTRIAL ALLIANCE ECOFLEX "M" MONEY MARKET FUND $ → C No RSP S CMM

Manager: Industrial Alliance

MER: 1.36%

About three quarters of the portfolio is invested in federal T-bills with the rest in a variety of other short-term securities. Performance has been below average, due in part to the relatively high management expense fee.

INDUSTRIAL ALLIANCE ECOFLEX "H" MORTGAGE FUND $ → FI */No RSP S M

Manager: Industrial Alliance

MER: 1.86%

Weak performer in the mortgage category. Returns are well below average for the peer group. Five-year average annual compound rate of return was 5.3% to June 30/98.

LONDON LIFE FUNDS

THE COMPANY

London Life was acquired in 1997 by Winnipeg-based Great-West Life. However, their segregated funds continue to operate independently and, in fact, they have recently expanded their list of offerings considerably, adding 33 new funds to the list in mid-1998. Their new lineup resembles that of Great-West Life, with seven outside managers, including Mackenzie, AGF, and Maxxum, running some of the funds.

As I have said in the case of Great-West Life, I have a distinct feeling of overkill here — too many choices can be just as difficult for investors to deal with as too few. However, we'll see how this develops. All the new funds are obviously too young to be rated.

In the list below, all funds managed by London Life have no identifier attached. Those managed by outside companies are marked as follows:

AGF	(A)
Beutel Goodman	(B)
Great-West Life	(GWL)
Mackenzie	(M)
Maxxum	(Max)
Sceptre	(S)

THE DETAILS

NUMBER OF FUNDS:	40
ASSETS UNDER MANAGEMENT:	$6.3 BILLION
LOAD CHARGE:	BACK: MAX. 5%
SWITCHING CHARGE:	NONE
WHERE SOLD:	ACROSS CANADA
HOW SOLD:	THROUGH LONDON LIFE AGENTS
PHONE NUMBER:	1-800-FREEDOM (ENGLISH) OR 1-800-780-8941 (FRENCH)
WEB SITE ADDRESS:	WWW.LONDONLIFE.COM
E-MAIL ADDRESS:	N/A

FUND SUMMARY

$$$$ - NONE

$$$ - DIVERSIFIED, MORTGAGE, U.S. EQUITY

$$ - BOND, CANADIAN EQUITY, INTERNATIONAL EQUITY, MONEY

$ - NONE

NR - AMERICAN EQUITY (MAX), AMERICAN GROWTH (A), ASIAN GROWTH (A), BALANCED (B), BALANCED (S), CANADIAN BALANCED (MAX), CANADIAN EQUITY (GWL), CANADIAN EQUITY GROWTH (MAX), CANADIAN OPPORTUNITY (M), DIVIDEND (MAX), EQUITY (M), EQUITY/BOND (GWL), EUROPEAN EQUITY (S), GLOBAL EQUITY (MAX), GOVERNMENT BOND, (GWL), GROWTH EQUITY (A), GROWTH & INCOME (A), GROWTH & INCOME (M), INCOME (M), INCOME (MAX), LARGER COMPANY (M), MID CAP CANADA (GWL), NATURAL RESOURCE (MAX), N.A EQUITY (B), PRECIOUS METALS (MAX), REAL ESTATE (GWL)

BEST CHOICES: DIVERSIFIED, MORTGAGE, U.S. EQUITY

BEST FOR RRSPs: DIVERSIFIED, MORTGAGE

BEST UNRATEDS: TOO SOON TO JUDGE

FUND RATINGS

CANADIAN EQUITY FUNDS

LONDON LIFE CANADIAN EQUITY FUND $$ → G * RSP S CE

Manager: London Life Investment Management

MER: 2.35%

Veteran manager Rohit Sehgal, who had been running this fund since 1982, decamped in mid-'98 to move over to Dundee Capital where he is heading a new group known as the Power Funds. That leaves a big gap here that will be hard to fill. Under Sehgal's direction, the fund had been doing quite well, with above-average returns for all time periods. However, we'll have to see what happens now. The portfolio focuses on mid-size to large companies represented on the TSE 300 Index. In the first half of '98, the portfolio was well diversified, with the financial services sector the largest single component. London Life guarantees a death benefit of not less than the total value of your contributions to any of their funds. There's also a maturity guarantee of at least 75% of the value of all contributions.

U.S. AND INTERNATIONAL EQUITY FUNDS

LONDON LIFE INTERNATIONAL
EQUITY FUND $$ → G * £ S IE

Manager: Jardine Fleming Canada, since 1997

MER: 2.50%

This has been the weak link in the London Life chain so in November, 1997 the management was moved over to Jardine Fleming, an international organization with offices in 44 countries. Investors hope they will be able to breathe some life into this one, and the early results were encouraging — the fund was ahead 17.5% in the first six months of '98, a tremendous improvement over previous results. But six months isn't long enough to warrant any more than a $$ rating. We'll give the new folks another year or so and then look again.

LONDON LIFE U.S. EQUITY FUND $$$ ↓ G * £ S USE

Manager: Jeff Brown, since 1995

MER: 2.55%

This fund has been looking very strong ever since Jeff Brown assumed responsibility for the portfolio in '95. Over the past three years, to June 30/98, the fund has produced an average annual return of better than 30%, which is outstanding. It's unlikely to continue at that pace, of course, but those results are very good even in the context of a hot U.S. stock market during that time. The well-balanced portfolio favoured financial and technology stocks in the first half of '98, and those sectors have been the keys to success for Brown over the past couple of years. I promised last year that one more round of good results would produce a rating upgrade. Brown delivered, and so am I. Good safety record is a bonus.

BALANCED FUNDS

LONDON LIFE DIVERSIFIED FUND $$$ → FI/G * RSP S CBAL

Manager: Robert Badun, since 1993

MER: 2.35%

This is a fund of funds, investing in units of other funds in the London Life family. Asset mix will vary, depending on the economic climate. As other London Life funds have improved their results, this one has gained as well. Return for the year to June 30/98 was a solid 14.6%. Three-year results have also improved to above average. As of the first half of '98, the holdings were: Canadian Equity Fund (42%), Bond Fund (42%), U.S. Equity Fund (10%), International Equity Fund (6%).

FIXED INCOME AND MONEY MARKET FUNDS

LONDON LIFE BOND FUND $$ → FI * RSP S CB

Manager: Grant McIntosh, since 1997

MER: 1.75%

This is a diversified portfolio which emphasizes government issues but also has some high-quality corporate bonds mixed in. Nothing special; returns tend to be about average. New manager took over in '97.

LONDON LIFE MONEY FUND $$ → C * RSP S CMM

Manager: Audrey Cole, since 1988

MER: 1.20%

Good long-term results, although most recent returns have slipped to below average because of the relatively high MER. The portfolio is a mix of federal and provincial notes and bankers' acceptances.

LONDON LIFE MORTGAGE FUND $$$ ↓ FI * RSP S M

Manager: Grant McIntosh, since 1995

MER: 2.00%

How about a mutual fund that hasn't had a losing calendar year going all the way back to 1975! Will that help you sleep at night? This one managed to keep its record intact by escaping a loss (by the skin of its teeth) in '94, when many other mortgage funds were hitting the red ink. Since then, it has chalked up four years of slightly better than average gains. Return for the 12 months to June 30/98 was 6.7%. Perhaps that doesn't seem like a lot, but by mortgage fund standards it was near the top of the heap. ATP analysis shows only a 4% chance of suffering a loss in any given 12-month period. This is a fund to use as a core holding in a conservative portfolio. It's less vulnerable than the companion Bond Fund to movements in interest rates, so the risk is lower here.

MANULIFE FINANCIAL

THE COMPANY

Manulife is one of Canada's leading insurance companies, and it has been making major changes in its product line in recent years.

The Vista Funds were the original segregated fund group. However, they were withdrawn from sale at the end of December, 1997 so are no longer covered here.

The NAL line was formerly the segregated fund group of North American Life, which was taken over by Manulife in 1995. These products have also been taken off the market, effective June 30, 1998. So coverage has also been discontinued in this *Buyer's Guide*, since they can no longer be purchased. (Existing unitholders may still find performance numbers in the media.)

The Guaranteed Investment Funds (GIFs) are a brand-new line, and have become the focus of Manulife's seg fund sales. These are well-known funds run mainly by outside managers, such as Trimark and Fidelity, that have been dressed up in seg fund clothing and marketed for their guarantees, creditor protection, etc. They are not rated individually as they are clones of other funds. However, their returns will vary somewhat from the underlying fund because of the difference in management fees and the timing of purchases.

Manulife also offers a non-segregated fund group, the Cabot Funds. You'll find them in the regular mutual funds section.

THE DETAILS - GUARANTEED INVESTMENT FUNDS

NUMBER OF FUNDS:	35
ASSETS UNDER MANAGEMENT:	$2.9 BILLION
LOAD CHARGE:	FRONT: MAX. 3%; BACK: MAX.5.5% (REDUCED CHARGES FOR MONEY MARKET AND BOND FUNDS)
SWITCHING CHARGE:	FIVE FREE TRANSFERS PER YEAR
WHERE SOLD:	ACROSS CANADA
HOW SOLD:	THROUGH LICENSED LIFE INSURANCE AGENTS AND BROKERS
PHONE NUMBER:	1-888-MANULIFE OR 1-888-626-8543
WEB SITE ADDRESS:	WWW.MANULIFE.COM
E-MAIL ADDRESS:	N/A

FUND SUMMARY

All the funds in this group are segregated versions of existing mutual funds, most of which have well-established track records. The rating for each of the underlying funds can be found in the section on the parent company elsewhere in this book. The Manulife version of these funds is designed to allow investors to obtain the benefits of creditor protection, loss guarantees, and estate planning that are not available by investing in the underlying funds themselves. For these added benefits, you'll be assessed an extra management fee, over and above the one applied to the underlying fund. Ask a Manulife representative for full details.

The funds used in this group are: AGF Canadian Bond, AGF Canadian Equity, AGF Dividend, AGF Global Government Bond, AGF Growth and Income, AGF High Income, AGF International Group Limited American Growth Class, C.I. Harbour, C.I. Harbour Growth and Income, Dynamic Dividend Growth, Dynamic Global Bond, Dynamic Partners, Elliot & Page American Growth, Elliott & Page Balanced, Elliot & Page Equity, Elliot & Page Money Market, Elliot & Page Value Equity, Fidelity Canadian Bond, Fidelity Canadian Asset Allocation, Fidelity Capital Builder, Fidelity Growth America, Fidelity International Portfolio, Fidelity True North, GT Global Canada Fund, Canada Growth Class, GT Global Fund, America Growth Class, Manulife Canadian Equity Index, Manulife U.S. Equity Index, O'Donnell Canadian, O'Donnell Select, Talvest Cdn. Asset Allocation, Talvest/Hyperion Value Line U.S. Equity, Talvest Income, Trimark Select Balanced, Trimark Select Canadian Growth, Trimark Select Growth.

MARITIME LIFE FUNDS

THE COMPANY

Maritime Life began operations in Halifax in 1922. Initially, the company only provided services to the Atlantic provinces, but in the early 1970s it expanded operations across Canada. In 1969, the firm was acquired by John Hancock Mutual Life Insurance Company of Boston, although it maintained its original name and identity. In 1995, the firm took over the individual life and health business and the segregated funds of bankrupt Confederation Life. Today, it is one of the top 10 largest insurance firms in Canada, with assets under administration of $5.5 billion.

Note the three purchase options for these funds. The Series A and Series B units are essentially the same, except that the B units are sold on a deferred sales charge basis. Choose A units if it comes down to a decision between those two. The C units are also sold on a deferred sales charge basis, declining to zero after 10 years, but they offer a bonus payment if they are held for 15 years or more. Ask a Maritime Life representative for details. If you know you're definitely going to be in for the long haul, they may be the best choice.

In March, 1998, Maritime Life announced it was enhancing the guarantees on its Stock Market Guarantee Funds to 100% of the value of deposits and 100% of market gains achieved 10 years or more prior to the plan's maturity date. However, there was a price attached: the MER of the funds involved increased by about 20 basis points in most cases. These funds feature an automatic daily reset, which means their guaranteed value is updated every day to reflect new deposits and market gains. For full details on how this works, speak to a company representative.

THE DETAILS

NUMBER OF FUNDS:	15
ASSETS UNDER MANAGEMENT:	$2.2 BILLION
LOAD CHARGE:	THREE PURCHASE OPTIONS: SERIES A - NO LOAD
	SERIES B - BACK: MAX. 6%
	SERIES C - BACK: MAX. 10%
SWITCHING CHARGE:	NONE
WHERE SOLD:	ACROSS CANADA
HOW SOLD:	THROUGH BROKERS, DEALERS, AND FINANCIAL PLANNERS
PHONE NUMBER:	(902) 453-7116 - DAVID STAR
WEB SITE ADDRESS:	WWW.MARITIMELIFE.CA
E-MAIL ADDRESS:	CPA@MARITIMELIFE.CA

FUND SUMMARY

$$$$ - NONE

$$$ - BALANCED, CANADIAN EQUITY

$$ - AMERICAN GROWTH & INCOME, BOND, DIVIDEND INCOME, GLOBAL EQUITIES, GROWTH, S&P 500

$ - MONEY MARKET, PACIFIC BASIN EQUITIES

NR - AGGRESSIVE EQUITY, DISCOVERY, DIVERSIFIED EQUITY, EURASIA, EUROPE

BEST CHOICES: BALANCED, CANADIAN EQUITY

BEST FOR RRSPs: BALANCED

BEST UNRATEDS: EURASIA

FUND RATINGS

CANADIAN EQUITY FUNDS

MARITIME LIFE CANADIAN EQUITY FUND

$$$ → G */No RSP S CE

Manager: Richard F. Crowe (J.R. Senecal), since inception (1995)

MER: 2.55%

This fund employs a sector rotation style, with manager Richard Crowe seeking to identify those industries that are likely to do best in the current economic environment and then weighting the portfolio towards them. In the first part of '98, financial services companies dominated the mix (27% of the total) with oil and gas next (18%). So far, Crowe has done well with his selections and this fund shows above-average gains over all time periods out to three years. One-year return to June 30/98 was 14.8%. We'll start this one off at $$$ in its first appearance here.

MARITIME LIFE DIVIDEND INCOME FUND $$ → G/FI */No RSP S INC

Manager: John H.G. Dustan (Genus Capital Management), since inception (1995)

MER: 2.25%

This fund seeks to generate a combination of high dividend income and modest capital appreciation. About two thirds of the portfolio is in blue-chip common stocks, with the rest in preferreds, fixed-income securities, and cash. Recent returns have been quite good: 22.1% for the year to June 30/98. However, three-year results are slightly below par for the dividend category. Debuts at $$.

MARITIME LIFE GROWTH FUND $$ → G */No RSP S CE

Manager: Multiple

MER: 2.55%

Maritime Life now offers a number of Canadian equity fund options, some of which are too new to rate. This is the oldest one in the group. It was a long-time sub-par performer before the company changed its approach in late '92 to implement a multi-manager style. This involves dividing the fund into two segments. Segment one approximates the return on the TSE 300 Index (about 60% of the portfolio). Segment two is growth oriented. Four managers are involved in the process: Bolton Tremblay, Knight, Bain, Seath & Holbrook, Genus Capital Management, and Nesbitt Burns. It took some time, but results have shown improvement, although the most recent numbers are only average. Three-year average annual compound rate of return for the year to June 30/98 was quite strong at 17.9%. However, the Canadian Equity stablemate has been better lately.

U.S. AND INTERNATIONAL EQUITY FUNDS

MARITIME LIFE AMERICAN GROWTH & INCOME FUND $$ ↓ G */No £ S USE

Manager: John F. Snyder III (Sovereign Asset Management), since inception (1994)

MER: 2.55%

This fund invests in high-quality U.S. stocks and limits its selection to companies that have increased their dividends annually for a minimum of 10 years. Some of the companies that qualify are General Electric, Johnson & Johnson, and Pitney Bowes. You'd expect a blue-chip portfolio like that to have been shooting out the lights in recent years but the returns, while certainly respectable, have been just average for the U.S. equity category. Average annual compound rate of return for the three years to June 30/98 was 23.7%. That was bang on the average for the peer group, as reported by *The Globe and Mail*. One big factor in this fund's favour is a great safety record to date.

MARITIME LIFE GLOBAL EQUITIES FUND $$ → G */No £ S IE

Manager: Miren Etcheverry (John Hancock Advisors), since 1997

MER: 2.75%

This is a growth-oriented fund in which stocks are selected on the basis of the outlook for the company itself and for the industry in which it operates. Lead manager Miren Etcheverry is senior vice-president of the John Hancock funds in the U.S. The portfolio is well diversified geographically, with Europe and the U.S. being the dominant regions in the first half of '98. Recent results have been above average for the international category (gain of 14.8% for the year to June 30/98), but three-year returns are sub-par.

MARITIME LIFE PACIFIC BASIN EQUITIES FUND

$ ↑ G */No £ S FEE

Manager: Miren Etcheverry (John Hancock Advisors), since 1997

MER: 2.75%

This fund's mandate allows it to invest throughout the entire Pacific Basin. That is defined very broadly so as to include not just the Far East but also the U.S., Canada, and Mexico. Unfortunately, that didn't help a lot last year, as the fund lost 43.4% over the 12 months to June 30/98. Major weightings were in Hong Kong, Japan, and Australia in the first part of '98. The fund is modelled after the John Hancock Freedom Pacific Basin Equities Fund, one of the oldest international stock funds in the U.S.

MARITIME LIFE S&P 500 FUND

$$ → G */No RSP S USE

Manager: Bill Chinery (Yield Management Group), since inception (1994)

MER: 2.20%

This is a fully eligible RRSP fund that is designed to replicate the return of the U.S. Standard & Poor's 500 Index. This is done by investing in Canadian money market instruments (typically T-bills), which are pledged against the purchase of S&P 500 futures contracts. So this is basically a derivatives-based index fund. Index funds are all the rage these days but, interestingly, this one underperformed the average for U.S. equity funds as a group, gaining 24.7% over the year to June 30/98. Three-year results are slightly above average, however. Debuts at $$.

BALANCED FUNDS

MARITIME LIFE BALANCED FUND $$$ ↓ FI/G */No RSP S CBAL

Manager: Multiple

MER: 2.45%

This fund employs eight (count 'em!) money management companies to direct the investments. The portfolio is divided among Canadian stocks, bonds, Treasury bills, foreign stocks, and U.S. stocks for maximum diversification.

Stock and bond holdings may never exceed two thirds of the total assets, so the portfolio is never too heavily over-weighted in any direction. The managers make good use of their foreign content allotment. Results have improved to above average for the balanced category; gain to June 30/98 was 13.2%. Very good safety rating improves its attraction. Rating moves up to $$$ this year.

FIXED INCOME AND MONEY MARKET FUNDS

MARITIME LIFE BOND FUND $$ → FI No RSP CB

Manager: John Braive (T.A.L. Investment Counsel), since 1997

MER: 1.80%

The multimanager approach that was being used for this fund was abandoned in September, '97 with Braive, one of the most highly respected fixed-income managers in Canada, given sole responsibility. (He had been one of the managers previously involved so he is not new to the fund.) As well, the mandate was amended to allow the fund to hold up to 20% of its assets in high-yield bonds, with no more than 1% in any single position. This was a clear effort by Maritime Life to improve the below-average returns. So far, it seems to be working; the fund posted an 8.6% advance in the year to June 30/98, which was right on the average for the bond fund category as reported by *The Globe and Mail*. Most of the assets are in federal, provincial, and municipal government bonds, but the corporate holdings have been significantly increased since Braive took over. No increase in the rating yet, but this fund seems to be headed in the right direction.

MARITIME LIFE MONEY MARKET FUND $ → C No RSP S CMM

Manager: Juanita Flynn, since 1985

MER: 1.00%

The good news here is that Maritime Life has reduced the MER for the second year in a row. Two years ago it stood at 1.75%, now it is down to 1% and the manager has a fighting chance to bring the returns up to at least average for the money market category. The portfolio is a mix of T-bills and bankers' acceptances. Returns are still sub-par so the rating doesn't go up yet, but there's hope.

METROPOLITAN LIFE M.V.P. FUNDS

Metropolitan Life sold its Canadian business to the Mutual Life Assurance Company of Canada in Spring, 1998. The MetLife MVP family of segregated funds was part of that deal. Sales of these funds were suspended on May 1, 1998 and their future is uncertain, although they continue to be actively managed. They may at some point be merged with other funds in the Mutual group. Since they are not available for purchase at this time, I've suspended the ratings until further developments are announced.

NATIONAL BANK OF CANADA

THE COMPANY

Like many other organizations with regular mutual fund families, National Bank of Canada has moved into the segregated fund business as well, with a family called InvesNat Protected Funds. This group of five funds was launched in January, 1998.

Although several of the funds have the same name, general mandate, and manager as regular mutual funds in the InvesNat lineup, they are not clones of those funds. The portfolios are expected to be somewhat different, so the returns will vary as well.

None of these new funds has been in existence long enough to receive a rating.

THE DETAILS

NUMBER OF FUNDS:	5
ASSETS UNDER MANAGEMENT:	$75 MILLION
LOAD CHARGE:	NONE
SWITCHING CHARGE:	NONE
WHERE SOLD:	QUEBEC AND NEW BRUNSWICK
HOW SOLD:	NATIONAL BANK BRANCHES
PHONE NUMBER:	N/A
WEB SITE ADDRESS:	N/A
E-MAIL ADDRESS:	N/A

FUND SUMMARY

$$$$ - NONE
$$$ - NONE
$$ - NONE
$ - NONE
NR - CANADIAN BOND, CANADIAN EQUITY, GROWTH BALANCED, INTERNATIONAL, RETIREMENT BALANCED

BEST CHOICES: N/A
BEST FOR RRSPs: N/A
BEST UNRATEDS: CANADIAN BOND

FUND RATINGS

The funds in this group have not been in existence long enough to qualify for a rating.

NATIONAL LIFE FUNDS

THE COMPANY

National Life is a member of the Industrial-Alliance Group. However, it offers its own line of five segregated funds to investors. There was some controversy about their performance-reporting method in the past, but that has now been cleared up and the funds in this group use the same reporting standard as most of the industry.

THE DETAILS

NUMBER OF FUNDS:	5
ASSETS UNDER MANAGEMENT:	$600 MILLION
LOAD CHARGE:	BACK: MAX. 5%
SWITCHING CHARGE:	FOUR FREE TRANSFERS PER YEAR, $50 THEREAFTER
WHERE SOLD:	ACROSS CANADA
HOW SOLD:	THROUGH LIFE INSURANCE BROKERS
PHONE NUMBER:	(416) 585-8094 OR 1-800-977-2116
WEB SITE ADDRESS:	WWW.NATIONAL-LIFE.CA
E-MAIL ADDRESS:	N/A

FUND SUMMARY

$$$$ - NONE
$$$ - BALANCED, EQUITIES, FIXED INCOME
$$ - GLOBAL EQUITIES
$ - MONEY MARKET
NR - NONE
BEST CHOICES: BALANCED, EQUITIES
BEST FOR RRSPs: BALANCED, FIXED INCOME
BEST UNRATEDS: N/A

FUND RATINGS

CANADIAN EQUITY FUNDS

NATIONAL EQUITIES FUND $$$ ↓ G * RSP S CE

Manager: Michael Weir, since 1997

MER: 2.40%

The management style of this fund is top-down, which involves identifying industry sectors that will outperform the market and then selecting companies that should be among the leaders in that area. In the first half of 1998, the portfolio was weighted towards the industrial sector and financial services, but about a quarter of the assets were in resource issues. You would have expected that to be a drag on returns, but the fund managed to turn in yet another above-average year, gaining 15.3% for the 12 months to June 30/98. Longer term results, which pre-date Weir's arrival on the scene, are also above average. Very good safety record adds to this fund's attractiveness.

U.S. AND INTERNATIONAL EQUITY FUNDS

NATIONAL GLOBAL EQUITIES FUND $$ → G * £ S IE

Manager: James Fairweather (Martin Currie Investment Management), since inception (1993)

MER: 2.75%

This fund's a bit of a cheat. It invests entirely in units of another mutual fund, the Edinburgh-based Martin Currie International Growth Fund, run by James Fairweather. The fund had been going along just fine when all of a sudden it hit a wall. Gain for the year to June 30/98 was a meagre 1.7%, way below average for the international category. A contributing factor was a relatively heavy weighting (24%) in Asia and Latin America in the first half of '98. Unfortunately, that bad performance pulled all the longer term results out to three years to below average, although the five-year return is still good. Rating drops a notch while we await a return to past glories.

BALANCED FUNDS

NATIONAL BALANCED FUND $$$ ↓ FI/G * RSP CBAL

Managers: Nang Cheung, since inception (1992); Michael Weir, since 1997

MER: 2.40%

The portfolio of this fund offers a blend of Canadian stocks, foreign mutual funds, bonds, mortgages, and T-bills, so there's a little something of everything. The portfolio was fairly evenly balanced in the first half of '98, with about 53% of the holdings in stocks and the balance in bonds, mortgages, and short-term notes. Gain for the year to June 30/98 was a good 11.6%, and the results for all time periods out to five years are above average. Excellent safety record; historically, there is only an 8% chance of loss in any given 12-month period.

FIXED INCOME AND MONEY MARKET FUNDS

NATIONAL FIXED INCOME FUND $$$ → FI * RSP S CB

Manager: Nang Cheung, since 1985

MER: 2.00%

This fund offers a good mix of bonds, with a fairly even balance between federal, provincial, and corporate issues. The manager uses a highly disciplined approach to assess interest rate trends and determine the correct mix of maturities for the portfolio. Returns have been above average. Gain for the year ending June 30/98 was 9%. Ten-year average annual compound rate of return was 9.8%, just a touch above the average for the bond fund category.

NATIONAL MONEY MARKET FUND $ ↓ C * RSP S CMM

Manager: Antony Krosel, since inception (1992)

MER: 1.60%

Sound portfolio, about equally divided between government T-bills and corporate notes. However, returns are below average for the money market category, due in part to the relatively high MER.

NN FINANCIAL

THE COMPANY

NN Financial was established in 1989 through the merger of Halifax Life and MONY Life of Canada. It is a member of the ING Group, a large, Netherlands-based multinational financial corporation that operates in 58 nations worldwide. The company has been aggressively expanding its segregated fund line in this country over the past few years.

The guarantee here is not up to the standard now being set by many other seg fund groups, providing protection for just 75% of your total investment at maturity or death. Many companies now offer 100% guarantees, so if this is important to you, check around.

This company did not provide the names of individual fund managers, only the corporations that handle the responsibilities.

THE DETAILS

NUMBER OF FUNDS:	14
ASSETS UNDER MANAGEMENT:	$1.3 BILLION
LOAD CHARGE:	BACK: MAX. 6% ON ALL FUNDS EXCEPT MONEY MARKET
SWITCHING CHARGE:	FOUR FREE TRANSFERS PER YEAR, $25 THEREAFTER
WHERE SOLD:	ACROSS CANADA
HOW SOLD:	THROUGH LICENSED LIFE INSURANCE BROKERS
PHONE NUMBER:	(416) 391-2200
WEB SITE ADDRESS:	WWW.INGFIN.COM
E-MAIL ADDRESS:	THROUGH WEB SITE

FUND SUMMARY

$$$$ - NONE

$$$ - ASSET ALLOCATION, BOND, CAN-EURO, MONEY MARKET

$$ - CAN-AM, CANADIAN GROWTH, CANADIAN 35 INDEX, DIVIDEND

$ - CAN-ASIAN, ELITE, T-BILL

NR - CAN-DAQ 100, CAN-EMERGE, CAN-GLOBAL BOND

Best Choices: Asset Allocation, Bond
Best for RRSPs: Asset Allocation, Bond
Best unrateds: Can-Daq 100

FUND RATINGS

CANADIAN EQUITY FUNDS

NN CANADIAN GROWTH FUND $$ → G * RSP S CE

Managers: RT Capital Management and Jones Heward Investment Counsel, since 1992

MER: 2.80%

This fund uses a dual manager system to cover all the investment bases. One (RT Capital Management) focuses on large corporations with good growth potential. The other (Jones Heward) concentrates on small-cap stocks. For a time it seemed to be an uncomfortable blend, as this fund's returns tended to be below average. However, the year ending June 30/97 signalled the beginning of an improvement, with a gain of 27.3%. And the team followed that up with another above average gain of 14.8% for the year to June 30/98. So we're now looking at a fund on the upswing, with a three-year average annual compound rate of return of 17.4%, slightly better than the norm for Canadian stock funds as a group. Rating moves ahead a notch as a result.

NN CANADIAN 35 INDEX FUND $$ → G * RSP S CE

Manager: ING Investment Management, since inception (1989)

MER: 2.55%

This is an index fund, designed to track the TSE 35 Index. So if the blue-chips do well, so will you. Lately, the Canadian market has been strong, and so has this fund, with an average annual compound rate of return of 18.7% for the three years to June 30/98. Even though the companion Canadian Growth Fund is improving, this one continues to put up the better returns. It remains the better bet, at least for now.

NN DIVIDEND FUND $$ → G * RSP S INC

Manager: ING Investment Management, since 1994

MER: 2.60%

Trying to compare one dividend fund with another is often an apples and oranges situation. In recent years, those funds that have heavy weightings in high-yield common stocks, such as the banks, have turned in very impressive total returns. But that has been due to the big price advances for those stocks in the marketplace. More traditional dividend funds that invest a large portion of their assets in preferred shares, such as this one, have lagged behind on the total return side. But in terms of income distribution, they have usually performed much more effectively. This fund is an example of that investment approach, ranking in the high first quartile in income distribution over the past three years. This makes the fund a good choice if you're looking for tax-advantaged income, as NN offers the option of receiving any distributions in cash if the fund is held outside a registered plan.

U.S. AND INTERNATIONAL EQUITY FUNDS

NN CAN-AM FUND $$ → G * RSP S USE

Manager: Newcastle Capital Management, since inception (1992)

MER: 2.65%

This is one of the growing number of funds that uses derivatives to retain full RRSP eligibility while providing increased foreign exposure. In this case, S&P 500 stock index futures are used to produce results that will replicate the rise (or fall) of that key U.S. index. Results to date have been good, with an average annual return of 19.3% for the five years to June 30/98. But that was only slightly better than average for U.S. equity funds as a group. And keep in mind that those were good years for the U.S. stock market. When it goes south, this fund will follow.

NN CAN-ASIAN FUND $ ↑ G * RSP S FEE

Manager: Newcastle Capital Management, since 1995

MER: 2.65%

This fund uses derivatives to provide exposure to the major Far East markets without using foreign content room in an RRSP. Like all other Far East funds, it got rocked by the Asian crisis, losing just under 35% in the year to June 30/98. Still, that was better than average for the Far East category, if that's any consolation. In my view, Asian funds are too speculative for RRSPs.

NN CAN-EURO FUND $$$ → G * RSP S EE

Manager: Newcastle Capital Management, since inception (1995)

MER: 2.65%

NN offers several RRSP-eligible funds that use index futures contracts to provide international exposure without taking up foreign content room. This one focuses on six major European markets: the U.K., France, Germany, the Netherlands, Switzerland, and Italy. Those markets have been hot in recent years and the fund's numbers reflect that, with an average annual compound rate of return of 30.5% over the three-year period to June 30/98.

BALANCED FUNDS

NN ASSET ALLOCATION FUND $$$ ↓ FI/G * RSP S CBAL

Manager: RT Capital Management, since 1992

MER: 2.65%

Invests primarily in a mix of TSE 300 issues and high-quality bonds. At no time will any asset class exceed 75% of the portfolio, or be less than 25%, except for money market securities, which are capped at 25% maximum. The performance of this fund has been steadily improving; it produced another good gain of 13.9% for the year to June 30/98. All returns out to five years are now above average for their time period. Good safety record adds to its attractiveness.

NN ELITE FUND $ ↓ FI/G RSP S D

Manager: Newcastle Capital Management, since inception (1994)

MER: 2.30%

You won't find many entries like this in seg fund family lineups. It's a hedge fund, designed to provide returns that are independent of the broad movements of stock and bond markets. If you buy into it, you'll be acquiring an unusual portfolio that includes discounted bank debt, distressed securities, long/short equity positions, and various arbitrage plays. If you understand all that stuff and want to be part of it, fine. Most people don't. For all this complexity, the returns are not impressive; average annual gain for the three years to June 30/98 was 7.5%.

FIXED INCOME AND MONEY MARKET FUNDS

NN BOND FUND $$$ → FI * RSP S CB

Manager: ING Investment Management, since 1992

MER: 2.30%

This fund continues to produce above-average returns for its investors. The gain of 12.6% in the 12 months to June 30/98 was comfortably above average for the bond fund category. Longer term results are also better than average. Portfolio is mainly invested in federal and provincial bonds, with a few corporates mixed in. A good choice if you're a client of NN.

NN MONEY MARKET FUND $$$ → C No RSP S CMM

Manager: ING Investment Management, since 1994

MER: 1.00%

Portfolio is a mix of corporate notes and T-bills. Much better returns than the companion T-Bill Fund, due in part to a lower management fee. This should be your preferred choice between the two funds.

NN T-BILL FUND $ ↓ C * RSP S CMM

Manager: ING Investment Management, since inception (1986)

MER: 1.30%

Invests only in federal and provincial T-bills, giving it a high degree of safety. Returns are well below average, however. The companion Money Market Fund is a better choice.

NORTH WEST LIFE

THE COMPANY

The funds offered by North West Life are the same Ecoflex family that is available through Industrial Alliance. See the Industrial Alliance entry for complete information.

ROYAL & SUN ALLIANCE INVESTMENT FUNDS

THE COMPANY

In 1996, Royal Insurance merged with Sun Alliance to form Royal & Sun Alliance Life Insurance Company, a U.K.-based firm with over 40,000 employees in more than 100 countries. The Canadian seg funds changed their name in March, 1998 to reflect that merger.

All Royal & Sun Alliance funds guarantee you won't get back less than you invested on death or at policy maturity, so there's solid downside protection.

THE DETAILS

NUMBER OF FUNDS:	9
ASSETS UNDER MANAGEMENT:	$430 MILLION
LOAD CHARGE:	NO LOAD OR BACK-END LOAD OPTIONS: MAX. 4.5%
SWITCHING CHARGE:	FOUR FREE TRANSFERS PER YEAR, $50 THEREAFTER
WHERE SOLD:	ACROSS CANADA EXCEPT NORTHWEST TERRITORIES
HOW SOLD:	THROUGH REGIONAL OFFICES, MANAGING GENERAL AGENCIES, OR INDEPENDENT BROKERS
PHONE NUMBER:	1-800-263-1747
WEB SITE ADDRESS:	WWW.ROYALSUNALLIANCE.CA
E-MAIL ADDRESS:	N/A

FUND SUMMARY

$$$$ - NONE
$$$ - BALANCED, EQUITY, INCOME, MONEY MARKET
$$ - INTERNATIONAL EQUITY
$ - NONE
NR - CANADIAN GROWTH, DIVIDEND, GLOBAL EMERGING MARKETS, U.S. EQUITY

BEST CHOICES: BALANCED, EQUITY
BEST FOR RRSPs: BALANCED, EQUITY, INCOME
BEST UNRATEDS: U.S. EQUITY

FUND RATINGS

CANADIAN EQUITY FUNDS

ROYAL & SUN ALLIANCE
EQUITY FUND $$$ → G No/* RSP S CE

Manager: John Smolinski, since inception (1990)

MER: 2.30%

This is a value-oriented fund that uses a bottom-up approach for stock selection, emphasizing corporate fundamentals. Conservatively managed, with blue-chip issues favoured, although smaller growth stocks may also be included. The portfolio was weighted towards the financial services sector (24%) and the oil and gas sector (11%) in the first half of '98, with good diversification across other areas of the economy. Performance continues to be strong, with a gain of 16.1% for the year ending June 30/98. Five-year average annual compound rate of return was 15.1%, much better than average for the Canadian equity category. A good choice for clients of this company.

U.S. AND INTERNATIONAL EQUITY FUNDS

ROYAL & SUN ALLIANCE
INTERNATIONAL EQUITY FUND $$ → G No/* £ S IE

Manager: Ken Spry, since inception (1994)

MER: 2.57%

The mandate of this fund is long-term capital appreciation through investments in countries outside North America. In addition to common stocks, the manager may invest in convertibles, warrants, options, and other derivatives. Currency management also plays an important role in the overall strategic approach. In the first part of '98, about a quarter of the portfolio was in Japan and the Far East, with most of the balance in Europe. Results have tended to be about average for international funds that are excluded from the North American market. Average annual compound rate for the three years to June 30/98 was 12.2%.

BALANCED FUNDS

ROYAL & SUN ALLIANCE
BALANCED FUND $$$ ↓ FI/G No/* RSP S CBAL

Managers: John Smolinski and Rob Rublee, since inception (1990)

MER: 2.30%

This is one of those funds that manages to produce profits most of the time, with a relatively low level of risk. The equity side of the portfolio is selected on the basis of a conservative, value-oriented methodology. The fixed-income side is run using an "interest rate anticipation approach". The mandate puts a cap of 75% on the proportion of the fund that can be in stocks or bonds at any given time, but usually the ratios are kept in closer balance. In the first part of '98, for example, about 55% of the portfolio was in bonds, 42% in stocks, and the rest in cash. Returns have been steadily improving in recent years. Gain for the year ending June 30/98 was a better-than-average 12.4%. Five-year average annual compound rate of return was just a touch above the norm for the balanced fund category, at 11.1%. Good safety record. Rating moves up to $$$ this time around.

FIXED INCOME AND MONEY MARKET FUNDS

ROYAL & SUN ALLIANCE
INCOME FUND $$$ → FI No/* RSP S CB

Manager: Rob Rublee, since inception (1990)

MER: 1.80%

Manager Rob Rublee uses a two-pronged investment approach here. Two thirds of the portfolio is structured to mirror the ScotiaMcLeod Universe Bond Index. The other third uses an "interest rate anticipation" approach, which simply means the manager trades actively to attempt to benefit from moves in the bond/interest rate market. As with other funds in this group, returns have been improving. Gain for the year to June 30/98 was a healthy 9.6%. Three-year average annual compound rate of return was 10.4%, above average for the bond fund category. Rating moves to $$$.

ROYAL & SUN ALLIANCE
MONEY MARKET FUND $$$ → C No/* RSP S CMM

Manager: Dale McMaster, since inception (1993)

MER: 1.00%

This fund invests entirely in corporate issues to enhance performance. Returns have been comfortably above average.

STANDARD LIFE IDEAL FUNDS

THE COMPANY

Standard Life offers two families of funds. This is the segregated group, known as the Ideal funds. For details on the non-segregated funds, see the Standard Life entry in the Mutual Funds section.

THE DETAILS

NUMBER OF FUNDS:	4
ASSETS UNDER MANAGEMENT:	$828 MILLION
LOAD CHARGE:	BACK: MAX. 3.5%
SWITCHING CHARGE:	NONE
WHERE SOLD:	ACROSS CANADA
HOW SOLD:	THROUGH LICENSED AGENTS AND BROKERS
PHONE NUMBER:	1-888-841-6633
WEB SITE ADDRESS:	WWW.STANDARDLIFE.CA
E-MAIL ADDRESS:	N/A

FUND SUMMARY

$$$$ - NONE
$$$ - BALANCED, EQUITY, MONEY MARKET
$$ - BOND
$ - NONE
NR - NONE

BEST CHOICES: BALANCED, EQUITY
BEST FOR RRSPs: BALANCED, MONEY MARKET
BEST UNRATEDS: N/A

FUND RATINGS

CANADIAN EQUITY FUNDS

STANDARD LIFE IDEAL EQUITY FUND $$$ → G * RSP S CE

Manager: Standard Life Portfolio Management

MER: 2.00%

A good performer, but don't confuse it (and it's easy to do) with the Standard Life Equity Mutual Fund, which is not a segregated fund. This fund gained 20.1% last year, well above average for this category. Returns right out to 10 years are also above average. Strategy is to focus on a small core group of about 25 companies. A very good choice among seg funds. Formerly called Standard Life Equity 2000 Fund and before that Standard Equifund.

BALANCED FUNDS

STANDARD LIFE IDEAL BALANCED FUND $$$ → G * RSP S CBAL

Manager: Standard Life Portfolio Management

MER: 2.00%

This is a well-diversified balanced fund that offers a mix of high-quality bonds, blue-chip Canadian equities, and some U.S. stocks. The aim is to provide capital appreciation and income while limiting risk. Returns have improved significantly in recent years. Gain for the 12 months ending June 30/98 was 14.7%, much better than the norm for the balanced category. Looking farther back, results for all time periods out to 10 years are also better than average. This fund would be a very good choice for a segregated RRSP plan with this company. Rating moves up to $$$ this year. Formerly called the Standard Life Balanced 2000 Fund and before that known as the Standard Diversifund.

FIXED INCOME AND MONEY MARKET FUNDS

STANDARD LIFE IDEAL BOND FUND $$ → FI * RSP S CB

Manager: Standard Life Portfolio Management

MER: 2.00%

This is a conservatively managed bond fund that invests almost exclusively in government issues. The bulk of the portfolio was in short- to mid-term bonds in mid-'98, a strategy that limits risk but also lowers return potential. As a result, latest returns have been a bit below the norm for the bond fund category. Gain for the year to June 30/98 was 8.3% (versus an average of 8.6% as reported by *The Globe and Mail*). Long-term record is also slightly below average. Formerly known as Standard Life Bond 2000 Fund.

STANDARD LIFE IDEAL
MONEY MARKET FUND $$$ → C * RSP S CMM

Manager: Standard Life Portfolio Management

MER: 1.00%

Most of this portfolio is invested in corporate notes, which helps to boost returns a bit. Performance has been comfortably above average for the money market category. A good spot for parking cash.

SYNCHRONY FUNDS

In early September, 1998, Talvest Fund Management and Maritime Life joined forces to create a brand-new line of segregated fund portfolios under the name Synchrony. The concept offers a different approach to segregated fund investing, and has been dubbed "Seg Wraps" by the two companies. The idea is to combine some of the best Talvest Funds with the top offerings from Maritime Life into five distinct packages, each of which is tailored to a specific investor need. The makeup of the portfolios will be determined by Talvest using tactical asset allocation principles.

The Synchrony Funds feature the usual seg fund guarantees, with an extra kicker: an automatic daily reset feature that allows unitholders to lock in market gains on a daily basis.

These portfolios are too new for any meaningful analysis and full details were not available at press time. However, investors interested in seg funds may wish to take a look at this new venture before making a purchase decision.

TRIMARK SEG FUNDS

A number of mainstream mutual fund companies have created segregated lines of their products recently. Trimark is one such organization, with a family of 13 funds that was launched in late June, 1998 in partnership with AIG Life Canada.

These seg funds all mirror existing Trimark mutual funds, and will invest in units of the underlying fund on which they are based. The returns may vary somewhat, but that will be due to differences in the MERs and in the timing of purchases. Therefore, these seg funds will not be reviewed and rated as independent funds. For details on the Trimark funds, consult the section that deals with the company's mutual funds.

WESTBURY LIFE

THE COMPANY

Westbury Life is owned by the Royal Bank and is part of RBC Insurance. It is not a big player in the seg fund market, with only three active funds.

THE DETAILS

NUMBER OF FUNDS:	3
ASSETS UNDER MANAGEMENT:	$123 MILLION
LOAD CHARGE:	BACK: MAX. 7%
SWITCHING CHARGE:	ONE FREE TRANSFER PER YEAR, $25 THEREAFTER
WHERE SOLD:	ACROSS CANADA
HOW SOLD:	THROUGH INDEPENDENT INSURANCE AGENTS
PHONE NUMBER:	(905) 528-6766 - DENNIS CRAIG
WEB SITE ADDRESS:	N/A
E-MAIL ADDRESS:	N/A

FUND SUMMARY

$$$$ - NONE
$$$ - BALANCED, EQUITY GROWTH
$$ - NONE
$ - BOND
NR - NONE

BEST CHOICES: BALANCED, EQUITY GROWTH
BEST FOR RRSPs: BALANCED, EQUITY GROWTH
BEST UNRATEDS: N/A

FUND RATINGS

CANADIAN EQUITY FUNDS

WESTBURY LIFE EQUITY GROWTH FUND $$$ → G * RSP S CE

Manager: Donald C. Conner (Yield Management Group), since 1998

MER: 2.41%

The aim of this fund is to track the performance of the TSE 100 Index (it used to be the TSE 35), and it is doing a good job at it. The portfolio is well diversified and consists mainly of mid-size and large-cap companies. Returns have been steadily improving. Gain for the year ending June

30/98 was 15.9%, and that came on the heels of an advance of almost 30% the year before. Three-year average annual compound rate of return was a very good 18.6%. Like all other equity funds, this one was hit over the summer of 1998. However, there is no reason to believe it will not perform well over the long haul. A new manager took charge in April, 1998, but the overall direction remains in the hands of the Yield Management Group. Rating advances to $$$.

BALANCED FUNDS

WESTBURY LIFE BALANCED FUND $$$ → FI/G * RSP S CBAL

Manager: Michael C. Doran (Yield Management Group), since inception (1991)

MER: 2.42%

This is a somewhat unusual balanced fund in that most of its stock exposure has been through TIPs and index futures on the TSE 35. However, that may change as a result of the appointment of Donald Conner in April, '98 to handle the equities side of the portfolio. The fixed-income portion invests in Government of Canada bonds and T-bills. Results have improved to above average. Gain for the year to June 30/98 was 12.9%. Three-year annual compound rate of return was 14.7%.

FIXED INCOME AND MONEY MARKET FUNDS

WESTBURY LIFE BOND FUND $ → FI * RSP S CB

Manager: Art Yeates (Yield Management Group), since 1995

MER: 2.07%

This fund offers a mix of government and corporate issues, and some mortgage-backed securities. Return for the 12 months to June 30/98 was below average for the bond fund category, at 8.1%. The manager reported this "was due entirely to the unanticipated and ongoing dispute involving the right of B.C. Tel to redeem one of its debentures at an unfavourable price. The adverse impact of this one event was approximately 0.6%". These are the kinds of stories you never hear about in the media, but that have an impact on your wallet!

LABOUR-SPONSORED FUNDS

It's been a rough road for Canada's labour-sponsored venture capital funds since the federal government's 1996 budget. That was when Finance Minister Paul Martin decided that too much money was flowing into these tax-advantaged offerings. Investors had gone crazy in the previous RRSP season, pumping in $700 million in Ontario alone, the province that offers the most fund choices. With a fat federal tax credit of 20%, which was matched by Ontario and several other provinces, the cost to federal and provincial treasuries was becoming onerous.

So the minister took action. The federal tax credit was cut to 15% from 20%. The maximum amount eligible for a credit in any year was dropped from $5,000 down to $3,500. Holding period restrictions were tightened. The participating provinces played follow-the-leader in their budgets and suddenly labour funds didn't look like such a great tax shelter any more.

Predictably, sales slumped. The 1997 RRSP season saw them tumble back to $200 million in Ontario. Things got even worse in 1998, with new investments down to $125 million. The whole concept appeared to be on its way out the door, another footnote in the long history of tax-advantaged investments that became too popular with the public. Mr. Martin had done his work well.

Too well, it turns out. The government didn't really want to shut down the funds: they've been very useful in channelling venture capital to young and growing enterprises, creating jobs in the process. Mr. Martin just wanted to slow things down a bit. So in September Ottawa announced some changes designed to make labour funds more appealing in the 1999 RRSP season. The 15% federal credit (matched by several provinces) was left intact. But the maximum annual amount eligible for the tax break was restored to $5,000, effective with the 1998 tax year. That means investors can now obtain a federal tax credit of up to $750, instead of a limit of $525 as before. Assuming the participating provinces make a similar change, the maximum total tax credit from a $5,000 investment for the 1998 tax year will rise to $1,500.

As well, the three-year "cooling off" period is to be eliminated. This is a rule that prevented anyone who redeems shares in a labour fund from making a new purchase and claiming a tax credit within three years. The change is important, because people who bought units back in 1993 when the holding period was five years (it is now eight) are now able to cash them in. Without a rule change, some funds were looking at potentially large redemptions. The prospect of a new tax credit may be enough to persuade a significant number of people who cash in to re-invest their money.

That's not the end of the story. As of this writing, in early September, there was another change in the works that may have an even bigger impact on the future fortunes of these funds. Amendments passed in June, 1998 to the Income Tax Act in the form of Bill C-28 will allow shares in labour-sponsored funds that are held in RRSPs to be classified as qualifying small business assets for purposes of calculating your allowable foreign content. Changes to the appropriate regulations still had to be promulgated as this was written, but that process was expected to be completed during the fall and had the approval of the Department of Finance.

Assuming everything proceeds as planned, you'll be able to increase the foreign content in your RRSP to above the 20% limit if you hold any labour fund units. The additional allowable foreign content is three times the value of the labour fund assets. However, your total foreign content may not exceed 40% of your plan.

For example, suppose you buy $5,000 worth of labour fund units for your RRSP. That will entitle you to an additional $15,000 in foreign content, over and above the 20% limit. For those who have been buying labour funds for some years and have large RRSPs, this change could open up many thousands of dollars of foreign content room.

To illustrate, a $350,000 (book value) RRSP would normally be limited to $70,000 in foreign content under the 20% rule. But if you've bought $22,000 worth of labour funds over the past five years, you will be able to add another $66,000 to that, bringing your total foreign content maximum to $136,000, or 38.9% of your plan.

There are three points to be aware of, however.

1) Some labour funds were advising investors in September that they could proceed on this basis immediately. However, a prominent lawyer I spoke to who has been tracking the progress of the amendments advises waiting until the regulations are formally approved and announced. Otherwise, if the federal cabinet changes its mind, you'd have no recourse.

2) RRSP administrators will have to figure out how to adjust their computers to calculate the new foreign content limits for affected accounts. The process has started, I am told, but it may take some time.

3) New labour fund purchases do not immediately qualify for the full foreign content extension. There is a three-month phase in period. For example, suppose you buy $5,000 worth of new units in January. No additional foreign content is allowed in that month. However, over the next three months (February, March, and April), you can add an additional $5,000 a month in foreign holdings until you reach the extra $15,000 total that you're allowed.

Of course, labour funds are not confined to RRSPs, but most people have been purchasing them that way. If you invest the maximum amount eligible for a tax credit in an RRSP under the recently revised rules, here's how it will work out for someone with a 50% marginal tax rate:

Amount invested	$5,000
Federal tax credit	750
Provincial tax credit*	750
Cost before RRSP deduction	3,500
RRSP deduction @ 50%	2,500
Net cost	1,000

* Where applicable. May vary in some provinces.

Of course, your tax bracket will be a major factor in deciding whether this is a sensible choice. If you're in a 27% bracket, for example, the net cost of a $5,000 investment increases to $2,150. The 15% federal and, where applicable, provincial credits are the same no matter what your tax bracket, but the tax saving generated by the RRSP contribution is less for low-bracket taxpayers. If this is your situation, you should ask yourself whether there are better investment choices available.

That's because the performance of labour-sponsored funds to date has left much to be desired. The tax breaks are attractive, true. But you give up a lot to get them.

Here are some comparative returns. I've used small- to mid-cap Canadian equity funds as the yardstick, as they are closest in concept to the labour-sponsored funds. All the figures are as published in *The Globe and Mail* and cover the period ending June 30, 1998. LS denotes a labour-sponsored fund.

	1 YEAR	2 YEARS*	3 YEARS*
Canadian Medical Discoveries (LS)	2.4%	0.5%	3.6%
Capital Alliance Ventures (LS)	1.2%	-3.2%	3.3%
VenGrowth (LS)	5.7%	7.9%	6.6%
Working Opportunity (LS)	8.5%	6.2%	7.9%
Working Ventures (LS)	3.4%	1.3%	2.5%
Altamira Special Growth	2.5%	10.6%	14.4%
Ivy Enterprise	13.6%	17.3%	18.2%
Guardian Enterprise	-4.6%	12.2%	22.4%
Average all Small- to Mid-Cap**	3.8%	10.5%	14.9%
Average all Labour Funds**	1.1%	2.3%	3.0%

*Average annual compound rate of return
** *The Globe and Mail*

As you can see, you're giving away a lot in terms of return. If you'd invested $5,000 in the average labour fund three years previously, your units would have been worth $5,463 on July 1, 1998. The same investment in the average Canadian small- to mid-cap fund would have been worth $7,585.

However, three years ago you would have earned $2,000 worth of special tax credits by investing in a labour fund because the combined federal and provincial credits at that time were 40%. (The RRSP credit would be the same in either case.) So when you factor that into the equation, the labour-sponsored fund does better, even with the poor rate of return.

Of course, if the average labour-sponsored fund continues to underperform the average small- to mid-cap mutual fund, the tax credit advantage will eventually disappear. However, that's not a given. Returns on labour funds are starting to show some improvement. Earl Storie and David Ferguson of VenGrowth, one of the better funds in this category, point out that venture capital investments by definition take some time to mature. Now that is starting to happen, however, and looking ahead they have set a target annual rate of return in the mid-teens. If they can pull it off, labour funds will start to look very attractive to investors, especially with the tax credit sweeteners.

If you are considering investing in these funds, here are some of the issues to look at:

See what tax credits the fund qualifies for. All funds get the federal credit but, outside of Ontario, all won't necessarily get a provincial tax credit. Some provinces offer no provincial tax credits at all; others (such as Quebec, Manitoba, and B.C.) restrict them to just one or two provincially sponsored funds. Ask before you invest.

Ask if the fund is eligible for direct RRSP purchase. Some investors have adopted a strategy of buying labour-sponsored funds inside an RRSP, using "old" money to generate a tax credit outside the plan. This can be done with no problem in provinces such as Ontario. But the rules are different across the country. If you're interested in this approach, ask a sales rep whether it is allowed where you live.

Remember that the credits can only reduce your tax to zero. The tax credits generated by labour-sponsored funds aren't refundable. So if you don't owe enough tax to make full use of them, you won't get the maximum benefit from this strategy.

Recognize that the units are above-average risk. The mandate of all these funds is to invest in small to medium-size companies that are usually not publicly traded. Such companies may have above-average growth potential — but they're also higher risk than more established firms.

Don't forget that you can't get your money out. All labour-sponsored funds have a minimum holding period of eight years.

If you take your money out before then, you'll have to repay your tax credits — up to 30% of the value of your total investment! There are no exceptions to the eight-year rule. So these funds are not suitable for RRIFs or for people who are likely to need access to their cash within eight years.

Take into account the fact your returns may be below average. As I've pointed out, these funds have yet to prove they can generate decent returns over the long term, although results are improving.

Here's a strategy that will help make a labour fund investment more effective. If you invest in one of these funds and put the units in an RRSP, calculate your tax savings and re-invest that amount outside your registered plan. A solid mutual fund with strong capital gains potential is a good choice. This will provide a cushion in the event the labour-sponsored fund underperforms. For example, had you invested the $2,000 tax credit from a labour fund purchase three years ago in the Ivy Canadian Fund, it would have grown to about $3,400, before taxes, by June 30, 1998.

Another good strategy if you live in a province where several funds are available is to diversify. Ontario residents are especially blessed in this regard, as they have the widest range of funds available to them. There's no way of knowing which funds will perform best over the long term. So instead of putting all your money in just one, spread it around among three or four.

Here is a rundown of the labour-sponsored funds now available. Only those with a three-year record have a rating. "NR" in the legend means the fund doesn't yet qualify. Most of the funds are shown to have a higher-than-average risk factor because of their venture capital approach, however a few use strategies that reduce the risk inherent in this type of investing.

FUND REVIEWS

B.E.S.T. FUND   NR ↑ G #/* RSP LAB

Manager: Trinity Capital Securities, since inception (1996)

MER: 4.33%

B.E.S.T. stands for Business, Engineering, Science, and Technology. That gives you the focus of this fund in a nutshell. The management company is a highly respected

Toronto-based venture capital firm that invests some of its own money in every security selected for the fund. The screening process zeros in on firms that already have significant sales ($3 million – $15 million) and the capability to go public within two years. The fund has only been operational since early '97, so results to date are not indicative of future potential (the fund lost 2.9% in the year to June 30/98). Sold in Ontario only, through brokerage firms and financial planners. Call (416) 214-4616 for information.

CANADIAN MEDICAL DISCOVERIES FUND $$ ↑ G * RSP LAB

Manager: Dr. Calvin Stiller, since inception (1995)

MER: 4.91%

When this fund was first launched, I tipped it as one of the best prospects in the labour-sponsored universe. It operates in an area of rapid growth (medical technology) and the principals are extremely well connected in the medical world (the chairman and CEO, Dr. Calvin Stiller, is a renowned physician and scientist, one of Canada's leaders in the field of organ transplants, and the co-founder of Diversicare). The fund also has the advantage of being associated with MDS, the leading medical services company in Canada. Returns so far have been modest, with an average annual compound rate of return of just 3.6% for the three years ending June 30/98. However, I expect to see improvement down the road as some of the investments the fund is holding come to fruition. Residents of Ontario, Nova Scotia, and New Brunswick who buy these units will qualify for a provincial tax credit as well as a federal one. In all other provinces, only a federal credit is available. The fund is distributed by Talvest and available through brokers and financial planners. Call 1-800-268-8258 for more information, or consult a broker or planner.

CANADIAN SCIENCE AND TECHNOLOGY GROWTH FUND NR ↑ G * RSP LAB

Manager: Peter Day

MER: 5.50%

This is a promising new entry to the labour fund field. The managers seek investment opportunities in the technology sector, working in partnership with the National Research Council, the Natural Sciences and Engineering Research Council of Canada, and the Canadian Space Agency. The fund also benefits from a blue ribbon advisory board that includes some of the top names in Canada's research community. It is still too new to get any real feeling for future performance (the fund lost 1.4% in the year to June 30/98), but conceptually it looks appealing. A provincial tax credit is available to investors in Ontario and Nova Scotia. The units are distributed by Talvest and sold through brokers and financial planners. Call 1-800-268-8258 for more information.

CANADIAN VENTURE OPPORTUNITIES FUND $ ↑ G * RSP LAB

Manager: Goodman and Company, since 1997

MER: 6.37%

Although this fund has technically been in existence long enough to acquire a rating, this is really a case of starting over. In its original manifestation as the Integrated Growth Fund, this was a sad performer, recording big losses for investors. It has now been renamed and the management responsibility placed in the hands of Goodman & Company, who run the successful Dynamic Funds. About two thirds of the fund's assets are in publicly traded small-cap companies. It has been a tough year for small-cap stocks, and that is reflected in the fund's latest returns, which show a loss of 9.4% for the 12 months to June 30/98. This one must show some significant improvement before I can recommend it. Available only in Ontario through brokers and financial planners. Call 1-888-527-4811 for information.

CAPITAL ALLIANCE VENTURES INC. $$ ↑ G No RSP LAB

Manager: Richard Charlebois, since inception (1994)

MER: 4.04%

This is another fund that specializes in technology issues, with special emphasis on companies in the Ottawa area, where it is based and where most of the shareholders live. The fund's goal is to reach $75 million in assets and then close the doors to new money. However, the slowdown in new investments that followed the reduction in the federal and provincial tax credits indicate it will take some time to reach that goal. Average annual compound rate of return for the three years to June 30/98 was 3.3%, slightly above average for the labour fund category. The fund is available through brokers and financial planners in Ontario and Quebec. Call 1-800-304-2330 for additional details.

CENTERFIRE GROWTH FUND   NR ↑ G * RSP LAB

Manager: Normand Lamarche, since inception (1997)

MER: 1.60%

This fund will invest in a broad range of industries (no sector focus here) with strong growth potential and what is known in the venture capital business as a clear "exit strategy". That means the manager must be able to foresee a way of cashing in on an investment and taking profits within a reasonable period of time. This could be achieved by taking the company public or selling the fund's interest to a third party. Manager Norm Lamarche is a former Altamira fund manager, so he has experience in running this type of operation. He is backed by a team of seasoned business people. The plan is to cap this fund when it reaches $50 million. By limiting the number of investments, the managers feel they can concentrate more effectively on improving performance. Initial results have been impressive; the fund gained 4.3% for the year to June 30/98, well above average for the labour category. Available only in Ontario. Call (416) 777-0707, ext. 222 for information.

C.I. COVINGTON FUND $$ ↑ G * RSP LAB

Managers: Grant Brown, since inception (1995) and Chip Vallis, since 1996

MER: 4.40%

This labour-sponsored venture capital fund is distributed through C.I., but operates on an independent basis. This has been one of my top labour fund recommendations from its inception. Grant Brown has established a sound reputation in the venture capital business over the years and Chip Vallis has a wealth of experience. The focus is on early-stage companies and one of the big successes to date has been a $2.5 million stake in Playdium Entertainment Corporation. That company now operates a high-tech video games emporium in Mississauga, Ont. that is exceeding all revenue projections. This fund's 5.5% average annual compound rate of return for the three years to June 30/98 may look modest, but investors in labour-sponsored funds shouldn't expect big returns at this early stage. In fact, that result is better than average for the category. If you're interested in a labour fund, this is one of the better choices available. The fund is distributed through the C.I. organization (Ontario residents only). Or you can contact them directly at (416) 365-0060 for more information.

CROCUS INVESTMENT FUND $$$ ↑ G No RSP LAB

Managers: James Umlah, Janice Lederman, Joyce Rankin, John Culligan, Natalie Braun, Brad Peacock

MER: 3.78%

This fund was created to promote industrial development in Manitoba and is only open to residents of that province. It does not limit itself to any specific sector of the economy. The fund has been quite successful in raising money from its limited base ($87 million to date). Performance has been among the best in the labour category. The fund scored the best one-year advance over the period to June 30/98, gaining 12.5%. That pulled the five-year average annual compound rate of return up to 6.2%, not the top but very good. The folks in Manitoba have a winner here. Units can be purchased through brokers, some mutual fund dealers, credit unions, and directly from Crocus Capital. Call 1-800-361-7777 or (204) 925-2401 for more details.

DGC ENTERTAINMENT VENTURES CORP. $$ ↑ G * RSP LAB

Manager: EVC Management Inc., since inception (1993)

MER: 5.60%

This is your chance to invest in the exciting world of movies, TV, the Internet, pop music, and just about any other entertainment venture you can think of. The fund is sponsored by the Directors Guild of Canada (the DGC in the name) and the board of directors includes several high-profile show biz personalities. The good news is that performance to date has been pretty good, too. The fund produced an average annual compound rate of return of 5.7% for the three years to June 30/98, one of the better results in this category. Sold in Ontario only.

ENSIS GROWTH FUND   NR ↑ G * RSP LAB

Manager: Bill Watchorn, Don Martin, John Liddle, Ken Bicknell, since inception (1998)

MER: 2.00%

Manitoba now has a second venture capital fund, to compete with that province's original Crocus Fund. The fund invests in small to medium-sized businesses based in the province and favours companies with high value-added products or services. No specific area is targeted; the managers will look at companies in all sectors of the economy. The company that oversees the money, ENSIS Management, was once named one of Canada's 50 best private managed companies by *The Financial Post*. Obviously, it's way too soon to forecast how this fund will do, but the Crocus Fund has been one of the best performers in the labour-sponsored category so it's clear that there are lots of opportunities in Manitoba. Distribution is being handled by the BPI Funds.

FESA ENTERPRISE VENTURE CAPITAL FUND $ ↑ G * RSP LAB

Managers: Eduard J. Mayer and Rob Mayer (Acorn Ventures), since inception (1995)

MER: 6.20%

FESA stands for the Federation of Engineering and Scientific Associations, but the fund's investment mandate does not limit it to those types of companies. Eduard Mayer is well experienced in venture capital funds, with more than 15 years of experience in the business. This fund is quite small ($7.4 million in assets) and the performance to date has not been particularly good. Net asset value declined 10.9% in the year to June 30/98 and the three-year average annual compound rate of return over that time was -4.1%. Available in Ontario only, however no new money is being accepted at this time. Call (416) 216-5356 for more information.

FIRST ONTARIO FUND $$$ ↓ G * RSP LAB

Managers: First Ontario Management, Crosbie Capital Management, and Co-operators Investment Counselling, since 1995

MER: 4.75%

This fund invests in a wide range of Ontario-based companies involved in everything from packaging to high-tech research. It is set apart from other labour-sponsored funds by its commitment to socially responsible investing. That makes this fund a good choice for those who are interested in putting their money into companies that are committed to environmental protection, good labour relations, and community support. As well, the managers adopt an investment strategy that is designed to reduce the risk normally inherent in venture capital funds by structuring most of their deals as senior ranking debt securities. About a quarter of the portfolio will always be invested in government bonds, which further reduces risk. Returns have been good for such a conservatively managed fund. Gain for the year to June 30/98 was 7.1%, one of the best results in the labour fund category. Three-year average annual compound rate of return was a more modest 3.8%, but that was also better than the norm for the peer group. Sold in Ontario only. Call 1-800-777-7506 or (416) 487-5444 for details.

QUEBEC SOLIDARITY FUND $$ → G * RSP LAB

Manager: Team

MER: 1.60%

This is the oldest and biggest of the labour-sponsored venture capital funds, with assets of more than $2.3 billion in mid-'98. Open only to Quebecers. Investments can at times be politically motivated. Average annual rate of return for the decade to June 30/98 was a modest 5.8%. Recent returns have been weaker; the fund gained only 3.9% over the past 12 months. The risk factor here is lessened by the size of the fund, which allows for greater diversification.

RETROCOMM GROWTH FUND

$$ ↑ G * RSP LAB

Manager: Black Investment Management, since inception (1995)

MER: 4.26%

The focus of this fund is on the construction industry, but it also will invest in firms involved in energy conservation and the environment. Investments are mainly in the private sector, with very few publicly traded companies held. Returns have been improving. Gain for the year to June 30/98 was above average, at 5.4%. However, the three-year average annual compound rate of return is under par for the labour category, at 2.6%. This fund is expanding its distribution base. It used to be available in Ontario only, but is now registered in Nova Scotia as well. Residents of Saskatchewan and New Brunswick may also be able to buy units in time for the 1999 RRSP season. Check with a broker or financial planner in your area or call 1-888-743-5627 or (905) 848-2430 for more information.

SPORTFUND

$$ ↑ G * RSP LAB

Manager: Joel Albin, since inception (1994)

MER: 4.85%

As you might guess from the name, the focus here is on industries involved in sports. That can cover everything from pitch-and-putt operations to snowboard manufacturers. The fund receives counsel from an advisory board that includes a number of well-known sports personalities. Three-year returns are above average, although latest results are weak. Closed to new investors and unlikely to reopen.

TRIAX GROWTH FUND

NR ↑ G * RSP LAB

Manager: Susan Coleman, Altamira, since inception (1995)

MER: 5.70%

This fund was an immediate hit with investors when it was launched just in time for the 1996 RRSP season. The dual attraction was Susan Coleman's reputation as a sound small-cap manager with Altamira and the fund's stated intention to focus on companies that already had a public listing or would soon be in a position to come out with an IPO. The result was an astonishing inflow of $135 million within six weeks of the fund's launch. But that flood has since been reduced to a trickle; the fund's assets stood at $188 million in mid-1998. Performance to date has been above average for the labour fund category, although it's nothing to get excited about. Return for the year to June 30/98 was 5.4%. One advantage this fund does offer is wide distribution; it is now available in all parts of the country except Saskatchewan and the Territories. For more information, call 1-800-407-0287 or visit the Triax web site at www.triaxcapital.com.

TRILLIUM GROWTH CAPITAL INC. $ ↑ G * RSP LAB

Managers: Richard Kinlough and John Hague, Ontario Corporate Funding Inc., since inception (1994)

MER: 5.60%

This fund employs a highly diversified approach to its investing strategy, with no more than 25% of the placements in any one industry sector, and no more than 10% in any single company. The parent company of the management firm is Canadian Corporate Funding Ltd. (CCFL), one of the country's leading merchant banking operations since its establishment in 1979. Results to date have not been impressive. The fund shows an average annual compound rate of return of -3.6% for the three years ending June 30/98. Available only in Ontario. Call 1-800-328-5988 for information.

VENGROWTH INVESTMENT FUND $$$ → G * RSP LAB

Managers: Earl Storie, David Ferguson, Allen Lupyrypa, Michael Cohen, since inception (1995)

MER: 3.90%

This is one of the better bets in the crowded labour-sponsored funds marketplace. The management team is well experienced in the venture capital field (they've been in the business since 1982) and they bring a highly disciplined approach to the difficult task of analyzing the profit potential of small operations. This fund focuses on companies that are already up and running, with annual sales of at least $3 million. That reduces the investment risk to some extent and increases the possibility of an early, profitable exit from their positions. Returns have been above average for the labour fund group, with average annual gains of 6.0% for the three years to July 31/98. If you are in the market for a labour-sponsored fund, this is certainly one you should look at. The units are distributed through BPI and are available through brokers and financial planners in Ontario only. Call 1-800-937-5146 for more information.

WORKING OPPORTUNITY FUND $$$ → G * RSP LAB

Manager: Mike Phillips

MER: 2.70%

This is a labour-sponsored venture capital fund just for British Columbia residents. Investment focus is on B.C.-based industries in the biotechnology, manufacturing, high-tech, tourism, and knowledge-based sectors. To be eligible, a firm must have less than $35 million in assets and be 80% located in B.C., with at least half the salaries and wages paid to B.C. employees. Started slowly and returns in the early years were low because most of the assets were held in short-term notes while investment opportunities were reviewed. However, returns have looked better recently. The fund gained 8.5% over the 12 months to June 30/98. Five-year average annual compound rate of return of 5.6% is slightly better than average for the labour fund category. The asset base has now grown to almost $200 million, making this one of the top five labour funds in Canada in terms of size. Sold by brokers and planners throughout B.C. Call 1-800-563-FUND for details or visit their web site (www.wofund.com/wof).

WORKING VENTURES CANADIAN FUND $$ → G * RSP LAB

Manager: Jim Hall, since inception (1990)

MER: 2.41%

This was the first labour-sponsored fund to be offered outside a single province, and money came flooding in faster than anyone could have imagined (current assets are about $750 million). That created big problems for fund president Ron Begg and his senior vice-president of investments, Jim Hall. Federal and provincial legislation requires that money flowing into these funds be invested in qualifying fledgling companies according to a set timetable. Working Ventures had accumulated too much cash to enable it to meet those requirements while exercising the appropriate due diligence on new proposals. As a result, the fund suspended new sales for the 1997 and 1998 RRSP seasons. However, they have announced their intention to reopen for business in time for 1999 RRSP sales. Returns to date have been low (average annual yield of just 2.9% for the five years ending June 30/98). However, they have shown recent improvement and should continue to do so now that a significant percentage of the assets have been deployed. The risk factor here is relatively low for this type of fund, because of its size and the large cash position. This is one of the few funds that is available throughout Canada. However, provincial tax credits are only available in some jurisdictions. Call 1-800-268-8244 for information or visit their web site at www.workingventures.ca.

THE BEST FUNDS AT A GLANCE

Here is a summary of all the funds that have earned a $$$ or $$$$ rating in this year's *Buyer's Guide*. This doesn't mean you should confine yourself to these funds. At times, there may be good reason to add some $$ funds to your portfolio; for example, for defensive purposes. However, the funds on the pages that follow should be considered first before selecting lower-rated alternatives.

CANADIAN EQUITY FUNDS

$$$$
ABC FUNDAMENTAL VALUE FUND

AIC ADVANTAGE FUND

BISSETT CANADIAN EQUITY FUND

BISSETT DIVIDEND INCOME FUND

BPI DIVIDEND INCOME FUND

ETHICAL GROWTH FUND

IVY CANADIAN FUND

PHILLIPS, HAGER & NORTH DIVIDEND INCOME FUND

ROYAL DIVIDEND FUND

$$$
AGF CANADIAN GROWTH FUND

AGF DIVIDEND FUND

AIC DIVERSIFIED CANADA FUND

AIM GT CANADA GROWTH CLASS

ALTAMIRA DIVIDEND FUND

ALTAMIRA NORTH AMERICAN RECOVERY FUND

ALTAMIRA SPECIAL GROWTH FUND

ASSOCIATE INVESTORS LTD.

ATLAS CANADIAN LARGE CAP GROWTH FUND

BANK OF MONTREAL FIRST CANADIAN DIVIDEND INCOME FUND

BANK OF MONTREAL FIRST CANADIAN GROWTH FUND

BANK OF MONTREAL FIRST CANADIAN SPECIAL GROWTH FUND

BEUTEL GOODMAN SMALL CAP FUND

BISSETT SMALL CAP FUND

BNP (CANADA) EQUITY FUND

BPI CANADIAN EQUITY VALUE FUND

CANADA TRUST STOCK FUND

CANADIAN ANAESTHETISTS MUTUAL ACCUMULATING FUND

CHOU RRSP FUND

CLEAN ENVIRONMENT EQUITY FUND

COLONIA SPECIAL GROWTH FUND

CO-OPERATORS CANADIAN EQUITY FUND

COTE 100 EXP

COTE 100 REER

CUNDILL SECURITY FUND

DESJARDINS DIVIDEND FUND

DESJARDINS ENVIRONMENT FUND

DYNAMIC DIVIDEND FUND

FIDELITY CANADIAN GROWTH COMPANY FUND

GBC CANADIAN GROWTH FUND

GREEN LINE CANADIAN EQUITY FUND

GREEN LINE DIVIDEND FUND

GREEN LINE VALUE FUND

GUARDIAN ENTERPRISE FUND

GUARDIAN GROWTH EQUITY FUND

GUARDIAN MONTHLY DIVIDEND FUND

HONGKONG BANK DIVIDEND INCOME FUND

HONGKONG BANK EQUITY FUND

HONGKONG BANK SMALL CAP GROWTH FUND

INDUSTRIAL DIVIDEND GROWTH FUND

INDUSTRIAL HORIZON FUND

INVESNAT SMALL CAPITALIZATION FUND

INVESTORS DIVIDEND FUND

INVESTORS SUMMA FUND

IVY ENTERPRISE FUND

LEITH WHEELER CANADIAN EQUITY FUND

LOTUS CANADIAN EQUITY FUND

MANULIFE CABOT BLUE CHIP FUND

MANULIFE CABOT CANADIAN EQUITY FUND

MANULIFE CABOT CANADIAN GROWTH FUND

MARITIME LIFE CANADIAN EQUITY FUND

MAWER CANADIAN EQUITY FUND

MAWER NEW CANADA FUND

MAXXUM DIVIDEND FUND

McLEAN BUDDEN EQUITY GROWTH FUND

MILLENNIUM NEXT GENERATION FUND

MUTUAL EQUIFUND

MUTUAL PREMIER BLUE CHIP FUND

NATIONAL EQUITIES FUND

OPTIMA STRATEGY CANADIAN EQUITY SECTION

OPTIMUM STOCK FUND

PHILLIPS, HAGER & NORTH CANADIAN EQUITY FUND

PHILLIPS, HAGER & NORTH CANADIAN EQUITY PLUS FUND

PHILLIPS, HAGER & NORTH VINTAGE FUND

PURSUIT CANADIAN EQUITY FUND

QUEBEC GROWTH FUND

ROYAL & SUN ALLIANCE EQUITY FUND

SAXON SMALL CAP FUND

SAXON STOCK FUND

SCOTIA CANADIAN DIVIDEND FUND

SCOTIA CANADIAN MID-LARGE CAP FUND

SPECTRUM UNITED CANADIAN EQUITY FUND

SPECTRUM UNITED CANADIAN INVESTMENT FUND

SPECTRUM UNITED DIVIDEND FUND

STANDARD LIFE CANADIAN DIVIDEND MUTUAL FUND

STANDARD LIFE EQUITY MUTUAL FUND

STANDARD LIFE GROWTH EQUITY MUTUAL FUND

STANDARD LIFE IDEAL EQUITY FUND

STRATEGIC VALUE DIVIDEND FUND

TALVEST/HYPERION SMALL CAP CDN. EQUITY FUND

UNIVERSAL CANADIAN GROWTH FUND

UNIVERSAL FUTURE FUND

WESTBURY LIFE EQUITY GROWTH FUND

U.S. AND INTERNATIONAL EQUITY FUNDS

$$$$

AIC VALUE FUND

CANADA LIFE U.S. AND INTERNATIONAL EQUITY FUND (S-34)

FIDELITY INTERNATIONAL PORTFOLIO FUND

PHILLIPS, HAGER & NORTH U.S. EQUITY FUND

TEMPLETON GROWTH FUND

TEMPLETON INTERNATIONAL STOCK FUND

TRIMARK FUND

$$$

AGF AMERICAN GROWTH CLASS

AGF EUROPEAN GROWTH CLASS

AGF GERMANY CLASS

AGF INTERNATIONAL VALUE FUND

AGF RSP INTERNATIONAL EQUITY ALLOCATION FUND

AIC WORLD EQUITY FUND

AIM AMERICAN PREMIER FUND

AIM EUROPA FUND

AIM GLOBAL HEALTH SCIENCES FUND

AIM GT GLOBAL TELECOMMUNICATIONS CLASS

AIM INTERNATIONAL FUND

ALTAMIRA EUROPEAN EQUITY FUND

ALTAMIRA SELECT AMERICAN FUND

ATLAS AMERICAN LARGE CAP GROWTH FUND

ATLAS EUROPEAN VALUE FUND

BANK OF MONTREAL FIRST CANADIAN U.S. GROWTH FUND

BANK OF MONTREAL FIRST CANADIAN NAFTA ADVANTAGE FUND

BISSETT MULTINATIONAL GROWTH FUND

BPI AMERICAN EQUITY VALUE FUND

BPI GLOBAL EQUITY VALUE FUND

CANADA TRUST AMERIGROWTH FUND

CANADA TRUST EUROGROWTH FUND

CANADA TRUST NORTH AMERICAN FUND

CENTREPOST FOREIGN EQUITY FUND

CHOU ASSOCIATES FUND

C.I. GLOBAL FUND

CIBC GLOBAL EQUITY FUND

CLEAN ENVIRONMENT INTERNATIONAL EQUITY FUND

CO-OPERATORS U.S. EQUITY FUND

DYNAMIC AMERICAS FUND

DYNAMIC EUROPE FUND

DYNAMIC INTERNATIONAL FUND

DYNAMIC REAL ESTATE EQUITY FUND

ELLIOTT & PAGE AMERICAN GROWTH FUND

ELLIOTT & PAGE GLOBAL EQUITY FUND

EQUITABLE LIFE INTERNATIONAL FUND

ETHICAL NORTH AMERICAN EQUITY FUND

FIDELITY EUROPEAN GROWTH FUND

FIDELITY GROWTH AMERICA FUND

FIDELITY SMALL CAP AMERICA FUND

GBC NORTH AMERICAN GROWTH FUND

GLOBAL STRATEGY DIVERSIFIED EUROPE FUND

GLOBAL STRATEGY DIVERSIFIED WORLD EQUITY FUND

GLOBAL STRATEGY U.S. EQUITY FUND

GLOBAL STRATEGY WORLD COMPANIES FUND

GLOBAL STRATEGY WORLD EQUITY FUND

GREAT-WEST LIFE INTERNATIONAL EQUITY FUND (P)

GREEN LINE EUROPEAN GROWTH FUND

GREEN LINE GLOBAL SELECT FUND

GREEN LINE SCIENCE AND TECHNOLOGY FUND

GREEN LINE U.S. MID-CAP GROWTH FUND

GREYSTONE MANAGED GLOBAL FUND

GUARDIAN AMERICAN EQUITY FUND

HONGKONG BANK EUROPEAN GROWTH FUND

HONGKONG BANK U.S. EQUITY FUND

INVESNAT EUROPEAN EQUITY FUND

INVESTORS GLOBAL FUND

INVESTORS GROWTH PORTFOLIO

INVESTORS NORTH AMERICAN GROWTH FUND

INVESTORS SPECIAL FUND

INVESTORS U.S. GROWTH FUND

IRIS GLOBAL EQUITY FUND

LONDON LIFE U.S. EQUITY FUND

MAWER U.S. EQUITY FUND

MAWER WORLD INVESTMENT FUND

MAXXUM AMERICAN EQUITY FUND

MAXXUM GLOBAL EQUITY FUND

McLEAN BUDDEN AMERICAN GROWTH FUND

MONTRUSCO SELECT NON-TAXABLE U.S. EQUITY FUND

MUTUAL AMERIFUND

MUTUAL PREMIER AMERICAN FUND

MUTUAL PREMIER INTERNATIONAL FUND

NAVIGATOR AMERICAN VALUE INVESTMENT FUND

NN CAN-EURO FUND

OPTIMA STRATEGY U.S. EQUITY SECTION

OPTIMUM INTERNATIONAL FUND

ORBIT WORLD FUND

PH&N NORTH AMERICAN EQUITY FUND

ROYAL U.S. EQUITY FUND

SPECTRUM UNITED AMERICAN EQUITY FUND

SPECTRUM UNITED EUROPEAN GROWTH FUND

SPECTRUM UNITED GLOBAL EQUITY FUND

SPECTRUM UNITED GLOBAL TELECOMMUNICATIONS FUND

STANDARD LIFE U.S. EQUITY MUTUAL FUND

STRATEGIC VALUE EUROPE FUND

TALVEST/HYPERION EUROPEAN FUND

TALVEST/HYPERION VALUE LINE U.S. EQUITY FUND

TRIMARK SELECT GROWTH FUND

UNIVERSAL EUROPEAN OPPORTUNITIES FUND

VISION EUROPE FUND

ZWEIG STRATEGIC GROWTH FUND

BALANCED FUNDS

$$$$

ABC FULLY-MANAGED FUND

AGF AMERICAN TACTICAL ASSET ALLOCATION FUND

BISSETT RETIREMENT FUND

COMMON SENSE ASSET BUILDER FUND I

COMMON SENSE ASSET BUILDER FUND II

COMMON SENSE ASSET BUILDER FUND III

COMMON SENSE ASSET BUILDER FUND IV

COMMON SENSE ASSET BUILDER FUND V

GLOBAL STRATEGY INCOME PLUS FUND

MAWER CANADIAN BALANCED RETIREMENT SAVINGS FUND

SCEPTRE BALANCED GROWTH FUND

$$$

AGF CANADIAN TACTICAL ASSET ALLOCATION FUND

AGF EUROPEAN ASSET ALLOCATION FUND

AGF WORLD BALANCED FUND

AIM GT GLOBAL GROWTH & INCOME FUND

ATLAS CANADIAN BALANCED FUND

BPI GLOBAL BALANCED RSP FUND

CANADA TRUST BALANCED FUND

CAPSTONE BALANCED TRUST

C.I. CANADIAN INCOME FUND

C.I. INTERNATIONAL BALANCED FUND

C.I. INTERNATIONAL BALANCED RSP FUND

CIBC BALANCED FUND

CLEAN ENVIRONMENT BALANCED FUND

CO-OPERATORS BALANCED FUND

ETHICAL BALANCED FUND

FIDELITY CANADIAN ASSET ALLOCATION FUND

FIDELITY GLOBAL ASSET ALLOCATION FUND

GLOBAL STRATEGY INCOME PLUS FUND

GREAT-WEST LIFE INCOME FUND (G)

GREEN LINE BALANCED GROWTH FUND

GREEN LINE BALANCED INCOME FUND

GREYSTONE MANAGED WEALTH FUND

HONGKONG BANK BALANCED FUND

INDUSTRIAL PENSION FUND

INVESTORS ASSET ALLOCATION FUND

INVESTORS GROWTH PLUS PORTFOLIO

INVESTORS MUTUAL OF CANADA

IVY GROWTH AND INCOME FUND

JONES HEWARD AMERICAN FUND

LEITH WHEELER BALANCED FUND

LONDON LIFE DIVERSIFIED FUND

LOTUS BALANCED FUND

MARITIME LIFE BALANCED FUND

MAWER CANADIAN DIVERSIFIED INVESTMENT FUND

MAWER CANADIAN INCOME FUND

McLEAN BUDDEN BALANCED FUND

MILLENNIUM DIVERSIFIED FUND

MONTRUSCO SELECT BALANCED+ FUND

MUTUAL DIVERSIFUND 40

NATIONAL BALANCED FUND

NN ASSET ALLOCATION FUND

PHILLIPS, HAGER & NORTH BALANCED FUND

ROYAL & SUN ALLIANCE BALANCED FUND

ROYAL TRUST ADVANTAGE BALANCED FUND

ROYAL TRUST ADVANTAGE INCOME FUND

SCOTIA CANADIAN BALANCED FUND

SCOTIA TOTAL RETURN FUND

SPECTRUM UNITED DIVERSIFIED FUND

STANDARD LIFE BALANCED MUTUAL FUND

STANDARD LIFE IDEAL BALANCED FUND

TEMPLETON BALANCED FUND

UNIVERSAL WORLD BALANCED RRSP FUND

WESTBURY LIFE BALANCED FUND

FIXED INCOME AND MONEY MARKET FUNDS

$$$$

ALTAMIRA BOND FUND

INDUSTRIAL CASH MANAGEMENT FUND

PHILLIPS, HAGER & NORTH BOND FUND

PHILLIPS, HAGER & NORTH CANADIAN MONEY MARKET FUND

PHILLIPS, HAGER & NORTH $U.S. MONEY MARKET FUND

SCEPTRE MONEY MARKET FUND

$$$

AGF CANADIAN BOND FUND

AGF GLOBAL GOVERNMENT BOND FUND

AGF HIGH INCOME FUND

AGF U.S. DOLLAR MONEY MARKET ACCOUNT

AIM GT GLOBAL BOND FUND

ALTAMIRA INCOME FUND

ATLAS AMERICAN MONEY MARKET FUND

ATLAS CANADIAN HIGH YIELD BOND FUND

ATLAS CANADIAN MONEY MARKET FUND

BANK OF MONTREAL FIRST CANADIAN MORTGAGE FUND

BEUTEL GOODMAN INCOME FUND

BEUTEL GOODMAN MONEY MARKET FUND

BISSETT BOND FUND

BISSETT MONEY MARKET FUND

BNP (CANADA) BOND FUND

BPI GLOBAL RSP BOND FUND

BPI T-BILL FUND

CANADA TRUST BOND FUND

CENTREPOST SHORT TERM FUND

C.I. CANADIAN BOND FUND

C.I. GLOBAL BOND RSP FUND

C.I. MONEY MARKET FUND

C.I. U.S. MONEY MARKET FUND

CIBC CANADIAN BOND FUND

CIBC PREMIUM CANADIAN T-BILL FUND

CIBC U.S. DOLLAR MONEY MARKET FUND

CO-OPERATORS FIXED INCOME FUND

ELLIOTT & PAGE MONEY FUND

EQUITABLE LIFE CANADIAN BOND FUND

ETHICAL INCOME FUND

GBC CANADIAN BOND FUND

GREAT-WEST LIFE MORTGAGE FUND (G)

GREEN LINE CANADIAN BOND FUND

GREEN LINE CANADIAN MONEY MARKET FUND

GREEN LINE CANADIAN T-BILL FUND

GREEN LINE U.S. MONEY MARKET FUND

GUARDIAN INTERNATIONAL INCOME FUND

GUARDIAN U.S. MONEY MARKET FUND

HONGKONG BANK CANADIAN BOND FUND

HONGKONG BANK MONEY MARKET FUND

HONGKONG BANK MORTGAGE FUND

ICM SHORT TERM INVESTMENT FUND

INDUSTRIAL BOND FUND

INVESNAT BOND FUND

INVESNAT CORPORATE CASH MANAGEMENT FUND

INVESNAT INTERNATIONAL RSP BOND FUND

INVESNAT MORTGAGE FUND

INVESNAT TREASURY BILL PLUS FUND

INVESNAT U.S. MONEY MARKET FUND

INVESTORS CORPORATE BOND FUND

INVESTORS GOVERNMENT BOND FUND

IRIS BOND FUND

IVY MORTGAGE FUND

JONES HEWARD MONEY MARKET FUND

LEITH WHEELER FIXED INCOME FUND

LEITH WHEELER MONEY MARKET FUND

LONDON LIFE MORTGAGE FUND

LOTUS BOND FUND

LOTUS INCOME FUND

MAWER CANADIAN BOND FUND

MAWER CANADIAN MONEY MARKET FUND

MAXXUM INCOME FUND

MAXXUM MONEY MARKET FUND

McLEAN BUDDEN FIXED INCOME FUND

McLEAN BUDDEN MONEY MARKET FUND

MONTRUSCO SELECT INCOME FUND

MONTRUSCO SELECT T-MAX FUND

NATIONAL FIXED INCOME FUND

NAVIGATOR CANADIAN INCOME FUND

NN BOND FUND

NN MONEY MARKET FUND

OPTIMA STRATEGY CANADIAN FIXED INCOME SECTION

OPTIMUM BOND FUND

OPTIMUM SAVINGS FUND

PHILLIPS, HAGER & NORTH SHORT TERM BOND AND MORTGAGE FUND

PURSUIT MONEY MARKET FUND

ROYAL & SUN ALLIANCE INCOME FUND

ROYAL & SUN ALLIANCE MONEY MARKET FUND

ROYAL BOND FUND

ROYAL $U.S. MONEY MARKET FUND

SCEPTRE BOND FUND

SCOTIA CANADIAN INCOME FUND

SCOTIA CANAM U.S. $ INCOME FUND

SCOTIA CANGLOBAL INCOME FUND

SCOTIA MORTGAGE INCOME FUND

SCOTIA PREMIUM T-BILL FUND

SPECTRUM UNITED LONG-TERM BOND FUND

SPECTRUM UNITED U.S. DOLLAR MONEY MARKET FUND

STANDARD LIFE BOND MUTUAL FUND

STANDARD LIFE IDEAL MONEY MARKET FUND

STANDARD LIFE INTERNATIONAL BOND MUTUAL FUND

STANDARD LIFE MONEY MARKET MUTUAL FUND

STRATEGIC VALUE INCOME FUND

TALVEST BOND FUND

TALVEST FOREIGN PAY CDN. BOND FUND

TALVEST/HYPERION HIGH-YIELD BOND FUND

TALVEST INCOME FUND

TALVEST MONEY FUND

TRIMARK ADVANTAGE BOND FUND

TRIMARK CANADIAN BOND FUND

TRIMARK INTEREST FUND

TRANS-CANADA MONEY MARKET FUND

YMG MONEY MARKET FUND

LABOUR-SPONSORED VENTURE CAPITAL FUNDS

CROCUS INVESTMENT FUND

FIRST ONTARIO FUND

VENGROWTH INVESTMENT FUND

WORKING OPPORTUNITY FUND

THE 1999 MUTUAL FUND AWARDS

Every year we nominate our choices for the best, and worst, performers in Canada's mutual funds industry. This idea has now been picked up and formalized by the organizers of the annual Mutual Funds Awards Gala, held every year in December. Sometimes our choices agree, sometimes they don't. See what you think.

Some of these categories are intended to be serious, some humorous, but all are designed to make a point.

And now, for 1999, the envelopes, please!

THE BIGGIES

Fund of the Year: Altamira Bond Fund. 1998 was a rough year for stocks. All the outstanding equity funds that would have been candidates for the Fund of the Year honour were hammered in July and August, with most suffering double-digit losses. They will eventually recover, but it's hard to hand out an award of this type to a fund that has just taken a blow to the chin. Fortunately, there was an outstanding candidate in another category ready to step forward.

Altamira's Robert Marcus is a man of strong convictions. He has fervently believed for several years that long-term interest rates are heading down, and has managed his bond portfolios accordingly. This fund gave him the best opportunity to put those views into practice, since its mandate is to be more aggressive than its stablemate, Altamira Income. That means Altamira Bond carries more risk — if interest rates rise, as they did in 1994, it will be hard-hit. But when long-term interest rates are dropping, Marcus's strategy of loading up with bonds of long maturity will pay large dividends for investors.

Marcus also uses some little-known bond techniques, such as large option positions, to enhance returns, and lately these have paid off well. But he doesn't venture into the field of junk bonds to boost performance. That's outside the mandate of this fund. Assets in the portfolio are very high quality, usually confined to federal and Ontario government bonds. Marcus wants to keep his portfolio highly liquid and is proud of saying that if interest rates start to rise he can liquidate all his assets "with two phone calls".

You can't argue with the results. The returns from this fund outclass everything else in the Canadian bond category. Over the year to June 30/98, the fund gained an astonishing 22.9%. That was more than most Canadian equity funds, and this was before the stock markets went south. Over the summer, while equity funds were in freefall, this one held steady as a rock, with only a slight loss.

A long bond strategy won't work forever. Sooner or later, rates will turn and we'll see how nimble Marcus is in those circumstances. But the superior performance of this fund in recent years deserves recognition. Altamira has had its problems lately, but this fund is an example of the excellence that still exists in that organization.

Fund Company of the Year: AIM GT Investments. Two companies that were drifting got together because of events that took place in other parts of the world and, presto! A new force on the Canadian mutual funds scene was born.

It all unfolded on the international stage, where mergers and acquisitions are running big these days. A London-based company, Invesco PLC, had taken control of the small Canadian fund company, Admax, which was originally founded by Lou Voticky, an ex-Air Canada pilot. Shortly thereafter, Invesco merged with a U.S. mutual fund giant, AIM, which is based in Houston. The Canadian operation took on the AIM name, but not a lot happened beyond that (total assets under management at the time of the merger with GT Global were about $500 million).

AIM and Invesco are controlled by a holding company called Amvescap PLC, which is based in the U.K. Amvescap moved early in 1998 to acquire the worldwide assets of GT Global. That purchase had the effect of pulling the two Canadian operations into a single company, now known as AIM GT Investments.

In Canadian terms, it looked like another "minnow swallows whale" story. The tiny AIM Funds, which few people have ever heard of, took over the GT Global operation at the beginning of June, 1998, absorbing a company that was six times larger in asset terms.

But GT Global was floundering. It had been one of the shooting stars of the Canadian mutual fund firmament, a company that had burgeoned past the $2-billion mark in assets in record time. However, that was under the direction of hard-driving Joe Canavan. When he shocked the financial community by stepping down as GT Global president in mid-1997, the company was left rudderless. Growth continued, but the spark seemed to be gone.

The merger changed all that. The revamped lineup now offers an impressive array of funds, including seven that qualify for $$$ status in this year's *Buyer's Guide*. A number of others are showing improvement under new direction and should be in a position to move up soon.

The revamped organization is still weak on the domestic side — all but one of the $$$ entries are foreign content funds for registered plan purposes. But the company now appears to have the strength and the will to remedy that deficiency.

Watch out for these folks. They look like real players.

Manager of the Year: Jerry Javasky. When Gerald Coleman shocked the Mackenzie organization early in 1997 by suddenly decamping to join the rival C.I. group, there was great consternation. Mackenzie had created a brand-new fund line for Coleman and his associate, Jerry Javasky, when the two had come to the company from the

United funds. The new Ivy funds were Mackenzie's saviour in the mid-'90s when old warhorses like Industrial Growth and Industrial Horizon faltered. Coleman was the key man, the manager of the successful Ivy Canadian fund that had pulled billions of dollars into Mackenzie. Suddenly, he was gone.

It was a logical move to name Javasky to replace him. The two had worked together for years and shared the same conservative value approach to stock selection. But Javasky was not as well known to the investing public and there was some doubt as to whether he could deliver the same level of performance.

The past year has assuaged all those doubts. Javasky has done an outstanding job with Ivy Canadian. He retained the Coleman style, but with his own personal stamp. His first move was to dump some stocks chosen by his predecessor that he didn't like. He then reshaped the Ivy Canadian portfolio in his own image, building a large cash reserve to cushion the blow from the market correction he expected was coming. Over the 12 months to June 30/98, which roughly corresponded with Javasky's first year at the helm, Ivy Canadian gained 17.4%, way above average for the Canadian equity category, despite the drag of all that cash.

Some of that was given back over the summer, but the damage wasn't as bad as that suffered by other funds. Ivy Canadian was 35% in cash at the beginning of August. That helped a lot. While the TSE 300 index was falling more than 20% in August, and the blue-chip TSE 35 was losing over 21%, Ivy Canadian's NAV dropped only about half that.

Meanwhile, Javasky's other fund, the balanced Ivy Growth and Income, fared even better, losing only 7.5% in August. It too has been a leading performer in its category since he assumed control.

The best fund managers are those who can produce above-average returns to investors in good times while minimizing losses when things turn sour. Jerry Javasky has proven his ability to do that and is a worthy recipient of the Fund Manager of the Year Award.

Rookie of the Year: Synergy Asset Management. Joe Canavan had it all. He headed up a rising star of a mutual fund company that had just passed $2 billion in assets in record time. He enjoyed widespread respect in the financial industry for his imagination, drive, platform presence, and marketing skills. And he chucked it. Threw it all away. Handed in his resignation as the head of GT Global in the spring of 1997 and walked out, jolting Bay Street and leaving financial observers groping for some answers.

No one ever got any, beyond the fact that Joseph Canavan seems uncomfortable working for other people. He had caused a stir a few years earlier with a surprise departure from Fidelity Canada. Again, the reasons were never clear but there was suspicion that what Joe really wanted was to run the show without interference — from anyone.

Well, now he has his wish and he says he's settled in for the long haul. The Royal Bank may be a major partner in his new firm, Synergy Asset Management, but their 40% stake comes with no voting rights. Joe's in command and the new company is strictly his baby.

As with GT Global, this is definitely a different kind of fund company. It's hard to believe that, in such a crowded marketplace, someone can come forward with a new idea, but Joltin' Joe has done it.

Synergy's funds are structured in what most people would regard as an unorthodox way. Instead of the traditional equity, fixed-income, and balanced funds, the company offers five Canadian stock funds that are differentiated purely by management style (there is also a money fund, but it's just a parking place for cash).

He says it's an approach he's wanted to implement for a long time. Now he's done it.

Synergy offers four management styles in its funds: value, growth, momentum, and small-cap. Each fund is a pure embodiment of the style, with a manager who is an industry expert in the approach. They are all covered by an umbrella fund, so that money can be moved around among them without attracting capital gains tax, the same approach that was used at his former company, GT Global.

For investors who can't make up their minds which style to select, Synergy offers a traditional Canadian compromise: the Canadian Style Management Class. This fund of funds combines all four styles under one roof.

The obvious question is, what's next? Certainly Canavan isn't going to sit still with a company that has no international funds, no balanced funds, no fixed-income funds.

No, he isn't. But neither is he in a rush to add more horses to the stable until the existing ones have established a track record and gained investor acceptance, even if that takes three years. This time, he plans to stay the course.

Comeback of the Year. International bond funds. Some fund categories are always in favour. No time is the wrong time for a balanced fund or for a well-balanced international stock fund. But other fund categories are in and out like the seasons. Emerging markets and Far East funds are in the depths of winter right now. European equity funds may be in the autumn phase. But international bond funds are currently basking in the full heat of summer.

For several years, this was no place for your money. The Canadian dollar was strong and international interest rates looked like they would move higher as economic growth accelerated, which would be bad news for bond funds. Returns were very unimpressive.

But last year was a different story. The sliding Canadian dollar and the whiff of deflation from the Far East suddenly put the wind back into the sails of international bond funds. Over the 12 months to July 31/98, the average fund in this category posted a healthy 9.6% return, while Canadian bond funds as a group could do no better than 5.4%.

Some international bond funds were outstanding. The Universal World Tactical Bond Fund, which has been focusing on only three markets (Germany, the U.S., and the U.K.) posted an 18% one-year gain, outstanding for a bond fund. Standard Life's International Bond Fund was a close runner-up at 17.6%, while the small Guardian Foreign Income Fund gained 17.4%.

Most international bond funds will lose their lustre if the loonie makes a determined upward surge in '99. But for much of '98, they were among the shining stars.

Best no-load fund company: Phillips, Hager & North. This award recognizes long-term achievement, whereas the Fund Company of the Year is intended to focus more on the rising stars of the industry. PH&N claimed the top no-load company title for the first time in the 1997 edition and retained it last year. This year, it faced a serious challenge from the fine Calgary firm of Bissett & Associates. However, PH&N wins again, by an eyelash.

Bissett's Canadian stock funds are superior to those of PH&N at this time. But Bissett doesn't have the overall balance and consistency that the Vancouver company brings to the table.

Again this year, PH&N placed five funds in the top $$$$ category. No other company has ever done that (Bissett has three). As well as excellent results, the firm continues to provide low management fees, no sales commissions, a conservative investing style, high ethical standards, and top-flight management.

The only weakness in their lineup continues to be the International Equity Fund, which has struggled and which is in need of a major overhaul. But stay within North America and you won't go wrong, no matter which fund you select from this top-notch group.

Best load fund company: Mackenzie Financial Corporation. This was a difficult choice. Trimark has held this honour for many years, but the poor performance of their Canadian equity and balanced funds and their apparent reluctance to do much to address the problem have knocked them off the perch.

All the other pretenders had flaws. Fidelity offers a fine lineup of international funds, but their domestic offerings are generally weak with the exception of True North. The same can be said for Templeton and AIM GT. The AIC funds have been great performers, but the organization is thin. AGF has too many holes. Investors Group would be a decent choice, but several of their funds are coming off indifferent years and they lost the services of star manager Larry Sarbit.

That leaves Mackenzie, but it's not by default. The company has made a lot of positive moves over the past couple of years. You have to pick and choose carefully, but you can build yourself a very respectable fund portfolio with this company's products.

The Ivy funds head the list, of course. Ivy Canadian is Mackenzie's only $$$$ equity fund entry, but the Enterprise, Growth and Income, and Mortgage funds all weigh in at $$$ in this year's edition.

The Industrial funds offer the $$$$ Cash Management Fund and four $$$ choices: Bond, Dividend Growth, Horizon, and Pension. Industrial Horizon is worth a special mention; after languishing for years it is once again a very sound choice under the guidance of Bill Procter.

The Universal funds are very much a mixed bag, with a lot of mediocrity and worse. But a few are stick-outs, including the $$$ Canadian Growth, European Opportunities and Future funds.

As a bonus, Mackenzie absorbed the two Cundill funds into their vast lineup in mid-1998. Both are managed using a deep value approach to stock selection. Cundill Security, a Canadian equity fund, has looked especially good in recent years.

As well as their wide array of offerings, Mackenzie has always been a favourite among financial advisors because of their good marketing and strong back shop. It has taken the company a long time to regain the prominent position it held during the 1980s, but it's back and well-poised for the 21st century. Well done!

THE NOT-QUITE-SO-BIGGIES

Most Improved Fund Group: AGF. Eight of their funds were worthy of a rating upgrade this year. They now boast one $$$$ fund and 14 that merit a $$$ ranking. Too bad about the 10 that are still only worth $.

Most Disappointing Fund Group: Trimark. Investors and financial advisors were stunned by the sharp decline in performance from the company's core Canadian equity and balanced funds. The problem was made even more acute by the fact there were very few places within the Trimark lineup to switch to, especially within registered plans. Other than the company's bond funds, the only decent performers were restricted by foreign content limitations. Some brokers were telling clients to bite the bullet and pay the redemption fees needed to move their assets to another company. I cannot believe this will continue; this is a proud and classy organization. But a lot of damage control is needed quickly.

Best Group with No Ratings: Scudder Funds. There are lots of impressive performers in this company's lineup, but no fund has the three-year track record needed to qualify for a rating in this edition (next year will be different). But don't ignore them for that reason. There are some good choices here.

Takeover of the Year: Scotia Funds/National Trust. The absorption of the old National Trust funds into the Scotia lineup was one of the major developments of the year. The new, merged group looks a lot stronger than the two parts that went into it. Scotia's acquisition of Cassels Blaikie, who managed many of the National Trust funds, was another move that strengthened this good fund line.

Most Imitated Fund Group: Manulife Financial. When Manulife launched their GIF line of funds in late 1996, many people were skeptical. Would investors really pay premium prices to buy regular mutual funds from companies like Trimark and Fidelity repackaged in a seg fund wrapper? Yes indeed they would — to the tune of billions of dollars. That was good enough to convince the industry that Manulife was on to something big. Over the past year, C.I., BPI, Trimark, National Bank, Templeton, and Talvest have all jumped on the same bandwagon. There will be more to follow.

Underrated Fund Group of the Year: Standard Life. Most people don't even realize that Standard Life offers a line of non-segregated funds. Even fewer investors know how good they are. How good are they? Good enough that eight of the 10 funds they offer earn a $$$ rating in this year's edition. Very few companies can claim an 80% ratio of $$$ and $$$$ entries. Check them out.

Reorganization of the Year: Global Strategy Funds. We have too many small funds around. They don't pay their own way and in many cases they force investors in larger funds to subsidize those with money in the "tiddlers". However, most companies are unwilling to kill off these parasites for fear of losing a marketing advantage. Global Strategy, to their credit, bit the bullet and did some head-chopping. By the time all was said and done, seven funds had taken the gas pipe, trimming Global Strategy's lineup by almost a third and making it much more comprehensible to the ordinary investor. Good for them. May others follow suit.

Explosion of the Year: London Life. From seven funds to 40 in one sudden August burst! Wow! I cannot ever recall 33 new funds exploding onto the scene all at the same time. Nor is it something I ever want to see again. How are investors supposed to absorb something like that?

Segregated Fund Group of the Year: Co-operators General Insurance. They're way out there in Regina, a long way from the fast pace of Bay Street. Their roots are in the credit unions and co-operatives of the Prairies. Not exactly a place where you'd expect to find a family of top-performing seg funds. But Canada is full of surprises, and here's another one. It's not a big group, just six funds, but four of them get a $$$ rating in this year's edition. The other two don't make it because they haven't been around long enough to be ranked.

Dog of the Year: AIM Korea Fund. Just because you're the Fund Company of the Year doesn't make you immune from serving up a dog. Here's the evidence. Sure it was a bad time for anything associated with the Far East. But a 12-month loss of 66.2%? What ever happened to cash in bad times? Ugh. This fund has got to go.

THE REST

Most Confusing Fund Groups: Great-West Life, London Life. This isn't a surprise because Great-West Life has won this not-so-coveted award in the past and recently acquired control of London Life, which they have moved in the same direction. The problem is not the fact that both groups offer a huge selection of funds — many other companies do also.

The difficulty is that many of the funds have exactly the same name except for a different initial at the end to designate the company that manages them. Great-West has a computer program called Discovery to help you sort your way through this maze, but investors would be better served by clearer brand distinction. Look at the Mackenzie organization for an example of a better way.

The Small Investor Award: Atlas Canadian Large Cap Growth Fund. Many investors would like to have some money in the high-performance Bissett Canadian Equity Fund but can't afford the $10,000 admission fee. Here's your answer: $500 invested here buys you the same manager (Fred Pynn) and the same investing style. You'll pay a higher MER this way, but, hey, nothing's perfect.

The "I've Got a Secret" Prize: Spectrum United Canadian Investment Fund. Whenever investors think about Spectrum United's Canadian stock funds, they usually think of Kiki Delaney, who runs their Canadian Equity Fund. Television commercials will do that. But this lesser-known entry, run by Kim Shannon, actually has a better record over the past three years, with an average annual compound rate of return of 20% to July 31/98. Kiki still pulls in the money, however; her fund is five times the size of this one. Look again, folks.

The Fund I'd Most Like to Have Invested in 10 Years Ago Prize: AIC Advantage Fund. Yes, it was hit hard in the August meltdown. Yes, it is vulnerable in declining markets. But we're looking back, not ahead, and these folks were in exactly the right place at the right time. Average annual compound rate of return over the decade to July 31/98 was 22.6%. Awesome!

The Fund I'd Least Like to Have Invested in 10 Years Ago Prize: Cambridge Special Equity Fund. The Sagit funds have a reputation for volatile swings, both up and down. But over time, you hope it all evens out and you come away with a nice profit. Unfortunately, it didn't happen in the case of this small-cap fund. It lost an average of 3.7% a year over the 10 years to July 31/98. Perhaps that doesn't seem like a large number, but think of it this way: for every $1,000 invested a decade ago, you would have $686 today. Not $686 profit. Just $686.

Catch of the Year: Dundee Mutual Funds. The people who run the Dynamic Funds went out and snagged veteran manager Rohit Sehgal from London Life and set him up with his own brand line, known as Power Funds. At the time, they made a big splash about all this, featuring Sehgal prominently in their promotion. What's ironic about this star approach is that Dynamic Funds is one of the groups that no longer tells investors the name of their funds' lead managers, preferring to hide behind the "Team" designation. Only when it suits us, I guess.

New Fund Group to Watch: Artisan Funds. Fund packages are becoming the new rage in the business. Winnipeg-based Artisan has launched an impressive collection of funds of funds that includes offerings from such companies as Fidelity, Dynamic, BPI, C.I., and AGF. The portfolio selections are made by Loring Ward, one of the up-and-coming companies in this business.

The Condolences Prize: Altamira. Things were already bad enough at Altamira, what with a bitter ownership battle and declining performance numbers. Then star manager Frank Mersch got into trouble with securities regulators and resigned his position. Shortly after, veteran bond manager Will Sutherland also left (not because of any regulatory problems, however). The loss of two top managers within a few weeks left the company reeling. The next year will be crucial.

The Welcome Back Award: Veronika Hirsch. This headline-maker bounced from AGF to Fidelity to nowhere in the space of a few months back in 1996 after encountering her own problems with the securities people. Now she's back with her own fund line, under the name Hirsch Asset Management. Early results aren't exciting, but give it time. She's made lots of money for investors in the past.

GENERAL INDEX

FUND INDEX